OXFORD SHAKESPEARE STUDIES

*

THE DIVISION OF THE KINGDOMS

SHAKESPEARE'S TWO
VERSIONS OF *KING LEAR*

OXFORD SHAKESPEARE STUDIES

The Division of the Kingdoms

Shakespeare's Two Versions of *King Lear*

EDITED BY

GARY TAYLOR

AND

MICHAEL WARREN

CLARENDON PRESS · OXFORD

Oxford University Press, Walton Street, Oxford OX2 6DP

Oxford New York Toronto
Delhi Bombay Calcutta Madras Karachi
Kuala Lumpur Singapore Hong Kong Tokyo
Nairobi Dar es Salaam Cape Town
Melbourne Auckland

and associated companies in
Beirut Berlin Ibadan Nicosia

Oxford is a trade mark of Oxford University Press

Published in the United States
by Oxford University Press, New York

© Oxford University Press 1983

First published 1983
Reprinted new as paperback 1986

British Library Cataloguing in Publication Data

The Division of the Kingdoms.—(Oxford Shakespeare studies)
1. Shakespeare, William. King Lear
2. Shakespeare, William—Criticism, Textual
I. Taylor, Gary II. Warren, Michael
822.3'3 PR2819
ISBN 0-19-812950-5 Pb

Library of Congress Cataloging in Publication Data

The Division of the Kingdoms.
(Oxford Shakespeare studies)
Bibliography: p. Includes indexes.
Contents: Introduction/Stanley Wells—"The base
shall to'th' legitimate"/Steven Urkowitz—The folio
omission of the mock trial/Roger Warren—[etc.]
1. Shakespeare, William, 1564–1616. King Lear—
Criticism, Textual—Addresses, essays lectures.
I. Taylor, Gary. II. Warren, Michael (Michael J.)
III. Series.
PR2819.D55 1983 822.3'3 82—24647
ISBN 0-19-812950-5 Pb

Set by Macmillan India Ltd.
and printed in Great Britain
at the University Printing House, Oxford
by David Stanford
Printer to the University

PREFACE

THIS collection had its origins in the Annual Meeting of the
Shakespeare Association of America in Cambridge, Massachusetts,
in April 1980. On that occasion the Textual Seminar, under the
benevolent and judicious guidance of Professor G. Blakemore Evans,
was devoted to 'The Textual Problem in *King Lear*'. The debate
turned almost exclusively upon the differences between the Quarto
and Folio texts, and upon the possibility that they preserve two
separate and successive stages in the creation of *King Lear*. For many
members of the seminar the conventional conflated text, far from
recovering the true Shakespearian perfection in form and content,
had come to seem an unauthoritative creation of eighteenth-century
editors. Out of that debate this volume was conceived, although only
one of the essays printed here bears any direct relation to those
discussed at the seminar; several are by scholars not present on that
occasion. Our aim in commissioning contributions was to produce a
comprehensive study of several outstanding issues pertinent to the
hypothesis that both texts represent independent Shakespearian
versions of *King Lear*, and to bring to bear on these problems a
variety of expertise and method. In particular we sought to produce a
volume which, by drawing on the disciplines of literary, theatrical,
and textual criticism, would demonstrate their necessary interdependence – and which would demonstrate too, we hope, that textual
studies need not be unintelligible to literary critics. All of the
following essays – with the single exception of Paul Werstine's
analysis of corruption in the Folio text – deal in whole or part with
issues of interpretation relevant to any reader of *King Lear*.

The book's title is taken from the second speech of the play and,
appropriately enough, the Quarto and Folio contain different
versions of the quoted phrase. In the Folio text, accepted without
discussion by all subsequent editors, Gloucester speaks of 'the
diuision of the Kingdome' (TLN 7); in the Quarto, of 'the diuision of
the kingdomes' (B1). Though this variant could easily result from an
accident of transmission in either text – addition or omission of
terminal *s* being among the commonest of all errors – the despised
Quarto reading in fact makes good sense, and in the absence of the

Folio might never have been emended. Until later in the seventeenth century the noun *kingdom* could mean 'kingly function, authority, or power' (*OED*, *sb.* 1), so that a Jacobean audience could easily have understood the Quarto phrase to mean 'the division of powers'. Alternatively, Gloucester might be using 'kingdomes' proleptically. Lear intends to divide the unified kingdom of Britain into three territories, each of which will remain 'perpetuall' and 'hereditarie euer' in the possession of one daughter and her descendants: Lear is thus effectively creating three 'kingdomes', in the division of which he has shown no partiality to either Albany or Cornwall. Since, in order for Kent and Gloucester to speak of them, the territorial divisions must clearly have been decided, the three 'kingdomes' in some sense already exist. Moreover, to a Jacobean audience, the names of the two Dukes would have strongly suggested two British 'kingdomes' with which they were thoroughly familiar. Albany, the old name for all of Britain north of the Humber, was eventually identified, more loosely, with Scotland; it was one of the three territories into which the legendary Brutus had divided the island. Cornwall was a separate kingdom until the tenth century; from the fourteenth century the Duke of Cornwall was also always the Prince of Wales, thereby uniting the two western territories under one nobleman. (This in turn would have immediately suggested that the 'third, more opulent' which Lear intended for Cordelia was England.) To an audience of 1605, for whom the reunification of 'the kingdomes' was an immediate political issue, the Quarto's plural should not have caused any perplexity. And for Shakespeare, clearly working with the anonymous *King Leir* in his mind (and probably on his desk), there would have been yet another reason for writing *kingdomes* – because in his source Leir's sons-in-law were not Dukes but the sovereigns of neighbouring kingdoms, so that the division of Leir's own kingdom amounted to a re-division of the boundaries of three kingdoms. Shakespeare could thus easily have written the plural, under the influence of *Leir*, even if it made no sense in his own context. But of course it does make sense. There is thus no reason to deny the authority of either the Quarto's plural or the Folio's singular. We have, after some vacillation, chosen the Quarto variant for our own title, partly because this book is largely devoted to the defence of hitherto neglected or rejected readings, and partly too because we are seeking to effect a kind of textual devolution, the re-division of two separate 'authorities', two independent 'kingdomes' spuriously

joined since the eighteenth century: the Quarto and Folio texts of
King Lear.

In planning this collection, we were guided by two fundamental
decisions about its purpose and scope. First, we chose to focus upon
the Folio text. We knew from the outset that Peter W. M. Blayney
was preparing a two-volume study (half of which has since appeared)
which concentrates heavily upon the Quarto, exhaustively investigating the printing of that text and the great variety of non-literary
evidence that points to its having been set up from Shakespeare's own
draft manuscript. It would have been foolish – and unhelpful – to
attempt to duplicate Blayney's research. All of the following essays,
by defending the independent dramatic integrity of the two texts, do
offer 'literary' defences of the Quarto; some of them – notably those
by Taylor and Jackson – address themselves directly, in part, to an
examination of the Quarto's authenticity. Nevertheless, the bulk of
this collection focuses upon the Folio.

Secondly, it seemed to us that any adequate evaluation of the Folio
had to combine critical exegesis with historical research. The
traditional editorial conflation of the two early texts of *King Lear* has
always depended upon a belief that both are corrupt; but different
kinds of deficiency have been alleged for each text, and consequently
each requires a different kind of defence. In the Quarto, editors have
denigrated the 'inferiority' of many individual readings, and have
alleged an irregular process of textual transmission; consequently any
comprehensive defence of the Quarto's authority would have to
provide – as Blayney has set out to do – a detailed critical
consideration of many individual variants, in addition to more
general evidence for the text's direct derivation from an authorial
manuscript. In the Folio, by contrast, most individual readings have
been generally regarded as Shakespearian and satisfactory, but the
authority of larger alterations – major omissions, additions, and
changes in staging – has been doubted. Any proper critical approach
to the challenged Folio variants must therefore be macroscopic, must
deal with problems of structure, character, and interpretation rather
than with, primarily, 'an exagmination round the factification' of
isolated readings. Likewise, a scholarly defence of the Folio text must
be based less on an intensive study of the derivation of a single text
than on a wide-ranging examination of certain basic questions. How
did the compositors and editor(s) who worked on the First Folio
corrupt or contaminate other texts – and therefore how much and

what kind of printing house corruption can we expect in Folio *Lear*? Can we distinguish authorial variants from those due to other agents of transmission (inefficient actors or annotators), and if so do the variants in *King Lear* look authorial? Did theatrical adaptation differ, in this period, from authorial revision, and if so how? Could the Folio text represent an adaptation by some other author? The collection therefore moves from critical essays which immediately address aspects of Folio *Lear* to others which approach *Lear* through a survey of the practices of authors, players, and printers.

A short bibliography of the more important twentieth-century investigations of the text(s) of *King Lear* appears on pp. 469–70. Five works in particular, published since 1978, have provided the initial demonstration and justification of a new way of thinking about *King Lear*. References to these works (Blayney, *Origins*; Stone, *Textual History*; Taylor, 'War'; Urkowitz, *Revision*; M. Warren, 'Albany and Edgar') have been placed, wherever possible, directly in the text, not in the notes. We have also supplied an index of passages discussed in our volume (pp. 478 ff.), and also (pp. 471–8) in the works mentioned above (with the exception of Blayney's *Origins*, which contains its own extensive index). These indexes will make it easier for both editors and critics to survey the recent controversy, in so far as it affects any particular variant.

Reference to the texts of *King Lear* is at present hampered by the fact that, although editions of the conflated modern text are legion, neither the Quarto nor the Folio is available in an edited text. Blayney will provide an edited old-spelling reference text of Q in Volume II of *Origins*; the forthcoming Complete Oxford Shakespeare (to be published in both original and modern spelling) will provide edited texts of both Q and F. However, as none of these conveniences is yet available, we have employed an improvised system of reference. Quotations from the First Quarto are from *King Lear 1608* (Pied Bull Quarto), ed. W. W. Greg, Shakespeare Quarto Facsimiles No. 1 (1939); quotations from the Folio are from *The Norton Facsimile: The First Folio of Shakespeare*, ed. Charlton Hinman (New York and London, 1968). Press variants in Q are reproduced from Greg's *The Variants in the First Quarto of 'King Lear': A Bibliographical and Critical Inquiry* (Oxford, 1940); press variants in F, from Hinman's *The Printing and Proof-Reading of the First Folio of Shakespeare* (Oxford, 1963). The Quarto text can also be consulted in *Shakespeare's Plays in Quarto: A Facsimile Edition of Copies*

Primarily from the Henry E. Huntington Library, ed. Michael J. B. Allen and Kenneth Muir (Berkeley and Los Angeles, 1982). Although most quotations from Q and F transcribe the texts typographically, some of the essays quote the originals photographically (as on pp. 14–16); such 'photo-quotations' are not necessarily to a uniform scale. Unless otherwise stated photographs of the First Quarto (1608) are from the Shakespeare Quarto Facsimile; those of the First Folio (1623) and the Second Quarto (1619) are from the Royal Shakespeare Theatre's copies in the Shakespeare Centre Library, by permission of the Governors of the Theatre. All quotations from *King Lear* are followed by at least two references: the first the signature of the Quarto page and/or the Folio Through Line Number; then the conventional act-scene-line notation as it appears in *The Riverside Shakespeare*, ed. G. Blakemore Evans (Boston, 1974). This same edition includes 'A Glossary of Selected Bibliographical Terms' (pp. 41–4), which may assist readers unfamiliar with the conventional terminology of modern textual studies.

Although each contributor remains finally responsible only for his or her own essay, the neat attribution of names to pages in the Table of Contents to some degree misrepresents what has been, at least in part, a collaborative venture. Contributors have read drafts of one another's essays, and we have all profited from the criticism of our colleagues.

Many people have given us help and encouragement, directly or indirectly. We wish particularly to thank Richard Proudfoot, Peter W. M. Blayney, Philip Gaskell, Richard Knowles, and John Jowett. Michael Warren wishes to acknowledge the support afforded him by Faculty Research funds granted by the University of California, Santa Cruz; Gary Taylor, in addition to the many debts recorded in his footnotes, has also profited from the labour and learning of Jenny Wormald, Robert Ashton, Keith Thomas, and Jean Fuzier, who all helped in his fruitless effort to track down 'the wisest foole in Christendome'. The staffs of several libraries have given us indispensable help: our thanks to the Folger Shakespeare Library, the Henry E. Huntington Library, the British Library (especially for permission to reproduce photographs of *The Fleire*), the Bodleian Library, the Shakespeare Institute Library (University of Birmingham), the Shakespeare Centre Library (Stratford-upon-Avon), and the Oxford University English Faculty and Radcliffe Science libraries. We thank Kate Howells for drafting the indexes.

We are deeply grateful for the invaluable assistance we have received from Christine Avern-Carr and Louise Pengelley in Oxford, and from Phyllis Halpin, Charlotte Cassidy, Wallie Romig, and Julie Reiner in Santa Cruz. Of course, none of these benefactors is responsible for the errors and misjudgements which, undoubtedly, remain.

We wish also to express our gratitude to the families of our contributors, for their tolerance of the strains that we may have imposed upon them. And – 'Although the last, not least in our deere loue' – we wish especially to acknowledge our great debt to our own families – Rebecca, Isaac, and Daniel Taylor; Susan, Kate, and Adam Warren – for their patience and forbearance.

GARY TAYLOR

MICHAEL WARREN

PREFACE TO THE 1986 REPRINT

IN this reprint we have corrected half a dozen trivial errors, but have not attempted any revision or reformation of the substance of the original. Readers interested in pursuing the issues considered in this book may wish to consult several works published since 1983:

R. A. Foakes, 'Textual Revision and the Fool in *King Lear*', *Essays in Honour of Peter Davison*: Trivium 20 (Lampeter, Wales, 1985), 33–47

T. H. Howard-Hill, 'The Challenge of *King Lear*', *The Library*, VI, 7 (1985), 161–79

Philip C. McGuire, *Speechless Dialect: Shakespeare's Open Silences* (Berkeley and Los Angeles, 1985), esp. pp. 97–121 ('Open Silences and the Ending(s) of *King Lear*')

Kenneth Muir, 'The Texts of *King Lear*', in *Shakespeare: Contrasts and Controversies* (Brighton, 1985), 51–66

Annabel Patterson, *Censorship and Interpretation* (Madison, Wisconsin, 1984), esp. pp. 58–73

Gary Taylor, 'Folio Compositors and Folio Copy: *King Lear* and its Context', *PBSA*, 79 (1985), 17–74

Sidney Thomas, 'Shakespeare's Supposed Revision of *King Lear*', *SQ*, 35 (1984), 506–11

Michael Warren's *The Complete 'King Lear'* (forthcoming from University of California Press) will provide facsimiles of Q1, Q2, and F, and parallel texts of Q1 and F, using photo quotation.

G.T. and M.W.

CONTENTS

CONTRIBUTORS

THOMAS CLAYTON, University of Minnesota

BETH GOLDRING, University of Chicago

MACD. P. JACKSON, University of Auckland

JOHN KERRIGAN, St. John's College, Cambridge

RANDALL MCLEOD, University of Toronto

GARY TAYLOR, Associate Editor, The Oxford Shakespeare

STEVEN URKOWITZ, Maritime College, State University of New York

MICHAEL WARREN, University of California, Santa Cruz

ROGER WARREN, University of Leicester

STANLEY WELLS, Balliol College, Oxford; General Editor, The Oxford
Shakespeare

PAUL WERSTINE, King's College, London, Ontario

M. William Shak-ſpeare:

HIS
True Chronicle Hiſtorie of the life and
death of King LEAR and his three
Daughters.

With the vnfortunate life of Edgar, *ſonne*
and heire to the Earle of Gloſter, and his
ſullen and aſſumed humor of
TOM of Bedlam :

THE TRAGEDIE OF
KING LEAR.

INTRODUCTION
The Once and Future *King Lear*
STANLEY WELLS

POETIC plays may give much pleasure to readers, and some poets have adopted a dramatic form while not writing for the theatre. But plays written for performance are not fully realized until they reach the stage, and critics who treat such plays purely as literature are choosing to work in blinkers. Increasing recognition of these facts during the past two or three decades has resulted in the growing acknowledgement among critics of drama of the need to experience plays in performance and to read them with an awareness of the theatrical dimension, both imagined and actual. Nevertheless, readers, directors, and actors must all take the text as their starting point. To this extent, in reading and performing plays of the past they depend on the work of textual critics. Usually, the literary critic, in writing about a novel, poem, or play, can ignore textual problems. Sometimes, as Fredson Bowers amply demonstrated in his *Textual and Literary Criticism* (Cambridge, 1966), he does so at his peril. And there are some works in relation to which textual questions obtrude so insistently that even the critic most purely concerned with literary values must take notice of them. No one can write seriously about Dickens's *Edwin Drood*, or about Marlowe's *Hero and Leander*, without mentioning that they are unfinished. Criticism of Shakespeare's *Timon of Athens* has become particularly tentative in face of the hypothesis that the only surviving text is an incomplete draft. *Pericles* is self-evidently a damaged text, and for that reason resists standard critical procedures. Even in the theatre, with its many freedoms, textual problems cannot be wholly ignored. Directors may – though they rarely do – slavishly follow the edition they are working with; but editors do not solve all the problems that must be faced in the theatre; so, for example, a director must either supply the song called for by Titania in the final episode of *A Midsummer Night's Dream* or must cut the lines in which she mentions it.

Problems are especially acute when a work has survived in more than one form. It is possible to write about the 1805 text of *The*

Prelude without mentioning Wordsworth's revision of it, but it is not possible to take a comprehensive view of Wordsworth's poetic art without comparing the two. Here, at least, we know what the relationship is. The textual scholar can tell the critic that the version published in 1850 represents the poem as Wordsworth finally revised it, and that the 1805 text – preferred by most readers – is an earlier, distinct version. The editor can print the texts side by side, and the critic can exercise his art with as much or as little comparison between them as he finds appropriate to his purposes. In some cases, indeed, the art of the literary critic is indistinguishable from that of his textual colleague. This is true of Keats's 'Hyperion' poems. The scholar (if for the moment I may sustain a distinction which, though unreal, is convenient) can tell the critic that 'Hyperion' was included in the volume of Keats's poems published in 1820, and that 'The Fall of Hyperion' did not appear until some thirty-five years after the poet had died, but the relationship between them is not one that can be fruitfully discussed in bibliographical terms. It is a matter in which the literary critic may discuss, and even solve, problems that are more often the preserve of the textual critic.

There are also some works, including the subject of the present volume, which pose problems that are of equal importance to the textual and the literary critic, and which can be tackled only by their joint efforts. It is perhaps relevant that the current reinvestigations of the textual problems of *King Lear* come at a time in which Shakespeare critics have not only become increasingly aware of the need to write about plays as works to be performed, but have also become more alert than most of them once were to the need to allow for uncertainties in the texts which they study. It is an amateurish critic who writes of a Shakespeare play without knowing something about the state of its text: which words are suspected of corruption, which are emendations, which stage directions are editorial, which passages differ significantly in collateral texts, or are omitted from one or the other of them. We all know that there are important differences between, for example, the 'good' Quarto and Folio texts of *Hamlet*, *Othello*, and *Troilus and Cressida*. We know, too, that there are differences between the Quarto and Folio texts of *King Lear*, but we have been accustomed to believe that these texts can be reconciled to produce a composite version that we can read as Shakespeare's *King Lear*, even if we may have to tread warily from time to time before accepting the authority of particular readings.

Nevertheless, and although *King Lear* is widely regarded as the greatest tragedy written by the greatest dramatist of the post-classical world, and as one of the monuments of Western civilization, good critics have from time to time expressed serious dissatisfaction with it, and sometimes with aspects of it which relate to the conflation of the Quarto and Folio texts. A. C. Bradley found the play 'as a whole . . . imperfectly dramatic' and was greatly worried by what he regarded as its dramatic and structural defects.[1] Allardyce Nicoll, describing it as 'one of the finest and most comprehensive of Shakespeare's productions', was 'compelled to admit that in its function as a work of dramatic art it fails when compared with [*Hamlet*, *Othello*, and *Macbeth*] . . . and that it is not planned with that all-pervading subtlety which characterises those others'.[2] In 1957 Margaret Webster described *King Lear* as 'the least actable of the four' great tragedies because of its 'lack of this fundamental theatre economy'.[3] And more recently Maynard Mack has expressed dislike of Act Four, Scene Three (found only in the Quarto), in which 'Kent and a Gentleman . . . wrap Cordelia in a mantle of emblematic speech that is usually lost on a modern audience's ear and difficult for a modern actor to speak with conviction'.[4] Granville-Barker, too, had been critical of this scene, regarding it as 'a carpentered scene if ever there was one', which he 'could better believe that Shakespeare cut . . . than wrote'.[5] It is interesting that this man of letters who was also a man of the theatre should have anticipated much recent thought in his dissatisfaction with editorial conflation of the Quarto and Folio texts. He comments that 'the producer is confronted by the problem of the three hundred lines, or nearly, that the Quartos give and the Folio omits, and of the hundred given by the Folio and omitted from the Quartos. Editors, considering only, it would seem, that the more Shakespeare we get the better, bring practically the whole lot into the play we read. But a producer must ask himself whether these two versions do not come from different prompt books, and whether the Folio does not, in both cuts and additions, sometimes represent Shakespeare's own second thoughts. . . . Where Quarto and Folio offer alternatives, to adopt both versions may make for redundancy or confusion.'[6]

Since Granville-Barker wrote there have, of course, been advances in the textual study of Shakespeare which permit a clearer view of the situation than he was able to take, and it may be helpful at this point

to offer a sketch of the basic facts as they are seen at present, before
going on to discuss some of their implications.

Like most plays of the time, *King Lear* had been performed before it
appeared in print. It was entered in the Stationers' Register on 26
November 1607 as 'A booke called M[r] Willm̃ Shakespeare his historye
of Kinge Lear as yt was played before the Kinges Maiestie at
Whitehall vppon St Stephans night at Christmas Last by his Ma[ties]
seruantes playinge vsually at the globe on the Banksyde'.[7] The
statement does not, of course, imply that the performance before
James I was the first; rather is it a boast, designed for reproduction on
the title-page, that this is a work considered good enough for the
court. When the manuscript was put into print, someone was careful
enough to allow for the passage of time by altering the phrase 'at
Christmas Last' to 'in Christmas Hollidayes'. The resulting volume,
dated 1608 and printed for Nathaniel Butter, was 'to be sold at his
shop in *Pauls* Church-yard at the signe of the Pide Bull neere S[t.]
Austins Gate'. So it has come to be called by the picturesque label of
the 'Pied Bull quarto', mainly in order to distinguish it from another
quarto with a similar but not identical title-page, on which the imprint
reads simply 'Printed for *Nathaniel Butter*. 1608'. Until 1866 it was
not known which of these editions, both bearing the same date, was
printed first, but in that year the editors of the Cambridge edition,
W. G. Clark and W. Aldis Wright, demonstrated that the Pied Bull
quarto was the earlier, and between 1908 and 1910 W. W. Greg, A. W.
Pollard and others showed that the second edition, though dated
1608, was one of a group of plays printed by William Jaggard for
Thomas Pavier in 1619. The false date may be an attempt to
circumvent an order of 3 May 1619 forbidding unauthorized printing
of plays belonging to the King's Men.[8]
    The first quarto is, by general agreement, badly printed even by the
low standards normally applicable to Elizabethan and Jacobean play
quartos. Much of what is obviously verse is set out as prose; prose is
sometimes broken up as if it were verse; verse is often misaligned. The
punctuation is sketchy and often misleading. As P. W. K. Stone writes
in his detailed study *The Textual History of 'King Lear'* (1980),
'Questionable readings meet the eye on nearly every page, many of
them obviously wrong, and some of them egregious nonsense (e.g.
accent teares; *flechuent*; *Mobing, & Mohing*)' (p. 2). The degree to
which these faults reflect the nature and state of the manuscript from

which the Quarto was printed, rather than resulting from incompetence in the printing-house, is important. Are the obvious errors due to the printer's incompetence, to non-authorial corruption in the manuscript from which he was working, or to Shakespeare's own illegibility? Does the light and in many ways peculiar punctuation reflect Shakespeare's own practice or the inexperience of the printer Okes (who had never before printed a play) combined with his shortage of certain important types (full stops and colons, for instance); or might it stem from both causes?[9] Do a number of peculiar spellings reflect Shakespeare's own idiosyncrasies, or are they aural errors which might testify to unauthoritative transmission?

It is fair to warn the reader that statements about the quality of the Quarto text have often been coloured by views of its relationship to the Folio. Peter W. M. Blayney quotes a clear example of such fallacious reasoning from no less an authority than W. W. Greg, who wrote:

When, in the line:

> That iustly think'st, and hast most rightly said: [TLN 197]

the Quarto transposes the words 'iustly' and 'rightly', the blunder is perhaps not beyond the range of original sin latent in a copyist.[10]

As Blayney comments, 'Historically speaking, the Folio transposed the Quarto's words, and we cannot begin to suggest why it may have done so until we have decided on the nature of the text which it altered. Greg's tone shows that he has himself decided – but that decision does not appear to have been based on the evidence presented.'[11] Steven Urkowitz offers a similar instance from the same source:

Greg . . . claims that many speeches are misassigned in the Quarto (*First Folio*, p. 378). His prime example is 5.3.81, TLN 3026, where Regan, in the Folio, says, 'Let the Drum strike, and prove my title thine.' Greg argues that this 'appears absurdly perverted and misassigned in Q as '*Bast.* Let the drum strike, and prove my title good.' But there is nothing at all absurd about the Quarto's reading. Greg confuses readings that are merely different with those that are wrong.[12]

Reprints of the Quarto are accessible;[13] it is worth reading as a text in its own right. An exhaustive study of its press variants by W. W. Greg, based on a collation of the twelve surviving copies, concludes that 148 changes were made during the printing process, resulting in variant readings between one copy and another which show that the printers were not without some sense of responsibility, and which have the incidental advantage of providing clues to the process of transmission of later editions.[14]

There is no dispute that the second quarto reprints the first without recourse to the authority of an independent manuscript, though the printers tried to improve spelling, punctuation, and lineation. They also introduced many new substantive readings, some correcting obvious misprints, some aimed at improving the style, and a few attempting to emend difficult words and phrases. At the same time, new errors crept in.[15]

The title-page of each quarto labels the play as Shakespeare's '*True Chronicle Historie of the life and death of King Lear . . .*'. In the Folio of 1623, however, the play appears among the tragedies and is headed 'The Tragedie of King Lear'. The change in designation may or may not be significant. The Folio offers a far better-printed text, more regular and consistent in spelling and punctuation, more accurate in distinguishing between verse and prose, better in its alignment of verse, and fuller in its stage directions. It divides the play carefully into acts and scenes. (The Quarto's failure to do this is, of course, quite normal: there are no such divisions in any of the early quartos of Shakespeare's plays.) There are other, more important differences. The most striking is the presence of short passages amounting to more than 100 lines of text which are not in the Quarto. The Folio also lacks close on 300 lines which *are* in the Quarto; several speeches are differently assigned; and there are more than 850 verbal variants, some of them obviously the correct version of manifest errors in the Quarto, others offering an alternative sense. Again, the reader should be warned that views of the relative authority of the two substantive texts appear sometimes to have caused critics to regard as corrections what may more properly be looked upon simply as alternative versions. Some of the Folio variants affect not just what is spoken on stage, but the accompanying action. Although, in those passages where direct comparison is relevant, the Folio text is generally better printed than the Quarto, it has its own obvious 'errors and problematical readings, some echoing the mistakes of Q1, others diverging with doubtful accuracy, others again arising strangely where Q is manifestly correct'.[16]

From 1623, then, two basic texts were available to editors of *King Lear*. Each text could be reprinted independently, though a conscientious editor who knew both would inevitably draw on one in the attempt to correct manifest corruption in the other. It was also possible to conflate the two, introducing into one text some or all of the passages found only in the other. For a century after the publication of the First Folio, no conflation was attempted. The second quarto was reprinted in 1655. The Folio was reprinted three times, and in 1709 Nicholas Rowe, in what is, by our standards, the first edited text of the complete works, depended entirely on the Folio. Steven Urkowitz, in an essay printed in the following pages, traces the process by which the composite version established itself. Pope, in 1723, basing his text largely on Rowe's revised edition of 1714, made some additions from the Quarto and omitted a few lines found only in the Folio. Ten years later Theobald added to the additions, providing the version which, with minor variants, has been standard ever since. Although Theobald's text is based on the Folio, it is evident from his note on the play's final speech that he regards this as a theatre-derived text which might well display corruption. He writes 'This speech from the authority of the Old 4to is rightly plac'd to *Albany*: in the Edition by the players it is given to *Edgar*, by whom, I doubt not, it was of Custom spoken. And the Case was this: He who play'd *Edgar*, being a more favourite Actor, than he who personated *Albany*; in Spight of Decorum, it was thought proper he should have the last word.' We may be sure that Theobald knew no more than we do about the relative popularity of the original impersonators of Albany and Edgar, and that this is mere rationalization. Theobald's assumption is that the Quarto offers the more 'literary' text. On the so-called mock trial, not present in the Folio, he remarks that 'Mr *Pope* had begun to insert several Speeches in the mad way, in this Scene, from the Old Edition', and that he – Theobald – has 'ventur'd to replace several others, which stand upon the same Footing, and had an equal right of being restor'd'. Dr Johnson, as Urkowitz shows, was more respectful of the Folio's authority as being 'probably nearest to Shakespeare's last copy', even though he believed that revision was 'carelessly and hastily performed'; but Capell, whose edition appeared in 1767, reverted to Theobald's low view of the Folio, supposing Shakespeare quartos in general to derive from 'the Poet's own copies', however badly printed, and accusing the 'player editors' of the Folio of denigrating the quartos, and even of deliberately departing from them 'to give at once a greater currency to their own lame edition, and support the charge which they bring against the quarto's' (I, 10–11).

Though he found some evidence of Shakespearian revision in the Folio text, he blamed most of its omissions of lines found in the Quarto on compositors or editors. Edmond Malone, whose edition first appeared in 1790, adopted essentially the same position; nevertheless he included all the Folio-only lines. The practice of conflation had acquired the status of orthodoxy; but it had done so by a process of haphazard accretion over half a century, with no agreement on a textual theory which would satisfactorily explain the differences between the Quarto and the Folio texts.

It is fair to notice once again that the play represented by the composite text has not been regarded as entirely satisfactory, and that objections have been raised specifically to the grafting on to the Folio text of passages found only in the Quarto. Granville-Barker, whose comments I have quoted, had been anticipated most notably by the Victorian editor Charles Knight, who believed in the integrity of the Folio text while stating that Quarto-only passages should be preserved, 'upon the principle that not a line which appears to have been written by Shakespeare ought to be lost'; so his 'copy is literally that of the folio, except that where a passage occurs in the quartos which is not in the folio, we introduce such a passage, printing it, however, in brackets'.[17] Alfred Harbage followed a similar practice in his Pelican edition (1958). Other editors from time to time betrayed some concern with the question of whether the Folio represented Shakespeare's revision. So, in 1940, Kittredge wrote 'The differences between the Quarto and the Folio by no means warrant the theory that Shakespeare ever rewrote his *King Lear* or subjected it to a substantial revision';[18] and twenty years later, G. I. Duthie in the New Cambridge edition expressed a similar view: 'There is no basis for any theory of a Shakespearian revision separating Q1 and F (apart from whatever share Shakespeare may have had in the work of abridgment)' (p. 124).

Until recently, then, the general opinion has been that Shakespeare wrote one play about *King Lear*; that this play is imperfectly represented in both the Quarto and the Folio texts; that each of these texts contains genuinely Shakespearian passages which are missing from and should have been present in the other; that comparison of the variant readings of the two texts must form the most important basis for the correction of errors of transmission; and that conflation of the two texts, along with such correction, will bring us as close as we can hope to get to the lost archetype which each is supposed imperfectly to represent. This is the position to which the contributors to the present volume are opposed. To understand why, we need to look more closely at the question of the origins of the Quarto and Folio texts, and of the relationship of the one to the other.

I have said that the second quarto of *King Lear* is essentially a reprint of the first. It can, therefore, offer no independent information about the underlying manuscript. But such a reprint may affect the transmission of a text which draws also on a manuscript of independent authority. This has happened with *King Lear*. W. W. Greg, discerning influence of the first quarto on the Folio, believed that the Folio text was printed from a copy of the first quarto 'that had been brought into general though not complete conformity' with the (manuscript) prompt-book.[19] Other studies have demonstrated that the Folio text was influenced by the second quarto as well, and that this was the only printed text used in the setting-up of the Folio.[20] Gary Taylor argues, in this volume, that the specific influence of the first quarto identified by Greg came by way of the prompt-book – an argument which entails the interesting consequence that this manuscript postdates the publication of the first quarto, which itself postdated the play's earliest performances. It follows that a prompt-book influenced by the quarto cannot have been used for the original performances, but must have been the prompt-book of a revised text. This argument, only recently advanced, has not yet been subjected to scholarly scrutiny. But its logic, though ingenious, seems undeniable. In any case, there is no dispute that whatever printed copy was used for the Folio had been extensively annotated and supplemented by comparison with a manuscript different from that lying behind the original quarto. The influence of such a manuscript is most evident in the one hundred or so lines not present in the Quarto, but shows itself too in the many additional and variant stage directions, as well as at numerous points in the dialogue. So it is clear that, to a considerable degree, the Folio represents actual theatrical practice. This entails the possibility of theatrical corruption, on top of whatever other corruption or unnatural sophistication the text may have suffered in the course of its transmission into print. Stone (p. 127) believes that the alterations as a whole are not by Shakespeare but, possibly, by Massinger. Though this is an extreme position, it grows out of the traditional belief that Shakespeare could not have been responsible for any of the Folio omissions, or for some of its changes in stage directions and dialogue. Many of the essays in this volume directly address the problem of possible theatrical or transmissional corruption in the Folio; they challenge not only Stone's ascription of all the changes to a hand other than Shakespeare's, but also the conventional view that many changes derive from anonymous compositors, scribes, and actors rather than from Shakespeare himself.

However, the conventional view not only denies the authority of many individual Folio alternatives; it also, more systematically, denies the authority of the Quarto by claiming that it represents, in whole or in part, a memorial reconstruction. If this is true, it would be reasonable to argue that the manuscript behind it was a version of Shakespeare's *King Lear* which had been corrupted during the memorizing or reporting process. This would give far superior authority to the Folio's variants from the Quarto, even when the Quarto made sense. Yet this hypothesis has always been open to two major objections which have not been successfully resolved. First, the Quarto text clearly differs in important ways from the other texts generally regarded as 'bad' quartos. Secondly, if the Quarto has been influenced by memories of performance, and the Folio was printed from a prompt-book, why are they so different? As Greg wrote in 1955, 'Had there been a report of a stage performance it would almost certainly have given us a garbled version of F rather than anything resembling Q.'[21]

The alternative possibility is that the Quarto derives directly from a Shakespearian manuscript. The state of the text as printed suggests that if this was so the manuscript was not a prompt-book but one which, like those deduced to lie behind many other quartos – *Love's Labour's Lost, A Midsummer Night's Dream, Much Ado About Nothing, Hamlet* (1604–5), for instance – represented the play in a more-or-less final state of composition, before the author handed it over to his company of players. If this were so, the editor's position would be very different. In some ways, the Quarto's status would be raised. Those of its variants which make sense would have independent authority. But if they were not seen as corruptions of the text that lies behind the Folio, we should have to explain how it came about that equally intelligible variants found their way into the Folio text. The most obvious hypothesis would be that they represent a deliberate rewriting of the text printed in the Quarto. Whether the reviser was Shakespeare or someone else might be debated, but we should clearly be faced with two versions of the play, each consciously and distinctly fashioned, which it would be wrong to confuse. And we should be justified in an initial assumption that the Folio alterations were Shakespeare's own. As with all the other texts printed in the First Folio, the burden of proof rests upon those who wish to deny Shakespeare's authorship. We should thus have a first *King Lear* and a second one, as we have an 1805 *Prelude* and an 1850 *Prelude*. The first would be a text representing the play before it was acted. We should not know for certain whether this script had been put into production; it would be possible that Shakespeare's revisions, resulting essentially in the text as printed in the Folio, were made before the play reached the stage, and that the Quarto title-page's statement of performance referred to the revised state. Steven Urkowitz makes this assumption in his book (pp. 146–7). It seems inherently unlikely to me. If Shakespeare were revising before performance I should expect him to have used the papers of his earlier draft in the process, not to have released them (voluntarily or not) for publication. And Gary Taylor, in the second of his contributions to this volume, persuasively argues that the play did reach performance in its earlier version, that the revision was made on a copy of the Quarto that had been printed in 1608, and that it can be dated 1609–10.

The importance of the nature of the printer's copy for the Quarto makes it particularly regrettable that this has proved to be one of the most intransigent problems in textual scholarship. A. W. Pollard, in the first systematic study of good and bad quartos, published in 1909, counted *Lear* among the good quartos, and maintained this view later.[22] But in 1930 E. K. Chambers wrote 'I think that the characteristics of Q point to a reported text', and since then many scholars, including some of the most distinguished textual critics of this century, have laboured mightily in the attempt to solve the problem.[23] So far, no consensus has been achieved, and some even of those who, having worked intensively on the problem, have arrived at an hypothesis have later abandoned it. Thus W. W. Greg, in 1933, endorsed Chambers's view of the Quarto as a reported text, stating that 'If it is indeed a reported text it must have been taken down by shorthand'.[24] He repeated this opinion in 1942, though with less confidence: 'I cannot but conclude that some kind of shorthand was employed, however little I like the conclusion.'[25] In 1949 G. I. Duthie demonstrated to Greg's satisfaction that no contemporary system of shorthand could have been responsible for the Quarto text, and by 1955 Greg thought that 'any theory that Q is essentially a report of a stage performance, however obtained, has to meet objections as formidable in their way as the theory of revision'.[26]

Duthie had argued that the Quarto was still a reported text, made not from shorthand but from the memories of actors: in the Cambridge edition of 1961 he wrote that he had 'thought of the company as being in the provinces, temporarily deprived of its prompt-book, and desirous of producing a new one; and I imagined its personnel gathered round a scribe, each actor dictating his own speeches in a kind of performance without action' (p. 131). But by 1961 he had abandoned that theory in favour of a modified version of Alice Walker's hypothesis that the text had been arrived at by 'transcription from foul papers by dictation, the persons involved having had some memorial knowledge of the play' (Duthie, 1961, p. 135). Specifically, Dr Walker had suggested, somewhat tentatively, that the boys playing Goneril and Regan provided the manuscript and that 'the scenes in which both were on the stage are most heavily contaminated because their joint recollection of the matter enabled them to concoct the text without constant reference to the foul papers'.[27]

The manner in which opinion has fluctuated is illustrated by the fact that in one book published in 1980 Steven Urkowitz could write that the 'only two theories . . . now seriously considered as possible explanations for the derivation of the Quarto' were 'Alice Walker's proposal that the Quarto is printed from a surreptitiously made copy of Shakespeare's foul papers' and 'the theory that it was derived from his foul papers' in a confused state (pp. 8–9), yet in the same year P. W. K. Stone, in his long and ambitious study, produced yet another version of the reported-text theory, claiming that 'It cannot but be concluded, upon any thorough examination of the evidence, that the text of Q1 derives from a theatrical report', and postulating a reporter who wrote out the play in longhand after 'attending repeated performances of the play, acquiring more of the text on each occasion until, presumably, he judged it complete, or as nearly so as he could make it' (p. 35).

The alternative theory, that the Quarto derives from Shakespeare's foul papers, received a notable statement in 1931, in an intensive study by Madeleine Doran; in *The Text of 'King Lear'* (Stanford), she argued that the Quarto was printed from Shakespeare's autograph, a manuscript already confused and illegible from much correction and alteration, and thrown aside as worthless when, as a result of a further thorough revision, the play had taken final shape in the prompt-book. In 1941, however, Miss Doran expressed doubts about her position, though she has continued to maintain that 'the text of Q . . . must represent an earlier form of the play than the Folio'.[29] Alice Walker's theory, already mentioned, is an ingenious attempt to combine the 'reported-text' theory with the 'foul-papers' theory. More recently, there has been support for a return to Miss Doran's original position. G. K. Hunter writes that 'in the main it [Q] gives the impression of being quite closely derived from an authoritative original' while giving qualified assent to Alice Walker's theory to account for 'the film of corruption' which keeps the Quarto 'from being satisfactory'.[30] Urkowitz, arguing against Greg's and Alice Walker's interpretations of the evidence, uses Miss Doran's hypothesis to 'justify a working presumption that the Quarto text is at least an approximation of Shakespeare's draft of the play before it was adapted for the stage' (p. 11). Peter W. M. Blayney, in the prospectus to his two-volume study *The Texts of 'King Lear' and Their Origins*, concludes that copy for the Quarto 'was a much altered autograph manuscript containing the "unpolished" but probably near-final text of a play differing in some important respects from the play as we know it'. Blayney's study is announced by the publishers as 'without exception, the most exhaustive bibliographical investigation of a Shakespeare Quarto ever to have been attempted'. Certainly the first volume, *Nicholas Okes and the First Quarto* (1982), in itself represents a unique and valuable account of the printing of the Quarto of *King Lear* and, more generally, of the working methods of a Jacobean printer. The publication of Blayney's second volume, which will directly address the problem of the printer's copy for the Quarto, and its relationship to the Folio, must be awaited with the keenest interest. But already, even in advance of the publication and assessment of Blayney's evidence, it is fair to claim that those who regard the Quarto as a reported text have, by their own admission, not yet offered a satisfactory explanation of how such a report came into being; that Urkowitz has persuasively challenged much of the supposed evidence for that position; and that several essays in this volume contribute new arguments and evidence to support the hypothesis that the Quarto derives directly from a holograph manuscript.

Even if their arguments are not accepted, so long as the problem remains open there is no logical obstacle to pursuing the hypothesis that the differences between the Quarto and the Folio arise because the Folio represents Shakespeare's revision of the text printed in the Quarto. Essentially this is not a new position. It resembles that stated by Granville-Barker which I have already quoted. It is adumbrated by E. A. J. Honigmann in *The Stability of Shakespeare's Text* (1965), when he remarks that if Alice Walker and Duthie are right in proposing 'that Q, though contaminated by knowledge of the play as performed, goes back not to the prompt-book but to a copy taken by dictation from Shakespeare's foul papers . . . some QF variants could . . . represent first and second thoughts' (p. 121). But the 'revision' theory was not seriously pursued in public until 1976, when Michael Warren delivered to the International Shakespeare Congress in Washington a paper, 'Quarto and Folio *King Lear* and the Interpretation of Albany and Edgar', which has proved to be of seminal importance.[31] It is worth quoting at some length the assumptions upon which he works, because they are those of all the contributors to the present volume. He writes 'that in a situation where statements about textual status are never more than hypotheses based upon the current models of thought about textual recension, it is not demonstrably erroneous to work with the possibility (a) that there may be no single "ideal play" of *King Lear* (all of "what Shakespeare wrote"), that there may never have been one, and that what we create by conflating both texts is merely an invention of editors and scholars; (b) that for all its problems Q is an authoritative version of the play of *King Lear*; and (c) that F may indeed be a revised version of the play, that its additions and omissions may constitute Shakespeare's considered modification of the earlier text, and that we certainly cannot know that they are not' (pp. 96–7). Most of Warren's essay consists of an examination of the differences in characterization of Albany and Edgar which, he claims, 'go beyond those which may be expected when two texts descend in corrupted form from a common original; they indicate that a substantial and consistent recasting of certain aspects of the play has taken place' (p. 99). He precedes this with an example of variant dialogue which it will be useful to cite here as an illustration of the problem.

In Q, it reads thus:

> *Lear.* No.   *Kent.* Yes.
> *Lear,* No I fay,   *Kent.* I fay yea.
> *Lear.* No no,they would not.   *Kent,* Yes they haue.
> *Lear.* By *Iupiter* I fweare no;they durft not do't,

(E3ᵛ)

In F, thus:

> *Lear.* No.
> *Kent.* Yes.
> *Lear.* No I fay.
> *Kent.* I fay yea.
> *Lear.* By *Iupiter* I fweare no.
> *Kent.* By *Iuno*, I fweare I.
> *Lear.* They durft not do't:

(TLN 1291–7)

Normal editorial procedure is to conflate, so that the dialogue then runs:

> *Lear.* No.
> *Kent.* Yes.
> *Lear.* No, I say.
> *Kent.* I say, yea.
> Q { *Lear.* No no, they would not.
>   { *Kent.* Yes, they have.
> *Lear.* By Jupiter, I swear no.
> F { *Kent.* By Juno, I swear ay.
> *Lear.*   They durst not do't . . .

(2.4.15–22)

Indisputably this produces, as Warren says (p. 98), 'a reading that has *no* authority'. If the Folio simply included words not in the Quarto the theory of a lost archetype would be tenable: reporters might easily omit such speeches. But the fact that the Folio also lacks words that *are* in the Quarto would suppose coincidentally independent omissions in both texts, or invention by the alleged Quarto reporters in a passage that did not require it, and this, though not impossible, is inherently less likely. Another example of the same problem occurs early in Act Three, Scene Six. The Quarto reads:

> *Foole.* Prithe Nunckle tell me, whether a mad man be a Gentleman or a Yeoman.
> *Lear.* A King, a King, to haue a thoufand with red burning fpits come hifzing in vpon them.
> *Edg.* The foule fiend bites my backe,
> *Foole.* He's mad, that trufts in the tamenes of a Wolfe, a horfes health, a boyes loue, or a whores oath.

(G3ᵛ)

In the Folio this is changed to:

> *Foole.* Prythee Nunkie tell me, whether a madman be
> a Gentleman, or a Yeoman.
> *Lear.* A King, a King.
> *Foole.* No, he's a Yeoman, that ha's a Gentleman to
> his Sonne : for hee's a mad Yeoman that sees his Sonne a
> Gentleman before him.
> *Lear.* To haue a thoufand with red burning fpits
> Come hizzing in vpon 'em.
> *Edg.* Bleffe thy fiue wits.

(TLN 2007–14)

The Quarto is coherent in itself. Lear does not offer a direct answer to
the Fool's question so, after Edgar's marginal interjection, the Fool
answers it himself. The Folio alters this so that the Fool picks up
directly on the King's indirect answer, but omits the Fool's illustrations of mad behaviour. Conflation results in the following:

> *Fool.* Prithee, nuncle, tell me whether a madman be a gentleman or a
> yeoman?
> *Lear.* A king, a king!
> *Fool.* No, he's a yeoman that has a gentleman to his son; for he's a mad
> yeoman that sees his son a gentleman before him.
> *Lear.* To have a thousand with red burning spits
> Come hizzing in upon 'em—
> *Edgar.* The foul fiend bites my back.
> *Fool.* He's mad that trusts in the tameness of a wolf, a horse's health, a
> boy's love, or a whore's oath.

(3.6.9–19)

This offers no motivation for the Fool's second statement, which is
rendered redundant by the fact that he has already responded to the
King's answer. In the absence of certainty that the Quarto is a
reported text it is more in accordance with genuine conservatism of
editorial principle to print one or the other version of both these
passages than to create a passage of dialogue which there is no
evidence that Shakespeare ever wrote.

When Warren's paper appeared in print he remarked in a footnote
(p. 95) that as a consequence of delivering it he had learnt that three

other scholars – Georgia Peters Burton, Steven Urkowitz, and Peter W. M. Blayney – were working on 'dissertations arguing for the distinction of the Quarto and Folio texts', and that each had 'arrived at the same major conclusion independently of the others'. Clearly a *zeitgeist* was at work, and it has manifested itself with increasing liveliness and substantiality in the years since 1976. In 1980 at the Cambridge, Massachusetts, meeting of the Shakespeare Association of America the issue was keenly debated during a seminar chaired by G. Blakemore Evans. One of the papers presented was Gary Taylor's 'The War in *King Lear*', later published in *Shakespeare Survey 33* (Cambridge, 1980), which demonstrates that the two texts 'present coherent but distinct accounts' of the military actions of the fourth and fifth acts. It provides an excellent introduction to the critical implications of the debate by illustrating within a short space that conflation muddies our understanding of Shakespeare's artistry and that textual disentangling must increase our respect for it. Later in the same year Steven Urkowitz's dissertation, to which Michael Warren had referred, was published in revised form as *Shakespeare's Revision of 'King Lear'*. Although Urkowitz does not offer a systematic and comprehensive discussion of variants, he tilts vigorously against Greg's and Alice Walker's arguments that the Quarto was not set entirely from author's papers. He offers a spirited defence of the Folio version as a revision which is also, theatrically, a great improvement on the Quarto text. Though not everyone has been persuaded,[32] George Walton Williams, reviewing the book in *Shakespeare Survey 35*, writes: 'The logic of Urkowitz's thesis is undeniable. It is impossible to disagree with his basic premise that there are two texts, that the effects in each are distinguishable, and that "the script of *King Lear* . . . in the Folio is Shakespeare's final version" (p. 147); the corollary is abundantly clear: "The modern composite version diminishes the intensity of the action . . . , confuses the plot line . . . , makes trivial the relationship [between characters] . . . , and blurs the delicately indicated expectations" (p. 78).'[33] In short, 'this is not *Lear*'.

As the published work of Warren, Urkowitz, Blayney and Taylor is supplemented by additional studies – including those collected in this volume, and those forthcoming from Blayney – the shift in attitude to *King Lear* which is already apparent is bound to become more general and to take various forms. Past criticism based upon the composite text will not, of course, be generally invalidated, but it will need to be read with some caution, especially when it concerns the plays' scenic structure and episodes not included in the Folio. Future criticism must acknowledge the existence of two authoritative texts. It need not be primarily comparative, but when it is not it will have to base itself upon one or the other – though, as with other plays, responsible literary criticism will take account of textual variants or uncertainties which might affect its argument.

Opinion about the relative merits of the two texts will vary, for agreement does not entail endorsement of the superiority of the revised text. Some readers may prefer the earlier version just as most readers prefer the earlier version of *The Prelude*; but they will find it hard to deny that the second, Folio *King Lear* gives us Shakespeare's later thoughts, just as readers of Wordsworth must agree that, however misguidedly, the author preferred the 1850 version of *The Prelude*. So far, most of those who have studied the two versions of *King Lear* in detail are agreed that the later is the better play, even though it omits admired passages from the earlier version.

The work of the critics will wait to some degree on that of the editors. New editions must be prepared – are, indeed, already in preparation – attempting to restore each text to an authentic, independent state. It will not be easy, for many individual variants will be disputed. But this is no new situation. It is true already of – to name only the most conspicuous examples—*Richard III, Hamlet, Troilus and Cressida, Othello*, and indeed *King Lear*, for editors presenting a composite text differ in the respective authority they allow to the primary sources of evidence for variants in passages common to both texts. In some ways, indeed, editors will find it an advantage to be required to make sense of each text in its own terms rather than to bring a conflation into conformity with a non-existent, hypothetical ideal.

Among those who accept that the Folio is a revised text – and who thus align themselves with no more revolutionary a figure than Granville-Barker – heart-searchings may be felt about the Quarto passages omitted in the Folio. A text based upon the belief that the revisions in the Folio are Shakespeare's, and in particular that its omissions from the Quarto were not, as has often been supposed, forced upon the author by vulgar theatrical exigencies – length, censorship, theatrical practicality – would deprive us of such passages, admired by many, as the Gentleman's description of

Cordelia's grief at her father's plight ('her smiles and teares, | Were like a better way . . .'), the compassion of Gloucester's servants after his blinding (which Peter Brook was castigated for omitting from his 1962 production), and Lear's mock trial of Goneril and Regan. But these passages would not be lost for ever. They could still be read – and acted – where they belong, and where, it may be argued, they make their fullest and most proper impact, in the Quarto text, properly edited in its own right. This text, indeed, may be the more attractive to those who like their Shakespeare as close as possible to the point of conception – and, on the evidence of recent editions, this includes a number of his editors. For this reason, it seems proper that editions of the complete works should include both texts. The two works may then be independently enjoyed, just as music-lovers may enjoy both the original and the revised version of Bach's *Magnificat* or (to take a more Shakespearian example) Tchaikovsky's *Romeo and Juliet*, recently recorded in an earlier and substantially different form from that which we know and love. If the play is to be presented for reading in a single text then, on the principle that an editor should seek to represent his author's final thoughts, it should be in a text based on the Folio, though it would seem proper for the editor to make the more substantial Quarto-only passages available in notes or appendices, since there is no reason to doubt that they are by Shakespeare. It would not, however, be fair to the reader to include them within the text, even within square brackets (as Harbage does) and even if the text otherwise were Folio-based; for this would represent an implicit subversion of the Folio's integrity. An analogy is presented by a very different play, Oscar Wilde's *The Importance of Being Earnest*; Russell Jackson, basing his text on the edition of 1899 prepared by Wilde himself, adds as appendices three substantial episodes which Wilde wrote but did not finally include (New Mermaids edition, 1980).

We must also hope that the new attitudes will be represented in theatre practice. It would probably be over-optimistic to expect professional directors to give us either the Quarto or the Folio text uncut, but it would be perfectly easy for a director to base his production on one or the other text, not admitting any degree of conflation. And it would be especially valuable to have such a production based on the Folio as a way of testing, in the only way that is ultimately valid, the belief that the revisions are theatrically justified, and that *King Lear* is a better drama in its later state.[34] A director who took this course would be following Granville-Barker's recommendation: 'On the whole then – and if he show a courageous discretion – I recommend a producer to found himself on the Folio. For that it does show some at least of Shakespeare's own reshapings I feel sure' (p. 332).

Those of us who have lived long with the traditionally conflated text of *King Lear* are likely to experience a subconscious resistance to what may appear to be a disintegrationist movement. Acceptance of its implications requires a mental adjustment that may prove painful. But we must, if we really care about what Shakespeare wrote, ask ourselves whether our resistance is logical or whether it proceeds, perhaps, from mental inertia, from mere dislike of change. Even in writing these paragraphs I have found that my natural tendency was to write of reversion to the Folio text as involving the 'omission' of passages found only in the Quarto, whereas the truth is that we have good reason to believe that they were never there. The case, it seems to me, is established. The Quarto and Folio texts of *King Lear* are distinct. There is no valid evidence that they derive from a single, lost archetype. The burden of proof rests not upon those who would keep the two texts asunder but upon those who would merge them into one. If those who support the eighteenth-century practice of conflation can prove that the Quarto and Folio texts are based upon a lost archetype, then a composite text is what we should read. But just as those who wish to emend a single word must first establish that the original requires emendation, so those who wish to produce an editorial conflation of *King Lear* must first demonstrate that both of the original documents seriously misrepresent Shakespeare's intentions. Until then the proper, conservative scholarly procedure is to suppose that the Quarto gives us Shakespeare's first thoughts and the Folio the text in its revised state. The matter of whether any of the Folio's revisions are not by Shakespeare may remain a topic for debate. Debate is likely to continue, too, about the merits of the revisions and about their philosophical implications. The process of investigation will disturb our reactions towards a greatly loved masterpiece; but it may vindicate the plays against some of the adverse criticisms based on the conflated text which I have cited. To split asunder the two texts of *King Lear* is a work of restoration, not of destruction. We shall lose by it no more than a wraith born of an unholy union; we shall gain a pair of legitimate – though not identical – twins.

NOTES

1. *Shakespearean Tragedy* (1904), p. 247.
2. *Studies in Shakespeare* (1927), p. 138.
3. *Shakespeare Today* (1957), p. 214.
4. *'King Lear' in Our Time* (Berkeley and Los Angeles, 1965), p. 9.
5. *Prefaces to Shakespeare* (1927; two-volume edition, 1958), I, 332.
6. *Prefaces to Shakespeare*, I, 328–9.
7. From the photographic facsimile in S. Schoenbaum, *William Shakespeare: Records and Images* (1981), p. 218.
8. The facts are summarized by E. K. Chambers, *William Shakespeare: A Study of Facts and Problems*, 2 vols. (Oxford, 1930), I, 133–7.
9. Peter W. M. Blayney establishes that *Lear* was Okes's first play in *The Texts of 'King Lear' and their Origins*, 2 vols. (Cambridge), I (1982), pp. 10, 129. Information on Okes's punctuation is from Blayney's 'Shakespeare's Punctuation: a Study in Pointlessness', a paper given to a New Cambridge Shakespeare conference at the University of York, 5 April 1978. (Peter Alexander, in an unpublished paper dating from the 1950s, argued that the punctuation of Q resembles that of the Shakespearian 'good' quartos: see Kenneth Muir's new Arden edition (1952; rev. 1972), p. xvii, n. 2.)
10. 'The Function of Bibliography in Literary Criticism Illustrated in a Study of the Text of *King Lear*' [1933], in *The Collected Papers of Sir Walter W. Greg*, ed. J. C. Maxwell (Oxford, 1966), p. 287.
11. *Origins*, I, 7.
12. *Shakespeare's Revision of 'King Lear'* (Princeton, 1980), p. 131.
13. See Preface, pp. viii–ix.
14. *The Variants in the First Quarto of 'King Lear': A Bibliographical and Critical Inquiry* (1940); now supplemented by Blayney, *Origins*, I, pp. 207–57, 592–7.
15. See, for example, Stone, *Textual History*, p. 5.
16. Stone, *Textual History*, p. 6.
17. *The Pictorial Edition of the Works of Shakespeare*, ed. Charles Knight, 8 vols., [1839–] 1843, VI, 392.
18. *King Lear*, The Kittredge Shakespeares (Boston, 1940), p. viii.
19. *The Editorial Problem in Shakespeare* (Oxford, 1942; third edition, 1954), p. 100.
20. Gary Taylor, 'Folio Copy for *Hamlet, King Lear*, and *Othello*', *Shakespeare Quarterly*, 34 (1983), 44–61.
21. *The Shakespeare First Folio: Its Bibliographical and Textual History* (Oxford, 1955), p. 381.
22. *Shakespeare Folios and Quartos* (1909), p. 76; *Shakespeare's Fight with the Pirates* (Cambridge, 1920), pp. 50–1.
23. *William Shakespeare*, I, 465.
24. 'The Function of Bibliography', p. 289.
25. *Editorial Problem*, p. 96.
26. G. I. Duthie, *Elizabethan Shorthand and the First Quarto of 'King Lear'* (Oxford, 1949); W. W. Greg, *The Shakespeare First Folio*, p. 381.
27. *Textual Problems of the First Folio* (Cambridge, 1953), p. 49.
28. Greg's summary: *Editorial Problem*, p. 89.
29. See Urkowitz, *Revision*, p. 11.
30. New Penguin Shakespeare edition (Harmondsworth, 1972), pp. 314–15.
31. In *Shakespeare, Pattern of Excelling Nature*, ed. David Bevington and Jay L. Halio (Newark and London, 1978), pp. 95–107.
32. See the reviews of Urkowitz's book by Philip Edwards (*Modern Language Review*, 77 (1982), 694–8) and by Richard Knowles (*Modern Philology*, 79 (1981), 197–200). On the other hand, E. A. J. Honigmann (among others) accepts Urkowitz's

thesis and argues for Shakespeare as the reviser: see 'Shakespeare's Revised Plays: *King Lear* and *Othello*', *The Library*, VI, 4 (1982), 142–73.

33. 'The Year's Contributions to Shakespearian Study, 3: Textual Studies', p. 180.
34. Since this essay was written a semi-professional production of the unedited Folio text has taken place in Santa Cruz, California. Playing in July and August 1982, it was directed by Audrey Stanley, with Tony Church as Lear and Julian Curry as the Fool.

The Base Shall to th' Legitimate
The Growth of an Editorial Tradition

STEVEN URKOWITZ

WE all learned our *King Lear*s from edited texts which we believed trustworthy, believed trustworthy long before we knew anything about textual criticism, long before our teachers directed us toward bibliographical discussions of the *Lear* problem. Our teachers, in turn, also learned from texts edited in the same tradition; and so did the editors who have prepared the generations of modern printings of this play. Shakespeare's *King Lear* was not a questionable construct. It was there, open for analysis and discussion.

But our modern texts descend from printed versions of *King Lear*, the 1608 Quarto and the 1623 Folio, which give surprisingly different readings for many speeches and stage actions. Because almost all editors over the last two hundred years have believed that the Quarto and the Folio themselves descend from a single, 'authorial' antecedent of the two earliest printed texts, our modern editions blend the two into a third, or actually into a multiplicity of descendant-third versions. The fundamental premise of a lost original justifying this traditional practice of conflation is at once so simple and so unquestioningly accepted that it is rarely examined and almost never thoroughly analysed in modern editions.

An alternative to this premise – one which explores the possibility that Shakespeare composed *Lear* in stages, an earlier draft represented in the Quarto followed by a revision reproduced in the Folio – has been suggested intermittently since the eighteenth century. Unlike the single-antecedent premise, this alternative has had little observable consequence in printed editions, in literary criticism, or in stage productions. In recent years, however, Shakespearian revision as the source of variants in the two early texts has been argued with increasing frequency.

The fundamental premise of a single antecedent text for *King Lear* may perhaps prove valid. Many old and new arguments in favour of and in opposition to it should be advanced and tested. But the very familiarity, the virtual universality, of texts based on the single-antecedent premise has, until recently, inadvertently closed off any discussion of its suitability, or any consideration of alternative treatments of the texts of *King Lear*. If we are to gain some perspective on our familiar texts so that we may with fresh insight judge both them and the Quarto and Folio from which they derive, we must first re-examine the editorial tradition leading to the modern *King Lear* to understand how we arrived where we are. That tradition began and grew in the successive editions printed in the eighteenth century.

After 1623 the Folio text of *King Lear* was reprinted – with minor compositorial errors, omissions, changes in lineation, spelling, and punctuation – in successive Folio editions of 1632, 1663, and 1685. The Quarto text was reprinted in 1619 and again in 1655, with the same kinds of small textual differences.

Our earliest example of textual work on the *Lear* problem after the Quarto and Folio is found in the handwritten collations of material from the Quarto on pages of a Third Folio which may have been prepared as a prompt-book for Dublin's Smock Alley Theatre in the 1670s. The job of collation is incomplete, diminishing and finally ceasing altogether towards the end of the play, but it is clear that the collator knew he had two versions of *King Lear* to reconcile. 'To loue my father all' (B2; 1.1.104), a half-line found only in the Quarto, is written into its corresponding place on the Folio page, and the Folio's 'pray you let vs sit together' (TLN 328; 1.1.303–4) is altered to include the Quarto's 'hit' (C1) in place of the Folio's 'sit'. Showing the same awareness of the two texts, Nahum Tate painstakingly collates Quarto and Folio lines for those parts of his 1681 adaptation of *King Lear* which are closely derived from Shakespeare's play.[1] For example, where the Quarto has a line reading 'They traueled hard to night, meare Iustice' (E4; 2.4.89), and the Folio reads 'They haue trauail'd all the night? meere fetches' (TLN 1363), Tate patches the two together and prints 'They have travelled hard to Night——meer fetches'. Of course today we think of Tate's wholesale rewriting as an antique perversity, but he confesses openly that he is cutting an old author's fabric to fit the patterns of a new fashion. Shakespeare's editors in the eighteenth century, however, will insist that they are reclaiming the 'originals' when they impose, through conflation and radical emendation, their own new readings.

Nicholas Rowe edited the first collected works of Shakespeare to break from the seventeenth-century folio format.[2] A successful poet and playwright, Rowe was no textual scholar. His edition follows only the 1685 Folio text, but his editorial credo and practice depart sharply from those underlying the Folios.[3] Rowe promises to adopt for Shakespeare's texts the time-honoured methods of textual scholarship: 'I have taken some Care to redeem him [Shakespeare] from the Injuries of former Impressions. I must not pretend to have restor'd this Work to the Exactness of the Author's Original Manuscripts: Those are lost, or, at least, are gone beyond any Inquiry I could make; so that there was nothing left, but to compare the several Editions, and give the true Reading as well as I could from thence' (I, A2–A2ᵛ).

Rowe assumes that only a singular 'true Reading' could exactly reflect the lost 'Author's Original', a unique composition in a singular text. Although the methods of recovering true readings from badly-transmitted originals are well suited to texts for which there was only a single original, the same methods are extraordinarily unreliable when applied to variant texts produced by a revising author. But since Rowe works only from the Folio version of *King Lear*, he has no problems with an embarrassment of rich and contradictory textual variants.

The next editor, Alexander Pope, begins the analysis of Quarto and Folio alternatives. Pope argues that the vision of Shakespeare writing flawless copy in a single draft is only a mirage: '. . . it was thought a praise to *Shakespear*, that he scarce ever *blotted a line*. This they [his fellow actors] industriously propagated, . . . there never was a more groundless report, or to the contrary of which there are more undeniable evidences. As, the Comedy of the *Merry Wives* of *Windsor*, which he entirely new writ; the *History of* Henry *the 6th*, which was first published under the Title of the *Contention of* York *and* Lancaster; and that of *Henry the 5th*, extreamly improved.'[4] Pope believes that many variants in plays such as *King Lear* represent 'The Alterations or Additions which *Shakespear* himself made' (I, xxii), but many corrupt 'trifling and bombast passages' as well were inserted in all texts by the actors (I, xvi–xvii).

In the variants between the Quarto and Folio of *Lear*, Pope most often concludes that what he regards as a corruption occurred when the script was brought into the theatre. It may be that Pope's feelings about theatrical degradation of a play come from the fluent changes and adaptations practised by his contemporaries in their theatres. In any case, textual variants in Shakespeare's plays lead Pope to declare that in the Renaissance theatres 'many speeches also were put into the mouths of wrong persons, where the Author now seems chargeable with making them speak out of character: Or sometimes perhaps for no better reason, than that a governing Player, to have the mouthing of some favourite speech himself, would snatch it from the unworthy lips of an Underling' (I, xix). With this feral image of actors at work Pope begins an anti-theatrical bias still potent even among some contemporary editors of Shakespeare's plays. He lists the kinds of 'low and vicious parts and passages' brought into the early printed texts: 'arbitrary Additions, Expunctions, Transpositions of scenes and lines, confusion of Characters and Persons, wrong application of Speeches, corruptions of innumerable Passages by the Ignorance, and wrong Corrections of 'em again by the Impertinence, of his first Editors', especially Heminges and Condell (I, xxi).

Pope also suggests that Shakespeare's poetic artistry suffered from his association with the theatre. 'Players are just such judges of what is *right*, as Taylors are of what is *graceful*. And in this view it will be but fair to allow, that most of our Author's faults are less to be ascribed to his wrong judgment as a Poet, than to his right judgment as a Player' (I, vii–viii). Shakespeare's flaws as a dramatic poet arise from his excellence as an actor. Players, like tailors, are in Pope's estimation only the tradesmen of taste or 'right judgment', not the inventors or arbiters of art like poets or true critics. Shakespeare himself admits as much in Sonnet 111 where he bewails the 'publick manners' he has learned by having to provide for his living through 'publick meanes'. Because Shakespeare's poetic judgement is almost 'subdu'd | To what it workes in, like the Dyers hand', proper judgement between alternative authorial readings or between an authoritative reading and a proposed emendation should not rely on the taste of the poet-player Shakespeare, but rather upon that of the poet-critic, Pope. Faced with contrary Quarto and Folio readings in *King Lear*, Pope will himself decide which is the better. And he will be free to invent new readings, creatively 'improving' the text without regard to the careful principles of emendation which are derived from analysis of the process of textual transmission. In one passage from *King Lear*, for example, 3.1.17–42 (F3^v; TLN 1626–38), Pope freely adjusts words and rhythms of the Quarto and Folio to suit his taste: 'be' becomes 'is', 'cunning' is changed to 'craft', 'secret feet' appears as 'secret sea', and 'bemadding' is reduced to 'madding'. 'And from some knowledge and assurance, | Offer this office to you' reappears in

Pope's text as 'And from some knowledge and assurance of you, |
Offer this office'.

The Folio remains Pope's basic text; but although he includes only
about half the lines unique to the Quarto, at many points he finds the
1608 text superior to the Folio. Like the collator of the Smock Alley
prompt-book, Pope sees that in the opening scene the Quarto has a
half-line not in the Folio at the end of a speech for Cordelia:

> Happely when I shall wed, that Lord whose hand
> Must take my plight, shall cary halfe my loue with him,
> Halfe my care and duty, sure I shall neuer
> Mary like my sisters, *to loue my father all.*
> (B2; TLN 107–10; 1.1.100–4: words in italics appear
> only in the Quarto)

Pope incorporates the half-line from the Quarto into his text, noting
'*These words restor'd from the first edition, without which the sense was
not compleat.*' But the Folio here is as complete as the Quarto, and as
sensible. It is shorter, more declarative and (arguably) less redundant
than the Quarto, but it is not demonstrably inferior, as Pope asserts.

For longer passages found only in the Quarto Pope appeals to
narrative 'necessity', poetic beauty, and Shakespearian authenticity
as justifications for their inclusion. All of 4.3 enters Pope's text from
the Quarto because it is '*manifestly of* Shakespear's *writing, and
necessary to continue the story of* Cordelia, *whose behaviour here is most
beautifully painted.*' In his desire to give readers all that Shakespeare
wrote, Pope fails to consider that Shakespeare also may have cut this
scene and other significant passages missing in the Folio. Pope's
claim for the scene's authenticity is valid, but that 4.3 is '*necessary to
continue the story of* Cordelia' must be proved rather than simply
declared. Cordelia's immediate appearance onstage, the alternative
found in the Folio, may be a *better* continuation of Cordelia's story
than the report of her behaviour in 4.3, however beautiful the report
may be.[5]

Pope had good justification for printing this and other passages
unique to the Quarto.[6] They had not been reprinted since the 1655
Quarto, they display the dramatic and poetic fluency and style we
associate only with Shakespeare, and they should be made available
to readers and actors. The question is: do they belong in the Folio
version of *King Lear*, or should they instead only be included in an
edition of the Quarto text? Pope never explicitly considers the second

possibility; implicitly he rejects it, in claiming that certain passages absent from the Folio are 'necessary' to it. But, though he speaks of necessity, Pope in fact seems to include lines for their poetic appeal, without regard to dramatic alternatives or theatrical consequences. Pope is the first editor to grapple with the major textual crux at 3.1.17–42, problematic lines that still exercise critics today. In both the Quarto and the Folio Kent is telling a Gentleman about political discord between Albany and Cornwall: 'There is diuision | (Although as yet the face of it is couer'd | With mutuall cunning) 'twixt Albany, and Cornwall' (TLN 1628–30; F3ᵛ). In the Quarto only, Kent goes on to reveal that a French power is coming to England, and he asks the Gentleman to report the king's suffering to friends gathering in Dover. In the Folio, however, Kent instead goes on to talk about spies who are reporting news of this discord to France, but he is prevented from continuing when the Gentleman cuts him off abruptly in mid-sentence. Both versions yield satisfying dramatic action. Pope prints the version from the Quarto in his text with the lines unique to the Folio in a footnote. He chooses the Quarto because its lines *'seem necessary to the plot, as preparatory to the arrival of the* French *army with* Cordelia *in Act* 4. . . . *The lines which have been put in their room* [*in the Folio*] *are unintelligible, and to no purpose.*' But the lines in the Quarto are *not* 'necessary', at least not for any reason here given by Pope: the army supporting King Lear is mentioned prior to Act Four at other points in the play aside from this passage. And the lines from the Folio *are* intelligible. They form part of an 'interrupted speech', a disjointed rhetorical figure commonly found in dramatic scripts. (Interrupted speeches are often mistaken for errors by editors more comfortable with the regularities of non-dramatic verse.)

On other occasions Pope seems to fear that some of his editorial decisions may be supported by neither taste nor reason. He rather diffidently includes only nine of the fourteen speeches from the mad trial of Goneril and Regan which appears only in the Quarto version (G3ᵛ–G4; 3.6.16–56): '*There follow in the old edition several speeches in the mad way, which probably were left out by the players, or by* Shakespear *himself. I shall however insert them here, and leave 'em to the reader's mercy.*' In the Quarto this mock court and two later passages of gentle reflection about the king spoken by Kent and Edgar provide a momentary relaxation of dramatic tension. The Folio text, with cuts and revisions, instead accelerates the tempo.[7]

Pope, and every later editor who conflates the two texts here, fails to see that we have two equally valid and alternative designs for staged action.

After Pope few editors doubt that their primary function is to assemble a single 'more Shakespearian' *King Lear* from Quarto and Folio pieces. Later editors will collate more carefully, emend more judiciously and conflate more consistently than Pope, but they will work at essentially the same task.

Lewis Theobald, whose edition of Shakespeare's works in 1733 follows Pope's, was a thoroughly competent editor of classical texts.[8] He was also, in many respects, a good editor of Shakespeare—most of whose works survive in only one substantive edition, in which as a consequence issues of revision seldom arise. Theobald's attitude toward Shakespearian two-text plays may derive from his classical editing, or from his own commercial experience writing and adapting plays for the eighteenth-century English stage; certainly, neither of these influences can have equipped him to cope with the radically different problems of Shakespeare's text and stage. Theobald does grant the playwright's life in the theatre a more benign influence on his art than Pope allows: 'his Employment, as a *Player*, gave him an Advantage and Habit of fancying himself the very Character he meant to delineate.'[9] But theatrical and transmissional corruption of Shakespeare's text still is for Theobald, as it was for Pope, the major source of variants in Quartos and the Folio: 'many Pieces were taken down in Short-hand, and imperfectly copied by Ear, from a *Representation*: Others were printed from piece-meal Parts surreptitiously obtain'd from the Theatres, uncorrect, and without the Poet's Knowledge' (I, xxxvii–xxxviii). Unlike Pope, who often chooses between and 'improves' what he feels are multiple authoritative versions of Shakespeare's plays, Theobald works to preserve or to restore what he assumes is a single authorial composition underlying any variant texts: 'His genuine Text is religiously adher'd to, and the numerous Faults and Blemishes, purely his own, are left as they were found. Nothing is alter'd, but what by the clearest Reasoning can be proved a Corruption of the true Text; and the Alteration, a real Restoration of the genuine Reading' (I, xl). For *King Lear* in particular, Theobald does not consider Shakespeare as a possible source of any variant readings. Instead, he seems to believe that one 'genuine' and 'true' script existed prior to the Quarto and Folio.

Extremely confident in his ability to detect corruption, Theobald corrects 'errors' rigorously. For example, the speech announcing the entrance of France and Burgundy at 1.1.188 (B3^v; TLN 204) is given to Gloucester in the Quarto but assigned to *Cor.*, i.e. Cordelia or Cornwall, in the Folio. Each of the three would work effectively in a stage presentation.[10] Rowe and Pope follow the Folio; Theobald uses the Quarto, explaining: 'The Generality of the Editions, antient and modern, stupidly place this Verse to *Cordelia*. But I have, upon the Authority of the old 4to, restor'd it to the right Owner, *Glo'ster*; who was, but a little before, sent by the King to conduct *France* and *Burgundy* to him.' All subsequent editors print Theobald's choice of Gloucester, although Cornwall and Cordelia have at least an equal authority and theatrical viability.

Other variants for which either early version has dramatic validity also call forth similarly fierce defences of one of the readings and strenuous assertions of corruption in the other. Theobald argues that the speech appearing at the end of the Quarto text of 3.6 was omitted from the Folio in error. 'The Soliloquy of *Edgar* is extreamly fine; and the Sentiments of it are drawn equally from Nature and the Subject. Besides, with Regard to the Stage, it is absolutely necessary: For as *Edgar* is not design'd, in the Constitution of the Play, to attend the King to *Dover*; how absurd would it look for a Character of his Importance to quit the Scene without one Word said or the least Intimation what we are to expect from him?' But no canon of Renaissance stagecraft requires a sententious soliloquy for Edgar at this moment. Theobald's 'absolutely necessary' simply inflates Pope's claims that other passages unique to the Quarto are 'necessary'. Both men try to impose their own visions or theories of dramaturgy on to Shakespeare's scripts.[11] And because Theobald does not consider possibilities of authorial revision, he must attack one (or sometimes both) of the alternative readings found in the early texts.

Theobald is the first editor to conflate the two versions of Kent's problematic speech to the Gentleman in 3.1. Rejecting Pope's preference for the Quarto, and pleased to demonstrate his superior understanding, Theobald notes that the lines unique to the Folio 'were degraded by Mr. *Pope*, as unintelligible, and to no purpose. For my part, I see nothing in them but what is very easie to be understood; and the Lines seem absolutely necessary to clear up the Motives, upon which *France* prepar'd his Invasion: nor without them is the Sense of the Context compleat.' In Theobald's version the sentence fragment dramatically cut off in the Folio:

> What hath bin seene,
> Either in snuffes, and packings of the Dukes,
> Or the hard Reine which both of them hath borne
> Against the old kinde King; or something deeper,
> Whereof (perchance) these are but furnishings
> (TLN 1634–8; 3.1.25–9)

dangles lamely in the middle of what is now a rambling discourse.[12] Yet Theobald's conflation has supplanted the two alternatives from the Quarto and Folio in virtually all modern literary analysis of this moment in *King Lear*.

After Theobald, the next significant edition is that of Samuel Johnson, published 1765–8.[13] Johnson was not a particularly careful collator of the texts, and in the opinion of modern editors the emendations he offered lack brilliance, yet alone among editions printed in the eighteenth century Johnson's shines with wit and sensibility. His general preface and his notes still yield valuable insights into problems of editing and into the practical decisions faced by playwrights. More than any other eighteenth-century editor he notices and evaluates the theatrical consequences of Quarto and Folio alternatives. For example, a line for Goneril appearing only in the Folio momentarily interrupts Albany at TLN 3035 (5.3.89): '*Gon.* An enterlude.' Johnson suggests, 'This short exclamation of *Gonerill* is added in the folio edition, I suppose, only to break the speech of *Albany*, that the exhibition on the stage might be more distinct and intelligible.'[14] Johnson implies that the Quarto works dramatically without the line and that the Folio reflects an effort to make the moment more theatrically effective. Similarly, where nine Quarto lines of a descriptive speech at 3.1.7–15 (F3–F3ᵛ, 'teares his white haire', etc.) are cut from the Folio, Johnson suggests that 'The whole speech is forcible, but too long for the occasion, and properly retrenched.' In Johnson's view the dramatic occasion, here a storm on the heath only a few moments before Lear makes his grand entrance, must be considered along with questions of authenticity or literary worth. And Johnson concludes that the lines cut from the Folio should be relegated to a footnote. Nevertheless he leaves them in the main body of his text. It appears that Johnson steps momentarily into the trap which entices editors to save from obscurity all lines of the poet's composing, even those he seems to have discarded, in effect thrusting into the reader's consciousness lines which a revising author apparently elected to suppress. (Charles Jennens, in his 1770 edition of *King Lear*, comments derisively on two similar lapses in Johnson's text:[15] 'this passage [C3; 1.3.16–20] that J[ohnson] thinks *should not stand* in the text, he has put there; as, a while ago, he neglected to insert a passage which he thought *should stand* in the text. A very reasonable way of proceeding!')

In any case, Johnson then goes on to reject Theobald's conflation as an adequate solution to the problems of Kent's long speech at 3.1.17–42 (F3^v; TLN 1626–38). Instead he prints the five lines common to both versions, then he prints in italics the lines unique to the Folio followed by the lines unique to the Quarto enclosed in brackets. He gives the notes which had been offered by Pope, Theobald and Warburton, and then he lays out the problem as he sees it for his readers: 'The true state of this speech cannot from all these notes be discovered. As it now stands it is collected from two editions: . . . if the speech be read with omissions of the *Italicks*, it will stand according to the first edition; and if the *Italicks* are read, and the lines that follow them omitted, it will then stand according to the second. The speech is now tedious, because it is formed by a coalition of both.' Johnson's method is cumbersome, of course, but he here encourages his readers to reconstruct and read through *both* authoritative sources of this passage. Johnson asks his readers to observe what he believes is Shakespeare's revising process: 'The second edition [i.e. the Folio] is generally best, and was probably nearest to *Shakespeare*'s last copy, but in this passage the first is preferable; for in the folio, the messenger is sent, he knows not why, he knows not whither.' Here Johnson points to one of the possible ways out of this tangle of variants (although whether the Gentleman is actually being *sent* to meet Cordelia is made clear only in the Quarto; in the Folio an errand may only be implied). Assuming that his author's revisions were at least purposeful, if not perfectly executed, Johnson concludes: 'I suppose *Shakespeare* thought his plot [concerning an army coming to rescue Lear] opened rather too early, and made the alteration to veil the event from the audience; but trusting too much to himself, and full of a single purpose, he did not accommodate his new lines to the rest of the scene.'

Other cuts which Johnson attributes to Shakespeare he also regards as hasty or ill-considered. 'The omission of them [i.e. speeches missing at the end of 3.6] in the folio is certainly faulty: yet I believe the folio is printed from *Shakespeare*'s last revision, carelesly and hastily performed, with more thought of shortening the scenes, than of continuing the action' (G4ᵛ; 3.6.97–115). He gives similar notes for the Folio's omissions of 4.3 and of speeches at the end of 4.7.

Alone among editors of his century and rare among textual critics of any era, Johnson repeatedly draws his readers to look at the evidence in the Quarto and the Folio when other editors instead point their readers towards an editorial reconstruction which they usually claim is 'what Shakespeare undoubtedly wrote'. Johnson is fully caught up in the effort of distinguishing authorial revisions from compositorial errors, and although in particular instances we may agree or disagree with his findings, we are always encouraged to involve ourselves as alert participants in the process.

Working at roughly the same time as Johnson, Edward Capell brought out his edition of Shakespeare's works in 1767–8. Capell asserts that all the quarto editions of Shakespeare's plays were authentic, but badly printed from 'the Poet's own copies'.[16] In his opinion, Folio versions of quartos corruptly reprint the earlier texts. And where Pope imagines forms of corruption produced by actors in performance and Theobald postulates errors made by surreptitious stenographers, Capell speculates that the Folio has many spurious or counterfeit revisions: 'who knows, if the difference that is between them [the Quarto and Folio versions], in some of the plays that are common to them both, has not been studiously heighten'd by the player editors, – who had the means in their power, being masters of all the alterations, – to give at once a greater currency to their own lame edition' (I, 11). Without any supporting evidence, Capell supposes that because Heminges and Condell probably had a commercial interest in selling the Folio, the text they provided may have had faked 'corrections'. His supposition seems more appropriate to the editorial competition of the eighteenth century than to the theatrical world of Heminges and Condell.

Capell uses many quartos previously unavailable to eighteenth-century editors, and he collates his texts very accurately.[17] Unfortunately, however, from the alternative texts of any play Capell assembles only a single composite version. 'It . . . became proper and necessary to look into the other old editions, and to select from thence whatever improves the Author, or contributes to his advancement in perfectness, the point in view throughout all this performance: that they do improve him, was with the editor an argument in their favour;

and a presumption of genuineness for what is thus selected, whether additions, or differences of any other nature; and the causes of their appearing in some copies, and being wanting in others, cannot now be discover'd, by reason of the time's distance, and defect of fit materials for making the discovery' (I, 21–2). He draws his text of *King Lear* from Q1, Q2, and F; the Folio 'was both corrupted and mutilated; it's only real original is in the quarto's; which have also their differences one from the other, but not very considerable, and both are corrupt; but in such manner that they assist at times to heal each other's corruptions, and the corrupt folio is assistant at other times to heal the wounds of them both'.[18]

Like Pope and Johnson, Capell identifies some variants as authorial revisions. For example, a catalogue of astrologically predicted disasters appears only in Edmund's part in the Quarto (C2^v; 1.2.144–9), while the Folio has instead a similar but somewhat altered catalogue spoken by Gloucester, about thirty lines earlier (TLN 439–44; 1.2.109–14). This revision, Capell indicates, 'was probably of the Author's directing' (*Notes*, I, pt. 2, 147). Again, for the complex variants surrounding the words '*Lears* Shadow' (Dl^v; TLN 744; 1.4.231), Capell finds that the Folio's 'advantages appear so strong to this editor, that he thinks the same of this passage as of one a little before it, namely – that 'tis of Shakespeare's own mending' (*Notes*, I, pt. 2, 152).

Capell sometimes invents extraordinary chains of circumstance to account for differences between the Quarto and the Folio.[19] Here is a small part of his derivation of the Fool's prophecy, which appears only in the Folio (TLN 1734–49; 3.2.79–96): 'The Fool was doubtless a favourite character; and this speech of his (or these speeches) a superfœtation, calculated, like one before it, to make his exit more *gracious*, in Shakespeare's sense of that word . . . It is conceiv'd he wrote two for him: one comprizing the whole of that prophecy which relates to things *present*; it's conclusion a waggery, at which the speaker might face about and be going, but return to speak the lines about "*Merlin*;" . . . it is conceiv'd further, that these seperate prophecies were at first spoken seperately, or on seperate nights; or one drop'd for the other, . . . that both were found in his manuscript, standing irregularly', etc. (*Notes*, I, pt. 2, 165–6). Such speculation without the taint of evidence makes up a vivid and all-too-enduring branch of *King Lear's* textual history.

Aside from the few variant readings charged to the playwright,

Capell ascribes most of the significant differences between the Quarto and Folio to compositorial negligence and editorial tampering. For example, three Quarto speeches for Edgar and Albany on L2ᵛ–L3 (5.3.205–22) 'are left out by the folio editors; a more ill-judg'd omission is not found in their work' (*Notes*, I, pt. 2, 186). Capell also rejects several brief additions found only in the Folio version of Edgar's speeches throughout 3.4. For example, 'Humh' (TLN 1828; 3.4.47), 'O do, de, do, de, do de' (TLN 1839; 3.4.58–9), and 'Sayes suum' (TLN 1879; 3.4.99), according to Capell, 'must have been the issue of the proper brain of those editors, or some one of their comrades, who was wise enough to think that stuff without meaning might suit a madman; and he has accordingly fitted him with what is void of it absolutely . . . : But Shakespeare was of another opinion; his real nor his counterfeit madman [*sic*] throw out nothing that has not vestige of sense, nothing quite unintelligible' (*Notes*, I, pt. 2, 167).

For the crux at 3.1.17–42, Capell is the first editor to comment on the interrupted grammatical structure of Kent's last sentence in the Folio. Although he notices other interrupted speeches in textual variants earlier in the play, Capell here proposes that the irregularity results from a complex interaction of editorial interference and compositorial error. In Capell's explanation the Quarto compositor accidentally omitted the eight lines of Kent's speech – TLN 1631–8, 3.1.22–9 – that are printed only in the Folio, and an unknown number of others, now lost, that included the ending of the interrupted sentence. Then, fifteen years later, 'From this scene are subtracted by the folio editors two several passages, both beautiful in themselves, and both necessary [i.e. 3.1.7–15 and 30–42]; and (as 'twere in recompence for it) one addition is made by them [3.1.22–9], of less beauty than their omissions, but of equal necessity' (*Notes*, I, pt. 2, 162). Capell proposes that the Folio editors, while they excised two long passages, lines 7–15 and 30–42, perversely restored only *part* of the passage which had been left off originally by the Quarto compositor.

These and other ingenious theories invented by Capell assume the intermittent intervention of editors, compositors, actors, and playwright carefully correcting and simultaneously botching both a lost original manuscript and the copy used to set the Folio. In sum, despite his careful textual collation, Capell's work loses much of its potential value because he fails to consider the relative merits of his manifold theories, and he only rarely checks to see if a hypothesis generated for one textual crux may be applied elsewhere or, more seriously, if it may be contradicted by an explanation he has offered elsewhere.

Unlike the editors who produced the complete editions so far discussed, Charles Jennens edited only six of Shakespeare's plays. *King Lear* was the first. His 1770 edition of the play is the first attempt to provide readers with a complete collation, on the page, of all the variants between the early editions, and with a full record of the editorial decisions of his eighteenth-century predecessors. Jennens also tries to use italic type to indicate material found only in the Quarto or Folio (though he is not consistent in this, and his use of italics for material unique to *either* text can be confusing, because of overlapping additions, cuts, and revisions).

Jennens offers two reasons for his careful collation. The first is a refreshing statement of editorial responsibility: 'No editor that I know of has a right to impose upon every body his own favourite reading, or to give his own conjectural interpolation, without producing the readings of the several editions' (p. ix). The second is more questionable: 'it is evident that one edition, though the best, may be in many places corrected by another, though a worse edition; and the several editions are a mutual help to each other; or why do editors collate?' (p. ix). To this rhetorical question there are possible answers unforeseen by Jennens: editors *could* collate in order to identify points at which an author has revised his own work, as indeed Pope and Johnson had intermittently done in their editions. (Capell's similar remarks, unpublished until 1779, were not available to Jennens.) Without a theory which accommodates the possibility of authorial revision, Jennens inserts all the lines unique to either of his early texts. And he must necessarily dismiss as a corruption whichever one of a pair of alternative readings he happens to reject.

For example, King Lear in the storm cries out to the 'elements': 'Heere I stand your Slaue' (TLN 1674; F4; 3.2.19), and so – though there could hardly be any doubt about this point – we, and certainly the actor playing Lear, realize that he is standing upright. A few moments later, though, he cries out, 'No, I will be the patterne of all patience, | I will say nothing' (TLN 1689–90; F4; 3.2.37–8). A vigorous actor who, like Shakespeare himself, finds iconic ways to amplify words and ideas could very well sit down on this line, thereby assuming a posture appropriate to a 'patterne of all patience'.[20] The Quarto text seems to require this interpretative movement with

Kent's question to Lear: 'Alas sir, *sit* you here? (F4; 3.2.42; my italics). The Folio reads, 'Alas Sir *are* you here?' (TLN 1694; my italics), thereby giving us no clue as to whether Lear is sitting or standing. Jennens explains: 'This seems to be an alteration made for the ease of the actors, that he who acted *Lear* might not have the trouble of sitting down on the ground, and rising again.' Jennens implies that such a change could result only from the theatrical corruption of Shakespeare's original, and so he prints 'sit' in his text. But Lear might be sitting, even in the Folio; the change of verb in Kent's question might be designed simply to emphasize 'here' (in the storm, out of doors), rather than Lear's posture ('sit'-ting). Moreover, even if the variant did reflect a change in Lear's actions, we have no way of knowing that the change resulted from laziness or even arthritis rather than from a desire to keep Lear dramatically 'standing up' to the elements.

Jennens, like other eighteenth-century editors, occasionally emends what he feels are his poet's rough spots: he transforms

> *Kent.* Is this the promis'd end?
> *Edg.* Or image of that horror.
> *Alb.* Fall and cease.
> (TLN 3224–6; L3ᵛ; 5.3.264–5)

into

> *Kent.* Is this the promis'd end?
> *Edg.* O image of true honour!
> *Alb.* Fair and chaste.

(The fair and chaste image of true honour being, it appears, the corpse of Cordelia.) But it would be unfair to judge him on the basis of occasional lapses like these. His real contribution lies in the respect he paid to the problems of presenting the complex and detailed evidence of the early texts.

Considered the father of modern Shakespearian criticism, Edmond Malone develops a text of *King Lear* which becomes a standard of editorial decorum.[21] In the preface to his edition, Malone repeats the commonplace appeal to the principles of textual study: 'for though to explain and illustrate the writings of our poet is a principal duty of his editor, to ascertain his genuine text, to fix what is to be explained, is his first and immediate object: and till it be established which of the ancient copies is entitled to preference, we have no criterion by which the text can be ascertained' (I, xii). Malone generally prefers Shakespearian quarto texts over their Folio equivalents because, he says, 'the editors of the folio, to save labour, or for some other motive, printed the greater part of them [the plays which were earlier printed in quartos] from the very copies which they represented as maimed and imperfect, . . . in some instances with additions and alterations of their own' (I, xii–xiii). In many of his notes on variants in *Lear* Malone will point to alterations he suspects were due to one particularly ignorant editor who prepared the Folio text.

Like Theobald and Jennens, Malone assumes without discussion that only a single authorial original lies behind the variant testimony of the early texts. This 'original' was particularly vulnerable to distortion after it left Shakespeare's direct control: 'Even in the first complete collection of his plays published in 1623, some changes were undoubtedly made from ignorance of his meaning and phraseology. They had, I suppose, been made in the playhouse copies after his retirement from the theatre' (I, lxv). Like some of his predecessors, Malone ascribes variants to the blunders of an anonymous editor of the 1623 Folio:

To shield thee from diseases *of the world*;] Thus the quartos. The folio has *disasters*. The alteration, I believe, was made by the editor, in consequence of his not knowing the meaning of the original word. . . .

[TLN 188; B3; 1.1.174]

Your old kind father, whose frank heart gave you *all,*—] I have already observed that the words, *father, brother, rather*, and many of a similar sound, were sometimes used by Shakspeare as monosyllables. The editor of the folio, supposing the metre to be defective, omitted the word *you*, which is found in the quartos.

[TLN 1800; G1^v; 3.4.20]

And, commenting on the stage direction at the beginning of 4.7 in the Folio, '*Enter Cordelia, Kent, and Gentleman.*' (TLN 2744), where the Quarto reads, '*Enter Cordelia, Kent and Doctor.*' (K1^v), Malone reasons, 'I suppose, from a penury of actors, it was found convenient to unite the two characters [i.e. the Gentleman and the Doctor], which, we see, were originally distinct. Cordelia's words, however, might have taught the editor of the folio to have given the *gentleman* whom he retained the appellation of *Doctor*'.

Malone particularly scorns his hypothetical Folio editor's ignorance of Shakespearian verbal habits. Malone prints at 1.1.105 the Quarto reading of Lear's speech, 'But goes this with thy heart?' (B2; TLN 111), and comments: 'Thus the quartos, and thus I have no doubt Shakspeare wrote, . . . The editor of the folio, not understanding this kind of phraseology, substituted the more common form – But goes *thy heart with this?* as in the next line he reads, Ay, *my good* lord, instead of – Ay, *good my lord*, the reading of the quartos, and the constant language of Shakspeare.'[22] Again, in a note explaining the second of two omissions of the word 'cold' in the Folio at TLN 1828 (3.4.48), Malone addresses the editor's folly: '*Humph! go to thy cold bed, and warm thee.*] Thus the quartos. The editor of the folio 1623, I suppose, thinking the passage nonsense, omitted the word *cold*. This is not the only instance of unwarrantable alterations made even in that valuable copy [i.e. the Folio]. That the quartos are right, appears from the Induction to *the Taming of the Shrew*, where the same words occur.' Indeed, Christophero Sly says, 'goe to thy cold bed, and warme thee' (*Shrew*, TLN 11–12; Induction 1.9–10), but this parallel does not prove that Folio *Lear* is corrupt. It does, however, forcefully demonstrate Malone's tendency to treat Shakespeare as if he were incapable of introducing variety in his language, even in such a small matter and even over plays separated by years in time.

Along with other editors, Malone argues that the Folio text was cut by the actors. Commenting on dialogue only in the Quarto text at the end of 4.7 (K2ᵛ–K3; 4.7.85–96), Malone first reprints Johnson's note: '[The passage] was omitted by the authour, I suppose, for no other reason than to shorten the representation.' Malone then rejects Johnson's exposition of Shakespeare as a revising artist by offering a further recension of the theatrical-corruption myth: 'It is much more probable, that it was omitted by the players, after the authour's departure from the stage, without consulting him.'[23] Continuing in the same note, Malone then broadens his theatrical disapproval to include modern performances and their audiences: 'His plays have been long exhibited with similar omissions, which render them often perfectly unintelligible. The loss however is little felt by the greater part of the audience, who are intent upon other matters.'

But serious difficulties arise where Malone prints, without any note of contradiction, some of Johnson's ascriptions of variants to Shakespeare's revising hand. Although it is a mark of his sense of editorial responsibility that he gives his readers Johnson's views,

Malone (like Jennens) fails to see that if Johnson even occasionally is correct about authorial revision then doubt is cast upon virtually all of his own confident pronouncements about textual corruption. If, as Johnson's notes propose, in the interval between the preparation of the manuscript that was used to set the Quarto and the preparation of whatever document was later used to set the Folio, Shakespeare himself could have cut four lines, or three speeches, or an entire scene, couldn't he also have altered a word or two? or a hundred? or a thousand? A revising author imposes obligations on his editors quite out of keeping with their traditional reconstructions of 'a lost original'. He demands texts, not a text.

Malone's extraordinary scholarly labours earn a genuine and deserved respect from later editors, but the strength of his reputation also seems to have validated the unproven hypothesis of a lost original manuscript for *King Lear*, and to have lent authority to the composite texts that try to reproduce it. The work of Theobald and Jennens might not have commanded acceptance of a conflated version of *King Lear* by later editors who doubted its theoretical justification, but after Malone the composite is so strongly established that no major editor deviates from it. For example, in his 1839–43 edition, Charles Knight argues that significant variants in *Lear* reflect purposeful and artistically valuable improvements in the Folio.[24] Knight believes in the artistic superiority of the Folio in much the same way that Malone believes in the artistic integrity of the lost original. Despite his belief, Knight prints the composite text. Similarly, the editors of the important Cambridge edition of 1863–6 print Edgar's soliloquy at the end of 3.6 with this note: 'Every editor from Theobald downwards, except Hanmer, has reprinted this speech from the Quartos. In deference to this consensus of authority we have retained it, though, as it seems to us, internal evidence is conclusive against the supposition that the lines were written by Shakespeare.'[25]

Texts of *King Lear* printed today offer not much more bibliographical proof of the existence of a lost original *King Lear* than the undemonstrated assertions given by eighteenth-century editors. Texts printed today offer only slightly more agreement in editorial decisions over the placement of stage directions, choices between alternative speech prefixes and single word variants than those printed in the latter part of the eighteenth century. Texts printed today still give all the lines unique to both the Quarto and Folio – so that not a line written by Shakespeare may be lost – without evident regard of the possibly distorting effects this conflation has upon our perception of *King Lear*.[26]

Dr Johnson sets the high calling of the editor as a guardian of literary culture: 'the history of our language, and the true force of our words, can only be preserved, by keeping the text of authours free from adulteration' (I, lxii). What has been a well-meaning quest after a quite-possibly-nonexistent lost original may have promulgated a two-hundred-year usurpation of our greatest play by an adulterated text.

> . . . fine word: Legitimate.
> Well, my Legittimate, if this Letter speed,
> And my inuention thriue, *Edmond* the base
> Shall to'th' Legitimate: I grow, I prosper:
> (TLN 352–5; Cl; 1.2.18–21)[27]

NOTES

1. Nahum Tate, *The History of King Lear. Acted at the Duke's Theatre. Reviv'd with Alterations* (1681; Cornmarket Press facsimile, 1969), p. 19. For a demonstration and discussion of Tate's indebtedness to both texts, see James Black's edition, Regents Renaissance Drama Series (1975), pp. 97–100.
2. Nicholas Rowe, ed., *The Works of Mr. William Shakespear; in Six Volumes, Revis'd and Corrected, with an Account of the Life and Writings of the Author* (1709; repr. New York, 1967). *Lear* is in Volume V of Rowe's edition.
3. Rowe's dependence on the Fourth Folio was established by Capell; this has been confirmed by subsequent scholarship, though some trial pages of *The Tempest* were set from the 1632 edition (for which see S. Schoenbaum, *Shakespeare's Lives* (Oxford, 1970), p. 130). R. B. McKerrow dismisses Rowe's edition as being, in respect to collation of the early texts, 'little more . . . than a revision of the Fourth Folio' ('The Treatment of Shakespeare's Text by his Earlier Editors, 1709–1768', reprinted in *Studies in Shakespeare: British Academy Lectures*, ed. Peter Alexander (Oxford, 1964), p. 110).
4. Alexander Pope, ed., *The Works of Shakespeare in Six Volumes, Collated and Corrected by the Former Editions by Mr. Pope* (1723–5; repr. New York, 1969), I, viii. *Lear* is in Volume III of this edition.
5. I and others have argued that the play works better without this scene. See, for example, Urkowitz, *Revision*, pp. 53–4, and Taylor, 'War', p. 30.
6. As McKerrow says, 'Pope with all his shortcomings was the first editor of Shakespeare to make a genuine attempt to collect all the available material and to use it for the construction of what he regarded as the best possible text' (p. 119).
7. See Roger Warren's essay below, pp. 48–9.
8. McKerrow has some illuminating reflections on the distorting influence, for early Shakespeare editors, of traditions of editing inherited from classical texts (pp. 120–1).
9. Lewis Theobald, ed., *The Works of Shakespeare: in Seven Volumes* . . . (1733 [-4]), I, xvi. *Lear* is in Volume V of this edition.

10. See Beth Goldring's essay, below.
11. Although Theobald is a better editor than either Pope or Warburton, it is *not* true, as Brian Vickers claims, that 'one looks in vain [in Theobald] for the kind of disabling contemporary attitudes expressed in the high-handed decisions of a Pope or a Warburton' (*Shakespeare: The Critical Heritage*, 6 vols. (1974–81), II (1974), 17).
12. For further discussion of this speech see Urkowitz, *Revision*, pp. 67–79, and Taylor, 'War', pp. 31–2.
13. The editions of Sir Thomas Hanmer (Oxford, 1743–4) and William Warburton (1747) are of no real importance. As McKerrow says, 'Hanmer seems to have known little and cared less about such matters as early editions or the language of Shakespeare's time, and attempted to reform the text by the light of nature alone . . . [Warburton's edition] is a compound of Theobald's text . . . with Pope's scene-numbering . . . Much of Warburton's best work on Shakespeare is contained in the notes which he contributed to Theobald's edition . . . The new matter contributed by his own edition is relatively unimportant' (pp. 126–7).
14. Samuel Johnson, ed., *The Plays of William Shakespeare, in Eight Volumes* . . . (1765–8), VI, 148. *Lear* is in Volume VI of this edition. For Johnson's editing as a whole see Arthur Sherbo, *Samuel Johnson, Editor of Shakespeare*, Illinois Studies in Language and Literature, XIII (Urbana, Illinois, 1956); for his editing of *Lear* in particular, S. W. Johnston's 'Samuel Johnson's Text of *Lear*: "Dull Duty" Reassessed', *Yearbook of English Studies*, 6 (1976), 80–91. Though some of Johnston's conclusions are invalidated by her simple assumption of the validity of modern theories of the derivation of the Quarto and Folio texts, she does make the useful point that Johnson was 'far less permissive of emendation' than any of his predecessors (p. 88).
15. *King Lear. A Tragedy. By William Shakespeare. Collated with the old and modern editions* (1770).
16. Edward Capell, ed., *Mr. William Shakespeare: His Comedies, Histories, and Tragedies* . . . , 10 vols. (1768). I, 10. *Lear* is in Volume IX of this edition.
17. Vickers concludes that Capell's edition and notes represent 'in many ways the best scholarship of the century' (VI, 32), and *The Riverside Shakespeare* accepts more emendations from Capell than from any other editor.
18. Edward Capell, *Notes and Various Readings to Shakespeare*, 3 vols. (1779; repr. New York, 1970), I, part 2, 140. Hereafter cited in the text as *Notes*, these volumes containing detailed commentary on his edition were published posthumously.
19. McKerrow describes Capell's edition as 'the climax . . . of the selective theory of editing – the idea that if an editor likes a reading, that reading is (a) good, and (b) attributable to Shakespeare' (p. 130). The inverse of this principle is that if an editor doesn't like a reading, it is (a) bad, and (b) to be explained away by any means, however far-fetched. It is hardly surprising that Alice Walker, the modern editor who most doggedly defended and applied these principles herself, should have chosen Capell as the subject of her own British Academy Lecture ('Edward Capell and his Edition of Shakespeare', in *Studies in Shakespeare*, pp. 132–48).
20. Viola in *Twelfth Night* evokes just such an image of her pining 'sister' who 'sate like Patience on a Monument' (TLN 1003; 2.4.114); Shakespeare might also have wished to exploit the indecorum of a royal figure sitting on the ground, as he does with Constance in *King John* (TLN 990–6; 3.1.68–74) and Richard II ('For Gods sake let vs sit vpon the ground', F2ᵛ; 3.2.155).
21. Edmond Malone, ed., *Plays and Poems of Shakespeare in Ten Volumes* . . . (1790); *Lear* is in Volume VIII. The editions of George Steevens (1778, 1785) are primarily valuable for their commentary, particularly in citing parallels for words and phrases, rather than for any development in the theory and practice of editing.

22. In the first fifteen plays in Marvin Spevack's *The Harvard Concordance to Shakespeare* (Cambridge, Mass., 1973), 'my good lord' occurs 40 times and 'good my lord' 34 times; *both* phraseologies are clearly 'the constant language' of Shakespeare. Malone's ignorant Folio editor apparently understood 'good my lord' on the eight occasions on which it appears in Folio *Lear* itself.

23. On the historical improbability of this, see Gary Taylor's discussion below, pp. 415–22.

24. Charles Knight, ed., *The Pictorial Edition of the Works of Shakespeare*, 8 vols. ([1839–] 1843), VI, 392–3.

25. William G. Clark, John Glover, and W. Aldis Wright, eds., *The Works of Shakespeare*, The Cambridge Shakespeare, 9 vols. (Cambridge, 1863–6), VIII, 433. I do not mean to imply that the Cambridge editors are right in doubting the authenticity of this passage.

26. It should be noted that the warning implied by square brackets, used by many editors to indicate departures from their copy-text, has been in this respect universally ignored by readers of modern texts – students, scholars, and theatre artists. All these users believe that there is only *one* text of *King Lear*, responsibly given them by a modern editor.

27. For a defence of the QF reading, usually emended to 'top' (Capell), see Thomas Clayton's 'Disemending *King Lear* in Favour of Shakespeare: "Edmund the Base Shall *to* th' Legitimate" (1.2.21)', forthcoming in *Notes and Queries*.

The Folio Omission of the Mock Trial Motives and Consequences

ROGER WARREN

IN the climactic scene of his madness, Lear provides two vivid images of human injustice. First, those who administer justice are indistinguishable from those whom they try:

> See how yond Iustice railes vpon yond simple theefe. Hearke in thine eare: Change places, and handy-dandy, which is the Iustice, which is the theefe:
>
> (TLN 2595–8; I4; 4.6.151–4)

Second, the robes of the judge can conceal vices whereas the rags of the offender cannot:

> Thorough tatter'd cloathes great Vices do appeare: Robes, and Furr'd gownes hide all.
>
> (TLN 2606–8; I4; 4.6.164–5)

These two images form the basic idea for the mock trial of Goneril and Regan in the Quarto, where Lear sets up an imaginary courtroom in which a naked beggar, a fool and a serving-man sit in judgement on his daughters, the powerful representatives of justice. In the Folio, this sequence is cut. If, as I assume, the Folio cuts, additions, and rewordings represent Shakespeare's own second thoughts, 'as a result of difficulties at rehearsal and, perhaps, dissatisfaction with performance',[1] why was Shakespeare so dissatisfied with the episode as to omit it entirely?

The most striking feature of the Quarto version of 3.6 is its use of the elaborate theatrical device of a kind of ensemble of madness: Shakespeare makes Lear imagine a dramatic situation in which his sane and powerful daughters are arraigned in a courtroom by people who are not only destitute but are also, or appear to be, 'mad' in ways that differ from Lear himself and from each other. In this way Shakespeare externalizes the chief preoccupations of Lear's mad mind, the cruelty of his daughters and the injustice of those who wield power; it is appropriate to his vision of a world where accepted values are reversed that an apparent bedlam beggar should become a 'learned Iustice', and should seem a robed judge precisely because he is naked; and that another man whose profession is folly should be his 'yokefellow of equity', a 'sapient sir'. Later, when Lear imagines that Regan has escaped, he blames 'corruption in the place' and accuses a 'False Iusticer' (G3ᵛ–G4; 3.6.20–56). The whole topsy-turvy situation seems intended to express Lear's vision of injustice, what he later calls 'the great image of Authoritie' (TLN 2602; I4; 4.6.158). But if this is the starting-point for the mock trial, the episode as a whole turns out somewhat differently. Lear attempts to follow the judicial processes: seating the justices, arraigning the prisoners, bringing evidence. But no sooner has he seated them than those whom he has cast as judges go off at tangents: Tom/Edgar interrupts Lear's address to his daughters to indulge his familiar obsession with devils: 'Looke where he stands and glars' (G3ᵛ; 3.6.23). In his next phrase, 'madam' presumably refers to Goneril or Regan, but this only leads him off at another tangent, to sing a popular song, to which the Fool improvises an obscene refrain, after which he returns to the fiends once more. Lear attempts to bring the court to order by reseating the judges and calling for evidence. Tom/Edgar promises to 'deale iustly', but immediately reverts to his songs and his devils; and when Lear arraigns Goneril, the Fool explodes the whole situation with a joke which reduces Lear's imagined courtroom to the bathetic reality: 'I tooke you for a ioyne stoole' (G4; 3.6.52). And this leads Lear to imagine his court broken up in confusion at Regan's escape. The total effect of this scene is that Lear's attempt to express his obsession with the injustice of his daughters by establishing the processes of a trial is sabotaged by the 'judges', who lapse from their 'judicial' roles to the other roles which they habitually play – Edgar to the bedlam beggar obsessed by devils, the Fool to his songs and jibes which bring everything down to earth.

It could be argued that this very state of confusion is in itself an appropriate image of Lear's view of injustice, a *tour de force* of technical dexterity which combines various elements from the preceding scenes – Lear's madness, the Fool's professional folly, Edgar's mock-possession – in an elaborate climax. I think that such a climax may well have been Shakespeare's aim in writing the scene, but that in rehearsal or performance it became clear that the focus of the scene had shifted from Lear's mock-justice to eccentric individual detail – the Fool's joint-stool joke, Edgar's songs and devils – leading to a generalized sense of chaos. Certainly the effect in performance more often than not seems to amount to no more than the eccentric tricks of a stageful of madmen; but Shakespeare obviously goes far beyond mere eccentricity and chaos in these mad scenes to express what Edgar calls 'Reason in Madnesse' (TLN 2617; I4; 4.6.175). But if an audience is to grasp this idea, they must pay attention to what the characters are saying in detail; and the difficulty here is that audiences tend to respond to madness on stage merely as a general effect: when they see a character go mad they assume that, being mad, he can't have anything to tell them, and that therefore they need to concentrate line-by-line even less than they usually do. This question of audience reaction to a mad character seems to me to highlight the main problem facing the actor of Lear. In 3.6, at the half-way point of the play, when an audience is beginning to tire anyway, a Lear has to take them step-by-step with him into his madness, and to retain their attention upon the details of what he says in order to make them comprehend his 'mad' view of the 'sane' world – that what appears a distorted image is in fact a true reflection.

The precise theatrical difficulty here can perhaps be clarified by two comments about the related problem of Ophelia's madness in performance. Robin Phillips stresses that 'the text is important, and she has something desperately important to say to Gertrude'; but because she is mad, 'our attention [has] to be arrested firmly enough for us to want to listen to what she has to say'.[2] And Hugh Leonard, reviewing Glenda Jackson as Ophelia, remarked how 'one could hear the click of numerous minds snapping shut all over the auditorium'.[3] This might simply have been a rejection of Glenda Jackson's stridency – 'Pray you MARK!' bawled at Gertrude to ensure that she paid attention – were it not that the sensation he describes is so familiar. And if audiences react like that to the relatively simple presentation of Ophelia's madness ('simple' in the sense that only one character is involved), it is hardly surprising that, confronted with the way in which the mock trial's combination of real and assumed madness keeps pulling the scene in different directions, they should lose concentration on Lear's sense of mock-justice because they are so distracted (and perhaps bewildered) by the eccentricities, songs and jokes of Tom and the Fool.

Perhaps Shakespeare attempted to concentrate the audience's attention, not by snipping passages here and there, but by one big bold cut. One consequence is to streamline Act Three; for the audience's response to the mad ensemble is not the only problem with the mock trial; another is its positioning. After all, Shakespeare could have decided to shorten, for instance, Edgar's very extended mock-madness in 3.4. Indeed, Donald Sinden, who has played Lear and is obviously aware of the practical problems of sustaining audience attention in this part of the play, recommends exactly that: 'the Poor Tom material in the hovel scene', he says, is 'totally incomprehensible for the first time of seeing; when you know the play, marvellous stuff. As an actor, Edgar is better off to have half the things to say; then he can work harder on hitting those home.'[4] It might seem that Shakespeare is working on this principle in thinning out the mad scenes; but in fact he cut nothing from 'the hovel scene', and indeed *added* a few lines (TLN 1807–8, 1819; 3.4.26–7, 37). He seems to have felt that this scene needed to be extensive, because it is dramatically so important; it is the scene in which Edgar establishes his performance as Tom, a performance which gives Lear the final shock that turns his mind and brings him to his awareness of 'vnaccommodated man'.

It was not this scene but 3.6 which was condensed. The Folio version of 3.6 is a different kind of scene from the Quarto version, not only shorter but sharper, more urgent and rapid. In cutting the trial, it abridges those features of the Quarto scene which look backwards, like Edgar's mock-possession and the Fool's jokes, while emphasizing those which look forward. The Folio's omission of the whole of Kent's and Edgar's speeches at the end of the scene helps to intensify the urgency of Gloucester's point that even half an hour's delay could result in the death of Lear and his supporters; and it immediately follows Gloucester's solicitous concern for the King's well-being with its disastrous consequences for his own. And although the Folio's much shortened, speeded-up 3.6 omits the mad enactment of injustice, it rushes on instead to show us the thing itself in its most violent form, as Cornwall and Regan sadistically go through the processes of interrogation before inflicting the horrible punishment:

> *Reg.* Wherefore to Douer?
> Was't thou not charg'd at perill.
> *Corn.* Wherefore to Douer? Let him answer that.
> (TLN 2122–4; H1^v; 3.7.52–3)

Another important dramatic consequence of the cuts in 3.6 is that they bring closer together the crises of Lear's and Gloucester's ordeals, the cracking of Lear's mind as he sees Poor Tom, and Gloucester's realization of the truth about Edmund and Edgar as his second eye is put out. This strengthens the dramatic structure of the play, and it also helps to prepare for the climactic meeting of the mad Lear and the blind Gloucester in 4.6.

Most of the Folio changes to 3.6 are cuts; but Shakespeare also added two speeches for the Fool, 'No, he's a Yeoman, that ha's a Gentleman to his Sonne: for hee's a mad Yeoman that sees his Sonne a Gentleman before him' (TLN 2010–12; 3.6.12–14) and, notably, 'And Ile go to bed at noone' (TLN 2043; 3.6.85). These can also be explained in practical theatrical terms. Kent's remark to the Fool, 'Come helpe to beare thy maister, thou must not stay behind' (G4^v; 3.6.100–1) is lost in the process of condensing the end of the scene; and with the mock trial omitted, only one reference to the Fool remains from the Quarto's version of the scene: 'Prythee Nunkle tell me, whether a madman be a Gentleman, or a Yeoman' (TLN 2007–8; G3^v; 3.6.9–10). But this is the last time we see the Fool, and the natural supposition that Shakespeare wanted to give him a more effective final appearance would explain the Folio's additions to an otherwise severely abbreviated scene.

The two biggest omissions from 3.6, the mock trial and Edgar's closing soliloquy, both cut material which is given more effective (and, in the Folio, expanded) treatment later in the play. While the Folio omits Edgar's soliloquy at the end of 3.6, it extends the one which opens 4.1 in compensation, so that Edgar paradoxically 'gains in prominence' by losing a soliloquy (M. Warren, 'Albany and Edgar', p. 103): Shakespeare here seems to be applying to the 'sane' Edgar the practical treatment recommended by Donald Sinden for the 'mad' one, giving him 'half the things to say' in a dramatically more advantageous position in the play. It seems to me that Shakespeare does precisely the same with Lear's vision of mock-justice: the next time we see him after 3.6 is for his most extended scene of madness, 4.6, in which he develops at great length his two central obsessions in the mock trial: the corruption of his daughters and of human justice. Just as the omission of the mock trial abridges the repetition of effects from the previous scenes, it also avoids anticipating important elements of 4.6. Shakespeare could have decided to eliminate the less successful treatment of mock-justice in its dramatically weaker position in 3.6 in order to guarantee it maximum impact by concentrating it all in one place in 4.6, at the same time intensifying its effect in a dramatically stronger position by making various additions to it there.

The big difference between the technique of 3.6 and 4.6 is that the mock trial presents an arraignment of the daughters and of false justice in terms of an ensemble of madness, whereas 4.6 does so by concentrating on Lear's mad mind alone. This scene provides the most effective presentation of the way his mind works, of the logical connections which underlie the mad remarks and which make the speeches effective in both dramatic and psychological terms. These connections help to provide a concentration, a focus, upon the mad remarks which the eccentric digressions of the mock trial tend to dissipate: 4.6 gives a very strong sense of two people in a specific situation. It brings together the mad Lear and the blinded Gloucester for the first time since the crises of their sufferings, which themselves were brought closer together by the extensive cutting of 3.6; and it is a decisive factor in the success of 4.6 that Lear's verbal arraignment of women and justice arises out of the details of their dramatic relationship, rather than through the elaborate creation of an imaginary courtroom. The reunion of Lear and Gloucester in 4.6 is a much simpler, more human scene than 3.6 – a major reason, I think, for its greater impact in performance.

The verbal differences between the Quarto and Folio versions of 4.6 are often tiny, but the Folio readings sharpen the immediacy and impact of Lear's 'mad' remarks by strengthening the basic technique: Lear's own preoccupations are clearly revealed by tying them in as closely as possible to the facts of the situation on stage. In the Quarto, for instance, Lear's cry 'Ha *Gonorill*, ha *Regan*' (13ᵛ) of course reflects what is uppermost in his mind; the alteration in the Folio to 'Ha! *Gonerill* with a white beard?' (TLN 2543; 4.6.96) makes it clear that Lear is reacting specifically to the sight of the white-bearded Gloucester in front of him: this in turn leads Lear to think of his daughters' flattery of his own 'white hayres in [his] Beard' (TLN 2544–5; 13ᵛ; 4.6.97–8) and thence to his experience of a storm which by contrast refused to flatter him.

When, a little later, Shakespeare makes Lear use the technique of mock-arraignment, it is in response to another specifically human moment in the scene, Gloucester's recognition of his voice: 'Is't not the King?' (TLN 2553; 13ᵛ; 4.6.107). Lear demonstrates that he is 'euery inch a King' by acting out a situation in which he presides over an imaginary trial:

> When I do stare, see how the Subiect quakes.
> I pardon that mans life. What was thy cause?
> Adultery? thou shalt not dye: dye for Adultery?
>   (TLN 2555–7; I3ᵛ; 4.6.108–11)

The grounds for this clemency are that illicit copulation has had
happier consequences than his own 'legal' issue:

> For Glousters bastard Son was kinder to his Father,
> Then my Daughters got 'tweene the lawfull sheets.
>   (TLN 2560–1; I3ᵛ; 4.6.114–16)

This speech vividly points the contrast between this 'mock trial' and
the one in 3.6. There, the whole situation is an imaginary one, in
which Lear attempts to get everyone on stage to act out his
obsessions, with some distracting results. But here, the dramatic
situation is not imaginary; and the other characters intensify Lear's
vision of mock-justice rather than distracting from it, because that
vision is specifically, acutely related to their own experience, since
Lear's remark about Edmund must obviously cause bitter pain to the
listening Gloucester. Shakespeare thus roots Lear's mad utterances
in an individual human context.

When Lear takes up the other chief preoccupation of the mock
trial, justice and injustice, this too is firmly rooted in the dramatic
situation. Gloucester's movingly trenchant statement that he sees
without eyes by experiencing and understanding – 'I see it feelingly' –
leads Lear to his topsy-turvy image of justice: 'A man may see how
this world goes, with no eyes. Looke with thine eares: See how yond
Iustice railes vpon yond simple theefe' (TLN 2593–6; I4; 4.6.149–
52). At this point in the Folio Shakespeare again seems to have made
a tiny but significant alteration. The Quarto goes on: 'harke in thy
eare handy, dandy, which is the theefe, which is the Iustice' (I4). But
the Folio reads: 'Hearke in thine eare: *Change places, and* handy-
dandy, which is the Iustice, which is the theefe' (TLN 2596–8;
4.6.152–4, italics mine). Such tiny changes might seem to provide
slender ground to build upon: it might be objected that 'Change
places, and' simply got missed out of the Quarto. But since the
passage has apparently been retouched, with the justice and the thief
reversed, presumably to throw doubt primarily upon 'Iustice', it
seems quite likely that 'Change places, and' was deliberately added.
What it achieves is to spell out more clearly and decisively the

implications of 'handy-dandy', that the justice and the thief are interchangeable – the basic image of the mock trial.

Lear associates guilty women with 'corruption in the place' and the 'False Iusticer' at the end of the mock trial, and also in the next passage:

> Thou, Rascall Beadle, hold thy bloody hand: why dost thou lash that Whore? Strip thy owne backe, thou hotly lusts to vse her in that kind, for which thou whip'st her.
>
> (TLN 2603–6; I4; 4.6.160–3)

Lear's perception that underneath the robes the justice is as guilty as the ragged offender who cannot conceal his sins is expressed in the mock trial by treating the naked Tom as a 'robbed' (i.e. robed) 'man of Iustice' (G4; 3.6.36), and in this scene by the sharply phrased

> Thorough tatter'd cloathes great Vices do appeare: Robes, and Furr'd gownes hide all.
>
> (TLN 2606–8; I4; 4.6.164–5)[5]

Perhaps in compensation for omitting the mock trial's statement of this idea, Shakespeare adds a passage in the Folio which develops the theme:

> Pla[t]e sinnes with Gold, and the strong Lance of Iustice, hurtlesse breakes: Arme it in ragges, a Pigmies straw do's pierce it.
>
> (TLN 2608–10; 4.6.165–7)

So Lear pardons the offenders – 'None do's offend, none, I say none' – but he does so as a representative of corrupt justice:

> Ile able 'em; take that of me my Friend, who haue the power to seale th' accusers lips.
>
> (TLN 2610–12; 4.6.168–70)

This addition strengthens Lear's arraignment of justice, his 'Reason in Madnesse'; but it does not simply make this general point, for when it connects with the Quarto version again, it is at the phrase 'Get thee glasse-eyes', returning once more to the physical situation which set off this verbal re-creation of the mock trial in the first place, Gloucester's ability to see without eyes. This again emphasizes the important distinction between the two mock trials: whereas the elaborate technique of 3.6 'opens out' Lear's vision of mock justice to involve other kinds of 'madness', 4.6 by contrast *narrows* the focus to the underlying logic of Lear's own extended speeches, and to the very intimate dramatic situation. While the use of apparently related forms of 'madness' in the mock trial distracts attention from Lear's view of injustice, the very contrast between Gloucester's and Lear's experiences (a physical ordeal and a mental one) serves to heighten the impact of Lear's own vision. Contrasted and yet closely linked, the physically maimed Gloucester and the mentally maimed King communicate on a level of instinctive human sympathy which moves audiences in a way that the more elaborate contrivance of the mock trial does not:

> If thou wilt weepe my Fortunes, take my eyes.
> I know thee well enough, thy name is Glouster.
>   (TLN 2618–19; I4; 4.6.176–7)

So it seems to me that this very powerful scene expresses in a much more successful manner the 'mad' insights of the mock trial. Perhaps Shakespeare originally intended the trial's treatment of mock-justice to pave the way for that of the later scene, but then the experience of rehearsal or performance made him change his mind. Several critics (Taylor, 'War'; Urkowitz, *Revision*; M. Warren, 'Albany and Edgar') have demonstrated that the whole trend of the Folio revisions is towards streamlining and simplification: to concentrate the presentation of mock justice all in one scene, adding new passages to intensify it, would be in line with the other revisions.

Although theatre evidence is inconclusive since no major modern production has used the Quarto or Folio text exclusively, it does confirm the interdependence of 3.6 and 4.6. The only modern production to omit the mock trial, Glen Byam Shaw's at Stratford in 1959, did not follow the Folio cuts consistently in 3.6: the whole of Kent's speech at the end of the scene was retained except for the phrase 'helpe to beare thy maister', as well as five lines of Edgar's soliloquy (which seems like the worst of both worlds). But Muriel St Clare Byrne clearly felt that the omission of the mock trial, and the staging of what was left of the scene, worked specifically to the advantage of 4.6: 'in view of its inherent difficulties [3.6] may well have gained by being played at a greater distance from the audience than usual [on an upper level], while, by contrast, the mad scene of Act IV gained in power by having the action concentrated as far downstage as possible' to strengthen the impact of 'an old, dishevelled man whose wits wander intermittently, sitting on a farm cart, his only audience a blind man and a beggar to whom he leans forward in familiar talk'.[6]

The interdependence of the two scenes was illustrated very differently by Peter Brook's 1962 Stratford production. This was the only time I have found the mad scenes (including the mock trial) entirely persuasive, and their conviction led directly to an outstanding treatment of 4.6. Two exceptional aspects of the production achieved this. The first was that Paul Scofield's performance as Lear possessed what Irving Wardle called 'a continuity . . . that carries him from the rational world of the first acts into madness'.[7] Harold Hobson described the process: in 1.5, Lear and the Fool

> sit side by side upon a plain bench at the corner of an empty stage, and talk quietly about mankind and jokes and life and other weighty matters. . . . 'Let me not,' [Lear] says suddenly, almost as if speaking to himself, 'let me not be mad.' Now I have seen Lears, with wildly tossing hair . . . , looking as though they were at home in Stonehenge, to whom madness seems only a natural extension of their personalities . . . But Mr Scofield's Lear is so strong, so normal, so healthily weather-beaten that the vision of madness starts both compassion and terror; it is like an intimation of death on a sunny morning.[8]

By this means Scofield lured the audience into following him into madness, substantially because he was not an obviously Titanic hero, and therefore managed to keep the audience's attention on the details of what he was saying, so that, as T. C. Worsley reported in his review, 'one could see what people meant in the interval when they said that the play had never been so clear'.[9]

The second major contribution to this clarity was that, in the central mad scenes, the Fool and Edgar 'unite with Mr Scofield's Lear in a masterly ensemble which forces one to take a huge imaginative leap into their company'. Irving Wardle here provides an exact summary of the mock trial's demands on both actors and audience: it requires an 'ensemble' of madness which compels the audience's attention and involvement. With this kind of preparation, 4.6 seemed the inevitable climax to which the earlier mad scenes had built: the mad Lear and the blind Gloucester squatted at the front of a huge white empty stage, as in the earlier scene with the Fool, to talk quietly about mankind and life. It seemed so truthful and above all so simple: a simplicity into which a great deal of very complex, very hard-won experience had been distilled – which seems to me exactly the impression given by the text at this point.

It might be argued that the success of this production vindicated

what seems to have been Shakespeare's original intention of preparing for the climactic treatment of mock-justice in 4.6 with the
mock trial; but the fact that one exceptional production has
overcome the difficulties of the trial scene does not alter the general
position that its difficulties usually defeat performers. If they defeated
the original cast also, this *could* have given a strong practical motive
for making the cut. Moreover, as I have tried to show, the omission
has other dramatic and structural consequences. What Brook's
production chiefly made clear was that the retention of the mock trial
demands quite exceptional ensemble acting, and sustained continuity
in the performance of Lear, in order to establish the reason-in-
madness; and that the theatrical realization of the complex simplicity
of 4.6 depends directly on establishing this.[10] Just how difficult
this is to achieve was by contrast demonstrated the hard way
by a production on a comparable level of professional com-
petence.

Trevor Nunn's 1968 Stratford production concentrated on 'the
stripping of Lear': Irving Wardle called this 'an uncomplicated
progression from . . . cloth-of-gold [to] rags' and nakedness.[11] 'As
he stands naked, . . . his descent is complete', said Trevor Nunn in
the programme: 'For Lear, further discovery can occur only in
madness.' But that is where the trouble starts – and in this case
started. These near-naked madmen, especially a Lear with his tights
down around his feet, seemed *merely* absurd, almost to the point of
slapstick. This in itself is not necessarily at odds with the way in which
the individual members of the court in the mock trial keep slipping
out of their 'judicial' roles into their individual eccentricities: in fact,
Irving Wardle thought that Tom/Edgar and the Fool were, individually, 'performances of shape and intelligence', but that taken
together, they did not 'generate the intensity that these scenes
demand, and nothing less than that will do'. Clearly what he missed
here was what he received from the mad scenes in the Brook version,
that sense of a 'masterly ensemble which forces one to take a huge
imaginative leap into their company'. It is, of course, a lot to ask; but
he is right that nothing less will do, and this underlines the practical
difficulty of the mock trial; for if the actors do not succeed here in
holding the audience's attention and concentration upon the details
of the mad speeches, it becomes virtually impossible for Lear
subsequently to communicate the logical connections in his mad
speeches in 4.6. G. K. Hunter remarks that 'Looke, looke, a Mouse'

(TLN 2535–6; I3ᵛ; 4.6.88–9) interrupts a 'tissue of ideas' in Lear's speech;[12] but in this production it became merely a piece of mad rambling. Because the parade of naked madmen earlier had seemed merely chaotic, the audience could not suddenly alter its response and start concentrating on the 'tissue of ideas': not merely 'looke, a Mouse', but all Lear's speeches, began to seem inconsequential. And if that happens, the mock trial, far from preparing for the mock-justice in 4.6, actually decreases the later scene's chance of being effective.

If something of the kind happened in the original production, Shakespeare may have felt that it would be better to cut (in more senses than one) his losses and reduce the mock trial scene so that its view of mock-justice could be concentrated into one decisive scene later, making small but significant revisions to ensure that it worked as strikingly as possible. In my experience only Brook's production achieved that effect of a mad ensemble which the mock trial demands; it remains to be seen whether a production following the Folio revisions, which reduce the need for that ensemble effect, would achieve more successful results.

NOTES

1. Stanley Wells, 'First and second shots', *The Times Literary Supplement*, 13 February 1981, p. 176.
2. Ralph Berry, *On Directing Shakespeare* (1977), pp. 100–1.
3. *Plays and Players*, October 1965, p. 33.
4. *Shakespeare Survey 33* (Cambridge, 1980), p. 84.
5. The Quarto has 'through tottered raggs, smal vices', another tiny but interesting difference pointing to Shakespearian revision: the Folio's replacing of 'raggs' by 'cloathes' was almost certainly to avoid repetition, since the passage added to the Folio text at this point includes 'Arme it in ragges'; so perhaps, while revising the phrase, Shakespeare altered 'smal' to 'great', though there is no obvious dramatic gain: the contrast is still between the rags which cannot conceal vices and the robes which can.
6. '*King Lear* at Stratford-on-Avon, 1959', *Shakespeare Quarterly*, 11 (1960), 197–9.
7. *The Times*, 13 December 1962.
8. *The Sunday Times*, 11 November 1962.
9. *The Financial Times*, 13 December 1962.
10. Although Brook did not cut anything from the mock trial itself, he did make some cuts in the mad scenes of Act Three, particularly some of the repetitive mad Tom material in 3.4 and 3.6. Not all of his cuts followed the Folio's: indeed, he omitted a Folio addition, the Fool's prophecy at the end of 3.2. Kent's 'All the powre of his wits, haue giuen way to his impatience' (TLN 2001–2; G3ᵛ; 3.6.4–5), which emphasizes Lear's complete insanity, was presumably omitted specifically to avoid

encouraging the audience to assume that Lear was about to talk gibberish before the mock trial had even begun. Brook basically followed the Folio's cuts which tighten the ending of the scene, omitting a line and a half from Kent's last speech and the whole of Edgar's final soliloquy.

11. *The Times*, 11 April 1968.
12. New Penguin Shakespeare (Harmondsworth, 1972), p. 285.

The Diminution of Kent

MICHAEL WARREN

I

CRITICS using the conventional conflated text called *King Lear* accept Kent's importance within that text; the role is acknowledged as vital primarily in that Kent functions as the faithful servant to Lear throughout the play, and speaks the penultimate speech of the play, declaring that he expects soon to join Lear in death. However, consideration of Kent in the Quarto and Folio texts separately leads one to perceive not that qualities of character differ from text to text, as they do in the cases of Albany and Edgar,[1] but that the role functions differently in each text, just as the play itself displays different elements of plot in each. The significance of the variation in the role of Kent lies in the notable diminution that it undergoes between the Quarto and the Folio. In the process of revision a major reduction was made in the prominence of the role in the last half of the play.

Although numbers have only a limited capacity for revealing the differences between masses of verbal material in a theatrical text, there is something to be learned from them; and since lines of speech are a relatively imprecise measure when one is dealing with material printed variously in verse and prose in the two texts, and in different lengths of prose line and often with irregular verse lineation in each, the safest measure is the number of words spoken. At the same time another revealing measure to be used in connection with the numbers of words is the number of cues for speech that a role has; Kent's cues and words for each act are as follows:[2]

Act	Quarto		Folio	
	Cues	Words	Cues	Words
1	29	567	27	560
2	35	912	36	903
3	29	582	27	505
4	19	304	4	56
5	12	147	13	152
Totals	124	2512	107	2176

Even when these figures are broken down by scene they give only a very limited sense of the variations in the role that result from transfer of speeches, presence or absence of words, contracted and expanded forms of words. Unfortunately they can conceal significant variation as easily as they can reveal it: for instance, the figures for 3.1 (Q 6 cues, 242 words: F 6 cues, 215 words) give no sense of the divergence of language between the two texts. However, the relative proportions of the figures for the first three acts and for the last two give some sense of how concentrated the role is in the first three acts in both texts; and the discrepancy between the figures for the fourth act in each text signals a major difference – the absence from F of two sequences of dialogue featuring Kent in Q – which alters the perception of Kent in the last two acts of the play in F.

It is on the modification of the role in the last part of the third act and in the fourth and fifth acts that I wish to focus attention. I wish to suggest that, whether as a central aim of the revision or as an incidental consequence of revisions with other major objectives, the part of Kent undergoes such substantial change between Quarto and Folio in the last two and a half acts that in the Folio he becomes a marginal figure until his entrance just prior to Lear's final scene. To show the change I shall initially comment briefly upon the characteristics of Kent's part in the first half of the play, then discuss in general terms the alteration in function that the part undergoes between Q and F, and then proceed to the examination of particular elements in detail, relating them to other alterations in the design of the play.

II

Although textual variants between Q and F abound in Kent's speeches in the first two acts,[3] Kent's role functions in the same way in each text. In each he makes his protest against Lear's folly, and, refusing to keep his honest vision to himself, is exiled for the blunt expression of his clear perceptions; in this he is immediately associated with Cordelia as a spokesman for truth, fearless in his honesty and rashly brave. Assuming a disguise, established theatrically by the adoption of a new voice and the removal of his beard (C3–C3^v; TLN 531–4; 1.4.1–4), and presumably by a change of clothes (K1^v; TLN 2753–5; 4.7.6–8), he is the first person in the play to be brought low from high estate, and in becoming Lear's servant presents that powerful image of love, loyalty, and fidelity in service to his king that proves a vivid contrast to the dubious love that the sisters show and to the opportunistic loyalty of the hundred knights. With the Fool, whose attachment to Cordelia is established even before his first entrance, Kent-as-Caius maintains the link with Cordelia in the abstract – they are both honest and faithful individuals – and in the concrete – he proves to be in correspondence with her at the end of 2.2 (E3; TLN 1240–5; 2.2.163–8). In this capacity Kent, an earl disguised as a servant, is the solitary figure of active virtue in Britain, the sole source of hope. As a heroic servant Kent undergoes the indignity of the stocking at the hands of Cornwall, an act that has a particular sharpness when his former aristocratic status is recalled; by his readiness to suffer for his master Kent gains admiration. Like the Fool, Kent-as-Caius is able to speak candidly to his superiors; it is he who insists that Lear recognize that it is Cornwall and Regan who have stocked him, and that that action bodes ill for Lear's future. His disguise proves the means by which the dog Truth can avoid going to kennel in the vicinity of Lear. However, it is clear to the audience that the price that Kent pays for his loyalty is high, and he is admired as an isolated figure of virtuous devotion in the first two acts.

These functions remain in the beginning of the third act also. Despite the substantial variants between Q and F in 3.1, variants whose different dramatic significances have already been well documented by both Urkowitz (*Revision*, pp. 67–79) and Taylor ('War', pp. 31–2), both scenes present Kent in the role of active protector of the king, indeed as prime preserver of the king's well-being. And in 3.2 and 3.4 Kent appears as the one companion who can give Lear sane and sensible advice in the midst of the storm; it is he who presses Lear insistently towards the hovel in both scenes, anxious to protect Lear from the rigours of the weather; it is he who persuades Gloucester to accede to Lear's apparently crazy desire to have his 'Athenian' with him: 'Good my Lord sooth him, let him take the fellow' (G3; TLN 1960–1; 3.4.177). Up to this point in the play, the close of 3.4, Kent is a vital figure in both texts. He is the only support that the King has apart from the Fool, who is a passive rather than an active comfort to him; Gloucester has only just intervened. Whatever modification Kent's role may have undergone thus far between the two texts, it has not suffered in relation either to scale or to major function.[4]

III

However, after Lear loses his wits in 3.4, there begins to be a significant quantitative distinction between Kent's parts in the texts. The large pattern of alteration between the texts has already been well described in print by Urkowitz and Taylor. The ample, relatively loose structure of the Quarto is tightened in the Folio; passages of moral commentary are removed, some speaking parts are eliminated, particularly characters with no identifiable name; the whole movement of the play is streamlined and sharpened, and the action concentrated. Notable abbreviation occurs near the beginning of the fourth act: Taylor points out that 'between the beginning of III, vi and the end of IV, iii it [the Folio] omits 157 lines, while adding only seven. To put it another way, the Folio cuts *one-third* of the Quarto text in these five scenes; *half* of the approximately three hundred lines omitted by the Folio are from these scenes' ('War', p. 29). Urkowitz comments that the reductions in length in F promote 'important theatrical values – concision, contrast, and surprise' (*Revision*, p. 55). Many of the passages that are removed, passages that Taylor calls 'eminently dispensable' ('War', pp. 29–30) and which Urkowitz regards as superfluous, are passages that involve Kent. I do not wish to argue that the diminution of Kent's part was the major focus of the revision, since the range and extent of the revisions in the last two and a half acts are so great that the modification of Kent's role is intimately bound up with other changes. Nevertheless, before dealing in detail with specific passages that relate to Kent, I shall address the broad issue of Kent's role in the second half of the play to suggest that the severity of its modification between Q and F may have been a response to a particular feature of its function in Q, a function distinctive to the dramaturgy of Q.

A shift occurs in Kent's role after 3.4 in Q; Kent simply plays a far less prominent part in the play's action than earlier. Each of the functions that he performs in the first part of the play either ceases to bear much significance or else becomes a major property of another character. For example, after Lear has lost his reason Kent can no longer serve the function of presenting the truth to Lear; in the trial scene in 3.6 he is left conspicuously outside the main action, which engages Lear, Edgar, and the Fool; among these 'madmen' the sane Kent is concerned solely with protecting Lear.[5] However, in this regard Gloucester begins to take a far more conspicuous part at this point; having determined that 'though I die for't, as no lesse is threatned me, | The King my old master must be releeued' (G1; TLN 1768–9; 3.3.17–19), Gloucester intervenes to take the major initiative in the preservation of Lear, providing the litter in which Lear is carried to Dover. In so doing he risks more than the disguised Kent, and in the succeeding scenes is subjected to cruel treatment that eclipses Kent's earlier experience; and henceforth in the play Gloucester draws to himself all the dramatic attention as the suffering servant of the play, punished unjustly for his fidelity to human values. Similarly, while Kent's disguise ceases to have real importance in the plot, Edgar's becomes of great dramatic interest as he guides his father to Dover, attempting to sustain the old man's spirits; in his various disguises he slowly develops his own powers until he restores himself and becomes Edgar once more in the last scene. The promise of Edgar coupled with the reintroduction of Albany and Cordelia as moral forces in the fourth act also means that Kent is no longer the solitary source of hope. Thus during and after 3.6 in the Quarto all Kent's major plot functions are taken from him; a previously dynamic figure, Kent-as-Caius becomes static. It is not that Kent loses any of his basic qualities of character; he merely is not seen in crucial action. Instead he becomes primarily an emblematic figure: his succeeding appearances before the last moments of the play are in relatively undramatic contexts. Kent is no longer interesting for what he does so much as for what he says: he becomes a spokesman for humane values, acting an almost choric role. Although regular reference is made to his disguise, it ceases to be a powerful focus of dramatic action since little depends upon it, and becomes instead an object of artificially sustained curiosity that is satisfied at the close.[6]

In the Quarto, then, the role of Kent has a distinct but surprisingly limited theatrical function in the second half of the play: he remains an independent voice but not a centre of dramatic action, while other figures, by contrast, become more vitally integrated into the plot, acting forcefully and speaking with authority. Kent retains presence in the Quarto, but not much dramatic significance. The more concentrated dramaturgy of the Folio, however, has no room for Kent's choric utterances or for the maintenance of serious interest in his functionless disguise. By being narrowed Kent's part in F is focused more precisely. Little attempt is made to maintain dramatic interest in him in the last two acts of the play; instead, after a brief appearance in 4.7 he and his disguise are simply and audaciously reintroduced in the last scene.

Such is the general outline of the diminution of Kent. In examining specific passages I shall illustrate the alterations in Kent's role and show how they coincide with three distinguishable qualities of the Folio text in its relation to the Quarto text: the reduction in the number of passages of static speech or dialogue about moral issues in the play, an alteration in the presentation of the role of Cordelia, and an enhancement and development of the role of Edgar.

IV

It is a characteristic of the Quarto text that it includes a number of soliloquies and brief dialogues, often at the ends of scenes, and especially of those of high tension, that slacken the pace before the action plunges on. In these passages moral reflections are made on past events, or else crucial moral decisions are made verbally; in them there is always a display either of judgement or of moral or humane concern. The most notable of these is probably the dialogue of the two servants at the end of the third act, after the dying Cornwall and the blinded Gloucester have been removed from the stage. In that brief exchange the servants express their horror at the actions of Cornwall and Regan, and decide to help Gloucester. For a moment the ferocious movement of the play halts and a moral insight is presented; characters comment upon the events in a way that reflects common human feeling confronting enormity; the audience is reminded of the existence of pity and kindness by hearing moral outrage and charitable sentiments expressed. On one notable occasion such a passage shows a character making a deplorably evil decision: the Captain in 5.3 who agrees to kill Lear and Cordelia reveals a total misperception of what it means to be man: 'I cannot draw a cart, nor eate dride oats, | If it bee mans worke ile do't' (K4ᵛ; 5.3.38–9). The absence of other passages of moral reflection or decision from the Folio text entails a reduction of Kent's presence. Each deletion may not be great in itself, but the sum of the deletions amounts to much of Kent's part in the last two acts of the Quarto text.

For instance, the Folio text closes 3.6 with a ten-line speech in which the fearful and agitated Gloucester urges a hasty departure for Kent and the Fool, telling Kent to 'Take vp thy Master' (TLN 2051;

G4^v; 3.6.92), and repeating his 'Take vp, take vp' soon after to move Kent to action (TLN 2054; G4^v; 3.6.95). In the Quarto, by contrast, Gloucester's speech is not a single unit, and he does not have the last word in the scene. Before Gloucester utters his final 'Come, come away' in the Quarto, a speech of Kent's intervenes, a speech of calm tenderness and human warmth that offsets Gloucester's urgency and anxiety. While Gloucester is quite justly concerned with the strategies of survival, Kent is concerned with the pathetic circumstance of the deranged but sleeping king:

> Oppressed nature sleepes,
> This rest might yet haue balmed thy broken sinewes,
> Which if conuenience will not alow stand in hard cure,
> Come helpe to beare thy maister, thou must not stay behind.
> (G4^v; 3.6.97–101)

Amid the frenzy of the action there is a moment of stasis, an expression of loving-kindness. But the establishment of a moment of sympathy does not end there; in the last line Kent addresses the Fool, who has spoken only five times during the scene and not for thirty-six lines at this point, asking him to help carry Lear offstage, and refusing to allow him to linger behind. The Fool is therefore seen not only as an object of concern for Kent, who in insisting that he come along is assuming Lear's recently adopted protective role towards the Fool, but also as participating in the common act of preserving the king. Thus the Fool, whose part in the Folio closes with 'And Ile go to bed at noone' (TLN 2043; 3.6.85), a line not in the Quarto, and with an unspecified exit, is last seen in the Quarto bearing the burden of his mad master. In the Quarto the lowly are seen physically supporting the king in his distress. Where the Folio stresses the dangers and moves straight into them, the Quarto presents a cameo of the world of patient and loving refugees from hostility, of which Kent appears to be the major spokesman, although it should be noted that the scene in the Quarto actually closes on Edgar's soliloquy, in which he expresses his sense of the sufferings of others. Such cameos, in which the progress of the plot is briefly arrested and an image of moral life is presented, are a distinctive feature of the dramatic technique of the Quarto, a readiness to allow the action to pause so that the moral impact of events can be demonstrated verbally and visually; in F, by contrast, the plot just takes its mighty course.

It is in scenes like these that Kent appears in the fourth act in the Quarto; he is present as a still point of moral life, for when he appears the scene is always charged with benevolence and selfless concern for others' well-being. In this context the absence of 4.3 from the Folio is particularly revealing because it shows an alteration not merely in relation to pace of action, but in relation to the functions of characters, and specifically to the functions of Kent and Cordelia. Of course, the absence of 4.3 from the text may be considered as part of a modification relating strictly to plot, in particular the reduction of identification of Cordelia's army with France in the Folio.[7] However, the scene's distinctive quality in the Quarto is its concentration upon the psychological and moral states of Lear and Cordelia. The conversation of Kent and the Gentleman presents a very kindly interpretation of human nature after the animal imagery of the conversation of Goneril and Albany in 4.2 in the Quarto; each presents his subject sympathetically. Kent is the means by which the audience of the Quarto learns of the state of Lear's mind in what must be a brief moment of lucidity upon arrival at Dover; he presents a Lear filled with 'A soueraigne shame', a 'burning shame' that 'detaines him from *Cordelia*', a Lear who is grappling with the moral consequences of those earlier acts of his that 'sting his mind' (I1; 4.3.42–7).[8] The same sympathy informs the Gentleman's description of Cordelia. He presents her exemplary qualities, evoking pathos by the description of her emotions; in his speech she develops almost emblematic status in her joyful suffering, for her 'smiles and teares' are presented in an elaborate static figure by the Gentleman:

> those happie smilets,
> That playd on her ripe lip seeme not to know,
> What guests were in her eyes which parted thence,
> As pearles from diamonds dropt . . .
>   (H4^v–I1; 4.3.19–22)

Moreover, he presents her as a paragon of sensitivity, tenderness, and forgiveness:

> Faith once or twice she heau'd the name of father,
> Pantingly forth as if it prest her heart,
> Cried sisters, sisters, shame of Ladies sisters:
> *Kent*, father, sisters, what ith storme ith night,
> Let pitie not be beleeft there she shooke,
> The holy water from her heauenly eyes,
> And clamour moystened her, then away she started,
> To deale with griefe alone.
>   (I1; 4.3.25–32)

It is in response to this speech that Kent utters his general commentary upon heredity, one which in the light of the horrific behaviour of Regan and Goneril in previous scenes serves to reinforce the hyperbolical image of Cordelia as a figure of transcendent virtue:

> It is the stars, the stars aboue vs gouerne our conditions,
> Else one selfe mate and make could not beget,
> Such different issues.

(Il; 4.3.32–5)

This scene is representative of Kent's function in the Quarto as spokesman for deep human feeling and profound moral concern. The absence of this scene from the Folio diminishes our awareness of Kent and removes this function; the Folio text is not only more rapid and more vigorous, but also more objective and more challenging, because less overtly moral. The Folio text does not risk the sentimental, as the Quarto does.[9] But the absence of 4.3 from the Folio is also part of a profound difference in the presentation of Cordelia. When Cordelia finally enters in the Quarto after the introduction that Kent and the Gentleman afford her, the stage direction reads 'Enter Cordelia, Doctor and others' (Il; 4.4.0). By contrast in the Folio Cordelia makes her entrance with no prior introduction and as head of her armed forces: 'Enter with Drum and Colours, Cordelia, Gentlemen, and Souldiours' (TLN 2349–50; 4.4.0). The Folio presentation of Cordelia maintains her virtuous qualities but, without Monsieur la Far as general, she is presented as a commander; her humane qualities are apparent in her speeches in this scene and later scenes, but she is neither sentimentalized nor glorified in advance by the hyperbolic static imagery of the Gentleman. She is known by her action and speech, not idealized by report.

Kent's importance is markedly diminished by Cordelia's re-entry. It is a commonplace of criticism to observe that the Fool enters the play after Cordelia's banishment and leaves it before she returns from exile, as if the Fool were a substitute object for Lear's tenderness in Cordelia's absence. Kent's diminution similarly gives a distinctive feature to the role of Cordelia; with Kent reduced in the fourth act from a residual figure of honesty and loyalty to almost a cipher, Cordelia, who has suffered exile for honesty and candour just like Kent, is given the stage more prominently in the Folio text, and not obliged to share with Kent the role of representative in the play of their distinctive virtues – honesty, fidelity, forgiveness, and tenderness of human love.

V

If the diminution of Kent can be seen as bringing into prominence, or at least reducing any possible obscuring of, Cordelia, Folio alterations in the role in the last two acts may be seen as enhancing the role of Edgar. During the third and fourth acts Kent and Edgar perform similar functions: the old Kent, disguised in servant's clothes, cares for his master Lear; the young Edgar, disguised in a variety of clothing, cares for his father Gloucester. Each endures the heroic trek across the south of England to Dover, and each delays the revelation of his identity presumably in anticipation of what he conceives as the perfect movement. If these parallel actions can be discerned in both texts, it is nevertheless true that the parallelism is reduced in the Folio. Without 4.3 the audience is less conscious of Kent's attendance upon Lear during the journey, while Edgar remains conspicuous in his heroic efforts with Gloucester. Little attempt is made to sustain interest in Kent's disguise and his anticipated revelation. By contrast, in the Quarto Kent's far-from-large part in the fourth act gives a disproportionate amount of attention to his concealment: at the end of the conversation with the Gentleman in 4.3 he volunteers to the Gentleman that he will one day disclose his identity to him; at the end of 4.7 a Gentleman engaging Kent in conversation about current events and personalities refers to a rumour that Edgar is with Kent in Germany, and Kent gives an evasive reply. The Folio includes only the brief reference to disguise early in 4.7 just after Kent has received such thanks from Cordelia for his completed service to Lear that he appears at that moment to be about to be dismissed from the play; to Cordelia's request that he 'Be better suited', he replies

> Pardon deere Madam,
> Yet to be knowne shortens my made intent,
> My boone I make it, that you know me not,
> Till time and I, thinke meet.
> (TLN 2753, 2756–9; K1ᵛ; 4.7.6, 8–11)

The Folio text obviously reminds us of Kent's disguise, but it can hardly be said to accentuate it, not least because this speech is one of only four that Kent has in the Folio between 'Here Sir, but trouble him not, his wits are gon' (TLN 2046; G4ᵛ; 3.6.87) and his final entrance in the last scene at TLN 3182 (L3; 5.3.230).

When he makes that entrance amid the confusion created by the deaths of Goneril and Regan it is sudden and unexpected in either text. However, in the Folio it is particularly so because by this time Kent is also a 'Great thing of vs forgot.' It is not just the absence of periodic conversations with Gentlemen that has diminished our awareness of him; alterations in the part of Edgar also have deleted references to Kent which in the Quarto serve as a prelude to his entry. Part of the modification of the role of Edgar in the Folio involves the omission of the report that he gives in the Quarto to the assembled company, telling (over the protest of Albany) of the tearful meeting that he had with Kent beside the dead body of Gloucester. This speech is rich in parallels: it is the great moment when the three devoted servants are all in one place, one dead, one dying, and one just about to go off to reclaim his identity; it brings together the two men who have lived in disguise; it associates Kent with Gloucester, in conversation with whom he had begun the play, in his nearness to death. An emblematic moment, a static image of a kind of common fulfilment, it has a distinctive histrionic exemplary power; but it also appears to tie up loose ends of whose unravelling the audience was otherwise unaware. Coupled with the preceding speech of Gloucester's death it halts the play's action in the Quarto, and delays the climactic revelations of the deaths of the sisters and the moment of Lear's entrance. Without it the Folio text moves with greater swiftness than the Quarto. And without it also Edgar appears a stronger, more commanding figure; but Kent is left with his heroic career uncelebrated and no introduction beyond Edgar's 'Here comes *Kent*' (TLN 3181; L3; 5.3.230), a terse remark that ensures that the audience will recognize Kent when he enters, no longer dressed as Caius, upon the chaotic scene. When Kent speaks it is a language of death: 'I am come to bid my King and maister ay good night, | Is he not here?' (L3; TLN 3189–91; 5.3.235–7). In the Quarto he is prophesying his own death; Edgar has informed us that under the strain of telling his tale Kent's 'strings of life, | Began to cracke' (L3; 5.3.217–18). In the Folio he may be prophesying his own death also – he is old, it has been a long journey, he may have been wounded in the battle – but we are provided no explicit reason; on the other hand he may be anticipating Lear's. Certainly he is not at this point a major focus of the dramatic action even though he restores

Lear's predicament to the audience's consciousness in both texts. The Folio's omission of Edgar's speech about Kent can be seen as part of a larger pattern of alterations in the last scene. The Folio focuses on Edgar as the youth of the realm, not, as does the Quarto, on Albany and the generation that has already known power; it concentrates upon Edgar's survival in disguise and on the relative success of his revelation of his identity to his father, presenting Edgar as the inheritor of responsibilities in the shattered realm. The parallels in Kent's behaviour are played down, to emphasize Edgar's triumph.

VI

Between 3.6 and the middle of 5.3 Kent atrophies, ceasing to have a clear dramatic purpose or unique function in the play's action. The Folio severely curtails his role in that part of the play. But at the end, when he returns undisguised to face Lear one last time, he has again a reason for being, both dramatically and personally. After Lear's entrance he participates in the final moments similarly in both texts (with one exception). He is part of that chorus of witnesses to the last devastating moments of Lear's life, and acts toward Lear with his characteristic solicitude. In both texts Lear's failure to recognize him as Caius is briefly powerful; in both texts Kent is denied the reward and recognition he has waited for, and has so clearly merited; in both texts Kent's frustration is a minor example of the 'inexplicable defeat of the deserving' (Taylor, 'War', p. 31), of which the major example is the death of Cordelia.[10] In Q Kent's earlier repeated references to his disguise arguably make the audience more aware of the degree of his investment in this moment; in F, on the other hand, the very unexpectedness and bad timing of his arrival can make their own comment. After all, as his first words reveal, Kent had expected Lear to be here. Kent makes his long-relished re-entrance only to discover that the one crucial spectator is absent, and that in fact no one is expecting him. In Q we may be more aware of Kent's investment in his moment of self-revelation, but he at least receives more attention and sympathy before and upon his entrance; in F the entrance is as anticlimactic, for Kent, as the reunion with Lear will be.

Far from being diminished, at the very end of the play Kent's role is expanded. The Folio gives him an extra speech which beautifully reinforces the quality of his tender devotion to Lear even as its transfer from Lear himself is part of a radical alteration in the quality of Lear's death. When Lear dies in the Quarto he asks for the button to be undone, offers his thanks, groans 'O,o,o,o' as he swoons, and then after Edgar's 'He faints my Lord, my Lord' utters his last words 'Breake hart, I prethe breake' (L4; 5.3. [311], 312–13), desiring death in the desolation of Cordelia's death. The Folio text does not include the groan, but instead has the lines of Lear's deluded vision at his death, 'Do you see this? Looke on her? Looke her lips, | Looke there, looke there' (TLN 3282–3; 5.3.311–12), followed by the explicit stage direction '*He dies*'; it then gives the words 'Breake heart, I prythee breake' to Kent. As Kent's last line it may be Kent asking for Lear's release from life, or (as Bradley suggested) for his own.[11] However it is regarded, and I prefer the former interpretation, it certainly gives to Kent an opportunity for one last climactic demonstration of his loving fidelity before his final utterance 'My Master calls me, I must not say no' (TLN 3297; L4; 5.3.323). At the same time it suggests a more intimate involvement in Lear's death than in the Quarto, and could permit theatrically an increased physical closeness between Kent and Lear. Indeed, it can lead to a new consideration of the earlier line 'Pray you vndo this Button. Thanke you sir' (TLN 3281; L4; 5.3.310), which presents interpretative problems in either text, since it is not clear from 'you' who undoes the button, or even, given the range of possible states of Lear's mind, whether the button is actually undone. In either text someone, perhaps Kent, may undo the button; but if Kent is to speak the line 'Breake heart, I prythee breake' he becomes a particularly likely person to serve Lear's request; it may even be he rather than the assembled company whom Lear asks to 'see this'. Such observations lead to speculation about the quality of Lear's interaction with Kent at and after his moment of actual acknowledgement, 'are you not *Kent*?' (TLN 3247; L3ᵛ; 5.3.283), a matter of importance in stage performance in either text. However, it is enough for the non-theatrical interpreter to observe that after suffering considerable diminution Kent's role in the Folio actually concludes in a way which provides for greater prominence than in the Quarto and which, if anything, increases the opportunities for richness of theatrical interpretation.

NOTES

1. See M. Warren, 'Albany and Edgar', *passim*, and Urkowitz, *Revision*, esp. pp. 80–128.
2. I am grateful to Linda Charnes for compiling these figures.

3. Gary Taylor presents a precise study of many variants in the first act in a book entitled *To Analyze Delight: A Hedonist Criticism of Shakespeare* (as yet unpublished).
4. It could be argued, however, that the diminution of Kent's function in F begins as early as 3.1. In the F version of the long speech to the Gentleman, Kent tells him that France has spies who have presumably already transmitted information about division between the dukes and their mistreatment of Lear; thus Kent has no special news to send, as he has in Q (F3ᵛ; TLN 1628–38; 3.1.19–42).
5. The editorial tradition beginning with Capell customarily includes Kent with the Fool and Edgar in Lear's 'court' by intruding the direction 'To Kent' before the concluding phrases of Lear's speech: 'you are ot'h commission, sit you too' (G4; 3.6.38–9). But this is not the only reasonable interpretation of these words, which I believe should be addressed to the Fool. The passage in question reads '& thou his yokefellow of equity, bench by his side, you are ot'h commission, sit you too'. Although the shift from the familiar 'thou' to the more formal 'you' may appear to indicate a shift in addressee from the Fool to Kent-as-Caius, it affords no security to the interpreter. To this point in Q Lear has used 'thou' consistently to Kent-as-Caius except in the speech when he sends him ahead with a letter (D2ᵛ; TLN 876–9; 1.5.2–5), when he uses 'you' and 'your'. Moreover, Lear is not in his right mind at this point; it is possible that to a new prospective member of his commission he uses the more polite 'you', but it is equally possible that the change of pronoun reflects a new attitude to the person he is already addressing, an impatience with the Fool who is not responding quickly enough (see E. A. Abbott, *A Shakespearian Grammar*, 3rd edn., 1870, §232). I favour the latter reading of the lines. Kent does not participate in Lear's fantasy as the others do; I believe that he stays separate from Lear's 'court', acting as a commentator upon the mad action. However, even if the conventional interpretation is adopted and Kent is bidden to be a member of that 'court', he plays no part in its activities.
6. In his scornful summary of its plot of *King Lear*, Tolstoy draws attention frequently to the artificiality of the maintenance of Kent's disguise. Although his view is prejudiced, he points to a real issue (see Leo Tolstoy, *Tolstoy on Shakespeare*, trans. V. Tchertkoff and I. F. M., New York and London, 1907). More recently Bertrand Evans has written a severe critique of the operation of Kent's disguise: see *Shakespeare's Tragic Practice* (Oxford, 1979), pp. 154–66. Gary Taylor informs me that John Shrapnel, who played Kent in the 1982 BBC production, strongly favoured all the Folio cutting of his role, feeling that it removed theatrical dead weight which made audiences stop listening to Kent at all. Many of the relevant Folio cuts were adopted, although some passages were later restored at the insistence of the Gentleman.
7. See Taylor, 'War', pp. 30–2, for a discussion of the French presence. W. W. Greg addressed this issue but with limited success because he believed in the conflation of the texts; see 'Time, Place, and Politics in *King Lear*', *Modern Language Review*, 35 (1940), 431–46, reprinted in *Collected Papers*, ed. J. C. Maxwell (Oxford, 1966), pp. 322–40.
8. Urkowitz (*Revision*, pp. 53–4) raises important questions about the relation of statements in this scene to later details in the plot; he calls Kent's description of Lear's 'shame' a 'major anomaly'.
9. In *The Pictorial Edition of the Works of Shakespeare* (8 vols., [1839–]1843), Charles Knight wrote of 4.3: 'the greater part of the scene is purely descriptive; and, exquisite as the description is, particularly in those parts which make us better understand the surpassing loveliness of Cordelia's character, we cannot avoid believing that the poet sternly resolved to let the effect of this wonderful drama entirely depend upon its action' (VI, 393).

10. In *The Lear World: A Study of 'King Lear' in its Dramatic Context* (Toronto, 1977), John Reibetanz presents an illuminating discussion of the particular disguise convention within which Kent and Edgar operate (pp. 91–2).

11. A. C. Bradley, *Shakespearean Tragedy* (1904), p. 309: 'It is of himself he is speaking, perhaps, when he murmurs, as his master dies, "Break, heart, I prithee, break!"' With the exception of the New Temple edition edited by M. R. Ridley (1935) I have found no edition of *King Lear* that takes the Quarto reading seriously; the Folio stage direction commands too great respect. For example, in the new Arden edition (1952, rev. 1972) Kenneth Muir notes that 'Q, impossibly, gives the words to Lear who is already beyond speech' (p. 205 n.). However, in the New Variorum edition (Philadelphia, 1880) H. H. Furness quotes Richard Grant White (1861): 'I am not sure that this speech does not belong to Lear. The stage direction "He dies," at the end of Lear's foregoing speech, may be only a timely warning to the prompter, such as is constantly to be found in our old dramas. Possibly Lear was supposed to expire during Kent's next speech' (p. 348). Thomas Clayton also discusses this passage in his essay (see pp. 128–39 below).

Monopolies, Show Trials, Disaster, and Invasion
King Lear and Censorship

GARY TAYLOR

I T has been widely accepted that the Folio text of *King Lear* was set, directly or indirectly, from a theatrical manuscript; such a manuscript would have represented the text after it had been seen and approved by the Master of the Revels; as a result certain variants between Quarto and Folio may be the consequence of nothing more than political censorship.

This possibility exists whether or not one believes that there are two versions of the play. But if, as has been assumed, both texts are defective representations of a lost 'fine, full, perfect' original, then it becomes rather difficult to explain which text has been censored, when, and where.[1] According to the traditional theory, Q is a memorial report of the play as performed, and F a prompt-book of the play as performed; therefore, if the text was censored before it was staged, the uncensored original of any passage so affected *should* appear in *neither* text. In order to dismiss certain Folio cuts or alterations as the results of censorship, one must presume that the play was resubmitted to the Master of the Revels some time after the performances upon which Q was based; but there would have been no need for such resubmission unless the play had in the meantime been significantly revised or adapted. Attempts to support the traditional one-text theory by explaining certain Folio variants as the result of censorship thus lead inevitably to the assumption that the play must have been substantially revised at some time after its first performance. In other words, an attempt to prove that there was only ever one text eventually postulates that there were two.

I

Censorship imposes the political restraints of a particular time and place upon a potentially timeless work of art; to understand it we must understand both the political context it works within and the artistic context it works upon. The historian can determine if (or when) a particular passage might have been considered objectionable in the light of contemporary events; the critic must then decide whether the variant can be plausibly explained on dramatic or literary rather than political grounds. The bulk of this essay will therefore be devoted to an historical and critical analysis of four major differences between the two texts of *King Lear*, differences often or always attributed to political interference. But because the circumstances under which *King Lear* might have been scrutinized by the Master of the Revels are themselves of some importance in determining the relationship of the Quarto and Folio texts, before I can begin the analysis of specific passages something must be said about the procedures of Jacobean theatrical censorship.[2] Those procedures have an immediate pertinence to the larger problem of whether *King Lear* was, at some point between 1605 and 1623, adapted or revised.

If Quarto *Lear* contains material which has apparently been removed from the Folio at the censor's request, then either the Quarto represents the text as it stood before being submitted to the censor, or the Folio version of the play was subjected to a second phase of censorship. The first of these alternatives forces us to the conclusion that the Quarto and Folio must represent different versions of the play, because no one imagines that censorship can account for all of the differences between them. But in order to entertain the other option, we must identify when, and for what purpose, the text of *King Lear* might have been submitted to the censor a second time.

We possess no evidence that, before 1633, revived plays were automatically resubmitted to the Master of the Revels, *unless* they had been adapted or revised; indeed, the reaction of the actors on that specific occasion in 1633, and the details of Henry Herbert's letter to them, make it quite clear that Herbert was changing the rules.[3] Before 1633, revival without revision apparently required no resubmission. Therefore we cannot assume that *King Lear* was resubmitted simply because it was revived. Nor can we explain the resubmission by postulating that the original licensed prompt-book was somehow lost, and that a new one had therefore to be prepared and submitted for approval. In 1623, in just these circumstances, Herbert himself approved a new prompt-book of *The Winter's Tale* without even looking at it, after receiving verbal assurances that nothing had been altered since his predecessor George Buc had approved it more than a decade before.[4] Nor will it help to suppose, as did Alice Walker, that the Quarto was set from a heavily contaminated transcript of Shakespeare's foul papers, prepared by two actors who often relied on their own memories instead of looking at the manuscript in front of them.[5] The implausibility of this hypothesis was recognized, by W. W. Greg among others, almost as soon as Walker formulated it.[6] But even if Walker's hypothesis were credible, it would not resolve the specific difficulty of accounting for the apparent censorship of F but not Q, since it would force us to suppose that the two actors deliberately included material which they *knew* had been censored – and that George Buc subsequently *approved* the publication of a text which disregarded his own demands for the removal of sensitive passages.[7]

The presence in the Quarto (supposedly corrupted by memories of the play as performed) of passages absent from the Folio (apparently because of censorship) thus creates a considerable difficulty for the traditional conflationist hypothesis. One could only escape this apparent contradiction by conjecturing that further cuts were made at a later date, either by the actors themselves or in circumstances where the Master of the Revels may have felt compelled to examine yet again a text he had already approved once. These two possibilities need to be separately considered.

The King's Men might, on their own initiative, have excised certain passages which – though innocent enough in 1605 – had become dangerously topical at some later date.[8] Such scrupulous self-regulation would, however, plausibly explain the variation between Q and F only if particular passages, omitted from the Folio, could be convincingly related to political or religious developments later in James's reign. The only variant in *Lear* clearly attributable to such subsequent interference is the Folio omission of the single word 'Fut'.

as if we were Villaines by necessitie, Fooles by heauenly compulsion . . . Drunkards, Lyars, and Adulterers by an enforst obedience of planitary influence, and all that wee are euill in, by a diuine thrusting on, an admirable euasion of whoremaster man, to lay his gotish disposition to the charge of Starres: my Father compounded with my Mother vnder the Dragons taile, and my natiuitie was vnder *Vrsa maior*, so that it followes, I am rough and lecherous, Fut, I should haue beene that I am, had the maidenlest starre of the Firmament twinckled on my bastardy
    (C2–C2ᵛ; TLN 450–61, reading 'a Starre' and 'bastardizing', and omitting 'Fut'; 1.2.121–33)

OED records *fut* as a variant of the exclamation *foot* (*sb.* 1b), meaning 'Christ's foot'; E. A. M. Colman suggests it may also have been influenced – as *foot* on occasion demonstrably was – by French *foutre* ('fuck').[9] The word thus compounds profanity with obscenity, and G. I. Duthie was probably right in suggesting that the Folio omitted it in deference to the 'Acte to Restraine Abuses of Players' in May 1606 (*3 Jac. I*, c. 21).[10] Of course, the omission might result from compositorial or scribal error, especially as Folio *Lear* shows no other signs of having been edited to remove profanity;[11] on the other hand, since 'Fut' is undoubtedly the most profane word in a play remarkably un-profane (verbally), it does seem rather disingenuous to blame its disappearance on fortuitous error. Authorial second thoughts seem equally unlikely. The exclamation emphatically marks an important transition in Edmund's argument; its sexual and religious meanings draw upon and sustain the imagery of his whole speech; its omission contributes to no discernible larger pattern of Folio alterations affecting this scene or Edmund's role in general. Censorship therefore seems to me likely here; it also seems to me likely that *King Lear* was originally submitted to the censor before the 1606 Act had been passed. In this single instance, then, a Folio variant probably does derive from later attention to the play, either by the King's Men themselves (voluntarily bringing the play into conformity with the new legislation) or by the censor (reading the revised text when it was resubmitted, or rereading the original for some special occasion). But, although this conclusion justifies an editor in restoring 'Fut', it does not tell us anything about the larger problem of the Quarto's relation to the Folio. This single omission can be credibly attributed to the influence of censorship whatever our view of the nature of the two texts.

This cut, and others, might have been made for a known specific performance, that at Court on 26 December 1606. That performance provides an obvious occasion for which the Master of the Revels might have examined yet again a text he had already approved once. Certainly, if the Court performance was *not* the play's première (which it might have been), then Buc would have been wise to look at the text again, and carefully, before King James saw it;[12] he might well, for the safety of himself and the actors, have recommended a few more cuts. However, these new recommendations – if they were ever made – would have been intended either to modify the Court performance only (in which case they should not have affected the company's licensed book for public playing) or, more likely, to regulate *all* subsequent performances. Since Buc himself licensed the publication of Q, eleven months later, one might expect him to have checked that significant new cuts, earlier insisted on, had indeed been made.[13] But even if Buc had not bothered, the newly-censored passages should still not have appeared in any text derived, in whole or part, from memories of performance – unless, that is, we further assume that the memorial reconstruction behind Q was itself compiled *before* the Christmas of 1606, even though it was not sold until almost a year later. We might well ask what happened to the manuscript in that interval, and why the indigent soul or souls driven to the laborious expedient of pirating a text for the sake of pecuniary gain were then so unaccountably tardy in unloading their treasure. This series of assumptions – of public performances before Christmas, of further cuts at court, of Buc's considerable carelessness in licensing the Quarto, of an eleven-month gap between Q's unauthorized compilation and its authorized entry in the Stationers' Register – must be constructed simply in order to answer one of a multiplicity of objections to the conflationist hypothesis. Moreover, even this pyramid of assumptions will not suffice if one or more of the passages absent from the Folio is so offensive that Buc could not be credibly supposed to have *ever* let it pass.

It is thus doubly important to determine whether any extended passages were omitted from the Folio because of political censorship. If any were, then the presence of those passages in the Quarto might seriously undermine the traditional hypothesis (that Q in some way reflects the play as remembered from performance) and to the same degree bolster recent claims that Q was set from Shakespeare's own foul papers. If it was, then many of the differences between it and the Folio presumably result from deliberate alteration in the Folio rather than inadvertent corruption in the Quarto. But on the other hand, if Shakespeare's foul papers lie behind the Quarto, then the manuscript which lies behind the Folio must have undergone at least one and possibly two submissions to the censor—in which case several significant differences between Quarto and Folio might be due to political rather than artistic intervention. The authority of both texts is therefore inextricably bound up with the evidence for political interference in the Folio.

II

Four major differences between Quarto and Folio *Lear* have sometimes been attributed to censorship.

The first of these involves a whole series of alterations and omissions. The Folio consistently eliminates references to France in Acts Four and Five, and to a lesser extent in Act Three. W. W. Greg insisted that the foreign invasion was a 'ticklish business' which created a 'patriotic dilemma';[14] Madeleine Doran was confident that the Folio omissions and alterations affecting the nationality of Cordelia's army resulted from censorship.[15] But this seems most implausible. The old *Leir* play had been much more explicit in dramatizing the French invasion than Shakespeare was, even in the Quarto; *Leir*, moreover, dates from a period (*c*. 1590) when invasion of England by a continental power was a real and feared possibility. James I had little to worry about on that score: England had been officially and actually at peace since 1604. The real threat to the Stuarts was not foreign invasion but domestic discontent, and the Folio alterations to Acts Four and Five metamorphose the former into the latter.[16] Moreover, Jacobean censorship of references to foreign powers always involves *negative* portrayal of *contemporary* figures.[17] We know, for instance, that the French ambassador objected to the portrait of the contemporary French court in Chapman's *Charles, Duke of Byron*;[18] but in *Lear* the unnamed, pre-Christian French King, who twice intervenes on the side of truth, justice, and an audience's sympathies, bears no resemblance to the corrupt and scheming modern politicians who populate Chapman's play.

Nothing in the Quarto's references to France could possibly have offended either the English or the French authorities. Nor can I lend much credence to Greg's later suggestion that thirteen lines of Kent's speech to the Gentleman (F3^v; 3.1.30–42) were censored because they alluded, dangerously, to 'neglect of port defences'.[19] But these lines, and the other references to France, might well have been consciously sacrificed to an altered dramatic vision of the last half of the play. Neither Greg nor Doran considered the possible structural or thematic implications of these Folio changes, but they have recently been defended – independently, and on purely artistic grounds – by both Steven Urkowitz (*Revision*, pp. 71–4, 93) and myself ('War'). As one of the proponents of this interpretation I can hardly pass an objective judgement on its merits; but a number of more disinterested readers have evidently found it persuasive.[20] In any case, since censorship seems, on the historical evidence, extremely unlikely, conscious artistic alteration remains the only currently available explanation for this apparently interrelated set of variants.

III

The Folio's altered presentation of Cordelia's army entails changes throughout the second half of the play; much less important critically, but equally unlikely as a candidate for censorship, is a short passage in 1.2 present in Q but not F. (The Folio omits the lines I have bracketed.)

> *Bast.* I am thinking brother of a prediction I read this other day, what should follow these Eclipses.
> *Edg.* Doe you busie your selfe about that?
> *Bast.* I promise you the effects he writ of, succeed vnhappily, [as of vnnaturalnesse betweene the child and the parent, death, dearth, dissolutions of ancient amities, diuisions in state, menaces and maledictions against King and nobles, needles diffidences, banishment of friēds, dissipation of Cohorts, nuptial breaches, and I know not what.
> *Edg.* How long haue you beene a sectary Astronomicall?
> *Bast.* Come, come,] when saw you my father last?
>
> (C2ᵛ; TLN 469–74; 1.2.140–52)

Edmund's 'Eclipses' are 'These late eclipses in the Sunne and Moone' (C2; TLN 433; 1.2.103), and almost certainly allude, extra-dramatically, to the extraordinary juxtaposed eclipses of September and October 1605. This lends Edmund's 'prediction I read this other day' a potential topicality which certainly might have led the censor to scrutinize it carefully. But, though modern editors all apparently agree in blaming the censor for this cut, no one has explained what George Buc found dangerously topical about such hoary generalities as 'death', 'dissolutions of ancient amities', or 'needles diffidences, banishment of friēds, dissipation of Cohorts' – not to mention 'and I know not what'. If he had objected (as he well might) to the more openly political 'diuisions in state, menaces and maledictions against King and nobles', he could easily – as he did on similar occasions elsewhere – have struck through those ten words, without touching the rest of the passage.[21] In fact, even if – as seems most unlikely – Buc had ordered Edmund's entire catalogue to be cut, Edgar's reply would still have been perfectly sensible; yet it too has disappeared. In short, more has been omitted here than can be plausibly attributed to even the most paranoid of censors. What unites all the material omitted is its mocking tone, not topical significance or possible political controversiality. This in itself strongly suggests that any convincing explanation of the Folio omission must begin with the passage's tone, rather than its liability to political objections directed at particular items.

I stress this point because specific objections might conceivably have been made to three more of the items in Edmund's catalogue. The 'dearth' of 1608 was associated with disturbances in the Midlands, and led to a bad outbreak of plague the following year; James I, not always on the best of terms with his son and heir Prince Henry, might have been sensitive to allusions – however vague – to 'vnnaturalnesse betweene the child and the parent'; and the 'nuptial breach' between Lady Frances Howard and the Earl of Essex, in 1613, was one of the most notorious court scandals of James's reign. Lady Howard's marriage to Essex was annulled by a special commission packed with royally-appointed judges; her marriage to Robert Carr – the King's favourite, with whom she had been having an affair – followed with predictable and indecent haste. Moreover, the King's 'breaches' with his own wife caused him some personal and political embarrassment.

A censor might well, for these particular reasons, have objected to 'vnnaturalnesse betweene the child and the parent', 'dearth', and 'nuptial breaches'. But the Lady Howard divorce could hardly have influenced the censor before 1613 or late 1612;[22] Prince Henry died, after many weeks of illness, on 6 November 1612, thereby removing any danger of further 'vnnaturalnesse' between him and his father. On the other hand, not until 1610–11 did Henry's initial political activities bring him into open conflict with his father.[23] Most of the gossip about rifts between Queen Anne and James comes, instead, from early in the reign.[24] As for 'dearth', that of 1608 of course postdates the 1606 Court performance of *Lear*, but precedes the Lady Howard affair, or the major conflicts with Prince Henry; before 1608 there had been six good harvests in a row (1601–6) followed by an 'average' one (1607). After 1608 'The next really bad harvest came in 1622', leading to dearth the following spring.[25]

In short, though *each* of these phrases might have been impolitic at certain times, one cannot easily pinpoint a time when the censor would have objected to *all* of them.[26] Moreover, though the Lady

Howard affair makes 'nuptial breaches' the likeliest candidate for
censorship, that scandal cannot have influenced the censor until later
in the reign; and if Edmund's speech was not censored early, there
would be little reason to censor it at all. The further we move from
1605 the less topical Edmund's speech necessarily becomes.[27] In 1605
or 1606, with 'These late eclipses in the Sunne and Moone' prominent
in the public memory, any prognostication of terrestrial consequences might easily be taken – might easily be intended – as a
transparent allusion to current political gossip. But as those eclipses
themselves receded in time, Edmund's predictions would to the same
degree begin to lose their extra-dramatic, topical self-consciousness,
subsiding gradually into the time and place and plot of the fiction as a
whole. In short, 'these Eclipses' would lose the quotation marks
which must have surrounded them in performances of 1605 or 1606,
so that by 1610–13 the whole passage would have become markedly
less censorable, whatever its specific content. It would also, of course,
have lost much of its initial dramatic *raison d'être*. The very
diminution of topicality which makes censorship *less* likely after 1606
makes deliberate excision for purely artistic motives *more* so.

The venereal immorality of the Countess of Essex thus seems
unlikely to have depraved the Folio text of *King Lear*. On the other
hand, Edmund's allusions to 'dearth' and 'vnnaturalnesse betweene
the child and the parent' *might* have been censored as early as 1608. If
so, however, what the playwright apparently added to replace
Edmund's 'censored' lines can hardly have pleased the censor. (The
Folio adds the lines I have bracketed.)

Glou. These late Eclipses in the Sun and Moone portend no good to vs:
though the wisedome of Nature can reason it thus, and thus, yet Nature finds
it selfe scourg'd by the sequent effects. Loue cooles, friendship falls off,
Brothers diuide. In Cities, mutinies; in Countries, discord; in Pallaces,
Treason; and the Bond crack'd, 'twixt Sonne and Father. [This villaine of
mine comes vnder the prediction; there's Son against Father, the King fals
from byas of Nature, there's Father against Childe. We haue seene the best of
our time. Machinations, hollownesse, treacherie, and all ruinous disorders
follow vs disquietly to our Graues.] Find out this Villain *Edmond*,
(TLN 433–44; C2; 1.2.103–15)

If this bracketed passage is indeed an addition to the original text,
Edmund's 'vnnaturalnesse betweene the child and the parent' can
hardly have been eliminated to avoid offending the King, because
Gloucester's added lines make an uncomplimentary allusion to King
James even easier to infer.

However, it might be maintained that Shakespeare originally
included *both* passages, and that *both* were censored; that the Folio
compositor made the required cut in Edmund's lines, but overlooked
or ignored a similar instruction to cut Gloucester's.[28] But since this
Folio page seems to have been set from marked-up Quarto copy,
whoever prepared that marked-up copy would have had to *insert* into
the printed text lines which had been marked for omission in his
manuscript, while at a later point *deleting* lines which stood in the
printed text – though (allegedly) both passages stood in his
manuscript, and both were marked for similar treatment.[29] This
seems most implausible. Besides, this hypothesis also requires us to
suppose that most of the rest of Gloucester's speech – 'In Cities,
mutinies; in Countries, discord; in Pallaces, Treason; and the Bond
crack'd, 'twixt Sonne and Father' – should also have been omitted,
but was again spared by the annotator or compositor. Such a bundle
of assumptions hardly recommends itself, especially when a further
bundle must be borne in order to explain the absence of Gloucester's
lines from, or the presence of Edmund's in, Q. The Quarto should,
according to this reconstruction, either have contained both passages
(if it was set from the uncensored foul papers), or neither (if it was
contaminated in some way by memories of the performed play).[30]
Madeleine Doran conjectured that the omission of Gloucester's lines
resulted from compositorial eyeskip in Q, from 'This villaine' (TLN
439) to 'this Villain' (TLN 444); although relatively unusual, eyeskip
across so many lines does occasionally happen. But such an error
would have left out two words which do appear in Q ('find out').
Anyone who noticed that the resulting lines did not make sense, and
then went back to the manuscript in order to retrieve 'find out', could
hardly have failed to find out that more than two words had been left
out. Q's 'omission' of Gloucester's lines can thus hardly result from
mere mechanical error: to dismiss the absence of these lines from Q as
a printer's accident, we must presuppose an unusual eyeskip,
followed by an unusually incompetent resort to copy, in order to
half-correct the original error. All this must be presumed simply in
order to account for the absence from Q of Gloucester's lines, which
should have been present if (1) Q was set from foul papers, and (2)
Edmund's speech was omitted from the Folio because of censorship.
But even more difficult to account for than the absence of
Gloucester's lines is the presence of Edmund's, which should never
have appeared in Q if indeed (1) Q was set from memorially

contaminated copy, and (2) both references to 'vnnaturalnesse betweene the child and the parent' were censored.

The simpler conclusion, in every way, is that neither passage was censored. Moreover, one important detail in Gloucester's catalogue strongly suggests that the lines added by the Folio are indeed a later addition to the dialogue. Gloucester ruminates about what 'comes vnder the prediction', but in fact no prediction has yet been mentioned. The first reference to 'a prediction I read this other day, what should follow these Eclipses' comes almost forty lines later (C2^v; TLN 469–70; 1.2.140–1), *immediately before Edmund's omitted lines*. It would therefore have been exceptionally easy for anyone excising Edmund's later lines to turn back to Gloucester's speech and, in the process of inserting a similar catalogue there, to include in it an offhand allusion which had not yet actually been explained at the time Gloucester speaks. I cannot prove that this is what happened, but this explanation at least accounts, relatively simply, for a real anomaly in the dialogue. It also accepts at face value the evidence of the two texts themselves, which show one passage omitted from a text which adds a rather similar passage elsewhere.

The censor, in 1605 or 1606, could thus hardly have objected to more than twelve words ('diuisions in state, menaces and maledictions against King and nobles . . . nuptial breaches') out of the fifty omitted by the Folio. Even if the play was resubmitted at a later date, or voluntarily censored by the actors in the light of subsequent political developments, only another seven words can have been affected ('vnnaturalnesse betweene the child and the parent'). In order to believe that any of these words were censored, we must ignore or explain away the fact that the Folio adds material similar to that allegedly removed by the Master of the Revels. Likewise, even if we reject the apparent evidence that Gloucester's extra lines were added at the same time that Edmund's were removed, there still remain two obvious dramatic motives for the Folio's omission: to play down the mocking tone (which unites all of the omitted material), and to remove a frankly topical exchange, once its dramatic currency had been devalued by the passage of time.

Two additional artistic motives might easily be inferred, one specific to this passage, the other characteristic of a number of other Folio omissions. In Q, Edmund's list of effects which 'succeed vnhappily' consists almost entirely of disasters relevant to the play. However, though the relevance of some of these items announces itself immediately, the pertinence of others ('dissipation of Cohorts, nuptial breaches') could hardly be discerned until much later – by which point audiences are unlikely to remember all the verbal details of this relatively inconspicuous speech. The Folio by contrast substitutes a dramatic irony which can be immediately perceived:

> *Baſt.* I promiſe you, the effects he writes of, ſucceede
> vnhappily.
> When ſaw you my Father laſt?

In changing the Quarto's 'writ of' to 'writes of' the Folio strongly implies that Edmund actually has a book in hand—at least, in fifteen of Shakespeare's twenty-one other uses of 'writes', a letter, paper, or book is present onstage. (The six exceptions all involve clear uses of the continuous present: he writes himself Armigero, he writes verses, he writes brave verses, the Turk writes so tedious a style, the bill writes them all alike, he that writes of you.) This book might be one Gloucester has left behind, or—even better—one that Edmund theatrically pulls from his own pocket when Edgar enters: 'Pat: he comes like the Catastrophe of the old Comedie: my Cue is villanous Melancholly, with a sighe like *Tom* o' Bedlam.——O these Eclipses do portend these diuisions' (TLN 463–6; C2ᵛ; 1.2.134–7). Edmund's book, like Hamlet's, would be an aptly conventional stage accessory for a melancholic. The Folio's apparent provision of a book for Edmund thus makes good dramatic sense, and though editors fail to note its presence productions often supply it. But the added prop may be more than a fortuitous practical improvement. In late 1605 or early 1606 the actor of Edmund may not have needed a book, because his audience could be expected to interpret 'These late eclipses' by the light of their own recent double darkness, and so to interpret 'a prediction . . . he writ' in terms of the spurt of ephemera, of broadsides and ballads, which almost certainly followed in the eclipses' wake. But by, say, 1610, an onstage book would be much more useful to the actor, who could by then no longer rely upon an audience's automatic, knowing response to 'the effects he writ of'. Just as, with the passage of time, 'These late eclipses' would move out of the spectators' world into the character's, so too 'a prediction' might naturally begin as a deliberately unspecified allusion to the world outside the theatre, and then eventually be tied down to a particular book carried in a particular actor's hand.

Besides implying an onstage appearance for Edmund's book, the

Folio's change of 'writ of' to 'writes of' also has a subtle effect upon the following 'succeede', lending it a suggestion of futurity less evident in its Quarto counterpart. In fact, the Quarto's 'succeed' might even be the past tense, as it must apparently be once in *Titus Andronicus* (A3ᵛ; TLN 48; 1.1.40). And instead of a list of generic— and rather fancifully phrased—disasters, what does in the Folio 'succeede vnhappily', and immediately, is the beginning of Edmund's deception of Edgar. As Gloucester had predicted, 'Brothers diuide'. This is a joke Edmund, and an audience, might well relish.

The Folio's version of this moment creates an apparent disjunction between Edmund's statement and his question. The question looks like a *non sequitur*; it therefore invites both actor and audience to fill in the apparent vacuum. The actor can do so, in part, with the prop the Folio supplies him: I think almost any Edmund, given a book and the Folio text of this passage, would snap the book shut before abruptly changing the subject. An audience, on the other hand, is invited to find a psychological explanation for the abrupt dislocation of behaviour—and this invitation of course increases its chances of perceiving Edmund's joke. This procedure, whereby an audience is encouraged to explain an apparent disjunction or obscurity, seems to inform at least three other Folio changes in Act One. One of these is discussed by John Kerrigan (below, pp. 219–20).

> Who is it that can tell me who I am?
> *Foole.* Lears shadow.
> *Lear.* Your name, faire Gentlewoman?
> (TLN 743–5; 1.4.230–6)

As Kerrigan says, the Folio 'opens a gap . . . which is both painful and unignorable. The poetic space can scarcely be played across.' Another such dramatic lacuna occurs in the first scene, with Cordelia's enigmatic 'Sure I shall neuer marry like my Sisters' (TLN 110; 1.1.103). Without the addition of the Quarto's 'to loue my father all' (B2; 1.1.104), the Folio leaves the exact import of Cordelia's insult damningly undefined, and so contributes to its tougher, harsher characterization of Cordelia herself.[31] A third example occurs earlier in this second scene, where the Quarto's

> *Glost.* He cannot be such a monster.
> *Bast.* Nor is not sure.
> *Glost.* To his father, that so tenderly and intirely loues him, heauen and earth! *Edmund* seeke him out,
> (C2; 1.2.94–7)

is transformed into the Folio's

> *Glou.* He cannot bee such a Monster. *Edmond* seeke him out:
>
> (TLN 427-8)

In both texts, between 'monster' and 'Edmund' Gloucester apparently decides that his eldest son might indeed be such a monster. But the Folio communicates this reversal by simple juxtaposition, and by the pause that presumably intervenes between the two sentences, rather than verbally and explicitly; it therefore allows, indeed forces, an audience to attend to the unspoken mental processes of the character. In none of these passages can the cutting have been seriously intended to reduce the length of the play; in all of them it does serve a discernible artistic purpose. More important, since censorship cannot possibly have dictated these other, similar cuts, the passage at 1.2.144–52 also presumably owes its omission from the Folio to artistic rather than political sensitivity.

IV

The so-called 'mock trial' (G3^v–G4; 3.6.17–56) offers, at first sight, a rather more tempting target for censorship: the image of legal action as the accusation of a joint-stool by a mad plaintiff, before a 'bench' presided over by a fool and a madman in a hovel, might not recommend itself to someone paid to preserve the authority of Authority. But, as with the passage in 1.2, more has been omitted from the Folio than can be attributed to the censor. The first three lines of the omitted passage actually precede Lear's decision to 'arraigne them straight'; these lines have nothing to do with the trial, or with anything else to which the censor might have taken umbrage.

> *Edg.* The foule fiend bites my backe[.]
> *Foole.* He's mad, that trusts in the tamenes of a Wolfe, a horses health, a boyes loue, or a whores oath.
>
> (G3^v; 3.6.17–19)

Even in the mad trial itself, most of what has been omitted in the Folio contains no political or social comment whatsoever; aside from 'corruption in the place, | False Iusticer why hast thou let her scape[?]' (G4; 3.6.55–6), nothing directly alludes to any fallibility in the legal system. And the composition of Lear's 'commission' is less satirical than might appear. The plaintiff is a king; the madman not mad but the sane, good, legitimate son of a nobleman, who will eventually become the champion of justice; the Fool no simple fool, but a commentator who repeatedly passes judgements which the audience is clearly expected to endorse. Kent, who may or may not be one of the judges, likewise endorses traditional moral and social values.[32] Moreover, the entire trial sequence resembles a play-within-the-play, a recognizable dramatic convention which regularly exploits the discrepancy between a dramatic representation and its real counterpart. The Fool's joke about the joint-stool, for instance, like Prince Hal's joke about the joint-stool in the play-scene in *1 Henry IV* (E2; TLN 1337–9; 2.4.380–2), presumes that the inadequacy of the stage surrogate will amuse an audience. The absurdity of Lear's 'commission' need therefore cast no aspersions on legal dignity – at least, no more than Falstaff's portrayal of Henry IV casts upon regal dignity. The Duke of Cornwall's violent abuse of justice, in the very next scene, dramatizes a much more damning and objectionable instance of political 'legality' at work than anything even hinted in 3.6 – and both texts contain that scene. In fact, those who suggest that 3.6.17–56 suffered from censorship have been able to provide no examples of political interference in scenes or passages of a similar nature.[33] Many contemporary plays satirize justices: dramatic exemplars of the legal profession include daft Adam Overdo in *Bartholomew Fair*, senile Shallow and Silence in *2 Henry IV*, corrupt Angelo in *Measure for Measure*, Justice Greedy in *A New Way to Pay Old Debts*, the drunken lecherous Justice Tutchim in *Ram Alley*, the greedy lecherous Justice Falso in *The Phoenix*, Picklock in *A Staple of News*, the bribed judge in *A Looking Glass for London and England*, the unjust judges in *The Fatal Dowry*, the duped Sir Paul Either-Side in *The Devil is an Ass*, the duped judges at the end of *The Atheist's Tragedy*, and the duped judges 'more hard than stones' in *Titus Andronicus*. Moreover, as Roger Warren points out (above, pp. 52–3), the Folio compensates for this omission in 3.6 with an addition in 4.6, one which directly and explicitly formulates the criticism of legal institutions only, at most, implicit here.[34] If the censor had objected to 3.6, he would have been furious about what apparently replaced it.

The historical evidence is in this case straightforward and unequivocal, and I suspect that censorship has been entertained as an explanation for this cut only because no other obvious explanation presents itself. Whatever its merits or motives, the omission of the mad trial is, without question, the Folio's most surprising cut. Any apologia for Folio *Lear* must explain why anyone would have wanted to remove a passage which most modern readers regard as an epicentre of the play's meaning. Moreover, if we are to believe that Shakespeare himself did the cutting, most of us will need to be persuaded that the omission actually improves, rather than defaces, the play.

The passage as it stands in the Quarto can hardly have offended the censor; but the passage may eventually have been omitted because Shakespeare decided that, in part, it failed, and failed primarily because of constraints which the political regulation of the drama had from the beginning placed upon his freedom of imaginative manoeuvre. In trying to detect the influence of censorship upon dramatic texts editors have naturally and necessarily concentrated upon known or probable cases of the censor's direct interference with an author's manuscript, post partum; such damage can normally be undone. But the anticipation of censorship must have influenced, far more pervasively, what dramatists attempted, and such aborting inhibitions cannot be retrospectively removed. In writing a play so intrinsically political as *King Lear* Shakespeare must sometimes have had half a mind's eye on the censor, and in composing 3.6 – the scene most heavily influenced by *Eastward Ho*, which earlier that year had landed two of its authors in prison – he could hardly have overlooked the potential sensitivity of his material.[35]

Of course, I cannot prove that such mental constraints did influence Shakespeare's original composition of the scene. But speculation about how differently Shakespeare *might* have handled the trial, if he had not needed to worry about the Master of the Revels, at least helps further to define, by contrast, how uncontroversial, and how unlikely to be censored, is the Quarto as it stands. For instance, Lear's kangaroo court easily *could* have become the vehicle for two deeply subversive ideas – ideas subversive because they challenge the entire social institution of the law, rather than (like Justice Falso and the others) simply satirizing the failings of particular fictitious practitioners. Lear's mad trial could have directly portrayed legal ceremony, procedure, and decorum as a theatrical farce, in which madmen and fools operate the levers of a claptrap machinery of justice; it could also have demonstrated, dramatically, that the economically and politically powerless, deprived of any resort to real justice, must content themselves with fantasies of legal retribution, must vent their anger upon senseless surrogates.

It seems to me no accident that the scene dramatically articulates neither of these ideas. To be sure, its dramatic procedure – mute defendants tried on a ridiculous charge (kicking a father) before judges who betray a complete inability to stick to the point and who are themselves (one of them at least, and perhaps two) fugitives from justice – might to a modern reader sound like something out of Genet; but Genet's parodies derive their force from the obsessive verisimilitude of the impersonations. If Edgar and the Fool could put on robes and wigs, pound their gavels, interrogate a witness (even a joint-stool) in some approximation of a dock, then the element of legal parody in their compulsive digressions – and so the structure of the whole 'trial', with its repeated collapse and reimposition of decorum – could be made immediately clear. Shakespeare instead obsessively re-iterates the scene's irreality: the legal 'bench' a literal homely bench, the robed justice nearly naked, the accused a stool who 'cannot deny' her name, who is told to 'Come hither' and asked 'wan[t]st thou eyes'. After Lear's initial speech setting up the trial, Edgar does not formally announce a session, but instead exclaims – either of one of his hallucinated fiends, or as an aside describing Lear himself – 'Looke where he stands and glars'. Then, after only six words which (if emended) refer to a 'tr[i]al', Edgar himself abandons the legal structure; the next three speeches – by the Fool, Edgar, and Kent – also ignore it. Shakespeare does not set up the decorum of a courtroom, and then knock it down, or reveal its underlying absurdity; instead, he never allows any initial pretence of verisimilitude to establish itself. If Shakespeare had dramatized the trial as Genet might have done, its structure would be more evident; but by making it more evident he might also have made it susceptible to censorship. What he has done runs, by contrast, no risk at all of censorhip – but some risk of obscuring its own structure.

In the same way, Caius (the servant who had been ignominiously and unjustly stocked) or Poor Tom (lowest of the low, pariah and untouchable) might easily have focused an audience's attention upon the social implications of Lear's farmhouse trial; so might a crowd of huddled indigents, sharing with Lear's party this temporary shelter from the storm. But Shakespeare, unlike the film directors Grigori Kozintsev and Peter Brook, did not provide such a backdrop of oppressed humanity, though in this part of the play he had actors available who could have done so. Kent takes little or no part in the trial, and has in any case long ceased to exploit his Caius personality: by 3.6 author and audience have stopped attending to any discrepancy between Kent's real and assumed personality or social status. Edgar participates, but rather than launch himself with relish into Lear's fantasy of retribution – a game with obvious attractions for the innocent fugitive, condemned without a hearing – he instead carries on a kind of tit-for-tat struggle with the Fool, and then pulls back from his adopted persona in order to tell us how painfully affecting he finds Lear's madness. The contest between Edgar and the Fool helps to structure the dialogue of a scene otherwise often marked by disconnection rather than dramatic interplay; but however useful in context, or interesting in terms of the Fool's characterization, this mini-conflict does not focus or contribute to the symbolism of the scene, or to the larger structures and themes of the play. Edgar's asides – perhaps beginning, in Q, with 'Looke where he stands and glars' (G3^v; 3.6.23) – likewise distract attention from the scene's symbolic or social content. Shakespeare marshals his dramatic resources in order to signpost our emotional responses to Lear, rather than to communicate a vision of political reality. As a consequence, by not directing our attention to one subversive idea or the other, or to the relationship between them, the scene confuses the two in a way which prevents either idea from achieving an intelligible dramatic embodiment. Does the joint-stool represent a political victim condemned in her absence by a court the plaintiff himself appoints, or does it represent instead a pathetic substitute, the closest political impotence can get to punishing its oppressors? Does the charge – that she 'kickt the poore king her father' (G4; 3.6.47–8) – parody the trumped-up accusations of a corrupt legality, or does it symbolize the real nature of Goneril's offence, and if so does this symbol mitigate or magnify what she has done? The scene does not allow us to answer these questions; more important, it does not clearly direct us to ask them, or guide us toward a vantage where we see, intuitively, that the joint-stool symbolizes, simultaneously and rightly, both the oppressor and the oppressed. If it did so, the scene *might* have been censored; since it does not, its omission from the Folio cannot plausibly be blamed directly on George Buc. On the other hand, one might feel that the scene, to some degree, fails to articulate its own form (or its own formlessness), fails to organize a structure of perception that will guide an audience to a recognition of its range of meanings – and one might suspect that this structural uncertainty derives from Shakespeare's anticipation of a censor's objections. The uncertainty of focus is apparent in the scene's detail as well as its structure. For instance, to whom does Lear speak when he asks, 'False Iusticer why hast thou let her scape[?]' He must address someone, but the question gains nothing by being addressed to Kent, or the Fool, or Edgar; indeed, it actually loses significance as soon as we attempt to identify the specific 'False Iusticer' to whom Lear speaks. Even as an accusing question to the heavens – which are, in any case, usually plural in this play – it simply duplicates the more powerful imprecations of previous scenes. Lear's earlier identification of Edgar and the Fool (and perhaps Kent) as justices strongly encourages us to seek for a specific 'False Iusticer' here; yet any such identification we make lacks the force and irony of those earlier invocations of a naked beggar as a robed man of justice (G4; 3.6.36), or of a fool as 'most learned Iustice | Thou sapient sir' (G3ᵛ; 3.6.21–2).[36]

Likewise, how has this 'her' of Lear's imagination escaped? Peter Brook's film could place the entire sequence in a real shed and show us a real rat scurrying into a corner, thereby providing both an objective stimulus for Lear's mad misinterpretation and an objective correlative for Goneril; but the theatre – Shakespeare's least of all – could hardly have supplied such effects. A real rodent would be too funny, too unpredictable, too distracting. Marvin Rosenberg describes two modern performances in which Lear managed the transition by suggesting 'a man seeing something disappear before his eyes; he saw Regan, and suddenly he was looking at emptiness – the actor's art made both unrealities tangible'.[37] This would be strikingly dramatic; it also provokes the thought that 'False Iusticer' might be directed at Lear himself, an interpretation which lets the line resonate with accumulated meaning.[38] But though I suspect that this may have been what Shakespeare intended, how is an actor to communicate that intention? Elsewhere, when Lear apostrophizes his 'old fond eyes' (D2ᵛ; TLN 820; 1.4.301) or tells himself to 'beat at this gate that let thy folly in' (D2; TLN 784; 1.4.271), we know he is addressing himself. Here, neither actor nor audience is given such clues to comprehension – and here, of course, in a scene where Lear repeatedly addresses imaginary figures, and in which he has specifically identified for us two or even three other characters whom he calls justices, we desperately need those clues.

And why a joint-stool in the first place? Partly, no doubt, because it was a property readily available on the Jacobean stage. But so, too, were many other properties. The divided map, the divided coronet, the throne Lear sits on, in 1.1; the chair he wakes in, at Dover; the chair Gloucester is bound and blinded in; the torch Gloucester carries; the stocks Kent is punished in; the armour Edgar wears for his dramatic entry in 5.3; the pin Lear pricks himself with – these, too, are commonplace properties, but Shakespeare transforms them into sharp foci of dramatic significance. The joint-stool, for me, never suffers such a memorable 'Sea-change | Into something rich, & strange'. (In fact, the stools in *Coriolanus* 1.3 stand out much more clearly in my memory, epitomizing as they do a whole domestic world in counterpoint to the world of war and politics.)

Partly, too, joint-stools were used in order to set up the Fool's witticism. 'Cry you mercy I tooke you for a ioyne stoole' was itself a proverbial joke, a facetious apology for having overlooked someone. The proverbial joke depends upon a pretence of non-recognition; the Fool plays a joke on the joke, by using it in a situation where the comic non-recognition is comically justifiable. But this is a joke-within-a-joke Shakespeare has already used before, in *1 Henry IV*. What moral do we extract from it here? That Lear was justified in not recognizing Goneril's true nature? This seems a most out-of-the-way conclusion now; besides, the rest of the play emphatically contradicts it. That things indeed are what they appear to be? If so, how is Goneril like a joint-stool? I do not see how this property adequately typifies or symbolizes or encapsulates or even suggests Goneril's nature. What do the two have in common, besides hardness? And is hardness the essential, or even the most obvious, attribute of joint-stools?[39] When Launce, in *The Two Gentlemen of Verona*, has his shoe stand for his mother, the comic incongruity of the substitute is its sole function. The same is essentially true of the folk plays which influenced this scene (and others) in *King Lear*:[40]

> The pot-lid kicked the ladle,
> Up jumped spit jack
> Like a mansion man
> Swore he'd fight the dripping pan
> With his long tail,
> Swore he'd send them all to jail.
> In comes the grid iron, if you can't agree
> I'm the justice, bring um to me.

Here, the absurd application of legal procedure to kitchen utensils is still primarily funny, but it also suggests that the rigours of the law are grossly disproportionate to the nature of the offence (and the offenders). But when Lear does to furniture what Launce and the folk play have done to footwear and tableware, we surely expect a greater complexity of resonance. Goneril, after all, unlike Launce's mother, is a major character in the play, one whose 'nature' Lear and the play and the audience repeatedly grope to understand; when, here, we are given a dramatic image of that character, we can hardly fail to wonder how this vehicle illuminates its tenor. One might claim that Shakespeare raises such expectations precisely in order to thwart them; but if so one would expect that frustration to be sharply structured, as it is when Shakespeare gradually and insistently raises our expectations of Cordelia's victory, only to dash them, baldly and abruptly, in four words: 'King *Lear* hath lost' (K4; TLN 2929; 5.2.6).[41] The inadequacy of the joint-stool as an image of Goneril is, by contrast, never focused, never made the object of a structural preparation and resolution.

That other joint-stool, the one in *1 Henry IV*, is again instructive. There, Shakespeare organizes the play-scene around the comic inadequacy of its surrogates – properties and actors – until at the end Hal's impersonation of his father electrifies us because of the very adequacy of his performance, its convincing reality. Hal's initial joke about the unpersuasive joint-stool masquerading as a throne thus sets the stage for a climactic performance which reminds and persuades us that Hal will indeed someday become what he now only impersonates. Lear's joint-stool serves, so far as I can see, no such structural function, in the scene or the play. In 3.6 as in 1.1, Lear attempts to mount a play, and fails; but the structure of the two scenes, the nature and personnel of the two 'plays', the reasons for their failure, differ so fundamentally that in performance the parallel does little to illuminate the particular difficulties of 3.6. Kent, for instance, appears in both 'plays', but Shakespeare never defines his role in the second. He might be one of the judges, but if so his very commonsensical sanity jars with the symbolic madness of Lear's court; he might not be one of the judges, in which case he has literally – and, in the theatre, awkwardly – nothing to do.

Edgar unmistakably participates in Lear's imaginary trial; he also, more than any other character on stage, is still playing a part, inside and outside the trial. But in other respects Edgar's uneasy blend of participation and non-participation raises as many questions as Kent's. Edgar's asides not only conspicuously fail to direct our intellectual perception of the trial; they also betray Shakespeare's anxiety about how audiences will respond to the whole spectacle. Kenneth Muir suggested that the trial may have been omitted because audiences laughed at it.[42] Audiences could hardly be blamed for having done so. The scene is unfocused emotionally as well as politically; it at times provokes the uncertain, uncomfortable laughter of painful embarrassment. Wilson Knight perceived this, and perceived too that the effect must have been quite deliberate: *King Lear* repeatedly wrenches pathos from 'vnsightly tricks', snatches tragedy from the edge of risibility.[43] But until now the play has seemed confident of our reactions; its characters have not stepped out of the frame in order to tell us (just in case we might be inclined to laugh) that we should cry. In writing 3.6, Shakespeare appears to have wanted to be absolutely sure that we responded sympathetically, and appears also to have worried that we might not. This anxiety seems to me justified. Audiences inevitably and properly perceive 3.6 as the culmination of the storm sequence, and since we will not see Lear again for six scenes, the emotional impact of this single episode pivotally affects our perspective on Lear during and after the storm. If repeated performances justified Shakespeare's initial anxieties about the scene, he might well have decided that the risk of misunderstanding – even with an actor as great as Burbage – was simply too great.

Certainly, similar alterations in at least three other scenes imply a deliberate retrenchment of anything which might too directly suggest senility, the comic *senex iratus*, or the doddering old man, 'tottering about the stage with a walking-stick', who so embarrassed Charles Lamb. In the first scene, Quarto Lear exclaims 'Goe to, goe to, mend your speech a little' (B2; TLN 100, 1.1.94), and 'Goe to, goe to, better thou hadst not bin borne, | Then not to haue pleas'd me better' (B4; TLN 256–7; 1.1.233–4). These testy interjections suggest a figure at least fitfully reminiscent of old Capulet, or Polonius. The Folio not only removes these telltale exclamations; it also, by a series of additions and alterations, makes Lear's crucial second speech (TLN 41–59; B1^v; 1.1.36–54) both much longer and more complex, intellectually and syntactically. As a result, Lear dominates the scene even more dramatically, marshalling his subjects and his thoughts with the same authority.[44] Having eliminated Lear's interjections here, the Folio also removes Goneril's later description of him as an 'idle old man', and her impatient 'now by my life old fooles are babes again' (C3; 1.3.16–20).[45] Likewise, Q Lear cries out, 'You see me here (you Gods) a poore old fellow' (F2ᵛ; 2.4.272); F offers a more dignified 'poore old man' (TLN 1572). All these changes reduce the danger of an audience finding Lear, on occasion, merely embarrassing.

If, as this suggests, omission of the mad trial does a service to Lear's own role, it also, even more clearly, does a service to the play's structure. In John Barton's words:[46]

I've always felt in the theatre that in the middle section of the play something goes on too long somewhere. There's an insistence on all forms of madness, between 'Blow, wind, and crack your cheeks' [F4; TLN 1656; 3.2.1] and the flax and eggs sequence [H2; *not in F*; 3.7.99–107], which becomes, on stage, rather repetitive. The three mad scenes – Lear on the heath, Edgar in the hovel, and then the mock trial – suspend the action unhelpfully: it's very difficult for actors to sustain dramatic momentum.

The most dispensable of the three scenes which create this difficulty is 3.6, and in particular the trial itself. In 3.2, Lear and the Fool begin the scene alone, eventually to be joined by Kent; in 3.4 these three encounter Edgar (as Poor Tom), then Gloucester. These two scenes pose no problems of structural monotony, and the Folio does not abbreviate them; on the contrary, it actually expands them, not only with a more dramatic entrance for Edgar but also with a long speech, direct to the audience, from the Fool – something, again, both new and striking, a dramatic variation on the surrounding material. But 3.6, as it stands in Q and thus in conflated editions of the play, essentially gives us more of the same. The omitted passage – with Lear mad, poor Edgar playing Tom, the Fool fooling, and Kent trying to be reasonable – contains no new dramatic ingredients. All the new elements in the scene the Folio keeps, brings forward, or introduces: Lear's movement out of the storm, into bed, and off to Dover; Edgar's asides, as compassion for the King begins to endanger his play-acting; Gloucester's last and most important act of moral heroism, witnessed by his son, and leading directly to his blinding in the next scene; the Fool's enigmatic exit (this last not present in Q at all).

But the Folio abridgement of 3.6 not only improves the structure of the play; it also improves the structure of 3.6 itself. The scene remains, after three centuries, so unfamiliar in its Folio form that it is worth quoting in full.[47]

Enter Kent, and Gloucester.

Glou. Heere is better then the open ayre, take it thank-
fully: I will peece out the comfort with what addition I
can: I will not be long from you.

Kent. All the powre of his wits, haue giuen way to his
impatience: the Gods reward your kindnesse.   [*Exit Gloucester*]

Enter Lear, Edgar, and Foole.

Edg. *Fraterretto* cals me, and tells me *Nero* is an Ang-
ler in the Lake of Darknesse: pray Innocent, and beware
the foule Fiend.

Foole. Prythee Nunkle tell me, whether a madman be
a Gentleman, or a Yeoman.

Lear. A King, a King.

Foole. No, he's a Yeoman, that ha's a Gentleman to
his Sonne: for hee's a mad Yeoman that sees his Sonne a
Gentleman before him.

Lear. To haue a thousand with red burning spits
Come hizzing in vpon em.

Edg. Blesse thy fiue wits.

Kent. O pitty: Sir, where is the patience now
That you so oft haue boasted to retaine?

Edg. [*aside*] My teares begin to take his part so much,
They marre my counterfetting.

Lear. The little dogges, and all;
Trey, Blanch, and Sweet-heart: see, they barke at me.

Edg. Tom, will throw his head at them: Auaunt you
Curres,
Be thy mouth or blacke or white:
Tooth that poysons if it bite:
Mastiffe, Grey-hound, Mongrill Grim,
Hound or Spaniell, Brache, or Hym:
Bobtaile ti[ke], or Trou[n]dle taile,
Tom will make him weepe and waile,
For with throwing thus my head;
Dogs leapt the hatch, and all are fled.
Do, de, de, de: sese: Come, march to Wakes and Fayres,
and Market Townes: poore Tom thy horne is dry[.]

Lear. Then let them Anatomize *Regan*: See what
breeds about her heart. Is there any cause in Nature that
make[s] these hard-hearts. You sir, I entertaine for one of
my hundred; only, I do not like the fashion of your garments. You will say they are Persian; but let them bee
chang'd.

Kent. Now good my Lord, lye heere, and rest awhile.
Lear. Make no noise, make no noise, draw the Cur-
taines: so, so, wee'l go to Supper i'th' morning.
Foole. And Ile go to bed at noone.
[*Enter Gloster.*]
Glou. Come hither Friend: Where is the King my Master?
Kent. Here Sir, but trouble him not, his wits are gon.
Glou. Good friend, I prythee take him in thy armes;
I haue ore-heard a plot of death vpon him:
There is a Litter ready, lay him in't,
And driue toward Douer friend, where thou shalt meete
Both welcome, and protection. Take vp thy Master,
If thou should'st dally halfe an houre, his life
With thine, and all that offer to defend him,
Stand in assured losse. Take vp, take vp,
And follow me, that will to some prouision
Giue thee quicke conduct. Come, come, away. *Exeunt*
(TLN 1997–2056)

The mad trial's fuzziness of detail has vanished. Lines like 'Then let
them Anatomize *Regan*: See what breeds about her heart', or 'To
haue a thousand with red burning spits | Come hizzing in vpon 'em',
or 'Make no noise, make no noise, draw the Curtaines', or 'Ile go to
bed at noone' attain an immediate impact, a multi-faceted rightness
which echoes in the memory. We can instantly register the painful
ambiguity of 'A King, a King': an outburst of self-definition from
Lear's depths – like his much earlier 'so kind a Father' (TLN 906; D3;
1.5.32) or 'To tak't againe perforce' (TLN 912; D3; 1.5.39) – which at
the same time provides a cruelly appropriate, unexpected answer to
the Fool's question. And even if we don't catch the echoes of betray,
blanch (with horror), and Cor-delia in 'Trey, Blanch, and Sweet-
heart', or don't catch the etymological aptness of '*Fraterretto*', we do,
I think, instinctively sense the field of significant resonance in such
details – in, for instance, the allusion to incestuous '*Nero*', the
notorious parent-killer, 'angling' in a dark, infernal lake. Tom's
earlier arias of sexual loathing and demonic possession give these
images a satisfying feel of meaning, even if we fail to make all the
possible connections. Likewise, Lear's hallucination of the three
'little dogges', with their ladylike names, barking at him, offers the
audience an emotion-charged image of domestic betrayal, even if
spectators overlook the specific appropriateness of the three names,

or fail to catch the echo of 'Truth's a dog must to kennell, hee must bee whipt out, when the Lady Brach may stand by'th' fire and stinke' (TLN 641–3; C4^v; 1.4.111–13). The quality of spontaneous resonant aptness which the stage image of the joint-stool and the accusing cry 'False Iusticer' lack, these images and speeches possess in abundance. The Folio not only keeps all the new dramatic elements in the scene; it also keeps most of its best poetry.

It also gives the scene a perceptible, emotionally and intellectually satisfying structure. Unlike the Quarto, the Folio brings on Kent and Gloucester alone, beginning the scene with a moment of sanity and calm – and giving the trio of Lear, Poor Tom, and the Fool a separate, emblematic group entrance. Kent has warned us that 'All the powre of [Lear's] wits, haue giuen way to his impatience', and in the Folio we see exactly that: Edgar's obsessed demonic patter, the Fool incongruously persisting with his riddles, Lear's two exclamations – first 'A King, a King' and then the unmistakable demonic violence of 'To haue a thousand with red burning spits | Come hizzing in vpon 'em'. The unbalanced savagery of this shakes even Edgar out of his self-absorption, and prompts Kent's attempt to calm Lear. And gradually Lear calms. The vision of the dogs is self-pitying, not enraged. Edgar's aside makes it clear that his rhyming exorcism of the dogs is directed – as nothing else so far has been – selflessly outward, in an effort to help someone else. Edgar attempts to distract Lear, and this time he does so not in order to conceal himself, but to turn the King's attention away from 'things would hurt [him] more'. And Lear's instruction that they anatomize Regan seems, to me, a quietly philosophical resolution, an insane 'modest proposal' that will help finally resolve this puzzling matter of Regan's hard heart. Admittedly, this is my own interpretation of the tone of the lines; others might read them differently. But certainly Lear is no longer doubling exclamations, or breaking off in mid-sentence from a vision hizzing with the imagery of hell. We have settled into the universe of pet dogs, doctors anatomizing a corpse (rather than fiends tormenting one), logical connectives ('Then'), vague impersonal imperatives ('let them'), Persian garments, bed curtains, supper. Lear begins the scene dangerously insane, and ends it going off to sleep; he begins entirely self-absorbed, addressing no one on the stage, and ends entertaining Tom for one of his hundred knights, telling his companions to close the curtains and make no noise, promising them supper in the morning. Almost inevitably, in performance his three companions gather round him at this moment, a triumvirate of solicitude guarding a defenceless, sleeping, calmed old man who has gone out of his mind. Then Gloucester enters.[48] As he promised at the beginning, he has returned; closing the formal circle of the scene's structure, exploding the moment of tranquility, driving them relentlessly on to Dover. And so the scene ends, not with Edgar's soliloquy, but with a striking, prophetic image: Kent carrying the sleeping Lear in his arms, as Lear later will carry Cordelia.[49] At least, the Folio strongly encourages such a staging, while the Quarto specifically rules it out. For in the Quarto Kent tells the Fool 'Come helpe to beare thy maister', a line omitted from the Folio, which therefore gives us only Gloucester's repeated injunctions to Kent to take Lear 'in thy armes . . . Take vp thy Master . . . take vp, take vp'. As if to compensate for Kent's diminution in Acts Four and Five (where he has little function), the Folio heightens the impact of his exit here, just as it will expand his role in the play's final moments (as Michael Warren notes above, pp. 70–1). Kent's Folio exit with Lear in his arms emblematically sums up, as it concludes, his role in the first half of the play.

Why should Shakespeare not have been responsible for this elegant, moving, memorable Folio scene?

There is always something disconcerting, for reader and writer alike, in the suggestion that any passage in Shakespeare's mature work in any way or for any reason 'fails', and that the play might be better without it. The mad trial is so good, by the normal standards of this world, that perhaps no one but Shakespeare could have been dissatisfied with it. I may have erred in guessing at the sources of that dissatisfaction, or in suggesting that they spring from the mental constraints imposed by the author's anticipation of censorship; but, whatever our explanation for the Folio's omission of the trial, it cannot plausibly be attributed to objections made by the Master of the Revels to the scene as it stood in Q. That much, at least, is clear.

V

So far, disregarding 'Fut', we have identified only a line and a half in 3.6 and twelve to nineteen words in 1.2 to which (at different times) the censor might reasonably have taken exception; in each case these words occur in the context of a much longer passage omitted by the

Folio, for what appear to be admirable (or at least sensible) artistic motives. As a result none of the omissions so far discussed can be credibly attributed to political interference. The same cannot be said, however, of a major Folio omission in Act One, Scene Four. (The bracketed passage is not in F.)[50]

Lear. A bitter foole.
Foole. Doo'st know the difference my boy, betweene a bitter foole, and a sweete foole.
Lear. No lad, teach mee.
[*Foole.* That Lord that counsail'd thee
　　　　to giue away thy land,
　　　Come place him heere by mee,
　　　　doe thou for him stand,
　　　The sweet and bitter foole
　　　　will presently appeare,
　　　The one in motley here,
　　　　the other found out there.
Lear. Do'st thou call mee foole boy?
Foole. All thy other Titles thou hast giuen away, that thou wast borne with.
Kent. This is not altogether foole my Lord.
Foole. No faith, Lords and great men will not let me, if I had a monopolie out, they would haue part an't, and ladies too, they will not let me haue all the foole to my selfe, they'l be snatching;] giue me an egge Nuncle, and ile giue thee two crownes.
Lear. What two crownes shall they be?
Foole. Why, after I haue cut the egge in the middle and eate vp the meate, the two crownes of the egge

(C4ᵛ–D1; 1.4.136–59)

This omission has, since at least the time of Dr Johnson, usually been attributed to censorship, because the Fool's reference to the granting of monopolies would, without a doubt, have been politically sensitive. The King's granting of monopolies was debated in Parliament in 1604 and 1606 (as well as in 1610, 1614, and 1621).[51] But this allusion affects only three of the omitted lines. In fact, the grounds for censorship are much more extensive, and involve the entirety of the omitted material. Even without the reference to monopolies, the Master of the Revels would almost certainly have objected to the Fool's characterization of 'Lords and great men' and of 'ladies . . . snatching' – just as he objected to similar remarks about courtiers in *The Second Maiden's Tragedy, The Honest Man's*

Fortune, Eastward Ho, and *Cynthia's Revels,* and to similar remarks about the promiscuity of 'ladies' in *The Second Maiden's Tragedy* and *The Honest Man's Fortune.*[52] And since the Fool is clearly punning on 'all the foole' in the sense 'all the custard' (*OED sb.*[2]1), the censor may also have detected – and Shakespeare might well have intended – a reference to the quite incredible competitive gluttony which had already become a notorious feature of banquets at the court of King James.[53] The censor may also have been offended by the Fool's jibe about the king's giving away of titles, which might be interpreted as a sneer at James's own wholesale dispensation of titles. There are satirical allusions to new titles in *Eastward Ho,* which probably antedates the composition of *Lear,* and which so infuriated James that Jonson and Chapman were imprisoned for it (and feared worse than imprisonment).[54] The censor's suspicion that similar criticism might be intended here could easily have been compounded by the presence in this scene – and the criticism by Goneril – of some of Lear's '100. knights'. James was especially notorious for giving away knighthoods – having created more knights in the first four months of his reign than Queen Elizabeth had in the entirety of hers.[55]

James I was widely criticized for his attitude toward monopolies, for his extravagant dispensation of titles, for the incompetence of the 'Lord[s] that counsail'd' him, and for the corruption, greed, and promiscuity of his court. He was also criticized and rebuked for being more interested in hunting than governing. As early as September 1603 Count Beaumont wrote to Henri IV of France that James was 'so passionately addicted to the chase, that he for the sake of it postpones all business, to great scandal'.[56] In December of 1604 an anonymous note was attached to one of James's favourite hunting dogs, asking the dog to speak to the King, 'for he hears you every day, and so doth he not us'.[57] The same month the Archbishop of York wrote to Lord Cranborne of the Privy Council urging 'lesse wastening of the treasor of the realm, and more moderation in the lawfull exercise of hunting'; transcripts of this letter were widely circulated.[58] In June 1607 the Venetian ambassador reported that 'it pleases [the King's subjects] still less that he leaves all government to his Council and will think of nothing but the chase', and that for the sake of hunting 'he throws off all business, which he leaves to his Council and to his Ministers. And so one may say that *he is Sovereign in name and in appearance rather than in substance and effect*' (my italics).[59] Some indication of the King's obsession with hunting can be seen in his itinerary from November 1604 to December 1605:[60]

Late in November 1604, he was at Royston . . . [he] came to Whitehall for Christmas, which became his invariable custom. But by the middle of January 1605, the disorderly revels at Whitehall having ended, he was again at Royston, then at Huntingdon and Hinchinbrook. He came to London early in February but soon returned to Royston, travelled thence to Ware, Newmarket and Thetford, then back to Newmarket and Royston, then to London about the middle of March. For some four months he remained in the vicinity of the capital, moving between Greenwich, Richmond, Windsor and Oatlands, hunting as he went. A progress in July and August took him towards Oxford. Thence he came to Windsor and to Hampton Court for part of September. In October he was again at Royston, Huntingdon, Hinchinbrook and Ware, and though he came to London to open Parliament in November, he returned to Royston for most of the remainder of the year.

Shakespeare probably began composition of *King Lear* in the last three months of this period. In electing to dramatize Lear's reign, Shakespeare was presumably paying James a compliment, for James (whose great ambition was to unite the island of Britain into one kingdom) pictured himself as the anti-type to Lear (who had divided it).[61] But the very existence of such a perceived relationship between Lear and James opened up the possibility of other, less flattering comparisons between them. In this scene, Lear has just returned from hunting; like James when the hunting went badly, he proceeds on his arrival to upbraid and then physically attack a servant.[62] In the passage omitted from the Folio, the Fool addresses a series of potentially objectionable remarks to a king who has given up his political responsibilities in order, apparently, to spend his time (like James) hunting.

Any one of these features – the abdicated king hunting, the knights, the jokes about monopolies, or courtiers, or promiscuous ladies, or bad advisers, or giving away titles – *might*, in isolation, have passed unnoticed; their conjunction, in one brief passage, even the blindest censor could hardly overlook. But even if Buc were half asleep when he first read the submitted manuscript of *King Lear*, one line alone would have been enough to wake him up: 'Do'st thou call mee foole boy?' The King's licensed fool calls the king, to his face, a fool. Such sentiments would have been dangerous in any circumstances, but particularly so in 1605–6. To begin with, *King Lear* almost certainly came to the censor at a time when he must have been particularly sensitive to political indiscretion, following a series of increasingly serious theatrical scandals: *Sejanus* and *Philotas* in 1604, *The Dutch Courtesan* and *The Fawn* in 1604–5, *Eastward Ho* in 1605, *The Isle of Gulls* in February 1606.[63] James himself had been the perceived object of satire in the last four of these, and Buc would have been well advised to start paying intense attention to any possible implied criticism of James in plays submitted to him in 1606. Secondly, when King James ascended the English throne he brought with him a licensed royal fool, thereby reviving an institution which had languished throughout Elizabeth's reign.[64] Archie Armstrong became the most famous royal fool since Henry VIII's Will Sommers. Finally, James himself was by 1606 beginning to be characterized as less than astute in his managing of political affairs. He may already have been memorably epitomized as 'the wisest foole in Christendom';[65] but even if that witticism dates from later in the reign, it simply articulates the disparity, obvious soon enough, between James's much-vaunted learning and his relative political ineptitude. In politics as in the theatre, the paying public relishes any demonstration that those who most boast of their own mental powers are in fact fools, and James I set himself up for such debunking. In early 1606, it would have been hard not to see the Fool's jibe at Lear as a reflection of King James's own royal fool commenting on the folly of James himself.

For all these reasons, I find it difficult to believe that this passage, omitted by the Folio, could have withstood the attentions of the censor in 1605–6. If I am right, the Quarto text of *King Lear* must have been set from a manuscript which contained material the censor had ordered to be removed. This manuscript might have been foul papers, or even, theoretically, a prompt-book (in which the censor's marginal instructions might conceivably have been ignored by the printer); the characteristics of the Quarto text make prompt-book copy intrinsically unlikely. In any case, the lines present in the printed text should not have been present in any manuscript based upon a report or memory of the play as performed, for the lines seem most unlikely ever to have been performed.

The probability of political interference in this passage thus undermines the traditional assumption that the Quarto represents a 'bad' or reported text. However, the Folio omission raises at least one serious question about the nature of the manuscript underlying the Folio. The problem, essentially, is that the Folio retains the question which prompts the Fool's omitted answer. We would expect the three lines preceding the omission (TLN 667–9; 1.4.137–9) to have been omitted too. On the basis of this anomaly, P. W. K. Stone argues that 'the passage was omitted neither by the compositor nor even by the reviser but cut by the book-keeper in the theatre' (*Textual History*, p. 234). Stone notices that the Folio changes Quarto 'sweete foole' to 'sweet one' (TLN 668; 1.4.138);[66] he decides that this change must be an editorial adjustment, rather than a compositorial error; he concludes that the three lines must, therefore, have stood in the prompt-book. Having decided that the three lines should have been omitted with the rest of the passage, he infers that, if *they* were present in the manuscript, so must the rest have been. Since he believes (as I do) that the Folio represents the prompt-book of a revised version of the play, he concludes that this particular cut must have been made *after* that revision had taken place.

Stone does not even consider the possibility of censorship in this passage; he regards the Folio omission as no more than an unauthorized abridgement of the dialogue. My own investigation leads me to believe that the impetus for the cut came from the Master of the Revels. If Stone is right, and the entire passage stood (marked for deletion) in the prompt-book consulted in the printing of the Folio, then either the passage was not censored until the play was resubmitted to the Master of the Revels, or no new prompt-book was ever prepared (the old one simply being marked up and amended). As I have already said, the nature of the omitted passage gives us every reason to suspect that its deletion dates from the play's first submission for licensing, and the nature of the widespread Folio changes from the Quarto makes the idea of a 'marked-up' revised prompt-book decidedly unattractive. I am therefore inclined to reject Stone's interpretation of the evidence. If Stone is wrong, the survival of the three introductory lines ('Do'st thou know . . . teach me') can only mean one of three things: that the Folio compositor accidentally omitted (as compositors occasionally, though rather infrequently, do[67]) several lines, which contained a revised and abbreviated answer to the Fool's question; or that an annotator, marking up a copy of Q2 to serve as printer's copy for the Folio, began his deletion mark three lines lower than he should have, and that the compositor subsequently and independently set 'one' in error for copy 'foole'; or that Shakespeare intended the passage to stand just as it does in the Folio. Since both the first and second of these explanations involve intrinsically implausible kinds or combinations of error, it seems to me most likely that the third is correct.

To those acquainted with the full Quarto text, the Folio's train of thought appears nonsensical;[68] but, considered in its own right, it seems to work in much the same way that some of the Fool's other exchanges do.

> *Foole.* Do'st thou know the difference my Boy, betweene a bitter Foole, and a sweet one.
> *Lear.* No Lad, teach me.
> *Foole.* Nunckle, giue me an egge [*why? what does this have to do with two fools? or with 'sweet' and 'bitter'?*], and Ile giue thee two Crownes.
> *Lear.* What two Crownes shall they be?
> *Foole.* Why after I haue cut the egge i'th' middle and eate vp the meate, the two Crownes of the egge[*why? as symbols of what?*]: when thou clouest thy Crowne i'th' middle, and gau'st away both parts . . .
>
>   (TLN 667–76, reading 'Crownes' in the last line)

None of the subsequent seventeenth-century folios shows any sign of dissatisfaction with this passage; nor does Rowe. Even more significantly, whoever prepared the Smock Alley prompt-book some time after the Restoration – who on the evidence of changes elsewhere had access to lines preserved only in the Quarto – left this passage as it stands in the Folio. In fact, the difficulty here is entirely of a piece with the difficulty of the Fool's speech elsewhere: the promise of meaning followed by deliberate obfuscation, sudden changes of direction, reliance upon and frustration of the expectations and suspicions of his audience. 'Do'st thou *know* the difference my Boy, betweene a bitter Foole, and a sweet one[?]' can easily be no more than a rhetorical question; Lear answers it like a literal one (thereby, as it were, retracting the accusation in his preceding speech); the Fool pauses and then says something which appears completely out of the way. But is it? With the Fool we (like Lear) never know. The request for an egg can look, easily enough, like a request for a comic prop, something he will use to demonstrate a ridiculous analogy (as he had used his coxcomb earlier). In particular, the pun on 'custard' in 'Foole', and the culinary imagery in 'bitter' and 'sweet', would have made the request for an egg seem entirely natural – for at the time (as OED attests) eggs were a normal ingredient for 'fools'. Eggs were also, proverbially, dirt cheap: in 1605 a hundred of them sold for as little as 3 shillings 10 pence.[69] The Fool's offer to pay Lear two crowns – ten shillings – for a single egg is, therefore, an action entirely appropriate for an idiot. The Fool appears to be an innocent half-wit, easily cheated of his money. But he then proceeds to turn this offer into an acid pun at Lear's expense, thereby demonstrating that he is more satirical than naive – or, if you like, more bitter than sweet.

The Folio change almost certainly originated in censorship, in external constraints beyond the artist's control. But the artist could have substituted something less offensive politically which would have made the same dramatic points (a lord counselling Lear to abdicate or divide his kingdom, Kent's seconding the Fool); even more easily, he could have omitted the whole of the exchange, skipping straight from Lear's 'A bitter foole' to the Fool's 'giue me an egge Nuncle' (which *would* have been a complete *non sequitur*). Instead, the text which appears in the Folio manages the transition in a way entirely characteristic of the peculiar dramatic style Shakespeare created for the Fool. Moreover, one other variant earlier in the dialogue seems fairly clearly related to F's omission. The omitted passage contains Kent's last speech in the scene ('This is not altogether foole my Lord'); F gives Kent an alternative last speech, 'This is nothing Foole' (TLN 658; C4ᵛ; 1.4.128), which Q attributes to Lear. Either character could reasonably speak the line, but without it Kent, in F, would have nothing at all to say after the Fool's entrance.[70]

If my own analysis of the possible political significance of the omitted lines is correct, then their deletion must have been instigated by the Master of the Revels. But Shakespeare may not have resisted the change too vehemently; in fact, once it was suggested he may have welcomed the deletion. The omitted lines contain the play's only allusion to 'That Lord that counsail'd thee | to giue away thy land' (a hangover from the *Leir* version of the story); the Folio, in its handling of 1.1, more clearly makes Lear himself singly responsible for the decision to abdicate, and the omission here fits that revised conception of the abdication. It also removes a minor difficulty created by the fact that Kent's 'This is not altogether foole my Lord' – the comment of a newly-hired retainer – apparently provokes no response at all from Lear. If Lear reacts so strongly to his allowed and intimate jester calling him a fool, why does he not react at all when a hireling stranger endorses that accusation? Beyond eliminating these two minor difficulties, the omission also serves the laudable dramatic function of abbreviating the fairly repetitive exchanges between Lear and his Fool here. The omitted lines are hardly the Fool's most brilliant: we know at once that the bitter fool is going to be Lear's counsellor (in the person of Lear himself), and as the riddle was prompted by Lear's calling his jester 'A bitter foole', it doesn't take much audience ingenuity to guess who the sweet one will prove to be. The Fool elsewhere exploits the obviousness of the answers to some of his questions, but here alone is an obvious answer drawn out at length, rather than simply and quickly turned to comic effect. Shakespeare's own impulse to comment upon contemporary abuses may have led him to write at greater length than the play required. The censor, by curbing that impulse, may actually, in applying the restraints of a particular time and place, have done the timeless work of art a service.

VI

Only one word ('Fut') and one passage (1.4.140–55) seem to have been omitted from Folio *Lear* under the influence of censorship. The omission of 'Fut' tells us nothing about the larger issue of textual transmission in the two texts, but the omission of 1.4.140–55 was almost certainly called for at the time of the play's initial submission or, at the latest, before the Christmas performance of 1606; this in turn establishes that the Quarto text, which contains that passage, almost certainly cannot represent the text as remembered from performances. Equally important, both the ready availability of dramatic motives for all the other omissions discussed, and the implausibility of censorship as a factor in any of those omissions, drastically weaken the case for conflation, by removing one allegedly important cause of unauthoritative variation between the two texts.

Should an editor replace what censorship displaced? In the case of 'Fut' I see no reason not to. The word could have been removed in deference to the 1606 Act on any one of six occasions: by the King's Men themselves, voluntarily, soon after the Act was passed; by George Buc, rereading the text before the court performance of Christmas 1606; by Shakespeare, when revising the play, in the knowledge that 'Fut' would now be – as it was not when he originally wrote it – censorable; by a scribe, preparing or revising a prompt-book for resubmission, and anticipating the censor's demand; by Buc, reading the resubmitted revised text; or by an editor in Isaac Jaggard's printing shop, in 1623.[71] 'Fut' stood little chance of running those half a dozen gauntlets unscathed. Even if it had survived censorship, its omission is of a kind that could easily arise from simple inadvertence, by a scribe or by a compositor. The probability of unauthoritative omission is thus staggeringly high. And there is no reason to suspect deliberate authorial revision here: the Folio omission serves no discernible dramatic purpose, either locally or in terms of the larger characterization of Edmund. With 'Fut' the editorial problem is as simple as the expletive itself; the passage omitted from 1.4, which serves a variety of artistic functions, poses editorial questions correspondingly complex. It seems to me highly likely that the original impetus for the omission of part or all of the affected passage came from the Master of the Revels in 1605–6. But Shakespeare had at least one and probably two opportunities to recast the passage in a less objectionable form; he did not do so. As abbreviated the passage makes good dramatic sense, not only in its immediate context but in relation to the larger pattern of Folio alterations; and the omission has apparently resulted in at least one other dramatic variant elsewhere. At all the motives of the omission we can only guess (although, in this case, censorship almost certainly *influenced* the decision); that it happened, in a text which shows other evidence of extensive authorial revision, is a fact. Should an editor rescue an author from the constraints imposed by history?[72] Should we revert from Falstaff to Oldcastle? Should the guess displace the fact?

NOTES

1. E. K. Chambers proposes, within the course of three sentences (*William Shakespeare*, 2 vols. (Oxford, 1930), I, 467), that three 'omissions' from Q and three from F were due to censorship. (All three omissions from F are discussed above: see Sections III, IV and V.)
2. On the subject of theatrical censorship generally I am indebted to the recent thorough survey by Janet Clare ('Art made tongue-tied by authority: a study of the relationship between Elizabethan and Jacobean drama and authority and the effect of censorship on the plays of the period', unpublished Ph.D. thesis, University of Birmingham, 1981). Anne Lancashire has also given generous and helpful advice.
3. For *The Tamer Tamed* (also known as *The Woman's Prize*) affair – particularly the reaction of the actors – see G. E. Bentley, *The Profession of Dramatist in Shakespeare's Time, 1590–1642* (Princeton, 1971), pp. 155–7; for transcripts of Herbert's memorandums, see *The Dramatic Records of Sir Henry Herbert*, ed. J. Q. Adams (New Haven, 1917), pp. 20–1.
4. 'For the king's players. An olde playe called *Winter's Tale*, formerly allowed of by Sir George Bucke, and likewyse by mee on Mr. Hemmings his worde that there was

nothing profane added or reformed, thogh the allowed booke was missinge; and therefore I returned it without a fee, this 19 of August, 1623' (*Records*, p. 25). For another similar memorandum see Bentley, p. 159.

5. *Textual Problems of the First Folio* (Cambridge, 1953), pp. 37–67.

6. *The Shakespeare First Folio: Its Bibliographical and Textual History* (Oxford, 1955), pp. 382–3. See also MacD. P. Jackson's critique (below, pp. 325–8).

7. Buc began licensing plays for publication from 16 November 1606 onwards (almost exactly a year before *Lear* was so licensed). See W. W. Greg, 'Entrance, Licence, and Publication', *The Library*, IV, 25 (1945), 1–22, and Elias Schwartz, 'Sir George Buc's Authority as Licenser for the Press', *Shakespeare Quarterly*, 12 (1961), 467–8. Buc had, in all but name, succeeded Tilney as Master of the Revels in 1603 (for which see E. K. Chambers, *The Elizabethan Stage*, 4 vols. (Oxford, 1923), I, 96–9); he therefore must have licensed both the performance and (separately) the publication of *King Lear*. In theory, material censorable in the theatre need not be censorable in print, if its offensiveness results from an actor's mimicry of the appearance, gestures, or voice of a particular public figure. But such a distinction would not apply to any of the suspected passages in *Lear*; besides, in practice I doubt that Buc would have felt that something unfit to stage was fit to print.

8. Examples of such scrupulousness are, however, hard to find. It has been suggested that the so-called 'clock passage' in *Richard III* (I1ᵛ–I2; 4.2.98–116; not in F) was omitted because it might have offended the Duke of Buckingham; but Antony Hammond, in his new Arden edition (1981) rightly protests at the implausibility of this hypothesis (pp. 334–5). A more attractive example is the alteration, in the Folio text of *The Merchant of Venice*, of 'the Scottish Lorde' to 'the other lord' (B1ᵛ; TLN 267; 1.2.77); this change almost certainly postdated the accession of James I, seven years after the play's original performances (which can be fairly confidently dated in 1596). However, *The Merchant of Venice* was performed at court twice in February 1605; Buc might have asked to see the manuscript again before the court performance, in which case even this change might have been initiated by the censor rather than the actors.

9. *The Dramatic Use of Bawdy in Shakespeare* (1974), pp. 194–5. W. J. Craig, in the old Arden edition of *King Lear* (1901), lists six parallels for 'fut' in Marston's plays, most in contexts of sexual innuendo.

10. G. I. Duthie, *Shakespeare's 'King Lear': A Critical Edition* (Oxford, 1949), p. 170. The Act is reprinted in Chambers, *The Elizabethan Stage*, IV, 338–9. MacD. P. Jackson reports to me that in his own survey of the Middleton canon, he discovered the related profanity 'sfut' in eight plays certainly or putatively by Middleton written in or before 1606, and in no such 'Middleton' play thereafter – which certainly suggests that at least one dramatist of the period felt that 'God's foot' fell within the jurisdiction of the Act.

11. Only three other potentially objectionable asseverations in the Quarto have been omitted by the Folio, and in each case the asseveration disappears as part of a much larger cut: 'faith' in the midst of 1.4.140–55 (C4ᵛ – D1; discussed above, pp. 101–9), 'by my life' in the midst of 1.3.16–20 (C3), and 'heauen and earth!' in the midst of 1.2.95–7 (C2; discussed above, pp. 87–8). In each case, moreover, none of the other occurrences of the asseveration has been altered (though such inconsistency does occur in other censored texts). The 'faith' at 1.4.152, coming as it does immediately before the jibe at 'Lords and great men', might be included among the variety of objectionable features in that whole passage (see above, pp. 102–5).

12. It seems to me most likely that the play was composed in the winter of 1605–6, and consequently that it had been performed publicly before Christmas 1606. (See

my 'A New Source and an Old Date for *King Lear*', *Review of English Studies*, 33 (1982), 396–413.) However, the later in 1606 that the play was completed and licensed, the less likely it becomes that Buc would wish to re-examine the manuscript. He seems to me unlikely to have done so, for the simple reason that he would rely on the actors themselves to be especially wary of anything which might offend the King. (*The Merchant of Venice*, by contrast, had been licensed nine years earlier, by a different censor, under a different monarch; Buc would have been much more likely to want to examine it again personally. See n. 8.)

13. For a photographic reproduction of the Stationers' Register entry (26 November 1607), see S. Schoenbaum's *William Shakespeare: Records and Images* (1981), p. 218. Some negligence on Buc's part must in any case be assumed, if we believe that even a single passage present in Q had indeed been censored in the licensed copy (see above, pp. 102–5). However, the more censorship we suspect, the less plausible Buc's negligence becomes. If only one or two passages had originally caught his eye, he might be excused for forgetting about them, and for remembering only that the text had been essentially uncontroversial and acceptable; but if (as has been argued) the play had been rather heavily censored, and/or had required further special attention before its Court performance, then Buc would have been decidedly unwise to authorize the publication of an unexamined manuscript. Likewise, if Buc knew that the King's Men had themselves sold that manuscript to Nathaniel Butter, he might well have approved it with little thought, assuming either that the company would have taken care to follow his earlier instructions, or that – if they had not – any subsequent embarrassment could be blamed on their negligence, not his. In short, Buc's possible negligence, in licensing for publication a manuscript which contained passages he had asked to be omitted from performance, can be most plausibly explained if (1) the original play had required little censorship, and (2) the King's Men clearly approved of the manuscript's publication. Either of these assumptions undermines the case for conflation of Q and F, which must therefore postulate considerably more negligence on Buc's part.

14. 'Time, Place, and Politics in *King Lear*' [1940], in *Collected Papers*, ed. J. C. Maxwell (Oxford, 1966), p. 333.

15. *The Text of 'King Lear'* (Stanford, 1931), pp. 73–6. Doran's explanation has been accepted by at least some other editors: see for instance G. K. Hunter's New Penguin edition (Harmondsworth, 1972), p. 319.

16. Aside from the Gunpowder Plot of 1605, there were enclosure riots in the Midlands in 1607–8, the continued resistance of Parliament to James's union of the two kingdoms, discontent with the extravagance of James's court (see p. 103), and Protestant unease about James's religious toleration (see Kerrigan, below, pp. 221–3). None of these posed a major threat to James, but the King's political problems were clearly domestic, not foreign.

17. Bentley includes in his list of the objects of dramatic censorship 'Unfavorable presentations of *friendly* foreign powers or their sovereigns' (p. 167; Bentley's italics). Examples include *Barnavelt, The Game at Chess, Marquis D'Ancre* (lost), *Believe as You List*, and Walter Mountfort's *The Launching of the Mary, or the Seaman's Honest Wife*. For a full discussion of these and other examples, see Bentley, pp. 170–7.

18. For a full account see Chambers, *Elizabethan Stage*, III, 257–8; II, 53–4.

19. Greg presents no evidence that this issue much exercised contemporary critics of the government: neither C. D. Penn's *The Navy under the Early Stuarts* (1913) nor Herbert Richmond's *The Navy as an Instrument of Policy, 1558–1727* (Cambridge, 1953; pp. 160–71) even mentions this aspect of Jacobean naval policy. Although there were enquiries into financial corruption and naval maladministration in 1608

and 1618, these were prompted by and dwelt upon the deterioration in the fleet itself, and the only apparent mention of 'port defences' was a single brief query in 1618 about the river defences of Chatham. (See *The Jacobean Commissions of Enquiry, 1608 and 1618*, ed. A. P. McGowan, Publications of the Navy Records Society, Vol. 116 (1971), p. xxii.) The possible infiltration of foreign saboteurs or spies – to which Kent more specifically refers – seems never to have been discussed. In any case, for most of James I's reign the Folio's added lines about spies in noble households (TLN 1631–4; 3.1.22–5) would have been decidedly more dangerous than those the Folio omits; the added lines might be thought to allude to the extensive Spanish bribery of members of the court (including James himself). (See Garrett Mattingly, *Renaissance Diplomacy* (1955, repr. 1973), pp. 246–9.) Even if Greg were right about the censor's sensitivity to port defences, such sensitivity could only account for the omission of two lines of Kent's speech ('alreadie | Wise in our negligēce, haue secret feet | In some of our best Ports, and'). More generally, even at its most expansive Greg's suggestion, unlike Doran's, explains only one of a whole series of Folio alterations concerning the nationality of Cordelia's army, and therefore must leave those other alterations unexplained, or invoke additional hypotheses to explain them.

20. See for instance George Walton Williams, *Shakespeare Survey 34* (Cambridge, 1981), p. 194. Clare, who accepts that the Folio represents a revised version of the play (but does not refer to 'War'), suggests that Shakespeare himself removed the references to France, in deference to James I's known pacifist views (pp. 232–4). I find it difficult to believe that the man who, at about this time, wrote *Macbeth* and *Coriolanus* believed that his duty as a subject demanded such an abstention from military material; nor is it clear why James would find armed rebellion more palatable than foreign invasion. But, in any case, since the censor clearly did not insist that dramatists refrain from treating such subjects, it hardly matters whether Clare is right about Shakespeare's motives for the revision, since she agrees that a revision did take place.

21. Greg recognized this: after singling out these two phrases as the potentially objectionable part of Edmund's catalogue, he concedes that 'objection to particular phrases need not have involved extended omissions' (*First Folio*, p. 387). Anne Lancashire advises me that 'The manuscript of *The Second Maiden's Tragedy* contains a few places where some words have been cut by mistake and/or the beginning or end of a given cut is not clear' (private communication). But it remains unlikely that an instruction to cut ten continuous words would be misinterpreted as an instruction to cut fifty. Lancashire also notes that in places 'someone seems to have taken advantage of a censorship cut to cut a bit more as well'. But such changes cannot themselves be blamed on the censor; they had other motives, which the critic rather than the historian must attempt to discern and evaluate.

22. 'By early 1613 it was common talk at court that the young Essexes wanted a divorce' (G. P. V. Akrigg, *Jacobean Pageant: or, the Court of King James I* (Cambridge, Mass., 1962), p. 181.) Akrigg also notes that there is no real evidence for any earlier sexual scandals involving Frances Howard (p. 131). However, on 25 July 1610 Samuel Calvert wrote to William Trumbull, 'My Lord Cranborne begins to look sour upon his wife. So hath my Lord of Essex cause, for they say plots have been laid by his to poison him' (Historical Manuscripts Commission, *Report of the Manuscripts of the Marquess of Downshire*, ed. E. K. Purnell and A. B. Hinds, II (1936), p. 328). According to evidence in the later trial of Frances Howard and Robert Carr, they were lovers by early 1612 (T. B. Howell, *A Complete Collection of State Trials*, II (1816), p. 973); but John Chamberlain had heard nothing about it until June 1613 (*The Letters of John Chamberlain*, ed.

114   *The Division of the Kingdoms*

Norman E. McClure (Philadelphia, 1939), I, 456, 458, 461). Therefore, though it is possible that some people at court knew about a 'breach' between Essex and his wife as early as 1610, knowledge of the link between Frances Howard and the King's favourite could not have been widespread until much later. Not until the breach with Essex led to a notorious divorce scandal, involving the King himself, would the censor be likely to take care over any potential allusions to it. (For fuller discussion see Anne Lancashire's forthcoming '*The Witch*: Stage Flop or Political Mistake?', in '*Accompaninge the Players': Essays Celebrating Thomas Middleton, 1581–1980*, ed. Kenneth Friedenreich (New York, 1983).)

23. Akrigg, pp. 132–3. As early as June 1607, the Venetian ambassador reported that James was not 'overpleased to see his son so beloved and of such promise that his subjects place all their hopes in him; and it would almost seem, to speak quite frankly, that the King was growing jealous' (*Venetian State Papers, 1603–7*, pp. 513–14). Such diplomatic inferences about the King's private feelings toward his twelve-year-old son are, however, markedly less significant than the incident, also described by a Venetian ambassador, on 4 May 1611, when the King and his sixteen-year-old, politically active son publicly quarreled, James threatening Henry with his cane (*V.S.P., 1610–13*, p. 142). The Master of the Revels might well object to 'vnnaturalnesse betweene the child and the parent' after this later incident; it is harder to believe he would have done so in 1607.

24. Akrigg, p. 265. 'The King is for ever following the chase in order to divert his spirit, saddened and discomposed by the misconduct of the Queen' (8 July 1604, Count Beaumont to Henri IV; reprinted by Frederick von Raumer, *History of the Sixteenth and Seventeenth Centuries, Illustrated by Original Documents*, 2 vols. (1835), II, 207). Another contemporary comment to the same effect, dated 16 June 1603, is reprinted in Edmund Lodge, *Illustrations of British History*, 3 vols. (1791), III, 163–4. See also Robert Ashton, *James I by his Contemporaries* (1969), p. 86. Alfred Hart, in a conjecture not taken up by subsequent investigators, suggested that the Folio's omissions in 4.2 stemmed from anxiety over possible offence to 'James and his queen' who 'agreed little better than Albany and Goneril; the quarrel . . . between the latter may have been a politic omission because Albany bore a Scottish title' (*Stolne and Surreptitious Copies: A Comparative Study of Shakespeare's Bad Quartos* (Melbourne, 1942), p. 148). But the play makes nothing of Albany's Scottishness, and his name never even occurs in the dialogue after 3.1; any parallel with James in 4.2 would be most indirect, especially since (as noted above, p. 104) the play clearly encourages comparison of James with Lear himself. In 4.2, the couple clearly quarrel, in both texts; the passages not present in F contain no discernible links with James, while those retained include gibes at Albany's 'Milke-Liuer'd' nature and 'Cowish' spirit. Like Oswald's later observation that Goneril 'is the better Souldier' of the two (TLN 2388; 4.5.3), these hits at Albany's pacifist nature would be more likely to offend anyone alert to parallels between Albany and James than would any of the lines omitted by F. The Folio also retains the adultery of Albany's wife, her plot to poison her husband, and her retort 'the Lawes are mine . . . Who can araigne me for't?' (TLN 3116–17; 5.3.159–60) – all more objectionable, if a link with Queen Anne were suspected, than the omitted lines in 4.2. The Folio also adds Goneril's sneer dismissing Albany's arraignment of Edmund for treason as 'An enterlude' (TLN 3035; 5.3.89); Queen Anne was much criticized for her enthusiasm for dramatic entertainments. Perceived comparisons between Albany's marriage and James I's thus seem most unlikely to have influenced the Folio text.

25. See W. G. Hoskins, 'Harvest Fluctuations and English Economic History, 1480–1619', *Agricultural History Review*, 12 (1964), 28–46, and 'Harvest Fluctuations and English Economic History, 1620–1759', *AHR*, 16 (1968), 15–31. The most

severe periods of dearth relevant to the composition or publication of Shakespeare's plays occurred in 1587–8, 1597–8, and 1623; for those see Andrew B. Appleby, *Famine in Tudor and Stuart England* (Stanford, 1978), pp. 95–154.

26. If the Folio does represent a deliberate redaction of the play, one or more of these phrases might have been censored when this new version was submitted for licensing, depending on when that resubmission took place. Stone argues that the redaction dates from after 1617 (*Textual History*, pp. 120–6); John Kerrigan (below, pp. 221–3) points out that Stone's evidence would in fact accord equally well with redaction before 1612; I present other evidence for dating Shakespeare's revision of the play in 1609 or 1610 (below, pp. 354–95). If the resubmission took place before 1611, F's omission of 'nuptial breaches' seems unlikely to be due to concern for its possible relevance to the Essex marriage, but 'vnnaturalnesse . . . parent' might have been omitted in deference to James and Henry. One might then speculate that 'nuptial breaches' had already been censored at the play's first submission (because of possible relevance, then, to James and Anne). This still leaves the omission of 'dearth' – and, of course, the remainder of the passage – unexplained.

27. There was another lunar eclipse in July 1610, and a solar eclipse at the end of May 1612; it would be rather stretching things to refer to these together, since they were separated by twenty-three months. Otherwise the only eclipses between 1605 and the publication of the Folio were two lunar eclipses in June and December 1620. See S. J. Johnson, *Historical and Future Eclipses* (1896), pp. 58–9, 77.

28. Doran in fact offers a somewhat similar explanation (inadvertence) for the fact that the Folio does not remove all of the Act Three references to French invasion (*The Text of 'King Lear'*, p. 73, n. 48).

29. For the most recent account of the evidence that part at least of Folio *Lear* was set from annotated Q2 copy, see my 'Folio Copy for *Hamlet, King Lear, and Othello*' (*Shakespeare Quarterly*, 34 (1983), 44–61). Although Compositor B, who set this Folio page (qq3^v), may have worked from manuscript elsewhere in the play, two factors point to Quarto copy here: the use of the Quarto's consistent prefix '*Bast.*' for '*Edm.*', and the peculiar indentation of Edmund's 'When saw you my Father last?' (immediately after the omitted passage). The Folio substitutes '*Edm.*' in the prefixes of the first scene, and this practice resumes on page qq4; the Folio therefore switches, in the middle of 1.2, from the Quarto's preferred prefix to one apparently taken from a manuscript. This suggests that qq3^v was *not* set directly from manuscript. For the peculiar spacing around the Folio cut, see the photoquote above (p. 86); this strongly suggests that the copy from which B was working contained the full version of this passage, with the excised lines crossed out. My own guess is that both B and E worked from marked-up printed copy till near the end of rr3, and that B then took over (at TLN 1853; 3.4.72), setting the next 6½ Folio pages (900 lines) directly from manuscript; Q2's influence clearly resumes in column b of rr6^v, and on the next page E resumed work, setting the remainder of the play from annotated Q2 copy. Certainly, the 'various highly irregular exchanges of copy between B and E' described by Charlton Hinman (*The Printing and Proof-Reading of the First Folio of Shakespeare*, 2 vols. (Oxford, 1963), II, 272–3) – 'exchanges that are almost without parallel elsewhere in the Folio' – make it extremely unlikely that, for quire qq at least, two separate blocs of copy were prepared in advance for the two compositors. Moreover, the effect of these exchanges of copy is that 'Compositor E did not set three pages of *King Lear* – qq3^v, qq5, and qq2 – that would else have fallen to him'. These three pages contain virtually all the major Folio additions in quire qq: eleven lines on qq2, six on qq3^v, thirteen on qq5. Such additions, by interleaving or annotation, would have

produced much messier copy, and Compositor B might well have been given the affected pages for that reason.

30. Both authors and theatrical scribes sometimes anticipated likely objections before they submitted a manuscript to the censor. For a possible example of authorial self-censorship, see my Oxford Shakespeare edition of *Henry V* (1982), p. 16; for the scribal equivalent, see Herbert's note when returning *The Tamer Tamed*: 'In many things you have saved mee labour . . .' (*Dramatic Records*, p. 21). However, even if the foul papers had received such preliminary cautious attention by Shakespeare or a theatrical scribe, anyone who cut one of these passages for such reasons could hardly have overlooked the other.

31. The last line of a speech is relatively unlikely to have been omitted by accident. For the altered presentation of Cordelia, see Goldring (below, pp. 148–50).

32. For the difficulty about Kent's participation, see Michael Warren (above, p. 72, n. 5).

33. The censorship of parts of the trial scene in *Barnavelt* was clearly motivated by its portrayal of the Prince of Orange, and so falls under the rubric of 'Unfavorable presentation of *friendly* foreign powers'.

34. Greg himself recognized this contradiction (*First Folio*, p. 387).

35. For the influence of *Eastward Ho* on this scene, see 'A New Source and an Old Date', pp. 397–9.

36. Q actually reads 'robbed man'; *OED* recognizes 'robbe' as a sixteenth-century spelling of modern 'robe'. Editors usually assume that 'most learned Iustice' and 'sapient sir' are addressed to different characters, but all agree in directing one of the two to the Fool.

37. *The Masks of King Lear* (Berkeley and Los Angeles, 1972), p. 235.

38. If Lear did address the question to himself, then it might conceivably have been censorable after 1616, when another king (James I) had 'let . . . scape' (by pardoning, after her conviction for the murder of Sir Thomas Overbury) another 'her' (Lady Frances Howard, after her divorce from Essex and marriage to Somerset), in what was widely perceived as a miscarriage of justice. See Godfrey Davies, *The Early Stuarts, 1603–1660* (1937, rev. edn. 1959), pp. 19–20. However, the excision of the line and a half, even if ordered or voluntarily undertaken at that time (and I find the connection with James decidedly far-fetched), need not have affected the remainder of the scene.

39. The Quarto text, however, at least makes better use of the stool's hardness than do conflated editions. In Q, Lear asks for Regan to be anatomized in order to determine whether there is 'any cause in nature that makes this hardnes'; conflated editions retain the mad trial, but follow F in reading 'these hard-hearts' (silently removing the hyphen) for Q's 'this hardnes'. But 'this hardnes' makes perfectly good sense, since Lear can, by simply tapping on the stool, identify the phrase as a reference to the hardness of the stool, which he has equated with Regan. This not only draws attention to the stool's one relevant attribute, but also provides an ironic answer to Lear's question – for there is, clearly, a cause in nature which makes the hardness of the stool. Conflation produces a text less satisfactory than either early edition.

40. For the influence of the folk plays see particularly Carol E. Dixon's '*King Lear* and the Popular Tradition: Dialectic of the Inversion Metaphor' (Shakespeare Association of America conference paper, 1978); also Thomas McFarland, *Tragic Meanings in Shakespeare* (New York, 1966), 127–71. The passage quoted is from E. K. Chambers, *The English Folk-Play* (Oxford, 1933), pp. 46–7.

41. I have discussed this 'aggressive disappointment' of an audience's expectations in 'War', pp. 27–8.

42. See his new Arden edition of *King Lear* (1952, rev. edn. 1972), p. xliii.

43. G. Wilson Knight, '*King Lear* and the Comedy of the Grotesque', in *The Wheel of Fire* (1930, rev. edn. 1949), pp. 160–76. More sympathetic modern attitudes toward madness have drastically diminished our perception of the tension (and consequently, some of the difficulties of staging the trial scene): Jacobean Englishmen, it must be remembered, visited madhouses for amusement.

44. For a fuller analysis of the changes in Lear's presentation in the first scene, see Thomas Clayton and MacD. P. Jackson (below, pp. 123–6, 332–9).

45. See also Randall McLeod's discussion (below, p. 174).

46. Private communication, 13 May 1982.

47. In addition to the bracketed emendations, I have omitted F's redundant and unmetrical 'Or' before 'Bobtaile' (as in Q), and relined Tom's exorcism of the dogs, so that the first rhymed line begins 'Be' rather than 'Curres, be', and so that the last two lines of the speech are prose (as in Q), rather than verse (as in F). F sets Gloucester's penultimate speech as two half-lines, divided after ' Friend:'.

48. Like other editors I follow Q in postponing Gloucester's entrance until just before he speaks; F places it before Kent's preceding speech. Gloucester's urgency makes it unlikely he would stand by silently during this interval, and his first question makes it clear that he has not seen or heard Lear going to bed. The Folio contains a number of such anticipatory stage directions, which are often a feature of contemporary prompt-books.

49. Gloucester specifically tells Kent to 'take [Lear] in thy armes'; the litter is ready, but presumably not on the stage, since if it were Gloucester need not tell Kent about it. The fact that Gloucester says 'driue toward Douer', and the inference that the litter is offstage, strongly suggest that Shakespeare was thinking of 'a vehicle . . . containing a couch shut in by curtains' (*OED, sb.* 2a) rather than the simpler, more portable modern object.

50. I have accepted Capell's arrangement of the Fool's rhyme; Q prints as four verse lines instead of eight.

51. See Davies, *The Early Stuarts*, p. 25.

52. For an account of known or probable censorship in all of these plays, see Clare. For censorship in *The Second Maiden's Tragedy*, see also Anne Lancashire's Revels edition (Manchester, 1978), Appendix A. For *snatch* meaning 'a hasty act of copulation', see Colman, *The Dramatic Use of Bawdy*, p. 214. Qa reads 'lodes', but Qb's 'Ladies' has been universally accepted as a necessary correction (though the capitalization presumably does not reflect copy).

53. 'A Court banquet, so decorously conducted in Elizabeth's time, became an indecent scramble for free food and drink which quickly degenerated into a debauch' (William McElwee, *The Wisest Fool in Christendom: The Reign of King James I and VI* (1958), p. 174.) This excessive banqueting began with James's journey south into England (McElwee, pp. 108–10; see also pp. 167, 172, 175). Sir Dudley Carleton wrote to a friend that, after the masque on 6 January 1605, 'The Night's Work was concluded with a Banquet in the great Chamber, which was so furiously assaulted, that down went Table and Tresse[l]s, before one bit was touched' (*Memorials . . . Sir Ralph Winwood*, ed. E. Sawyer (1725), II, 44). Of revels a year earlier Dudley noted that the banquet 'was dispatched with the accustomed confusion' (*State Papers, Domestic, Jac. I*, VI. 21). For Harington's description of a notorious banquet in 1606, see Ashton, *James I by his Contemporaries*, 242–4.

54. 'I ken the man weel; he's one of my thirty-pound knights' (4.1.197–8); see R. W. Van Fossen's Revels edition (Manchester, 1979). Chambers points to similar satiric references in the anonymous *Nobody and Somebody*, Chapman's *Monsieur D'Olive*, *Bussy D'Ambois*, and *The Widow's Tears*, Barry's *Ram Alley*, and Middleton's *The Phoenix* and *Michaelmas Term* (*Elizabethan Stage*, III, 215, 252, 253, 255, 257, 439, 440; IV, 37). All these plays date from 1603–7, six from 1604–6.

55. Lawrence Stone, *The Crisis of the Aristocracy, 1558–1641* (Oxford, 1965), pp. 74, 81–2. In the course of his reign James created sixty peers (as opposed to eight during Elizabeth's much longer one). See Davies, *The Early Stuarts*, pp. 1, 266.
56. See von Raumer, *History of the Sixteenth and Seventeenth Centuries*, II, 201.
57. A letter recounting this event (written by Edmund Lascelles to the Earl of Shrewsbury) is reprinted in Lodge, *Illustrations of British History*, III, 245.
58. Lodge, *Illustrations of British History*, III, 252. Cranborne's reply, in February 1604, mentions the circulation of transcripts of this letter (III, 262).
59. *Venetian State Papers, 1603–1607*, pp. 513, 510.
60. D. Harris Willson, *King James VI and I* (1956), p. 179.
61. See Glynne Wickham, 'From Tragedy to Tragi-comedy: *King Lear* as Prologue', *Shakespeare Survey 26* (Cambridge, 1973), 33–48. (I do not necessarily subscribe to Wickham's other theories, about *Lear* or the late plays.) For some other specific parallels with James, see Margaret Hotine's 'Lear's Fit of the Mother' (*Notes and Queries*, 226 (1981), 138–41) and 'Two Plays for St. Stephen's Day' (*Notes and Queries*, 227 (1982), 119–21).
62. Count Beaumont's letter of 12 September 1603 notes that James 'was yesterday a little disturbed by the populace, which ran together from all sides to see him. He fell into such anger . . . he cursed every one he met, and swore that if they would not let him follow the chase at his pleasure, he would leave England' (von Raumer, II, 202). In 1608 the French ambassador reports on a play in which the actors 'brought forward their own King, and all his favourites . . . They made him curse and swear . . . and beat a gentleman because he had called off the hounds from the scent' (II, 220).
63. For a full account of this sequence of scandals see Clare, pp. 202–31.
64. See Enid Welsford, *The Fool: His Social and Literary History* (1935), pp. 170–1; for more on Armstrong, see *The Dictionary of National Biography*.
65. Though commonly attributed to Henri IV, the description of King James as 'the wisest foole in Christendome' apparently first occurs in Antony Weldon's 'Character of King James' (printed 1650; not written till after Weldon's disgrace in 1618). Weldon there attributes the witticism (p. 186) to 'a very wise man'. (The whole passage is conveniently reprinted in Ashton's *James I by his Contemporaries*, p. 15.) If Henri IV, or his chief minister Sully, indeed coined the phrase, it could be confidently dated early in James's reign, since Henri was assassinated in 1610 and Sully disgraced by the next year. However, Maurice Lee, Jr., in his comprehensive account of relations between Henri and James (*James I and Henri IV: An Essay in English Foreign Policy, 1603–1610* (Urbana, 1970)), never mentions the remark, though he does note how relations were permanently soured by Henri's early jibe that James might well call himself the Scottish Solomon, since he was the son of David who played on the harp (p. 10). In fact it seems possible that the 'wisest foole' remark has been attributed to Henri *because* of this earlier witticism at James's expense. One cannot be confident, therefore, that the remark dates from before 1610 (or, for that matter, before 1623).
66. Even the 'foole/one' variant could, in this context, be compositorial; however, if we assume that it is we must further assume that the compositor also erred in omitting too much or too little of the following dialogue, and this combination of error seems relatively unlikely. The only other variant in the three lines – Folio's 'Do'st thou' for Quarto's 'Doo'st' – could more easily be an error, especially since the Folio follows the reading in Q2, which was almost certainly the compositor's copy at this point. (See p. 115, n. 29, above.)
67. For what appears to be a compositorial omission of a number of lines, see *Love's Labour's Lost* 3.1.84–92, present in Q but not F (C4ᵛ; between TLN 856 and 857). The Folio is, for *Love's Labour's Lost*, essentially a reprint of the Quarto, and

without the omitted lines the passage does not, in any way I or others have been able to see, make sense. For another example see *Troilus and Cressida* TLN 1257–61 (not in Q).

68. Even Urkowitz calls this 'one of the few clumsy cuts in the Folio text' (*Revision*, p. 155, n. 21), where the compositors had 'to resort to the setting of nonsense' (p. 13). Tony Church and Julian Curry (Lear and the Fool respectively) were also uncomfortable with it, in the 1982 Santa Cruz production based on the Folio text.

69. James E. Thorold Rogers, *A History of Agriculture and Prices in England* (Oxford, 1866–1902), V (1887), pp. 373–4. See also *OED* 'egg' *sb.* 4, and M. P. Tilley, *A Dictionary of the Proverbs in England in the Sixteenth and Seventeenth Centuries* (Ann Arbor, 1950), E90 ('To take eggs for money') and E83 ('As dear as an egg for a penny').

70. The Quarto gives Kent one other speech after the Fool's entrance, 'Why Foole?' (C4^v; 1.4.98); but the Folio attributes the line to Lear instead ('Why my Boy?', TLN 628). Editors often prefer Q, but F makes good dramatic sense, being part of the shifting of interlocutor or audience which characterizes the Fool's comic technique.

71. For evidence that some at least of the purging of profanity in Folio texts was editorial rather than theatrical in origin, see Greg, *The Shakespeare First Folio*, pp. 151–2, 171–2, 264.

72. For a discussion of the editorial problems created in some modern texts, where outside constraints coincide with the author's own recasting of his text for personal or artistic reasons, see Hans Zeller, 'A New Approach to the Critical Constitution of Literary Texts', *Studies in Bibliography*, 28 (1975), pp. 245–9.

'Is this the promis'd end?'
Revision in the Role of the King

THOMAS CLAYTON

I

SHAKESPEARE'S King Lear undergoes his tragic passion, fulfils his dramatic destiny, and articulates some of the play's profoundest themes and most searching images and perceptions in Quarto and Folio alike. He is physically present during nearly half of the play's action in the Quarto, and the only extensive reduction in his part in the Folio is in the mad trial scene (G3ᵛ–G4; 3.6.17–56).[1] In fact, since the Folio's *King Lear* is about 200 lines shorter than the Quarto's, the King has proportionately more dialogue, both on that account and by virtue of the few and brief but important additions; his presence is increased especially in the later acts, where most of the cuts were made.[2] The content, quality, and effects of the additions are quite another story.

It is significant that few 'key' passages, philosophical statements, and questions of theodicy have been cut, and Lear of course has many of them. Thus the purposes of revising did *not* include radical abbreviation of dialogue or simplification of philosophical issues, and the Folio *King Lear* is still 'about' most of what it had been in the earlier, longer Quarto version, still focusing thematically on such quintessential speeches as the Janus-like apostrophic reasoning of the respective needs of low and high estate in

> Poore naked wretches, where so ere you are
> That bide the pelting of this pittilesse storme,
> How shall your House-lesse heads, and vnfed sides,
> Your lo[o]p'd, and window'd raggednesse defend you
> From seasons such as these? O I haue tane
> Too little care of this: Take Physicke, Pompe,
> Expose thy selfe to feele what wretches feele,
> That thou maist shake the superflux to them,
> And shew the Heauens more iust.
> (TLN 1809–17; G1ᵛ, reading 'night' for 'storme';
> 3.4.28–36)

In no case are the additions or revisions in Lear's part without dramatic purpose, theatrical effect, and thematic significance, and even the numerous 'minor' changes in wording are almost never 'indifferent variants'. But here I shall confine myself to the most significant revisions in the dialogue and action: the 'add-omissions'[3] and changes made in his final speeches and earlier as significant components of a pattern of preparations for an ending altered from the 'image of that horror' in the Quarto to the more systematically 'promis'd end' of the Folio.

The passages concerned occur, appropriately, at the beginning (B1ᵛ; TLN 43–58; 1.1.38–53), the middle (G2ᵛ; TLN 1888–9; 3.4.108–9), and the end (TLN 3282–3, [not in Q], 5.3.311–12; and L4, TLN 3285, 5.3.313). These alterations are part of an evident, emphatic, and functional pattern that combines the progressive peeling away of layers of attire, appearance, affectation, and at last anatomy itself with an ultimate regression (or progression) to a state of 'second childhood'. This state may be seen by turns as 'this great decay', as clinical senility with the 'patient' technically as well as otherwise 'sundowning',[4] as childlike – or childish – innocence, as grace through forgiveness, as age transfigured by traces of the white radiance of eternity, or as a moment of simple – and fleeting – reunion and reconciliation of the long and agonizingly separated father and daughter.[5]

The first 'component' centres especially on clothing and body, and the actions of divesting, the second on the paradoxes of simultaneous youth and age. Both lines of developing figures arouse expectations of a kind of deliverance and rebirth, and in essential dramatic terms it scarcely matters whether the 'rebirth' is an imaginative and conceptual matter of re-entering the nitrogen cycle and being rolled round in earth's diurnal course with rocks and stones and trees, or of an immediate and extraterrestrial reunion of Lear with Cordelia and translation to beatitude: either way, an order of relief at Lear's release is built into his passing, however bleak and pessimistic the overall spectacle or conclusion 'is' or is taken to be. And one cannot reasonably ignore the reverberations of 'So be my graue my peace as here I giue, | Her fathers heart from her' (B2ᵛ; TLN 133–4; 1.1.125–6), and 'The Gods to their deere shelter take thee Maid, | That iustly think'st, and hast most rightly said' (TLN 196–7; B3–B3ᵛ; 1.1.182–3);[6] or the much later and still more complex preparatives:

Lear. You do me wrong to take me out o'th'graue,
Thou art a Soule in blisse, but I am bound
Vpon a wheele of fire, that mine owne teares
Do sca[ld], like molten Lead.
  Cor. Sir, do you know me?
  Lear. You are a spirit I know, where did you dye?
     (TLN 2794–9, reading 'scal'd' for 'scald'; K2;
     4.7.44–48)

     Vpon such sacrifices my *Cordelia*,
     The Gods thēselues throw incense. . . .
          (K4; TLN 2961–2; 5.3.20–1)

These all point to a culmination inextricably involved with 'justice',
poetical or otherwise, and to traditional sources of comfort that
cannot prevent but do temper grief, for spectators within the
dramatic action and theatre audience alike. They are expressed in
such ancient notions as 'whom the gods love die young' and – since
theoretically there may be no gods and the old die, too – all are 'cur'd
| By'th' sure Physitian, Death' (*Cymbeline* TLN 3041–2; 5.4.6–7),
notions that have a basis in how persons actually have died and how
their deaths are taken by their survivors.[7] R. F. Hill aptly remarks
that 'clearly the mystery of Divine dispensation is an important factor
in Shakespeare's pattern, but what seems doubtful is the value of
giving that mystery theological habitation and name.'[8]

II

The first brief complex of additions initiates a pattern culminating in
the altered end. The Quarto's nine and a half lines (notable
differences in the parallel passages italicized and QF-italicized names
in roman),

    . . . tis our *first* intent,
  To shake all cares and busines of our *state*,
  Confirming them on yonger *yeares*,
  The *two great* Princes France and Burgundy,
  Great ryuals in our youngest daughters loue,
  Long in our Court haue made their amorous soiourne,
  And here are to be answerd, tell me my daughters,
  Which of you shall we say doth loue vs most,
  That we our largest bountie may extend,
  Where *merit* doth most challenge it[?]

become the Folio's fifteen and a half lines,

> . . . 'tis our *fast* intent,
> To shake all Cares and Businesse from our *Age*,
> *Conferring* them on yonger *strengths, while we*
> *Vnburthen'd crawle toward death.* Our son of Cornwal,
> *And you our no lesse louing Sonne of Albany,*
> *We haue this houre a constant will to publish*
> *Our daughters seuerall Dowers, that future strife*
> *May be preuented now.* The Princes, France & Burgundy,
> Great Riuals in our yongest daughters loue,
> Long in our Court, haue made their amorous soiourne,
> And heere are to be answer'd. Tell me my daughters
> (*Since now we will diuest vs both of Rule,*
> *Interest of Territory, Cares of State*)
> Which of you shall we say doth loue vs most,
> That we, our largest bountie may extend
> Where *Nature doth with merit* challenge[?]
>
> (B1ᵛ; TLN 43–58; 1.1.38–53)

None of the variants is 'indifferent', and there is every appearance of a unified conception in the effects of the changes. The major differences are the additions, 'while we . . . preuented now' and '(Since now . . . Cares of State)';[9] the lesser variants are correlatives of these. The complex of effects is threefold. First, there is anticipation of Lear's characteristic firmness as it proves to be in due course, becoming obdurately 'hideous rashness' at some crucial moments (1.1) but making him 'the patterne of all patience' at others. This is accomplished by redirection and substitution of terms, particularly in the added 'We haue this hour a *constant will*' and in the change from 'first' to 'fast' intent; and 'first' by itself is essentially inert (what is the second 'intent'?) – although in the revising process it may have suggested a second motive, which the Folio in fact adds. This effect is complemented still more minutely by the change from the Quarto's 'cares and busines' con*firm*ed on 'yonger yeares' to the Folio King's 'Conferring them on yonger strengths'; the former emphasizes 'Confirming' on the receiver, youth, while the latter emphasizes the bestower's act of giving. In addition, the Quarto's 'yonger yeares' involve merely the age of the recipients, whereas the Folio stresses an important attribute not confined by age: 'yonger strengths' logically entail older strengths, and the reformulation tacitly holds Lear's peculiar 'strength' in reserve to be revealed and developed. These differences can hardly be explained as mere errors in transmission, and their very subtlety and apparent slightness suggest a reviser with a circumspect and careful eye, or at any rate one not given exclusively to the easy strokes of wholesale cutting. Second, the Folio version lays a strong foundation for the development of sympathy and admiration by providing Lear with a creditable, rational, and regal motive for his division of the kingdom, namely 'that future strife | May be preuented now'. This clause, not incidentally, contains the ominous subliminal irony that strife is indeed to be 'preuented' – in a strong etymological sense of the word – by being brought on sooner than it might have come without the division and partial abdication. Lear's other motive, to 'retire' (his sole stated motive in the Quarto), remains prominent in the Folio but is significantly modified: his will to 'shake all Cares and Businesse from our *Age*' stresses his vulnerability in the strain of years rather than his relinquishing the weight of office in the Quarto's '[busines] of our state'. The Quarto's 'state' is, however, retained in the addition of the later lines concerned with 'Rule, | Interest of Territory, Cares of *State*'.

Third, there are notable contributions to the integral patterns of images centring on clothing and nakedness, as on the manifestations and relationships of youth and eld already mentioned, both shared with a difference by *Macbeth*.[10] Lear's 'while we | Vnburthen'd crawle toward death' in the Folio adds in itself a complex and theatrically striking image; in paradoxical combination with the royal 'we', it gives a proleptic hint of decay and infancy concurrently regnant. But the most emphatic contribution, especially following 'Vnburthen'd crawle', is 'we will *diuest* vs', which has its ultimate fulfilment at the end of the play in 'pray you vndo this button' and Lear's death. This addition also gives by antecedence a special piquancy and significance to Lear's rueful subsequent acknowledgement that 'I lou'd her most, and thought to set my rest | On her kind nurcery' (B2ᵛ; TLN 131–2; 1.1.123–4). And it is also intimately related to Lear's

> Thou must be patient; we came crying hither:
> Thou know'st, the first time that we smell the Ayre
> We wawle, and cry. I will preach to thee: Marke. . . .
> When we are borne, we cry that we are come
> To this great stage of Fooles. . . .
> (TLN 2620–2, 2624–5; I4, prose, reading 'wayl' and
> 'marke me'; 4.6.178–80, 182–3)

The differences between Quarto and Folio in this relation, slight as they are quantitatively, result in an altered tragic pattern in the Folio, in which the rounds of birth and death, womb and tomb, investment and divesting, are emphasized not by frequency or relentless harping, but by being set in relief in their contexts – now 'I doe inuest you [Albany and Cornwall] ioyntly with my power' (TLN 138; B2ᵛ, reading 'in' for 'with'; 1.1.130), for example – and connected with a profoundly compassionate and unflinching vision of poverty and riches of flesh and spirit.

III

The second major change is almost microscopic in the perspective of the play as a whole.

> *Lear.* Thou wert better in a Graue, then to answere with thy vncouer'd body, this extremitie of the Skies. Is man no more then this? Consider him well. Thou ow'st the Worme no Silke; the Beast, no Hide; the Sheepe, no Wooll; the Cat, no perfume. Ha? Here's three on's are sophisticated. Thou art the thing it selfe; vnaccommodated man, is no more but such a poore, bare, forked Animall as thou art. Off, off you Lendings:
> (TLN 1881–8; G2–G2ᵛ, with 'thy' for 'a [graue]', 'but' for 'then [this]', and 'leadings' for 'lendings' in the uncorrected state; 3.4.101–8)

In the Quarto this speech concludes either 'come on bee true.' (Qa) or 'come on' (Qb). 'Come, vnbutton heere.' is the reading of the Folio, where the imagery of divesting introduced in the addition to the first scene (TLN 43–58; 1.1.38–53) is thus further emphasized, and the positive force of the endplay's 'Pray you vndo this Button. Thanke you Sir' (TLN 3281; L4; 5.3.310) is intensified by this added anticipation, a 'minute' but major departure from the Quarto's readings.

Much ink has been shed in trying to make Quarto and Folio reflect the same hypothetical original, but the respective readings, though both integral, are clearly alternative and have been so treated by editors, who cannot and do not conflate readings but invariably adopt the Folio reading. P. W. K. Stone argues that

> we must eliminate the reading in Qb ['come on '] which is merely the result of an accident to the type. The full stop after *bee true* in Qa having disappeared in Qb along with the words, it is unlikely that the compositor removed them deliberately. We should also probably discount *heere* in F as an interpola-

tion. The remaining *Come, unbutton* may easily represent a more accurate decipherment of the manuscript reading which yielded *come on bee true* in Q. The latter, however, makes sense and is perfectly consistent with the idea expressed in the context. Lear, exhorting himself, and perhaps his companions, to the honesty of 'vnaccommodated man', may well say: 'Off, off, you lendings! Come on, be true!'

(*Textual History*, pp. 225–6)

Qb's 'come on ', though wanting terminal punctuation, in fact makes dramatic as well as syntactical sense in itself, and Stone's conviction that it 'is merely the result of an accident to the type' seems unwarranted. It is at least as likely that 'come on ' represents an attempt to 'correct' a reading not in need of correcting but appearing to be so on account of the ellipsis: 'come on bee true [to the condition of "unaccommodated man"].' The most obvious explanation is that 'bee true.' puzzled the corrector and was proof-marked for deletion *with* the period included (or apparently so), and that the compositor removed types accordingly. This possibility is consistent with internal evidence strongly suggesting that the Quarto corrector consulted the copy for few of his 'corrections', which were apparently made rather on the basis of common-sense reading and corresponding alteration as perceived necessary.[11]

But Stone's analysis represents in part a notable advance over Greg's, which shows his confidence to better advantage than his critical acumen: 'Faced with nonsense [i.e. 'come on bee true.'] and a copy he could not read the corrector threw up the sponge and merely deleted what obviously could not be right. F is undoubtedly correct, but the last word was evidently either wanting or wholly illegible in the quarto copy: for the rest, "come on be true" is a fairly easy misreading of "come vnbutton"!' !'[12] Especially noteworthy are four points. First, Qa's reading is very doubtfully 'a fairly easy misreading' of 'come vnbutton'; Stone's interpretation here is considerably more circumspect than Greg's. Second, Greg's 'undoubtedly correct' is a judgement of value rather than an interpretation of the process of transmission; the presumed soundness of that – universally shared – judgement argues for the superior dramatic value of the Folio's revised reading, but it does not prove that it ever stood, or should have stood, in the manuscript from which Q was printed. Third, 'heere' is of course a problem for both Greg and Stone. For Greg 'heere' was 'either wanting or wholly illegible in the quarto copy' but clearly Shakespeare's word, not because it is necessary or a marked improvement but simply because it was taken from what Greg regarded as the authoritative source; for Stone it is 'probably . . . an interpolation', not because there is anything wrong with it but simply because it was taken from a text Stone distrusts. Fourth and finally, by the test of Occam's razor the Folio's 'Come, vnbutton heere' would seem to be neither a restoration nor an interpolation but a genuine revision, one related – importantly – to other revisions.

In the Folio, this first explicit and literal 'vnbutton'ing in 3.4 is made also a symbolic divesting associated with becoming painfully and self-knowledgeably human, and learning that 'the thing it selfe', 'vnaccomodated man', is 'no more but such a poore bare forked Animall' as poor Tom is (G2–G2ᵛ; TLN 1886–8; 3.4.106–8). Thus Lear's final divesting – 'Pray you vndo this button' – is made by extension the ultimate divesting – death and disembodiment, with suggestions of reference to spiritual be(com)ing, whether illusive or 'real', or, alternatively, to nothingness, whatever that is but what is not.

IV

Especially as anticipated in the added antecedents and as shaped by the changes made in the context, the most significant revisions in the dialogue and action of the King are the changes made in his final speech (5.3.306–14, my underlining emphasizing differences):

QUARTO:
Lear. And my poore foole is hangd, no, no life, why should a dog, a horse, a rat of life and thou no breath at all, O thou wilt come no more, neuer, neuer, neuer, pray you vndo this button, thanke you sir, O,o,o,o. *Edg.* He faints my Lord, my Lord.
   Lear. Breake hart, I prethe breake. *Edgar.* Look vp my Lord.
Kent. Vex not his ghost, O let him passe, . . .

(L4)

FOLIO:
    Lear. And my poore Foole is hang'd: no, no, no life?
Why should a Dog, a Horse, a Rat haue life,
And thou no breath at all? Thou'lt come no more,
Neuer, neuer, neuer, neuer, neuer.
Pray you vndo this Button. Thanke you Sir,
Do you see this? Looke on her? Looke her lips,
Looke there, looke there.   *He dies.*

Edg. He faints, my Lord, my Lord.

<u>*Kent.*</u> Breake heart, I prythee breake.

Edg. Looke vp my Lord.

Kent. Vex not his ghost, O let him passe, he hates him, . . .

　　(TLN 3277–87; in the uncorrected state Lear's penultimate
　　line reads 'this, looke')

The evident superiority of the Folio reading is attested by the consensus of adopting editors and the declared or implicit agreement of critics, and it ordinarily goes unnoted and perhaps sometimes even unnoticed that Lear's death in the Quarto is intelligible and dramatically satisfactory in its own way; it must be regarded as substantially Shakespeare's earlier version. Certainly 'pray you vndo this button, thanke you sir, O,o,o,o', with or without '*Lear.* Breake hart, I prethe breake', is coherent and conclusive, and in fact it better accords with the gloomier interpretations of the play and of Lear's passing than the Folio conclusion (incorporated in the composite texts) that such commentary is in effect addressed to.[13] But 'Breake hart, I prethe breake' also can be thought of as *as* Lear's, as it is in the Quarto, with Lear passing – in Donne's terms in 'A Valediction: Forbidding Mourning'[14] –

> As virtuous men passe mildly'away,
> 　And whisper to their soules to goe,
> Whilst some of their sad friends doe say,
> 　The breath goes now, and some say, no . . .

Since the speech has generally not been thought of as Lear's, much remains to be said of it as his last line. In any case, the Folio's ascription to Kent alters Lear's passing substantially and 'dramatically': whatever the details and timing of the process by which '*He dies*', in the Folio there is a striking and significant contrast between Edgar's youthfully urgent attempts to revive King Lear – he has already lost his father ('(O fault)', TLN 3155; L2ᵛ, reading '(O Father)'; 5.3.193) – and the older and wiser Kent, speaking for Lear's release.

The direction and effects of the revised form of Lear's concluding speech become clearer in the context of the process of his dying, a more complex, accomplished, and affecting dramatization of a similar situation involving father and child in *1 Henry VI*:

Enter with Iohn Talbot, borne.

Seru. O my deare Lord, loe where your Sonne is borne.
Tal. Thou antique Death, which laugh'st vs here to scorn,
Anon from thy insulting Tyrannie,
Coupled in bonds of perpetuitie,
Two *Talbots* winged through the lither Skie,
In thy despight shall scape Mortalitie.
O thou whose wounds become hard fauoured death,
Speake to thy father, ere thou yeeld thy breath,
Braue death by speaking, whither he will or no:
Imagine him a Frenchman, and thy Foe.
Poore Boy, he smiles, me thinkes, as who should say,
Had Death bene French, then Death had dyed to day.
Come, come, and lay him in his Fathers armes,
My spirit can no longer beare these harmes,
Souldiers adieu: I haue what I would haue,
Now my old armes are yong *Iohn Talbots* graue.   *Dyes*
(TLN 2247–63; 4.7.17–32)

Two points require stressing here. First, although they 'demonstrate' neither that such things actually happen nor that Shakespeare himself believed they did, in context such lines as 'Two *Talbots* winged through the lither Skie, | In thy despight shall scape Mortalitie' are evidently designed to convey, and in theatrical experience ordinarily *do* convey, the emotional conviction that what Talbot says is 'true', not only for him but *in some sense* for all.[15] And this 'dramatic optimism' has a bearing on how one reads Lear's hallucinating, delusional, visionary, or extrasensory-perceptive state as he passes. Second, the pertinence and similarity to King Lear's speech of Talbot's 'Speake to thy father, ere thou yeeld thy breath' and 'Poore Boy, he smiles, me thinkes' are obvious. A significant difference is that Lear is made to seem to detect signs of life of which there is no other evidence (TLN 3227, 3235–6, 3282–3; L3ᵛ, [L4]; 5.3.266, 272–3, 311–12), and therefore either to hallucinate or actually to see and hear what we cannot – and be it noted that the distinction between delusion and perception, and even between biological life and death, has been shown by modern science to be less certain than it is conventionally thought to be.[16] The parallel in *1 Henry VI* conveniently emphasizes the real comfort of 'he smiles' even as no more than a matter of self-recognized 'me thinkes'; Shakespeare goes further in the Quarto *King Lear* and very much further still in the Folio.

V

Henry VI provides an illuminating early parallel with the representation of the process of dying in the two *King Lears*. *Antony and Cleopatra*, probably written not long after the original composition of *King Lear*, is still more illuminating. It is structurally and theatrically close to *King Lear* in at least two prominent ways, especially in the way the deaths of Lear (in the Folio) and Cleopatra are presented: a primary design in both cases seems to be to convey the emotional conviction that we are witnessing one side of a sort of mystical communion transcending death.

The plays are strikingly similar, first, in the way they frame the protagonists and introduce their prospective tragic passions. In *Antony and Cleopatra*, Philo's prologue-like, ten-line anamorphic 'character' of Antony (and Cleopatra) is terminated in mid-line by '*Flourish. Enter Anthony, Cleopatra, her Ladies, the Traine, with Eunuchs fanning her*' (TLN 4–14, 15–16; 1.1.1–10), which prompts his ironical judgement and prophetic annunciation,

> Looke where they come:
> Take but good note, and you shall see in him
> The triple Pillar of the world transform'd
> Into a Strumpets Foole. Behold and see.
> (TLN 17–20; 1.1.10–13; F's parentheses
> round 'The . . . World' omitted)

Immediately Cleopatra and Antony oblige and perform, with their opening stichomythic quatrain on the imaginative leaps and bounds of passionate love in 'new Heauen, new Earth'. In *King Lear*, following the opening colloquy between Gloucester and Kent, the theme and plot of the play as *Bildungsspiel* are adumbrated in Gloucester's dramatic epitome, 'the King is coming' (B1ᵛ; TLN 36; 1.1.33). This is followed immediately by '*Sound a Sennet, Enter one bearing a Coronet, then Lear, then the Dukes of Albany, and Cornwell, next Gonorill, Regan, Cordelia, with followers*' (B1ᵛ; TLN 37–8, with variants); then by Lear's first speech, a ceremonious 'one-liner', in which he simultaneously asserts royal authority, propriety, and hospitality in 'Attend my Lords of France and Burgundy, *Gloster*' (B1ᵛ; TLN 39, reading 'the' for 'my'; 1.1.34); and finally by the division of the kingdom (in one perspective the subject of *Antony and Cleopatra*, too). In both plays a royal progress is heralded in a theatrical and literary complex of similar ways, with differences according to the characters of the respective rulers and the progresses and tragic passions befitting each.

   In the parallel deaths, Cleopatra has her Kent-counterparts in Iras and especially Charmian, whose 'O breake! O breake!' (TLN 3564; 5.2.310) is noticeably similar in context, content, and speaker to *Kent's* 'Breake heart, I prythee breake' (TLN 3285; L4 [spoken by Lear]; 5.3.313). Both Cleopatra and Lear give signs – or appearances – of being in communion with the dead (physically present in the case of Cordelia). Through half-implicit dramatic action and one-sided 'dia'logue, the 'living' presence of an indestructible animating force is powerfully suggested.[17] First Lear:

> This feather stirs, she liues . . .
> (TLN 3227; L3^v, unpunctuated; 5.3.266)

> *Cordelia, Cordelia*, stay a little, ha,
> What ist thou sayest[?] her voyce was euer soft,
> Gentle and low . . .
> (L3^v; TLN 3235–7; 5.3.272–4)

> Do you see this? Looke on her? Looke her lips,
> Looke there, looke there.   *He dies.*
> (TLN 3282–3; 5.3.311–12)

Now Cleopatra:

> Yare, yare, good *Iras*; quicke: Me thinks I heare
> *Anthony* call: I see him rowse himselfe
> To praise my Noble Act. I heare him mock
> The lucke of *Caesar*, which the Gods giue men
> To excuse their after wrath. Husband, I come. . . .
> (TLN 3534–8; 5.2.283–7)

> This proues me base:
> If she first meete the Curled *Anthony*,
> Hee'l make demand of her, and spend that kisse
> Which is my heauen to haue. . . .
> (TLN 3552–5; 5.2.300–3)

> As sweet as Balme, as soft as Ayre, as gentle.
> O *Anthony*! Nay I will take thee too.
> What should I stay——   *Dyes.*
> (TLN 3565–7; 5.2.311–13)

In *Antony and Cleopatra* the intimations of reunion are more explicit than those in *King Lear*: 'O *Anthony*!' suggests the kiss of reunion, and 'What should I stay——' the beginning of the answer, anticipated in TLN 3552–5. But *King Lear* is working in the same suggestive mode, by far the more so in the King's revised last lines as we have them in the Folio.

In the dialogue shared by both versions, Lear's higher senses tell or show him that Cordelia lives, whether 'we' regard this persuasion as a matter of spiritual recognition, optical perception, or stark delusion. There is in any case a transitory lightening before death in 'This feather stirs, she liues', and rather more in '*Cordelia, Cordelia*, stay a little, ha, | What ist thou sayest[?] her voyce was euer soft, | Gentle and low'.[18] But in the Quarto the prevailing emphasis is on Lear's desolation, his conviction that 'shees gone for euer' (L3ᵛ; TLN 3234; 5.3.260), that 'my poore foole is hangd', and that Cordelia has 'no, no life' (L4; TLN 3277, with three 'no's; 5.3.306) and will 'come no more, neuer, neuer, neuer' (L4; TLN 3279–80, with five 'neuer's; 5.3.308–9). His immediately following 'pray you vndo this button, thanke you sir' (L4; TLN 3281; 5.3.310) has a courtesy and gentleness about it that contributes much to the pathos of the passing in either text, but 'O,o,o,o' expresses an ineluctable nullity as darkly and as deeply as the most pessimistic could wish, for a nihilistic final turning of misfortune's wheel to close the circle of Lear's mortality. These groans of agony speak to the heart of a desolated Lear whether he dies at once or survives a little longer to speak his final Quarto line, a regal imperative and a personal entreaty, 'Breake hart, I prethe breake', an issue of some consequence in its own right.

P. W. K. Stone asserts that 'F's ascription [to Kent] is obviously correct . . . since Kent expresses the same sentiment, or something very close to it, in his next speech: "Vex not his ghost. Oh, let him pass . . .".'. The attribution to Lear is, in any case, highly implausible: he has clearly spoken his last words by this time' (*Textual History*, p. 230).[19] One might sympathize with his view, but Lear's line cannot be made Kent's by fiat, and it is more likely to be his by design than by default in the Quarto; in that case Lear has 'clearly' *not* 'spoken his last words by this time'. Stone identifies Lear's 'final words in Q' as 'pray you vndo this button, thanke you sir', and it is not clear how he regards Lear's subsequent 'O,o,o,o', which he seems to ignore.[20] We may think that 'O,o,o,o' looks and sounds final enough, but it need not be so. Othello's two last-scene 'O,o,o,o's could represent heart-breaking terminal cries, but they do not.[21] And there is similar death-wishing self-address in *Antony and Cleopatra*. Receiving the report of

Cleopatra's death, which has been greatly – and tragically – exaggerated, Antony exhorts himself,

> Oh cleaue my sides.
> Heart, once be stronger then thy Continent,
> Cracke thy fraile Case.
>
> (TLN 2872–4; 4.14.39–41)

The contexts are different and the parallels perhaps loose between Antony and the Quarto's Lear in this connection, but the shared situation and address are suggestive. Lear may well implore his heart to break and render him deliverance such as Antony receives when finally 'my Spirit is going, | I can no more' (TLN 3069–70; 4.15.58–9). His last words in the Quarto are as they are. The important fact is that 'O,o,o,o' and 'Breake hart, I prethe breake', though very different in specific resonance and significance from each other, are still more different, both and each, from Lear's last lines in the Folio.

VI

Anticipated and prepared for by the Folio additions in 1.1 and 3.4, 'Pray you vndo this Button' (TLN 3281; L4; 5.3.310) is a kind of terminal preparation, as a loosening, with release and relief in prospect. 'Do you see this? Looke on her? Looke her lips, | Looke there, looke there. *He dies.*' (TLN 3282–3; 5.3.311–12). P. W. K. Stone writes that

> it is difficult to see these lines as anything more than an *attempt on the reviser's* [i.e. Massinger's?] *part to provide Lear's speech with a more dramatic ending.* His final words in Q (*pray you vndo this button, thanke you sir*) certainly reach the limit of dramatic understatement (but are all the more effective for that, we may now think). *The reviser, however, unable to supply anything original, reverts weakly* to an idea that has already been exploited to moving effect (V. iii. 265–67 and 271–72), *viz.* that Lear fancies Cordelia may still be alive. There is even reason to argue that, in doing this, he has misunderstood the drift of the scene. It appears from Q that Lear, as his vitality ebbs, loses his grasp of the reality outside him. . . .
>
> (*Textual History*, p. 247, emphasis mine)

Stone's argument contains debatable – and on some points definitely refutable – assertions, but he accurately points to the central motive of any adapter or reviser in such a case, 'to provide . . . a more dramatic ending'; it thus becomes a matter for critical evaluation whether, how, and how far the new ending *is* more dramatic or, for example, less 'original'. Since virtually *all* critical commentary, from the most Christian-sacramental to the most atheistic, has taken these words of the received text to be Shakespeare's, the play's, and Lear's, it is reasonable to wonder whether Stone's critical judgement was affected here by his genealogical hypothesis. The relations between the passage, its antecedents in the immediate context, and the whole play help to give it a range and power as well as subtlety mostly lacking in the ending of the earlier version: the passage is imaginative and dramatic in itself, and full of significance and histrionic potentialities.

Whatever specifically may be done in performance with Lear's last Folio speech, the first two 'Looke's are addressed to Cordelia's person, and the last two immediately follow, whether Lear's attention stays directed to her face or turns away from her.[22] Stanley Wells writes that 'the intensity of his emotion over her body is the play's final paradox. Bewildered, despairing, nakedly true to his emotions, giving out pure and merited love, he is at his best; he is, if we wish to use the theological term, redeemed. Through feeling he has been brought to see. "Look there, look there." Whether or not it is expressive of delusion, it shows sight well directed, and reminds us of what goodness has achieved. Fully human, Lear dies.'[23] *That* is an 'affirmative' characterization of Lear's passing, one that many do not accept, but such an interpretation of the tonality, emphasis, and focus of the play and its conclusions is surely right, as much without as with the sacramental attachments. What Shakespeare has done in revising is to transfer Lear's ultimate Quarto line ('Breake hart, I prethe breake') to Kent, thus utterly altering action, character, context, and significance; and to strike out the 'O,o,o,o' that appears a hollow death rattle at the end of the dance of death begun in 'Howle, howle, howle, howle' and continuing through the 'neuer, neuer, neuer' in the Quarto *King Lear*. By contrast, TLN 3280 in the Folio reads 'Neuer, neuer, neuer, neuer, neuer', and this full line of falling-rhythmical trochaics – in context perhaps the profoundest expression of human grief and loss in all literature – is counterpointed by the rising thythm of Lear's concluding iambics, 'Looke there, looke there', his speech ending in mid-line and prospectively *in medias res*.[24]

VII

The balance of ambivalence equipoising gain and loss, relief and sorrow, is as pronounced in *King Lear* as it is in any of Shakespeare's

sad stories of the death of kings and peers of tragic stature, and it is
inevitably shared, with a difference, by dying dramatis personae and
living theatrical spectators and readers: our loss of valued great ones
is their gain, in fictional deliverance – and our gain, too, in theatrical
'catharsis'. Their gain – in the peace that passeth all understanding –
is also their loss of what they loved on earth, except for hypothetical
recovery hereafter. This tragi(comi)c equilibrium is expressed with
(tragi)comical deception in *Measure for Measure* by the Duke,
consoling Isabella on the supposed death of Claudio:

> . . . peace be with him,
> That life is better life past fearing death,
> Then that which liues to feare: make it your comfort,
> So happy is your Brother.
> (TLN 2782–5; 5.1.396–9)

This sentiment may be construed as 'Christian', but nothing in it
would be unfamiliar to elegiac poets of any time and any faith or
none. It is integrated into *King Lear* by Edgar, with greater
prominence in the Folio because many of Edgar's apophthegmatic
Quarto lines have been omitted: 'O our liues sweetnesse, | That we the
paine of death would hourely dye, | Rather then die at once' (TLN
3147–9; L2ᵛ, reading 'with' for 'we'; 5.3.185–7).

Soon after follows Edgar's account of Gloucester's death, which
came quickly as Edgar at last revealed himself, to seek his father's
blessing:

> . . . his flaw'd heart
> (Alacke too weake the conflict to support)
> Twixt two extremes of passion, ioy and greefe,
> Burst smilingly.
> (TLN 3159–62; L2ᵛ; 5.3.197–200)[25]

'This speech of yours hath mou'd' Edmund, who speaks also for an
audience effect that is, on balance, uplifting: with the 'burst', the last
and best is 'smilingly'. Edgar's subsequent Quarto account of his
meeting with Kent is not in the Folio, nor, therefore, is his narration
of Kent's

> most pitious tale of *Lear* and him,
> That euer eare receiued, which in recounting
> His griefe grew puissant and the strings of life,
> Began to cracke[.   T]wice then the trumpets sounded,
> And there I left him traunst.
> (L2ᵛ–3; 5.3.215–19)

Deletion of these lines has notable accelerating and other effects on the action and significance of the endplay.[26] Three such effects are to defer reference to the King (the reference here is auxiliary and essentially inert), to give special prominence by the abridgement of context to the 'burst[ing] smilingly' of Gloucester's heart, and to precipitate the movement from Gloucester's death to Lear's and explicitly prepare for it. Gloucester's heart had 'burst smilingly' in his son's retrospective narration. With Cordelia in his arms or near, Lear dies in prospective attitude and action prepared for by the manner and details of Gloucester's death, the later function and effects of which are different in the Folio, with its addition of Lear's 'Do you see this? Looke on her? Looke her lips, | Looke there, looke there.' One cannot be sure that Lear's 'flaw'd heart . . . burst smilingly', but one does not *see* Lear's heart and certainly cannot be sure it doesn't. Probably it is a coincidence that the last line describing Gloucester's death ('Burst smilingly.') and Lear's last line 'Looke there, looke there.' are both conspicuously short – tetrasyllabic – lines, but it is undeniable that the final show of lightening at Lear's death, however interpreted, in the Folio has been brought closer to Gloucester's.

VIII

To return to the parallel with *Antony and Cleopatra*: the Folio Lear's last lines are much nearer Cleopatra's than the Quarto's are. Each speaker's final line is a dimeter the sense of which looks beyond itself for fulfilment and halts on a rising note: 'What should I stay⸺', and 'Looke there, looke there'. Both plays end in a hallucination, delusion, transcendent vision, or extrasensory perception of life's being where death but seems. Lear is made to say he sees a sign on Cordelia's lips, and dies; Cleopatra is made to imply that she sees Mark Antony himself, and dies. In both plays (di)vesting is profoundly consequential, too, though in complementary not identical ways: Cleopatra requires her robe and crown, her 'best Attyres', to prepare to satisfy her 'immortall longings', for she is 'againe for C[y]d[n]us, | To meete *Marke Anthony*'. By contrast necessarily, Lear must go the other way. Again but young in deed, he has come to see feelingly, too late for the dearest purposes and the creature comforts of Cordelia's kind nursery, that 'Robes, and Furr'd gownes hide all' (TLN 2607–8; I4; 4.6.165). He therefore divests himself, as translated king of the 'Poore naked wretches', ready now for reconciliation, at least peacefully with his mother earth if not with his daughter Cordelia. Hence his Folio 'Pray you vndo this Button. Thanke you Sir', a line given much of its conclusive dramatic value, thematic significance, and heart-rending poignancy by the Folio's anticipatory addition, earlier, of 'In Boy, go first. You houselesse pouertie, | Nay get thee in; Ile pray, and then Ile sleepe' (TLN 1807–8; 3.4.26–7), and more focally, then, of 'Come, vnbutton heere' (TLN 1888–9; 3.4.108–9). That Lear in his own way outlives his life, every inch a king and with that in his countenance that Kent would fain call master still, Kent reminds us in his own last lines: 'I haue a iourney Sir, shortly to go, | My Master calls me, I must not say no' (TLN 3296–7; L4, reading 'cals,and'; 5.3.322–3).

Lear's passing is a moment of extraordinary dramatic intensity and complexity; we who would take upon's the mystery of things must reckon with its very different representations in the Quarto and the Folio. Shakespeare's editors have done so in effect, and it is not surprising that they have preferred the Folio's readings. At the time and for the purpose of his revisions, Shakespeare evidently preferred them, too.

NOTES

1. Lear has 22% of the play's words in the composite text of *The Riverside Shakespeare*, according to *A Complete and Systematic Concordance to the Works of Shakespeare, Vol. III: Drama and Character Concordances to the Folio Tragedies*, ed. Marvin Spevack (Hildesheim, 1968).
2. Overall, the play is shorter by about 5%. Act One is virtually the same length in Q and F (though there are numerous differences otherwise), and Act Two is longer in F than Q (by about 2.5%). But in F Acts Three to Five are shorter, Act Three by 47 lines (8%), Act Four by 104 lines (15%), and Act Five by 34 lines (9%).
3. I use 'add-omissions' for additions and omissions taken together. Archibald A. Hill coined the term to identify neutrally passages that are present in some 'variant texts' but not in others, to avoid the question-begging use of 'addition' and 'omission' alone; see 'Some Postulates for Distributional Study of Texts', *Studies in Bibliography*, 3 (1951), 63–95.
4. 'Sundowning' is a term used in hospitals to describe the radical disorientation and hallucinations frequently experienced by elderly patients immediately upon admission for periods of varying duration.
5. In recent years readings of *King Lear* have come to be seen as polarized between 'existentialists' and 'redemptivists'; such terms are reductive (and often pejorative) in both directions. Dame Helen Gardner gives an impressive balanced view in her John Coffin Memorial Lecture, *King Lear* (1967). Interpretations of the darker kind are represented by Jan Kott's influential '*King Lear*, or Endgame', in *Shakespeare Our Contemporary* (1964), trans. Boleslaw Taborski (1965, rev. edn., 1967), and very recently in the essays in *Shakespeare Survey 33* (Cambridge, 1980) by James Black, Frank McCombie, and Derek Peat. Black, for example, concludes

his essay, 'Perhaps this, then, is the shape or pattern of *King Lear*: not the wheel, not rising action-peak-falling action, not even an up-up-up movement; but a pattern which overturning all conventions, justice, expectations and hopes takes us down and down and down' (*'King Lear*: Art Upside Down', p. 42). The 'positive' position, represented by A. C. Bradley, is found more recently in Maynard Mack, *King Lear in Our Time* (Berkeley and Los Angeles, 1965), Paul A. Jorgensen, *Lear's Self-Discovery* (Berkeley and Los Angeles, 1967), and John Reibetanz, *The Lear World: A Study of 'King Lear' in Its Dramatic Context* (Toronto, 1977), and in Stanley Wells's essay in *Shakespeare Survey 33*; in the same volume G. R. Hibbard's '*King Lear*: A Retrospect, 1939–79' helpfully surveys positions and other important and representative exponents (pp. 1–12). Mack's summing up in 1965 holds in 1983: 'to say, with an increasing number of recent critics, that "the remorseless process of *King Lear*" forces us to face the fact of its ending without any support from systems of moral . . . belief at all' is to indulge the mid-twentieth-century *frisson du néant* at its most sentimental. We face the ending of this play, as we face our world, with whatever support we customarily derive from systems of belief or unbelief' (p. 116).

6. TLN 196–7 differ from Q1 in reading 'deere shelter' for 'protection', 'thee' for 'the', and 'iustly . . . rightly' for 'rightly . . . iustly'.

7. In his chapter on 'Death' in *The Past and the Present* (1981), Lawrence Stone notes 'a structure of belief which runs unaltered among the masses right up to the nineteenth century . . . The key ritual is the deathbed scene: a public display of repentance and calm acceptance of the end. Death is not particularly frightening, and the fate of the individual is subordinated to the future of the collectivity, the society, the status group and the family. Life after death is no more than a kind of sleep, for an indeterminate period' (p. 246). There is something of this kind of assimilation at the end of *King Lear*.

8. Review article, 'The Year's Contributions to Shakespearian Study, 1: Critical Studies', *Shakespeare Survey 31* (Cambridge, 1978), p. 170.

9. In *Textual History* (p. 238) P. W. K. Stone says of the first that 'this (a) completes a line left short in Q and (b) serves to call attention to Albany and Cornwall soon after their entrance. They do not speak at all in the course of the scene, and are not identified in Q until addressed by Lear a good deal later' (1.1.127); and of the second that it 'repeats what Lear has previously said (lines 39–40), but in more precise terms. The reviser may have thought the earlier announcement too vague.' This attenuating description of the changes makes it easier for Stone to look to Massinger as their possible author.

10. The classic studies of the pattern are, for *Macbeth*, Cleanth Brooks's essay, 'The Naked Babe and the Cloak of Manliness', in *The Well-Wrought Urn: Studies in the Structure of Poetry* (New York, 1947), pp. 21–46; and, for *King Lear*, Robert B. Heilman's *This Great Stage: Image and Structure in 'King Lear'* (Baton Rouge, 1948). Also see Maurice Charney, ' "We Put Fresh Garments on Him": Nakedness and Clothes in *King Lear*', in Rosalie L. Colie and F. T. Flahiff, eds., *Some Facets of 'King Lear': Essays in Prismatic Criticism* (Toronto, 1974), pp. 77–8. Charney cites related earlier studies by Dean Frye, Thelma Nelson Greenfield, and Emily W. Leider (p. 88, n. 1).

11. Quarto correction is discussed in connection with a critical analysis of a three-way-variant line in Thomas Clayton, 'Old Light on the Text of *King Lear*', *Modern Philology*, 78 (1981), 347–67. Paul Werstine writes me that, 'if there is no evidence of the loosening of type in outer G beyond the absence of "bee true." ', and there seems to be no such evidence (as one would infer from Greg's silence on the matter), then 'Stone's explanation of the variant is as close to impossible as any scholar's hypothesis can ever be. While parts of words or whole words have been

shown to have fallen out of badly locked up formes, it seems most unlikely that two words could fall out at the same time without the whole page falling apart.'

12. W. W. Greg, *The Variants in the First Quarto of 'King Lear': A Bibliographical Inquiry* (1940), pp. 164–5.

13. In *The Masks of King Lear* (Berkeley and Los Angeles, 1972), Marvin Rosenberg finds the 'four heartbreaking *O*s' a 'more human equivalent to the howls' of 5.3.258 (L3ᵛ; TLN 3217); see pp. 312, 319. As Rosenberg aptly notes, '*Pray you undo this button* may refer to Cordelia's dress [or, more generally, attire]; but almost universally it is taken to reflect the constricting of Lear's throat' (p. 319) – or in any case to refer to Lear's button, not Cordelia's. An important study of implied action and stage-business during Lear's passing is John C. Meagher, 'Vanity, Lear's Feather, and the Pathology of Editorial Annotation', in Clifford Leech and J. M. R. Margeson, eds., *Shakespeare 1971: Proceedings of the World Shakespeare Congress, Vancouver, August 1971* (Toronto, 1972), pp. 244–59.

14. *John Donne: 'The Elegies' and 'The Songs and Sonnets'*, ed. Helen Gardner (Oxford, 1965), pp. 62–4.

15. Such designs are pervasive in Shakespeare. For example, also in tragic vein, in Richard's last lines in *Richard II*: 'Mount mount my soule, thy seate is vp on high, | Whilst my grosse flesh sinckes downeward here to die' (Kl; TLN 2783–4; 5.5.111–12). And, in comic vein, in 'The most lamentable comedy and most cruell death of *Pyramus* and *Thisby*' (*MND*, B2; 1.2.11–12), burlesquing in effect some of his own – mostly later – profound and powerful effects:

> Come teares, confound, out sword, and wound
> The pappe of *Pyramus*:
> I, that left pappe, where heart doth hoppe.
> Thus dy I, thus, thus, thus.
> Now am I dead, now am I fled, my soule is in the sky.
> Tongue loose thy light, Moone take thy flight,
> Now dy, dy, dy, dy, dy.
>
>   (H2ᵛ; 5.1.295–306)

16. Without Shakespeare's using overt *dei ex machina*, it is not reasonable to infer, with some of his more sacramentally-inclined critics, that he was writing latter-day Miracle Plays. It *is* reasonable to see him as working with similar effects not at all *necessarily* attributable to the same causes.

17. These causes and effects are discussed in some detail in Thomas Clayton, '"Mysterious by This Love": The Unregenerate Resurrection of *Antony and Cleopatra*', in a festschrift for S. C. Sen Gupta, *Jadavpur University Essays and Studies: Special Issue*, III: 1981, ed. Jagannath Chakravorty (Calcutta: Jadavpur University, 1982), 95–116.

18. Cordelia's 'answer' to Lear's 'What ist thou sayest[?]' is, again, 'Nothing my Lord' (B2; TLN 93; 1.1.87), with the profound difference that here that, too, with the rest of her kind nursery, is silence.

19. It should be noted that 'Kent expresses the same sentiment, or something very close to it, in his next speech' could be used to argue *against* (redundant) ascription to Kent, and that the argument from similarity could also point to Albany ('Fall and cease'; TLN 3226; L3ᵛ; 5.3.265). The Quarto ascription to Lear could be in error, the prefix perhaps having been caught from the '*Lear*' aligned directly above it in Lear's preceding speech in the Quarto, but this is not a usual or very likely kind of eyeskip, and it is the only hypothetical 'evidence' of erroneous ascription that is less subjective than Stone's '[*Kent* is] obviously correct'.

20. One would expect the omission to be noted on p. 238, as the last of the 'omissions' in F, but it may not be because 'only substantial cuts or interpolations of a half-line

or more are listed' (p. 233) in 'Appendix B2: Omissions and Additions in F' (pp. 233–48). Whether or not the four *o*'s are 'words', they constitute an utterance by Lear of some importance.

21. *Othello* 5.2.198 and 282; TLN 3484 and, with only two *o*'s, 3581. In 'Re-Enter the Stage Direction: Shakespeare and Some Contemporaries', *Shakespeare Survey 29* (Cambridge, 1976), pp. 117–25, E. A. J. Honigmann has an interesting discussion of 'crypto-directions', notably 'expletives, some of which appear to have served as short-hand directions for a great variety of noises' (p. 123). Tragic 'noises' of the kind T. S. Eliot immortalized as 'O O O O that Shakespeherian Rag' of course require sympathetic performance or reading to have their tragic effect; on paper not even 'Howle, howle, howle, howle' is free of risible potentialities for a susceptible readership (L3ᵛ; TLN 3217, with three 'howle's). Probably beyond saving, especially in a play otherwise 'Verry Badd', is the speech, '*O,O,O,O,O,O,O,O,O,O*', in the anonymous *Andronicus: A Tragedy* (1661); see Eric Rothstein, *Restoration Tragedy: Form and the Process of Change* (1967), p. 67.

22. In Peter Brook's production, Paul Scofield's Lear 'sat staring out blankly into the auditorium on his last "look there"' (Derek Peat, '"And That's True Too"', *Shakespeare Survey 33*, p. 45). In his film of *King Lear*, Brook's nihilistic reading asserted itself very early on: he made the King's first speech '[K]*no*[w]——that we haue diuided', etc. (TLN 42; B1ᵛ, omitting 'that'; 1.1.37; square brackets, italics, and dash mine).

23. '*The Taming of the Shrew* and *King Lear*', *Shakespeare Survey 33*, p. 65.

24. Although in a speech set as prose, Lear's 'O,o,o,o' in Q – in 'thanke you sir, O,o,o,o. *Edg*. He faints my Lord, my Lord.' – may be taken as the initial iambic feet of a pentameter line of 'heroic verse' completed by Edgar's 'He faints my Lord, my Lord' (TLN 3284, reading 'faints,'), an interpretation encouraged by Q's giving as one line, of blank verse, F's following *two* lines: 'Breake hart, I prethe breake. *Edgar*. Look vp my Lord' (L4; 3285–6, with '*Kent*' for '*Lear*'). Guided by this, one would take the Folio's 'Do you see this? Looke on her? Looke her lips' (3282) as an added line and 'Looke there, looke there' (3283) as a substitution for 'O,o,o,o'.

25. I am indebted to John Kerrigan for the suggestion that Enobarbus' death has some of the same effects in *Antony* that Gloucester's has in *Lear*. See, for example, 'This blowes my hart. | If swift thought breake it not[,] a swifter meane | Shall out-strike thought, but thought will doo't, I feele' (TLN 2615–17, reading 'doo't. I'; 4.6.33–5) and his last line, 'Oh *Anthony*! Oh *Anthony*!' (TLN 2720; 4.9.23).

26. M. Warren discusses other effects of the deletion in 'The Diminution of Kent', above (pp. 69–70).

Cor.'s Rescue of Kent

BETH GOLDRING

I

SMALL textual changes can have large effects in the dramatic structure of Shakespeare's plays. Two seemingly minor changes between the Quarto and Folio versions of the first scene of *King Lear*, both concerning the use of the *Cor.* prefix, have become issues in the discussion of the Folio as a possible revised version of the play. These are at 1.1.162 where, just as Lear is about to attack Kent, the Folio has '*Alb. Cor.* Deare Sir forbeare' (TLN 176), a line not in the Quarto, and 1.1.188 where the Folio changes the Quarto's '*Glost.*' (B3ᵛ) so that '*Cor.*' says 'Heere's *France* and *Burgundy*, my Noble Lord' (TLN 204). Why have these changes been made?

Both Peter W. M. Blayney and Steven Urkowitz see these changes as evidence of redaction in the Folio text, although they disagree about the alterations' merits. Blayney believes that the changes represent unsatisfactory attempts to give the sons-in-law speaking parts during the first scene. Having the *Cor.* prefix in both places, he says, 'possibly shows that the difficult question of which unsuitable line was least appropriate for Cornwall was never finally settled'.[1] Urkowitz takes a more positive view of the alterations, and stresses that the Quarto and Folio versions contain different dramatic events. He notices that the speaker who announces the suitors could in fact be Cordelia, 'since it is in her interest that Lear should deal with France and Burgundy', and he stresses the subtlety of effect the Folio achieves:

The Folio version, whether *Cor.* is Cornwall or Cordelia, enforces a complex 'subtext' on the interpretation of the line, since the characters who were onstage to watch the division of the kingdom may no longer view the arrival of the suitors as a simple ceremony. (*Revision*, p. 40)

If it were only a question of which character announces the suitors, one might wonder if an examination were worth the trouble. But the *Cor.* prefix which creates difficulty here creates a great deal more confusion where the rescue of Kent is concerned. As Marvin Rosenberg notices, this is an intensely dramatic and suspenseful moment, in which the 'advance of the furious king on his sacrilegious vassal is expected to end in blood or death'.[2] In the Quarto version, as Urkowitz points out (*Revision*, p. 32), no one intervenes. Kent himself stops Lear. Urkowitz sees the Folio as providing a more forceful set of events than the Quarto:

Because the Folio has Albany and Cornwall interpose themselves between Lear and Kent in some way, saying 'Deare Sir forbeare,' Lear may attack Kent much more forcefully than in the Quarto. The actor playing Lear may rush at Kent, confident that the actors playing Albany and Cornwall have their brief line as a cue to step in and stop him. (*Revision*, p. 32)

Both Urkowitz and Rosenberg cite evidence from productions exploiting the potential athleticism that the Folio line introduces.

There are, however, problems with this version of events. It is not clear that physically restraining a Shakespearian king is ever acceptable. Even if it were, Lear is hardly the king to be pacified by it – either by the force involved or by the offence to deference. And nothing in Lear's behaviour in the rest of the scene, his banishment of Kent and treatment of France and Burgundy, suggests that he has been forcibly made docile here. Nor does Kent's response sound as though Lear were physically helpless. 'Kill thy Physition, and thy fee bestow | Vpon the foule disease' (TLN 177–8; B3; 1.1.163–4) is a courageous challenge coming from an unarmed man to an attacker. But it is entirely unworthy of Kent as a taunt thrown at a king in restraint. One must either reassess Kent's character unfavourably or assume that Lear is at liberty here.

There are also certain difficulties in seeing Cornwall as Kent's defender. Blayney states these succinctly in objecting to the Folio line:

It beggars belief to accept that the Cornwall of Acts II–III would attempt to stop Lear punishing an inferior who has angered him, let alone that he would utter such a limp protest in chorus with Albany. Whatever the status and purpose of the line itself, I cannot believe that the second prefix has any authority.[3]

Moreover, 'Deare Sir forbeare' is as improbable for Cornwall's language as the heroic defence of an innocent party is for his character. Cornwall is capable of certain pieties of language, but they usually appear at morally inappropriate moments and are seldom evidence of strong emotion. He promises to be 'a deere Father' (TLN 1995; G3ᵛ; 3.5.25) to Edmund in response to Edmund's betrayal of

Gloucester, and he pledges his 'life and Honour' (TLN 1213; E2ᵛ; 2.2.133) to keeping Kent in the stocks. But his language of extreme emotion is not characteristically compassionate. Cornwall's language becomes vivid in calling Kent 'You stubborne ancient Knaue, you reuerent Bragart' (TLN 1204; E2ᵛ; 2.2.126) or in taunting Gloucester during the blinding: 'Out vilde gelly: | Where is thy luster now?' (TLN 2158–9; H2; 3.7.82–3). He is not likely to be eloquent in Kent's defence.

If we are to take the Folio line as deliberate, we need possibilities for staging which reconcile dramatic logic, character, and language with active intervention on Kent's behalf. Both Blayney and Urkowitz have noticed the ambiguity of the *Cor.* prefix in a situation where both Cornwall and Cordelia are on stage, and in his edition Jay L. Halio has silently assumed Cordelia's intervention, pairing her with Albany in speaking here.⁴ It is worth exploring the possibility that Cordelia, not Cornwall, intervenes.

II

The technical case for Cordelia as Kent's defender is suggestive if inconclusive. In the Folio *Cor.* is Cordelia's prefix, except at TLN 2366 (4.4.15) where she is *Cord.* Cornwall is *Corn.* 38 times, *Cornw.* once (TLN 1975; 3.5.5), and *Cor.* 14 times. Except for one justified line (TLN 1612; 2.4.308), all the instances where *Cor.* unambiguously represents Cornwall occur on two pages, qq6 and qq6ᵛ, both set by Jaggard's apprentice compositor E early in his stint on *King Lear*. It is possible that far from being genuine variants these settings are mistakes influenced by speeches in the first scene.

The quartos provide a basis for understanding the Folio speech prefixes. In Q1 *Cor.* (5 instances) and *Cord.* (24 instances) seem genuine variants for Cordelia. *Duke* is initially the almost exclusive prefix for both Cornwall and Albany, with one exception (*Corn.* on D4; 2.1.86). The situation changes suddenly at the blinding scene (G4ᵛ–H2; 3.7) just as the ambiguity in the *Duke* prefix is about to resolve itself spontaneously in Cornwall's death. Cornwall becomes *Corn.*, and Albany, at his next appearance, is *Alb.* (H3ᵛ–H4ᵛ; 4.2). These prefixes are then used exclusively until the final scene when Albany is *Duke* 10 times in his final 10 speeches (L3–L4; 5.3.237–319). At this point, of course, there is no longer a possibility of confusion with Cornwall. In summary, then, in Q1 Cornwall is *Duke*

26 times and *Corn.* 23; he is never *Cor.* Albany is *Duke* 16 times, and *Alb.* 39.

Q2 accepts the Q1 use and extends its differentiations. The prefixes for Cornwall's speeches remain unchanged while the use of *Duke* for Albany in the final scene is severely curtailed (2 instances instead of 10). Cordelia becomes *Cor.* at the beginning of the reconciliation (K1; 4.7) and, except for *C.* at 4.7.43 (K1ᵛ), remains *Cor.* She is also *Cor.* more extensively earlier in the play, so that she is *Cord.* 7 times and *Cor.* 21 times in Q2.

It appears that someone attempted to avoid confusion among Albany, Cornwall and Cordelia by using *Cor.* for Cordelia, *Corn.* for Cornwall, and *Alb.* for Albany. There is no evidence in the quartos that *Cor.* was considered acceptable for Cornwall, and – since the name occurs only in *King Lear* – there is no evidence elsewhere in Shakespeare.

The Folio decision regarding these prefixes appears to have been to accept the Quarto forms for the names and extend their usage from the beginning of the play. *Duke* no longer appears; Cordelia is *Cor.* from the beginning (except at TLN 2366; 4.4.15, set by Compositor B, where she is *Cord.*); Albany is *Alb.* throughout; and Cornwall, presumably, was to have been *Corn.*[5] Thus, the problem to be solved is not how E came to set *Cor.* for Cornwall when Cordelia is on stage, but rather how he came to set *Cor.* for Cornwall later, thereby creating retroactive confusion. Without the later pages, there would be no difficulty in our understanding that *Cor*delia comes to Kent's defence.

Quire qq, in which all of the prefix confusions exist, was the first quire of *King Lear* set, and it contains some anomalies. It was set as follows:

Compositor B	Compositor E
3ᵛ	4
	4ᵛ
	3
5	2ᵛ
2	5ᵛ
1ᵛ(*Hamlet*)	6
1 (*Hamlet*)	6ᵛ

B was apparently called away during the setting of the quire and E took over until he returned, during which time E set from both halves of the quire.[6] The two pages on which *Cor.* is unambiguously set for Cornwall are qq6 and qq6^v, both of which were set *after* E had set *Cor.* for Cordelia repeatedly on qq3 and qq2^v. Page qq2^v contains both the new line 'Deare Sir forbeare' and the *Cor.* prefix substituted for the crossed out *Glost.* prefix before 'Heere's *France* and *Burgundy*, my Noble Lord.'

It seems possible that this earlier correction from *Glost.* to *Cor.* influenced the later settings of *Cor.* for corrected prefixes on qq6 and qq6^v, especially since one of those corrections (TLN 1134; 2.2.61) was also from *Glost.* It is even conceivable that E, when he used *Cor.* on qq6 and qq6^v, thought that he was setting speeches for the same character he had called *Cor.* on qq2^v and qq3, or that an annotator (someone in Jaggard's shop who perhaps prepared a marked-up exemplar of Q2, to serve as copy for Compositor E) altered the prefixes under the same misconception. The six initial *Cor.* prefixes on qq6^v are for speeches in which Cornwall appears in his role as peacemaker between Kent and Oswald. The seventh (TLN 1165; 2.2.91) is a crowded line, and the eighth and ninth (TLN 1218, 1224; 2.2.138, 147) both have the word 'Sister' in adjacent lines. But the pages show ample evidence of incompetence, even without this level of misunderstanding. Page qq6 was repeatedly proof-read and corrected while in the press. It shows seven errors (two of which may have corrected themselves spontaneously).[7] Page qq6^v contains five corrected errors. E's setting was being carefully monitored at this point for reasons which are only too clear.

One further consideration needs to be urged here. The physical layout of '*Alb. Cor.* Deare Sir forbeare' tends to suggest Cornwall to the modern reader, especially since the sons-in-law have already been paired and contrasted. Anyone who has first read the play in a modern text, however, has first been exposed to this line as Albany and Cornwall's and not in its original form, and it is impossible to know what the prefixes would suggest if our habits of mind were not already fixed. McKerrow cautions against the 'simple and obvious things that we tend most easily to overlook because for generations everybody else has been doing the same'.[8] Our assumptions regarding the *Cor.* prefix are perhaps an excellent example of this kind of mistake.

The textual and bibliographical evidence, then, while inconclusive, only marginally suggests Cornwall as the speaker of either 'Deare Sir forbeare' or 'Heere's *France* and *Burgundy*, my Noble Lord.' The case for Cornwall must rest on dramatic logic, characterization, and appropriateness of language. As we have seen, these are not in his favour. The textual case for Cordelia as speaker is somewhat stronger, even with the retroactive confusion introduced by the *Cor.* prefixes on qq6 and qq6ᵛ. *Cor.* is Cordelia's standard prefix, even if an apprentice compositor also mistakenly uses it elsewhere. It is now time to see whether the dramatic evidence also supports her case.

III

Cordelia is admirably suited to speaking these lines and defending Kent. Her speech in this first scene is already marked by the combined formality and intensity of feeling which will characterize it throughout the play. She has already called Lear either 'my Lord' or 'my good Lord' or 'Good my Lord' four times in twenty-one lines (TLN 93–114; B1; 1.1.87–107), as well as 'your Maiesty' once (TLN 98; B2; 1.1.92). 'Sir' is her address to Lear in moments of most intense feeling. When he wakes from madness she will say 'Sir, do you know me' (TLN 2798; K2; 4.7.47) and 'O looke vpon me Sir, | And hold your hand in benediction o're me' (TLN 2810–11; K2ᵛ; 4.7.56–7). 'Deare Sir forbeare' is extreme language in her mouth, both in the intensity of its protest against Lear's action and the extremity of feeling it manifests towards Lear. Love and outrage combine in simple eloquence.

No character has more reason than Cordelia to come to Kent's aid. Even if Kent's primary concern is, as he says, with Lear's safety, it is still Cordelia's inheritance that he is defending, and some action on her part is demanded in response. We will learn more of the relationship between Kent and Cordelia as the play progresses, in hearing of their correspondence and witnessing their later meeting, but the foundations of that relationship should be visible here. We see Kent's side in his defence of her rights and hear it in his farewell address. Cordelia shows herself worthy of his regard through her attempt to restrain Lear. Rosenberg has noticed the prominence of Cordelia's 'shadow side'[9] in her conflict with Lear; heroic action here provides a necessary counterweight.

The courage required for this action is clearly within the bounds of Cordelia's character, and especially within the changes the Folio makes in it. Other changes in the Folio place Cordelia at the head of the invading army, rather than in its company, as she is in the Quarto.

The scene where Monsieur La Far is named as France's proxy (4.3) is excluded and the stage directions for her entrance in 4.4 (TLN 2349–50) specify a military presence (*Enter with Drum and Colours, Cordelia, Gentlemen, | and Souldiours.*). Cordelia will claim as her own virtues the capacity for taking action, 'since what I will intend, Ile do't before I speake' (TLN 247–8; B4; 1.1.225–6), and fortitude, 'For thee oppressed King I am cast downe, | My selfe could else out-frowne false Fortunes frowne' (TLN 2945–6; K4; 5.3.5–6). We see both of them at work here when, in the face of her own mistreatment, she steps in to intervene for Kent. We are accustomed to considering Cordelia totally courageous in defence of those she loves. We are simply not accustomed to recognizing that courage at work in this scene.

As a dramatic moment, Cordelia's defence of Kent would be both exciting and appropriate. If anyone could touch Lear at this point, she could. Her touch would neither constitute force nor offend deference, and her attempting to stop him would retain the excitement Urkowitz sees in the Folio version of the events. It would, however, redefine it, since the athleticism is not checked by force but restrained by Lear's recognition of the meaning of what he is doing. Moreover, if Cordelia led the protest and Albany joined her, we would also be given a microcosm for his later moral development.

The simplest and perhaps strongest staging would be for Cordelia to interpose herself physically between Lear and Kent, with Albany joining her at a slight distance. We would then *see* the polarization which is a central issue in this first scene: the three 'good' characters on stage, defenceless, standing up to Lear's rage, while the rest of the court looks on and waits. For a moment it could even look as though Cordelia were in danger. Kent's next line, 'Kill thy Physition, and thy fee bestow | Vpon the foule disease' (TLN 177–8; B3; 1.1.163–4), would then be both a challenge and an attempt to draw the danger back from Cordelia and on to himself. It is precisely the kind of challenge which would stop Lear, where physical force might only goad him instead.

A moment like this would reverberate throughout the rest of the play. Its meanings would resurface in two of Lear and Cordelia's most important later moments: first, in the exchange directly following Cordelia's acknowledgement of her identity, when Lear says

> If you haue poyson for me, I will drinke it:
> I know you do not loue me, for your Sisters
> Haue (as I do remember) done me wrong.
> You haue some cause, they haue not.
>   (TLN 2829–32; K3; 4.7.71–4)

and again, in Lear's speech over Cordelia's corpse: 'A plague vpon you Murderors, Traitors all, | I might haue sau'd her' (TLN 3233–4; L3ᵛ; 5.3.270–1). Lear's vision of himself as Cordelia's protector, like his vision of his culpability, gains added poignancy if he has also visibly been her danger.

What we have then, instead of a weak or simply athletic moment, is a moment emblematic of the whole first scene. Cordelia's and Kent's relationship; Albany's development; Lear's conflict with Kent; Cordelia's courage and Lear's conflict with her (both, finally, expressed in her death and his agony); and, centrally, Lear's alienation of himself from all love and loyalty – all these are physically realized in Cordelia's defence of Kent and the choice it presents to Lear. It is precisely the kind of moment we expect in Shakespeare's mature tragedies: intensely dramatic, psychologically complex, yet simply and powerfully presented. It is Lear, Cordelia, Kent and Albany's moment, and it cannot be realized, either critically or theatrically, if we substitute Cornwall for Cordelia.

NOTES

1. Peter W. M. Blayney, 'The Folio's Major Alterations' (a 1978 draft of a chapter from the second volume of *Origins*), p. 12 (privately communicated). I would like to thank Dr Blayney for extensive and generous technical assistance with this paper.
2. Marvin Rosenberg, *The Masks of King Lear* (Berkeley and Los Angeles, 1972), p. 72.
3. Blayney, 'Alterations', p. 12.
4. Jay L. Halio, ed., *King Lear*, Fountainwell Drama Texts (Edinburgh, 1973), p. 22.
5. The question of who made these decisions is tied up with the question of the compositors' copy for *King Lear*. Stone (*Textual History*) and Gary Taylor ('Folio Copy for *Hamlet*, *King Lear*, and *Othello*', *Shakespeare Quarterly*, 34 (1983), 44–61) have both argued that Compositor E, who set all the questionable *Cor.* prefixes, was setting from a copy of Q2 which had been annotated to embody the revisions made in the play. There is, however, at least one difficulty with the idea that E was setting from annotated Q2, and it occurs precisely at the point where he begins setting *King Lear*. Page qq4 begins with the completion of Edgar and Edmund's first scene together (TLN 485–504; 1.2.163–84). It contains three speeches of Edmund's, all of which have *Edm.* prefixes. The beginning of this encounter on qq3ᵛ (TLN 467–84; 1.2.138–63), presumably set by B simultaneously, uses *Bast.* for Edmund, as do both quartos universally. In other words, E began setting *King Lear* using prefixes which could only have come – directly or indirectly

- from an independent manuscript, most probably the one the playhouse had provided.

Two considerations regarding the *Cor.* prefix relate to this question of compositors' copy. First, it is likely that whoever annotated Q2 also standardized the prefixes. The standardization was not the compositors' doing. It is outside the scope of their ordinary responsibilities; it extends over both compositors' work; and the altered *Corn.* prefixes are most common in E's work. E retained 1 *Corn.* and changed 25 prefixes related to the name; B retained 21 *Corn.* prefixes and changed 5 related ones. This is exactly the opposite of what we would expect if the prefixes were the compositors' doing. Second, if E was working from annotated printed copy, then the physical condition of 'Deare Sir forbeare' (an entirely new line in the Folio) was not identical to his later settings of *Cor.* for Cornwall. Those were, with one exception, *Duke* prefixes which had been crossed out and written over. The exception (TLN 1134; 2.2.61) is the prefix to a speech which had, like 'Heere's *France* and *Burgundy*, my Noble Lord', originally been assigned to *Glost.*

6. Charlton Hinman, *The Printing and Proof-Reading of the First Folio of Shakespeare*, 2 vols. (Oxford, 1963), II, 272.

7. Hinman, *Printing*, I, 307–8, as the source of the figures; Blayney for the suggestion, privately communicated, that two of them were probably spontaneously corrected.

8. R. B. McKerrow, 'The Treatment of Shakespeare's Texts by his Earlier Editors, 1709–1768', Annual Shakespeare Lecture of the British Academy, 1933 (1933), p. 19.

9. Rosenberg, *Masks*, p. 59.

Gen. No more, the text is foolish.

RANDALL McLEOD

I

σώζειν τὰ φαινόμενα

THERE are two early substantive texts of Shakespeare's drama of King Lear, _The Historie of King Lear_, published in quarto in 1608, and _The Tragedie of King Lear_, published in the Folio of 1623. All the seventeenth-century editions derived from one or other of these first two, the source in each case apparently being determined by copyright rather than by any editorial sense of the relative merits of Q and F. A different attitude toward what came to be deemed the embarrassing multiplicity of authority for _Lear_ crystallized early in the eighteenth century, and still prevails two and a half centuries later: to conflate the two texts and to create a super-_Lear_ by selecting between variant readings those that are 'better'. The criteria of value seem to have been self-evident to each editor, but not to his predecessors or successors, and thus the historical collations of _Lear_ editions parade before us a long historie and tragedie of 'betters'. But the more the editions changed superficially, the more profoundly they became the same – testimonials of editorial commitment to eclectic conflation. The result is that virtually no one now experiences Q and F as independent texts.

This editorial procedure began in the days when bibliographical study was in its infancy; but as it came of age, the justification of textual manipulation was felt to need to rest less on taste than on textual authority. It may have been all right for Alexander Pope, an early eighteenth-century editor, to make the best art he could from the materials available, but by the mid-twentieth century the time had come to strive to recreate editorially what Shakespeare had actually written, whether it was good or not.

Thirty years ago George Ian Duthie sought to make such an edition (_Shakespeare's 'King Lear': A Critical Edition_, Oxford, 1949), and to base it on a rationalized editorial programme that proceeded on the small scale, crux by crux, with unprecedented attention to detailed textual argument. I say 'unprecedented' because the details of Shakespeare editions are traditionally laid down by editorial fiat without explanation. Even now, Duthie's edition remains the only thorough, editorially explicit commentary on the variants between Q and F *Lear*, and the most conscientious defence of the conflationist position. (I will turn to examples of his detailed arguments in the second part of this paper.) All his arguments, however, are governed by the idea that Q and F are mere derivatives (with relatively lesser and greater fidelity) of a single, complete, historical version of greatest authority; this version, X, now lost, would, if rediscovered, render the status of Q and F non-substantive, for where they differ from X they are deemed corrupt or incomplete. Duthie's global approach to the relationship of Q and F was not entirely new, but his own detailed research into Q and questions of textual transmission, and the then recent work of Madeleine Doran and W. W. Greg, had put him in a position to speak with new objectivity.

Duthie held that Q derived from memorial reconstruction by a group of actors of their staged version.[2] Memorial reconstruction necessitates that the 'accidentals' of Q cannot bear a close relationship to those of the original prompt-book (or of the actors' part-books). Given the tricks of memory, we are to suspect many 'substantives' as well. The Folio, by contrast, is alleged to derive by scribal transmission from a prompt-book, the same prompt-book from which Q circuitously derives, or possibly a copy of it. F is thus deemed generally to have greater fidelity in both 'accidentals' and 'substantives' to the lost X than does Q. And so Duthie adopts F as his copy-text, and asserts firmly that the ideal text is virtually identical with it, and that F needs correction only when it is manifestly in error, or when comparison of it with Q's *frequently* divergent readings leads one *occasionally* to detect some otherwise unobserved problem with F (p. 18). For convenience he regards Q as a report of the F text (p. 21).

There is much fine tuning to Duthie's arguments, which I cannot detail here. But we can now draw the essentials of his textual tree (p. 155, top). The dotted line is yet unexplained. Following P. A. Daniel's and W. W. Greg's discoveries, Duthie holds that the copy-text for F was an exemplar of Q marked up by Scribe E to bring it into agreement with the lost manuscript, X (or with a transcript of it, such as the prompt-book) (p. 13). Given the influence of Q press variation

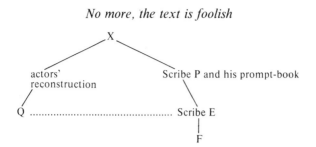

on the Folio text, the editor needs to allow for the possibility that through the scribe's negligence Q contaminates F elsewhere, where there is no press variation in Q to expose its influence. The corollary of this idea is one of the most ingenious notions of *Lear* editing: that when F and Q agree anywhere, we are to be less confident of the F reading than when they disagree – even when both make sense (pp. 17–18).[3] And so, unhappy Q becomes suspect not only when it agrees with F (and has corrupted it) but also when it differs (and betrays the faulty memory of the actors).

But there is another problem which confronts the editor when he focuses on Q, and which Duthie's reconstructionism cannot face squarely. If Q is so egregiously corrupt, how can we be sure that it is a corruption of X and not of some other stage of composition, Y – with X and Y possibly related by such trees as these?[4]

Duthie spends considerable effort (pp. 19–72) arguing with detailed examples against the idea that Q represents an early draft and F a revision. But for the moment let us stay on an abstract plane. We see from the challenge posed by Y that both aspects of Duthie's twofold definition of Q are essential to his position. For (a): if Q were a *good* memorial reconstruction, then its numerous divergences from F would throw suspicion on F, or on the notion that there could exist a single substantive version of the Lear story – an X which could supersede both Q and F, and be Shakespeare's final version. And (b): if one holds Q still to be a bad text, but of *scribal* rather than memorial transmission, then one casts doubt upon the very method of transmission that is supposed to guarantee the high quality of F.

Indeed, as it seems almost by definition that a bad scribal version cannot be as bad as a bad memorial version, respect for Q would have to increase. And if Q and F are both made respectable, their wide divergence is incompatible with the idea that they are both derivatives of the common ancestor, X, which was Shakespeare's finished version. Of course, at this point we may wish to postulate a contaminator or adapter who altered either Q copy or the prompt-book that lies behind the performance that lies behind Q. But the danger here is that Shakespeare himself might have been that contaminator or adapter. If this were true, there might be any number of Shakespearian aesthetic finalities, and the question of which finality is first in time and which last is obviously less important than what differentiates them. (Duthie does address the question of Shakespeare as abridger, but does not concede that he could have revised.[5]) And so we may come to see that 'bad' and 'memorial reconstruction' are mutually dependent attributes in Duthie's theory; together they constitute a self-fulfilling definition, which cannot be verified by external evidence (for the theory neatly deprives Q of external status).

There are some other possible definitions of Q that may drive us to doubt theoretically the existence of the X text as the final substantive version of the play. Perhaps Q and F are to be explained like this:

– in which Y and X are independent, lost, substantive versions, the former to be reconstructed largely from Q, the latter largely from F. (If these trees were correct, we would be right to object to the phrase, so often heard, that *Lear* has *divided* authority, and assert its authority as *multiple*.) Reconstructionists might accept such trees, with the proviso that there is a radical Z (or 'transcendent X') above it all:

Indeed, Z may be a necessarie letter, but even if it is, the problem is that there is no guarantee that it represents a complete play. After all, there cannot be an infinite regress of drafts, and at some point they may become scraps of speeches or scenes. The historical tree after pulling together in one trunk may branch out again as roots. Whoreson Zed may prove, to name one obvious possibility, to be a substantive version only of those scenes common to Q and F. (The scenes and episodes not common to Q and F could have been written for different runs.) If the reconstructionist were not after aesthetic unity, then his reconstruction of Z, an incomplete or unrevised draft, would pose no philosophic problem, however difficult it might be to achieve in practice. But, when we look at the rationale employed by Duthie in historical reconstruction, again and again we find that his eclectic editing depends upon faith in the aesthetic unity of X. Thus, the exaltation of X and the debasement of Q function as mutually self-constituting attributes. If the definition of either is changed, the system collapses. I reach the specific conclusion, therefore, that Duthie's postulation – that X is 'the full play' – is forced upon him; for if he allowed X to be an anterior draft he would threaten the notion of its completeness, and hence rob himself of the use of aesthetic argument in reconstruction. More generally, I fear that the editorial aesthetic serves as anaesthetic.

The direction of the next part of this essay will evolve heuristically simply from reading bits of the evidences as literary texts, without benefit of theories about their origins. I will have an eye constantly to the resistance editorial method and theory offer to such fundamental activity, for bare facts will be only as interesting to me here as the paradigms that raise them to consciousness, or that suppress them. The aim will be simply to detect whether, when we stand aside from editorial guidance, we find coherently differentiable aesthetic characteristics in Q and F. The extent to which we can bears an inverse relationship to the confidence we should owe the theory that Q is merely a corruption of X.

II

Ecce fructus myopiae

Editorial commentary typically contrasts single words from Q and F in a lemma, and continues with prose commentary leading to a choice of one word and rejection of the other. The following note in Duthie's edition for the crux at I i 299 (line 303 in Riverside) is more or less typical. Before I turn to its content, I wish to comment on the format, which, I believe, prejudices discussion. I promise eventually, however, to implicate the crux in larger and larger questions of editing and dramaturgy.

In addition to the note, it will be useful to select parallel stretches of Q and F texts as contexts for discussion of these cruxes, but I do not want to retypeset the text I quote, as is traditional. As the foundations of Shakespeare editing were laid prior to photography, we have inherited formats for textual discussion that neglect iconic detail, and thereby depress visual thinking, on which textual argument must often turn. Printing by photo-offset as in the present volume has recently made recovery of textual evidence *as an image* practicable, and I propose to take advantage of this photo-revolution. And so here 'photo-quoted' are the ends of the first scenes of *The Historie* and *The Tragedie*.[6] The cruxes under discussion are in the second line of each passage (C1; TLN 327–32; 1.1.302–8):

QUARTO:

> ⸀*Gono.* There is further⸍complement of leaue taking betweene
> *France* and him,pray lets hit together,if our Father cary autho-
> rity with such dispofitions as he beares,this last surrender of his,
> will but offend vs,
>   *Ragan.* We shall further thinke on't.
>   *Gon.* We must doe something,and it'h heate.   *Exeunt.*

FOLIO:

> *Gon.* There is further complement of leaue-taking be-
> tweene *France* and him,pray you let vs fit together, if our
> Father carry authority with such dispofition as he beares,
> this last surrender of his will but offend vs.
>   *Reg.* We shall further thinke of it.
>   *Gon.* We must do fomething,and i'th' heate.   *Exeunt.*

And here (likewise photo-quoted) is Duthie's note:

> I i 299 Q| hit   F| sit
>   The F reading makes sense: see Onions's *Shakespeare
>   Glossary*, p. 200 — '*sit*, 1, pregnantly = to sit in council,
>   take counsel together, hold a session'. But surely this
>   word would be more appropriate in the mouth of Regan,
>   who says 'We shall further thinke of it', than in the mouth

SHAKESPEARE'S 'KING LEAR'

of Goneril, who says 'We must do something, and i'th'heate'. This is an argument in favour of the Q reading; and there is another. 'Hit' meaning 'agree' is not pre-Shakespearian (see Onions, p. 106) and it is doubtful whether it would occur to a reporter, scribe, or compositor. That it is uncommon might be regarded as a possible reason for supposing that Scribe E emended it. I take it that Goneril wants the two of them to act together in agreement at once.

Let me start with the smallest details of the editor's lemma.

I i 299 Q | hit   F | sit

Duthie's note begins with roman and arabic numbers and with letters which identify not location*s* in the original evidences but *a* location in the editorial construct. Through its exclusive reference system, the ideal text may be seen to go before the debate about its nature like a fore-gone conclusion – just as the headline "SHAKESPEARE'S 'KING LEAR'", running through it, implies that there is only one Shakespearian *Lear*. I have thus spoken mistakenly hitherto of the 'crux at I i 299': at issue are the crux*es* of Q at line 9 of page C1 and of F at page qq3, column b, line 38 (TLN 328). The editorial numbering system is a numbing system; it facilitates no access to the historical evidences, and thus effectively neutralizes whatever resistance Q and F contexts might offer to editorial manipulation, rendering the texts of their alleged cruxes submissive to the logic of eclecticism.[7]

Perhaps I may seem too concerned with irrelevant matters of convention and mechanical details; but it is interesting at the beginning of any foray into criticism to ask how certain parts of a critical text achieve uncritical status – for thus we perceive that some parts of text are more equal than others.

The next examples may seem to demonstrate more weightily that editorial reference is not neutral. The editor contrasts 'Q | hit' with 'F | sit'. But a glance at the photo-quoted cruxes shows that the modern typographic format has transformed the evidence.

hit   ſit

The F crux, for example, exhibits no dot over the i, and this is evidence that, as was usual in contemporary composition, a single type, a ligature in f and i, was set instead of a separate type for each letter. One can immediately and decisively reason that neither Q's h nor F's f can be a typographic error for the other.[8]

This problem does *not* have the structure, then, of the following notable cruxes which look like this in Q and F (H1ᵛ; TLN 2135; 3.7.63):

deαrne   ſerɒe

and which are misidentified by Duthie's modernized typesetting like this:

Q | dearne   F | sterne

In the earliest known lay of the English case the compartment for the ligature in f and t is very near that of the d.[9] Therefore, either reading in the lemma could easily be a typo for the other, and this material observation frustrates those who automatically prefer the rarer of the two synonyms for the abstract reason that it is a 'more difficult' reading. Duthie regards the Q reading as original and the F reading as a sophistication. He cannot think, he says, that 'dearne' is 'the sort of word likely to have been substituted by reporter or compositor: reporters and compositors do not generally substitute readings more satisfactory from the literary point of view than the genuine ones' (p. 194). The problem with this line of reasoning is that if a typo is involved in either Q or F, the error does not come from a compositor's substitution of a *word* for another, but of one piece of *type* for another, and therefore need have nothing to do with literary understanding.

The perception that such a typo as is possible in the 'dearne'/'sterne' cruxes cannot be involved in the 'hit'/'sit' cruxes radically informs our knowledge of the transmissional processes of each text, and thereby refines our notions of relative probabilities of accuracy and error. If 'sit' is to be regarded as a typo, it may readily be a mis-setting of 'fit' – for fi (one of the few old ligatures still in use, as in the fount of this volume) was adjacent to the ligature in f and i in the old lay of the case. Conversely, if 'hit' is to be the typo, it would not be for 'sit' (or 'fit') but for a three-sort word like 'pit' (which can be ruled out as anachronistic in context) or 'wit' (which can be ruled in, in the absolute sense of the *OED*'s 'wit', *v*. B. I. 3. c.). All this speculation does not lead us automatically to right answers, but it is surely part of an intelligent method guided by the precise typographical evidence which inheres in the text because it is text. We see here that editorial argument is biased toward literary issues to the extent that it neglects literal aspects of text. In such cases photo-quotation brings speculation immediately to heel.

So, a typo seems not to be involved. Let us shift our search for a source of supposed error to such issues as compositorial or scribal mis-hearing or mis-remembering. To understand such issues necessitates analysing a mass of detail; and a limited confrontation between Q and F in a single lemma hardly augurs adequate preparation for editorial decision. On the question of mis-hearing, however, we can quickly make some progress with a limited amount of evidence, if only in sophisticating our scepticism.

Editors habitually choose the graphically isolable word as the basis of textual citation. But the lexical divisions so rigidly part of our graphic conventions rarely coincide with pauses in speech, which are paramount in staging, and which may weigh heavily with a dramatic author with an ear for speech. What if the editor's lemma were attuned to the continuum of sound, and, contrasting Q and F like this, rendered that which the eye hath not heard?

s hit t   s fit t

Here the lexical is somewhat integrated into the phonetic context, and we are able to group it with the following, in which phonetic and graphic seem at odds:

in fight   incite

(I1ᵛ; TLN 2379; 4.4.27)

with the   we the

(L2ᵛ; TLN 3148; 5.3.186)

a dogge, fo bade in office,   a Dogg's | obey'd in Office.

(I4; TLN 2602–3; 4.6.158–9)

If the graphic convention of h in 'hit' does not reflect aspiration in speech, as was quite possible in Shakespearian English,[10] there need have been no phonetic differentiation of 'hit' and 'sit' *in context*. This is not to say that the distinction could not have been made deliberately, but that in fast speech it might not be heard. Having argued that 'hit' and 'sit' were not then (as they are now) typographically confusable, I am arguing that in their contexts they were then (as they are not now) confusable by sound. There is thus some possibility of aural error in one text or the other, which is presumably a conclusion Duthie would be happy with (though my argument does not favour one reading more than another). But more importantly the example exposes also how strongly we are in the grip of our own graphic conventions, conventions that have no parallel in the relaxed state of English in Shakespeare's time. Much regulation of the language as we know it both in speech and writing came afterwards, and with it a shift in the relative roles of eye and ear. As the fluidity of Renaissance English was not a failure of our value system, we must not confuse pre-regular with ir-regular usage, or glean precision where it was not cultivated. The conventional modern neglect of the distinction between pre- and ir-regularity feeds quite easily in the 'hit'/'sit' cruxes into the editorial propensity to choose one reading and not the other – to choose the one because the other is a corruption of it. The present point is only indirectly related to whether Q and F derive from distinct authorial versions; I am here addressing rather an anachronistic notion of the graphic medium, one which facilitates the general idea, however it arises, that Q has suffered irregular transmission. (Paradoxically, in the present cruxes it is Q that is deemed to be right and F that is wrong.) It is true, perhaps, that irregular transmission was, as it were, regular in Renaissance texts, but these examples call in question the vocabulary and the senses through which we perceive what is regular. As Lear says to Gloucester, appealing to his insight, we must look with our ears to see how this world goes (4.6.151).[11]

Having questioned the implications of the format of the lemma, let us turn at last to the prose commentary, and proceed at a faster rate. Surprisingly, the editor concedes that both Q and F readings make sense. The prime issue for him, one he uses to justify his choice of one over the other, is that 'sit' is – not *in*appropriate to Goneril, but – *more* appropriate to Regan. To demonstrate 'appropriateness' the editor quotes a later F passage. This raises again the issue of context: Duthie suggests that subsequent speech establishes a criterion of appropriateness for prior speech, a notion that seems to deny the possibility of character development. Duthie's Goneril, it seems, is a woman of abrupt action, and 'sit' is too sedentary for her. But is it not reasonable to suppose that Goneril finally calls for action in the heat precisely because she is moved thither by Regan's hesitation even to 'sit' together? Duthie depends here on static notions of character; but as soon as characters interact the notion of appropriateness must become dynamic.

Furthermore, the quotations do not prove his point merely as words on the page. If, for example, when Regan says, 'We shall further thinke of it', her 'we' is royal, the editor's argument is supported; but if it is merely plural, and if she stresses 'shall', then he is contradicted. If when Goneril responds, 'We must do something', she stresses 'do' against her sister's 'thinke', Duthie is suppported; but if Regan stresses 'shall' and Goneril stresses 'must' or 'something', then Regan is quite eye to eye with her sister. By his neglect of the ambiguity inherent in the graphic medium, the editor gives evidence that he has his own way of reading, stressing and delimiting the meanings of text – in short, he has his own mental production of the play, which silently identifies *an* optional reading as *the* reading.[12]

I will conclude discussion of Duthie's note by analysing its second point. The editor offers another argument 'in favour of the Q reading' – by which curious phrase he must mean 'in favour of rejecting the F reading'. (But of course, praise of Q is not in itself a reason for dispraising the reading of another text. The issue of aesthetics is being irrationally crossed with that of textual authority.) The editor proceeds to imply that 'hit' here means 'agree', defending his choice by citing Onions's *A Shakespeare Glossary*. This reference work was created to 'supply definitions and illustrations of words or senses of words now obsolete or surviving only in provincial or archaic use' (Oxford, 1911; repr. 1941, p. iii). Onions in fact quotes the present F crux, and it is he who provides the convoluted epithet 'not pre-S[hakespearian]'. This phrase subtly implies that Shakespeare invented this usage – and we must be very hard-hearted if we would reject a Shakespearian neologism for plain old 'sit'. But that no use of 'hit' in this sense is recorded in the *OED* prior to Shakespeare does not really mean he gave the word this meaning – or even that it is new.[13] (Indeed, the *OED* gives a transitive usage from 1580 (*hit*, 15).) But more to the point, how can Duthie, Onions, or the *OED*, the ultimate source of the definition, prove that 'hit' here means only 'agree'? Why cannot 'hit' mean or also mean 'strike', as the *OED* says it has since 1205? One wonders whether the attractiveness to most[14] editors of 'hit' over 'sit' is the violence of this editorially unacknowledged definition – 'strike'.

But Duthie's argument is being directed not toward the content but toward the unfamiliarity of the word in this sense to 'reporter, scribe, or compositor' behind Q and to the scribe behind F, so that the former group could not have invented it, and the Folio scribe could plausibly have altered or 'emended' the reading of his copy, 'hit', to a more familiar word. Such an argument is suspicious. Why, for example, did the unfamiliarly defined 'hit' survive transmission in early times (1607–8) through the alleged reporter, scribe, and compositor (all of whom are taken to be unreliable), then survive the compositor of Q2 in 1619, and then *not* survive the single agent, Scribe E, who worked well after 1608 (when the alleged sense of 'hit' would have been better known, and when 'hit' was before him in both documents he collated, Q and the manuscript) – especially when Scribe E is considered a more competent workman than any behind the Q transmission? We should not trust an argument based on the strangeness of definition of 'hit' to justify its presence in Q and absence from F (as Duthie defines these two editions). It seems that the argument is worked backwards from the decision to eliminate divergent readings, and not forward from the evidence itself, which in this case offers no convincing rationale for selection even if it seems to offer one for preference, as Duthie feels, or for aural confusion in context, as I have suggested.

Let us come back to context. The editor's comment on 'hit' and 'sit', with which we began, might have been forced to take a different turn if he had argued from his lemma at the bottom of p. 216. Here is the relevant reading in the critical text for I i 299, and below it is the lemma.

pray you let vs hit

299 pray . . . hit] pray you let vs sit F.   pray lets hit Q.

If Duthie's note had discussed 'hit' and 'sit' in the contexts quoted in this lemma (instead of merely in that of F or of his critical edition), he would have had to deal with the obvious possibility that the verbal differences in the contrasted Q and F phrases were co-ordinate. One would want to know the relative distribution of vocative pronouns in imperatives (like 'pray you') or of contractions ('lets') in and between both texts. One would then wonder whether the laconic diction of the Q phrase connotes haste or impetuousness (and therefore suits the editor's concept of appropriateness, and suits 'hit'). But one might also feel that the slower pace of the whole F phrase is appropriate to 'sit'. And if so, how could the editor justify choosing the word but not the phrase? Contextualized lemmata would throw appropriately frustrating obstacles in the way of haste.

The last paragraph brought us to the notion of co-ordinate differentiation of Q and F, a particularly useful form of contextualizing, because it is open to structural considerations in ways impossible to atomized, single-word citations in a lemma, and because it opens itself to potentially relevant contexts. Of course, criticism could scarcely proceed with the ideal co-ordination – simply of all of Q with all of F; but practical criticism can still function by attending to the patterns of its own contexting, and so not be blind to the collational format and its implicit values. The literary-critical questions are unbegged then, as the textual critic continually searches out the bias of contextualizing. (I'll try to do it as I go.)

The idea of co-ordinate differentiation of Q and F may be sketched now by working back into their first scenes as far, say, as Lear's exit (B4^v; TLN 291; 1.1.266), and investigating the variations in all the speeches of Goneril and all those of Regan. As soon as we begin such a task with the photo-quotations before us, we realize that our criterion for designating the fields of comparison is suspicious. First of all, 'Goneril' and 'Regan' are names used in Duthie's commentary (and in most modern texts); but in Q we find 'Gonorill' and sometimes 'Ragan', whereas the Folio offers 'Gonerill' and 'Regan'. From here on, therefore, I will use the synthetic rather than the analytical terms, 'Ragan' instead of 'Regan in Q' (though with some awkwardness, I admit), in order not to allow the modern abstraction to eclipse the evidences, and to throw appropriately frustrating obstacles in the way of my own haste. In actuality the spelling of names varies within each text. In Q, for example, in 1.1 the shift in spelling 'Regan'/'Ragan' coincides with the end of a page (B4^v), and one habitually suspects a change of compositor at such a point. If I were aiming at greater subtlety, my spelling of the names should vary as I dealt with text of various pages or speeches; but let me limit myself to a milder form of confusion in this essay. If Duthie's note employed such awkwordness he would be driven to frame the concept of appropriateness in terms not only of the different diction of Q and F speeches, but also of the differently spelled names of the speakers.

Indeed, one could go farther than that, for look at these speech assignments (B4^v; TLN 301‑5; 1.1.276–9):

QUARTO:

> *Gonorill.* Prefcribe not vs our duties ?
> *Regan.* Let your ftudy be to content your Lord,
> Who hath receaued you at Fortunes almes,
> You haue obedience fcanted,
> And well are worth the worth that you haue wanted.

FOLIO:

> *Regn.* Prefcribe not vs our dutie.
> *Gon.* Let your ftudy
> Be to content your Lord,who hath receiu'd you
> At Fortunes almes,you haue obedience fcanted,
> And well are worth the want that you haue wanted.

One can proffer different kinds of explanation for the varying speech assignments. For example, if we consider the end of the scene, we see that in Q Gonorill and Ragan each have at least one long speech. Perhaps the distribution of long speeches between sisters serves to balance their stage presences in this episode. Perhaps, to state another kind of explanation for Q's distribution, the short burst in reply to Cordelia serves to characterize Gonorill's aggression. (And we note that Gonorill's speech 'hits off', as it were.) But in the Folio episode it is Regan who speaks in short phrases; it is she who flies at Cordelia with her second-person negative imperative ('Prescribe not'), whereas Gonerill 'sits' back with a third-(im)personal positive imperative ('Let . . . be.'), and is always more long-spoken in this episode. (In this explanation consistently contrasted characterization outweighs balancing.) However we figure it, such co-ordinations of differentiation immediately explode the idea that there is a simple Goneril and Regan to whom a simple notion of appropriateness can be simply applied.

Co-ordinate with the different ascriptions are differences in diction; Gonorill's 'Prescribe not vs our duties' (Q) contrasts with Regan's 'Prescribe not vs our dutie' (F). To my ear the former speech, with its plural 'duties', reads most easily as a speech on behalf of both the older sisters; if so, 'vs' is a simple plural form, though it could also be the royal 'us'. The royal 'us' is more the tone of Regan's 'vs', as I hear it, perhaps because of the singular 'dutie' in her version of the speech.[15] But I am also looking ahead to another way of contexting this crux, by comparing its (invariant) personal pronouns with those of the next speeches by these sisters, directly after Cordelia's exit.

QUARTO:

Gonor. Sifter,it is not a little I haue to fay,
Of what moft neerely appertaines to vs both,
I thinke our father will hence to night.
Reg. Thats moft certaine,and with you,next mon eth with vs

FOLIO:

Gon. Sifter,it is not little I haue to fay,
Of what moft neerely appertaines to vs both,
I thinke our Father will hence to night.   (with vs.
Reg. That's moft certaine,and with you; next moneth

It is quite possible to read this and all of Ragan's and Regan's remaining speeches in this episode as employing the royal distancing 'vs' in contrast to her sister's 'vs both'. Each text has its own range of ambiguity here; but I wish to suggest that in addition there is a differential structure for the ambiguity of each text that arises from 'reading between the texts'. We should hold back on the notions of appropriateness of characters until these differential structures are clearer.

Of course, I do not expect that every difference between the texts is either explicable or Shakespearian; but if, as we proceed with larger and larger ranges of text, we find more and more thematic consistency to the co-ordinate variation, we will naturally decrease our suspicion of accidents and agents of transmission, and have to speculate in earnest about purposeful differentation of Q and F.

There is another variant in this episode which the editor comments on, and which is of interest if we are contexting on the basis of all of Gonorill's and Gonerill's speeches. Look in the second lines (B4^v; TLN 315; 1.1.289):

QUARTO:

Gon. You fee how full of changes his age is the obferuation we haue made of it hath not bin little; hee alwaies loued our fifter moft, and with what poore iudgement hee hath now caft her off, appeares too groffe.

FOLIO:

Gon. You fee how full of changes his age is, the ob-feruation we haue made of it hath beene little;he alwaies lou'd our Sifter moft,and with what poore iudgement he hath now caft her off,appeares too groffely.

It is worth while again to devote a moment to criticizing Duthie's lemma.

I i 286 Q | not   F | om.

If F made good sense Q's 'not' would be easily explicable as a repetition from line 281. Schmidt accepts F, extracting from it the meaning – 'All our observation in the past is little in comparison with what we may expect in the future, to judge from Lear's treatment of Cordelia' (see Furness's note). We might accept F and say that in the past Goneril and Regan have not observed Lear's inconstancy much, though now they have striking evidence of it: but this is surely inconsistent with the fact that the sisters are able to make the statements, 'he hath euer but slenderly knowne himselfe' and 'The best and soundest of his time hath bin but rash'. It seems more likely that the F compositor has accidentally omitted 'not'.

                                                                    (p. 169)

'F/om.' must mean the Folio version has left something out which ought to be there. But, before we have seen the evidence, this is a prejudicial statement. It would be foolish to say, for example, that a man *omits* a womb. Closer to home, it would be wrong to say that *The Tragedie* omits Macbeth's speech 'Out, out breefe Candle'; for *Macbeth* and *Lear* are not trying to be the same play. And how do we know that *The Historie* is trying to be *The Tragedie* – or some hybrid of them both? Duthie does use 'omit' properly (though incorrectly, I think) at the end of his note, where he hypothesizes that the 'not' was left out of F by compositorial accident. It is true that the negative adverb has statistically a higher chance of coming and going during textual transmission than do nouns and verbs, the omission of which often conspicuously disrupts sense. (There are those seventeenth-century worldly-wise Bibles, for example, one of which commands,

Thou shalt commit adultery

– and another of which prophesies,

the unrighteous shall inherit
the Kingdom of God.)[16]

But we can reduce the plausibility of the suggestion that F omits 'not' here simply by exposing a contradiction in Duthie's argument; for he confuses Lear's inconstancy with both his lack of self-knowledge and his rashness, with neither of which it is logically identified or even associated. A person can be precipitous and self-ignorant, and yet be constant. Moreover, in their next speeches Gonorill and Gonerill say that the addition specifically of 'way-wardnesse' to Lear's 'long ingraffed' (or 'long ingrafted') 'condition' is something of his *age* (TLN 322–3; C1; 1.1.297–8).

This observation throws up before us a differential reading in the same speeches that might otherwise go unnoticed. Gonorill says that their observation of Lear's 'poore iudgement' 'appeares too grosse', but Gonerill says it 'appeares too grossely'. Q uses an adjective, F an adverb. F emphasizes that because the observation of Lear's inconstancy 'hath been little' it appears 'grossely' now. But in Q, where the observation 'hath not bin little', Lear's poor judgement appears 'grosse' among lesser examples to date. The subtle difference of adverb and adjective in these parallel passages may be seen to be co-ordinate with the differentiated interpretation of the sisters that arose from the previous divergent readings in Q and F.[17]

Duthie says that 'If F made good sense Q's "not" [in 286] would be easily explicable as a repetition from line 281' (*'Gonor:* Sister, it is not a little I haue to say'). As F has been shown to make good sense, might not Q's 'not' be wrong indeed, against Duthie's judgement? But if Q is wrong here, might it not be co-ordinately wrong in the 'grosse' that 'hits' with it? Again and again eclectic editing seems to proceed on the selective projection of error into the primary evidence whenever it is various, which editing then aims to 'correct' by elimination of variation.

We can now add these recent co-ordinate variants to the pictures presented by those considered earlier, and conclude discussion of this scene. In Q the imperious Gonorill comes out fighting and proceeds in the initial crux to 'hit'. The Q picture is consistently augmented by her observation in the last discussed crux of how her father's age has been and continues to be full of changes – the last being too gross. She appears to have premeditated her present scheme for power from consistent observation. But in F Gonerill is more reserved (in sharper contrast with pugnacious and perhaps haughty and aloof Regan), and she asks merely to 'sit' together with her in open discussion, without stipulating that they must agree or must strike. The latest co-ordinate variation shows Gonerill off balance, thinking on her feet in an attempt to grasp an unprecedented situation, which has erupted before her grossly and without notice. Regan's alleged delay in embracing Gonerill's plan could now be understood in F as a function not only of the general haughtiness and self-absorption I thought to attribute to her in that text, but also of the specific novelty of the problem for her and her sister.

Such subtleties of interpretation can scarcely come to us from the conflated *Lear*. Neither are they likely to occur to us from reading either text in isolation. They can reveal themselves readily, however, if we engage in differential reading of whole texts, if we bypass the atomized lemmata of the editorial tradition and the eclecticism they implicitly inculcate. And they seem to lead us to a startling, if tentative, conclusion: in the first scene Gonerill need not be such a bitch after all, though Gonorill may be.

To obtain an external fix on this question we might seek out co-ordinate variants in speeches to or about the sisters, such as those in Cordelia's first (and only) speech to them, just after Lear's exit and just before her own. Here in Q she bids them 'vse well our Father', whereas in F she bids them 'Loue' him well (B4ᵛ; TLN 296; 1.1.271). True, the different diction may reflect co-ordinate differentiation of Cordelia between Q and F, which would have to be detected by expanding the contexting of her speech and of speeches to her. (For example, Lear's first mention of 'his ioy' in Q (B2; 1.1.83) is as 'the last not least in our deere loue;' but in F (TLN 89) she is simply 'our last and least'.) The variants in her speech to her sisters suggest that in F, at least, they may indeed be capable of loving Lear – if Cordelia is any judge of character. But, of course, she may not be a good judge of character. Our disposition to think of her so may depend on questions we should not yet have answered, but whose answers may have come to us unbidden from our experience of the eclectic tradition in which we all first learned *Lear*. Citing the variant 'vse'/'Loue' in Cordelia's speeches, Duthie finds occasion to demonstrate Q's memorial confusion (with a much later passage) and to show that its reading is unsuitable to 'the context'; then he argues that it also has no claim to be the reading of a 'Shakespearian first draft', and that F's 'Loue' is the point of the line 'as initially conceived'. These extraordinary claims, especially the last, are not atypical of the editor's frequent assertions of the author's original intent. (It seems sometimes that 'original intent' and 'final draft' are synonymous in this edition – an equation which neatly excludes the possibility of intermediate drafts.) Here is Duthie's analysis (pp. 55–6):

I i 269 F | Loue well our Father:

Q | vse well our Father,

Cf. I v 14 –

F | Shalt see thy other Daughter will vse thee kindly,

Q | Shalt see thy other daughter will vse thee kindly,

The earlier and later passages could easily be confused in the memory: both concern the treatment of Lear by Goneril and Regan after the distribution of the kingdom. And it can be said quite confidently that in I i 269 the F reading is appropriate to the context while that of Q is not. The next line makes this clear – 'To your professed bosomes I commit him,' (the wording is the same in both texts). Cordelia is in effect saying to Goneril and Regan, 'You have said that you love our father – do so'. As Greg says (*Editorial Problem*, p. 93), 'she had yet no ground for supposing they would use the old man ill'. The person responsible for the Q reading was thinking ahead. (The fact that the Q reading is unsuited to the context militates, of course, against the theory that 'vse' is the reading of a Shakespearian first draft and 'Loue' that of a revision. The use of 'professed' in the next line shows quite definitely that the point of line 269 as initially conceived lay in the word 'Loue'.)

In general this argument makes the frequent editorial mistake of neglecting staging, which creates a 'context' for Cordelia's reaction, just as surely as does the dialogue. If to the audience the sisters have looked insincere or hypocritical, Cordelia will seem to have every justification to act as if they are so. But Duthie's argument can be more convincingly challenged here from philology, simply by observing that he neglects the irony that is part and parcel of the definition of 'professed' from well before Shakespeare's time. This example of his textual argument shows how editorial clairvoyance about the lost precursors can arise from not looking clearly at the present evidence.

However the variations relating to Cordelia impinge on previous discussion, we can observe that the initial presentation of Gonerill may be like that of Edmund and Edmond in both texts. Only after the Bastard's first appearance does the audience rethink him, gradually – and not necessarily until after his witty defence of bastardy – withdrawing sympathy and respect. That in both plays the elder sisters and the bastards are finally more sinning than sinned against is not in doubt; but the co-ordinate variation of the beginning of the texts suggests that F offers a vision of somewhat greater moral ambiguity than does Q, a subtlety that does not survive eclectic conflation.

At this point I wish to change scale again: instead of expanding the kinds of contexting, I shall sketch rapidly forward into the texts the contexting already begun. If the differentiation of Gonerill and Gonorill and the consequent slight shift of the moral tone of the tragedy is more than accident, we might search for a point where F and Q draw back together. If this comes as soon as the next scene, it will be hard to convince anyone that the small differences cited are more than accidental. But if the differentiation continues for some while, we will have to reconsider whether the tragic visions of *The Historie* and *The Tragedie* are the same.

Here with some contexts clinging to them are the third scenes of the plays (C3; TLN 502–32: 1.2.182–1.4.2).

QUARTO:

My practifes ride eafie, I fee the bufines,
Let me if not by birth, haue lands by wit,
All with me's meete, that I can fafhion fit.   *Exit.*
        Enter Gonorill and Gentleman.

Gon. Did my Father ftrike my gentleman for chiding of his
foole?,

Gent. Yes Madam.

Gon. By day and night he wrongs me,
Euery houre he flafhes into one grofle crime or other
That fets vs all at ods, ile not indure it,
His Knights grow ryotous, and him felfe obrayds vs,
On euery trifell when he returnes from hunting,
I will not fpeake with him, fay I am ficke,
If you come flacke of former feruices,
You fhall doe well, the fault of it ile anfwere.

Gent. Hee's coming Madam, I heare him.

Gon. Put on what wearie negligence you pleafe, you and your
fellow feruants, i'de haue it come in queftion, if he diflike it, let
him to our fifter, whofe mind and mine I know in that are one,
not to be ouerruld; idle old man that ftill would manage thofe
authorities that hee hath giuen away, now by my life old fooles
are babes again, & muft be vs'd with checkes as flatteries, when
they are feené abufd, remember what I tell you.

Gent. Very well Madam.

Gon. And let his Knights haue colder looks among you, what
growes of it no matter, aduife your fellowes fo, I would breed
from hence occafions, and I fhall, that I may fpeake, ile write
ftraight to my fifter to hould my very courfe, goe prepare for
dinner.   *Exit.*
        Enter Kent.

Kent. If but as well I other accents borrow, that can my fpeech
        C 3   defufe,

My practiſes ride eaſie : I ſee the buſineſſe.
Let me, if not by birth, haue lands by wit,
All with me's meete, that I can faſhion fit.   *Exit.*

Scena Tertia.

Enter Gonerill, and Steward.

Gon. Did my Father ſtrike my Gentleman for chi-
ding of his Foole?
  Ste. I Madam.
  Gon. By day and night, he wrongs me, euery howre
He flaſhes into one groſſe crime, or other,
That ſets vs all at ods : Ile not endure it ;
His Knights grow riotous, and himſelfe vpbraides vs
On euery trifle. When he returnes from hunting,
I will not ſpeake with him, ſay I am ſicke,
If you come ſlacke of former ſeruices,
You ſhall do well, the fault of it Ile anſwer.
  Ste. He's comming Madam, I heare him.
  Gon. Put on what weary negligence you pleaſe,
You and your Fellowes: I'de haue it come to queſtion;
If he diſtaſte it, let him to my Siſter,
Whoſe mind and mine I know in that are one,
Remember what I haue ſaid.
  Ste. Well Madam.
  Gon. And let his Knights haue colder lookes among
you : what growes of it no matter, aduiſe your ſellowes
ſo, Ile write ſtraight to my Siſter to hold my courſe; pre-
pare for dinner.   *Exeunt.*

Scena Quarta.

Enter Kent.

Kent. If but as will I other accents borrow,

The contexts of the quoted scenes – the concluding lines of the Bastard's and of Edmund's speeches, and the opening lines of Kent's – show that both groups of three scenes are concerned with dissimulations. To catch the right tones of each we would surely have to consider widely. But it may be enough to say (putting the theatrical appeal of the different characters aside) that, since Bastard Edmund has sounded a very low moral note, Gonorill and Gonerill would have to behave most wickedly not to shine relatively. The opening texts of the Q and F scenes show that if she thought to act in the heat (her last word), she has missed her cue – for Lear is a jump ahead of her. Unlike the Bastard, the Duchess is on the defensive; the attack on her Gentleman challenges both propriety and her own authority.

When John Keats read *Lear*, toward the end of the second decade of the nineteenth century, he left extensive underlinings, markings and annotations in his text. In the first scene he marked dozens of lines, including Gonerill's speech to Cordelia so assigned in F only ('Let your study | Be to content your Lord'), and he underlined the one in which she declares, in F only, that their observation of their father's changes has been little. When Keats came to the third scene, by contrast, he underlined only one phrase – 'weary negligence' (at the start of Goneril's third speech). The paucity of his underlining here is consonant with the fact that Keats's text was a facsimile of the First Folio;[18] there Gonerill's response to the report of Lear's violence to her gentleman is measured, and her behaviour is in keeping with the Gonerill whose speeches he had marked earlier. In Q, however, a different woman was appearing than the one Keats was heeding, as we see if we contrast the Duchess's last two speeches in the Q and F scenes; for Gonorill shrilly calls her father 'idle old man', and regards him as one among the old fools that turn babes again. There is, of course, more than a grain of truth in her charges, but her tone invites invidious comparison – in Q only – with her professed love for her father – 'Dearer then eye-sight, space or libertie' (B1^v; TLN 61; 1.1.56). Her hypocrisy in Q seems appropriate to the Gonorill who claimed in the first scene that she had observed many examples of her father's changes, and who asked Ragan to 'hit together' with her. Of this hypocrisy Keats's Folio revealed nothing; his noting of Gonorill's weary negligence in that text is indicative of Keats's eye not only for romantic idiom, but also (and unconsciously, I think) for the Folio characterization of the Duchess.

If we read either Q or F in isolation, we see in both that the Duchess is heading intentionally for confrontation with her father. As soon as we contrast the texts, however, we see that the plan to slack service in F is relatively cool; it reads like the reasoned tit for tat of a woman who is conscious of propriety and principle, and who responds to provocation slowly and in proportion. The Q Duchess by contrast seems to have lost her grip on herself, and her Q-only vituperations seem to offer an inner glimpse of a woman so insecure about the 'authorities that hee hath giuen away' that she is impelled to force his hand by 'breed[ing] from hence occasions'. When we contrast Q and F it seems that Gonerill the Bitch has yet to appear in *The Tragedie*; in *The Historie*, however, Gonorill is now taking on monstrous dimensions.

All the variants considered till now seem consistent with this conclusion, and suggest the hypothesis that there is purposeful differentiation of *Historie* and *Tragedie*. Duthie's policy is to conflate, adding the Q-only passages to the F text. This makes Gonerill more like Gonorill, as does the editor's adoption of 'not' and 'hit' in the first scene. The editor's Goneril is certainly a unified synthesis, but if we ground our notions of appropriateness in historical evidence, and read her against Gonorill and Gonerill, she seems schizoid, and the editorial *Lear* takes on the shape of a *cadavre exquis*.

In the next, the fourth scenes, the numerous variations need not concern us until well past Goneril's frowning entrance, in which, provoked, the daughter demands that Lear lessen his train. Speaking of the infection of 'this our court', she compares it with an inn (D2; TLN 753–65; 1.4.244–55):

QUARTO:

The Hiſtorie of King Lear.

like a riotous Inne,epicuriſme,and luſt make more like a tauerne
or brothell, then a great pallace, the ſhame it ſelfe doth ſpeake
for inſtant remedie, be thou deſired by her, that elſe will take the
thing ſhee begs, a little to diſquantitie your traine, and the remainder that ſhall ſtill depend, to bee ſuch men as may beſort
your age, that know themſelues and you.

 Lear. Darkenes and Deuils! ſaddle my horſes, call my traine
together, degenerate baſtard, ile not trouble thee, yet haue I left
a daughter.

FOLIO:

> Shewes like a riotous Inne; Epicurifme and Luſt
> Makes it more like a Tauerne, or a Brothell,
> Then a grac'd Pallace. The ſhame it ſelfe doth ſpeake
> For inſtant remedy. Be then deſir'd
> By her, that elſe will take the thing ſhe begges,
> A little to diſquantity your Traine,
> And the remainders that ſhall ſtill depend,
> To be ſuch men as may beſore your Age,
> Which know themſelues, and you.
>   *Lear.* Darkneſſe, and Diuels.
> Saddle my horſes : call my Traine together.
> Degenerate Baſtard, Ile not trouble thee;
> Yet haue I left a daughter.

That Gonorill should speak of a 'great pallace' but Gonerill of a 'grac'd Pallace' is consistent with the differentiations noted thus far; and so is her 'be thou desired' in Q as opposed to her 'be then desired' in F. One must admit the ease of phonetically or graphically confusing 'grac'd' and 'great', 'thou' and 'then', but the issue is whether one need postulate error in either text. Her thouing her father here in Q is the first such address to him in the play, and immediately precedes his first 'thee' to her, which it may be thought to provoke. In retrospect, her vaunting of herself, '*our* court', is as high as her 'thee' to Lear is low. We are impressed with how authority and its abuse continue to weigh on her mind. By contrast the 'then' in F may be interpreted as 'consequently', and thus may serve as an element of reasoning from evidence and allegations to conclusions, showing as before Gonerill's commitment to the rationale of her position, whereas Gonorill's interest seems to lie merely in her position. A corollary of these differences is that Lear's 'thee' to Gonerill registers as an aggressive escalation in F, not as the counter response of Q. Duthie follows F here completely and produces from his sources a milder Goneril than he had before.

After Lear's exit Albany begins to remonstrate with his wife. The stage business is much more complex in F, where his wife interrupts him with a speech addressing first him, then the Fool and her steward in rapid succession.[19] Though she seems generally more agitated in *The Tragedie*, her tone specifically to her husband, as Duthie also notes (p. 35), is softer and more respectful than in Q: 'Pray you content' rather than 'Come sir no more' (TLN 833; D2ᵛ; 1.4.312). Duthie holds that the Q reading is 'inappropriate in this context' – by which he means his own editorial context rather than those of Q and F. His Goneril speaks 'soothingly and in a conciliatory manner. Her attitude to Albany at this stage of the play is certainly not such as to warrant her being so rude as to say "Come sir no more" to him. Consequently, [he concludes,] I do not believe that Q gives the version of a first draft here' (I iv 298 in his edition, 313 in Riverside). I rather think that Duthie's eclecticism in the third scene *has* prepared us for 'rudeness without warrant', and that his assessment of Goneril is truer of F than of his own edition. But my main point is that the differences of Q and F continue to be appropriate to what we have observed in differential reading. The conclusion of Duthie's remarks is typical of his repeated assertions about the derivation of Q: a credo.

Of greatest interest in this scene is Gonerill's explosion when the Fool has followed Lear off stage, thirteen lines that occur only in *The Tragedie* (D2ᵛ; TLN 841–61; 1.4.321–38).

QUARTO:

followes after.
    Gon. What *Ofwald*, ho.   *Ofwald.* Here Madam,
    Gon. What haue you writ this letter to my fifter?
    Ofw. Yes Madam.
    Gon. Take you fome company, and away to horfe, informe
her full of my particular feares, and thereto add fuch reafons of

FOLIO:

So the Foole followes after.   *Exit*
    Gon. This man hath had good Counfell,
A hundred Knights?
'Tis politike, and fafe to let him keepe
At point a hundred Knights: yes, that on euerie dreame,
Each buz, each fancie, each complaint, difl ke,
He may enguard his dotage with their powres,
And ho'd our liues in mercy. *Ofwald*, I fay.
    Alb. Well you may feare too farre.
    Gon. Safer then truft too farre;
Let me ftill take away the harmes I feare,
Not feare ftill to be taken. I know his heart,

What he hath vtter'd I haue writ my Sifter:
If fhe fuftaine him, and his hundred Knights
When I haue fhew'd th'vnfitgeffe.

Enter Steward.

How now *Ofwald?*
What haue you writ that Letter to my Sifter?
Stew. I Madam.
Gon. Take you fome company, and away to horfe,
Informe her full of my particular feare,

These thirteen lines show her wrought in the extreme. At first she argues ironically for Lear's cause, but then, naming names, speaks – as she did earlier in this scene in both Q and F – of Lear's dotage (D2; TLN 805; 1.4.293), and comes at last to her fear, that he will hold their lives in jeopardy. (Here she is not using the royal singular 'our' as 'liues' shows, but seems to be including her husband.) Whether this speech testifies to paranoia, deceptive rhetoric, or recognition of a real danger, I will not argue; but differential reading is clear on one thing. If we compare the lines unique to Q in Scene Three, when Gonorill reacted to the striking of her gentleman, and the lines unique to F here in the fourth scene, we see that the latter lines show her wrought up, appropriately, only after the event, and even then self-possessed in her emotional extremity, trenchant in irony and rational in argumentation. This is not to judge her cause, of course, but it is to suggest that, unlike Gonorill, she is coming to the boil slowly.

That *The Historie* offers no address to the Duke corresponding to the F lines does not mean that there is a lack of information about Gonorill at this point. The fact that she exploded upon her father's striking merely her gentleman, but, now that he has cursed her, has absolutely nothing personal to say, merely turning to execute the next item of business, suggests a most perverse psychology: her response runs contrary to stimulus. Duthie, by adopting the Q-only lines in the third scene and the F-only lines in this scene, renders her continually volatile. He thus is true neither to the slow build in F nor to the 'manic depressive' alternation of Q.[20]

In the last variant to consider here, her address to Oswald, she refers to her 'particular feares' in Q but her 'particular feare' in F. These differences are minute but not necessarily trivial; like so many of the small details accumulated in this differential reading, they are consistent with Gonerill's self-control and the specificity of her grievance with her father in *The Tragedie*, and with Gonorill's general wildness in *The Historie*.

The next major variants arise in the scene in which the united sisters strip Lear of his retainers. We first hear of Gonorill and Gonerill from her sister; she counsels Lear to be patient and think better of his eldest daughter. In both versions Regan has received her sister's letter informing her, as Regan says, of the 'ryotous knights' (D4^v; TLN 1033; 2.1.94), on which advice she decided not to be at home if they came to sojourn with her. She has also read Lear's letter. As we have read neither, we have no reason to account Regan's behaviour as sinister *per se* in either text. Certainly in F she can scarcely be seen as a hypocrite in this particular instance, for she reveals to Lear (in F only) that she knows Gonerill 'restrained the Riots' of his followers (F1; TLN 1416–25; 2.4.138–46).

QUARTO:

> *Reg.* I pray fir take patience, I haue hope
> You leffe know how to value her defert,
> Then fhe to flacke her dutie.
> *Lear.* My curffes on her.

FOLIO:

> *Reg.* I pray you Sir, take patience, I haue hope
> You leffe know how to value her defert,
> Then fhe to fcant her dutie.
> *Lear.* Say? How is that?
> *Reg.* I cannot thinke my Sifter in the leaft
> Would faile her Obligation. If Sir perchance
> She haue reftrained the Riots of your Followres,
> 'Tis on fuch ground, and to fuch wholefome end,
> As cleeres her from all blame.
> *Lear.* My curles on her.

Now, neither Q nor F makes me think that I could ever see behind Regan's politic mask (as I feel I do behind Gonorill's in the Q-only lines in the third scene); but Regan's second F speech mitigates the bluntness of the first (her only one in Q), and so may render us less sympathetic to Lear's repetition of his curse on Gonerill, which it postpones.

When eventually Goneril enters, the texts vary strikingly. At the beginning and end of both the following quotations Lear demands to know who stocked his servant, as he has twice earlier in the scene (E3ᵛ, F1ᵛ; TLN 1286–8, 1467; 2.4.11–12, 182). And after Gonerill's entrance in F (in the middle of the excerpt), he asks again. But in Q the diction of the speech is different, and it is spoken by Gonorill, not by her father (F1ᵛ; TLN 1467–90; 2.4.182–98).[21]

QUARTO:

Lear. Who put my man i'th ſtockes ?
Duke. What trumpets that ?   *Enter Steward.*
Reg. I know t my ſiſters, this approues her letters,
That ſhe would ſoone be here,is your Lady come ?
L. ir. Th·s is a ſlaue, whoſe eaſie borrowed pride
Dwels in the fickle grace of her , a follows,
Out varlet, from my ſight.
Duke. What meanes your Grace ?   *Enter Gon.*
Gon. Who ſtruck my ſeruant, *Regan* I haue good hope
Thou didſt not know ant.
Lear. Who comes here ? O heauens !
If you doe loue old men, if you ſweet ſway allow
Obedience, if your ſelues are old,make it your cauſe,
Send downe and take my part,
Art not aſham'd to looke vpon this beard?
O *Regan* wilt thou take her by the hand ?
Gon. Why not by the hand ſir,how haue I offended?
Als not offence that indiſcretion finds,
And dotage rearmes ſo.
Lear. O ſides you are too tough,
Will you yet hold ? how came my man it'h ſtockes ?

FOLIO:

Lear. Who put my man i'th'Stockes ?
          Enter Steward.|
Corn. What Trumpet's that ?.
Reg. I know't,my Siſters : this approues her Letter,
That ſhe would ſoone be heere. Is your Lady come ?

Lear. This is a Slaue, whofe eafie borrowed pride
Dwels in the fickly grace of her he followes.
Out Varlet, fromimy fight.
   Corn. What meanes your Grace?
          Enter Gonerill.
   *Lear.*Who ftockt my Seruant? *Regan,*I haue good hope
Thou did'ft not know on't.
Who comes here ? O Heauens !
If you do loue old men , if your fweet fway
Allow Obedience ; if you your felues are old,
Make it your caufe : Send downe,and take my part.
Art not afham'd to looke vpon this Beard ?
O *Regan,* will you take her by the hand ?
   Gon. Why not by'th'hand Sir? How haue I offended?
All's not offence that indifcretion findes,
And dotage termes fo.
   Lear. O fides, you are too tough !
Will you yet hold ?
How came my man i'th'Stockes ?

In *The Historie* Gonorill strides in on the offensive, not even greeting her father, but demanding explanation of the wrong done her. She is harping on the same theme as in the third scene, the affront to her retinue. When in Q Ragan takes her sister's hand, she is seen by Lear, who thous her, and perhaps by us, to close ranks aggressively with a co-aggressor. In F, however, Gonerill, silent, may seem, by virtue of Lear's attempt at shaming her, to enter on the defensive; and we can thus easily read Regan as coming impulsively to her embattled sister's aid. Lear's respect for Regan seems to continue, as he yous her. The subsequent lines, leading up to Lear's distracted exit for the heath and the storm, are not themselves greatly differentiated. But these contrasting lines that initiate that confrontation can strongly swing our sympathies and horrors in different directions as we head into it. My main point is simply that F, by not having Gonerill press again the matter of her servant, by having Lear harp again and again on his servant, and by having Gonerill take Lear's abuse silently, argues her restraint relative to Gonorill's, in a way consonant with the earlier differential readings.

Duthie regards Q as corrupt here. His allegation of scribal error is one of his most convoluted and fantastic editorial flights, and makes interesting reading (in endnote) against the simple, contrasting drama of the Q and F lines.[22]

The next variant concerns Lear on the heath; he arraigns his elder daughters – but only in the mad trial scene unique to Q (G3ᵛ–G4; 3.6.17–56). Its fantastic visions of Gonorill – as a 'ioyne stoole' and as one who 'kickt the poore king her father' – offer us at this point a mad reminder (in Q only) of her agency in driving her father to distraction. After this, both Q and F mention Regan, and in the context of an anatomy of her heart. In Q we can see the initial trial metaphor as modulating into one of dissection; but I suspect most readers of Q (or of the conflation) see the anatomy as a continuation of the trial; in F, however, it cannot be a metaphor of trial, and must be taken literally. Perhaps to the reader of F the anatomical violence against Regan at this point becomes paired with the memory of Lear's curse of Gonerill in the fourth scene, when he invoked Nature to dry up her organs of increase. But in Q we link the anatomy of Ragan most readily with the immediately preceding arraignment of her sister. These different interpretative strategies can be spelled out theoretically: in the context of non-parallel portions of Q and F, portions of Q and F that do run parallel need not have the same meaning. This, I think, is the critical principle that invalidates Duthie's argument, widely echoed since by conflationists, that F is somehow incoherent because its 'omission' of the trial scene 'renders pointless the words "Then let them Anatomize *Regan:*" which it retains at III vi 74' (p. 8). Such theoretical questions of literary interpretation aside, the main points for this analysis are clear. Q adds to our stock of extreme pictures of Gonorill already culled from differential reading, and reminds us at the depths of Lear's madness of her responsibility. But F ignores Gonerill here to dwell on her sister, as if to give Regan her turn for Lear's wrath. Differential reading continues our sense that F presents a relatively less extreme picture of Gonerill's behaviour and of her perception by others than does Q.

I said 'relatively less extreme', as it would be perverse to hide the fact that by this point in the play any hope we might have had in Gonerill as a force for moderation has blown away in the great storm that closes Act Two. It is true that she does not, like her sister, participate in the actual blinding of Gloucester (3.7), but her grimly prophetic (or instigating) 'Plucke out his eyes' (G4ᵛ; TLN 2064; 3.7.5) brands her.

The next scene of strongly differentiated dialogue concerning Goneril, from the Q version of which the title of this essay is drawn, opens with a further damning revelation – of her adultery with the Bastard. Upon the exit of her lover and entrance of her husband, the two texts diverge widely. In Q Albany directs at his wife some thirty lines of thrilling denunciation not found in F (H3^v–H4; TLN 2301–13; 4.2.29–71).[23]

QUARTO:

Alb. O *Gonoril*,you are not worth the duſt which the
Blowes in your face,I feare your diſpoſition
That nature which contemnes ith origin
Cannot be bordered certaine in it ſelfe,
She that her ſelfe will ſliuer and disbranch
From her materiall ſap, perforce muſt wither,
And come to deadly vſe.
  Gon. No more, the text is foolish.
  Alb. Wiſedome and goodnes,to the vild ſeeme vild,
Filths ſauor but themſelues, what haue you done ?
Tigers, not daughters, what haue you perform'd ?
A father,and a gracious aged man

                                           Whoſe

The Hiſtorie of King Lear.

Whoſe reuerence euen the head-lugd beare would lick.
Moſt barbarous, moſt degenerate haue you madded,
Could my good brother ſuffer you to doe it?
A man, a Prince, by him ſo benifited,
If that the heauens doe not their viſible ſpirits (come
Send quickly downe to tame this vild offences,it will
Humanity muſt perforce pray on it ſelf like monſters of
  Gon. Milke liuerd man   (the deepe.
That beareſt a cheeke for bloes, a head for wrongs,
Who haſt not in thy browes an eye deſeruing thine honour,
From thy ſuffering,that not know'ſt, foolsdo thoſe vilains pitty
Who are puniſht ere they haue done their miſchiefe,
Wher's thy drum? *France* ſpreds his banners in our noyſeles land,
With plumed helme, thy ſtate begins thereat
Whil'ſt thou a morall foole ſits ſtill and cries
Alack why does he ſo ?
  Alb. See thy ſelfe deuill, proper deformity ſhewes not in the
fiend, ſo horrid as in woman.
  Gon. O vaine foole!
  Alb. Thou changed, and ſelfe-couerd thing for ſhame
Be-monſter not thy feature, wer't my fitnes
To let theſe hands obay my bloud,

They are apt enough to diflecate and teare
Thy flefh and bones, how ere thou art a fiend,
A womans fhape doth fhield thee.

 Gon. Marry your manhood mew---

 Alb. What newes.   *Enter a Gentleman.*

 Gent. O my good Lord the Duke of *Cornwals* dead, flaine by

FOLIO:

 Alb. Oh *Gonerill,*

You are not worth the duft which the rude winde
Blowes in your face.

 Gon. Milke-Liver'd man,
That bear'ft a cheeke for blowes, a head for wrongs,
Who haft not in thy browes an eye-difcerning
Thine Honor, from thy fuffering.

 Alb. See thy felfe divell:
Proper deformitie feemes not in the Fiend
So horrid as in woman.

 Gon. Oh vaine Foole.

    Enter a Meffenger.

 Mef. Oh my good Lord, the Duke of *Cornwals* dead,

Albany's speeches in Q form an impassioned catalogue of the Duchess's sins, and signal a major turn in the moral dynamic of *The Historie.* Lear, of course, has himself been able to anatomize his daughter's sins, but Gonorill's husband is a more impartial (and sane) spokesman than her father. Curiously the scene is written so as to inform us of Gonorill's adultery immediately before Albany's tirade; this juxtaposition drives home all the more strongly Albany's impartiality. If he knew of the adultery he would have the greatest personal reason to speak to her in the tone he now adopts, Albany's condemnation of her, however, is not as a husband, but as a moral man – and hence her pejorative 'morall foole'. She joins this barb to a taunt against his manhood and his patriotism, for French troops are landed. Her criticism sticks, of course (though it hardly justifies her savage reaction to Gloucester's 'treason'). In any case, Q documents the rising of moral indignation in Albany at this point as a deeply true but deeply non-practical response. Albany's truth may remind us somewhat of the wildly idealistic truth-telling of Cordelia or Kent. Moreover, we see him from some ironic distance, no matter how strongly we yearn for his attack: for he does not seem to see the horns on his own head. What a contrast is *The Tragedie*. The short exchange between Gonerill and Albany barely hints his future strength. We see his indignation aroused, but at what? He has relatively so little to say about her, before the messenger's entrance and his wife cut him off, that the audience's great relief in Q to find her monstrosity named can find no parallel in F, just as her arraignment in the mad trial found no parallel in F. He is so undefined by his own words here that our dominant sense of him may tend towards pity, as his cuckoldry bulks proportionately larger than it does in Q. Thus, through its first two acts, F seems to retard both the coming of our convictions of Gonerill's evil, and, thereafter, through the present scene, the cry of indignation against her; but Q speeds both along. As I commented at the end of discussion of the first scene, so in this present scene F offers a greater vision of moral ambiguity than does Q, and this subtlety does not survive conflation. The conflated version absorbs the Q-only lines into F and thus forces a turning of the moral tide before that text, in its own integrity, has revealed it. F continues to present relatively less extreme and irrational behaviour by Gonerill and perceptions of her than does Q.[24]

The variants do not stop here. From this point to the end of the play one's impression of Gonerill is that she is ever more self-possessed than her Quarto counterpart, but that her comparable perversity is paradoxically both more chilling and theatrically attractive – as was Edmund's – by virtue of wit. This element of Gonerill's characterization emerges quite late. When in 1.2.134 the Bastard wittily characterized his brother's approach – 'out hee comes like the Catastrophe of the old Co-|medy' (C2ᵛ; TLN 464) – he seemed almost to be a spectator of the play, like ourselves, rather than merely a character in it. So Gonerill's Folio-only line, 'An enterlude' (TLN 3035; 5.3.89), in which she tries to laugh off the allegation of adultery in Albany's speech to Regan, suggests a comparable (though less successful) manipulation of her opponent, by pretending that she is real, but he fictitious. Here she interrupts her husband (TLN 3033–6; 5.3.88–90):

> If you will marry, make your loues to me,
> My Lady is bespoke.
>   *Gon.* An enterlude.
>   *Alb.* Thou art armed *Glester*,

By contrast, Gonorill's silence in the Quarto (L1; 5.3.88–90) –

> If you will mary, make your loue to me,
> My Lady is befpoke, thou art arm'd *Glofter*,

– eloquently points up her vulnerability, and even perhaps her being wounded by her husband's charge. (I argued above in discussion of 1.4 that Gonorill's dark silence in response to her father's curse showed how deeply he had affected her.) Ironically, it is Gonorill's speaking here in 5.1, two scenes earlier, that reveals (as did her Quarto-only lines in 1.3) her continuing inner turmoil and anxiety in *The Historie* (K3; 5.1.16–20).

> *Baft.* Feare me not, fhee and the Duke her husband.
> *Enter Albany and Gonorill with troupes,*
> *Goxo.* I had rather loofe the battaile, then that fifter fhould loofen him and mee.
> *Alb.* Our very louing fifter well be-met

Her silence in F at this point (TLN 2863–5; 5.1.16–20)

> *Baft.* Feare not, fhe and the Duke her husband.
> *Enter with Drum and Colours, Albany, Gonerill, Soldiers.*
> *Alb.* Our very louing Sifter, well be-met :

– allows us to fix the strong image we have developed of her to the end of 4.2 in that version of the play, where she was unscathed by Albany's minimal challenge to her.

In the Folio, at 5.3 again, her wit reappears in variants in this aside; Q reads as mere villainy (L1; 5.3.95–6):

> *Reg.* Sicke, ô ficke.
> *Gon.* If not, ile nere truft poyfon.

By contrast, F reads as a villainous joke (TLN 3043–4; 5.3.95–6) –

> *Reg.* Sicke, O ficke.
> *Gon.* If not, Ile nere truft medicine.

– for 'medicine' was (and is) both a synonym and an antonym of 'poyson'. The full wit of her diction in F is to be detected by contrasting not merely Q with F 5.3, but also QF 5.3 with QF 4.7. For the word 'medicine' occurs there in its only other use in *Lear*, when

Cordelia exhorts Restoration to hang its medicine on her lips, and to
let her kiss repair the violent harms her sisters had made in Lear's
reverence (K2; TLN 2776–9; 4.7.25–8). Gonerill's ambiguous 'medicine' in F 5.3 is the middle ground, in *The Tragedie* only, that
connects the lips of restoration and the swollen lips of the corpse Lear
exclaims upon as he dies. Of course, Gonerill's wit here makes its
impact upon the audience in ways we cannot attribute to her intent, as
she did not hear Cordelia's reference to medicine, and will not live to
see her dead; but we in the audience hear the echo, and sound its
ironic depths. As differential reading of her speech in 5.3 leads us to
see the sophisticated ambiguity of her *Tragedie*-only diction, the wit
seems to redound (irrationally) to her credit.

Whether or not we detect an infusion of wit in Gonerill's character
at the end of *The Tragedie*, there is a very clear differentiation of
Gonorill and Gonerill around her final exit. This exit is implicated in
a variant, like that discussed in 2.4.188, which is made complex by
virtue of differently assigned speeches (L2; TLN 3112–20).[27]

QUARTO:

Alb. Stop your mouth dame, or with this paper shall I stople
it, thou worse then any thing, reade thine owne euill, nay no
tearing Lady, I perceiue you know't.   (me for't.
Gon. Say if I do, the lawes are mine not thine, who shal arraine
Alb. Most monstrous know'st thou this paper?
Gon. Aske me not what I know.   *Exit. Gonorill.*
Alb. Go after her, shee's desperate, gouerne her.

FOLIO:

Alb. Shut your mouth Dame,
Or with this paper shall I stop it : hold Sir,
Thou worse then any name, reade thine owne euill :
No tearing Lady, I perceiue you know it.
Gon. Say if I do, the Lawes are mine not thine,
Who can araigne me for't ?   *Exit.*
Alb. Most monstrous! O, know'st thou this paper?
Bast. Aske me not what I know.
Alb. Go after her, she's desperate, gouerne her.

In F, it is true, Gonerill leaves the stage challenged, but she is in a
position of strength, and asserts that she is above the law – even as
her dismissive 'An enterlude' asserted that she was real while her

husband was role-playing in a farce. Exactly what Gonerill will do after her exit eventually proves pitiful, of course; but at the moment the unknown is part of her strength. Seemingly about her defence, she exits with threats and taunts; she is still the owner of her face. Only when her suicide is announced, and the 'trifle' of her corpse revealed, do we fathom her bluff. In Q, however, Gonorill leaves the stage already defeated and shamefaced. Having claimed at first to stand above the law, she ultimately implies her guilt; not denying her husband's charge, she attempts merely to suppress it and run away from it. Her exit in defeat and her suicide, when it is revealed, do not contradict each other, as they do in *The Tragedie*.

What functions as Gonorill's weak exit line in Q ('Aske me not what I know.') is assigned to the Bastard in F, where, ironically, it serves him as a strong line; for all of what he knows (and we know too) counterpoises the mere carnal knowledge that weighs so heavily in Albany's scale of justice. It is the carnage that Edmund knows, that great thing of Albany forgot – the fate of Cordelia and Lear, whom Gonerill's accomplice in the ranks of death has sent to execution. The different speech assignments give us two very strong impressions of evil in F; two weaker ones in Q.

But enough. As Goneril's variants impinge on those of her husband and her lover, and as Q and F seem to be offering us distinct dramatic and moral visions, analysis of Goneril's variants in isolation becomes less compelling. Anyway, myopia yields to strabismus.

III

The essay began by questioning abstractly the editorial tendency to exalt by debasing – to enlarge its own freedoms at the expense of the evidence; to make a problem, in the case of *Lear* – and not of *Lear* alone – of textual variation. But the proof of such scepticism has to come – if it does come for the reader – in the close readings of my second section. Fraught with both the dead and the living weight of textual tradition, we need to ask rigorously how and what we read – I mean *exactly*. What are the physical objects – never mind the abstraction 'text' – that one's eyes perceive? Are we to look as low as a ligature, are we to see with our ears? And how is our awareness to arise from this basis?

Of course, I did not look at every variant relating to Goneril – this long paper is far too short for that; the reader will have to determine whether my selection has been fair. As the evidence seemed to point away from random differentiation, however, I saw growing something of great constancy, and thought to provide Theseus with the rational argument he may need. As the integral calculus for all the differentiation should have become apparent as I went along, I will not repeat here what separates Gonorill and Gonerill. Moreover, as the other characters we measure them against are also in flux, the attempt at a final statement is premature. But I will give a hard sell for the method that raised the question. Editors have had something of a free hand with *Lear* because they have controlled access to the rare evidence through their collations. But seeing is believing. Photography, by holding the mirror up to the copy-text, has ended their status as an elite, and a more appropriate role for them now is as commentators on the icon of the text rather than as atomizers of it, and as manipulators of its fragments.

By manipulating text, the editorial tradition has put supposed essence before known existences. When taste is the editors' motive, I cannot object to improving Shakespeare – if only the editors would state before their own names on the title pages (as I recently saw brazenly trumpeted in an eighteenth-century edition) 'SHAKESPEARE *as adapted for the stage by . . .*'. But when the historicism of the eighteenth, nineteenth, and twentieth centuries culminates in the same *Lear* as that of the tradition of taste, we are in the sleep of a settled idea, one that has enslaved rather than saved the phenomena. In so doing, the tradition may be said to have created great, but not likely Shakespearian, plays. By conflating contents, it has neglected form. If the difference between Q and F is the result of authorial revision, then the neglect of form for content is like the spurning of architecture for bricklaying. And if the difference stems from an adapter who is not Shakespeare, then the time has come to celebrate his artistic abilities, and not to meld them with another author's.

The editorial *Lear* of tradition has grown in Duthie's edition to be complexly simplistic: complex in the inordinate number of epicycles it requires to pull the evidences into the orbit of Truth; simplistic in its faith that this is the way of Art. As Blake says in his 'Proverbs of Hell' (*The Marriage of Heaven and Hell*, 10):

Improvent makes strait roads, but the crooked roads without Improvement, are roads of Genius.

NOTES

1. The Master Mistris of my passion is Rosalie Colie, to whose memory I dedicate this essay.

    Plato's admonition to students of astronomy 'to save the phenomena' is quoted from Simplicius's commentary on Aristotle's *de caelo* 492.30; his authority is Sosigenes, who quotes Eudemus (see also 488.23–4 and 493.3–4). My thanks to Plato scholar/businessman Ken Henwood for these references.

    I wish to thank Erindale College and the University of Toronto for granting me research leave in 1980/81 to work on problems of Shakespeare's text, and also the Social Sciences and Humanities Research Council of Canada for its research support during the leave.

2. Duthie later retracted this explanation: see Stanley Wells's discussion above (p. 12).

3. For when such an F reading differs from Q's, there is a strong presumption that it derives from the manuscript. But, of course, a divergent F reading can also derive from lapse or sophistication by scribe or by compositor; and for this reason the corollary cannot issue in practical editorial rules for handling specific cruxes. Its immediate practical consequence, however, is to defame Q, and to encourage editorial alteration of text.

4. The stemma on the left has actually been advanced (in a rather more complicated form) in Stone's *Textual History*: see Taylor's discussion below (p. 360).

5. Duthie faces the obvious possibility (a position, in fact, taken by Doran) as follows: 'I do not believe that Q represents a Shakespearian first draft and F a Shakespearian revision,' adding in a footnote, 'Unless Shakespeare was concerned in the cutting which produced the F abridgement. But even if he was (and he may not have been) it cannot in my opinion be maintained that he made any revisions apart from the cutting' (p. 21).

6. Photo-quotes of F are taken from the Yale facsimile, eds. Helge Kökeritz and Charles Tyler Prouty (New Haven, 1974). No press-variants are known in any of the F passages quoted; known press variants in Q will be detailed in the notes, where relevant. As the rules which form a conspicuous feature of the F page (see the photo-quote on p. 173) are not under discussion in this essay, they have for the most part been arbitrarily deleted.

7. Similarly, when Duthie quotes extensive parallel passages from Q and F (pp. 32–44), he assigns no line numbers to the Q passages; but he does assign line numbers from his own edition to the F passages, with which, by virtue of the editorial relineation appropriate for an X text, they do not always correspond.

8. I have treated ligatures and other typographic details generally in 'Spellbound: Typography and the Concept of Old-Spelling Editions', *Renaissance and Reformation/Renaissance et Réforme*, NS, 3 (1979), pp. 50–65. Application of ligatures specifically to literary interpretation can be found in my 'Unemending Shakespeare's Sonnet 111', *Studies in English Literature*, 21 (1981), 75–96.

9. Joseph Moxon's illustration of the lay in 1683 is the earliest English example. For a reproduction see my 'Unemending Shakespeare's Sonnet 111', p. 84.

10. The authorities on this aspect of contemporary pronunciation are Helge Kökeritz, *Shakespeare's Pronunciation* (New Haven and London, 1953), pp. 307–9; E. J. Dobson, *English Pronunciation 1500–1700*, 2 vols. (second edn., Oxford, 1968), II, 991–2; Fausto Cercignani, *Shakespeare's Works and Elizabethan Pronunciation* (Oxford, 1981), pp. 332–6. The later work is less confident than Kökeritz of the wide distribution of loss of prevocalic *h* in stressed syllables.

11. We can also look with our eyes, or at least our minds' eyes; for in contemporary hands, especially in mixed secretarial and italic, there may be granted the

possibility of confusion of letter shapes. R. B. McKerrow notes in his discussion of minuscules that the secretarial h with an unusual clockwise lower curve 'may . . . be not unlike a rather wide Italian ʃ' (*An Introduction to Bibliography for Literary Students* (Oxford, 1927), p. 347). But if his observation allows for the possibility of graphic confusability of 'hit' and 'sit' in manuscript, it does not inform us which must be the right and which the wrong version – or, indeed, whether there need be only one right version. Surely, if any of the hands involved in the transmission of the F text prior to its appearance in print offers confusion of s and h, as the general editorial rejection of 'sit' implies, then editors are obliged to scour the text for all such s/h cruxes before deciding conveniently in this instance. Not to do so is to edit impressionistically.

Another authority, W. S. B. Buck, agrees with McKerrow, but notes that secretarial h can also be confused with e, f, l, and g; and that secretarial f can be confused with f, j, and st (see his 'Table of Confusibilia', in *Examples of Handwriting: 1551–1650* (Chichester, 1973), pp. 66–8). Buck thus opens the door to speculation that 'hit' and 'sit' are confusable not only with each other, but also with 'fit'. Now 'fit' was one of the readings that just loomed before us out of the darkness of the Renaissance printing house, as it could easily be mis-set as 'sit' by virtue of error of case. It is, moreover, a literarily defensible reading. As soon as editors reject the reading of the respected Folio, then (as editors like Duthie, who trust in the badness of the quarto, continually argue) they are under no compulsion to discover right readings in the doubted quarto. Hence, 'fit' emerges as a reading as good as either 'sit' or 'hit' – if the fact of the variance of Q and F is taken to indicate corruption of F. Editorial argument that appeals to precise features of lost manuscripts inevitably is a two-edged sword.

12. Not all editors hide the influence of production on their texts. Kenneth Muir, the new Arden editor, reveals, for example, that his text is a revision of one he used in an amateur production before he became an editor of the play for publication (rev. edn., 1972, p. ix).

13. For the limits on *OED*'s reliability in identifying first usages see Jürgen Schäfer's *Documentation in the O.E.D.: Shakespeare and Nashe as Test Cases* (Oxford, 1980).

14. Most editors adopt F as their basic text, and all but six of the fifty editors who had access to Q – I am therefore excluding Rowe – whose editions are collated in the Furness Variorum edition, chose the Q reading here (Philadelphia, 1880; repr. New York, 1963, p. 41). The tradition also has a theatrical basis. The Smock Alley prompt-book known as 'Lear 1' (in Charles H. Shattuck, *The Shakespeare Promptbooks*, Urbana and London, 1965, p. 206), and which he dates from the 1670s, and therefore *before the editorial tradition of conflation*, is a Third Folio that has been annotated with many Q readings, especially early in the text. It too deletes 'Sit' and substitutes 'hit'. (It does not, however, insert the 'not' from Q in Gonerill's 'the obser-/vation we have made of it hath been little'.) In her discussion of this crux Alice Walker begins, 'If we reject, as of course we must, the Folio's "sit together" . . . for the quarto's "hit together" . . .' (*Textual Problems of the First Folio*, Cambridge, 1953, p. 63). Walker's theory of Q's derivation has special relevance to this paper: 'I have put forward briefly elsewhere what the evidence suggests to me: that the quarto was not based on an acting version of the play but on the foul papers and that these were surreptitiously dictated to a scribe by an actor who, for some reason we can only guess at (haste, over-confidence, laziness, inattention), relied on his memory instead of his script for dialogue with which he was familiar. The contaminating actor-reader was, I judge, a small-part actor, probably the boy who played Goneril. The scribe may have been an actor too. The memorial contamination is certainly heaviest in scenes involving both Goneril and

Regan, and it is in scenes where contamination is most marked that we must look for the actor, or actors, responsible for the quarto text' (p. 41).

15. Of course this variant might be due to compositorial error: Compositor E, who set this page of Folio *Lear*, was particularly prone to omission or addition of terminal *s*. (See Paul Werstine's discussion below, pp. 263–4).

16. Arthur Freeman, 'Inaccuracy and Castigation: The Lessons of Error', in Anne Lancashire, ed., *Editing Renaissance Dramatic Texts. English, Italian and Spanish: Papers given at the eleventh annual Conference on Editorial Problems, University of Toronto . . . 1975* (New York and London, 1976), p. 105, where Freeman cites A. S. Herbert, ed., T. H. Darlow and H. F. Moule, *Historical Catalogue of Printed Editions of the English Bible, 1525–1961* (London and New York, 1962), p. 162, and notes that a German Bible of 1731 is supposed to sanction the same licence in the seventh commandment as the 1631 English Bible; the Corinthians reading is from a Bible of 1651.

17. A word of caution. The contrasted passages could have registered as more synonymous than they do now. But they could also, I gather, have evoked the precise contrast they do for us, depending on the inflection of the respective sentences. See E. A. Abbott, *A Shakespearian Grammar*, third ed. (1870), § 1: 'Adjectives are freely used as Adverbs.' The reverse is also possible: 'It is characteristic of the unsettled nature of the Elizabethan language that, while . . . adjectives were freely used as adverbs without the termination *ly*, on the other hand *ly* was occasionally added to words from which we have rejected it' (§ 23).

18. Keats's 1804 'type' facsimile is now at Keats House, Hampstead. I discuss Keats's experience of *The Tragedie* extensively in 'UN *Editing* Shak-speare,' *Sub-Stance*, 33/34 (1982), 26–55. Keats did not, by the way, mark Gonerill's speech in 1.1 that contains the 'sit' crux.

19. For detailed discussion see Urkowitz, *Revision*, pp. 44–6.

20. W. D. Moriarty, 'The Bearing on Dramatic Sequence of the Varia in *Richard the Third* and *King Lear*', *Modern Philology*, 10 (1913), 451–71, was convinced of a 'causal relationship between the principle of dramatic sequence and the varia in . . . *King Lear*'. He held that the older Shakespeare was willing to cut characterizations of inner conflict (in Q) to expedite plot (in F). 'Two varia are produced when the folio (I, iv, 323–34) has Goneril explain to Albany instead of to her steward, as the quarto makes her in I, iii, 17–21, the pretended grounds upon which she treats her father as she does' (p. 457); and related to this, in Q 'Goneril explains to Oswald in vindictive fashion her theory of governing her father, but the folio omits this explanation and has Goneril use it expanded and more speciously stated in defending to Albany her actions toward her father' (pp. 452–3).

21. See Urkowitz, *Revision*, pp. 36–8.

22. These notes are from pp. 88 and 392–3. *Caveat scriba. Caveat lector.*

At II iv 184–5 the two texts run as follows:

Q | *Enter Gon.*
  Gon. Who struck my seruant, *Regan* I haue good hope
      Thou didst not know ant.
  Lear. Who comes here? O heauens!
F | *Enter Gonerill.*
  Lear. Who stockt my Seruant? *Regan*, I haue good hope
      Thou did'st not know on't.
      Who comes here? O Heauens!

The reconstructing actors may have given the text correctly as it appears in F. The scribe, looking over his work subsequently, may have misread his own 'stockt' as 'struck', and, remembering that Oswald had been struck, altered the speech-heading from '*Lear.*' to '*Gon.*', writing in '*Lear.*' in front of 'Who comes here? . . .' He may, going over his manuscript, have read 'stockt' correctly, but, remembering Oswald's being struck, and noticing that Goneril had just come on, he may have made the two alterations in speech-heading and dialogue on his own responsibility. Again, it is possible that the actor of Lear's part, dictating, pronounced 'stockt' as 'stuckt', that his '-t' was indistinct, that the scribe thought he was saying 'struck', took that down, and subsequently, looking over the manuscript, altered the speech-heading to conform with 'struck'. At any rate, I do not think it necessary to suppose that the reconstructing actors were responsible for the misassignation of the speech.

184 Q *Gon.* See p. 88. As regards the suggestion of misreading, it is quite
    Q struck   possible that 'stockt' was misread as 'struke' (i.e. 'struck'). Misreading of 'o' as 'r' is found elsewhere in Q – cf. III iv 6, where Q uncorr. has 'crulentious', a misreading of 'contentious' (F) (see Greg, *Variants*, p. 164). There are also examples of 'e' misread as 't': cf. III iv 115, where Q uncorr. has 'harte', Q corr. 'hare' (the compositor misread 'hare' as 'hart' and set up 'harte'), and IV ii 56, where Q uncorr. has 'noystles', Q corr. 'noyseles'. Examples of 't' misread as 'e' occur elsewhere: e.g. *Hamlet*, III ii 310, where Q2 has 'stare' for 'start', and *Othello*, I i 48, where Q1 has 'noughe' for 'nought'. Misreading of 'c' as 'u' is also possible: at I ii 130, where F reads 'my Cue', Q has 'mine', which does not make sense: this reading 'mine' may well be the result of the Q compositor having misread 'my cu' as 'myne' (cf. III iv 119, Q uncorr. 'thu', Q corr. 'the'): and if 'c' could be misread as 'n' it could also be misread as 'u', since 'n' and 'u' are frequently confused.

23. See Urkowitz, *Revision*, pp. 88–93. In the Folio, the 'seemes' in Albany's second speech agrees with the reading of the first state of Q1, which contains a number of press variants in this passage. Other variants affect the dialogue unique to Q, here reproduced in its second state. The first state reads 'it origin' for 'ith origin', 'beniflicted' for 'benifited', 'the vild' for 'this vild', 'Humanly' for 'Humanity', 'selfe' for 'self', 'know'st fools', for 'know'st, fools', 'noystles' for 'noyseles', 'slayer begin threats' for 'state begins thereat', 'Whil's' for 'Whil'st', 'horid' for 'horrid', and 'now' for 'mew'.

24. The treatment of Albany is taken up by M. Warren, 'Albany and Edgar', pp. 98–101, 105. Concerning Albany's tirade against Goneril in Act Four, Moriarty felt that 'The length of the speeches in the bombastic interchange of personality by Albany and Goneril in Act IV might indeed be considered as needlessly interfering with the rapid development of plot' ('The Bearing on Dramatic Sequence,' p. 459). The Q-only passages were 'evidently intended in the quarto version not merely to furnish mouth-filling lines, but to foreshadow the bitterness of the conflict and to prepare for Albany's final stand' (p. 460). Also, the foreshadowing of Albany's final stand against Goneril is discarded from F because it partakes 'too much of melodramatic declamation to produce the truest effect of tragedy' (p. 459).

27. See Urkowitz, *Revision*, pp. 112–14.

Revision, Adaptation, and the Fool in *King Lear*

JOHN KERRIGAN

WHEN Hamlet adapts *The Murder of Gonzago* for performance at
court, he does not subject it to a rigorous line-by-line revision.
Instead, he inserts into the old play 'a speech of some dosen lines, or
sixteene lines'[1] specially composed for the occasion. He substantially
interpolates; he does not tinker. Now while the Prince is in some ways
an atypical dramatic adapter (how many Elizabethan or Jacobean
plays were rewritten by royalty, and how many under such pressing
circumstances?), he does seem to work in a representative way. The
available evidence strongly suggests that when, in the early seventeenth century, one man of the theatre overhauled another's play, he
cut, inserted and substituted sizeable pieces of text without altering
the details of his precursor's dialogue.[2] Revising authors, by contrast,
though they sometimes worked just with large textual fractions,
tended to tinker, introducing small additions, small cuts and
indifferent single-word substitutions. A survey of rewritten plays
reveals two kinds of textual variation then, one rarely authorial in
origin, the other characteristically so. If *King Lear* is considered with
these categories in mind, its status quickly becomes clear: the
configuration of Q-F variants is such that the play falls firmly into the
category of authorial revision. But the argument cannot stop there:
external evidence needs internal support; textual analysis, its resolution in literary criticism. So, after discussing some dramatic
adaptations (works rewritten without authorial assistance) and some
revisions (texts reorganized by authors), this essay examines the role
of the Fool in Q and F *King Lear*.

I

In 1602, Thomas Pavier published a quarto entitled: 'The Spanish
Tragedie . . . Newly corrected, amended, and enlarged with new
additions of the Painters part, and others, as it hath of late been diuers
times acted.'[3] Whether or not the five passages printed for the first

time in Pavier's quarto[4] were composed by Ben Jonson, there can be little doubt that they were not penned by Kyd. The received view of the 1602 text – that it represents an adaptation of Kyd's original made in the late 1590s or early 1600s at Henslowe's behest – seems well-founded. (See Appendix I.) Significantly, Pavier's 'new additions' are substantial: 54, 10, 45, 185, and 49 lines in length. In scale, they resemble Hamlet's insertion in *The Mousetrap*. They are also discrete. Like the Prince, the adapter has not tinkered. It is true that Pavier's text sometimes strays from its basic copy (White's edition of 1599), but all the minor 1602 variants are explicable under the rubric 'Newly corrected, amended'. As Philip Edwards points out in his careful edition of the play, Pavier's text has undergone 'meagre and desultory "editing"'.[5] It includes four new stage directions;[6] but anyone who had seen the play in performance could have introduced them. It corrects some corruptions; but only obvious ones (while new errors are perpetrated).[7] It inverts two lines originally printed in the wrong order;[8] but, again, the change was easily made. Only once, it seems, did the adapter engage directly with Kyd's dialogue; and his engagement here was – to be paradoxical – distinctly detached. The fifth 'addition' (the one in which Hieronimo justifies his massacre to the Spanish court) is not, strictly speaking, an addition. It is a substitution.[9] The adapter has cut 23 lines from Kyd's dialogue, replacing them with 38 lines of his own. However, in the middle of the substitution, two pieces of original text (4 and 7 lines long), put into reverse order, recur. The most striking thing about this transferred material is its integrity. There are only two verbal changes – one quite possibly scribal or compositorial – in the 11 lines.[10] Evidently the adapter was content to appropriate Kyd's poetry, but not (whether from indifference or out of respect) to rewrite it.

Adaptation of the same kind can be discerned in the B-text of *Doctor Faustus*, though it should be conceded at once that the picture has been blurred there by corruption. It used to be thought that while the A-text of Marlowe's tragedy was published before the B (in 1604 rather than 1616) it nevertheless derived from it, and that the 'adicyones in docter fostes' prepared for Henslowe by William Birde and Samuel Rowley in 1602 had been lost for ever.[11] But the one-text theory has been discredited, and most Marlowe scholars now believe that B differs from A largely by virtue of its inclusion of the Birde-Rowley 'adicyones'.[12] Obviously, one consequence of the new view of *Doctor Faustus* is that any A-B divergence previously explained by cutting or corruption must now be considered, at least potentially, the product of rewriting. In practice, however, there is so much evidence of imperfection within each text (A, probably memorially contaminated, has certainly been trimmed for performance, while B has been censored, badly transcribed and infected by the 1611 edition of A) that most A-B variants immediately declare themselves the products of accumulated error.

The material which can be most securely ascribed to Birde and Rowley comes in eight passages unique to the B text.[13] Each 'new Addition' (to quote the title-page of the 1619 reprint of B) is substantial, the longest being 214 lines and the shortest – part of a larger movement of revision – 5. Similarly substantial, though not equally so, are the three B omissions which seem to stem from adapters' cuts.[14] Here we are dealing with losses of 14, 18, and 10 lines. The origin of a ninth piece of B-unique text – the short scene in which the Scholars find the hero's 'mangled limbs' (B2093–2112) – has been much disputed. It may be reinstated A material; or it may be an adapters' interpolation. I suspect the latter, but no conclusion is necessary here. The scene may have been excised in the theatre during the 1590s, or it may have been inserted in 1602; either way, its presence in B helps support the claim that non-authorial adapters worked with large units of text.

When Birde and Rowley recast old actions in new words they habitually operated at a great remove from the original dialogue. Their independence is most apparent at B1812–29, where the Old Man has a speech which bears absolutely no resemblance (even allowing for memorial contamination in A)[15] to its 1604 equivalent; but a similar degree of detachment is almost invariable with B substitutions.[16] Greg is a useful witness here because he lists, in support of his one-text theory, every conceivable verbal link between A and B. Looking at his apparatus for those parts of the tragedy in which the texts run apart but in parallel, one is struck by the dearth of echoes. Evidently, Birde and Rowley were sometimes influenced by the wording of the play which lies behind A; but only incidentally, while preparing a distinct (and inferior) version of its comic events. There seem to be only four points at which indisputably adapted material adheres to A.[17] At B1538–42, in the middle of a 21-line substitution, 5 lines of the old play turn up, varying from A by the narrow margin of 'sir', 'O', and 'ride him'. Once allowances have been made for memorial contamination in A and for scribal/compositorial error in both texts, comparison with the fifth 'addition' to *The Spanish Tragedy* becomes appropriate. What we find here at B1538–42 is a second example of non-authorial material engorging original lines in a virtually – perhaps wholly – unaltered form. The same thing happens at B1802–11, in the Scholars' vision of Helen. There, the first, second, sixth, ninth, and tenth lines (with two verbal changes, an inversion and a plural made singular) of A1291–1300 are incorporated. And, finally, at B1160–2 (in the heart of the second Robin-Rafe/Dick scene) and B1356–61 (where Faustus unhorns Benvolio), 3 and 6 lines of A recur, with a scattering of changes easily explicable by A and B error.

Can we be sure that such small changes do not derive from tinkering by Birde and Rowley? Not quite; but we can show that, since many of the minor A-B variants which fatten the collations of modern editions of *Doctor Faustus* cannot derive from adaptation, and since none must, it would be perverse to insist that more than a few do. In Appendix II, I take, as a hard case, Faustus's first soliloquy, arguing that nothing between B30 and B89 need derive from Birde and Rowley's 1602 adaptation. To carry the same point for the whole play, each minor A-B variant would have to be considered in detail; but I hope that the discussion of the soliloquy shows how Birde and Rowley can – as a rule – be absolved of responsibility for small A-B divergences without the postulation of an unreasonably large number of sources of textual error, and (which is more to the point) without the postulation of more sources of error than are necessary to account for self-evident corruption within each text.

In the British Library there is a marked-up first quarto of Sharpham's tragicomedy *The Fleire*[18] which shows us, with all the casual immediacy of pen-strokes across paper (see illustrations 1–3), a Jacobean or Caroline adapter at work. (See Appendix III.) To judge from his extensive cuts and economies, this adapter was preparing Sharpham's play for performance by a small company as part of a double-bill.[19] Perhaps a provincial tour prompted his work.[20] Certainly, special circumstances of some sort lie behind the adaptation. Because of this, it would be illegitimate to compare the adapted *Fleire* directly with the 1602 *Spanish Tragedy* or B *Doctor Faustus*, reworked in what seems to be the usual way, under few restrictions, with a drift towards expansion. Nevertheless, the British Library quarto is exceedingly useful at this point in the argument, for beleue this nowe?

Kni. I hope thee doth not,

Fle. No. no. no.

Gull. 1/2e: Come *Flair* shall we see thy Ladies?

Fle. I, I, loe, whose within there

Enter Seruingman.

Sern. What would you haue maister *Flein?*

Fle. Prethe shewe these Gentlemen vp into the great
Chamber, and giue my Ladies notice of their being there,
I haue a little businesse my Lord's, Heele conduct yes,
ye shall finde a couple of your acquaintance there.

Exeunt: maner Fleir.

Could I but worke Lord *Piso,* and my eldest daughter, to
make am both affect and loue each other, that marriage
might vnite their hearts togither: O then there were al-
fured hope wee might redeeme our honours lost, and
regaine our right in *Florence.* And for this Knight
though hee bee poore, yet would hee married were vnto
Felina.

For of a louing husbands awfull eye,
Sets right the womans steps that went awrie.
Heauen I know has grace ynough in store,
To make most chaste, a most lasciuious whore.

Enter the two wenches in boyes apparell.

How now? who haue we here a couple of footmen?

Sm. You see sir, we are not a horsbacke.

Fle. How eno ve my little fire-workes of witte? what?
flashes and flames? tell me true, were you neuer Vshers to
some great mans Coach-mares? did you neuer run bare
before them?

Nan, Neuer we fir.

Fle. Whither are you going?

Suf. Sir, we want a seruice, and are going to get a Ma-
fter.

Fr. Come, come Ile preferre you both, thou shalt serue
a Countrey-man of mine, hees going to trauaile; shalt
goe

E 2

---

which like to lightning appeares, and vanisheth ere one
can say tis come: but then repentance thicks close, There
was a fellow with one of my Ladies this morning, and the
poore slaue has but seauen shillings a weeke boord wages,
and yet he has giuen fixe can't for a bit of extraordinarye
flesh, well: God giue him the grace to pray, for a mustfast.
I askt the hot slaue why a did not marrie since a could not
bridle his lust? and a told me a had rather fal into the Surgions mercy, then the worldes beggery; well I see it cannot be denide, mercinarie women are necessarie members:
they plucke downe the pride of the flesh, yet are not proud
themselues, for their be as familiar with the men as with
the Masters. They doe as many good deedes as some Fryers
that puts one to penance for his sinnes, they put twentie
to painesthe out of charitie fends one to the Hospital once
a yeare, they send twentie to the Surgions once a month.
Say he bids men repent, they make am repent, yet for all
this some wil call am damn'd Puncks: well, if they bee
damn'd, theile not be damn'd *gratis* like your yong coistrie
Gentlemen, nor in hugger mugger like your Citizens
wife with her Prentise. They can practise with our an o-
uer fee: they scorne to haue a Suburbian Bawd lend am a
Taffaty gown, & they (like your common Players) let men
come in for two pence a peece, and yet themselues to haue
but the tenth penny, like the tenth Pigge, yet faith
the trade is a good trade: They for fweare not themselues,
in commendation of their wares, as your common Tradef-
men doe, swearing they cannot afford it at the price. They
are no prouerb breakers: beware the buyer say they, you
shall haue enough for your money, if halfe will not serue
your turne take the whole measure by your own yard, you
finall haue Winchester measure, I was some-what bold with,
one of their Ladiships this morning, & askt her why women went to the generating sport al the yere since beasts
themselues went not too but once And she answered me, because they were women, & had reason to know what was
good for themselues, and so had not beasts; but soft, here
comes Signor *Petrone.*

Exit

1. *The Fleire* E2   2. *The Fleire* C4

it amply confirms our main contention: that adapters worked with large units of text, eschewing minor alterations in dialogue.

Two important characters are removed: Piso, son to the Duke of Florence, and Susan, one of the two sisters who rival the Fleire's courtesan daughters in love. The adapter has excised the pair by a mixture of harsh cutting and deft conflation. At 1.191–242, Susan's important first exchange with her sister, Nan, is cut; similarly, one of the best speeches in the play goes when the adapter discovers that Piso's melancholy soliloquy in prison (5.57–87) cannot be accommodated in his version. So much conflation has been effected that there are a number of pages positively pestered by correction. At the opening B4ᵛ–C1, for example, the adapter has not only altered speech prefixes but glossed '*Peto, Knight*' in the stage direction 'both one' – much as, on E2 (illustration 1), he has replaced '*Enter the two wenches* [i.e. Susan and Nan] *in boyes apparell*' with the instruction 'Nan like a Boy'. As the text wears on, the adapter becomes less scrupulous; original names increasingly stand uncorrected in speech prefixes and stage directions. Perhaps the adapter expected to conduct rehearsals himself, rationalizing his inconsistent prompt-book as he went; more likely, he meant to return to the details of his version once the shape of the whole had been settled.²¹

Meanwhile, he inflicted substantial cuts. The first two scenes, for example, are sacrificed. Some sixty lines into Sharpham's text, on B2, the adapter has inscribed 'begin heare'. Elsewhere, 51, 71, 127, 37, and 72 lines of dialogue are excised.²² However, not all the cuts are on this scale. Typically, between six and two dozen lines go at a time. Entirely characteristic of the adapter's work are the cuts in Antifront's soliloquy against women (C4, illustration 2) and the excision of 2.258–64 (D3, illustration 3) discussed in Appendix III. At three points, the adapter, with shrewd theatrical sense, crops short a scene, making for pace in performance without much material loss. Illustration 3 shows him saving 15 lines of quarto prose around the carefully preserved cue, '*Fel.* Come sister will you in?' On E2ᵛ, at 2.494, a similar cut begins; trimming an exchange between Antifront and Nan already altered by the loss of Susan, the adapter saves some 7 lines. On the previous page, E2 (illustration 1), in what is perhaps his most inventive adjustment, the adapter excludes Sharpham's Servingman by bringing forward the exit of Piso/Knight, emending 'I, I, hoe, whose within there?' to '[I, I,] Sʳile lead you in', and cutting 16 lines of dialogue. In the original, Fleire summons a servingman to

Fle, Faith they say your Ladiships are a couple of stately Curtizans.

Flo, Faith that was not much amisse, said they no worse?

Flei, You'l not be angry with me.

Flo, No a my word.

Fle. By my troth they said stately whores.

Flo, What pagan rogues be these were they but roasted
Larkes for my sake, I would crush am bones and all.

Flo, Why are you so angry sister? you know they speak
truth.

Flo, Why are wee whores?

Fel, What are we else?

Flo. Why we are Curtizans.

Fel. And what difference pray?

Flei. O great [   ] madam, your whore is for euery raf-
call but your Curtizan is for your Courtier.

Flo, He has giuen you a difference now.

Flei, And indeed Mada I said so, for in truth I was very
agry with 'am, but they said you were for euery seruingmā
too.   *Flo,* Did they say so   (now.

Flei, Yes indeede Madam, I hope I haue touch'd you

Flo, Ile hold my life this slaue the Seruingman, that was
with me this morning, has brag'd of my kindenes to him.

Flei, Nay, thats likelie, neuer trust a fellow that wil flatter, fleire, and fawne for foure nobles a yeare.

Flo, Well, ile nere haue Seruingman touch anie linnin
of mine agen.

Flei, Yes Madam, a may touch't when tis at the Laundresses.

Flo, I at my Laundresses, or else not: but what a rascal's
this by this light, ile neuer suffer seruingman come neere
me agen.

Flei, Yes Madame, to deliuer you a letter or so.

F, By this hand, not vnlesse the Rogue kisse his hand first.

Flei, O Madam! why? since blew coates were left oft,
the kissing of the hand is the seruingmans badge, you shall
know him by't but Madam, I speake something boldly of
you now and then, when I am out of your hearing, to heare
what

what the world wil say of you, for you know thats the way
to pumpe filthie words out of their mouthes, if there bee
anie in them.

Fle, And doe so still, wee allow thee to say anie thing,
for thereby we shall know our friendes from our foes.

Flei, I assure your Ladiships, I loue you, and am sorrie
for you from my soule, although you know it not.

Flo, Wee doubt it not.

Fel, Come sister will you in?

Flo, I prithee *Fleire* informe vs how the tide of opinion
runs on vs, least we be drown'd in the slaunderous imagi-
nations of the world.

Flei, I shall be very vigilant of your reputations.

Amb, Be so.

Exeunt Sisters.

Enter Ruffell.

Flei, VVho comes heere a Godf-name? O, my gallant
ruffiest out in silke, where haue you bin all this while

Ruff, Faith at Court *Fleire,* when wert thou there?

Fl, Faith but yesterday, where I saw a Farmers Son fit
newly made a courtier, that fat in the presence at cardes, as
familiar as if the chayre of state had bin made of a peece of
his fathers barne-doore: O tis a shame: I would haue state-
be that in earnest and in game, I like your Courtier for nothing but often saying his praiers.

Ruff, What, I thinke thou seldome saist thy prayers,
since thou hast almost forgot thy Pater-noster,

Flei, Faith I pray once a weeke, doost thou pray oftner?

Ruff, I did pray oftner when I was an Englishman, but I
haue not praid often, I must confesse since I was a Brittaine:
but doost heare *Fleire?* canst tell me if an Englishman were
in debt, whether a Brittaine must pay it or no?

Flei, No, question lesse no.

Ruff, I'me glad of that, I hope some honest flatterer will
come shortlie, and wipe out all my scores.

Fl, But whats the newes now abroad Maister *Ruffell?*

Ruff, Why they say the Courtiers shall make the Citti-
zens no more Cuckolds.   *Fle,* Excellēt

C 3

3. *The Fleire* D2ᵛ–D3 (C3 is the printer's error for D3)

show Piso and the Knight off stage, 'into the great Chamber'; in the adaptation, he begins to exit with Piso/Knight, only to encounter 'Nan like a Boy'.

This is one of a very few points at which the adapter has altered Sharpham's dialogue.[23] At 1.318, in what he probably took to be a correction, he has changed 'And' to 'but'. At 3.46–7 he has prudently replaced 'first to take the Sacrament' with 'first to take an o[ath]'.[24] And at 5.89–90 he has redirected Fleire's 'Come, come, thou didst but dreame thou wert in hell' from Spark to Russell by substituting 'ha ha spark was adream'd that [thou wer(s)t in hell.]'[25] These changes are complemented by small cuts. 'Shall wee embrace?' goes at 2.87; so does 'O my good preferrer' at 2.332;[26] and at 2.354 'what said he' is trimmed from the repetitive question 'And what said the Knight, what said he?' All in all, then, the adapter's minor alterations are sparse. And they amount to an exception proving the rule: if revising dramatists tinker with their texts, adapters, having more immediate aims in view, don't bother.

The most detailed adaptation which I have been able to find – and it is something of a curiosity – is the five-act version of *1* and *2 Henry IV* preserved in the Dering Manuscript. This text, now in the Folger Shakespeare Library,[27] was written sometime after 1613 and annotated (probably by Sir Edward Dering) between 1622 and 1624. The bulk of the manuscript (1.1–4.8) reproduces Q5 *1 Henry IV*, omitting 2.1 and 4.4. *2 Henry IV* (from Qb) is huddled into the last twelve scenes, with the loss of most of Falstaff's lines, a good part of the archbishop's insurrection, Shallow, Pistol and the Lord Chief Justice. Reading through the collations in the Williams–Evans facsimile, one is immediately struck by the number of large textual adjustments: the removal of the long recruiting scene in *Part 2* (3.2), for example, or the annotator's addition of $5\frac{1}{2}$ lines – evidently stimulated by *Henry V* 1.2.222–33 – at the end of the manuscript:

> we will According to yow[r] strength & qualityes
>   as you shall deserue itt
> giue yo[w] Aduancement: ~~be it your charge my lord~~
> Now change our thoughtes for honour and renowne
> ~~to see performd the tenure of my word~~
> And since y[e] royal[t]y and crowne of Fraunce,
> ~~& thus set forward~~
> Is ~~Being~~ due to vs wee'll bring itt to our awe,
>   or breake itt all to peeces—Vanityes farewell
>   ~~Exeunt:~~

wee I'll now act deedes for Chronicles to tell.

(Fol. 55ᵛ; cf. *2 Henry IV* 5.5.69–72)

Nevertheless, there are some small adjustments to Shakespeare's text. In the very first lines of the play, the scribe has changed 'entrance' (Q5) to 'bosome', and the annotator replaced 'new broiles | To be cōmenc't in stronds afarre remote' with the two words 'sweete rest':

> *King* So shaken as we are, so wan with Care,
> Find we a time for frighted peace to pant,
> > sweete rest.
> And breath short winded accents of ~~new broiles~~
> ~~To be cōmenc't in stronds afarre remote~~.
> No more yᵉ thirsty bosome of this land
> > in
> Shall wash her self ~~with~~ her owne Childrens bloud.

(Fol. 1; cf. *1 Henry IV* 1.1.1–6)

There are perhaps 150 minor substantive variants between the manuscript and its copy.[28] Although this total is low compared with those for *Every Man in his Humour, Cynthia's Revels, Bussy D'Ambois* or, indeed, most of the authorial revisions we will examine below, it is significant, and it needs explanation. The key seems to be that Dering's *Henry IV* stands outside the theatrical tradition. The manuscript shows every sign of having been prepared for private performance in its owner's circle. Indeed, the annotator's most ambitious addition[29] has been written on the back of a torn cast-list for *The Spanish Curate*, inscribed with the names of Dering's family, friends, and neighbours. The scribe and annotator were evidently free from the commercial pressures which any 'man of the theatre' (p.195) would feel when preparing an adaptation (see below, pp. 215–17). If they felt inclined to tinker, no theatre manager or book-keeper would object. Looked at in this light, it seems remarkable that they made so *few* small changes over the five long acts – a tribute, no doubt, to the strength of the psychological constraints controlling adaptation (below, p. 217).[30]

No one has ever discovered which 'dosen lines, or sixteene lines' in *The Mousetrap* were composed by Hamlet. Perhaps they lie in the Player King's long speech about purpose, passion and memory; perhaps in the Player Queen's vow of fidelity; or perhaps Claudius breaks up the show before we get to them. We cannot be sure. Indeed, if we had not overheard the Prince's conversation with the First Player we would scarcely suspect that *The Murder of Gonzago* was a rewritten play. Many of the works which reach us from the Elizabethan and Jacobean theatre may be, like *The Mousetrap*, adaptations. After considering just this question, Gerald Eades Bentley concluded that 'almost any play first printed more than ten years after composition and known to have been kept in active repertory by the company which owned it is most likely to contain later revisions'.[31] As textual bibliography becomes more sophisticated, more adaptations will no doubt be discovered and divided. Indeed, Peter Berek has recently located two levels in *Locrine*, one from the hand of Charles Tilney in the mid-1580s, the other (including the dumb shows, the clowning and the rumbustious Senecanism) from an adapter working in the early 1590s.[32] But such analyses, however convincing, will never be able to contribute much to the kind of argument advanced here; for it is almost impossible to decide, with single-text adaptations, whether original dialogue has been altered or left intact.[33]

Authors sometimes worked, I said (p. 195), like adapters. The most recent editors of Middleton and Rowley's *A Fair Quarrel* both conclude, independently, that the 'new Additions of M^r. *Chaughs* and *Trimtrams* Roaring, and the Bauds Song' introduced (on three supplementary leaves inserted into gathering H) in the second issue of Q1 come from the hand of Rowley.[34] The 'new Additions' (comprising 4.4) match the rest of Rowley's work stylistically and in orthography. Moreover, they substantially expand a role which he probably played – that of the plump clown Chough.[35] No doubt 4.4 would be thought an interpolation even if the title-page and format of Trundle's 1617 quarto did not betray its belatedness; for although it locks into the original text thematically (braving and prostitution being prevalent concerns there), it indulgently introduces three characters found nowhere else in an otherwise tautly economical tragicomedy. By contrast, the fly scene (3.2), absent from the 1594, 1600 and 1611 quartos of *Titus Andronicus* and present in the First Folio, fits almost perfectly into the host text. It anticipates the dénouement by announcing the motif of the bloody banquet; it subtly develops a number of minor themes, such as handling, storytelling and remembrance; its verse is eloquently Shakespearian; and it features central rather than peripheral characters. That the scene is authorial has never been seriously questioned.[36] What has been suggested, however, is that it slots so neatly into F that it must be considered cut material reinstated rather than new text added.[37] I doubt this;[38] but I shall not insist, because, as in the case of *Doctor*

Faustus B2093–2112, both views of 3.2 advance our argument. If the scene was cut in the mid-1590s, Shakespeare, as company dramatist, would have at least acceded to its excision. If the scene was interpolated for one of the play's many revivals,[39] its authority can be deduced from internal as well as external evidence. Either way, we have an author making the kind of textual change associated above with non-authorial adapters.

Occupying the uncertain middle ground between authorial revisions like F *Titus Andronicus* and non-authorial adaptations like the 1602 text of *The Spanish Tragedy*, are the 1610 redaction of *Mucedorus* and the expanded (QC) version of *The Malcontent*. We do not know who wrote the original 'Most pleasant Comedie of *Mucedorus* the kings sonne of *Valentia* and *Amadine* the Kings daughter of *Arragon*' in the late 1580s or early 1590s, never mind who 'Amplified' it 'with new additions' during the first few years of King James's reign.[40] Conceivably, the same poet composed both texts. The original dramatist was probably skilful enough to supply the Prologue, the rudimentary overplot, the expanded clown part, Mouse's comic encounter with the bear and the rewritten Epilogue (to James rather than Eliza) which appear in Q3 (1610).[41] And yet, with the exception of Shakespeare (whose claim can be promptly dismissed), there is no candidate available for the double honour of authorship and amplification. Had Greene lived, the situation might be otherwise; but, as things stand, the 1610 text must be considered much more likely an adaptation than an authorial revision.[42] With *The Malcontent*, we can be more positive. We know that the tragicomedy was originally composed by Marston; and the QC title-page informs us that the author co-operated in his 1604 revision with John Webster.[43] The problems begin when we try to divide Malevole's extended kingdom between the poets. I think D. J. Lake right to ascribe six of the sizeable, discrete QC insertions (including the famous Induction and the passages dominated by the QC-unique character, the fool Passarello) to Webster, and the remaining half-dozen to Marston.[44] But, for the moment at least, the division is open to dispute.

II

As soon as we turn to the second category of dramatic reworking (that which includes plays which show, as a consequence of authorial revision, small adjustments from text to text), we confront the formidable and obsessive genius of Ben Jonson. All his early plays, from *Every Man in his Humour* (1598) to *Catiline* (1611), were overhauled before the publication of his *Works* in 1616 – most, if not all,[45] for the sake of their appearance in that volume. Generally speaking, the later the play the lighter Jonson's revision. Thus the Q (1601) and F1 versions of *Every Man in his Humour* differ at many points and on many levels. At one extreme are the revised accidentals (to which Jonson paid close attention in almost all his F1 plays). Then there are small, frequently indifferent, substitutions. One might cite, as a typical example, the first line: 'Now trust me, here's a goodly day toward' (Q), 'A Goodly day toward! and a fresh morning!' (F1).[46] But what follows would do just as well: '*Musco*, | Call vp my sonne *Lorenzo*: bid him rise: | Tell him, I haue some businesse to imploy him in' (Q), 'BRAYNE-WORME, | Call vp your yong master: bid him rise, sir. | Tell him, I haue some businesse to employ him' (F1). Beyond such small changes, there lies a full spectrum of textual variation, ranging through minor expansions (e.g. of Q 5.1.81–97) and contractions (e.g. of Q 4.3.145–57) to a big cut (Lorenzo Junior's eloquent defence of poetry in Q 5.3), a speech so different that it must called a substitution (Q 2.2.1–36, F1 2.5.1–66) and, in the case of the F1 Prologue, a substantial 'new addition'. In *Every Man out of his Humour*, where revision is less thorough, only the extremes of this spectrum are represented. Q (1600) and F1 differ over many details (e.g. 'my *Optique* instruments' becoming 'the organs of my sight' at 1.1.25) and in the location of Macilente's panegyric on Queen Elizabeth (exiled to an appendix in F1); but Jonson, evidently well pleased with his second humours play when preparing the *Works*, felt able to resist · the temptation to reorganize its dialogue. With *Cynthia's Revels* and *Poetaster* he was less temperate. In the former (a revision even in its first edition, 1601), 'Jonson's minute retouching'[47] produced indifferent variants (e.g. 'arteficially and deeply shadow'd' made into 'deeply and artificially shadow'd' at 2.3.34–5), significant but localized rewriting (e.g. 'Like a squeez'd *Orenge*, sower, sower' becoming 'Like a sea-monster, that were to rauish ANDROMEDA from the rocke' at 4.1.65–6), and numerous small additions (e.g. 'Pruning his clothes, perfuming of his haire' at 3.4.56). At the same time, F1 is a substantially expanded text, including not only belated interpolations (3.1.32–75 and 3.4.22–41) but, apparently, reinstated cuts (4.1.136–214, 4.3.159–203, presumably 4.5.76–100 and 142–51, and the first four scenes of Act Five). In *Poetaster*, roughly the same kind of work was done: tinkering substitutions are accompanied by a substantial interpolation (the dialogue between Horace and Trebatius, 3.5) and three non-Q passages which look very much like reinstated cuts (the 'apologeticall Dialogue', suppressed by authority in 1601, 1.2.98–136 and 3.4.306–13). The later Q–F1 plays,[48] *Sejanus, Volpone, The Alchemist* and *Catiline*, show less variation. But what, strikingly, persists, is Jonson's fussy insistence on fidgeting with single words and short phrases. Changes like 'For shee must feele/milke his *Epididimis*' (*Alchemist* 3.3.22) and 'Crowne/Swell mee my bowle yet fuller' (*Catiline* 1.499) betray the presence of a revising author in all four plays.

The same kind of tinkering is evident between the 1607 and 1641 quartos of *Bussy D'Ambois*. Peter Ure counted 'some 228 places where the B text differs from the A text in respect of word, phrase or single line of verse'.[49] Many of these variants are blandly indifferent: 'incessant/continuall stormes' (1.1.5);[50] 'gadding/ranging greatnes' (3.2.141); 'she who/that makes' (5.3.3); and so on. Others distinctly alter the lines in which they appear, as when Tamyra mourns Bussy's death 'kneeling' instead of 'sitting' (5.3.206) and when Henry calls Bussy's duelling not 'violent' but 'daring' (2.1.185). Significantly, such small divergences are not restricted to those parts of the play in which the A and B texts run along together. Thus, at 3.2.310a–22a, where the rewriter has replaced some 13 lines of Q1 by a 26-line substitution, the A lines turn up in the middle of the insertion sandwiched between 9 and 1 lines of clear B text in a much amended state. The passage recalls the fifth 'addition' in the 1602 text of *The Spanish Tragedy* and B *Doctor Faustus* 1160–2, 1356–61, 1538–42 and 1802–11 – until the density of revision in the borrowed pieces of 1607 text is noticed. 'This still hath made me doubt' becomes 'Put me in some little doubt'; 'Wilt thou doe one thing for me then syncerelie?' is, almost indifferently, 'Wilt thou doe one thing therefore now sincerely?'; 'Come, doe not doubt me, and command mee all things' is made more expansive and explicit, 'Then doe not doubt, | That there is any act within my nerves, | But killing of the King that is not yours'; 'and now by all my loue' becomes 'to prove which by my love'; and simple 'affection', in 'and by all fruits else | Alreadie sprung from that affection', turns into a vividly 'still flourishing tree'. As though this were not enough, three extra lines have been slipped into the displaced 1607 material: 'How most unseasonable thou playest the

Cucko, | In this thy fall of friendship?' and 'With whatsoever may hereafter spring'. This is not the only passage which might be cited; similarly altered pieces of 1607 text bracketed by bits of 1641 can be found at 1.2.87a–107, 4.2.0a–9b and 5.2.84a–88b. If Birde, Rowley, and the adapter of Kyd did not rework what they borrowed, the rewriter of *Bussy D'Ambois* evidently did. He seems to have been a compulsive textual meddler.

To prove this rewriter Chapman, it is necessary to make a move which, in a non-literary argument, might be illogical, but which is here, I think, acceptable. While, on the one hand, the reworking looks authorial because its small changes are (like those in early Jonson) frequently indifferent, on the other it seems so because it involves insertions which are pungently 'Chapmanesque'. Thus, we are told about the man 'That will not wind with every crooked way, | Trod by the servile world' (5.3.46a–b); and, in another characteristic by-blow, we hear Tamyra talking Platonist poetics: 'Papers hold | Oft-times the formes, and copies of our soules, | And (though the world despise them) are the prizes | Of all our honors' (4.1.197–8). It seems safe to say that only Chapman could have written such lines. And yet the honesty of the Q2 title-page, which declares the tragedy '*much corrected and amended by the Author before his death*', has sometimes been impugned.[51] If we ask how this can have happened, we find ourselves contemplating another part of the spectrum of textual divergences. For Q2 includes large as well as small to middling revisions. Most strikingly, there are additions in the part of the bumptious servant, Maffé (1.1.204a–c, 3.2.294p–302f), a soul-searching soliloquy lost and a dishonest dialogue gained for Tamyra (2.2.34–49, 3.2.130a–h), an insert showing Bussy as an ambitious flirt (1.2.87a–k), and a careful restructuring of the dénouement which leaves the play in the hands of Montsurry and Tamyra rather than Bussy and the Ghost of Comolet (5.2a.1–56f (5.3.1–56), 5.3.57–69f and 193a–g (268–74)). It has been said that such changes reduce the play as well as the protagonists, turning it away from tragedy towards melodrama. There is some truth in this charge, but the inferiority of Q2 does not prove the revision non-authorial. An author's second thoughts need not surpass his first. Most readers prefer the 1805 *Prelude* to the 1850, and many find the abandoned ending of *Great Expectations* truer to what precedes it than the one urged on Dickens by Lytton; but no one questions the authority of both versions of both books. In any case, as Albert H. Tricomi has shown in an important pair of essays,[52] it is unreasonable to judge Q2 *Bussy D'Ambois* simply in terms of Q1. *The Revenge of Bussy D'Ambois* also needs to be taken into account. For Chapman reworked his best play so that it could be produced alongside its sequel.[53] He debased Bussy deliberately, to make him a foil for the 'senecal' revenger Clermont; he made Tamyra's love more lustful and designing so that the virtue of the Countess of Cambrai would seem less tedious; and he opened out the end of *Bussy* to help the plot flow into *The Revenge*.

In about 1623–4 Dekker reworked his revenge play *The Noble Spanish Soldier* to produce a fashionable Fletcherian tragicomedy called *The Welsh Embassador*.[54] These two plays are ultimately very different. But because both rely on a love triangle and broken precontract to spring their main plots, similar material is used in their opening acts. Indeed, substantial slices of dialogue from 1.1, 1.2, 2.1 and 2.2 *The Noble Spanish Soldier* are carried into the corresponding scenes of *The Welsh Embassador*.[55] Dekker could simply have transcribed this dialogue. However, being a reviser rather than a non-authorial adapter, he refused to catch the nearest way. Instead, he cut, interpolated and substituted freely when redeploying the old dialogue. The sheer density of revision evident in a passage like *The Welsh Embassador* 1.3.74–96 (see overleaf) is startling. Nor can such rewriting be explained away as a simple consequence of a shift in genre. It would be absurd to argue, for example, that the changes made in the jest about powdering – 'ever' deleted, 'a' made 'anie', and 'your sex' replaced by plain 'you' – follow from Cornego's reduction to a Clown. They characterize Dekker rather than his altered antic. They reveal the presence of a fidgeting authorial reviser.

While the texts of early Jonson, *Bussy D'Ambois* and, we can add, *Troilus and Cressida*[56] vary because of revisions post-dating the first performance, [57] Q1 and Q2 *The Maid's Tragedy* apparently disagree because they derive from authorial manuscripts at different stages of composition. After carefully considering the 1619 and 1622 editions, Robert. K. Turner concluded that 'Q1 was printed from late-stage foul papers in Beaumont's hand, including Beaumont's rewriting of Fletcher's scenes', while 'Q2 was printed from a copy of Q1 into which had been introduced readings from a fair copy of the foul papers, probably also written out by Beaumont, who had made some changes in the process'.[58] A few of these 'changes' were substantial: of the seven pieces of text unique to Q2 (1.2.140–9, 1.2.234.1–248, 2.1.67–89, 2.2.7–10, 2.2.15–27, 3.1.203–6 and 4.1.81–6), three or

The Noble Spanish Soldier 1.2.165–203 (B4ᵛ–C1)

Onœlia. Here, as the dearest Iewell of my fame,
Lock'd I this parchment from all viewing eyes,
This your Indenture held alone the life
Of my suppos'd dead honour; yet (behold)
Into your hands I redeliver it.
Oh keepe it, Sir, as you should keepe that vow,   170
To which (being sign'd by heaven) even Angels bowe.
King. Tis in the Lions paw, and who dares snatch it?
Now to your Beads and Crucifix agen.
Onœlia. Defend me heaven!
King. Pray there may come Embassadors from *France*,
Their followers are good Customers.
Onœlia. Save me from madnesse!
King. 'Twill raise the price, being the Kings Mistris.
Onœlia. You doe but counterfeit to mocke my joyes.
King. Away bold strumpet   180

Onœlia. Are there eyes in heaven to see this?
King. Call and try, here's a whores curse,
To fall in that beleefe which her sinnes nurse.   *Exit.*

Enter Cornego.

Cornego. How now? what quarter of the Moone has she cut out
now? my Lord puts me into a wise office, to be a mad womans
keeper: why madam!
Onœlia. Ha! where is the King, thou slave?
Cornego. Let go your hold, or I'le fall upon you as I am a man.
Onœlia. Thou treacherous caitiffe, where's the King?
Cornego. Hee's gone, but not so farre gone as you are.   190
Onœlia. Cracke all in sunder, oh you Battlements,
And grind me into powder.
Cornego. What powder? come, what powder? when did you ever
see a woman grinded into powder? I am sure some of your sex
powder men and pepper 'em too.
Onœlia. Is there a vengeance yet lacking to my ruine?
Let it fall, now let it fall upon me!
Cornego. No, there has too much falne upon you already.
Onœlia. Thou villaine, leave thy hold, I'le follow him:
Like a rais'd ghost I'le haunt him, breake his sleepe,   200
Fright him as hee's embracing his new Leman,
Till want of rest bids him runne mad and dye,
For making oathes Bawds to his perjury.

The Welsh Embassador 1.3.74–96 (Fol. 5ᵃ)

[*Armante.*] Heere as the deerest Iewell of my fame
Lockt I this parchment from all couetous eyes.
This your Indenture holds alone the life
Of my sick wasted honor, yett behold,
Into your hands I redeliver it.

Kinge. So, it is ith lyons paw and whoe dares snatch it?

Armante. Ha, you doe but counterfeit to mock my ioyes.   80
Kinge. Awaie bould strumpit.
                    Enter Clowne.
Armante. Are there eyes in heaven to see this?

Clowne. Mad maudlin are you goeinge to bedlam?
Armante. Yes, lett mee haue fresh straw, I am mad.

Clowne. So am I, lett goe your catts nayles, or I'le fall
    vppon you as I'me a man.
Armante. Is the kinge gon, thou slaue?
Clowne. Hees gon but not so farr gon as you.
Armante. Rocks leape out of the sea to fall vppon mee
    And grinde mee into powder.   90
Clowne. What powder, come what powder, when did you see anie
    woman grinded into powder, I'me sure some of you powder men,
    & pepper em too.

Armante. Awaie, Ile bee a ghost & haunt this kinge

Till want of sleep bids him runne mad & dye
For makinge oathes bawds to his periury.   *Exit.*

four look like interpolations rather than reinstated omissions (presumably cuts marked in the foul papers reconsidered in the fair). Most of Beaumont's alterations were, however, quite small. Even if a large margin is allowed for compositorial error in both quartos, many of the over 400 minor substantive variants between the texts must be considered the result of revision. Consider Aspatia's lament in 2.2:

> Suppose I stand vpon the Sea, breach [sea-beach?] now
> Mine armes thus, and mine haire blowne with the wind,
> Wilde as the place she was in, let all about me
> Be teares [hearers?] of my story, doe my face,
> If thou hadst euer feeling of a sorrow,
> Thus, thus, *Antiphila* make me looke good girle
> Like sorrowes mount, and the trees about me
> Let them be dry and leauelesse, let the rocks
> Groane with conti[nu]all surges, and behind me
> Make all a desolation, see, see wenches,
> A miserable life of this poore picture.   (ll. 66–76, Q1)

Here, only one Q1–Q2 variant ('mount/monument') could be the product of compositorial error. All the other Q2 changes – the marginally inferior 'I stand vpon the sea breach now, and thinke', the doubly improved 'Wilde as that desart, and let all about me | Tell that I am forsaken', the slightly better 'striue to make me looke' and indifferent 'looke, looke wenches' – all these resemble the fidgeting changes made by Jonson, Chapman, and Dekker. The fingerprints of an anxious, revising author lie thick upon this passage, and upon the rest of the work.

The Maid's Tragedy is not the only play to be unstable in this way. The first two quartos of *Philaster* also derive – except for the first 93 and approximately the last 195 lines of Q1, which probably rest on a report – 'from different states of the authors' copy';[59] and, although about a third of the approximately 775 small substantive variants[60] between the central portions of the quartos are self-evidently the consequence of corruption (usually in the first edition), many others must be the result of revision. As both the play's recent editors point out, it is difficult to see how variants like 'silke-mans/Mercers' (2.2.24) and 'honest lookes' against 'tender youth' (3.1.275) could have arisen without authorial involvement. *Othello* is similarly unstable. Literary critics may not have seen this; they may not have realized that (to take a crucial instance) T. S. Eliot's influential interpretation of the Moor's suicide speech hangs on a variant reading;[61] but textual scholars have been aware for some time that there is no way in which the big Q and F divergences (amounting to $5\frac{1}{2}$ Q-only and about 160 F-only lines, and some 1,000 small substantive variants in common material)[62] can be explained without recourse to the idea of authorial revision.[63] Apparently, *Hamlet* was also overhauled by Shakespeare. In the deep 'sea of 1300 variants'[64] which lies between the Q2 (foul-paper based) and F (prompt-book secured) texts of this tragedy, many almost indifferent and paleographically incompatible alternatives lurk, such as 'no spirit dare sturre' against 'no Spirit can walke' (B3; TLN 160; 1.1.161) and 'heated/tristfull visage' (I2ᵛ; TLN 2433; 3.4.50). Their only plausible derivation is in authorial second thoughts. Beyond these small changes, there are brief and middling insertions, e.g. 'hide Fox, and all after' (TLN 2659–60; 4.2.30–1), 'Nature is fine in Loue . . . After the thing it loues' (TLN 2914–16; 4.5.162–4); similar-sized excisions, e.g. 'women feare too much, euen as they loue, | And' (H2; 3.2.[166]), 'Eyes without feeling . . . Could not so mope' (I3; 3.4.78–81); and, on a larger scale, bold but intelligent cuts and interpolations, e.g. Hamlet's encounter with the Captain and his sub-sequent soliloquy 'How all occasions doe informe against me' (K3-K3ᵛ; 4.4.9–66), and his conversation with Rosencrantz and Guildenstern about Fortune, Denmark, prison and the 'ayrie of Children' (TLN 1285–1316, 1384–1408; 2.2.239–69, 337–62). Significantly, the changes made between Q2 and F *Hamlet* resemble not only the revisions effected by Jonson, Chapman, Dekker, and Beaumont (with Fletcher?) in the texts already discussed but the alterations made by Middleton in the manuscripts of *A Game at Chess*. As R. C. Bald and E. A. J. Honigmann have shown in a fascinating pair of studies,[65] big changes – such as the late introduction of the Fat Knight and the amplification of satire against the White King's Pawn – and small, alike, can be traced through the Archdall, Trinity and Huntington manuscripts of this play. It is reassuring to learn, in view of the link made elsewhere in this essay between authors and small revisions, that, in *A Game at Chess* at least, Middleton persisted in making minor adjustments to the bitter end. Even when preparing one fair copy from another, he felt compelled to tinker.[66]

III

The pattern of variation between the two texts of *King Lear* looks, by now, rather familiar. As with *Every Man in his Humour*, or *Bussy*

D'Ambois, or *Hamlet*, there is a full spectrum of revision. F cuts the mock trial in 3.6, Edgar's account of his reunion with Kent over Gloucester's corpse (L2ᵛ–L3; 5.3.205–22) and the whole of 4.3; but it also interpolates substantially, as at TLN 1734–49 (3.2.79–96), the Fool's prophecy. There are modest cuts, too: Poor Tom's catalogue of fiends goes (H3; 4.1.58–63), and so do the brief exchange between the servingmen after Gloucester's blinding (H2; 3.7.99–107) and the anonymous Captain's grimly inhuman couplet, 'I cannot draw a cart, nor eate dride oats, | If it bee mans worke ile do't' (K4ᵛ; 5.3.38–9). There are insertions of roughly the same size: Lear's 'while we | Vnburthen'd crawle toward death . . . . that future strife | May be preuented now' (TLN 45–50; 1.1.40–5) is one example, 'In Boy, go first. . . . Ile pray, and then Ile sleepe' (TLN 1807–8; 3.4.26–7) another. Beyond these lie still smaller cuts, for example 'I and laying Autums dust' (I4ᵛ; 4.6.197), and a series of minute but telling additions, like the anticipatory 'vnbutton heere' (TLN 1888–9; 3.4.109; compare QF at 5.3.310) and the echoic 'Not an houre more, nor lesse' (TLN 2816; 4.7.60; compare QF at 1.1.93). Substitutions cover a similar range: there is the new version of Kent's long speech about the powers of France, near the start of 3.1; there is the reorganized argument between the stocked Kent and the King at TLN 1289–97 (E3ᵛ; 2.4.13–22); there are recast phrases, such as 'reserue thy state' for 'Reuerse thy doome' at TLN 159 (B3; 1.1.149); and there are a large number of single-word substitutions. Even if we treat the text conservatively, excluding from this last class any variant which could conceivably be – like 'The oldest haue/hath borne most' in the penultimate line of the tragedy – the consequence of casual corruption in one or other text, we are left with an impressively long list. Moreover, while some of F's single-word substitutions are significant, for example 'the bleak/high winds' (F3; TLN 1603; 2.4.300), many more are simply – 'authorially' we can surely say – indifferent: 'earebussing/ear(e)-kissing arguments' (D3ᵛ; TLN 936; 2.1.8); 'smite/Strike flat' (F4; TLN 1662; 3.2.7); 'you haue the captiues | That/Who were the opposites of this dayes strife' (K4ᵛ; TLN 2984–5; 5.3.41–2); and so on.

One kind of small variant common in *King Lear* we have not yet considered: substitute speech prefixes. Here, a few of the Folio changes might be straightforward corrections of Q. Thus, it is possible that Shakespeare never intended to attribute 'Breake hart, I prethe breake' to the King, after giving him 'O,o,o,o' at Q 5.3.310 (though I doubt it); clearly, the F prefix '*Kent.*' is, even within Q, a *workable* substitute for Q's '*Lear.*' (L4; TLN 3285; 5.3.313). Yet most of the F reattributions do seem self-evidently the result of rewriting. It is clear, for example, that the donation of Albany's words at 5.3.223, 224, 252 and 324–7 to Edgar forms part of a larger movement of revision designed to radically reshape the two roles. (See M. Warren, 'Albany and Edgar', pp. 101–5.) If the evidence of other authorial revisions can be trusted, reattributions need not complicate our argument. Changes similar to those found in *King Lear* occur in *Bussy D'Ambois, The Maid*'s *Tragedy, Philaster, Othello, Troilus and Cressida*, and *Hamlet.*[67]

While the evidence collected above allows us to say that *The Tragedie of King Lear* (F) looks, overall, like an authorial revision of the *Historie* (Q), it does not enable us to date the rewriting with any assurance. If Q is based on foul papers and F on a copy of Q2 marked up from a prompt-book,[68] we cannot determine, simply on the basis of our survey of revised and adapted plays, whether F represents the play as first performed or as rewritten for a revival – whether, that is, we are dealing with a case like *The Maid's Tragedy* or with a full-blooded belated revision like *Bussy D'Ambois*. To show that *King Lear* was overhauled about 1609–10, it is necessary to advance literary and bibliographical evidence of quite another kind.[69] Yet there is one important consideration forced upon us by our survey. *The Tragedie of King Lear* is significantly shorter than the *Historie*. While F adds about 120 lines to Q, it cuts about 285. This imbalance recalls *Hamlet*, rewritten and trimmed for performance,[70] rather than the frankly amplified *Bussy D'Ambois* and *A Fair Quarrel*, revised for revival. Such a parallel encourages critical caution. It is important to remember, while reading Q and F *King Lear*, that some of the revisions not published till 1623 – and especially the cuts – might have been made in a fair copy or prompt-book of the play before its first performance about 1606.

Before turning to a close analysis of one set of variants in *King Lear*, it seems wise to consider two potential objections to the distinction I have here proposed between revision and adaptation. I shall deal with them in turn. First, can we be sure that the printing history of plays like *The Spanish Tragedy* has not concealed the fact that adapters fidgeted with texts as freely as did revisers? After all, the Elizabethan and Jacobean book trade worked for profit, and the most profitable formula for publishing a revised play would be to reprint an old edition, incorporating only big changes from a new manuscript, for costs would escalate if, in order to reproduce small alterations, compositors worked from manuscript (or, at the least, if an old quarto had to be annotated with such alterations), and the public would hardly cover a printer's increased expenses if all they got for their money was a string of indifferent and semi-indifferent new readings. So it might be in the interests of publishers and printers to suppress small textual changes whenever they could. This would explain why Pavier's printer, William White, set most of his 1602 edition of *The Spanish Tragedy* from the 1599 quarto, taking only the 'new additions' from manuscript.

The objection is much less coherent than it seems. Gravely embarrassed by the publication of texts so unremittingly variant as A and B *Doctor Faustus* (and B could have lifted shared material wholesale from an edition of A), it entirely fails to explain why so many revised plays were, in practice, published with small alterations. Are we to assume that publishers and printers accepted trifling changes from authors because they were particularly keen to handle authorial rewriting? It seems most unlikely that the Q1–Q2 variants in *The Maid's Tragedy* had greater commercial value than the Painter's scene added to *The Spanish Tragedy* in Q 1602, or even that they were more saleable than hypothetical non-authorial tinkerings preserved in Henslowe's early seventeenth-century prompt-book of Kyd's play. Might it not be the case, though, that authors – naturally caring more about their texts than non-authors – would have bullied publishers and printers into respecting revisions in their entirety, commercially unattractive though they were? The trouble with this argument is that it exposes a fatal flaw in the objection which it seeks to support. If publishers and printers found small textual changes unattractive, we can be sure that the company managers who commissioned non-authorial adaptations in the first place would have regarded them with distaste; for, if the reading public would not pay good money for minor alterations, neither, it can be safely assumed, would theatre audiences; and, if the publication of small changes involved at least the expense of annotating quarto copy, their performance would require the troublesome and costly emendation of both actors' parts and the prompt-book, and, in some cases, fresh learning by actors returning to old roles. So, if we claim that commercial pressures excluded small changes from printed adaptations, we must at the same time concede that such pressures would have kept small changes out of staged adaptations.[71] Following the logic of the first objection, we reach the somewhat paradoxical conclusion that, if an adapter ignored the logic of laziness (which encourages us to leave things alone unless they must be altered) and the natural instincts of authorship (which make us much more likely to fidget discontentedly with our own work than with other people's) in order to indulge in some textual tinkering, his changes would have been blocked in the theatre before the publishers and printers even had a chance to reject them. Unplayed and unprinted, such changes would fall stillborn from the pen. Excluded from the public realm of dramatic discourse, they could hardly – even if we knew of them – detain us here. Though written by adapters, they would have no role in adapters' adaptations.

The second objection which might be made against the case advanced above is rather stronger: how can we be sure that *King Lear* was not revised by Shakespeare and then adapted by someone else? Or, to vary the question: how can we be sure that Shakespeare did not co-operate in his revision (rather as Marston did over QC *The Malcontent*) – with, say, Middleton (who probably helped write *Timon of Athens*),[72] or Fletcher (who almost certainly contributed to *The Two Noble Kinsmen*)?[73] Either way, could not Shakespeare be responsible for the tinkering and another man for the big cuts and interpolations? Obviously, a thorough defence of every sizeable F revision would be needed to answer this objection, and only a limited defence is possible in the remainder of this essay. However, by justifying that part of *The Tragedie of King Lear* which looks – in the light of our survey – the least likely to be fully authoritative, I hope to unfold an argument with more than limited implications. Time and again we have seen adapters amplify jesting and clownage. There are the enlarged Robin–Rafe/Dick, Horse-Courser and Obtuse Knight (i.e. Benvolio) scenes in B *Doctor Faustus*, there is Strumbo in *Locrine*, almost certainly the expanded Mouse of the 1610 *Mucedorus*, and Passarello, the bitter fool[74] in QC *The Malcontent*. So many adjustments between Q and F *King Lear* affect the part of the Fool that one inevitably wonders whether he has suffered the same fate as his comic fellows. Might an adapter not have added such F-only passages as Merlin's prophecy (TLN 1734–49; 3.2.79–96), cutting from the Q text disconcerting jests like 'Cry you mercy I tooke you for a ioyne stoole' (G4; 3.6.52)? Certainly, if the integrity and authority of anything in the Folio *King Lear* is doubted, the Fool's part will fall under suspicion.

IV

A general point first. The F Fool's role has not been crudely expanded, farced out, like those of Robin, Rafe and Mouse. While F adds some 32 lines to the part, it cuts about 22 from Q, so that the Fool has little more to say in the *Tragedie* than in the *Historie*. Evidently, reorganization rather than amplification was the motive behind the rewrite. A second point should also be registered. In B *Doctor Faustus*, *Locrine* or QC *The Malcontent*, the added clowning is clearly meant to divert. It is designed to please the audience, not intensify the drama. '*Media inter carmina poscunt | aut ursum aut pugiles*' mocks Horace (*Epistles* 2.1.185–6); happy to indulge such tastes, the 1610 *Mucedorus* provides a bear as well as comic fisticuffs. The alterations in *King Lear* are altogether different. There is nothing opportunistic about them. The F Fool would not woo many groundlings away from the Red Bull. He is not particularly funny – no more a stand-up comic than his counterpart in Q. Nevertheless, there are striking differences between the pair. Interpretations of the Fool based on the received text have swung wildly between the extremes represented by Empson's blathering natural and Orwell's canny rationalist.[75] In neither version of the play is the character uncomplicated; but, broadly speaking, the Empsonian view of him rests on those elements in the conflated text which derive from Q, while the Orwellian interpretation depends on ingredients drawn from F. Between Q and F comes a substantial rewrite – involving some 54 lines of a part only about 225 lines long when conflated – which significantly alters the Fool's personality and quite changes the direction of his dramatic development.

Political factors may have contributed to the first textual adjustment affecting the Fool: the cut of 9 Q lines at 1.4.140–55 (C4^v – D1). Censorship has long been suspected.[76] But, as Gary Taylor observes above (pp. 105–9), there are good grounds for thinking that if Shakespeare did not initiate this excision he eventually became reconciled to it. Several considerations lead towards the conclusion that Shakespeare meant the F version of 1.4 to stand as it does, that no replacement for Q 1.4.140–55 has been lost. For the moment, though, let us examine two purely literary motives for the cut. There is, first, the question of pacing. In Q, the long set-piece between Lear and the Fool is, despite two interjections by Kent, a little too long and set (1.4.95–188). F restructures the sequence, partly by cutting

ll. 140–55, but partly, too, by granting Kent's 'Why Foole?' – as
'Why my Boy?' – to Lear (l. 98) and Lear's 'This is nothing foole' to
Kent (1.128). F is Q's superior because it decisively marks the Fool's
first appearance in the play by establishing a King-jester duologue
which runs unbroken for 32 lines, while (by placing Kent's interjection centrally in an altogether shorter sequence) ensuring that the
exchange does not become monotonous. Secondly, the cut seems to
have been prompted by the reviser's changing – or the adapter's
novel – view of the Fool's psychology. In F, the Fool is consistently a
wise and worldly jester, more urbane and more oblique than his
precursor. Both Fools are interested, in 1.4, in land holdings, lawyers'
fees and rent; but this side of the Fool's character predominates and
persists in F, ultimately changing the play. That is why F produces –
as Gary Taylor points out – a jump in the rewritten dialogue from
sweet and bitter folly to egg custards, crowns and kingdoms. The
disjunction is the first of several increasingly violent dislocations
working to distance and finally divorce the revised or adapted Fool
from the Folio King.

The second alteration which we must consider is slighter than the
first. It gives point to a single exchange rather than reshaping an
entire sequence. At 1.4.230–38, Q reads:

> [*Lear.*] . . . who is it that can tell me who I am? *Lears* shadow? I would learne
> that, for by the markes of soueraintie, knowledge, and reason, I should bee
> false perswaded I had daughters.
>   *Foole.* Which they, will make an obedient father.
>   *Lear.* Your name faire gentlewoman?
>   *Gon.* Come sir, this admiration is much of the sauour of other your new
> prankes . . .   (D1ᵛ)

F gives '*Lears* shadow' to the Fool; it cuts 'I would learne that . . . an
obedient father'; and it alters Goneril's reply, excising 'Come sir,' to
produce 'This admiration Sir, is much o'th'sauour | Of other your new
prankes' (TLN 743–7; see Q and F at 1.4.219 or 1.4.313, and pp. 175–9
above). It is possible that Shakespeare always intended the Fool to say
'*Lears* shadow' (elsewhere in the tragedy the King is baffled by his own
questions), but it is not, I think, very likely. A misattribution in Q
would presuppose not one but two omitted prefixes. And the Q
reading is strikingly close to the play's main source: at *King Leir*
1111, Lear's precursor tells Perillus, 'think me but the shaddow of my
selfe'. Moreover, F's reattribution seems to complement its cut, in

that it gives the Fool a replacement for 'Which they, will make . . . '
and so foregrounds '*Lears* shadow' by shifting it from the King that it
makes what follows in Q redundant. Of course, Q is excellent in itself.
It draws attention to Lear's growing derangement most cunningly, by
having him invoke the very 'knowledge, and reason' which he lacks.
And it shows him groping towards an understanding of himself as he
concedes that he has become his own shadow. But F surpasses Q. It
opens a gap between '*Lears* shadow' and 'Your name . . . ' which is
both painful and unignorable. The poetic space can scarcely be
played across. Within it, the Fool's words resonate, and (if the actor
performing Lear has the right instincts) the King takes a silent step
towards self-discovery.

The first addition affecting the Fool occurs in 2.4. Almost as
though making up for the cut at 1.4.140–55, which had disposed of
the rhyme 'That Lord that counsail'd thee to giue away thy land', F
gives the Fool a new jingle:

> (way,
> *Foole.* Winters not gon yet, if the wil'd Geese fly that
> Fathers that weare rags, do make their Children blind,
> But Fathers that beare bags, shall see their children kind.
> Fortune that arrant whore, nere turns the key toth' poore.
> But for all this thou shalt haue as many Dolors for thy
> Daughters, as thou canst tell in a yeare.
>   (TLN 1322–7; 2.4.46–55)

As Gary Taylor points out (below, p. 396), the imagery here is so
Shakespearian that the authority of the passage can hardly be
questioned. That makes it the more significant that the alteration
complements those made in 1.4. 'Fathers that weare rags . . .' has
clearly been added, as 'That Lord . . .' cut, to reshape a duologue. In
Q, Kent has a two-hander with the King which runs uninterrupted for
36 lines; by inserting the Fool's rhyme, F disrupts the exchange,
preventing predictability. Still more strikingly, F emphasizes the
Fool's hard-headedness. The new lines resemble the 1.4 quips about
unfe'd lawyers and rent. Only, whereas such observations were then
to the point, they now seem distressingly irrelevant. The Fool's first
few jokes may not have helped Lear recover his kingdom, but they did
make him 'See better' what he had done when he gave his crown
away. At TLN 1322–7, by contrast, the Fool's sallies are disengaged
from the King. The two characters no longer speak the same
language, because Lear is losing touch with the way things are. As a

result, 2.4.56, 'O how this mother swels vp toward my hart . . .', harrowing enough in Q, becomes, in F, almost unbearable. Originally an anguished but clearly motivated response to Kent's long speech about Oswald, Cornwall and Regan, the King's words are, in the *Tragedie*, the spontaneous cry of a soul in agony; and the distance which Lear has travelled towards the insanity of Act Three is clearly defined, in the later text, by the discrepancy between the Fool's worldly notion that dollars lost are dolors gained and the King's inward sense of 'climing sorrow'. In the *Tragedie* 2.4 the King and his jester are on different wavelengths. They are beginning to drift apart, something which never really happens in the *Historie*.

The Fool has already – in the way fools do – established a rapport with the audience, leaving QF 1.4 with the jingle 'a fox when one has caught her . . .' (ll. 317–21; D2ᵛ; TLN 837–41), and concluding 1.5 with the jest: 'Shee that is [F, that's a] maide now, and laughs at my departure, | Shall not be a maide long, except [F, vnlesse] things be cut shorter.' Q and F fleetingly return to this device at 3.4.65–6,[77] but F adds, meanwhile, the Fool's prophecy at the end of 3.2 (TLN 1734–49), a speech which marks an important stage in the Fool's extrication of himself from the action. Before considering its dramatic function at large, it is necessary to dispose of an objection to its authority recently advanced by P. W. K. Stone. Correctly observing that the fifth to tenth lines of the prophecy refer to contemporary events (see below, p. 225), Stone insists that one couplet in that part of the speech, 'When Nobles are their Taylors Tutors, | No Heretiques burn'd, but wenches Sutors',[78] cannot have been composed until after Shakespeare's death in 1616. 'The last heretics to be burned in England', he writes, 'went to the stake in 1612. . . . It was not, in fact, until 1618 that a royal reprieve confirmed the final abandonment of a barbarous practice' (*Textual History*, p. 121). But the last burnings in Jacobean England were also the first. Until 1612, James had a quite extraordinary record of religious toleration. In particular, he refused to be swept up in the great wave of anti-Catholic hysteria which followed the discovery of the Gunpowder Plot in 1605.[79] His *Proclamation charging all Jesuites, Seminaries &c. to depart the land*, published in the wake of the Plot, urges Catholics not to provoke him to violence; James says that he passionately wants 'to avoid the effusion of blood'.[80] Three years later, under pressure because of his policy of toleration, James told Parliament:

I neuer found, that blood and too much seueritie did good in matters of Religion: for, besides that it is a sure rule in Diuinitie, that God neuer loues to plant his Church by violence and bloodshed; natural reason may euen perswade vs, and dayly experience prooues it trew, That when men are seuerely persecuted for Religion, the gallantnesse of many mens spirits, and the wilfulnes of their humors, rather then the iustnesse of the cause, makes them to take a pride boldly to endure any torments, or death it selfe, to gaine thereby the reputatio[n] of Martyrdome, though but in a false shadow.[81]

In May 1610, Henry IV of France was assassinated, apparently by extreme papists. James's initial response was fierce; evidently, he feared for his life. 'I will let you know thus much,' he told Parliament:

their aim was not at him alone but at other princes too, whereof I assure you I was one. Look these weeds do not overgrow the corn, that papistry be not increased by one thing too much used amongst them; they send out their kinsmen, children, and servants to Douai and such like places; these after they have been there nourished come daily over and with their poison infect many others. This one day will make us smart if it be not prevented. . . .[82]

Parliament was as anxious as the King. The Lords and Commons jointly petitioned James to deal severely with the recusants.[83] But the King's tolerance survived this crisis at least. The *Proclamation for the due execution of all former Lawes against Recusants*, James's considered response to Henry's death and the parliamentary petition which followed it, is harsher in tone than its 1606 predecessor; but it does no more than its title suggests, insisting on the application of the relatively enlightened laws introduced four years before. Characteristically, it begins with an eloquent disquisition on clemency:

Though the principall care that a Religious and wise King ought to have, should be for the maintenance and propagation by all godly lawfull and honest meanes, of the true Catholique [i.e. Protestant] and Christian Religion, and to that effect as he must plant good seed with the one hand, so to displant and to roote out with the other as farre as he can, the Cockle and Tares of Heresie that doe ordinarily grow up amongst the Lords Wheat; Yet hath Our nature bene ever so enclined to clemencie, especially we have ever bene so loath to shed blood in any case that might have any relation to conscience, (though but of a deceived & disguised conscience,) . . .[84]

For many, this decree did not go far enough.[85] They had seen for themselves the slack application of earlier laws against 'Heresie'.

They wanted the 'weeds' growing in the 'corn', the 'Cockle and Tares' harboured by the 'Lords Wheat', to be punished promptly, not 'burned in the fyre . . . in the end of this worlde'.[86] I am not suggesting that James's speeches and proclamations constitute a new source for *King Lear*. I simply want to establish that in 1609–10 – the most likely date, it seems, for a substantial reworking of *King Lear*[87] – James's tolerant attitude towards 'Heresie' was widely remarked. It was a matter of great public interest, and in some quarters of grave concern, that there were then 'No Heretiques burn'd, but wenches Sutors'.

As for the unfortunate Legate and Wightman, burned in 1612: they suffered the displeasure of a King goaded beyond endurance by the 'Dutch Arminians'. James's patience frayed when, engaged abroad in a fierce controversy with the theologian Vorstius, he found unorthodox opinions (in Wightman's case somewhat resembling those of his opponent) flourishing at home. As W. K. Jordan remarks in the standard study of religious toleration in England:

> The burning of Legate and Wightman represents an abnormal phase of James's policy which was wholly out of keeping with his known sentiments on the subject of heresy. James was a kindly and, on the whole, a merciful man. But the Arminian controversy had agitated him as did nothing else in the reign . . .[88]

So while Stone is right to say that the couplet about 'Nobles' and 'Heretiques' could not have been composed between 1612 and early 1618, he is wrong to imply that it could not have been written between about 1606 and 1611.

Nor is it possible to agree with Stone when he calls the Fool's prophecy 'self-evidently irrelevant' (*Textual History*, p. 119).[89] The speech dramatizes, most relevantly, the F Fool's growing sense of his own irrelevance. The reviser or adapter has turned a stilted convention, according to which the stage fool can move easily between engagement with a play and engagement with its audience, to profound dramatic effect. As he recites Merlin's prophecy,[90] the F Fool begins to leave Lear. The general, rather than the specific, relevance of the speech to its speaker becomes apparent if the two are regarded historically; for in Jacobean England the ancient association between folly and prediction still held good.[91] The flippancy of the speech also becomes comprehensible if it is considered in an historical perspective. So highly regarded was the genre of spoof prophecy in the Renaissance that a contemporary of Shakespeare's would have had no difficulty in accepting the inclusion of the Fool's speech in a serious tragedy.[92] As for the relevance of the prophecy to *King Lear* as a whole, it is difficult to see why it should be thought less crucial to the play than Gloucester's speech (significantly expanded in F) about the consequences which must follow from the 'late eclipses in the Sunne and Moone' (C2; TLN 433–44; 1.2.103–14) or Edmund's sarcastic 'prediction' of 'diuisions' a few lines later (C2ᵛ; 1.2.136–49; TLN 465–73). Stone has failed to perceive the degree to which *King Lear*, like *Macbeth*, is preoccupied with prophecy. The similarity between the tragedies is in this respect striking, for both use prediction ironically. But whereas in *Macbeth* irony flows from the fulfilment of apparently impossible prophecies (Birnam wood *does* come to Dunsinane, Macbeth *is* finally killed by a man not 'of woman borne'), in *King Lear* irony flows from the disappointment of reasonable hopes. For example, at the start of Act Four, Edgar predicts that he has reached the nadir of his fortunes, that what follows must be better: 'The worst returnes to laughter' (H2; TLN 2184; 4.1.6). F emphasizes his optimism by a three-line addition: 'Welcome then, | Thou vnsubstantiall ayre that I embrace: | The Wretch that thou hast blowne vnto the worst, | Owes nothing to thy blasts.' But Edgar's prediction is immediately frustrated; his father enters, blind, in the care of a poor countryman. 'O Gods,' he cries (in both texts), 'who ist can say I am at the worst, | I am worse then ere I was. . . . And worse I may be yet, the worst is not, | As [F, So] long as we can say, this is the worst' (H2ᵛ; TLN 2207–11; 4.1.25–8). Another example: when Edgar leaves Gloucester just before the battle, he predicts 'If euer I returne to you againe ile bring you comfort' only to return after the '*Alarum and retreat*' with 'Away old man, giue me thy hand, away, | King *Lear* hath lost, he and his daughter taine . . . ' (K4; TLN 2923–9; 5.2.3–6). Again, at 5.3.71, in a line clearly linked to the Fool's prophecy, Regan says that she will marry Edmund. Hearing Goneril (Albany in F) mockingly remark that Edmund could only be made Albany's equal through her power 'if hee should husband you', Regan replies, 'Iesters doe oft proue Prophets' (L1; TLN 3012–13). But the joke is on her, not Goneril or Albany. Her ironic prediction goes ironically wrong. She never weds Edmund. It is in quite another sense that the Bastard, Goneril and she all 'marie in an instant' (L3; TLN 3180; 5.3.230).

It is not only the characters whose reasonable hopes are dashed in

King Lear. The play constantly provokes its audience to predict a return from 'the worst', only to disappoint. The return of Kent (1.4), the news of Cordelia's mustered army (3.1), Cornwall's and Oswald's deserved deaths (3.7, 4.2, 4.6), the 'Sun shine and raine at once' of Q 4.3.18 (H4ᵛ), the arrival of Cordelia (4.4) and the suggestion that she 'redeemes nature from the generall curse which twaine hath [F, haue] brought her to' (I4ᵛ; TLN 2648–9; 4.6.206–7), Kent's happy anticipation of that 'meete' time when he will reveal himself to Lear (K1ᵛ; TLN 2759; 4.7.11), and then, in the last act, the triumph of Edgar over Edmund (with the dying man's good deed), the murder and suicide of Regan and Goneril, and Albany's final disillusionment with the forces of evil: all these prompt us to expect a turn towards tragicomedy (as in *King Leir*); but it never comes. Indeed, at the end of the play tragicomedy is travestied: by revealing his identity, Edgar kills his father (5.3.182–200); Kent's reconciliation with the King – unlike, say, Camillo's with Leontes – is left incomplete, a sad end to his long and faithful service (5.3.268–95); and the play's Perdita is brought in dead. Critics sometimes say that the conclusion of *King Lear* is tragic because it defies poetic justice. But this notion rests on the very neo-classical misconceptions which it seems to flout. Poetic justice is not even negatively relevant to the play's profound sleight of hand, its tragic duplicity. *King Lear*, though not lifelike, shows us what life is like; in itself it makes no concessions to what we would like life to be. Yet, because it also reminds us that (being drama) it could at almost any moment resolve its tragic action in comedy, it makes us think that (since it shows us what life is like) life need not after all be what it is (like), and that its mere being what it is is desperately unfair.

The Fool's wisdom at TLN 1734–49 should by now be apparent. What he tells us, the play confirms: that the only safe prediction is not. For the Fool's prophecy is a studiously careful exercise in the avoidance of prophecy. The first four lines of the second-hand rhyme tell us what is happening *now*, in the 1600s:

> When Priests are more in word, then matter;
> When Brewers marre their Malt with water;
> When Nobles are their Taylors Tutors,
> No Heretiques burn'd, but wenches Sutors . . .

It takes no great wit to conclude from such abuses that the 'Realme of Albion' has 'come to great confusion'.[93] The Fool then gives us six lines of what will *never* be:

> When euery Case in Law, is right;
> No Squire in debt, nor no poore Knight;
> When Slanders do not liue in Tongues;
> Nor Cut-purses come not to throngs;
> When Vsurers tell their Gold i'th'Field,
> And Baudes, and whores, do Churches build . . . ·

The Fool does not hazard some secure impossibility to cap this sestet ('Then will the moon be made of green cheese', or suchlike). Rather, redoubling his caution about prediction, he opts for a dead certainty: 'Then comes the time, who liues to see't, | That going shalbe vs'd with feet.' In the clever last line, the rewriter ostensibly makes the Fool pile prophecy on prophecy with dizzying rashness, but actually draws attention to that truth inculcated throughout the tragedy, that the only sure knowledge is hindsight: 'This prophecie *Merlin* shall make,' says the Jacobean Fool, 'for I liue before his time.'

An important arrival in both versions of *King Lear*, Poor Tom has a slightly different impact in each text. Initially, the Q and F Fools are alike upstaged by him. It is particularly noticeable in performance that, after an abortive attempt to mediate between Lear and the newly-arrived Bedlam (3.4.39–113), the Fool lapses into silence (3.4.115–84). As the King talks to his 'Philosopher' (G3; TLN 1932; 3.4.154), his jester takes up a marginal role.[94] At this point the texts diverge. In Q 3.6 the Fool fights back, trying to oust Edgar from the King's favour. Hearing Tom's intriguing ramble about '*Freetereto*' and '*Nero*', the Fool puts in his own bid for Lear's attention: 'Prithe Nunckle tell me, whether a mad man be a Gentleman or a Yeoman' (G3ᵛ; 3.6.6, 9–10). In the mock trial which follows, the Fool tries even harder to please the King. He appropriates Poor Tom's idiom, answering his own riddle in the manner of Edgar at 3.4.85–100: 'He's mad, that trusts in the tamenes of a Wolfe, a horses health, a boyes loue, or a whores oath' (G3ᵛ; 3.6.18–19). He then goes further; not content with stealing Edgar's idiom, he deprives him of his lines. When Tom starts the popular song 'Come over the bourn, Bessy', the Fool interrupts him in the Bedlam vein:

> *Edg.* Looke where he stands and glars, wanst thou eyes, at tral madam come ore the broome [bourne] *Bessy* to mee.
> *Foole.* Her boat hath a leake, and she must not speake,
> Why she dares not come, ouer to thee.
> (G3ᵛ; 3.6.23–8)

Evidently, the Fool succeeds. The mad King is impressed enough to make him Edgar's 'yokefellow of equity' (G4; 3.6.37) in the arraignment of Goneril and Regan. Which success makes it the more surprising that, after contributing 'Come hither mistrisse is your name *Gonorill*' and 'Cry you mercy I tooke you for a ioyne stoole' (G4; 3.6.49–50, 52), the Q Fool should disappear from the play.

The Folio 3.6 is quite different from its Quarto equivalent. Whereas in the *Historie* 3.6 the Fool mimics Tom, in the *Tragedie* he declines the gambit. As a result, he retains the marginal position which had been his at 3.4.115–84 in both texts. True, he now has something to say; but his words seem far removed from the stormy centre of the action. In Q, 'Prithe Nunckle tell me, whether a mad man be a Gentleman or a Yeoman' registers as an appeal for attention; but in F it is rather the first half of a laboured and hard-headed jest. After Lear's 'A King, a King', the rewriter has inserted 'No, he's a Yeoman, that ha's a Gentleman to his Sonne: for hee's a mad Yeoman that sees his Sonne a Gentleman before him' (TLN 2010–12; 3.6.12–14). There is a sickening jolt in the later text as we shift from the worldly common sense of this – so reminiscent of the quips about lawyers and rent in 1.4 – to the madness of Lear's QF 'to haue a thousand with red burning spits come hiszing in vpon them [F, 'em].' The effect is a heightened form of that produced by the rewriting at TLN 1327–8 (see p. 220 above). Interestingly, the F addition relates not only to the rest of the tragedy (Lear is the yeoman outstripped by his son because he has given his lands to Albany and Cornwall and fallen lower than ever they were) but to Shakespeare's biography. In 1596, after his sunken fortunes had – apparently with his son's help – revived, the elderly John Shakespeare obtained a coat of arms. The man who had throughout his life been styled 'trades-man' and 'yeoman' on documents became, by a grant of the College of Arms, a 'gentleman'. Shakespeare was clearly not one of those who – like Andrew Lethe in Middleton's *Michaelmas Term* – forgot their parents to find a pedigree. He became a gentleman only as a consequence of his father's promotion. It is probably significant that, in 1602, shortly after John Shakespeare's death, the York Herald Ralph Brooke prepared charges against William Dethick and William Camden for granting gentility to more than a score of 'mean' individuals, including the dramatist's father.[95] We do not know what became of Brooke's complaint; but it may well be that during the 1600s Shakespeare had to justify his claim to the title which he used right up to his death. There are, then, excellent biographical grounds for connecting TLN 2010–12 with Shakespeare. But what I want to emphasize here is the compatibility of the added lines with the other F alterations of Q. At TLN 2010–12, as throughout, the F Fool is a court jester purveying worldly humour to an increasingly uncomprehending King.

The rewriter did not stop his work with the joke about the yeoman. Cutting the mock trial, he carried the Fool even further from the centre of the action than he had been at the end of QF 3.4. Instead of joining Edgar and Lear in a crazy ritual judgement, the F jester stands apart, watching in silence while the King and his grief-stricken 'Philosopher' cope with 'Trey, Blanch, and Sweet-heart' (TLN 2020–32; G4; 3.6.62–75). If Kent finds this spectacle pitiful, the Fool finds it unendurable. He announces his intention of abandoning Lear – that great wheel lying broken at the foot of Fortune's hill:

> *Lear.* Make no noise, make no noise, draw the Curtaines: so, so, wee'l go to Supper i'th'morning.
> *Foole.* And Ile go to bed at noone.
> > (TLN 2041–3; G4ᵛ, lacking the Fool's line; 3.6.83–5)

Those last seven words, added in F, are extraordinary. Strange, atmospheric, intensely suggestive, their significance seems to stem – as so often with the highly-charged language of *King Lear* ('No cause, no cause', 'Alack why thus', 'Fall and cease') – less from their inherent sense than from their being, somehow, entirely of their tragedy.

As the King settles down to sleep, drawing imaginary bed-curtains about him and promising to eat his missed evening meal in the morning, the Fool ostensibly endorses his master's odd timetable. 'Bed at noone' follows 'Supper i'th'morning' because sleep is natural after an evening meal. But the riposte is at least as critical as it is consolatory. It makes the audience keenly aware of the disorderliness of Lear's life. 'Supper i'th'morning' and 'bed at noone' are the world turned upside down, as surely as 'wise men' grown 'Fooles', and 'daughters' made 'mother[s]' (D1; TLN 680–1, 686; 1.4.166–7, 173). And there is nothing festive in Lear's disorderliness. His life has none of the crazy cheer of Falstaff's 'fat-witted' regime at Eastcheap: 'vnbuttoning thee after supper, and sleeping vpon benches after noone . . . What a diuell hast thou to do with the time of the daie?'[96] Indeed, there are sombre echoes of the Old Testament in the exchange which seem designed to underline the seriousness of the situation:

'They [the froward] mete with darkenes in the day time, and grope at noone day, as in the night' (Job 5: 14); 'Wo to thee, ô land, when thy King *is* a childe, and thy princes eat in the morning' (Ecclesiastes 10: 16).[97] What makes the Fool's line particularly serious is its witty accomplishment. Pursuing Lear's 'Supper i'th'morning' to its odd logical conclusion, the Fool cleverly quibbles on a proverbial phrase. As Hilda Hulme has observed,[98] early audiences would have understood 'go to bed at noone' in the sense 'be gulled, naively anticipate the impossible'. By using the phrase knowingly, the Fool implies something like Cleopatra's 'Ile seeme the Foole I am not.'[99] He knows how the world wags, which way the wild geese fly. That is why another sense of the phrase seems relevant:

Goates beard or Go to bedde at noone, hath hollow stalkes, smooth, and of a whitish greene colour, whereupon do grow long leaues crested downe the middle with a swelling ribbe . . . The flowers grow at the top of the stalkes consisting of a number of purple leaues, dasht ouer as it were with a little yellowe dust, set about with nine or ten sharpe pointed greene leaues; the whole flower resembleth a starre when it is spred abroade: for it shutteth it selfe at twelue of the clocke, and sheweth not his face open vntill the next daies sunne do make it flower anew, wherupon it was called Go to bed at noone . . .[100]

Goat's beard, like the marigold 'that goes to bed with'Sun, | And with him rises, weeping',[101] is as much an emblem as a plant.[102] It cannot bear to see the kingly sun decline; it closes up when 'the glorious planet Sol'[103] has passed its zenith. The Fool identifies himself with the flower, warning the audience that he can no longer follow the failing King. As this sense registers, another is unlocked. At the deepest level of significance (the point at which TLN 2043 most clearly means nothing without the play which contains it), 'Ile go to bed at noone' expresses the Fool's determination to leave *King Lear* with its course half run. The Fool sees the lineaments of Lear's tragedy only too well. And he sees that he can do nothing to help his master, now far beyond the reach of a jest. So he resolves to call it a day at 'noone', to abandon the action at its mid-point, to absent himself from half the story.

The changes in the Fool's part, large and small alike, form such a coherent pattern – and are of such consistent quality – that they must surely come from the hand of a single dramatist. That the writer in question was Shakespeare can be deduced from a number of diverse pieces of evidence. There is, first, the profound understanding of the play apparent in all the changes (but especially in the addition of TLN 1734–49, the Fool's prophecy, and TLN 2043, the resonant last line of the F Fool part). The new material is so unpredictable but right, so challenging yet appropriate, that it is difficult to imagine any dramatist who had not lived in the imaginative world of the play through a period of intense creativity composing it. The excellence of the new material helps support a second argument: the F Fool is dramatically superior to his Q equivalent; the only writer capable of surpassing Shakespeare at the height of his powers was Shakespeare; therefore the Fool's part was revised, not adapted. That the Fool's role is better in F than Q is, I think, indisputable. Frequently more effective line-by-line and in the handling of individual exchanges, it is more shapely overall, and its conclusion is clearly and movingly motivated. Moreover, the F Fool overlaps with Edgar and Lear much less than does the Q. Act Three of the *Tragedie* presents a full range of *folie* (the French word preserves what the English has lost), from the King's real and Edgar's affected insanity to the Fool's coolly rational riddling. In the *Historie*, where the Fool is less a court jester than a sage natural, covetous of his Nuncle's attention, the commonsensical kind of folly is sparsely represented. A third piece of evidence is provided by the distinctive image cluster at TLN 1322–7 (see p. 220, and 396 below). And a fourth by the biographical associations of TLN 2010–12 – that joke about the yeoman so indissolubly linked to the other changes in the F Fool's part that it could under no circumstances be considered an independent addition. In short, the changes in Fool's part are Shakespearian. Since this is so, since the most suspect strand in the apparently authoritative text (see above, p. 217) is demonstrably authorial, we can surely conclude with some confidence that *The Tragedie of King Lear* is a revision, not an adaptation, of the *Historie*.

NOTES

1. Q2, F4ᵛ; TLN 1581; 2.2.541–2.
2. Revision within collaboration (as in *The Booke of Sir Thomas Moore*) is another matter. As I suggest on p. 209, collaborators behaved like parts of a multiple author. Restoration adaptations, like Dryden's *All for Love* and Mrs Behn's *Abdelazer*, are consciously excluded from this study. Special circumstances obtain when half a century and a great shift in sensibility come between an author and his adapter. (See Gary Taylor's discussion below, pp. 408–9.)
3. *The Spanish Tragedy with Additions 1602*, ed. W. W. Greg for the Malone Society (Oxford, 1925).

4. 977–1030, which amplifies Hieronimo's reaction to Horatio's death; 1272–81, which intensifies the irony of the Knight Marshal's second encounter with Lorenzo; 1866–1910 (perhaps memorially contaminated), lamenting Horatio's loss to the two anonymous Portingales; 2063–2247, the famous Painter scene; and 3126–74, which is a version of Hieronimo's apology for his murderous playlet 'Soliman and Perseda'.

5. *The Spanish Tragedy*, ed. Philip Edwards, The Revels Plays (1959), p. xliii.

6. '*Draw his sword*' (677), '*Offer to kill him*' (687), '*They breake in, and hold Hieronimo*' (3115), and '*He bites out his tongue*' (3176).

7. See the list of variants on pp. xvii–xxv of *The Spanish Tragedy (1592)*, ed. W. W. Greg and D. Nichol Smith for the Malone Society (Oxford, 1948 [1949]).

8. At 2852–3. Previous quartos make Hieronimo's playlet sound like *Façade*: 'And I my selfe in an Oration, | That I will haue there behinde a curtaine, | And with a strange and wondrous shew besides: | Assure your selfe shall make the matter knowne.'

9. Schücking goes too far (in *Die Zusätze zur 'Spanish Tragedy'*, Leipzig, 1938), but one or two of the other 'additions' may also be replacements.

10. 'Speake' for 'But' (3142), 'reuenged' for 'auenged' (3151).

11. *Henslowe's Diary*, p. 206. The classic formulation of this view is Greg's, in the Introduction to *Marlowe's 'Doctor Faustus' 1604–1616: Parallel Texts* (Oxford, 1950). Greg's edition is used throughout.

12. See Fredson Bowers, 'Marlowe's *Doctor Faustus*: The 1602 Additions', *Studies in Bibliography*, 26 (1973), 1–18, and *Christopher Marlowe: The Complete Works*, 2 vols. (Cambridge, 2nd edn., 1981), II, 123–59; 'A Note on the Text' in Keith Walker's edition of the tragedy, Fountainwell Drama Texts, 26 (Edinburgh, 1973); Roma Gill's review of the first edition of Bowers's *Christopher Marlowe*, *Review of English Studies*, NS 25 (1974), 459–64; Constance Brown Kuriyama's excellent 'Dr. Greg and *Doctor Faustus*: The Supposed Originality of the 1616 Text', *English Literary Renaissance*, 5 (1975), 171–97; J. C. Maxwell's 'Note on the Text' in *Christopher Marlowe: Complete Plays and Poems*, ed. E. D. Pendry (1976); and Michael J. Warren's textually over-pessimistic '*Doctor Faustus*: The Old Man and the Text', *English Literary Renaissance*, 11 (1981), 111–47.

13. At B859–1072 Faustus arranges Bruno's rescue, and we see the Papal party depart to return in ceremony for its banquet; at B1181–1232 the B characters Martino, Frederick, and Benvolio are introduced, their dispute with Faustus being unfolded at B1362–6 and B1371–1522; at B1578–1636 and B1675–1768 the clowns meet in the tavern, interrupt Faustus's sorcery at Vanholt and are struck dumb; at B1894–1921 Lucifer, Mephostophilis and Belzebub gloat over the doomed hero; at B1983–2035 Faustus hears from Mephostophilis that it was he who first led him into sin, he has a final encounter with the Good and Bad Angels, and he endures a vision of hell.

14. A614–27, concerning Mephostophilis's book of knowledge; A930–47, the second speech of the Chorus; and A1377–86, the last speech of the Old Man.

15. And there is certainly something odd about A's combination of jog-trot regularity and frank illogicality: 'By which sweete path thou maist attaine the gole | That shall conduct thee to celestial rest', etc.

16. The other relevant passages are: the recast Robin–Rafe/Dick sequence (A948–1037, B743–76 and 1128–80); A870–1, B856–8 (a mere detail, designed to set up the B banquet scene); the Obtuse Knight–Benvolio scene (A1038–1133, B1234–1370); the Horse-Courser scenes (A1143–69 and 1175–1219, B1525–45 and 1553–68); the new start to the grape sequence (A1227–35, B1637–51) and the new conclusion to the scene (A1259–65, B1769–74); and the Scholars' vision of Helen (A1291–1301, B1802–11).

17. That we are not dealing here with lacunae in the B copy made good by an edition of A can be seen from the A-B variation, minimal though it is.

18. All quotations are taken from this text (British Library shelf-mark 11773 c. 8); references are to Hunold Nibbe, '*The Fleire*' *by Edward Sharpham, Nach der Quarto 1607* (Louvain, 1912), in *Materialien zur Kunde des älteren Englischen Dramas*, ed. W. Bang. The following paragraphs develop, partly through dissent, Clifford Leech's 'The Plays of Edward Sharpham: Alterations Accomplished and Projected' (*Review of English Studies*, 11 (1935), 69–74), apparently the only extended account of this fascinating document.

19. The cut play is, in all, some 20 pages shorter than the 56-page original. If the cut version were performed, it would probably run to about 90 minutes, as against 2½ hours for Sharpham's text (John Barton's estimates). In Sharpham's *Fleire* there are 21 characters; in the adapter's, 12. Leech judges that Sharpham's play 'could probably be acted by a company of sixteen, consisting of eleven men and five boys' (originally, of course, it was played at Blackfriars by the Children of the Revels), while the cut text 'could be performed by a company of seven men and four boys' (p. 73).

20. On provincial touring see Gary Taylor, *Three Studies in the Text of 'Henry V'* (Oxford, 1979), p. 109.

21. In view of the unchecked inconsistencies in the cut version, and especially the confusion produced at 5.289–302 (see Appendix III, p. 244), I agree with Leech that the adaptation was never quite completed and probably never performed.

22. At 1.191–242, 2.503–74, 3.65–192, 3.223–60 and 5.10–87.

23. Excluding those changes – such as 'Madam' for 'Ladies' – forced upon him by the conflation of characters, and the erratic modification of 'Fleire' to 'Antifront'.

24. The adjustment was probably made in deference to the 1606 *Act to Restrain Abuses of Players*, a law forbidding – among other things – profanity in theatrical performances. For similar cuts see Appendix II, p. 242 (*Doctor Faustus*), and Appendix III, p. 244 (*The Fleire*).

25. 'Adream'd' is a straightforward but nevertheless conjectural reconstruction of the annotator's 'ad re   an'd'. Spark has been removed from the stage direction at line 88, his prefix at 91 cut, and 93–5 plus 108–12 deleted.

26. But this should probably be excluded from any count of small adjustments because it forms a small part of something larger. As Leech observes: 'In the original Act I., scene iii., [1.59–188] "a Gentleman" applies to enter the service of the courtesans and is interviewed by their "waiting Gentlewoman." He does not appear again in the play, and Antifront is preferred to their service by one of the gallants. In the cut version, it is Antifront who applies to the waiting gentlewoman, and it has clearly been the object of the adapter to omit any reference to his being preferred' (pp. 71–2).

27. The reproductions in *William Shakespeare 'The History of King Henry the Fourth' as revised by Sir Edward Dering, Bart. A Facsimile Edition*, prepared by George Walton Williams and Gwynne Blakemore Evans for The Folger Facsimiles (Charlottesville, 1974), have been used throughout. I occasionally disagree with the editors' interpretation of the accidentals of the manuscript.

28. Ignoring evident errors, such as 'Rembring' for 'Remembred' at *Part 2* 1.1.103 (Fol. 43).

29. Inserted before *Part 1* 1.1.28–33:

> high
> ~~hault~~
> The ~~proud~~ aspiring Crescent of yᵉ Turke,
> Wee'll plucke into a lower ~~ob~~ Orbe. and then
> borrowed
> Humbling her ∧ horned Pride to th' English lyon,

With labor a[n]d with honore wee'le fetcht here
A sweating laurell from ye glorious East
And plant new iems on Éroyall Englands crowne.
Wee'll pitch our honores at ye sonnes vprise
and sell our selves or winn a glorious prize.

30. Interestingly, the annotator corrected a number of the scribe's errors and reversed certain alterations. (At *Part 1* 2.4.285, indeed, where the scribe begins a four-line cut, he has written the tart objection 'vide printed booke' (Fol. 18^v).) Prepared to 'improve' Shakespeare when he felt the urge, the annotator was at the same time possessed of a strong respect for copy. On one level he accepted and indeed initiated rewriting; on another, he resisted it.

31. *The Profession of Dramatist in Shakespeare's Time 1590–1642* (Princeton, 1971), p. 263.

32. '*Locrine* Revised, *Selimus*, and Early Responses to *Tamburlaine*', *Research Opportunities in Renaissance Drama*, 23 (1980), 33–54.

33. *Macbeth* is a possible exception to this rule. Shakespeare has left such large quantities of authoritative text that it is possible to sense how his verse should run when uncontaminated, and on the basis of that to judge whether his tragedy has suffered local non-authorial amending. It seems to me that the extreme positions adopted by J. Dover Wilson in the New Cambridge *Macbeth* (Cambridge, rev. edn., 1951), pp. xxii–xxviii, and J. M. Nosworthy in *Shakespeare's Occasional Plays* (1965), Chs. 1–3, are alike untenable. Associating metrical irregularity with the interfering hand of Middleton, Wilson finds rewriting wherever the verse becomes ruggedly expressive (as in 1.2, a scene which includes nothing more irregular, when the verse is properly printed, than the authoritative opening sequence of Q2 *Hamlet*). Nosworthy, anxious to rescue as much of the F text as possible for Shakespeare, produces a series of parallel passages which fail to rise above coincidence and the commonplace. The consensus view that – in the light of their links with *The Witch*, the introduction of Hecate, and (I would add) the form of the stage direction at TLN 1429–30 – TLN 1428–69 (3.5), 1566–75, and 1672–80 are interpolations by Middleton seems to me very reasonable. If this position is indeed correct, it is significant that the additions correspond in scale to those found in *The Spanish Tragedy* (1602) and the B-text *Doctor Faustus*. Here the through line numbering is deceptive. When the text of the songs '*Come away*' and '*Blacke Spirits*' (only alluded to by their titles in F) is included in the total for the first and second interpolations, they reach 81 and 28 actors' lines respectively. The third insertion is textually slighter: at 8 spoken lines it is roughly half the length of Hamlet's proposed interpolation and shorter than the shortest 'new addition' in Pavier's version of Kyd. However, since it contains directions for music and a Witches' Dance, it doubtless took at least as long to perform as the other interpolations and constituted an important and popular part of the audience's experience of the adapted play.

34. Ed. R. V. Holdsworth, The New Mermaids (1974), pp. xiv–xv, xliii; ed. George R. Price, The Regents Renaissance Drama Series (1977), pp. xiii–xiv, 111–12.

35. Holdsworth, pp. xii, 5 (n. 5).

36. E. K. Chambers's 'I have sometimes fancied that the fly episode might be Webster's' (*William Shakespeare: A Study in Facts and Problems*, 2 vols., Oxford, 1930; I, 321) can hardly be taken 'seriously'. Presumably Chambers was impressed by the resemblance between 'thy sight is young, | And thou shalt read, when mine begin to dazell' (*Titus* TLN 1538–9; 3.2.84–5) and 'Cover her face: mine eyes dazzle: she died young', Ferdinand's words over the dead Duchess of Malfi (ed. John Russell Brown, The Revels Plays (1964), 4.2.264). But Webster was a magpie, and if the similarity suggests anything it is that the fly scene was in

the repertory before the first performance of *The Duchess of Malfi* in 1613–14 – though it should be remembered that Webster's play was not published till 1623, and that some scholars believe that Okes's quarto presents a revised text (Revels edition, pp. xxv–xxvii). Joseph E. Kramer's sustained attack on the scene – in '*Titus Andronicus*: The "Fly-Killing" Incident', *Shakespeare Studies*, 5 (1969), 9–19 – rests on nothing more substantial than a critical dislike of its author's cold artfulness: 'Thou Map of woe, that thus dost talk in signes . . .'

37. See *Titus Andronicus*, ed. J. C. Maxwell, new Arden Shakespeare (1953). In the 1961 edition, Maxwell hedges.

38. Because: (i) the scene is not essential to the action; (ii) it defies the 'law of re-entry' (though that law is not binding) by having its characters exit only to return immediately for 4.1; (iii) it uses forms found nowhere else in Qq1–3 or F both in prefixes ('*An.*' for Titus) and the dialogue ('Tamira' for Tamora).

39. In the Induction to *Bartholomew Fair* (1614), Johnson cynically remarks the play's persistent popularity.

40. Quoting from the title-pages of Q1 (1598) and Q3 (1610).

41. The Prologue, 1.1, 1.2, 4.1, 5.2.92–109 and Epilogue 15–81 of the text printed by C. F. Tucker Brooke in *The Shakespeare Apocrypha* (Oxford, 1908). The longest addition is 66 lines, the shortest 15, the average about 37. Like the 1602 *Spanish Tragedy* (and like QC *The Malcontent*) the 1610 *Mucedorus* has been lightly edited. Richard Proudfoot informs me that, in the Epilogue of the text printed in 1606, a reference to King James replaces one directed at Queen Elizabeth.

42. Tucker Brooke's assertion that 'The additions are certainly not by the original author and are superior to the rest of the comedy' (p. xxv) cannot inspire complete confidence because it neglects the apparent memorial contamination of Qq 1–2. In his new Oxford edition of the Shakespeare Apocrypha (in progress), Richard Proudfoot argues strongly that the 1610 *Mucedorus* should be considered a non-authorial adaptation.

43. '*THE* MALCONTENT. Augmented by *Marston*. With the Additions played by the Kings Maiesties servants. Written by *Ihon Webster*.' The heading of the Induction appears to confirm this: 'THE INDVCTION TO THE MALECONTENT, AND the additions acted by the Kings Maiesties servants. Written by *Iohn Webster* '

44. In 'Webster's Additions to *The Malcontent*: Linguistic Evidence', *Notes and Queries*, 226 (1981), 153–8, Lake grants Marston 1.3.108–49 and 155–72, 1.4.43–89, 2.3.23–37, 5.3.66–97 and 5.6.137–58, and Webster the Induction, 1.8.1–62, 3.1.34–150, 5.1.1–55, 5.2.10–39, and 5.4.19–34 (using the lineation of *The Malcontent*, ed. G. K. Hunter, The Revels Plays (1975)).

45. E. K. Chambers's suggestion in *The Elizabethan Stage* (4 vols., Oxford, 1923; III, 359–60) that Jonson revised *Every Man in his Humour* in 1605 or 1606 still has its supporters, though I suspect that Herford and Simpson are right to postulate a revision *c*.1612 (*Ben Jonson*, 11 vols. (Oxford, 1925–52), I, 331–5; IX, 334–6). Certainly, as Gabriele Bernhard Jackson has shown in her Yale edition of the comedy (New Haven, 1969; pp. 221–3), the Prologue must be dated late.

46. Herford and Simpson, employed throughout.

47. Herford and Simpson, IV, 17.

48. *Epicoene* is an exception among the early plays in that its first extant quarto (1620) postdates F1 and has no independent authority.

49. 'Chapman's "Tragedy of Bussy D'Ambois"': Problems of the Revised Quarto', *Modern Language Review*, 48 (1953), 257–69, quoting p. 258.

50. Quotations from original quartos; references to *Bussy D'Ambois*, ed. Nicholas Brooke, The Revels Plays (1964).

51. By, for example, Berta Sturman, 'The 1641 Edition of Chapman's *Bussy*

D'Ambois', *Huntington Library Quarterly*, 14 (1950–1), 171–201, and Brooke in his edition; Robert P. Adams's vigorous literary attack on Q2 ('Critical Myths and Chapman's Original *Bussy D'Ambois'*, *Renaissance Drama*, 9 (1966), 141–61) is also relevant.

52. 'The Revised *Bussy D'Ambois* and *The Revenge of Bussy D'Ambois*: Joint Performance in Thematic Counterpoint', *English Language Notes*, 9 (1971–2), 253–62; 'The Revised Version of Chapman's *Bussy D'Ambois*: A Shift in Point of View', *Studies in Philology*, 70 (1973), 288–305.

53. Tricomi here builds on T. M. Parrott's 'The Date of Chapman's "Bussy D'Ambois"', *Modern Language Review*, 3 (1907–8), 126–40, and Peter Ure's 'The Date of the Revision of Chapman's "The Tragedy of Bussy D'Ambois"', *Notes and Queries*, 197 (1952), 1–2.

54. *The Noble Spanish Soldier* was printed in 1634; *The Welsh Embassador* apparently remained in manuscript until 1921, when it was edited for the Malone Society by H. Littledale. Line references to both plays are from *The Dramatic Works of Thomas Dekker*, ed. Fredson Bowers, 4 vols. (Cambridge, 1953–61), IV. The received text of *The Noble Spanish Soldier* may have been composed in the early 1620s or it may have been revised then from a collaborative play written twenty years before. Either way, as Cyrus Hoy declares in his authoritative commentary on *The Welsh Embassador*, 'the extant text of *The Noble Spanish Soldier* is certainly Dekker's unaided work' (*Introductions, Notes, and Commentaries to texts in 'The Dramatic Works of Thomas Dekker'*, 4 vols. (Cambridge 1980), IV, 140). The status of the tragicomedy is less secure. Dekker's hand is evident almost everywhere; but, as Bertram Lloyd observes in 'The Authorship of *The Welsh Embassador*' (*Review of English Studies*, 21 (1945), 192–201), there are some signs of Ford's manner in 3.3 and 5.1. Fortunately, only the early and undoubtedly Dekkerian scenes of the play are involved in our analysis.

55. There is a full list of these debts in Hoy (*Introduction, Notes and Commentaries*, IV, 167–8). In all, about 100 lines of *The Noble Spanish Soldier* are carried over.

56. On the priority of Q over F see Gary Taylor, '*Troilus and Cressida*: Bibliography, Performance, and Interpretation', *Shakespeare Studies*, 16 (1983), 99–136. On the approximately 500 small substantive variants between the texts see Kenneth Muir's Oxford Shakespeare edition of the play (Oxford, 1982), p. 3.

57. Which is not to say that all the revisions in all the plays postdate first performance. Since the first editions of these works were set from authorial rather than theatrical copy, some changes in the variant editions might stem from revision effected between the composition of this authorial copy and the settling of texts in early prompt-books. The same holds for Q and F *King Lear* (see p. 215). Indeed, the textual history of *Every Man in his Humour* seems very close to that of Shakespeare's tragedy if, as MacDonald P. Jackson and Gary Taylor argue (below, pp. 329–30, 354–67), the main revision of *King Lear* began on or from a copy of Q; for hints of Q accidentals in the apparently manuscript-based F1 *Every Man in his Humour* suggest that Jonson worked up his play from a copy of its 1601 Q (see '*Every Man in His Humour': A Parallel Text Edition*, by J. W. Lever, Regents Renaissance Drama Series (1972), pp. xxvii–xxviii), and that the bulk of the revision is, because of this, likely to postdate the first performance.

58. *The Dramatic Works in the Beaumont and Fletcher Canon*, gen. ed. Fredson Bowers (Cambridge, 1966–), II, 24. References throughout to the text, ed. Turner, in this volume; quotations from the original quartos. The only important consideration neglected by Turner is the echo of Jonson's 'On My First Daughter' in Q2-unique text at 2.1.78–9 (the lines cannot derive independently from Martial). Jonson's poem was not published until 1616, and the first

performance of *The Maid's Tragedy* must have taken place between 1609 and autumn 1611. But the difficulties introduced by the debt are not insurmountable; for the poem is usually put in the poet's Catholic period (i.e. dated to the 1600s), and if anyone was allowed to read it in manuscript it would have been Jonson's beloved Beaumont.

59. *Philaster*, ed. Andrew Gurr, The Revels Plays (1969), p. lxxviii.
60. Robert K. Turner, Textual Introduction to *Philaster*, in *The Dramatic Works in the Beaumont and Fletcher Canon*, I, 386–7. Turner's edition is used throughout.
61. 'I pray you in your Letters, |When you shall these vnluckie deeds relate, |Speake of me, as I am' (TLN 3650–2; 5.2.340–2) supports, much more readily than 'I pray you in your letters, |When you shall these vnlucky deedes relate, |Speake of them as they are' (N2), Eliot's claim that Othello is indulging in romantic self-deception: 'What Othello seems to me to be doing in making this speech is *cheering himself up*. He is endeavouring to escape reality, he has ceased to think about Desdemona, and is thinking about himself. Humility is the most difficult of all virtues to achieve; nothing dies harder than the desire to think well of oneself' ('Shakespeare and the Stoicism of Seneca' (1927), *Selected Essays* (3rd edn., 1951), p. 130).
62. W. W. Greg, *The Shakespeare First Folio: Its Bibliographical and Textual History* (Oxford, 1955), p. 358, and *Othello 1622*, ed. Charlton Hinman, Shakespeare Quarto Facsimiles, 16 (Oxford, 1975), p. xiv.
63. Alice Walker's stubbornly insensitive one-text theory (*Textual Problems in the First Folio* (Cambridge, 1953), Ch. 7; New Cambridge *Othello* (Cambridge, 1957), pp. 121–35) has been assaulted so often that I shall not linger to attack it here.
64. J. Dover Wilson, *The Manuscript of Shakespeare's 'Hamlet' and the Problems of its Transmission*, 2 vols. (Cambridge, 1934), I, 165.
65. R. C. Bald, 'An Early Version of Middleton's "Game at Chesse"', *Modern Language Review*, 38 (1943), 177–80; E. A. J. Honigmann, *The Stability of Shakespeare's Text* (1965), pp. 47–77.
66. This survey of revised plays is meant to be ample rather than exhaustive. Other works – such as *Love's Labour's Lost* or Fletcher's *The Woman's Prize* – might have been cited, other authors (like the disappointed dilettante William Percy) advanced.
67. For example *Bussy D'Ambois* 1.2.182–7, *The Maid's Tragedy* 1.1.140, *Philaster* 3.2.75 (but there are more than sixty reattributions in this text alone), *Othello* 5.2.171, *Troilus and Cressida* 5.2.69, *Hamlet* 3.2.320.
68. For F's dependence, in part at least, on Q2, see Gary Taylor, 'Folio Copy for *Hamlet, King Lear*, and *Othello*', *Shakespeare Quarterly*, 34 (1983), 44–61.
69. See Gary Taylor, 'The Date and Authorship of the Folio Version', below.
70. F cuts some 230 lines from Q2, and adds about 95.
71. It is surely highly significant that each of the authorial revisions probably or certainly made for theatrical revival which we have discussed above is the work of an established dramatist. Birde and Rowley, Chettle, and the young Dekker and Jonson can hardly have exerted the same authority over Henslowe as the reviser of *Troilus and Cressida* did over the King's Men. (See *Henslowe's Diary*, pp. 101, 175, 182, 187, 198, 200, 203, 206 and 216.) On the contrary: an author like Shakespeare would have been able to insist on the adoption of minor alterations, despite the cost; young impoverished poets would not.
72. See David J. Lake, *The Canon of Thomas Middleton's Plays* (Cambridge, 1975), pp. 279–86; MacD. P. Jackson, *Studies in Attribution: Middleton and Shakespeare*, Jacobean Drama Studies, 79 (Salzburg, 1979), pp. 54–66; and R. V. Holdsworth's 'Middleton and Shakespeare: The Case for Middleton's

Hand in *Timon of Athens*' (unpublished Ph.D. thesis, University of Manchester, 1982).

73. See Alfred Hart, 'Shakespeare and the Vocabulary of *The Two Noble Kinsmen*', *Review of English Studies*, 10 (1934), 274–87; Marco Mincoff, 'The Authorship of *The Two Noble Kinsmen*', *English Studies*, 33 (1952), 97–115; Kenneth Muir, *Shakespeare as Collaborator* (1960), Ch. 6; Cyrus Hoy, 'The Shares of Fletcher and his Collaborators in the Beaumont and Fletcher Canon (VII)', *Studies in Bibliography*, 15 (1962), 71–90. These studies of internal evidence all confirm the testimony of the title-page of the first edition (1634), which attributes the play to Shakespeare and Fletcher.

74. Compare *The Malcontent* 3.1.141 and *King Lear* 1.4.136.

75. *The Structure of Complex Words* (3rd edn., 1977), pp. 125–57; 'Lear, Tolstoy and the Fool', in *Shooting an Elephant* (1950).

76. Johnson seems to have been the first editor to propose this explanation for the cut.

77. 'Nay he reseru'd a blanket, else we had beene all sham'd' (G2; TLN 1846–7). 'Any decent actor', according to John Barton, 'would take that as an invitation to address the audience.' Certain other passages hover at the margin of audience address (3.2.27–36 and 3.4.78–9 are examples); a director – especially an F director – concerned to emphasize the Fool's ambivalent dramatic status might push such lines towards soliloquy.

78. That is, 'when noblemen tell their tailors how to make clothes, and the only heretics to be burned are lovers who [slang sense] catch VD'. Although the VD–burning connection is strong, that between the lover and the heretic is far from self-evident. It may therefore be significant that Shakespeare couples love and heresy elsewhere (see especially *Much Ado About Nothing* 1.1.230–7 and *Twelfth Night* 1.5.221–8).

79. See 'The Problem of the Recusants', pp. 141–60 of Wallace Notestein, *The House of Commons 1604–1610* (New Haven, 1971).

80. *Stuart Royal Proclamations*, Vol. 1, *Royal Proclamations of King James I 1603–1625*, ed. James F. Larkin and Paul L. Hughes (Oxford, 1973), p. 144.

81. *The Workes of the Most High and Mightie Prince, James*, ed. James Montagu (1616), p. 544.

82. *Proceedings in Parliament 1610*, ed. E. R. Foster, 2 vols. (New Haven, 1966), II, 106–7.

83. See *Parliamentary Debates in 1610*, ed. S. R. Gardiner (Camden Society, 1861 [1862]), pp. 42–4 for the petition and James's reply.

84. *Stuart Royal Proclamations*, I, 245–6.

85. The strength of feeling can be gauged from the *Petition of Ecclesiastical Grievances* delivered to James about a month after the publication of his *Proclamation*: ' . . . your Majesty therefore would be pleased, at the humble suit of your Commons in this present parliament assembled in those cases so highly concerning the glory of God, the preservation of true religion, of your Majesty and the state, to suffer your Highness' natural clemency to retire itself and to give place unto justice; and to lay your royal command upon all your ministers of justice, both ecclesiastical and civil, to see the laws made against jesuits, seminary priests, their receivers, maintainers and abettors, and all other popish recusants (of what kind, degree and sex soever) to be duly and exactly executed without dread, favor or delay' (*Proceedings in Parliament 1610*, II, 255).

86. Matthew 13: 40 (Geneva version). James's speech to parliament after the murder of Henry IV and his *Proclamation for the due execution of all former Lawes against Recusants* both invoke the parable of the tares and the wheat (Matthew 13: 24–30 and 36–43) in order to remind the people of Christ's desire that 'Heretiques'

should not be punished by man but left to God at the end of time. 'Let bothe [the tares and the wheat] growe together vntil the haruest, and in time of haruest I wil say to the reapers, Gather ye first the tares, and binde them in sheaues to burne them: but gather the wheat into my barne. . . .'

87. See especially Gary Taylor's '*King Lear*: The Date and Authorship of the Folio Version' (below, pp. 354–95).

88. *The Development of Religious Toleration in England*, 4 vols. (1932–40), II, 51.

89. Stone is not, of course, the first scholar to object to the prophecy. Grant White and Cowden Clarke also thought it an unauthorized interpolation. See H. H. Furness's New Variorum edition of *King Lear* (Philadelphia, 1880).

90. On the Fool's debt to Puttenham and pseudo-Chaucer here see Kenneth Muir's notes in the new Arden *Lear* (rev. edn., 1972), Gary Taylor's discussion (below, pp. 382–5), and Peter W. M. Blayney's forthcoming Commentary (*Origins*, II). Chapter 13 of Keith Thomas's *Religion and the Decline of Magic* (1971) provides a fascinating account of the sixteenth- and seventeenth-century standing of 'the dreamer Merlin and his prophecies' (*1 Henry IV*, Q1, F2; TLN 1680; 3.1.148).

91. Enid Welsford, *The Fool: His Social and Literary History* (1935), pp. 76–112, 128–81.

92. Mikhail Bakhtin, trans. Iswolsky, *Rabelais and His World* (Cambridge, Mass., 1968), pp. 232–9.

93. I agree with those editors, from Duthie on, who place TLN 1746 (divided into a couplet) after TLN 1739, breaking the prophecy into two roughly equal stanzas. But since TLN 1746 and TLN 1747–8 both state the obvious (England is always, as far as the English are concerned, in 'great confusion', and we always go 'with feet'), my argument would still operate if the three Folio lines were taken to be a single prophetic conclusion. Warburton's rearrangement (TLN 1747–8 after 1739, TLN 1746 where it stands) has not found much support among modern editors – rightly, I believe. If Shakespeare did mean TLN 1747–8 to follow 1739, the argument outlined above would have to alter in emphasis (towards the blatant obviousness of true prophecy), but not in direction.

94. Peter Brook in his film version of *King Lear* emphasized the Fool's alienation by having Paul Scofield push his jester aside at 'Let me aske you [i.e. Edgar] one word in priuate' (G3; TLN 1939; 3.4.160).

95. There is a lucid account in *The Riverside Shakespeare* (Appendix B, pp. 1829–31).

96. *1 Henry IV*, Q1, A3ᵛ; TLN 116–20; 1.2.2–6.

97. Geneva Version (where 'thy King *is* a childe' carries the marginal gloss: 'That is, without wisdome and coūsel'). See Rosalie L. Colie, 'The Energies of Endurance: Biblical Echo in *King Lear*', in *Some Facets of 'King Lear': Essays in Prismatic Criticism*, ed. Colie and F. T. Flahiff (Toronto, 1974), pp. 117–44, esp. p. 130. Several verses in Ecclesiastes 10 seem relevant to the tragedy:

> 4 If the spirit of him that ruleth, rise vp against thee, leaue not thy place: for gentlenes pacifieth great sinnes.
>
> 5 There is an euil *that* I haue sene vnder the sunne, as an error that procedeth frō the face of him that ruleth.
>
> 6 Folie is set in great excellencie, and the riche set in the lowe place. . .
>
> 12 The wordes of the mouth of a wise man *haue* grace: but the lippes of a foole deuoure him self.
>
> 13 The beginning of yᵉ wordes of his mouthe *is* foolishnes, and the latter end of his mouth *is* wicked madnes.

98. *Explorations in Shakespeare's Language* (1962), pp. 70–2.

99. *Antony and Cleopatra*, TLN 54, 1.1.42.

100. John Gerard, *The Herball* (1597), pp. 594–5. Christine Avern-Carr points out to me that 'Goates beard' thus resembles in its mix of colours the motley of Tom Skelton (white, blue, and yellow): see E. W. Ives, 'Tom Skelton – A Seventeenth-Century Jester', *Shakespeare Survey 13* (Cambridge, 1960), 90–105; p. 98. For an alternative floral interpretation see Edmund Blunden, 'Shakespeare's Significances', Shakespeare Association Pamphlets, 14 (Oxford, 1929), pp. 12–13.
101. *The Winter's Tale*, TLN 1918–19, 4.4.105–6.
102. There is a particularly striking example of a moralized marigold in Sonnet 25: 'Great Princes fauorites their faire leaues spread, | But as the Marygold at the suns eye, | And in them-selues their pride lies buried, | For at a frowne they in their glory die.'
103. *Troilus and Cressida*, B4, TLN 548, 1.3.89. That kings resemble suns is, of course, a commonplace of Shakespeare's plays and Elizabethan and Jacobean literature in general.

APPENDIX I

The Spanish Tragedy *Adapted*

IT is now generally agreed that Kyd cannot have been responsible for the additions. Several considerations have led scholars toward this consensus. First, Pavier tells us that his 'additions' are 'new', performed 'of late'; and Kyd died in 1594. Elizabethan title-pages should be approached with circumspection; but since the other claims made by Pavier are demonstrably true (his quarto does contain 'the Painters part, and others' and its text has been 'corrected' and 'amended', if only lightly) it seems reasonable to accept this one as well. Second, it is difficult to see why, if the 'additions' were written by Kyd, they did not appear in the good quarto of 1592, or (if they were composed at the end of his life) in the 1594 or 1599 quartos. Third, the 'new' matter is stylistically at odds with the original text which surrounds it, with *Soliman and Perseda*, and with Kyd's translation of Garnier's *Cornélie*. Eloquent, enquiring, and psychologically inward, the 'new' material feels closer to *Hamlet* (which it seems to echo at 1278–81) than the rhetorical revenge writing of the early 1590s. Moreover, as several scholars have observed, the 'additions' disrupt Hieronimo's carefully paced decline. Kyd leads the Knight Marshal slowly and painfully towards madness; the adapter makes him deranged from 2.5 (the discovery of Horatio's corpse) onwards. For all its brilliance (and partly because of its brilliance), the 'new' writing distorts the tragedy. Kyd's dramatic clarity, his structural articulacy, is sacrificed to the virtuosity of the adapter. Finally, two occasions have been found when the 'new additions' could have been composed, and both postdate Kyd's death. In 1597 Henslowe called the play 'ne', and in 1601 and 1602 he made two payments to Jonson 'vpon h[is] writtinge of his adicians in geronymo' and 'in earnestes of A Boocke called Richard crockbacke & for new adicyons for Jeronymo' (*Henslowe's Diary*, ed. R. A. Foakes and E. T. Rickert, Cambridge, 1961, pp. 55, 182, 203). The first chapter of Anne Barton's *Ben Jonson, Dramatist* (Cambridge, forthcoming) argues most persuasively, on critical as well as scholarly grounds, that Pavier's 'additions' are those commissioned by Henslowe in 1601–2.

APPENDIX II

Textual Variants in Faustus's First Soliloquy

THE most striking divergence between A31–93 and B30–89 consists in B's omission of three lines found in A: 'Seeing, *vbi desinit philosophus, ibi incipit medicus*', 'Is not thy common talke sound Aphorismes?', 'Nor can they raise the winde, or rend the cloudes' (A43, 49, and 89). Their absence in 1616 could be put down to Birde–Rowley cutting only if it could be shown that the adapters acted illogically elsewhere (which they did not); for the missing lines are neither difficult[1] nor irrelevant, and they can scarcely have been excluded on the grounds of sense since, inoffensive in themselves, they are not linked in subject-matter either with each other or with incontestably cut A material. Two alternative solutions confront us: either the lines were added by an actor reporting for A, or scribal/compositorial error behind B led to their omission. The former explanation seems to founder on the lines' literary merit, while the latter finds support in their syntactical subordination; but no choice between them is strictly necessary here.

The lesser variants can be dealt with more briskly. At A63, the erroneous 'And vniversall body of the Church' (B for the last word has 'law') is almost certainly the product of memorial corruption. The last line of the A soliloquy is more plausible ('Heere *Faustus* trie thy braines to gaine a deitie', B 'Here tire my braines to get a Deity'); but memorially-reconstructed lines often are plausible, and the fact that the words hang together by no means proves them accurate. I think A inferior to B and corrupt, though there could be transposed letters ('trie/tire') in either text. In any case, there is no need to invoke Birde and Rowley. Four A errors are more likely to be compositorial than theatrical. 'The deuill and illiberall for me' at A66 is manifest nonsense which no actor would have reported nor scribe set down; presumably Simmes's compositor found in his copy a semi-legible rendering of B's 'Too seruile a[n]d illiberall for mee'. At A52, 'easde' was probably set because 'cur'd' (B's reading) was written carelessly in the A copy. (Given 'cured' with a malformed 'r', the mistake is paleographically straightforward.[2]) Again, at A54, 'wouldst thou make man to liue eternally?' is unsatisfactory: 'man' is belied by the plural 'them' at A55/B52, and 'wouldst' queries Faustus's desire to perform marvels, where the context indicates that ability, not ambition, is in doubt. I take it that 'and a man' in A53 prompted the first error, while 'wouldst' was set from a manuscript 'Couldst' (B) by a compositor who either misread the word or misremembered part of a line he was carrying in his

---

[1] The first lost line includes Latin, but so do 7 lines preserved in the B soliloquy.
[2] I am grateful to Malcolm Parkes for confirming this judgement.

head.[3] 'His/This study' (A64, B61) is more difficult to classify, because although A seems inferior to B it is by no means unacceptable. However, the case is not so hard that rewriting need be invoked. 'His' and 'This' are close enough to make compositorial (perhaps scribal) error in A (conceivably B) a more attractive explanation for the variant.[4]

One of B's blunders is evidently inherited from earlier editions: A1 (1604) did justice to Faustus's ὄν καὶ μὴ ὄν, printing '*Oncaymæon*' (A42); but an officious house editor or assertive compositor, preparing the 1609 reprint (A2), emended this to '*Oeconomy*', and the reading passed through A3 (1611) into Wright's B text (1616). Two more B mistakes probably derive – like the omission of the three full A lines – from scribal/compositorial error. The added conjunction in 'and *Galen* come' (B41) is not just hypermetrical but out of character: everywhere else in the soliloquy, Faustus shifts impulsively from author to author, not with the consideration implied by 'and'. As for 'Lines, Circles, Letters, Characters' (B78): in the light of Birde and Rowley's verse styles elsewhere in the adaptation (regular to the point of 'jigging' and 'rhyming'),[5] this can hardly be their rewrite of A's 'Lines, circles, sceanes, letters and characters'. Five variants remain: 'thou hast attaind the/that end' (A40, B39); 'A pretty/petty case of paltry legàcies' (A60, B57); 'and theres no truth in vs' against 'and there is no truth in vs' (A73, B70); 'of/and omnipotence' (A84, B81); 'A sound Magician is a mighty god' against 'A sound Magitian is a Demi-god' (A92, B88). The provenance of the first four of these is as difficult to determine as the relative merit of the A and B readings in each instance. Memorial corruption could lie behind A40, A60, and A84 (A73 hardly counts); but scribal or compositorial error in either text is as likely to have caused the variation. Birde and Rowley, at least, need not be held responsible. With 'mighty god' and 'Demi-god', however, the provenance of the variant is as easily discovered as the superiority of A over B is manifest.[6] As we noted above (p. 197), B has been censored. It lacks not only A's vaunting blasphemies but many lines and phrases which, while they touch on religious concerns, could only be considered blasphemous by a

[3] For an instance of clear compositorial error creating such a variant, see Q7 of *Richard III*, which prints 'could' (D1) at 1.4.119 (variant in F) where all previous quartos have 'would' (D1ᵛ).

[4] For examples of a compositor setting 'this' for copy 'his', see Folio *Love's Labour's Lost* (TLN 2518; 5.2.566), Folio *A Midsummer Night's Dream* (TLN 258; 1.1.244), and Q6 *Richard III* (H1ᵛ; 3.7.190). For the same error in reverse, Folio *The Merchant of Venice* (TLN 1935; 4.1.30), Folio *A Midsummer Night's Dream* (TLN 262 and 1920; 1.1.248, 5.1.122), and *Richard III* Q2 (F1ᵛ; 3.1.87), Q6 (K1ᵛ; 4.4.343), and Q7 (E4ᵛ and I4ᵛ; 3.1.46, 4.4.185).

[5] *1 Tamburlaine*, Prologue. On the adapters' verse styles see Bowers, *Christopher Marlowe*, II, 133, and Kuriyama, 'Dr. Greg and *Doctor Faustus*', pp. 191–6.

[6] The B reading seems inappropriate for a Faustus (at this stage) so overweening, and hardly compatible with the words which succeed it. For a similar example of 'demie God' as a euphemistic version of 'God', see *Love's Labour's Lost* 4.3.76–8 (E3ᵛ; TLN 1412–14), where Berowne compares himself to the Deity in a Mystery Play.

precisian. Sometimes (as in Faustus's final soliloquy), censorship has left the text in self-evident disarray. Presumably this did not happen at B88 because the censor thought it sufficient to emend 'mighty god'. What prompted the emasculation of the B text? No doubt Greg is correct when he claims that, like many other plays current in the Jacobean repertory, *Doctor Faustus* was pruned to accord with the 1606 *Act to Restrain Abuses of Players* (see note 24 above, and Appendix III, p. 244).[7] If this is so, the only bit of text in the B version of Faustus's first soliloquy which has certainly been rewritten dates from after 1606. In short, Birde and Rowley need not be held responsible for any A–B variation in this section of text.

[7] *Marlowe's 'Doctor Faustus'*, pp. 85–6.

APPENDIX III

The Fleire *Adapted*

Q1 *The Fleire* was published in 1607, and Sharpham did not die until 22 or 23 April 1608 (G. C. Moore Smith, 'Edward Sharpham and Robert Hayman', *Notes and Queries*, 10 (1908), 21–4); so, in theory, the author could have annotated the British Library text. In practice, it is clear that he did not. Although there seems to be no paleographical evidence (and I am grateful to the Librarian of the Middle Temple for help in a fruitless search for Sharpham's signature), the following strong considerations lead towards that conclusion. First, the annotation fades out in the last scene of the play, as the reworker finds that the action cannot easily be resolved in the restricted form which his cutting has produced. Having trimmed the Florentine overplot and deleted allusions to Fleire's paternity of the two courtesans who are central to the action, the reworker found himself forced to leave 5.289–302 – in which Piso, learning that he has become the new Duke of Florence, praises Antifront (the Fleire's real name) so highly that the banished man declares himself and gives his daughters away in marriage – completely intact. Being familiar with the outcome of his own play, Sharpham would hardly have pursued a line of revision leading towards such an unhappy consequence. On the other hand, an adapter briefly acquainted with the play but eager to rework it might well feel that, in the last analysis, he could fudge the dénouement – only to find himself thwarted. Second, it is difficult to see why Sharpham, an established author by 1607–8, would abandon the 'Comicall discourses' projected in the preface to Q1 *The Fleire* to produce something which, for all its pragmatic theatrical accomplishment, is a travesty of his best play. Third, the cuts on D3 (see illustration 3, p. 201) conspire to suggest a date for the reworking rather later than 1608, the year of Sharpham's death. The deletion of 'since thou hast almost forgot thy Pater-noster' and questioning of 'a Gods-name' might have been done by any cautious man of the theatre after the 1606 *Act to Restrain Abuses of Players* (see note 24 above, and Appendix II, p. 242). The excision of 2.258–64 is another matter:

Ruff, I did pray oftner when I was an Englishman, but I haue not praid often, I must confesse since I was a Brittaine: but doost heare *Fleire*? canst tell me if an Englishman were in debt, whether a Brittaine must pay it or no?
Flei, No, questionlesse no.
Ruff, I'me glad of that, I hope some honest statute will come shortlie, and wipe out all my scores.

The context here – and it is one which also influenced *King Lear* – is James's proposal to the 1604 and 1606–7 sessions of Parliament that England and Scotland be united under the name 'Great Britain' or 'Brittany'. Controversy raged, the Commons stalled, and then a compromise was reached through the courts (Calvin's Case, 1607, which established that Scots born after the accession of James to the English throne were natural-born subjects of the King of England) and the matter was quietly forgotten.[8] Sharpham's jest, lively enough in 1607, would have been dull, if not dead, a decade later. By, say, 1615, 2.258–61 would have been ripe for excision.

Is it possible to establish a *terminus ad quem* for the adaptation? On C3^v the usual italic gives way, briefly, to secretary hand. 'A space' has been added, after 'Aect^e Ends', to mark a pause for Antifront to change into the '*new Suite*' required by the stage direction heading Act Two. This instruction may have been interpolated by a second hand, as Leech asserts,[9] or it may be an afterthought by an annotator fluent in two scripts. Either way, 'A space' helps date the adaptation to the first half of the seventeenth century. 'A space' is not a reader's comment; it is patently the work of someone regarding the quarto as a potential prompt-book. So these two words in secretary hand must coincide with or postdate the bulk of the annotation, which is in italic. This firmly places the italic work – which might in theory date from any period between about 1550 and 1750 – before the Commonwealth, because secretary hand had fallen out of general use into specialized legal and ecclesiastical employment by the start of the Civil War.

The adaptation dates, then, from the later Jacobean or earlier Caroline period.

[8] See Notestein, *The House of Commons 1604–1610*, pp. 78–85 and 211–54, and, on Calvin's Case, Samuel R. Gardiner, *History of England from the Accession of James I to the Outbreak of the Civil War 1603–1642*, 10 vols. (repr. New York, 1965), I, 355–6.

[9] 'The Plays of Edward Sharpham', p. 72.

Folio Editors, Folio Compositors, and the Folio Text of *King Lear*

PAUL WERSTINE

No amount of compositorial analysis can of itself determine whether there is one text of *King Lear* or – as Warren ('Albany and Edgar'), Urkowitz (*Revision*), Taylor ('War'), Stone (*Textual History*), and Blayney (*Origins*) have recently claimed – two. Nor can the textual bibliographer assume the role of Neoplatonic philosopher, intent on stripping away the veil of print from the extant texts of *Lear* to reveal the manuscripts behind these texts in their pristine forms. The bibliographer can, however, assess the textual variants in the light of his knowledge of the printing process and offer judgements about their probable sources: author, scribe, book-keeper, editor, compositor or proof-reader. The tradition of editing *Lear* as a single text derives ultimately from the suspicions of eighteenth-century editors that Shakespeare's printers were responsible for massive corruption introduced into the printed texts of his plays. It is, therefore, essential to an examination of this editorial tradition to study in detail the kind of corruption visited on the Folio *Lear* of 1623 in the house of its printer, Isaac Jaggard.

The agents at work in that printing house whose activities certainly or possibly influenced the 1623 text of *Lear* divide into three categories: the compositors who set the text into type; the editor or editors who might have prepared the printer's copy (whether an earlier printed text or a manuscript) from which those compositors worked; and the proof-reader or proof-readers who demonstrably intervened, as pages were being printed, to initiate stop-press corrections, and who may well have directed corrections to be made before press-runs began. Since stop-press corrections in the Folio have already been rather thoroughly analysed by Hinman,[1] I will concentrate on the compositors and the editor(s); and since whatever influence the editor(s) exerted, if any, can be discerned only after the characteristic activities of the type-setters have been discounted, I will first attempt to establish the kind and degree of corruption and sophistication typical of the compositors. This can be done by examining other texts set by the same workmen, where we know (as we do not for *Lear*) a good deal about what stood in the copy they were attempting to reprint, and so can determine the fidelity with which they carried out their task. For this reason, an evaluation of printing-house error in the Folio *Lear* cannot concentrate on *Lear* alone; indeed, it can turn to *Lear* only after the evidence of other texts has been collected and evaluated. From the point of view of textual bibliography, the printing of the Folio *Lear* is bound up with the printing of many other Folio texts edited and composed in the same shop at the same time. Hence it arises that the text which must be examined most carefully, in order to evaluate the Folio text of *Lear*, is the Folio text of *1 Henry IV*.

In what follows I will attempt to isolate and describe the kinds of error and sophistication perpetrated elsewhere by the two compositors ('B' and 'E') who set the Folio text of *King Lear*. A full list of Compositor E's errors, grouped into various categories, is provided in the Appendices (pp. 294–312), which also supplement the list of Compositor B's errors published elsewhere. By collecting these errors, by analysing their patterns of frequency and type (pp. 261–73), and by trying to distinguish editorial from compositorial interference, particularly in Folio *1 Henry IV* (pp. 248–60), I have sought to assemble the evidence that will enable us to answer (pp. 273–88) one elementary but crucial question: can much of the variation between the Quarto and Folio texts of *King Lear* be blamed upon corruption in the printing-house in 1623?

The answer is, very simply, no.

The Relevance of Folio '1 Henry IV'

Analysis of the quality of the work performed by Jaggard's compositors was begun almost thirty years ago by Alice Walker, before Hinman published his massive study of the Folio's printing. Only two compositors – A and B – were known to Walker, and her examination of the work attributed to them on a single Folio text, *1 Henry IV*, affected the reputation of both workmen for the next three decades.[2] In the nearly 1,800 lines of the Folio *1 Henry IV* assigned to Compositor B by Walker, she discovered 136 substantive departures from the compositors' quarto copy (Q5); only eighteen of these were restorations of readings from the authoritative first quarto (Q1), and only five more are generally accepted by modern editors as necessary corrections of readings common to Q1–5. The approximately 1,400 lines she attributed to Compositor A showed only thirty such departures; nine of them restored first quarto variants and three more are recognized as necessary corrections. Walker argued:

> the stints of the compositors were governed by mechanical reasons and bear no relation to any literary considerations or divisions in the text. Hence the division is textually arbitrary and can serve as pure evidence. What is common to the work of the compositors may therefore have been in their copy, but marked discrepancies between the number and character of the variants in their work are more likely to represent personal idiosyncrasies. . . . The only reasonable interpretation of the hundred and thirteen errors in B's pages of the Folio *1 Henry IV*, as against eighteen only in A's, is that they were for the most part due to the compositor's negligence.[3]

Compositor A emerged from Walker's study as a conscientious workman upon whose accuracy editors of the Folio plays could depend. He served as the foil to Compositor B who, according to Walker, deserved notoriety for 'habitual carelessness' and an inclination 'to take liberties with his copy'.[4] Since composition of the Folio *Lear* was then thought to have fallen to Compositor B alone, Walker's study had profound implications for editors of *Lear*:

> Since the average number of variants in the dialogue of *1 Henry IV* set by B is close on eight to a page, we are faced with the possibility that there may be at least two hundred errors in the Folio *Lear* and *Othello* for which compositor B was solely responsible.[5]

If Walker's argument were valid, it would provide bibliographical support for highly eclectic editions of *Lear* and perhaps even, according to Walker, for the traditional conflation of the Folio and Quarto texts of the play, since omission was the most frequent error in the work attributed to Compositor B in *1 Henry IV*.[6]

Scholars were initially slow to accept Walker's findings. W. W. Greg recognized the potential importance of her method, but was cautious about her conclusions:

> These figures are startling, and if *B* habitually introduced almost five times as many departures from copy as *A* and an average of nearly eight on each page, the textual implications for plays like *King Lear*, for which [Walker] assumes him to have been solely responsible, are serious. No doubt the figures given above must be accepted with some reserve till checked for other plays offering comparable conditions. Although nothing like full and reliable data are yet available, it is already apparent that a study of the habits of compositors will

in the future not only influence editorial procedure but may even affect basic assumptions respecting the nature of the text.[7]

G. I. Duthie remained unconvinced, believing that Walker had overestimated the amount of compositorial corruption in the Folio text of *Lear*.[8] For twenty years, however, no one heeded Greg's call for 'full and reliable data' on Compositor B's performance in the Folio. By 1974, when MacD. P. Jackson compiled a list of compositorial errors in *Much Ado*, Compositor B's reputation for carelessness in setting the Folio, left unexamined in the interval, had grown so strong that Jackson endorsed it in the face of clear evidence that in *Much Ado* 'Compositor B performed rather better than usual' – that is, rather better than Walker supposed he did in *1 Henry IV*.[9] Not until Compositor B's work on six more Folio plays had been examined did it become evident that the corruption attributed to him in his stint on *1 Henry IV* was not characteristic of his performance elsewhere in the Folio, especially in the tragedies.[10]

The following chart breaks down the numbers and kinds of errors that have been charged to B in *1 Henry IV* and those that can be assigned to him in the seven other Folio plays (both comedies and tragedies) during composition of which he again worked from lightly annotated quarto copy:[11]

	Comedies	*1 Henry IV*	Tragedies
lines	2037	1795	414
total errors	81	116	19
frequency of error	1/25.1 ll.	1/15.5	1/21.8
literals	31	27	2
frequency	1/68 ll.	1/67	1/207
substitutions	33	23	12
frequency	1/62 ll.	1/78	1/35
omissions	6	30	3
frequency	1/340 ll.	1/60	1/138
interpolations	5	28	2
frequency	1/407 ll.	1/64	1/207
transpositions	6	8	0
frequency	1/340 ll.	1/224	0

Obviously, Compositor B is guilty of many fewer errors in the comedies and tragedies than Walker laid at his door in *1 Henry IV*;

less obviously but just as significantly, the kinds of error differ radically between *1 Henry IV* and the other plays. In the history play, omission and interpolation are the errors discovered most frequently in Compositor B's work; these errors are rare in other plays. Substitutions, by contrast, increase sharply in the other plays, especially the tragedies. The 'full and reliable data' demanded by Greg indicate that Walker's analysis of Compositor B's performance in just one play seriously misrepresents him. Although he never approached the standard of accuracy in reprinting quarto copy achieved in the pages of *1 Henry IV* that Walker assigned to Compositor A, Compositor B proved more faithful to his copy in the comedies and tragedies than he appeared to be in *1 Henry IV* Clearly, we cannot apply Walker's characterization of Compositor B to editing the Folio text of *Lear*.

Walker's attempt highlights three major issues in the examination of compositorial accuracy: reliability of compositor identification, possible editorial interference between the compositor and his printed copy, and compositorial difficulties with cast-off prose copy in specific texts.[12] Compositor identification in *1 Henry IV* has never been adequately resolved: Hinman queried Walker's attribution of four of the fourteen and a half pages she assigned to Compositor B;[13] S. W. Reid's intensive study of the compositor's spellings failed to convince him that these four pages were indeed B's work;[14] and Jackson suggested that two of the pages, at least, should be reassigned from Compositor B to another as yet unidentified compositor.[15] It remains altogether possible that the 'personal idiosyncrasies' Walker found in B's work are not personal at all, but instead common to the work of two compositors – and therefore the responsibility of neither. T. H. Howard-Hill has recently suggested that such identification problems as Walker faced would still defeat anyone who set out to examine the quality of work produced by the major compositors of the tragedies, including *Lear*: 'It is difficult to see what value such a study would have when the stints of the two compositors [B and E] are not yet completely distinguished.'[16] But Hinman answered such an objection long before it was made. Although he too was aware of the need to solve 'certain identification problems . . . as decisively as possible', he insisted that

this does not mean that no further qualitative analysis can be undertaken until new spelling studies have been made. . . . There is plenty of material to work on; and there is no field of investigation more likely to produce significant gains, none more likely to throw new light on the peculiarities of the Folio text.[17]

The second problem Walker confronted, editorial preparation of the compositors' copy, is more challenging. Unlike the Folio compositors, the Folio editors have received almost no attention; they therefore remain shadowy figures.[18] Yet no play in the Folio is a simple reprint of an earlier printed text; no play thought to have been set from quarto copy contains only compositorial variants from printed copy.[19] Consequently a modern editor of any Folio play can ill afford to ignore the earliest of Shakespeare's editors. Greg remained convinced, even after he had read Walker's study, that the hand of a literary editor was evident in the Folio text of *1 Henry IV*, especially in the 'pruned and touched-up' stage directions found only in the portion of the text assigned to Compositor B by Walker.[20] Even Walker was forced to acknowledge some editorial interference in the preparation of Folio copy, although she sought to minimize its importance by claiming that

we cannot bridge the gulf between the number of errors in A's work and in B's without supposing that an 'improver' happened to have lost interest in the dialogue of Q5 whenever compositor A chanced to become responsible for the Folio text.[21]

In 1954, before Hinman had begun to publish his research on the printing of the Folio, Walker's position might have been justified; but it is difficult to accept today. Her statement implies that different compositors worked successively, not simultaneously, to compose the Folio. On this view Compositor B was thought to have begun *1 Henry IV* alone by setting pages d5^v–e3^v seriatim (i.e. in the order in which they were to be read); at page e4 Compositor A 'chanced to become responsible for the Folio text', setting pages e4–f1^v; Compositor B returned briefly for page f2, but then immediately deferred to Compositor A, who did pages f2^v–3^v; at last Compositor B finished the play with pages f4–6. Had the typesetting of the Folio proceeded in this way, the compositors alone, not the editor(s), would have to bear the responsibility for variations in the number of departures from printed copy between the compositors' stints, since Compositors A and B could and probably would both have used the same printer's copy, edited in the same way. Thanks to Hinman's work, we now know that the Folio was not composed seriatim, as

Walker believed, but instead by formes, with two compositors often at work on the same text at the same time. If we discount for a moment well-founded doubts about Walker's compositor identifications, the pattern of composition of *1 Henry IV*, as Hinman revealed it, can be easily described.[22] The first three pages (d5^v–6^v) were indeed the first to be set; these fell to Compositor B, who composed them seriatim while Compositor A was still at work on *Richard II*. Then Compositor A also turned to *1 Henry IV*, setting the last half of quire e (e4–6^v) at one type-case from one bloc of copy; at the same time, Compositor B set the first half of the quire (e1–3^v) at another type-case from his own bloc of copy. Composition of quire f followed essentially the same pattern, although this time Compositor B set the second half of the quire (f4–6), while Compositor A set most of the first half. Two distinct blocs of copy were thus required throughout the setting of quires e and f, with only one exception (forme f2:5^v, during composition of which Compositor B may have worked alone).

Therefore the possibility arises that the bloc of printer's copy given to Walker's Compositor B may have differed significantly from the copy used by Walker's Compositor A. Some of the variants between the Folio and Q5 that Walker regarded as errors and charged to Compositor B might instead derive from his copy; if so, they must be attributed to the editor who annotated the exemplar of Q5 used by Compositor B. The possibility of two different kinds of printer's copy for a single text would explain why the editorial alteration of Q5 stage directions noticed by Greg is confined to Compositor B's portion of the text. But it also has implications for an assessment of variants in dialogue. Before Walker dismissed as compositorial errors most of the dialogue variants between Q5 and the Folio text set by B, some of these variants had claimed serious attention from textual critics as possibly genuine Shakespearian readings. As Greg wrote,

Even in *1 Henry IV* there is always the possibility that a folio variant may be a fragment of an independent textual tradition, and moreover one which an editor, working within a few years of the author's death and in close touch with his fellow actors, thought superior to that of the quarto. This is no ground why we should necessarily prefer the folio reading, but it is a ground for giving it respectful consideration.[23]

Now that it has been established that, in both kind and number, many Folio variants in B's stints on *1 Henry IV* are not characteristic compositorial errors, they may again claim 'respectful consideration' as editorial annotations.

At best we can merely speculate about the identity of the Folio editor(s) and about how printer's copy (for *1 Henry IV* and other plays) was transmitted through the hands of the editor(s) to the Folio compositors. Bibliographical evidence can be marshalled to support two different hypotheses, each having special reference to Folio *1 Henry IV*. First, Jaggard may have received edited texts (manuscripts or annotated quartos) from the players themselves, who may then have filled the role of editors; or the players may simply have released materials to be assembled into printer's copy by editors in the printing house. We know that Jaggard sometimes made use of more than one text of a single play, one an edited version, the other unedited. *Troilus and Cressida* offers an example: the first three pages of the Folio text were apparently reprinted from a copy of the quarto with little variation, but the remainder (printed long after those first three pages) derives its authority from another source, an annotated first quarto.[24] As a result of Jaggard's use of two kinds of copy for *Troilus*, Compositor E's two pages there (χ2–2^v), set from unannotated quarto copy, differ sharply from most of the rest of the Folio text, set by Compositors B and H from different copy: Compositor E's pages correct some obvious errors, but contain no authoritative or editorial changes.[25]

Perhaps Jaggard also possessed two different copies of *1 Henry IV* Q5, one edited with cursory reference to a copy of Q1, the other containing heavier annotation that coincided only occasionally with Q1 readings. The first copy may have gone to the cases where Compositor A usually stood, the second to Compositor B's customary workplace. Thus in the pages assigned to Compositor A by Walker most of the variants from Q5 restore Q1 readings, but in the pages assigned to Compositor B few variants have parallels in Q1.

The analogy between *Troilus* and *1 Henry IV* is not exact, but neither is it arbitrary. There are important likenesses between the printing of Folio *1 Henry IV* and that of *Troilus*. Completion of *Troilus* was delayed until after work on the rest of the Folio was finished, even though the first three pages were initially printed to follow immediately after *Romeo*. The printing of Folio *1* and *2 Henry IV* was also delayed and did not take place until after *Henry V*, *1* and *2 Henry VI*, and the beginning of *3 Henry VI* had all gone to press; that is, the four plays which follow the *Henry IV* plays in the Folio preceded the *Henry IV* plays to the press.[26] In both cases – *Troilus and 1 Henry IV* – these delays in printing are thought to have arisen from Jaggard's difficulties with copyright for the plays.[27] The printing of *Troilus* was not completed until Jaggard had secured a text that varies significantly – and, editors believe, sometimes authoritatively – from the first quarto. In the delay that preceded composition of *1 Henry IV* might not Jaggard have acquired another text of that play as well? In the case of *1 Henry IV*, however, only the work of Walker's Compositor B may have benefited from the new acquisition.

We need not suppose, however, that the difference between the performances of the two compositors in *1 Henry IV* must be attributed entirely to their use of different kinds of copy. Instead, a printing-house editor may have introduced some of the variants found in pages assigned to Compositor B by Walker *after* the pages had already been composed. An instance of such editorial interference can be found on the last page of the Folio *Romeo*, another play set, as S. W. Reid has recently demonstrated, from quarto copy annotated by an editor.[28] This page was first set by Compositor E and printed as page *gg3, backing a first page of *Troilus* set by Compositor B (*gg3ᵛ). Although the leaf was later cancelled, at least one copy of it survived to be bound in a complete Folio.[29] Copies of it also survived to serve as printer's copy for subsequent composition of the end of *Romeo* (by Compositor B on page Gg1) and the beginning of *Troilus* (by Compositor H on page χ1ᵛ). Compositor H's page χ1ᵛ contains every variant introduced by Compositor B into page *gg3ᵛ, including even the obviously erroneous substitution of 'it' for 'her'. Compositor B's page Gg1, the second setting of the end of *Romeo*, reproduces two changes made in Compositor E's first setting of this text ('scarre' (Compositor E: 'scar') for 'scare' and 'raise' for 'raie'), but not two others ('for for' for 'for', nor 'the' for 'these' – this last not an obvious error in context). Page Gg1 also contains two substantively altered speech prefixes absent in Compositor E's page *gg3: '*Boy.*' for '*Balth.*', and '*Page.*' for '*Boy.*' In setting speech prefixes from lightly annotated quarto copy elsewhere in the Folio Compositor B made nothing other than literal errors; consequently, these two changes on a single page cannot be charged to him. Instead they must represent (together with the correction of Compositor E's substitution of 'the' for 'these') editorial interference with a compositor's copy – in particular, editorial interference *after* composition of a play was already in progress.

The most probable candidate for editor of Compositor B's copy for the last page of *Romeo* would be a Folio proof-reader. To a proof-reader should have gone a copy of the first setting of the page by Compositor E as page *gg3. Then, it would seem, the proof-reader not only corrected some of Compositor E's departures from printer's copy, but also may have introduced some fresh departures by altering the speech prefixes. Similar intervention by a proof-reader might explain why, in some pages of *1 Henry IV* assigned by Walker to Compositor B, there were so many departures from Q5 that are uncharacteristic of the compositor.

Textual critics may have been dissuaded from examining this hypothesis because of Hinman's insistence that the only method of correction used in the printing of the Folio was stop-press correction.[30] Since Hinman discovered few stop-press corrections in the entire Folio, few of the variants in Folio *1 Henry IV* can be dismissed as possible stop-press corrections, even if it is recognized that the record of such corrections remains incomplete.[31] But, *contra* Hinman, stop-press correction was probably not the only method of correction employed by Jaggard. D. F. McKenzie has demonstrated Jaggard's familiarity with the terms used by Moxon later in the seventeenth century to describe earlier stages of proof-correction used by printers.[32] According to Moxon,

> The *Press-man* is to make a *Proof* so oft as occasion requires. . . . The *Compositer* having brought the *Form* to the *Press*, lays it down on the *Press-stone*, and the *Press-man* . . . *Pulls* the *Proof-sheet* . . . carries the *Form* again to the *Correcting-stone* and lays it down: And the *Proof* he carries to the *Compositers Case*.[33]

'*Proof*' and printer's copy are then brought to the corrector, who, after proof-reading, directs the compositor to make the necessary corrections. After doing so, the compositor 'carries the *Form* to the *Press*, and lays it on the *Stone* for a *Second Proof*, and sometimes for a *Third Proof*. . . . After all this *Correcting* a *Revise* is made.'[34] It is during these early stages of proof-reading, the '*Proof-sheets*' and '*Revises*' or '*Reviewes*', as Jaggard termed them, that a proof-reader may have introduced — perhaps from consultation of a manuscript, perhaps on his own authority — some of the variants Walker charged as errors to Compositor B. The close working relationship between the individual compositor and the individual proof-reader described by Moxon might perhaps explain why so many variants in Folio *1*

Henry IV are located in the work of one of Walker's compositors, so few in the work of the other.

This explanation remains purely speculative, however, unless it can be grounded in evidence. In the search for evidence of proof-correction in the Folio, Moxon again proves useful, since he details the plight of a compositor forced to make corrections in a page already set in type, but not yet at press:

> If the *Compositor* is not firmly resolv'd to keep himself strictly to the Rules of good Workmanship, he is now tempted to make *Botches*; viz. *Pidgeon-holes*, *Thin-Spaces*, no *Space* before a *Capital*, *Short* &s, *Abbreviations* or *Titled Letters*, *Abbreviate Words*, &c. And if Botching is in any Case excusable, it is in this; for with too great *Spacing-out* or too *Close Setting*, he many times may save himself a great deal of Labour, besides the vexation of mind.[35]

Whatever '*Botches*' the compositor makes, Moxon insists that corrected lines must at least be justified with spaces so that they do not disintegrate at the press.[36] Of course, we would expect to find the irregularities listed by Moxon almost exclusively in long lines, since justification of short lines would cause few problems. But most of the *Botches* noted by Moxon as arising from proof-correction are too frequent in long lines set by Jaggard's compositors to provide certain evidence of interference due to proof-correction. In prose passages in the Folio we often discover such botches – '*Spacing-out*' (wide spacing between words), '*Close Setting*' (narrow spacing between words), no spaces before capitals, ampersands and abbreviations – where there is no reason to suspect proof-correction. The association of such ordinary botching with a substantial number of the variants in long lines set by Walker's Compositor B in *1 Henry IV* therefore cannot necessarily be cited as evidence that these variants arose from proof-correction, but the possibility remains that at least some did.[37]

Yet some variant lines in Compositor B's work contain such extraordinary botches that there may not be much doubt that they were reset, probably during proof-correction. Two will serve as examples. In TLN 276, the Folio version of Prince Hal's speech begins 'I, but' for Q5's 'Yea, but'; in this line the space between the speech prefix and the beginning of the speech is twice as wide as it is in any comparable line in Compositor B's pages in this play and certainly wide enough to contain 'Yea'. Here are two examples of the normal spacing after speech prefixes (TLN 283–4):

> *Prin.* But I doubt they will be too hard for vs.
> *Poi.* Well, for two of them, I know them to bee as

Here is the 'botch' at TLN 276:

> *Prin.* I, but tis like that they will know vs by our

And here is the same line with 'Yea' inserted (by me) in place of the Folio's 'I':

> *Prin.* Yea, but tis like that they will know vs by our

Probably in substituting 'I' for 'Yea' during proof-correction, Compositor B neglected to distribute extra spaces evenly throughout the line, or to reline the whole speech (as, ideally, he should have done), but instead crammed a single 'body' quad in between the speech prefix and the first word of the speech.[38] (As the photos make clear, the space after the prefix in TLN 276 is the same width as the space before the prefix in this and all other lines, so it clearly represented a standard-size quad.) A comparable spacing irregularity is found in connection with the Folio variant 'is' for Q5's 'to be' in TLN 649. This variant occurs in the exchange between the two carriers, who are invariably designated '1.*Car.*' and '2.*Car.*' in the speech prefixes:

> 2.*Car.* Peafe and Beanes are as danke here as a Dog, and this is the next way to giue poore Iades the Boxtes: This houfe is turned vpfide downe fince *Robin* the Ofiler dyed.
>
>   1.*Car.* Poore fellow neuer ioy'd fince the price of oats rofe, it was the death of him.
>
>   2. *Car.* I thinke this is the moft villanous houfe in al London rode for Fleas: I am ftung like a Tench.
>
>   1.*Car.* Like a Tench? There is ne're a King in Chriftendome, could be better bit, then I haue beene fince the firft Cocke.
>
>   2.*Car.* Why, you will allow vs ne're a, Iourden, and then we leake in your Chimney: and your Chamber-lye breeds Fleas like a Loach.

> **1.*Car.*** What Oftler, come away, and be hangd: come
> away.
> **2.*Car.*** I haue a Gammon of Bacon, and two razes of
> Ginger, to be deliuered as farre as Charing-croffe.

In each case (as here in TLN 643–60) the numeral, the period following it, and the abbreviation '*Car.*' are all set close-up – except in the variant line TLN 649:

> **2. *Car.*** I thinke this is the moft villanous houfe in al

Here, spacing intervenes between '2.' and '*Car.*', probably because again during proof-correction Compositor B simply wasted space after substituting 'is' for 'to be', the reading that he may have originally set. Again, we can see how the line might originally have been set up, with 'to be' but without the botch.

> **2.*Car.*** I thinke this to be the moft villanous houfe in

This does not prove that resetting created the botch, but it does show how easily it could have.

Beyond these two examples, it is impossible to demonstrate that variants in B's work on *1 Henry IV* originate with a proof-reader, rather than the compositor. Yet the two examples, however tiny a body of evidence, forbid exclusion of the hypothesis that a proof-reader may have been responsible for some of the variants Walker attributed to the compositor.

Neither of the hypotheses I have offered – two kinds of printer's copy, or a proof-reader's intervention – attempts to provide a definitive explanation of editorial influences on the Folio text of *1 Henry IV*. Instead both have been advanced to show that the distribution of variants in *1 Henry IV* can be explained without resort to Walker's hypothesis (gross inaccuracy on Compositor B's part). It seems necessary to investigate these alternative theories because Walker's hypothesis becomes highly improbable once we discover that nowhere else in Compositor B's pages of Folio texts set from lightly annotated quarto copy are there as many variants as we find in his stints of *1 Henry IV*.

In addition to problems with compositor identification and editorial interference, a third factor affecting the record of

Compositor B's performance in *1 Henry IV* was also largely ignored by Walker. As I have argued elsewhere,

> space was severely restricted during Compositor B's stints [on *1 Henry IV*] partly because copy for more than one quire had probably been cast off before he finished setting [the play] and partly because he set a great deal of prose in the first six pages of gathering e.[40]

Difficulties in justifying columns and lines of prose probably account to a significant extent for the sharp increase in omissions in Compositor B's stints on *1 Henry IV*, since a much higher proportion of this kind of error is evident in prose than in verse.[41] The concentration of prose in *1 Henry IV* also produced another change in Compositor B's fundamental habits: as Howard-Hill has observed, this history play marks the point in Folio production at which Compositor B began neglecting to space medial commas. As Howard-Hill also shows, Compositor B reverted to his habit of spacing medial commas when he encountered the predominantly verse tragedies – long before he set anything of *Lear*.[42] Thus the example of his total performance in *1 Henry IV* has much more relevance to his composition of the histories that followed *1 Henry IV* than to *Lear* and the other tragedies.

Walker's study thus reveals in aggravated form three problems which beset evaluation of the performance of Jaggard's type-setters: the problem of compositor identification, the confusion of possible editorial annotation with compositorial error, and the influence of cast-off prose copy on compositorial accuracy. Exclusive concentration on a single play, *1 Henry IV*, prevented Walker from appreciating the significance of the second problem; the other two did not become evident until later research had been published. Current recognition of these problems does not, however, constitute their solution. In identifying the work of individual compositors, in discriminating between editorial influence and compositorial inaccuracy, and in assessing the effects of cast-off copy on the quality of printed texts, we depend not on scientific demonstration, but instead on fallible human judgement. Yet a careful sifting of the variants found in a range of texts set by the compositors of Folio *Lear* ought to minimize distortions that might arise from possible misattribution of single pages to the compositors, from possibly erratic editorial intrusions, or from special circumstances affecting the transmission of individual Folio texts.

Patterns of Error in the Work of Compositors B and E

Compositor B was not, as Walker believed, the only compositor to work on Folio *Lear*. Shortly after Walker's study of B appeared, Hinman announced his discovery of another Folio compositor, the apprentice Compositor E, who set parts of *Lear* and several other tragedies.[43] In an edition of *Othello*, Walker flatly rejected Hinman's identification of the new compositor:

In a forthcoming article, which I have had the privilege of seeing in typescript, Dr. Hinman concludes that most of Act I of *Othello* was set by an apprentice. His evidence fails to convince me, as it is based on too narrow a range of spellings. In any case, his conclusion does not affect the editing of *Othello*, since the kinds of error that occur in what he believes to be apprentice work in the Tragedies are indistinguishable from those which are commonest in the work of B.[44]

Based on type-recurrence evidence – not just on a 'narrow range of spellings' – Hinman's identification of Compositor E has been widely accepted; it has recently been confirmed (and modified somewhat) by Howard-Hill.[45] Yet no one has responded to Hinman's long-standing appeal for a qualitative study of Compositor E's output;[46] nor has anyone tested Walker's claim that Compositor E's errors are indistinguishable from Compositor B's. This I shall now attempt to do.

Compositor E set portions of three Folio plays from lightly annotated quarto copy: *Titus*, *Romeo* and *Troilus*. Scholars agree that the printed copy for these plays consisted of the third quarto of *Titus* (1611), the third quarto of *Romeo* (1609), and the only quarto of *Troilus* (1609). There is also substantial agreement among scholars about the extent of Compositor E's stints in *Titus*, *Romeo* and *Troilus*. Hinman assigned to the apprentice all of *Titus* but the first page, and all of *Romeo* but the first page and the last, but only the second and third pages of *Troilus*, as well as the pre-cancellation setting of the first page (*gg3^v).[47] Howard-Hill would reassign from Compositor E to Compositor B pages dd3^v and ee2^v of *Titus* and page *gg3^v, the pre-cancellation first page of *Troilus*.[48] I have accepted Howard-Hill's reassignment of pages ee2^v and *gg3^v to Compositor B and included the errors on these pages in my summary analyses of Compositor B's work (together, of course, with the errors on pages of *Much Ado*, *Love's Labour's Lost*, *A Midsummer Night's Dream*, *Merchant*, *Titus* and *Romeo*, which everyone agrees were

Compositor B's). Page dd3^v (in *Titus*) I cannot accept as either Compositor E's or Compositor B's. The page cannot have been Compositor E's since it contains, as Howard-Hill has observed, a predominance of spaced medial commas, few of which Compositor E ever set. Yet it cannot be Compositor B's either, for (as Gary Taylor has noted) the spelling changes evident on dd3^v, and the acceptance there of nearly all the quarto-copy punctuation, both seem completely uncharacteristic of Compositor B.[49] Also foreign to this compositor's work is the paucity of emphasis capitals added to those in Q3 (which served as copy for one and a half columns of the page). Ordinarily Compositor B added many such capitals – for instance, 78 to part-page cc4, the first page of *Titus*, and 41 to part-page ee2^v, the last page of the play. To page dd3^v only one emphasis capital was added. The page, neither Compositor B's nor E's, is thus excluded from this study.[50] Since there is disagreement about the attribution of only a single page among those that have been assigned to Compositor E, and since that page has been excluded, compositor identification presents far less serious problems for a comparison of Compositors B and E than it did for Walker's study of *1 Henry IV*.

However, in two of the three plays set by Compositor E, *Titus* and *Romeo*, there are clear indications of the kind of sporadic editorial interference that is evident in B's work on *1 Henry IV*. Into both *Titus* and *Romeo* were introduced a significant number of readings also to be found in the first quarto of *Titus* or the first, second and fourth quartos of *Romeo*, but not in the quartos that served as printer's copy. Readings identical to those of the first quarto of *1 Henry IV* were, it will be recalled, one of the indications of an editorial hand in that Folio play. In an attempt to avoid confusing the Folio editors with the Folio compositors of *Romeo* and *Titus*, I have eliminated from the lists of the compositors' errors all readings in the Folio that might derive from quartos.[51] Excluded, too, are readings introduced into the Folio text which have been accepted into modern editions as necessary corrections.[52]

The Folio text of *Romeo* contains many more single variants paralleling readings in quartos that did not serve as printer's copy than does Folio *Titus*, although *Titus* contains a whole newly-printed scene, the 'fly scene' (TLN 1451–539; 3.2). We might then suspect that the kind of editorial attention received by the two texts differed markedly. As the following chart shows, however, the remaining departures from printed copy in Compositor E's stints differ

	Titus	Romeo	Troilus
number of lines	2385	3011	264
Literal Errors	50	59	9
Frequency	1/48 ll.	1/51	1/29
Substitutions	27	27	2
Frequency	1/88 ll.	1/112	1/132
Transpositions	1	8	0
Frequency	1/2385 ll.	1/376	0
Interpolations	9	12	3
Frequency	1/265 ll.	1/251	1/88
Omissions	14	27	5
Frequency	1/170 ll.	1/112	1/52
Total Errors	101	133	19
Frequency	1/23.6 ll.	1/22.6	1/13.9

significantly neither in number nor in kind from *Titus* to *Romeo*. The error rate in Compositor E's portion of *Titus* (1/23.6) is almost exactly the same as that for his pages in *Romeo* (1/22.6); in both, the most frequent errors are literals, followed by (in order of decreasing frequency) substitutions, omissions, interpolations, and transpositions. Such consistency seems to reflect the habits of a single workman, not a variation in editorial styles in the two plays. Fluctuations in kinds and numbers of errors in *Troilus* should probably be discounted because the sample of Compositor E's work in this play is only two pages; since these apparently-unedited pages contain mostly prose, the increase in the number of his errors may reflect difficulties with justification.

To test Walker's claim that Compositor E's errors are indistinguishable in number and kind from B's, we must compare the error rates of the two men. For such comparison, it seems desirable to separate the errors Walker charged to Compositor B in *1 Henry IV* from his errors in other plays. The chart reveals that the careless and high-handed Compositor B Walker characterized in her study of *1 Henry IV* bears scant resemblance to Compositor E. Instead, E appears much more similar to the Compositor B in evidence in the comedies and tragedies: neither compositor was guilty of many omissions, interpolations or transpositions, but both were guilty of numerous substitutions, literal or otherwise. However, more detailed comparison of the two shows that such resemblances are merely superficial. In the sections which follow, I first compare Compositor

E to the Compositor B of the comedies and tragedies, then compare the latter to Walker's Compositor B of *1 Henry IV*.

Substitutions   (For lists of Compositor B's alleged substitutions see Walker, '*1 Henry IV*', pp. 48–9, 52, and Werstine, 'Compositor B', pp. 244–7; for a list of Compositor E's, see Appendices I and II.)

Substitutions are usually divided into two major categories: first, literal substitutions involving deletion, addition or change of a single letter, or transposition of letters; second, substitution of one or more words orthographically dissimilar to copy readings. About two-thirds of E's substitutions (118 of 174) are of the first kind. This high proportion would appear to indicate that E had difficulty reading his copy accurately. Particularly striking among Compositor E's literal substitutions are his frequent deletions and additions of final -s. The error accounts for over one-third of E's literal substitutions and for a quarter of his total substitutions. One such error appears in his work for each full page of the Folio he set from quarto copy. So habitual is this error in his work that he would occasionally add a final -s to an adverb ('ersts', *Titus*, TLN 1607; 4.1.63), a name ('*Bassianuss*', *Titus*, TLN 1032; 2.3.274), or a noun already in the plural ('Prisonerss', *Titus*, TLN 280; 1.1.249). In contrast, Compositor B made this error only ten times, or once every second page. Literal errors constitute fewer than half of his substitutions (33 of 78). Instead Compositor B more frequently substituted words which are orthographically dissimilar to the words of his copy, but similar in meaning to the copy

	Compositor B		Compositor E[53]
	1H4	other plays	
number of lines	1795	2451	5660
Literals and Substitutions	50	78	174
Frequency	1/36 ll.	1/31	1/33
Transpositions	8	6	9
Frequency	1/224 ll.	1/409	1/629
Interpolations	28	7	24
Frequency	1/64 ll.	1/350	1/236
Omissions	30	9	46
Frequency	1/60 ll.	1/272	1/123
Total Errors	116	100	253
Frequency	1/15.5 ll.	1/24.5	1/22.4

words. Among the clearest examples of B's habit are the substitutions of 'smeered' for 'smirched' (*Much Ado*, TLN 1796; 4.1.133), 'end-lesse' for 'curelesse' (*Merchant*, TLN 2051; 4.1.142), and 'affraid' for 'a feard' (*Love's Labour's Lost*, TLN 2532; 5.2.579). Although the rate of substitution is about equal in the work of both compositors, the kind of substitution differs sharply.

Compositor B's substitutions would be far more difficult to identify in the absence of printer's copy than would Compositor E's. At least two-fifths (70) of E's substitutions result in obvious nonsense. Only about one-fifth (18) of Compositor B's erroneous substitutions reveal themselves by destroying the sense of a speech. Sometimes B will substitute a more difficult word for the clear reading of his copy, such as 'Broyles' for 'brawles' (*Romeo*, TLN 91; 1.1.89) or 'Beast-like' for 'beastly' (*Titus*, TLN 2703; 5.3.199). Sometimes his substitution will be the more common word, for example, 'pray' for 'bepray' (*Love's Labour's Lost*, TLN 2651; 5.2.696) or 'momentarie' for 'momentany' (*Midsummer Night's Dream*, TLN 153; 1.1.143). In contrast, Compositor E is dedicated to simplicity: he discards his copy's unusual spellings 'dririe' and 'yellowing' for 'sudden' and 'yelping' (*Titus*, TLN 436, 755; 1.1.391, 2.3.20), and he takes a literal understanding of Juliet's phrase 'heat of life', changing it to 'heat of fire' (*Romeo*, TLN 2497; 4.3.16). Without the quartos, Compositor E's nonsense and simplifications could be spotted more readily than B's sophistications.

The compositors do share some characteristics. Generally their substitutions affect only a single word. Only three times might Compositor B have done more: 'morall downe' for 'Moon vsed' (*Midsummer Night's Dream*, TLN 2010; 5.1.206), 'It is not' for 'Is it so' (*Merchant*, TLN 2174; 4.1.259) and 'was the' for 'am his' (*Titus*, TLN 11; 1.1.5).[54] One instance is all we find in E's stints: 'it action' for 'that accord' (*Titus*, TLN 2302; 5.2.18), perhaps an editorial insertion.[55] Fewer than half of B's non-literal substitutions (19 of 45) affect nouns, verbs, adjectives, and adverbs. More (26 of 45) change pronouns, pronominal adjectives, copula and auxiliary verbs, articles, prepositions, conjunctions, interjections or negative particles. Compositor E differs somewhat more in this respect, since his non-literal substitutions divide almost equally between the two categories mentioned. Thus, although B's substitutions are better concealed, his departures from copy may sometimes be less significant than those of his unsophisticated partner. Both are influenced by immediate context to about the same extent in making substitutions. One of six substitutions in both compositors' work is a recollection of a word just set or an anticipation of a word about to be set. Yet the differences in their work are greater than the similarities.

There are still greater differences, however, between Walker's Compositor B of *1 Henry IV* and the two workmen whom we have just assessed. At least seven of the substitutions charged to B by Walker resemble nothing found in his work on the other plays. Three of these, in successive lines, appear to represent an effort at coherent revision. In the fifth quarto of *1 Henry IV*, the passage reads:

> As he [Q1: is] deliuered to your Maiesty.
> Either enuy therefore, or misprision
> Is guilty of this fault, and not my sonne.
> (British Library copy, B2)

In the Folio, Northumberland's accusation against the King is not only more pointed, but also cast in the past tense:[56]

> As was deliuered to your Maiesty:
> Who either through enuy, or misprision,
> Was guilty of this fault; and not my Sonne.
> (TLN 348–50; 1.3.26–8)

A similar example is located at TLN 388, 1.3.66, where the fifth quarto reads, 'I answered indirctely [*sic*] (as I sayd)' B2[v]), but the Folio has, 'Made me to answer indirectly (as I said)'. These revisions may have been occasioned by discovery of the errors in the fifth quarto or by damage to the fifth quarto's pages, since both the cited passages occur right at the bottom of two pages constituting a single leaf of the quarto. Two other quarto passages were altered in a comparable manner on this same Folio page (e1): the fifth quarto's 'Albeit I make a hazard of my head' (B3[v]) becomes 'Although it be with hazard of my head' (TLN 449; 1.3.128), and 'Yea on his part' (B3[v]) is changed to 'In his behalfe' (TLN 455; 1.3.133). Associated with this last alteration is another substitution for 'Yea' on the preceding Folio page (TLN 276; 1.2.174). The contrast between these substitutions and what is found elsewhere in Compositor B's work, as well as the concentration of the changes on just two Folio pages, probably exonerates B from responsibility for the errors: sporadic editorial interference seems much more likely. Since the remaining sixteen non-literal substitutions in B's stint on *1 Henry IV* include some four multiple-word changes, a higher proportion than is evident in other plays set by B from quarto copy, some of these too may be editorial in origin; but in these cases no clear distinction is possible between compositorial and editorial variants. I have therefore included all four in the following summary assessment of Compositor B's work.

With the seven probable editorial substitutions eliminated, B's substitution rate in *1 Henry IV* is reduced to one substitution, literal or otherwise, for every forty-two lines, a lower rate than he managed in the rest of his stints on the Folio. A much higher proportion of substitutions than usual are literal errors (27 of 43), although only a few of these literals (6) result from the deletion or addition of final-s, as we have come to expect. A much higher proportion than usual also produce obvious nonsense (18 of 43), although this increase is probably a function of the larger number of literal errors. For non-literal substitutions in *1 Henry IV*, Compositor B again sometimes seems guided by the meaning of the copy word rather than its graphical shape: the substitution of 'haughty' for 'proud' is an obvious example (TLN 2902; 5.3.11).[57] Only six of the sixteen non-literal errors are nouns, verbs and adjectives, the remaining being pronouns, pronominal adjectives, prepositions, conjunctions, a copula verb and an article. (Each word in a multiple-word substitution is counted separately.) When probable editorial interference is discounted, inclusion of *1 Henry IV* in a study of Compositor B indicates only that B is capable of setting many fewer substitutions, most of them nonsensical literal errors, on this one occasion than on others.

Transpositions   (For lists of Compositor B's alleged transpositions, see Walker, '*1 Henry IV*', p. 53, and Werstine, 'Compositor B', p. 244; for a list of Compositor E's, see Appendix III.)

Compositor E transposed words less frequently than B, only once for every 629 lines compared to B's rate of one for every 409 lines. Compositor E's transpositions would also have been much easier to detect than B's without the quartos' authority. Four of E's nine transpositions make nonsense of the contexts in which he set them; a passage from *Romeo* is typical:

> *It is* more sin to wish me thus forsworne,
> Or to dispraise my Lord with that same tongue
> Which she hath prais'd him with aboue compare,
> So many thousand times?
>   (TLN 2286–9, 3.5.236–9; italics indicate the
>   words transposed)

Another transposition is unidiomatic (*Romeo*, TLN 2662; 4.5.82), another disturbs metre (*Romeo*, TLN 2884; 5.3.31), and yet another is betrayed by the faulty parallelism it introduces:

> A stone is *as soft* waxe,
> Tribunes more hard then stones.
> (*Titus*, TLN 1180–1; 3.1.45;
> italics again indicate the words
> transposed)

Without the quartos, seven of E's nine transpositions could have been detected and emended, but none of B's six could have been, since none obviously disturbs either sense or metre. Yet transposition remains the rarest of both the compositors' errors.

Essentially the same is true of Compositor B's transpositions in *1 Henry IV*. Although in this play transpositions are nearly twice as frequent, none of the eight impairs either sense or metre. Like most of Compositor B's transpositions throughout the Folio, most of these in *1 Henry IV* deal with verbs and their subjects or with verbs and the particle 'not'. If, as seems likely, the increase in transpositions in the history play should be attributed to an editor, his transpositions are indistinguishable from Compositor B's. For both editor and compositor, however, transposition must have been the least frequent alteration.

Interpolations   (For lists of Compositor B's alleged interpolations see Walker, '*1 Henry IV*', p. 51, and Werstine, 'Compositor B', p. 249; for Compositor E's see Appendix IV.)

The contrast between B's sophistication and E's naïvety, evident in their transpositions, appears again in their interpolations. Compositor E interpolated words at a higher rate than B, but without the authoritative quartos B's errors would often be difficult to uncover, while E's reveal themselves, for the most part, as mere nonsense. Dittography produced ten of Compositor E's twenty-four interpolations, while another four are equally senseless (*Titus* TLN 203, 1.1.174; *Romeo* TLN 386 and 2726, 1.3.35 and 5.1.4; *Troilus* TLN 272, 1.2.117), two of these marked by anticipation of words printed correctly later in the lines. Yet another – 'What booke?' (*Titus* TLN 1580; 4.1.36 + 1) – was set, according to W. W. Greg, in anticipation of the same words printed again five lines below.[58] Two more interpolations may have been designed to improve the metre of nine-syllable lines (*Romeo* TLN 1524 and 1700, 3.1.91 and 3.2.51), but four others clearly disturb metre (*Titus* TLN 1114 and 2208, 2.4.41 and 5.1.93; *Romeo* TLN 760 and 1281, 2.1.10 and 2.4.187). Again Compositor B proves more sensitive to verse, with six interpolations in verse, only three of them revealed by faulty metre. A small proportion of E's interpolations – two of twenty-four – are prompted by obvious corruption or omission in his copy; a much larger proportion of B's – three of seven – disguise errors in his copy. Like E, however, B interpolated only single words, most of them pronouns, articles, and copula and auxiliary verbs. Thus, although interpolation is nearly as rare as transposition in the work of both compositors, editors have more to fear from Compositor B's sophistication than from E's generally obvious bungling.

The twenty-eight interpolations in Compositor B's stint on *1 Henry IV*, one for every sixty-four lines, are therefore quite uncharacteristic of the compositor. Yet they would come as no surprise from the editor of B's copy, who is already known to have embellished the stage directions. There is no reason to believe that such an editor would subscribe to our modern distinction between stage directions and dialogue, whether he was emending on his own authority or from manuscript. Because Compositor B never added half-lines, adjectives, verbs, or expansions to his copy for the Folio, we may confidently assign to the editor interpolation of the redundant half-line 'And list to me' (TLN 536; 1.3.211 + 1), the two adjectives 'wond'rous' (TLN 605–6; 1.3.277) and 'worthy' (TLN 2881; 5.2.93), the verb 'light' (TLN 764; 2.2.28–9) and the expansion of 'christen' to 'in Christendome' (TLN 651–2; 2.1.17).

Coherent patterns are evident among other interpolations in *1 Henry IV* that are also at odds with the compositor's performance elsewhere. For example, characters are made to repeat themselves exactly through interpolation of words in their prose speeches. In the quarto version of the dialogue between the Prince and Poins near the end of 1.2, two of the Prince's speeches begin 'Yea, but', as he objects to Poins's plan to deceive Falstaff; but the Prince's first speech in the exchange is simply a request for information beginning 'How shall'. In the Folio, the three speeches are altered to begin 'But', 'I, but', and 'But' (TLN 270, 276, 283; 1.2.167, 174, 181), although the interpolation of 'But' at TLN 270 results in a tightly justified line from which the compositor was obliged to omit the second 'l' of 'shall'. (It should also be noted that there is plenty of room in both TLN 276 and 283 for the quarto word 'Yea'.) The same pattern is visible in the speeches of the drawer Francis, who is characterized by his responses to the inn's patrons: 'Anon, anon' or 'Anon, anon sir' or 'O Lord sir' (TLN 1000, 1007, 1012, 1026, 1034; 2.4.37, 44, 49, 64, 72). In the quarto, he is allowed to vary these replies slightly to 'Anone sir' and 'O Lord' (TLN 1015, 1022; 2.4.52, 60), but in the Folio these speeches at TLN 1015 and 1022 are made to conform exactly to those that precede and follow them. Such patterns of occasional repetition in the quarto would not have been apparent to a compositor working sequentially through his copy for single pages, and thus he could not have added to them. Even if the compositor's eye had skipped from one speech to a later one, he would have betrayed the eyeskip by omitting the intervening speeches. An editor, however, would have been free to work backwards and forwards in the text and could have developed (or reproduced from a manuscript) the patterns of comic repetition he observed.

Much in evidence in the Folio are the effects of an apparent impulse to impose formal, balanced syntax upon colloquial and elliptical prose speeches – an impulse that cannot be detected elsewhere in Compositor B's work. Where the quarto reads ' . . . is not my Hostesse of the Tauerne a most sweet wench? | *Prince.* As the hony of *Hibla*' (A4), the Folio has, for the second speech, ' . . . *Prince.* As is the hony' (TLN 155; 1.2.41). Then the quarto's 'poore iade is wrung' and '*Robin* Ostler' (C2) become in the Folio 'the poore Iade' and '*Robin* the Ostler' (TLN 640, 645; 2.1.6 and 10–11). The same fussiness can be seen in the Folio versions (with the interpolations italicized) of several speeches: (1) the Chamberlain's 'Nay, I thinke *rather*, you are more beholding to the Night, then *to* the Fernseed', (2) Falstaff's 'And 'twere not as good a deede as *to* drinke, to turne Trueman, and to leaue', and (3) Hotspur's 'our plot is *as* good a plot as euer was laid', where the quarto has 'a good plot as' (TLN 723–4, 757–8 and 864; 2.1.88–9, 2.2.22–3, and 2.3.17). By analogy the attempt at another infinitive construction – 'they pray continually vnto their Saint the Commonwealth; or rather, not *to* pray to her, but prey on her' (TLN 715–16; 2.1.79–81) – might also be attributed to the editor.[59] In fact, only two of the seventeen interpolations in the prose of *1 Henry IV* can be clearly attributed to the compositor. The addition of 'then' at the end of the last line of page e3 must have been his, since he had already set the proper word 'they' at the top of page e3ᵛ (already at press), and needed a substitution to fill the space in a line of prose. The dittographical 'great great', in the uncorrected state of TLN 3129 was also certainly his. Just as few of the eleven interpolations in verse may have been introduced by the compositor. Already identified as probably the editor's (p. 269) is the addition of one adjective ('worthy') to a metrically defective line of quarto verse; all but two of the additions to verse in the Folio might be his as well, for all seem designed, often mistakenly, to impose metrical regularity. Since occasionally in other plays Compositor B also attempted to repair metrically defective lines, it is not possible to separate his additions from the editor's. Nevertheless, it is nearly impossible to escape the conclusion that responsibility for the marked increase in interpolations in B's stints on *1 Henry IV* lies with the editor, not the compositor.

Omissions (For lists of Compositor B's alleged omissions see Walker, '*1 Henry IV*', pp. 49–50, and Werstine, 'Compositor B', pp. 248–9; for Compositor E's see Appendix V.)

Omissions are twice as frequent and often far more serious in E's work than in B's. Six times B omitted either the first or the last word(s) of a speech, sometimes apparently in an effort to save space in a line requiring justification. In contrast E omitted medial words through carelessness in no apparent effort to conserve space. Compositor B was much more sensitive to metre than E: only three of B's nine omissions occur in verse, only two of those disturbing the metre; twenty-seven of Compositor E's single-word omissions are found in verse (not always set as verse), twenty-four of them producing metrically deficient lines. Another two of these twenty-seven omissions might be naïve attempts to repair metre, while a third occurs in badly mislined verse. Compositor E's forty-six omissions include many adjectives and adverbs, and some verbs, as well as pronouns and prepositions, most of which are not essential to the preservation of some meaning (if not the author's meaning) in the passages from which they were omitted. Such compositorial error, according to John O'Connor, was probably memorial, suggesting the unwillingness of the compositor to refer to his copy sufficiently often.[60] Compositor B seems to have been much more careful, for his omissions are too few to classify. Compositor E, on the other hand, omits some eight full lines; none of these omissions is clearly the result of censorship, and only one is at the end of a page, where space may have been short. Three of the eight lines are omitted as a result of simple eyeskip. In contrast, apart from one instance of probable censorship, B omits but a single line.

Omissions are five times more frequent than usual in B's stints on *1 Henry IV*. Some of these thirty omissions, but by no means all, seem the responsibility of the editor (who also pruned the stage directions substantially). Three can be associated with interpolations already identified as editorial: the deletion of 'Yea' (TLN 283; 1.2.181) seems of a piece with the interpolated 'But' fourteen lines above it, also in a speech by the Prince. 'Yea' is again cut, probably by the editor, at TLN 2769 (5.1.130), when it again precedes the word 'but'. Associated with the editorial interpolation of 'is' (TLN 155; 1.2.41) is the omission of 'of *Hibla*' in the same line. Another deletion resembles the cuts made in some stage directions: '*Ned Poines*' is reduced simply to '*Ned*' (TLN 794; 2.2.61). On two occasions, more than a single word is omitted from the same line, although such concentrations of error are nowhere evident in Compositor B's labours on other plays (TLN 934 and 972; 2.3. 88 and 2.4.7–8). The errors in TLN 972 may, however, be the compositor's, for he is squeezing prose into the end of a column.

It is also difficult to make exact distinctions between the compositor's omissions in verse and the editor's. Only nine of the thirty omissions in B's section of *1 Henry IV* occur in verse, and only six of the nine result in metrically deficient lines; exactly the same ratio is found in B's work elsewhere. Yet not all of the nine are likely to be the compositor's, since the editor has already been identified tampering with the verse by interpolating words. At least eleven of the total of thirty omissions in verse and prose are doubtless the compositor's: nine make for obvious nonsense in context, and two others were produced by simple eyeskip. (It should be noted, however, that none of B's omissions elsewhere were eyeskips, nor did any result in nonsense.) The total number of omissions that can be charged to Compositor B in *1 Henry IV* probably thus cannot be more than twenty or fewer than fifteen; the range lies between one omission for every 120 lines and one for every 90, with a far denser concentration in prose than in verse – probably the result of the space constraints imposed in setting a great deal of prose. In conclusion, then, editors need not resort to the example of Compositor B's omissions in *1 Henry IV* unless their plays contain long stretches of tightly-set prose sprinkled with many obviously nonsensical single-word omissions.

With this detailed examination of the quality of workmanship in texts set from quarto copy by Compositors B and E behind us, we can now turn to a study of printing-house corruption in the text of Folio *Lear* itself.

Error and Sophistication in Folio 'Lear'

Copy for the Folio version of *Lear* was divided almost equally between Compositors B and E. To Compositor B, Hinman assigned pages qq2, 3^v, 5, $rr2^v$, 3^v–6^v, ssl and 3, and column $rr1^v$b; to Compositor E, $qq2^v$, 3, 4, 4^v, 5^v–6^v, rr1, 2, 3, $ss1^v$, 2 and 2^v, and column $rr1^v$a.[61] Howard-Hill has recently confirmed Hinman's attributions, but has also reassigned pages ss1 and 3 from Compositor B to Compositor E.[62] Inspired by Stone's discovery of Folio punctuation borrowings from the second quarto of *Lear* (*Textual History*, pp. 129–40), Taylor's analysis of Compositor E's borrowings suggests that Howard-Hill is correct, even though Howard-Hill's reassignments here and elsewhere appear to contradict Hinman's case identifications.[63] I have therefore accepted Howard-Hill's attribution of ss1 and 3 to Compositor E.

The work of Stone and Taylor also indicates that the Folio text of *Lear* was, at least in large part, set from an exemplar of the Second Quarto (Q2). Yet this printed copy was just as certainly annotated with reference to a manuscript and with reference, direct or indirect, to the First Quarto (Q1). The influence of Q1 has not been denied since Greg demonstrated the Folio's dependence on readings from both corrected and uncorrected states of Q1 sheets.[64] Thus the Folio text of *Lear* resembles those of *1 Henry IV*, *Titus* and *Romeo*: like them, it is based on printed copy from a derivative quarto annotated with reference to a source containing readings common to an earlier quarto or, in the case of *Romeo*, two earlier quartos and a later one (Q4). In Folio *Lear*, but not in Folio *1 Henry IV*, *Titus* and *Romeo*, however, we find agreement between Folio readings and printing-house errors from an earlier quarto (Q1), and so the analogy between Folio *Lear* and the other three Folio texts is not exact. Since the Folio text of *Lear* also differs from the three other Folio texts mentioned in containing a great many more departures from printed copy, there is all the more cause to examine Folio *Lear* for the possible influence of Folio editors on the integrity of its text.

The tests used in detecting such influence must be carefully selected. Without begging the question as flagrantly as Stone does, we cannot estimate editorial influence on Folio *Lear* simply by assessing the quality of substantive variants between the Quarto and Folio texts. Nor can we expect to find evidence of an editor's hand in the purely accidental features, such as punctuation and spelling, for these were generally the compositor's prerogative. Instead we must examine both stage directions and a class of variants that lies between substantives and accidentals – changes in verbal forms that affect meaning, if at all, only in so far as they alter the tone and, in the case of verse, the metre of a speech or line. This class includes contractions, elisions, expansions of contractions and elisions, and such substitutions as 'who' for 'that', 'hath' for 'has', 'if' for 'and', 'towards' for 'toward', or even the suffixes *ed* and *est* for *'d* and *'st*. (These examples illustrate the class but do not constitute an exhaustive description.) According to Madeleine Doran, such variants between Quarto and Folio *Lear* were almost entirely the choices of the Folio compositors;[65] according to Stone (*Textual History*, p. 105), almost none derive from the compositors. Examination of these variants in the context of other Folio plays set from quarto copy shows that neither critic was exactly right, and that such variants in Folio plays probably derive, in part, from Jaggard's compositors and, in part, from the Folio editor(s).

Compositors B and E differ sharply in the numbers of such variants they introduced. In setting some 2,037 lines of four comedies (*Much Ado about Nothing*, *Love's Labour's Lost*, *A Midsummer Night's Dream*, and *The Merchant of Venice*) in which little editorial interference with the text is suspected, Compositor B produced eighteen such variants, or one for every 113 lines of text. (Not included in the count are changes of the suffixes *ed* and *est* to *'d* and *'st* or *st*, or vice versa.[66]) In B's stints on *1 Henry IV*, there are twenty-seven such variants (not including the suffixes mentioned), or one for every sixty-seven lines—another clear indication of the editorial hand already identified in the compositor's copy.[67] In contrast, there are only thirty comparable variants in the 5,660 lines of the Folio set from lightly annotated printed copy by Compositor E; that is, one for every 189 lines. It is therefore in the work of E, who seems to have been more faithful to his copy, that we have the best chance to estimate editorial influence on this class of variants in the Folio.

To study this influence on E's pages both in *Lear* and in other Folio plays more fully, we must expand the range of variants to include the *d*, *de*, or *'d/ed* and *est/'st* or *st* variants which may affect syllabification or scansion.[68] The expanded class comprises eighty-six variants in Compositor E's 5,660 lines of *Titus*, *Romeo* and *Troilus*, or one for every sixty-six lines.[69] There can be little doubt that a substantial number of these are the editor's: Compositor E's pages of *Troilus*, where no editing is suspected, contain none;[70] of thirty-seven variants from printed copy in *Titus*, six are to be found in Q1, where parallels to Folio substantive variants introduced by an editor have also been located; of forty-nine variants in *Romeo*, fully twenty-one have parallels in Q1, Q2, and/or Q4—a clear indication that these derive from the editor, not the compositor.[71] Since there is no reason to assume that editorial annotation was confined to those Folio variants that might have been borrowed from the earlier quartos and that all the remaining variants in question must be the compositor's, we shall probably arrive at a liberal estimate of the rate at which Compositor E introduced such variants if we do charge all the rest to him. Upon such calculations, however, only fifty-nine variants in 5,660 lines could be his, or one variant for every one hundred or so lines.

Whether the variants in the class under discussion be editorial or compositorial in origin, the quality of these variants is not encouraging for a reader of the Folio. Of the eighty-six variants in *Titus* and *Romeo*, seventy-two may affect syllabification and, in verse, scansion; the other fourteen, such as *towards/toward* or *hither/hether*, seem altogether indifferent. Only six of the seventy-two still under consideration occur in prose speeches. Even if, among the sixty-six remaining variants (all in verse), we include those variants common to the earlier quartos, only two-thirds (forty-six) can be defended as necessary corrections.[72] Of the twenty erroneous variants, nine are found in *Titus* and eleven in *Romeo*; but three of *Romeo*'s eleven might have been borrowed from Q1 or Q4. Although most of the errors produce obvious metrical irregularities, six appear to have been introduced to make hypermetrical lines decasyllabic: in three of these cases, feminine endings are dropped; in three others extra syllables before or after the caesura disappear. If the Folio text of *Lear* fell prey to the same editor(s) who annotated printer's copy for the Folio *Titus* and *Romeo*, we should expect to find in Compositor E's pages of *Lear* something of the rate of error in this class of variants that we have discovered in the compositor's pages of *Titus* and *Romeo*.

In Folio *Lear* the category of variants under scrutiny is represented in an uncommon number of departures from Q2, an exemplar of which probably served as copy for the type-setters; there are about 200 in Compositor E's 1,877 lines alone.[73] Many of these variants have already been examined by scholars.[74] Doran noticed the Folio's preference for *besides* (TLN 1616; 3.1.1), *sometimes* (TLN 697, 1270; 1.4.184, 2.3.19) and *toward* (TLN 206, 494, 938, 2050, 2078; 1.1.190, 1.2.173, 2.1.10, 3.6.91, 3.7.19) to the quarto spellings *beside* (Q2: F1), *sometime* (Q2: C2ᵛ, E1) and *towards* (Q2: A4ᵛ, B4, G2ᵛ, G3ᵛ); these preferences she assigned to the compositors ('in one of the texts, at least, we are confronted with preferences of a compositor'). Possibly the first two are compositorial since they occur only in E's portion of *Lear* and may represent further examples of his habitual addition of final *s* to his copy's spellings. (As I will indicate below, there is double reason for charging the variant *sometimes* at TLN 1270 to Compositor E.) Yet the preference for *toward* cannot be assigned to a compositor: both B and E changed *towards* to *toward*, and, in one instance (TLN 938), E apparently followed manuscript copy in setting *toward*, since this line is missing from the second quarto. Thus the *toward* variants must derive from copy, not from the compositors.

Doran also attributed to the compositors or 'to the transcriber of the folio manuscript' the Folio's apparent preference for *has* (TLN 404, 632, 3206; 1.2.69, 1.4.102, 5.3.249), *do's* (TLN 738, 740, 892, 1165; 1.4.226, 227, 1.5.18, 2.2.91), *if* (TLN 1119, 1156; 2.2.45, 83), *he* (TLN 585, 897, 1473, 1947, 2215, 2515; 1.4.56, 1.5.23, 2.4.186, 3.4.167, 4.1.31, 4.6.70), and, before a vowel, *mine* (TLN 3201; 5.3.245) and *thine* (TLN 167, 181, 676, 1804, 2346, 2580, 2595, 2597; 1.1.156, 167, 1.4.161, 3.4.23, 4.2.96, 4.6.136, 151, 153); in these lines Q1 shows *hath*, *doth*, *and*, *a*, *my*, and *thy*. If, however, Q2 served as printer's copy for the Folio, as we now have good reason to believe, then a number of these variants disappear. The Second Quarto reads *if* at TLN 1156 (D3ᵛ) and *he* at TLN 585, 897, 1473, 1947 and 2215 (C1, 4ᵛ, E3ᵛ, G1, H1), as does the Folio. Of the remaining variants the last four examples of *thine* might be charged to Compositor B, who preferred *mine* to *my* in setting *Midsummer Night's Dream* (TLN 141; 1.1.131) and *Merchant* (TLN 2633; 5.1.209) from printed copy, and so may have changed Q2 *thy* (H3, I3) to *thine* here in Folio *Lear*. However, since the Second Quarto spellings *my* (L3) and *thy* (A4, C2, F3ᵛ) are also set as *mine* and *thine* five times in Compositor E's portion of *Lear*, the changes from *thy* to *thine* in B's stints cannot be assigned with any confidence to B's agency alone. But B may have been responsible for the single change from the Second Quarto's reading *a* (I2) to the Folio's *he*, for he made the same change from his printed copy in *Love's Labour's Lost* (TLN 2248, 2471, 2669; 5.2.323, 526, 714). None of the other readings charged to the compositors by Doran can be identified as the individual preferences of either. Both changed the Second Quarto's *hath* (B3, C1ᵛ, L3) to *has*; both set *do's* for their copy's *doth* (C3, C4, D3ᵛ). While E alone altered his copy's *and* (D3) to *if*, he is not likely to have done so on his own authority, since he never made the same change in using printed copy for *Titus*, *Romeo* and *Troilus*. Thus few of the readings cited by Doran as printer's changes can be demonstrated to be compositorial in origin.

E. A. J. Honigmann has analysed some of the variants in question in an attempt to show that the copy for Folio *Lear* may have benefited (or suffered) from the intervention of one of the editors or scribes whose work he suspected behind the Folio versions of *Love's Labour's Lost, Much Ado about Nothing, Richard II, 1 Henry IV, 2 Henry IV, Troilus, Titus, Romeo, Hamlet* and *Othello*. In groups of these Folio texts Honigmann charted consistent preferences for certain verbal forms, preferences that transcend the habits of individual compositors. For example, in the last half of Folio *Othello*, *hath* is consistently preferred to the quarto spelling *has*, but *has* is never substituted for *hath*; or in Folio *1 Henry IV, 2 Henry IV* and *Richard III*, quarto *yea* is omitted, or changed to *I* or *yes* (or, once each, to *ye* or *what*).

Naming such differences 'one-way variants', Honigmann charged them to scribes or Folio editors. He placed the following readings in Folio *Lear* within families of one-way variants also found elsewhere in the Folio (I list the Q2 reading first, then the Folio): *nought/naught* (D3ᵛ; TLN 1153; 2.2.80), *farther/further* (F1ᵛ, H1ᵛ, I1ᵛ, K3ᵛ; TLN 1639, 2241, 2467, 2931; 3.1.42, 4.1.52, 4.6.30, 5.2.8), *doth/do's* (C3, C4, D3ᵛ; TLN 738, 740, 892, 1165; 1.4.226, 227, 1.5.18, 2.2.91) *more/mo* (C4ᵛ, TLN 909; 1.5.34), *yon/yond* (I1ᵛ, 2ᵛ, 3; TLN 2453, 2563, 2596; 4.6.18, 118, 152), *a/he, Twas/It was* (D2; TLN 1047; 2.1.106), *ah(A)/Oh* (O) (H1, L3ᵛ; TLN 2202, 3230; 4.1.21, 5.3.268), *and/if, Yea/Ha?, O* (C3ᵛ, E2ᵛ; TLN 823, 1410; 1.4.304, 2.4.132). The first four categories are also found in Folio *Othello* and/or *1 Henry IV*, the next four in Folio *Troilus* or *2 Henry IV*, and forms of the last two in both *1* and *2 Henry IV*. Since Honigmann identified variants in *1 Henry IV* that conflict with variants in *2 Henry IV*, it is difficult to make sense of the similarities both have with *Lear* and with each other; and since authorial revision is suspected in Folio *Othello*, but not in *1 Henry IV*, the similarities between these two plays are equally puzzling.

Analysis of the variants discussed by Honigmann shows that none of them establishes editorial or scribal influence on Folio *Lear*. As Honigmann recognizes, the *nought/naught* variation is probably compositorial: 'One observes that it may have been one man, Compositor E, who was responsible for the (*n*)*aught* forms, since the three changes from (*n*)*ought* in *Lear* and *Othello* and the two instances of QF *naught* in *Lear* were all set by him.' The changes to *further* may also originate with the compositors. Although both Folio *Lear* compositors set *further* for Q2 *farther*, both demonstrate a preference for *further* in other Folio texts set from extant printed copy: Compositor B in *1 Henry IV* (TLN 952; 2.3.107), Compositor E in *Romeo* (TLN 986, 2887; 2.2.177, 5.3.34), although *further* in *Romeo* is common to Q1 and the Folio. Together with the preference for *further* in *Othello* (TLN 1021; 2.1.238), also set by Compositor E, these are the only Folio preferences for *further* recorded by Honigmann. Therefore neither *naught* nor *further* can be used to link the editing of copy for Folio *Lear* with the editing of *1 Henry IV* and *Othello*.

The single Folio alteration of *more* to *mo* occurs in a speech by the Fool, to whose speeches the Folio text is acknowledged to have restored many similar colloquialisms not found in the quartos; aesthetics, rather than the mechanics of editing, probably account for this substitution. No connection between Folio *1 Henry IV* and *Lear* can be supported by the *doth/do's* variants in the latter, since the single substitution in *1 Henry IV* is spelled *does* (TLN 2100; 3.3.93), not *do's*, and it replaces the misprint *dow* of the fifth quarto (G3ᵛ), not *doth*. Replacement of Q2 *yond* with *yon* in *Lear* is found in Compositor B's work alone, as is the single change of *a* to *he*, perhaps the compositor's preference, as I have already noted. While both compositors set *Oh* or *O* for Q2 *ah* or *A*, both show a preference for this change in other texts, Compositor B in *Titus* (TLN 2688; 5.3.184) and E in *Romeo* (TLN 1361; 2.5.50). Nor is the change a 'one-way variant', for Compositor B set *Ah* for Q2 *O* in Folio *Lear* (G1; TLN 1943; 3.4.163), as Honigmann has acknowledged. The alteration of Q2 *and* to *if* in Folio *Lear* is also not a one-way variant, as it is for example in *1 Henry IV*: twice in Folio *Lear* Compositor E set *and* for Q2 *if* (C2ᵛ, E1ᵛ; TLN 694, 1337; 1.4.181, 2.4.64). The substitutions of *Ha?* and *O* for *yea* in *Lear* differ sharply from those in the history plays cited by Honigmann, where *yea* is either omitted or replaced by the identifiably editorial preferences *I* or *Yes.* Moreover, the *yea/Ha?* *Lear* variant is, as Honigmann noted, no simple substitution, but entails the variant half-line containing it: 'yea is it come to this?' in the Second Quarto (C3ᵛ) becomes 'Ha? Let it be so' in the Folio. While Honigmann's method may yet prove fruitful, the variants he presented, taken together or singly, are insufficient to demonstrate a connection between the transmission of the Folio *Lear* text and that of other Folio plays he has cited, notably *1* and *2 Henry IV.*

The variants in *Lear* most suggestive of an editorial hand are the substitutions, before a vowel, of *mine* and *thine* for Q2 *my* and *thy,* five times by Compositor E and four times by Compositor B. The same changes are made four times in *Richard II,* four times in *2 Henry IV,* five times in *Richard III,* twice in *Troilus,* sixteen times in *Hamlet* and twice in *Othello.*[75] Yet we cannot absolutely deny Compositor B responsibility for the *thine* spellings in his stint, since, as I have indicated, he alone preferred such spellings in *Merchant* and *Midsummer Night's Dream.* Nor are the *thy/thine* variants in *Lear* one-way variants that suggest only mechanical editing; both compositors of Folio *Lear* also set *thy* for Q2 *thine* (I3, L1; TLN 2604, 3028; 4.6.161, 5.3.83).

Four pairs of specific variants tell against Honigmann's argument for the association of editorial or scribal practice behind Folio *Lear* with such practices in the Folio histories and in other Folio tragedies. While Honigmann noted one-way traffic in the variants *has/hath* from quarto to Folio *Othello,* in *Lear* there is two-way traffic. Both Folio *Lear* compositors set *ha's* or *has* for Q2 *hath* (B3, C1ᵛ, L3; TLN 404, 632, 3206; 1.2.69, 1.4.102, 5.3.249), but Compositor E also set *hath* for Q2 *has* (D3, F4; TLN 1143, 1835; 2.2.70, 3.4.54). According to Honigmann, in Folio *1* and *2 Henry IV, Hamlet* and *Othello,* quarto *you will* is contracted to *youle;* but in *Lear* Q2 *you'l* is expanded by Compositor B to Folio *you will* (G2ᵛ; TLN 2037; 3.6.80) – even though B preferred *you'l* to *you will* in *Much Ado about Nothing* (TLN 88; 1.1.93). The Folio *Lear* one-way preference for *toward,* already recorded, conflicts with the Folio *2 Henry IV* one-way preference for *towards* (charted by Honigmann). Finally, *Lear* is almost unique among the Folio tragedies in preferring *who[m],* *where,* and *which* to quarto copy *that* (B1, C2ᵛ, 3, 3ᵛ, D3, E1ᵛ, I3ᵛ, K3ᵛ, 4ᵛ, L3; TLN 235, 259, 724, 733, 781, 816, 1146, 1316, 1350, 2654, 2911, 2985, 3188; 1.1.214, 236, 1.4.213, 221, 268, 298, 2.2.73, 2.4.40,

78, 4.6.211, 5.1.64, 5.3.42, 235). The only similar variant is one found in Folio *Othello* (F1; TLN 1278; 2.3.161). Again the variation in Folio *Lear* is not just mechanical; Q2 *and* (Q1: *that*, D2) and *who*, as well as Q2 *that*, are also changed to *which* (C3, H1ᵛ; 761, 2232; 1.4.252, 4.1.45). Analysing these pronominal variants in the context of the use of relative pronouns in the Shakespeare canon, Doran argued that the Folio variants are probably authorial, but did not explain why similar changes are not found in other Folio plays in which authorial revision is suspected – *Troilus* or *Hamlet*, for example.

On what seems the most reasonable interpretation of the available evidence, we might attribute Folio *Lear*'s preference for *besides*, *sometimes*, and *naught* to Compositor E; its preference for *he* and *yon* to B; and its preference for *further* to both. On the other hand, the preference for *toward* most probably, and for *mine* and *thine* probably, derives from copy. On the evidence of the rest of the canon, Shakespeare himself preferred *toward* (97 to 70), so the variant here might be authorial;[76] likewise, an author preparing a fair copy of his work might be more solicitous about the euphonic use of *mine* and *thine* before vowels than he had been in working on the foul papers. Neither of these preferences, therefore, can be confidently ascribed to an editor or scribe. Nor can we attribute to such agents several other variants (*mo*, *ha*, *O*, *if*, *has*), where the Folio's practice is either inconsistent or adequately explained by the literary context. This leaves us with only two categories of one-way variant in Folio *Lear* which might derive from editorial or scribal interference: the preference for *do's* over Quarto *doth*, and the preference for *which*, *where*, or *who*[*m*] over Quarto *that*. Probably neither of these derives from a Folio editor. No other Folio text alters quarto *that* in this fashion, and other Folio texts – with the single seeming exception in *1 Henry IV*, already dismissed (p. 278) – consistently prefer *doth*, not *do's*. Both these preferences must therefore be either scribal or authorial. And since Shakespeare himself increasingly preferred *does* or *do's* in his later work, the Folio preference for *do's* in *Lear* could easily be authorial – especially if, as Gary Taylor argues below (pp. 354–95), Shakespeare's revision of *King Lear* took place several years after composition of the Quarto.[77] This leaves only the alterations to Quarto *that* as a potential scribal sophistication. However, even these changes might be related to the increasing grammatical complexity of Shakespeare's late style, a complexity which might have led to a heightened sensitivity to pronominal variation. Consequently, in the absence of a more detailed investigation of Shakespeare's developing use of *that, which, where,* and *who*[*m*], even this feature of Folio *Lear* cannot be confidently ascribed to scribal rather than authorial preference. In short, none of the recurring variants described by Doran and Honigmann can be securely identified as the result of interference by scribes or Folio editors.

This discussion may indicate the immense difficulty encountered in attempts to assign any significant number of specific variants in Folio *Lear* to an identifiable source – compositor, editor, scribe, or author – but it does not prevent us drawing inferences from the quantity and general quality of the variants. As already noted, Compositor E's stint on Folio *Lear* contains about 200 of the kinds of variants we are examining, far more than are found in any of the other plays in which I have examined his work. His habit in these other plays would suggest, according to our liberal estimate, that he could have introduced no more than twenty or so such variants in *Lear* on his own authority, that is, one for every hundred lines he set. Thus there remain in his stints about 180 variants that cannot be traced to the compositor. Many of these represent changes opposite to those found in Compositor E's portions of *Titus* and *Romeo.* In *Lear* contractions are often expanded; in the other two plays, expansions, when altered, are contracted, but contractions are never expanded, as Appendix VIII shows. Likewise, in *Titus* and *Romeo* 'thine' is once changed to 'thy', but in *Lear* 'thy' sometimes becomes 'thine', and 'my' 'mine', in Compositor E's stints. Most important, however, is the general correctness of the variants in Compositor E's sections of Folio *Lear.* Of the eighty-five Folio variants that may affect scansion in verse, only one has been emended by both Duthie and Evans.[78] On the basis of our study of this class of variants in Folio *Titus* and *Romeo,* we might predict that nearly a third of the eighty-five such variants in *Lear* would stand in need of emendation, had Folio *Lear* been edited according to the standard of Folio *Titus* and *Romeo.* There can be no denying that the editing of printed copy for the Folio *Lear* was far superior to the editing of copy for *Romeo* and *Titus.* The manuscript from which Folio *Lear* readings were adopted could have suffered little corruption in this respect.

Nevertheless, editors may have been too conservative in accepting as correct so many of the Folio variants from the class under discussion. As observed above, we might expect to find perhaps as many as twenty such variants of compositorial origin in E's portions of the text. Although not all of these would fall in the verse and not all would be identifiable errors, some would probably belong to the categories of error in verse already identified in E's work: omission of possible feminine endings and of possible extra unstressed syllables before or after the caesura. Editors might therefore consider emending the following three variants which fall into the first category, none of them beyond the compositor's capacity: 'lou'st' for Q1's 'louest' (TLN 536; 1.4.6), 'com'st' for 'comest' (TLN 1238; 2.2.161), and 'wear'st' for 'wearest' (TLN 1569; 2.4.269). No examples of the second category are found in E's work in *Lear*.

Stage directions in Folio *Lear* provide no more evidence of a literary improver's hand than do the variants we have already considered. Occasionally, as Greg has noted, the stage directions follow those from the quartos, but most are 'pruned to what is needed on the stage', and notations of stage noises and properties are added.[79] Greg may well have been correct in speculating that the omission of two necessary exits was the responsibility of the compositors, who occasionally made errors in stage directions.[80] There is no evidence in the directions in Folio *Lear* of the hand that annotated printer's copy for Compositor B's portions of *1 Henry IV*. That editor ignored stage properties and noises and also sometimes embellished stage directions (in addition to pruning them at other times). Therefore, Walker clearly exaggerated when she wrote: 'If there was conjectural interference with the copy for one play [*1 Henry IV*] there may have been tinkering with the copy for all.'[81] The style of 'tinkering' in Compositor B's copy for *1 Henry IV* was almost certainly not the style of annotation in Folio *Lear*. Since the handling of stage directions throughout Folio *Lear* is consistent, there is also no reason to suppose that different compositors used distinct blocs of printed copy which had received strikingly different kinds of annotation (as may have been the case in *1 Henry IV*).[82]

No matter how good the annotation of copy for Folio *Lear*, we must expect to find compositorial error in the text. From examination of B's work on *1 Henry IV*, Walker predicted some 200 compositorial errors in the Folio *Lear*:

we have strong reason to distrust in the Folio *Lear* . . . readings which may be due to the kind of carelessness evident in B's work in other plays: omissions (ranging from single words to a line or two), the occasional interpolation of an unnecessary word, and a wandering eye and inattentive mind which led to his repeating or anticipating words and substituting one word for another.[83]

Walker assumed, of course, that B alone set the text – or that, if E too worked on *Lear*, his errors resembled those she had found in B's pages of *1 Henry IV*. Walker's judgement of the compositors and her expression of it have been echoed by recent editors who have conflated the Folio and Quarto texts of *Lear*; for example, G. K. Hunter, editor of the New Penguin *Lear*, has written: 'Another reason for reserve about the Folio text derives from the fact that it was set up by two of the more incompetent compositors in the printing house, one an apprentice and the other a careless journeyman, . . . their eyes and their minds wandering from the line in hand.'[84] But now that Walker's assumptions have been disproved and her selection of evidence shown to be too narrow, we might predict, on the basis of B's rate of omission in other Folio plays, that he would have omitted no more than four or so words from his stint on *Lear* (unless we assume that copy for *Lear* was less legible than quarto copy for other Folio plays).

Yet the example of B's performance in the prose of *1 Henry IV* continues to have at least slight relevance for an estimate of his omission rate in the prose of Folio *Lear*. The conservative editor G. Blakemore Evans emends only three omissions in verse set by Compositor B.[85] All three emendations seem called for in the light of B's work on other plays. At TLN 73 (1.1.68), Evans finds the last word – 'speake' – omitted from a verse speech, an error B also committed in *Love's Labour's Lost* (TLN 2237; 5.2.312). At TLN 2228 (4.1.41), Evans interpolates two words – 'Then prethee' – to repair another omission probably committed by Compositor B, who dropped the first two words of a speech in *Midsummer Night's Dream* (TLN 142; 1.1.132) and, on three other occasions, omitted the first word of a speech.[86] Evans's third emendation in *Lear* repairs an obvious error: 'Would I could meet [him] Madam' (TLN 2426; 4.5.39). There is only one other obvious error in B's stint on *Lear*, this time in prose ('Poore Tom . . . who hath [had] three Suites to his backe' TLN 1914; 3.4.135), and just one error that probably resulted from eyeskip – 'foule fiend *fliberdegibek*', the quarto reading (G2ᵛ), becomes 'foule Flibbertigibbet' in the Folio (TLN 1895; 3.4.115) – again in prose.

These last two errors in Compositor B's share of the prose in Folio *Lear* resemble errors identified in his prose stints of *1 Henry IV*, where many other omissions (neither eyeskips nor obvious errors) can probably also be charged to him. Might we therefore anticipate a high rate of omission in the prose of *Lear* set by B? Probably not. On the basis of B's performance in *1 Henry IV*, where there are many obvious omissions and a pair of eyeskips, we can predict a large number of omissions in B's pages only when he is guilty of a large number of *obvious* omissions; we cannot therefore expect to find many more omissions in the Folio version of *Lear* where there are only two obvious ones and a single eyeskip. Evans is correct, I believe, in emending only two more omissions ('Fut' and 'Edgar') in B's stint on *Lear* (TLN 459, 461; 1.2.131, 133), both in prose.[87]

Qualitative study of B's pages in Folio plays set from lightly annotated quarto copy confirms the restoration of a few single words to the Folio text of *Lear*, but it cannot justify the free conflation of the Quarto and Folio texts of *Lear* traditional since the eighteenth century. Compositor B probably did not omit even a single line from his copy for the Folio version. Compositor E probably omitted only three lines, at least one the result of an eyeskip, and perhaps a dozen words or so – only a fraction of the 300 lines or part-lines from the Quarto text cut from the Folio version. Comparison of Q2 and Folio *Lear* suggests one occasion on which Compositor E's eye may have skipped from one line to another. At 1.3.22–6, Q2 (B4ᵛ) reads

> what growes of it no matter, aduife your fellowes fo, I would
> breed from hence occafions, and I fhall, that I may fpeake, Ile
> write ftraight to my fifter to hold my very courfe ; goe prepare

But the Folio (TLN 526–7) reads

>   . . . aduise your fellowes
>   so, Ile write straight. . .

Perhaps Compositor E's eye skipped from the 'I' of 'I would' directly to the word 'Ile' that is printed beneath 'would', thereby missing the intervening line. (It may be significant that Q1 reads 'ile' here, making the suggested error somewhat less probable if E had been working from that earlier quarto.)

Like the errors of omission of both compositors, all of E's errors can probably best be handled according to conservative editorial principles. In the Riverside edition, the application of such principles to E's stints in Folio *Lear* produces a text closely consistent with the demands E might be expected to make of an editor. Emended in E's stints are 39 literal errors, 14 non-literal substitutions, 8 single- or double-word omissions and a transposition.[88] On the basis of this study, I would not have predicted many more errors in Compositor E's 1,877 lines of *Lear*: 39 literal errors, 19 non-literal substitutions, a dozen or so omissions, 3 transpositions and 8 interpolations.

Reference to the lists of E's errors in the Folio texts of *Romeo*, *Titus*, and *Troilus* immediately suggests the possible validity of two additional emendations to the Folio text. At TLN 1270 (2.3.19) the Folio reads, 'Sometimes with Lunaticke bans, sometime with Praiers', while the Quarto reads: 'Sometime with lunaticke bans, sometime with prayers' (E3). As Duthie has pointed out, the Quarto's 'exact symmetry in this matter is not necessarily a guarantee of authenticity';[89] obversely, asymmetry alone in the Folio version is no guarantee of corruption. But asymmetry produced by the addition or deletion of final *s* in a line set by Compositor E almost guarantees that the Folio is here corrupt, since the addition or deletion of final *s* was habitual for the compositor. In the second example (TLN 3217; 5.3.258), the Folio reads, in a justified line, '*Lear*. Howle, howle, howle: O your [*sic*] are men of stones', while the Quarto reads, '*Lear*. Howle, howle, howle, howle, O you are men of stones' (L3ᵛ). The omission of the fourth 'howle' in the Folio closely parallels Compositor E's omission from quarto copy of the second repetition of 'hees dead' in *Romeo* at TLN 1684 3.2.37. There is double warrant for adopting the Quarto *Lear* reading into the Folio text: the shortness of space in the line and the parallel omission from *Romeo*.

Editors have had less success in applying conservative principles to Compositor B's portion of *Lear*. In the Riverside edition there are emendations of eighteen supposed literal errors, twelve non-literal substitutions and seven omissions. On the basis of this study, I would have predicted in *Lear* no more than twenty literal errors, and probably fewer, since the rate of literal error in B's stints fell off rapidly when he arrived at the tragedies. I would also have predicted many more non-literal substitutions (at least twenty-three, and perhaps more: B's rate of substitution increased sharply as he set the tragedies),[90] but no more than the seven omissions already discussed above, and very few interpolations or transpositions, even when B's pages of *1 Henry IV* are taken into consideration. It would appear that conservative editors have been too ready to detect literal errors in B's work, and (perhaps) not ready enough to detect his sophisticated non-literal substitutions. Non-literal substitutions for significant copy words have been suspected by conservative editors in Compositor B's stints on *Lear*; adjectives, nouns and verbs from the Quarto have been inserted into the Folio text, generally according to the principle *praestat difficilior lectio* ('the more difficult reading takes precedence'). There is some doubt, however, whether this principle is always applicable to B's pages, since B occasionally appears to have substituted a rarer word for his copy's reading. Such traditional emendations as the Quarto's 'rash', 'dearne', and 'distresse' for the Folio's 'sticke', 'sterne', and 'desires' (TLN 2130, 2135, 2369; 3.7.58, 63, 4.4.18) might be subjected to renewed scrutiny by editors of the Folio text since the majority of B's non-literal substitutions affect not verbs, adjectives and nouns, but connectives and minor modifiers. The latter often fail to claim much modern editorial attention. Only after the most intensive examination of syntactical patterns in Shakespeare (if then), can we hope to recover the Folio text from Compositor B's non-literal substitutions. On the other hand, editors might profitably re-examine the literal emendations admitted into B's stints on *Lear*, in the light of the rarity of literal errors in his pages of *Titus*, *Romeo*, and *Troilus*. Where the Folio makes good sense, it may not be necessary to emend: for example, F1 'qualities'/Q1 'equalities' (TLN 9; 1.1.5), F1 'opilent'/Q1 'opulent' (TLN 92; 1.1.86), F1 'sese' (TLN 2031; 3.6.74; *not in* Q1), F1 ''casion'/Q1 'cagion' (TLN 2688; 4.6.235), F1 'volke'/Q1 'voke' (TLN 2691; 4.6.238). (Duthie accepts the Folio reading in every case but the first.)

Although there may be difficulties with the consistent application of a conservative editorial policy to the whole Folio text, examination of a text edited in this manner, the Riverside, reveals significant correlations between the kinds and proportions of errors detected by a conservative editor in the compositors' stints on *Lear* and the kinds and proportions of errors identifiable as the compositors' in other texts. The conservative editor finds high proportions of substitutions (both literal and non-literal) in Folio *Lear*, but few omissions, interpolations, or transpositions; that is, without the benefit of any systematic analysis of the compositors' typical errors and even without correct compositor identifications in Folio *Lear*, he finds proportions of errors in *Lear* revealed by this study to be compositorial. For Compositor E the correlations are quite precise: both in *Lear* (according to the conservative editor) and in the tragedies set from lightly annotated quarto copy, there are twice as many literal substitutions as non-literal ones in E's stints, and about one-quarter of the substitutions result from the addition or deletion of final *s* (in *Lear*, 14 of 53; in *Titus*, *Romeo* and *Troilus*, 42 of 174). The correlations also hold for Compositor B, if not so precisely: proportionally fewer literal substitutions are found both in *Lear* and in the texts set from lightly annotated quarto copy (18 literals in 30 substitutions in *Lear*; 60 literals in 128 substitutions in the other texts); many fewer substitutions result from the addition or deletion of final *s* (2 of 30 in *Lear*; 17 of 128 in the other plays).

Of course, the Riverside edition also incorporates into the Folio text many passages found only in the Quarto, and in this respect it can hardly be called textually conservative; but for those parts of the text common to the Quarto and Folio, the emendations Evans makes in the Folio text accord reasonably well, in both number and kind, with the amount of compositorial corruption we would expect.[91] To account for nearly all the errors we find in the Folio *Lear*, we need hypothecate no stages of transmission beyond type-setting by the two different workmen, Compositors B and E.

Conclusion

The long-standing assumption, inherited from eighteenth-century editors, that printing-house agents were responsible for massive corruption of Shakespeare's *King Lear* finds no support in a detailed evaluation of Jaggard's Compositors B and E and of the editor(s) who prepared copy. Only a small proportion of the variants between the Quarto and Folio versions of *Lear* can be attributed to the two compositors. There is no evidence that the Folio text of *Lear* was corrupted by the officiousness of printing-house editor(s), such as may be discerned in some other Folio texts – *1 Henry IV*, *Titus*, or *Romeo*. Of course, no purely bibliographical investigation can rule out the possibility that a scribe may at some stage have interfered with the manuscript which was then used to annotate the quarto that served as printer's copy for Folio *Lear*. Yet if printer's copy for Folio *Lear* had been annotated by reference to a manuscript which had indeed suffered extensive scribal corruption, then we should expect to find in the printed Folio text a legacy of scribal error and other textual deterioration – a legacy which should obscure the patterns of error typical of Jaggard's compositors. Instead, we find in the printed Folio text errors typical of the compositors or errors derived from the quartos. While it cannot be demonstrated that no irresponsible or incompetent scribe interfered in the transmission of the Folio text, it certainly cannot be demonstrated that one did. If there is bibliographical evidence to show that the Folio text of *King Lear* is not a genuine Shakespearian version, that evidence remains to be discovered.

NOTES

1. Charlton Hinman, *The Printing and Proof-Reading of the First Folio of Shakespeare*, 2 vols. (Oxford, 1963). Although Hinman felt in 1963 that one man, probably Isaac Jaggard, was the Folio proof-reader, he admitted that 'we do not know and cannot know positively who the proof-reader for the Folio was, or even that there were not two or more readers' (I, 235–6). Compare J. G. McManaway, 'Another Discovery of a Proof Sheet in Shakespeare's First Folio', *Huntington Library Quarterly*, 41 (1977–8), 19–26.
2. In 'The Shrinking Compositor A of the Shakespeare First Folio' (*Studies in Bibliography*, 34 (1981), 96–117), Gary Taylor has argued that pages of *1 Henry IV* assigned to Compositor A by Walker or to Compositor A-or-C by Hinman should be attributed to neither, but instead to a compositor who was B's partner only for Folio *1* and *2 Henry IV*. Attribution problems for the remainder of the Folio text of *1 Henry IV* are discussed on p. 251.
3. Alice Walker, 'The Folio Text of *1 Henry IV*', *Studies in Bibliography*, 6 (1954), 45–59; pp. 46, 58.
4. Walker, p. 55.
5. Walker, p. 58.
6. 'We should also be prepared to conflate the two texts freely since it is evident that one of the most frequent causes of error in both the quarto and Folio was the accidental omission of words, phrases, short speeches and even longer passages': Walker, *Textual Problems of the First Folio* (Cambridge, 1953), p. 63.
7. W. W. Greg, *The Shakespeare First Folio: Its Bibliographical and Textual History* (Oxford, 1955), p. 466.
8. G. I. Duthie and J. D. Wilson, eds., *King Lear* (Cambridge, 1960), p. 137.
9. MacD. P. Jackson, 'Compositor C and the First Folio Text of *Much Ado About Nothing*', *Papers of the Bibliographical Society of America*, 68 (1974), 414–18; p. 418.
10. Paul Werstine, 'Compositor B of the Shakespeare First Folio', *Analytical and Enumerative Bibliography*, 2 (1978), 241–63.
11. The seven other Folio plays are *Much Ado about Nothing, Love's Labour's Lost, A Midsummer Night's Dream, The Merchant of Venice, Titus Andronicus, Romeo and Juliet*, and *Troilus and Cressida*. Totals in the chart for the 'Comedies' and 'Tragedies' are compiled from the lists of B's errors published in Werstine, pp. 244–9. Totals for *1 Henry IV* derive from the lists in Walker, '*1 Henry IV*', pp. 48–53. The totals reflect corrections to the published lists to be found in Appendix X to this essay.
12. 'Casting off' copy means 'determining in advance which parts of the text are to be accommodated in each of the various pages of the quire that is about to be composed and printed' (Hinman, I, 72).
13. Hinman, I, 373–4.
14. S. W. Reid, 'Some Spellings of Compositor B in the Shakespeare First Folio', *Studies in Bibliography*, 29 (1976), 102–38.

15. Jackson, p. 415.
16. 'New Light on Compositor E of the Shakespeare First Folio', *The Library*, VI, 2 (1980), 156–78; p. 156.
17. Hinman, II, 512.
18. The editors have recently been studied, however, by S. W. Reid, 'The Editing of Folio *Romeo and Juliet*', *Studies in Bibliography*, 35 (1982), 43–66; and by Eleanor Prosser, *Shakespeare's Anonymous Editors: Scribe and Compositor in the Folio Text of '2 Henry IV'* (Stanford, 1981). Professor Prosser, however, exaggerates the fallibility of Compositor B beyond even Walker's predictions of the compositor's capacity for error. Prosser's suggestions that B may have omitted as many as six lines at a time from Folio *2 Henry IV* cannot be supported by reference to similar omissions anywhere else in the Folio, and are thus not well founded (p. 84). I owe a large debt to the as-yet-unpublished work of S. W. Reid which emphasizes the importance of editorial interference in Folio *1 Henry IV*, though the hypotheses offered about the possible identity and function of the editor(s) are my own.
19. Scholars have long agreed that *Titus*, *Love's Labour's Lost*, *Romeo*, *Midsummer Night's Dream*, *Merchant*, and *Much Ado* were printed from quarto copy and that all but *Romeo* had received some editorial attention (Greg, pp. 204–8, 223, 243–6, 259–60, 279–81). Recently Reid has argued convincingly that quarto copy for *Romeo*, too, was edited ('The Editing of Folio *Romeo and Juliet*').
20. *The Shakespeare First Folio*, p. 264.
21. 'The Folio Text of *1 Henry IV*', p. 55.
22. Hinman, II, 74–91.
23. *Principles of Emendation in Shakespeare* (Oxford, 1928), p. 13.
24. On the copy for Folio *Troilus*, see, for example, Philip Williams, 'Shakespeare's *Troilus and Cressida*: the Relationship of the Quarto and Folio', *Studies in Bibliography*, 3 (1950), 131–43, and W. R. Elton, 'Textual Transmission and Genre of Shakespeare's *Troilus*', in *Literatur als Kritik des Lebens*, eds. R. Haas, H. J. Müllenbrock and C. Uhlig (Heidelberg, 1975), 63–82.
25. For compositor attribution in *Troilus*, see Taylor, 'Compositor A', pp. 98–103, and Howard-Hill, p. 159.
26. Hinman, II, 8–106, 326–40.
27. Greg, *The Shakespeare First Folio*, 443–9; Hinman, I, 27–8.
28. 'The Editing of Folio *Romeo*', passim.
29. *The Norton Facsimile of the First Folio of Shakespeare* (New York, 1968), pp. 916, 918.
30. Hinman, I, 228, n. 1 and n. 2.
31. For the current record of stop-press correction, see Hinman, I, 248–323; but also see Jeanne Addison Roberts, ' "Wife" or "Wise" – *The Tempest* I. 1786', *Studies in Bibliography*, 31 (1978), 203–8; Werstine, 'An Unrecorded Variant in the Shakespeare First Folio', *Papers of the Bibliographical Society of America*, 72 (1978), 329–30, and Werstine, 'An Unrecorded State in the Shakespeare First Folio', *PBSA*, 74 (1980), 133–4.
32. 'Printers of the Mind: Some Notes on Bibliographical Theories and Printing-House Practices', *Studies in Bibliography*, 22 (1969), 46; also see D. F. Foxon, 'The Varieties of Early Proof: Cartwright's *Royal Slave*, 1639, 1640', *The Library*, V, 25 (1970), 151–4. [Since my own investigation was completed, P. W. M. Blayney has provided a much more extensive demonstration that earlier stages of proofing took place, in *Origins*, I, 188–218.]
33. Joseph Moxon, *Mechanick Exercises on the Whole Art of Printing*, eds. Herbert Davis and Harry Carter (New York, 1978), pp. 302–3, as quoted by McKenzie, p. 42.
34. Moxon, pp. 238–9.

35. Moxon, p. 237.
36. Moxon, p. 235. Justification refers to the filling out of a line with types and/or spacing material so that the line fits securely into the chase.
37. Narrow spacing is found in TLN 270, 716, and 975; wide spacing (between at least two words or at least one word and one punctuation mark) in TLN 155, 168, 276 (a short line), 640, 644, 649, 715, 716, 724, 756, 794, 979, 1080, 2769 and 2931; no spacing before capitals in TLN 764 and 3052; and an ampersand in TLN 564. The lines cited account for 19 of the approximately 55 long lines in which Compositor B set variants charged as errors to him by Walker.
38. There is no alternative mechanical explanation for this botch. If the line had always read 'I', Compositor B could have fitted the first syllable of 'horses' into it, rather than carrying the whole word over on to TLN 277; he would not have had to mis-space the prefix. *Hor-ses* is divided twice on page pp6^v (TLN 3616–17 and 3626–7), a page that Compositor B may have set, according to T. H. Howard-Hill, 'Compositors B and E in the Shakespeare First Folio and Some Recent Studies' (Columbia, S.C., 1976; privately circulated typescript), p. 16.
39. Again, there is no alternative mechanical explanation, since B could have avoided the botch by spelling 'all' (the spelling of his Q5 copy, and his own overwhelming preference) instead of 'al'.
40. Werstine, 'Compositor B', p. 257.
41. 'Compositor B', pp. 258–9.
42. Howard-Hill, 'Compositors B and E'. That B may have been somewhat more careless in the Histories than elsewhere is suggested by his apparent omission of two lines from page d5 of *Richard II* (Hinman, I, 267).
43. 'The Prentice Hand in the Tragedies of the Shakespeare First Folio: Compositor E', *Studies in Bibliography*, 9 (1957), 3–20.
44. Walker and J. D. Wilson, eds., *Othello* (Cambridge, 1960), p. 132.
45. 'New Light on Compositor E', *passim*.
46. *Printing and Proof-Reading*, I, 226.
47. *Printing and Proof-Reading*, I, 380–91.
48. 'New Light on Compositor E', *passim*.
49. 'The Folio Copy for *Hamlet, King Lear*, and *Othello*', *Shakespeare Quarterly*, 34 (1983), 44–61.
50. Also excluded is most of column dd4a, the end of the 'fly scene' in *Titus*, first printed in the Folio, presumably from manuscript copy.
51. These readings in E's stints may be examined in Appendix VI; similar readings in B's portions are recorded in Appendix X. Critics disagree about whether, during the printing of Folio *Romeo*, other quartos, besides Q3, were consulted in Jaggard's shop. Brian Gibbons believes that Q4 was occasionally consulted (the new Arden *Romeo and Juliet* (1979), p. 2), but S. W. Reid argues, convincingly in my opinion, that occasional agreements between Q1 or Q4 and the Folio probably do not derive from consultation of these quartos during the printing of the Folio, but instead from an editor familiar with performance of the play ('The Editing of Folio *Romeo*', pp. 45–9).
52. For these readings see Appendix VII.
53. Excluded from the lists of E's changes and errors are all obvious typographical errors that do not result in a word; all errors in punctuation, including frequent erroneous uses of the apostrophe (for example, *intru'd* for intrude, *Titus*, TLN 582; 2.1.27); the many errors in spacing, such as *be friend* for befriend (*Titus*, TLN 1151; 3.1.16); variant spellings (*hether* for hither), turned letters; changes in the lining of verse (Compositor E divides many lines); the few changes, some admittedly substantive, in speech prefixes and stage directions (for these see Appendix IX); changes which affect only metre (for these see Appendix VIII); and corrections of

obvious errors in *Titus* Q3 and *Romeo* Q3. Included in the lists of E's errors are press variants, both corrected and uncorrected, recorded by Hinman. Also included in the counts are a number of variants which Reid has suggested originate with an editor of *Romeo*, not with Compositor E: literal variants at TLN 495, 1957, 1960, and 3035; substitutions at 1520, 1956, 1961, and 2497; and interpolations at 1524 and 2380. While I find Reid's suggestions attractive, they 'partake no doubt of some prejudice', as he puts it (p. 57), and I therefore have included the variants among Compositor E's errors. Exclusion of these variants, however, would not have affected the counts significantly. Jackson was the first to note E's many additions and deletions of final *-s* (p. 416).

54. The first of these variants is generally regarded as editorial: see H. F. Brooks, the new Arden *A Midsummer Night's Dream* (1979), p. 160.
55. J. C. Maxwell accepts the Folio version as authoritative: see the new Arden *Titus Andronicus* (1961), p. 110.
56. The second quoted line would be more metrical if, as Gary Taylor suggests, we read *thorough* (meaning 'through') for Folio *through*.
57. The substitution of 'haughty' also restores the metre, thereby 'correcting' an error in Q5, though probably unauthoritatively.
58. *The Shakespeare First Folio*, p. 206. It is worth noting, however, that the added words, though extra-metrical, do make some sense in context, and that their appearance five lines below occurs in the middle of a line (rather than at the beginning, as here) and is not capitalized, or followed by a question mark (as it is here). All these factors make Greg's explanation somewhat improbable, though not impossible.
59. Italics indicate the word interpolated.
60. 'A Qualitative Analysis of Compositors C and D in the Shakespeare First Folio', *Studies in Bibliography*, 30 (1977), 57–74.
61. *Printing and Proof-Reading*, I, 392–5.
62. 'New Light on Compositor E', p. 159.
63. 'The Folio Copy for *Hamlet*, *King Lear*, and *Othello*', 44–61. Thus we now know that Compositor B set TLN 1–94, 353–484, 735–863, 1426–91, 1618–744, 1862–2738 and Compositor E 95–352, 485–734, 864–1425, 1492–617, 1745–861, 2739–3302 (end). [See Addenda.]
64. W. W. Greg, *The Variants in the First Quarto of 'King Lear'* (1940), pp. 133–90.
65. *The Text of 'King Lear'* (Stanford, 1931), pp. 39–52.
66. Werstine, 'Compositor B', p. 250. The variant parfect/perfect (M5.2444) is not included in the count; the variants my/mine (N1ᵛ.141, Q2.2633) are included, although originally listed as substitutions (pp. 246–7).
67. Werstine, 'Compositor B', pp. 242–3.
68. Some problem may be perceived with the use of these variant suffixes in an assessment of the quality of editing and/or composition of Folio *Lear*. The First Quarto of *Lear*, which influenced the Folio text, does not generally observe a syllabic distinction between *ed* and *'d*, *d*, or *de*. The Quarto text is not, of course, alone among printed texts of English Renaissance drama in failing to observe this and other syllabic distinctions. Indeed, critics have long recognized that Renaissance actors were probably capable of rendering in metrical form texts in which syllabic distinctions were not marked, that Shakespeare may have depended on the actors' capacity to do so, and thus that Shakespeare may not have marked all syllabic distinctions in his own manuscripts. Therefore the authority of a printed text cannot be gauged according to whether or not syllabic distinctions are observed. It is not my purpose, however, to claim on such grounds greater authority for Folio than Quarto *Lear*. Instead this study merely (1) indicates that an effort was made in the editing of Folio *Romeo* and *Titus* to impose syllabic

distinctions on the texts and (2) compares the quality of this effort with the quality of the effort to do the same thing for Folio *Lear*. At issue then is neither the value of imposing syllabic distinctions on a text, nor even the thoroughness with which such distinctions are maintained in Folio *Lear*, but only the correctness with which distinctions were maintained to the extent that they were imposed on the Folio text.

69. See Appendices VI (under 'Other variants in dialogue') and VIII.

70. That E's pages of *Troilus* contain prose, not verse, might also explain the absence of such variants; those of his pages of *Romeo* and *Titus* in which such variants are found consist largely, but not exclusively, of verse. A few such variants (listed in Appendices VI and VIII), however, are found in the prose of *Romeo*.

71. See Appendix VI.

72. Counted as correct are all Folio variants common to the authoritative quartos (*Romeo* Q2, *Titus* Q1); all Folio variants that have been accepted as necessary emendations of the authoritative quartos in any of the following editions: New Cambridge, Alexander, Sisson, Riverside, the new Arden *Titus* and *Romeo*, and the New Penguin *Romeo*; and all Folio variants that indicate syllabic distinction necessary, in my view, to the proper scansion of lines in Q1 *Titus* or Q2 *Romeo*, but unmarked in these authoritative quartos. Such broad criteria for correctness should yield a liberal estimate of the quality of Folio variants in the class under discussion.

73. For evidence that Q2 served as printer's copy for Folio *Lear*, see, in addition to the work of Stone and Taylor already cited, T. H. Howard-Hill's 'The Problem of Manuscript Copy for Folio *Lear*', *The Library*, VI, 4 (1982), 1–24. Although Howard-Hill suggests the possibility that manuscript copy was used, he neither addresses nor refutes the striking punctuation evidence revealed by Stone and Taylor to show the dependence of Compositor E's section of Folio *Lear* on Q2; instead, Howard-Hill offers that, if printed copy were used for the Folio *Lear*, it was the Second Quarto, not the First.

I do not provide a complete list of the two hundred or so variants from Q2 counted in E's stint on *Lear* since most of these can be recovered from the collation in G. I. Duthie's *Shakespeare's 'King Lear': A Critical Edition* (Oxford, 1949). Although Duthie collated the First Quarto, not the Second, with the Folio, Q2 usually follows Q1, as far as the variants in question are concerned. I therefore list (in Appendix XI) only the 24 exceptions in which the Folio reads with Q2 against Q1, and the 39 exceptions in which the Folio reads with Q1 against Q2.

74. See Doran, pp. 39–52, E. A. J. Honigmann, 'On the Indifferent and One-Way Variants in Shakespeare', *The Library* V, 22 (1967), 189–204.

75. See Marvin Spevack, *A Complete and Systematic Concordance to the Works of Shakespeare*, 9 vols. (Hildesheim, 1968–80), IX (Substantive Variants). This work should prove valuable in the future in extending Honigmann's method to a larger class of variants.

76. It is also suggestive that, where substantive texts differ, *toward* is elsewhere preferred by the more authoritative: by Q2 *Romeo* at 2.2.157 (D3) and 4.1.17 (I2ᵛ), by Q2 *Hamlet* at 1.2.55 (B4) and 1.2.112 (C1), by Folio *Othello* at 1.3.39 (TLN 370), by Q *2 Henry IV* at 4.2.105 (G3ᵛ), and by Folio *Richard III* at 2.2.154 (TLN 1430).

77. For the chronological distribution of *doth* and *does*, see Frederick O. Waller, 'The Use of Linguistic Criteria in Determining the Copy and Dates for Shakespeare's Plays', in *Pacific Coast Studies in Shakespeare*, eds. Waldo F. McNeir and Thelma N. Greenfield (Eugene, Oregon, 1966), 1–19. Samuel Daniel provides a possible parallel for the Folio's alterations of Quarto *that*: 'By 1607, apparently, Daniel had come to prefer the relatives *which* and *who* to *that*, although in most cases the

[change] produces no significant difference' (*Samuel Daniel's Musophilus*, ed. Raymond Himelick (West Lafayette, Indiana, 1965), p. 45).

78. Duthie, *Shakespeare's 'King Lear'*, *passim*; Evans, *The Riverside Shakespeare*. The single Folio variant calling for emendation, 'hes' (TLN 3045, 5.3.97), is probably an inadvertent compositorial error – had Compositor E intended the contraction, he would almost certainly have included the apostrophe (of which he was fond).
79. Greg, *The Shakespeare First Folio*, p. 384.
80. For E's errors, see Appendix IX; for B's, see Werstine, 'Compositor B', pp. 251–2. But also see Taylor, 'Folio Copy', n. 49.
81. Walker, '*1 Henry IV*', p. 58.
82. It remains possible that Compositor B was working – as Stone, Taylor, and Jackson (below, pp. 346–8) suggest – at least in part directly from manuscript, while E worked from annotated Q2. If the annotation of Q2 were thorough, such a difference between B's and E's copy in *Lear* would not result in differences in their treatment of stage directions.
83. *Textual Problems*, p. 62.
84. (Harmondsworth, 1972), p. 319.
85. Collating the Folio against the Quarto text, I find little evidence of the compositors altering their copy to fit the space available when they were forced to depend on cast-off copy (in setting pages qq2–3ᵛ, rr1–3ᵛ, and ss1–3). Compositor B, of course, split a line of verse (TLN 1489–90) to stretch his copy at the bottom of rr1ᵛb, and E used the same device in quire ss. Yet beyond such obvious tinkering, I find no indication that the text of Folio *Lear* was cut by the compositors to solve difficulties presented by badly cast-off copy – certainly there is nothing in Folio *Lear* resembling what Prosser imagines the compositors of Folio *2 Henry IV* to have done (*Shakespeare's Anonymous Editors*, pp. 51–121). The alleged examples collected by J. J. Hogan in 'Cutting His Text according to His Measure: A Note on the Folio "*Lear*"' (*Philological Quarterly*, 41 (1962), 72–81) are, in comparison, minor, and deserve careful consideration.
86. It might be debated whether the interpolation of the two words from Quarto *Lear* – 'Then prethee' – adequately repairs the apparent error in the Folio. In the Quarto, the line reads in full: 'Then prethee get thee gon, if for my sake' (H2ᵛ); in the Folio, 'Get thee away: If for my sake'. Conflation of the Folio and Quarto versions of the line – 'Then prethee get thee away: If for my sake' – yields a metrically difficult line.
87. The first of these might be due to censorship: see pp. 77–8, above.
88. Excluded from these counts are the several errors in E's stints that are emended because they derive from uncorrected states of the First Quarto (i.e. 'the' for 'this' at TLN 1792; 3.4.12), or from probable misunderstandings of corrections of quarto readings marked by the annotator of the compositor's copy (i.e., according to Greg, 'miseries' for 'mysteries' at TLN 117; 1.1.110), or from errors in Q2, which probably constituted the compositor's printed copy.
89. *Shakespeare's 'King Lear'*, p. 143.
90. See the chart on p. 250.
91. I have not compared the record of emendation in an eclectic edition of *Lear* with the predictions for compositorial error in the play since an eclectic editor does not oblige himself to treat his copy-text consistently throughout, but resorts to a Quarto reading whenever he believes it, on whatever grounds, to be superior to a Folio reading. A conservative editor agrees to resort to the Quarto only when he believes the Folio to be in error, and thus a list of the readings he rejects is more likely to provide a record of error in the Folio than the list of rejected Folio readings in an eclectic edition.

APPENDICES

APPENDIX I

Literal Substitutions by Compositor E

(j indicates a justified line)

Titus		Quarto	Folio
cc4ᵛ	95	bowes	bowers (uncorr.)
	121	earthy	earthly
	130	sonne	sonnes
	155	ambitious	ambitions (uncorr.)
	157	looke	lookes
	191	fortunes	Fortune
cc5	253	sute	sure
	289j	you	your
	290	your	you (corr.)
	301	you	your
cc5ᵛ	401	vouch	vouch'd
	410	till	tell
	415	soule	soules (uncorr.)
cc6	543	swore	sware
	558	aboue	about
cc6ᵛ	617	durst	dar'st
	620	petty	pretty
	622	iet	set
	628	discords	discord
	693	lust	lusts
	696	streame	streames
	730	like	likes
dd1	793	Who	Whom
	811	swarty	swarth
dd1ᵛ	879	womans	woman
dd2	1074j	scrowle	scowle
dd2ᵛ	1191	prey	pray
dd3	1264	signe	signes
	1340	your	you
	1341	my	me
dd4	1563	*Hecuba*	*Hecubae*
	1605	friends	friend (uncorr.)
dd4ᵛ	1625	writ	writs
	1688	villaines	villanie's
	1699	*eget*	*egit*

	1723j	your	you
dd5	1822	as	at
dd5ᵛ	1914j	backs	backe
	1972	here's	her's
	1979j	sir	fir (uncorr.)
dd6	2011	vniustice	iniustice
	2042j	be Lady	ber Lady
	2073j	your	our
dd6ᵛ	2176	blacke nights	Blacke-night
	2199	Or	Ore
ee1	2272	what's	what
	2317	thy	the
	2342	*Epeons*	*Eptons*
	2366	ply	play
ee1ᵛ	2415	Feast	Feasts

Romeo

	148	other	others
ee3ᵛ	221	bide	bid (corr.)
	222	ope	open
ee4	314j	daughters	daughter
ee4ᵛ	395j	*Iule*	*Iulet*
	411	dispositions	disposition
	468	soule	soale
	473	so	to
ee5	495	you	your
	498	in	I
	516j	spider	Spiders
	516j	collers	coullers
	525j	dreame	dreamt
	535j	eare	eares
ee5ᵛ	672	two	to
	726	learnt	learne
ee6	837	What's	What?
	837	name	names
ee6ᵛ	891	laughs	laught
	1003	Friers	Fries
ff1	1101	housholds	houshould
ff1ᵛ	1167j–68	soly singular	sole-/singular
	1193	hide	hid
	1198j	for	or
	1218j	gĕtlemĕ	Gentleman (uncorr.)
ff2	1292	mans	man
	1314	heraulds	Herauld

	1321	Is	I
	1352j	leg	legs
ff2ᵛ	1501	loue	lou'd
ff3	1551	*Mercutio* is	*Mercutio's* is
	1582	name	names
	1602	*Tybalt*	*Tybalts*
	1638	out	our
ff3ᵛ	1760	*Tibalts*	*Tibalt*
ff4	1850	Howling	Howlings
	1909	Spakest	Speak'st
	1914	canceld	conceal'd
ff4ᵛ	1957	turne	turn'd
	1958	of	or
	1960	mishaued	mishaped
ff5	2157	wooe	woe
	2174	thy	the
	2188	hate	haue
ff5ᵛ	2214	gossips	gossip
	2219	bowle	bowles
	2223	tide	ride
ff6	2349	with this	with 'his
	2351	*Romeos*	*Romeo*
	2378	reekie	reckie
	2396	shuts	shut
gg1ᵛ	2742	liues	liue
gg2	2913	these	those
	2947	art	are
	2961	arme	armes
gg2ᵛ	2997	feare	feares
	3035	Tis is	'Tis in
	3065	our	out
*gg3	3137	scare	scar

Troilus

	176j	the	they
χ2	187	purblinde	purblinded
	191j	disdaine	disdaind
	227	nor	not
χ2ᵛ	323	it	is
	326	doe	does
	347j	iudgements	iudgement
	362	will	ill
	388j	note	not

APPENDIX II

Substitutions by Compositor E

Titus

cc4^v	144	their	the
	155	not	me
cc5	247	peoples	Noble
	267	thy	my (uncorr.)
	283	thy	my
cc5^v	436	dririe	sudden
dd1	755	yellowing	yelping
dd1^v	977	a	the
	984	this	the
dd2	1012	them	him
dd3	1277	misery	miseries
	1357	would	wilt
dd4	1584	for	to
dd4^v	1618	this	that
dd5	1798	ignomie	ignominie
	1825	no one	none
	1874	happily	haply
dd6	2088	feede	foode
	2107j	to	for
	2123	Be bolde	Behold
dd6^v	2242	the	few
	2250	their	the
ee1	2302	that accord	it action
	2318	thy	my
ee1^v	2491	may	might
	2506	I feare	If ere
ee2	2600	Then	This

Romeo

ee4	348	shall	shew (corr.)
	348	shew	shell
ee5^v	644	this	the
	656	my	the
	718	wedding	wedded
ee6	877	this	thy (uncorr.)
ff1	1062	and	rest
	1364	not	so
ff2^v	1520	Forbid	Forbidden
ff3	1642	but	not

ff3ᵛ	1775	with	which
ff4	1866	dispute	dispaire
	1868	thy	my
	1919j	deadly	dead
ff4ᵛ	1956	becomes	became
ff5	2149	that	this
ff6	2329	my	thy
	2332	now	own (uncorr.)
	2335	we	you
	2342	straines	streames
	2416	off eare	ofcare
ff6ᵛ	2497	life	fire
	2537	a	my
gg1	2652	should	shouldst
gg2	2852	aloofe	aloft
	2871	way	wayes
*gg3	3182	these	the

Troilus

χ2	163	chid	chides
χ2ᵛ	332j	Ilion	Illium

Readings censored in Compositor E's stints

dd5	1755	Zounds ye	Out you
ff2ᵛ	1480	zounds	Come
	1534j	sounds	What

APPENDIX III

Transpositions by Compositor E

Titus

dd2ᵛ	1180	soft as	as soft

Romeo

ff2	1296j	see a	a see
ff5	2067	²light it	itli ght
	2100	it is	Is it
ff5ᵛ	2286	Is it	It is
ff6ᵛ	2474	vp him	him vp
gg1	2662	vs all	all vs
gg2	2884	a Ring that	a that Ring (uncorr.)
gg2ᵛ	3089	is in	in is

APPENDIX IV

Interpolations by Compositor E

Titus

cc4^v	203	are alike	are all alike
dd2	1114	met	met withall
dd2^v	1192	and	and and
dd3	1345	for	for for
dd4	1579–81	deede. / Why	deed. / What booke? / Why
dd5	1827	the	the the
dd6^v	2200	to	to to
	2208	hands, and	hands off, and
ee2	2597	kind commiseration	kind hand Commiseration

Romeo

ee4^v	386j	a leuen	a eleuen
ee6	760	Cry but	Cry me but
ff1^v	1149j	the	the the
ff2	1281j	stay good	stay thou good
	1357	this	this this
	1364	that	that that
ff2^v	1426	such	such such
	1524	both houses	both the Houses
ff3^v	1700	determine my	determine of my
ff6	2380	his	his graue
gg1^v	2726	this day an	thisan day an
*gg3	3181	for	for for

Troilus

χ2^v	272	he so	he is so
	346j	hee's man	hee's a man
	349	him	him him

APPENDIX V

Omissions by Compositor E

Titus

cc5^v	409	not with himselfe	not himselfe
	422	and wise *Laertes*	And *Laertes*

cc6ᵛ	663–4	then / That both should speede? / *Chiron.*	then? / *Chi.*
	722	bene broad awake	bene awake
dd2ᵛ	1164	heare you not	heare not
dd4	1552	Feare her not	Feare not
dd4ᵛ	1687–8	news? / *Puer.* That you are both decipherd, that's the newes, / For	newes? / For
dd5	1759–60	mother. / *Aron.* Villaine, I haue done thy mother. / *Demet.*	mother. / *Deme.*
dd6	2095	to be our	to our
ee1ᵛ	2448–9	sure, / And stop their mouthes if they begin to cry. / *Chiron.*	sure, / *Chi.*
	2480	her owne increase	her increase
ee2	2551	hast thou doue	hast done
	2554–5	he, / To doe this outrage, and it is now done. / *King.*	he. / *Sat.*
	2613	am the turned	am turned

Romeo

ee4	289j	are here writ	are writ
ee5	512j	thē an Agat stone	then Agat-stone
	530j	with a tith-pigs	with Tith pigs
	571j	lie all in	lie in
	597	A hall, a hall	A Hall, Hall
ee6	766	dead, and I	dead, I
	775	it there stand	it stand
	888	loue me? I	Loue? I
ee6ᵛ	905	yonder blessed Moone	yonder Moone
ff1	1127j	minum rests, one	minum, one
	1133j	accent: by Iesu	accent: Iesu
ff1ᵛ	1154j	Pardon, good *Mercutio*	Pardon *Mercutio*
	1217j	is well said	is said
ff2	1355j	gentle as a	gentle a
ff3ᵛ	1684	hees dead, hees dead, hees dead	hee's dead, hee's dead
	1748	chide at him	chide him
ff4	1854	me a little speake	me speake
	1868	as I, *Iuliet*	as *Iuliet*

ff4^v	1976	all the night	all night
	2030j	so very late	so late
	2053	not the Larke	not Larke
ff5	2153	thee there a	thee a
	2192–3	not, / And yet not proud Mistrisse minion you? / Thanke	not. / Thanke
ff6	2411	come, and he and I / Will watch thy waking, and that	come, and that
ff6^v	2558	what is there	what there
gg1	2686–7	full: / O play me some merrie dumpe to comfort me. / *Minstrels.*	full. / *Mu.*
gg1^v	2765	abouts a dwels	abouts dwells

Troilus

χ2^v	301j	was a more	was more
	341j	I can tell you	I can you
	358	O a brave man.	O brave man!
	361j	iesting, thers laying on	iesting, laying on
	371j	you shall see *Troylus*	you shall *Troylus*

APPENDIX VI

Titus *and* Romeo: *Folio Agreements with the Quartos*

Titus: Agreements between the Folio and Q1
Substantive variants in dialogue

		Q3	Q1, F1
cc4^v	125	his	this
dd2^v	1170–2	me, or . . . marke, All bootlesse vnto them. . . . sorrowes bootles. . . .	me: oh . . . heare They would not pitty me. . . . sorrowes bootles. . . . (Q1: me, . . . marke, They would not pittie me, yet pleade I must, And bootlesse vnto them. . . . sorrowes. . . .)
ee1^v	2437	But	Tut
	2507	mine	my

eé2	2573	tempestious	tempestuous

Other variants in dialogue

cc4ᵛ	94	wayed	wegih'd (Q1: wayd)
	170	bretheren	Brethren
cc6	595	desprat	desperate
cc6ᵛ	651	*Saturnine*	*Saturnius*
			(Q1: *Saturninus*)
dd1	860	barberous	Barbarous
dd5ᵛ	1970	Emprour	Emperour

Stage direction variants

dd2	1081	[*omitted by Q3*]	*Exeunt.*

Romeo: Agreements between the Folio and Q1
Substantive variants in dialogue

		Q3	Q1, F1
ee4ᵛ	492	dùn	done
ee5	607	*Lucientio*	*Lucentio*
ee5ᵛ	725	tis . . . tis	this . . . this
			(Q1: *this . . . that*)
ee6ᵛ	902	trueloue	true Loues
ff2	1338	iaunce	iaunt (also in Q4)
ff3	1595	bloudy	[*omitted by Q1, F1*]
ff3ᵛ	1782	course	Coarse (Q4: corse)
ff4	1927	deuote	denote (also in Q4)
ff6	2437	selfe willde	selfe-wild
*gg3	3178	*Romeos . . .* Ladies	*Romeo . . .* Ladis [*sic*]
			(Q1: *Romeo . . .* Lady)

Other variants in dialogue

ee5	587	Vnplagued	Vnplagu'd
ee5ᵛ	626	nere	neuer
ee6	858	camest	cam'st
ee6ᵛ	986	farther	further
ff2ᵛ	1444	moued	mou'd
	1476	consortest	consort'st
			(Q1: consorts)
	1497	knowest	know'st (also in Q4)
ff3	1562	gauest	gau'st
ff5	2090	lookest	look'st
ff5ᵛ	2309	slowed	slow'd
gg2ᵛ	2887	farther	further

Speech prefix variants

ff1	1123	*Rom.*	*Ben.*
ff3	1645	[*omitted by Q3*]	*Iul.*

ff5	2087	*Ro.*	*Iuliet.* (also in Q4)
		(catch-word: *Iu.*)	
gg1ᵛ	2795	*Poti.*	*App.*
	2804	*Po.*	*App.*
	2806	*Po.*	*App.*

Stage direction variants

ff1ᵛ	1242	*Exeunt.*	*Exit. Mercutio, Benuolio.*
			(Q1: *Exeunt Benuolio,*
			Mercutio.)
ff3	1556	[*omitted by Q3*]	*Enter Tybalt.*
	1643	*Exit.*	*Exeunt.* (Q1: *Exeunt omnes.*)
ff6	2338	*Exit.*	*Exit Paris.*
ff6ᵛ	2465	*Exeunt.*	*Exeunt Iuliet and Nurse.*
			(Q1: *Exeunt Nurse and*
			Iuliet.)
gg1	2592	[*omitted by Q3*]	*Enter Mother.*
gg1ᵛ	2785	[*omitted by Q3*]	*Enter Appothecarie.*
gg2	2924	as stage direction	as speech assigned to *Pet.*
		O Lord they fight,	(Q1: assigned to *Boy.*)
		I will go call the	(Q4: assigned to *Page.*)
		Watch.	
gg2ᵛ	3035	[*omitted by Q3*]	*Kils herselfe.*
			(Q1: *She stabs herselfe and*
			falles.)
	3061	*Enter Capels.*	*Enter Capulet and his Wife.*
			(so Q4)
			(Q1: *Enter olde Capolet and*
			his Wife.)

Romeo: Agreements between the Folio and Second Quarto
Substantive variants in dialogue

		Q3	Q2, F1
ee4ᵛ	487	betakes	betake (also in Q4)
ee6	765	striueth	stirreth (also in Q4)
ff3ᵛ	1677	bring	brings (also in Q4)
ff5	2102	either	hither (Q4: hether)
	2153	happly	happily
gg2	2875j	the	that

Other variants in dialogue

ff3ᵛ	1743	Blistered	Blister'd
ff5	2116	slaughtered	slaughter'd
	2140	slaughtered	slaughter'd
ff5ᵛ	2280	maruailous	marue'lous (Q2: maruellous)

ff6^v	2456	hether	hither (also in Q4)
*gg3	3127	Returned	Return'd

Speech prefix variant

ee4	235	*Ro.*	*Ben.*

Romeo: Agreements between the Folio and the First and Second Quartos
Substantive variants in dialogue

		Q3	Q1, Q2, F1	
ee5	529j	dreame	dreames	(also in Q4)
ee6	767	the	thee	(also in Q4)
ee6^v	981	the	thee	(also in Q4)
ff1	1032	sence	sences	(also in Q4)
ff3^v	1686	hees is gone	hee's gone	(also in Q4)

Other variants in dialogue

ee5^v	629	hether	hither

Romeo: Agreements between the Folio and the Fourth Quarto
Substantive variants in dialogue

		Q3	Q4, F1
ff2	1363	iaunsing	iaunting
ff2^v	1416	is	in
	1420	musicke	musickes
	1427	sum	some
	1433	*Capels*	*Capulets*
gg2^v	3060	morning	mornings
*gg3	3174	raie	raise

Other variants in dialogue

ff2	1335	shamest	sham'st
ff3^v	1763	murdred	murdered
ff6	2452	becomd	becomed
			(Q4: becommed)

Stage direction variants

ee6	793	*Exit.*	*Exeunt.*
ff4	1881	*They knocke*	*Knocke*
gg1	2680	*Enter Will Kempe.*	*Enter Peter.*

Speech prefix variants

ff2	1325	*M.*	[*omitted by Q4, F1*]
gg2^v	3036	*Watch boy.*	*Boy.*

APPENDIX VII

Substantive Corrections in Compositor E's Stints

(These readings are accepted by the following editions: Kittridge, New Cambridge, Alexander, Sisson, and Riverside, the new Arden *Titus* and *Romeo* and the New Penguin *Romeo*.)

		Q3	F1
Titus			
cc5^v	443	*omit*	Yes, and will Nobly him remunerate
dd1	848	Ewe	yew
ddl^v	963	vnhollow	vnhallow'd
dd6	2093	yeares	eares

Romeo

Probably editorial is the omission of two lines from *Romeo* at TLN 1845, both lines constituting a Shakespearean second thought with the first shot almost immediately preceding. Modern editors also omit two of the lines, although they disagree among themselves and with the Folio in the choice of the omission (3.3.40 ff.).

Troilus

χ2^v	271	liste	lift
	359j	man	mans

APPENDIX VIII

Expansions, Contractions, Elisions, and Variants in Verbal Form

(See also Appendix VI under 'Other variants in dialogue')

		Q3	F1
Titus			
cc4^v	126j	brethren	Bretheren
	134	slaughtered	slaughtred
cc5^v	356	Emperesse	Empresse
	383	confederates	Confedrates
	476	honoured	Honour'd
cc6	574	Emperesse	Empresse
	583	knowest	know'st
	593	vnaduizd	vnaduised

cc6ᵛ	642	makes	mak'st
	693	shadowed	shadow'd
dd1	757	enioyed	enioy'd
	833	tyced	tic'd
dd1ᵛ	879	bearest	bear'st
	896	moued	mou'd
dd3	1323	withred	withered
dd4	1548	thine	thy
dd5	1755	ye	you
dd6	1829	to the	to th'
	2029	touched	touch'd
	2041	hanged	hang'd
	2047	trayterous	traytrous
	2049	butchered	butcher'd
	2058	gathered	gather'd
dd6ᵛ	2208	sawest	saw'st
	2223	mentioned	mention'd
ee1	2383	I will	Ile
ee1ᵛ	2438	hether	hither
	2495j	against	gainst
	2515	moe	more
ee2	2532	attired	attir'd
	2562	hether	hither

Romeo

ee3ᵛ	132	shunned	shunn'd
ee4	308	learned	learn'd
ee5	575j	loues	louest
ee5ᵛ	652	endured	endu'rd
ee6ᵛ	962j	toward	towards
ff1ᵛ	1195j	desirest	desir'st
	1277	shriued	shriu'd
ff2	1361	a	o
	1371	repliest	repli'st
ff2ᵛ	1500	iniured	iniur'd
			(Q2: iniuried)
ff3	1572	amazed	amaz'd
ff3ᵛ	1774	moued	mou'd
ff4	1909	Spakest	Speak'st
	1936	raylest	rayl'st
ff4ᵛ	1939	shamest	sham'st
	1955	slewest	slew'st
	1961	puts	puttest

ff6	2371	darest	dar'st
	2383	vnstaind	vnstained
ff6ᵛ	2462	there is	there's
	2483	knowest	know'st
	2545	crowed	Crow'd
gg1ᵛ	2798	fearest	fear'st
	2809	There is	There's
gg2	2879	hearest	hear'st
	2950	lyest	ly'st
	2953	thine	thy
gg2ᵛ	3011	where is	where's

APPENDIX IX

Compositor E's Errors in Stage Directions and Speech Prefixes

Titus		Quarto	Folio
cc4ᵛ	152	*Exit Titus*	['*Titus*' omitted]
		sonnes with Alarbus.	
	175	*Coffin*	*Coffins*
cc5ᵛ	409	3. *Sonne*	1. *Sonne*
	435	*Exit all but*	*Exit.*
		Marcus and Titus.	
cc6	528	*All.*	*Son.*
			(Q1 has no speech prefix)
dd1	743	*Enter Tamora*	['*alone*' omitted]
		alone to the	
		Moore.	
dd2	999	[*omitted by Q*]	*Boths fall in.*
dd2	1151	[*omitted by Q*]	*Exeunt*
dd4	1614	*mouth*	*mouths* (uncorr.)
dd6	2028	[*omitted by Q*]	*Aside.*
			(a half-line late)
	2107	*Exeunt.*	*Exit.*
ee1	2281	[*omitted by Q*]	*Flourish.*
			(one line too early)
ee1ᵛ	2452	[*omitted by Q*]	*Exeunt.*
ee2	2577	*Roman Lord.*	*Goth.*
Romeo			
ee4ᵛ	446	*Seruing*	*a Seruing man.*
ee5	567	*with napkins*	*with their napkins*
	568	*Enter* Romeo	*Enter Seruant*

	580	3.	1
	596	*they dance*	*the* dance
	612	*1. Capu.*	*3. Cap.*
ee6ᵛ	938	*[omitted by Q]*	*Cals within.* (one line late)
ff1ᵛ	1267j	*Rom.*	*Nur.*
ff2ᵛ	1417	*Ro.*	*Fri.*
ff4	1885	*Slud knocke.*	*Knocke.*
ff5ᵛ	2292	*Exit.*	*Exeunt.*
gg1	2675	*Exeunt.*	*Exeunt*
		manet.	

Some of the above errors may be editorial, especially those at TLN 446, 567, 568, 612, 938, and 1885, which Reid has already suggested are editorial ('The Editing of Folio *Romeo*', pp. 53–6).

Troilus

χ2ᵛ	383	*Troylus*	*Trylus*

APPENDIX X

Addenda to the Published Lists of Compositor B's Errors

Included in the tally of Compositor B's errors are the following, all introduced into page *gg3ᵛ, the cancelled first page of *Troilus*:

substitution

	Quarto	Folio
79j	her	it

interpolations

| 50j | must tarry | must needes tarrie |
| 60j | chance burne | chaunce to burne |

For completeness of the record, the following variants should also be added to the published lists of B's errors, although, since they are not substantive changes, they are not included in the counts of B's errors:

*gg3ᵛ	55j	leauening	leau'ning
	60j	yea	you
	62	suffrance	sufferance
	100j	in it	in't
	110j	a	¹on

Excluded from the counts are the following entries in lists of B's errors published in Walker, 'The Folio Text of 1 *Henry IV*', *passim*, and Werstine, 'Compositor B of the Shakespeare First Folio', *passim*.

		Quarto	Folio
ee3	7	and	if
	8–9	out of choller	out o'th Collar
	26	I will	and
	35	of *Mountagues*	of the *Mountagues*
Gg1	3178	*Romeos*	*Romeo*
		Ladies	Lady

(All six Folio readings are also found in the 'bad quarto' of *Romeo* and therefore may not be B's errors.)

ee2ᵛ	2676j	*Puer.*	*Boy.*

(*Puer.* is altered to *Boy.* throughout *Titus*, in Compositor E's portion as well as in Compositor B's.)

Gg1	3146	*Balth.*	*Boy.*
	3155	*Boy.*	*Page.*

(Nowhere else does Compositor B make wholesale alterations in the speech prefixes of his copy; the concentration of these two changes in just ten lines of *Romeo* suggests the interference of another agent between the compositor and his copy.)

d6	190j	similes	smiles

(Again the Folio reading is also the reading of a first quarto, this time the authoritative first quarto of *1 Henry IV*.)

N1ᵛ	141	my	mine
Q2	2633	my	mine

(Neither substitution is substantive.)

APPENDIX XI

Compositor E's Stints in King Lear: *Folio Agreement with the Quartos on Variants in Verbal Form*

TLN	Q1	Q2, F
174	swearest	swear.st (Q2: swear'st)
232	ashamed	asham'd

250	dishonord	dishonoured
303	receaued	receiu'd
553	thar't	thou art
585	A	He
676j	at'h	on thy
685j	vs'd	vsed
897	a	he
971	where is	where's
1135j	ruffen	Ruffian
1138j	you'l	you will
1156	and	if
1175	tak't	take it
1754j	desir'd	desired
1768j	for't	for it
3057	hether	hither
3079	saiest	saist (Q2: sayst)
3156	armed	arm'd
3178	poysoned	poyson'd
3196	beloued	belou'd
3197	poysoned	poison'd
3236	sayest	saist (Q2: sayst)
3256	You'r	Your are (Q2: You are)

TLN	Q2	F, Q1
600j	into it	intoo't
632j	of his	on's
660j	for it	for't
675j	in the	i'th'
694	If	And
889j	she is	she's
896j	side his	side's
953	against	'gainst
1015	fastened	fastned
1079	In the	I 'th'
1165	doth	do's
1189	to it	too't
1226	abused	abus'd
1283j–4j	by the	by 'th' (3 times)
1297–8j	do it	do't (twice)
1315	poisoned	poison'd
1337j	If	And
1387	indisposed	indispos'd
1399j	them	'em (Q1: vm)
1402	butterd	buttered

1410	adulteresse	Adultresse
1611	abused	abus'd
1789	thou wouldst	Thou'dst
1796	to it	too't
1823j	name is	name's
1846j	reserued	reseru'd
1847	shamed	sham'd
1860j	of the	o'th'
2760	be it	be't (Q1: beet)
2849	he is	he's
2959	by the	by th'
3117	for it	for't
3141	know it	know't
3219	she is	she's
3228	that	which
3256	hether	hither

Fluctuating Variation
Author, Annotator, or Actor?

MacD. P. JACKSON

Introduction

A NY attempt to determine the relationship between two or more texts must focus upon the *nature* of the variants, but their *distribution* may also be revealing. Almost all modern scholars believe that such 'bad' quarto texts as *Hamlet* (1603), *Romeo and Juliet* (1597), *The Merry Wives of Windsor* (1602), and *Henry V* (1600) are reports by actors of the plays as they remembered performing them; this conviction derives in part from our ability to identify the probable culprits, who – as comparison between bad and good texts of the same play reveals – recalled their own speeches more accurately than those of other characters, and floundered as they tried to re-create scenes in which they themselves had not participated.[1]

Variation between texts may be no less uneven when effected by a collator, annotating one text to bring it into agreement with another. For instance, the Folio text of Shakespeare's *Richard II* was printed from a copy of Q3 (1598), which had been corrected by reference to an authoritative manuscript, probably the prompt-book;[2] but correction was so sporadic that more than half the errors accumulated in two straight reprints (Q2 from Q1, and Q3 from Q2) were transmitted to F. The percentage of Q2–3 errors corrected in each act is 59, 54, 39, 33, and 55, which suggests that the collator-annotator grew progressively more careless and then improved as he neared the end of his task.[3] Stanley Wells has recently argued that the copy of the 1598 quarto of *Love's Labour's Lost* from which the Folio text was printed had been haphazardly checked against a manuscript.[4] The annotator evidently did some serious checking of speech prefixes and stage directions in the first three acts, but then skipped straight over to the last page.

Authors revising their work are likewise apt to concentrate their efforts on certain scenes. Chapman's *Bussy D'Ambois*, first published in a quarto of 1607, was reprinted in a second quarto of 1641, 'much corrected and amended by the Author', according to the title page.

The revisions may not all be Chapman's.[5] But whoever did the rewriting, the rate of alteration fluctuates dramatically: from 2.1 to 3.1 variants between the two texts are less than half as frequent as in the rest of the play, the average rate diminishing from one variant in seven lines to one in seventeen. The most densely variant act is the first.

In short, authors, actors, and annotators all create sundry patterns of textual variation, patterns which do not always unambiguously declare their origins. It is not surprising, therefore, that the incidence of variants between the two texts of *King Lear* fluctuates, and that scholars have disagreed about the identity of the agent or agents responsible for this fluctuation.

In 1952 Alice Walker drew attention to what she took to be the uneven quality of the Quarto text of *King Lear*.[6] At the time, orthodox opinion held Q to be a memorially corrupt version of the play preserved in F; G. I. Duthie postulated that Q copy had been reconstructed from memory by an entire acting company on tour in the provinces.[7] Walker suggested instead that for much of Acts Three and Four the variation between Q and F was sufficiently trivial to be blamed on compositors and scribes,[8] that Q shared many features with good quartos based on foul papers, and that its serious memorial contamination was concentrated into certain scenes, such as the first and last. Since corruption in Q appeared to her to be most severe in scenes that included Goneril and Regan, she proposed the engaging hypothesis that the two boy actors, one dictating to the other, had made a surreptitious transcript of Shakespeare's foul papers, but had unfortunately relied too heavily on their own memories of those portions of the play with which they were most familiar.

An alternative explanation of the fluctuation in the number of QF variants was advanced by J. K. Walton in 1955 and repeated with refinements in 1971.[9] He favoured either Duthie's hypothesis that behind Q lay a combined effort at memorial reconstruction, or the older hypothesis of shorthand piracy by a member of the audience (though both have been so decisively refuted that it is hard to understand anyone's continued adherence to either).[10] Assuming, as had Walker, that F was printed throughout from a copy of Q1 which had been corrected by reference to a prompt-book, he argued that the work of comparing that copy of Q1 with the manuscript had been performed with varying efficiency – that in Act Four, for example, where QF variants are few, the collator had worked perfunctorily, failing to make many of the necessary corrections to his exemplar of Q1.

Thus, whereas Walker assumed that Q varies in quality, Walton argued that the quality of Q is more or less constant, but that of F variable; more particularly, in respect to those parts of the play where variants are few, whereas Walker assumed that Q is comparatively good, Walton argued that F is comparatively bad. But the possibility of revision alters the terms of this crucial disagreement. If many of the QF variants result from revision – a possibility which, at the very least, must be seriously considered – then their rate of occurrence need not be connected with degrees of corruption in either text, but may primarily reflect the amount of rewriting. The issue has been further complicated by a change in scholarly opinion about the nature of the printer's copy for F. Both Walker and Walton believed that all of Folio *Lear* was set from annotated Q1 copy. The convincing new evidence that Jaggard's compositor E set his stint from a corrected exemplar of Q2, not Q1, must affect the detail, and might undermine the foundations, of their arguments.

The evident fluctuations in the rate of substantial variation between Q and F are thus inextricably related to three issues of fundamental importance: the character of Q, the relationship between Q and F, and the actual printer's copy from which the Folio compositors set their text. My aim here is to reconsider that pattern of variation between the two texts – a pattern which, as I hope to demonstrate, neither Walton's hypothesis nor Walker's can account for. The pattern can, in fact, only be plausibly explained as the result of authorial revision. In a final section I hope to reinforce this conclusion by an examination of selected variants in one scene, thus shifting the focus from the wood of statistics to a few of the individual trees.

Walton's Theory

In considering Walton's and Walker's theories it will be convenient, as a defence against circumlocution, to assume, as they did, F's use of Q1 copy, and to defer for the moment an evaluation of the validity of that assumption.

In support of his case Walton first examined the distribution of 325 pairs of variants drawn from two lists in Duthie's edition: namely, (1) a list of readings chosen to demonstrate the memorial character of Q, readings categorized by Duthie as actor's tags and interpolations, transpositions, anticipations, and recollections; and (2) a list of instances where Duthie was unwilling to accept Quarto readings preferred in most standard modern editions prior to his own.[11] If, as is generally assumed, Folio *Lear* was set from annotated Quarto copy, then the great majority of Folio readings in these two lists must have been introduced by the annotator-collator. Walton examined the incidence of these variants for each act. When he divided the number of lines in each act that are common to Q and F by the number of these variants, he arrived at the following proportions. (The higher the figure, the fewer the readings introduced by the collator.)

Table (g):   6.6   8.5   8.4   16.4   9.6

Walton interpreted this table as indicating that 'the collator tended to grow increasingly inefficient as he proceeded with his work, and regained something of his initial form only with the approach of the end of his task' (p. 274).

Walton next made his own independent count of *all* variants, but subtracted those 'of the kind a compositor is liable to introduce' (p. 275). The resultant table shows the following lines per variant within each act:

Table (h):   2.9   3.1   3.1   3.5   2.7

Even when Walton included in his calculations all variants except obvious F errors, Act Four showed proportionally fewer than the other acts:

Table (i):   2.4   2.5   2.5   2.8   2.5

My own check confirms these figures, apart from those for Act Five, where Walton may have overestimated the number of variants.[12]

Walton goes on to argue:

If the lesser incidence of variants in Act IV is due to the fact that Q is there of a better quality than elsewhere, we should expect that, provided the collator's efficiency was constant, Act IV would have fewer common errors [i.e. errors shared by both texts]. If, on the contrary, the fewness of variants is due to a greater inefficiency of collation, we should expect that the greatest number of errors common to Q and F would occur where Q and F variants are fewest. (pp. 276–7)

He shows that pertinent QF errors fall within the acts as follows:[13]

Table (j):   1   1   1   5   1

This table confirms him in his belief that the collator was at his least thorough in Act Four.

But Walton's evidence, growing to a plurisy, dies in its own too much; for his own theory renders his Tables (g) and (h) incompatible. If the incidence of Table (g) variation between Q and the manuscript authority behind F remained steady (varying efficiency of collation being alone responsible for the disparity between Acts One and Four), then in Act Four the collator was working at only 40 per cent $\left(\dfrac{6.6}{16.4} \times \dfrac{100}{1} \right)$ of the efficiency attained in Act One. But Table (h) presents a very different picture. Here we would have to take Act Five as a standard for the highest efficiency attained by the collator. If the incidence of Table (h) variation between Q and the manuscript authority behind F remained steady (varying efficiency of collation being alone responsible for the disparity between Acts Five and Four), then in Act Four the collator was working at *77 per cent* $\left(\dfrac{2.7}{3.5} \times \dfrac{100}{1} \right)$ of the efficiency attained in Act Five, or *83 per cent* $\left(\dfrac{2.9}{3.5} \times \dfrac{100}{1} \right)$ of the efficiency attained in Act One. This disparity between the two tables is so great that, even if we suppose that the collator's efficiency did fluctuate, we must also assume that the nature of the variation between Q and the collator's manuscript fluctuated too.

To make the point in another way, the proportion of Table (g) variants to Table (h) variants is uneven. The following table records, for each act, Table (g) variants as a percentage of Table (h) variants:

Table (w):   44   36   37   21   28

Thus the proportion of Table (g) variants among all the variants supposedly introduced by the collator is more than twice as high in Act One as in Act Four. Any satisfactory account of the variation between Q and F must explain this discrepancy. The most reasonable explanation is that the percentages simply reflect real act to act differences in the nature of the variation between Q and the manuscript authority behind F. The only alternative is to suppose that the collator, in working on Act Four (and to a lesser degree Act Five), actively discriminated against Table (g) variants in his manuscript – in other words, that the collator concentrated on introducing on to his copy of Q those variants that were *not* of the kind processed in Walton's Table (g).

I doubt that he could have managed to do this. As we have seen, Table (g) is based on two lists in Duthie's edition of 1949: the first records variants that Duthie regards as showing that Q was based on a report, and the second records instances where Duthie rejects Q readings that many earlier editors preferred to the corresponding F readings. Admittedly, few, if any, of the Q readings in either list are obviously wrong; indeed, most of the Q readings in the second list are attractive, which is why Duthie's predecessors preferred them to the F alternatives. But many of the Q readings that in Act Four, as elsewhere, the collator *did* correct are not obviously wrong either: the printer of Q2 was content to take over almost all of them, unchanged.

Walton might reply that his Table (g) gives only a sampling of variants, and that we should not expect a mere sample to conform precisely to the pattern of the more complete data presented in Table (h). But when the full count of QF variants supposed to have been introduced by the collator is separated into those belonging to Table (g) and those peculiar to Table (h), and the two distributions of variants per act are compared by a chi-squared test, the difference between them is found to be statistically significant far beyond the 0.001 level – which means that there is much less than one chance in a thousand that they could have been drawn from a single homogeneous population.[14] In other words, the discrepancy between Tables (g) and (h) cannot be simply the discrepancy between the sample and the whole; there must be some process or agent of discrimination at work.

There is a further point. Most QF variants, including virtually all those used for Walton's Table (g), reflect real differences between the printer's copy for Q and the printer's copy for F. However, some variants, which form a substantial group, result from the Q compositor's difficulties with a manuscript he could not easily read. The compositor's aptness to misread his copy is obvious enough from the Q press-variants and from the frequent resemblance in graphic outline between Q nonsense and F sense. About 275 words in Q seem safely attributable to misreadings or mechanical errors common in setting type. Only one or two of the more obvious of these errors were corrected in Q2; hardly any of the remainder could have been corrected except by somebody of great editorial or literary skill, or by someone with access to an authoritative manuscript. On the theory

that F was set from annotated Quarto copy, we have therefore to
suppose that each of these F corrections was individually introduced
by the collator. If Walton is right about the varying efficiency of
collation, this group of variants ought to display the same pattern as
Table (g) variants. But in fact it does not.
Depending heavily for guidance on the textual notes to Duthie's
1949 edition, in which cases of graphic similarity between Q
corruptions and good F readings are given detailed attention, I
compiled a full inventory of likely Q misreadings corrected in F.[15]
For the sake of argument, I accepted Walton's assumptions about the
nature of Q copy.[16] The distribution of these QF variants, expressed
as lines per variant in each act, is as follows:

	Table (x):	16.6	8.1	8.9	8.7	11

This table runs to a very different pattern from that of Walton's Table
(g). Whereas Table (g) variants are, in relation to the number of lines,
twice as frequent in Act One as in Act Four, variants apparently due
to misreading in Q are twice as frequent in Act Four as in Act One. If
Walton's Table (g) reflects a collator's efficiency, so that he corrected
not more than 40 per cent of Act Four errors, then misreadings in Q
must have occurred in Act Four at about *four* times the rate at which
they occurred in Act One, and there must have been some 160
misreadings in Act Four of Q, about 100 of which have persisted into
F and remain undetected to this day.[17] It is far easier to believe that
the tables indicate, however roughly, the true character of the
variation between Q and the manuscript authority behind F.

An obvious objection to my argument is that it assumes the
correctness of Walton's theory of Q copy. If F was partly or wholly
set from Q2, or if it was set from an exemplar of Q1 in which some
sheets were in a state different from that postulated by Walton, would
not the incidence of QF variants due to misreading in Q be greatly
changed? The short answer is that it would not. Compositorial
misreadings in Q that the press corrector corrected correctly form
fewer than 20 per cent of the total Q misreadings. If we were to
assume that F was set from Q2 copy throughout, or if we were to
include only variants between F and Q1 *in both its states*, Table (j)
would remain much the same.[18]

The paucity of misreading variants in Act One is especially
interesting in view of the fact that stop-press correction in Q
apparently began in earnest only with sheet D, about half-way

through 1.4. Sheet B is invariant and sheet C contains only two substantive alterations.[19] We might therefore have expected more misreadings, not fewer, to survive in the first act of Q, where there was little stop-press correction. Apparently, either Q underwent earlier stages of proofing that were conducted more thoroughly at the beginning of the play, or compositorial misreadings of Q copy occurred less often in the first few sheets (perhaps because the handwriting was clearer?)[20]

Synonym substitutions in F that bear no graphic resemblance to their Q counterparts are distributed much as Walton's Table (g) variants. My own figures, expressed as lines per variant within each act, are:

Table (y):   6.6   9   10.3   14.7   7.8

The act divisions are not, of course, clear-cut boundaries. Variants are more plentiful in the first half of the play up to and including 3.4, and then again in 4.6 and 5.3. From 3.5 to 4.5 the variants that Duthie cites as evidence of memorial corruption in Q occur at a quarter the rate of their occurrence elsewhere.

As with the other kinds of variation I have already discussed, the pattern of synonym substitution might reflect real differences in the manuscripts underlying Q and F: fluctuating memorial corruption in Q or fluctuating authorial revision in F. If, on the other hand, that pattern results only from the fluctuating attention of the collator, then we must explain why he became most lax in correcting synonym substitutions in the very pages where he became most scrupulous in detecting misreadings. Such a division of attention is not, perhaps, completely impossible, but it further complicates a picture already bewilderingly contradictory. And the entire appeal of Walton's hypothesis lay, of course, in its apparent simplicity: the fluctuating variation between Quarto and Folio *Lear* neatly reflecting the graph of one man's efficiency, as he descended from a morning peak of attentiveness into the valley of midday sloth, and then ascended to another (lower) afternoon peak of alertness. Behind Walton's numerical tables lies this simple image of the rhythms of work; but the tables in the end cannot be reconciled with each other, or with the hypothesis they were designed to prove.

To summarize: Walton's own tables grossly contradict one another; that contradiction cannot be plausibly explained as the result of conscious discrimination on the collator's part, nor can it be discounted on statistical grounds. Another table (of the incidence of apparent misreadings in Q, corrected by F) also contradicts Walton's account of the collator's fluctuating efficiency. Finally, the incidence of synonym substitution further complicates and confuses the alleged pattern of collator activity. All of these difficulties and contradictions in Walton's argument can be resolved by one assumption: that the fluctuating pattern of variation between Q and F results from real fluctuations in the manuscripts behind those texts.

But what finally decisively undermines Walton's hypothesis is Walton's own observation that the greatest number of errors common to Q and F occurs within Act Four. As I have said, he claims that Act Four has five such errors, whereas each other act has only one. His table, quite properly, includes only shared errors that he regards as having arisen from the collator's 'failure to compare conscientiously the quarto with a manuscript and to attempt correction accordingly' (p. 277). Given Walton's assumptions about F use of corrected Q1 copy, his classification of shared errors is sensible enough. His own arguments (p. 282, n. 2), however, require that he include F's 'prize' (TLN 1063; 2.1.120) as an example of an error taken over from the uncorrected state of Q (D4ᵛ); this would give two common errors in Act Two. But the real point of interest is that four of the five common errors in Act Four occur within the space of fifty lines in the conflated text of Scene Two; as the Folio does not include substantial passages present in Q in this scene, *the four common errors occur within a mere twenty lines or so of the Folio text.* Moreover, Walton's list of common errors includes, 'with one exception, all instances where Miss Walker holds that F has taken over an uncorrected reading from an uncorrected Q sheet' (pp. 152–3); *this single rejected instance also occurs within the same twenty lines of F:* 'whistle' (TLN 2300; 4.2.29), where Qb reads 'whistling' (H3ᵛ). Duthie in his New Cambridge edition of 1960, G. K. Hunter in his New Penguin edition of 1972, and G. B. Evans in the Riverside Shakespeare are among editors who agree with Walker that F's reading is an error.

This concentration of errors can hardly be a coincidence; nor does it suggest that a collator was working at minimal efficiency through-out Act Four, since if we were to exclude this obviously exceptional passage from our calculations, Walton's Table (j) would show the same number of F errors in each act (though it ought, I have argued, to show two, not one, in Act Two).

Why, then, is this passage in 4.2 so exceptional? The disproportionate number of shared errors in 4.2 may be connected with the fact
that this scene is heavily cut in F – if the omissions from F are cuts.
By far the most heavily cut scenes in F are 3.1, 3.6, and 4.2; only 4.2
affords three successive F omissions, between which short passages
intervene. As the Riverside edition numbers the lines in 4.2 (which
covers TLN 2267–347), both texts contain the first 25 lines, but Q
omits line 26; two shared errors appear in line 28, another appears in
line 29; the first F omission occurs at lines 31–50, the second at lines
53–9; then in line 60 there is another shared error; the third F
omission follows at lines 62–9; and the last shared error is at line 79;
the scene ends at line 97. (Shared errors are marked by an *.)

Oh, the difference of man, and man,	line altered
To thee a Womans seruices are due,	word added
* My Foole vsurpes my body.	word altered
Stew. Madam, here come's my Lord.	direction omitted
Enter Albany.	direction added
* Gon. I haue beene worth the whiftle,	
Alb. Oh Generill,	
You are not worth the duft which the rude winde	
Blowes in your face.	major omission
Gon. Milke-Liuer'd man,	
That bear'ft a cheeke for blowes, a head for wrongs,	word altered
Who haft not in thy browes an eye-difcerning	word altered
Thine Honor, from thy fuffering.	major omission
Alb. See thy felfe diuell:	
* Proper deformitie feemes not in the Fiend	major omission
So horrid as in woman.	
Gon. Oh vaine Foole.	major omission
Enter a Meffenger.	word altered
Mef. Oh my good Lord, the Duke of Cornwals dead,	prefix altered
Slaine by his Seruant, going to put out	
The other eye of Gloufter.	
Alb. Gloufters eyes.	
Mef. A Seruant that he bred, thrill'd with remorfe,	prefix and word altered
Oppos'd againft the act : bending his Sword	
To his great Mafter, who, threat-enrag'd	word altered
Flew on him, and among'ft them fell'd him dead,	
But not without that harmefull ftroke, which fince	
Hath pluckt him after.	
Alb. This fhewes you are aboue	
* You Iuftices, that thefe our neather crimes	word altered

If F was printed from annotated Q copy at this point (Q1 *or* Q2),
the collator, while conscientiously deleting from Q three passages of
Shakespearian dialogue that were not in his manuscript, and

inserting into his copy of Q one line that *was* in his manuscript, yet failed to make five corrections that the press corrector of Q had made. Even to have made the one-line addition and the three deletions accurately the collator would have been forced to compare Q with his manuscript rather carefully; moreover, if – as has been assumed – F was printed from an annotated copy of Q which, for lines 3–80, was in its uncorrected state (the other lines of the scene belong to the invariant outer forme), then the collator introduced at least thirteen substantive variants into the dialogue of 4.2, and made so many changes to stage directions, speech prefixes, and lineation, that he either deleted or in one way or another corrected no fewer than seventy of Q's ninety-seven lines. In fact, if Duthie is right – and his view is shared by almost every other modern editor – the collator examined his manuscript so attentively that at TLN 2285 (4.2.17) he convinced himself that his own misreading of that manuscript was superior to the true Shakespearian reading, 'armes', printed in Q. The collator, says Duthie, 'may easily have misread "armes" in the playhouse manuscript as "names" and altered Q accordingly' (p. 181). The collator could hardly, with the correct word 'armes' before him in Q, have altered it without giving the matter some thought; yet eleven lines later we find him, according to Walton, 'negligently' allowing two Q errors to stand. But we can hardly accuse the collator of negligence even at TLN 2297. F reads:

> To thee a Womans seruices are due,
> My Foole vsurpes my body.
> (TLN 2296–7; 4.2.27–8)

Qa omits 'a' from line 27 and reads in line 28 'My foote vsurps my body'. Qb reads 'A foole vsurps my bed'. Walton (p. 158) agrees with Walker and recent editors in regarding 'A foole vsurps my bed' as the Shakespearian version of the line, and I personally judge this to be the best and most plausible combination of the three variant words.[21] But if Qb preserves Shakespeare's text, and F was printed from annotated Qa copy, then the collator must have given the line some attention in order to change 'foote' to 'Foole'.[22] And he could scarcely have made this alteration without noting in both Q and his manuscript the word that preceded 'foote'/'Foole' and the three that followed: the five words have a line to themselves in Q and obviously form a sense unit.

We seem to be working our way towards an impasse from which

the only exit is some alternative to Walton's theory that F and Qa both read 'My' and 'body' only because a collator, editing a copy of Q for use in printing F, carelessly overlooked the readings in his manuscript.

It might be suggested that 'My' and 'body' are not errors at all. Duthie accepted them in his edition of 1949. Indeed, taken individually, any one of the five supposed errors common to F and Qa in this scene could, at a pinch, be judged the true reading, which the Q press-corrector had sophisticated. But of course the fewer common errors we are prepared to concede, the less evidence we have of F dependence on Q, let alone of the collator's inefficiency, and it cannot, I think, be coincidental that five words that Walker and other scholars have regarded as common errors all fall within twenty lines of F and are close to substantial F omissions.

The quantities of coincidence we are required to swallow become even more indigestible when we discover that proximity to a Folio omission or addition is a feature of nearly all probable QF errors in other scenes too. (I use 'omission' and 'addition' neutrally here and in what follows: by 'F addition' I mean simply a passage in F but not Q, and by 'F omission' a passage in Q but not F.) Walton (pp. 152–9) lists altogether fifteen F errors suggesting dependence upon Q, and all but two are close to F omissions or additions, most of them very close to additions or omissions of some length. Some such juxtapositions would certainly have occurred by chance, since F omissions or additions of half a line or so are fairly frequent, but – as statistical analysis makes clear – the overall tendency cannot be a matter of coincidence. Let us, for the sake of argument, define proximity to an F omission or addition as 'within ten lines either side of an F omission or addition of at least one full line in length'. Now out of 2,825 lines of *Lear* common to Q and F, (a) 760 lines are in this sense close to an F omission or addition, and (b) 2,065 are not. Of Walton's fifteen significant F errors, nine occur within the 760 lines of category (a) text, and six occur within the 2,065 lines of category (b) text. A simple statistical test, using the binomial theorem, shows that chance alone could produce such a result less often than once in a hundred times. This test is conservative, in so far as it does not, of course, take into account the fact that (1) other probable errors not dealt with by Walton occur close to F additions or omissions,[23] (2) four of those that do not qualify as close to F omissions or additions in the sense defined are nevertheless only just outside the ten-line range or are close to shorter F omissions or additions, (3) most of the significant errors are close to more than one F omission or addition, (4) several are within one or two lines of an F omission or addition, and (5) those close to an F omission or addition are always in the same scene as that omission or addition (although for my statistical test I regarded the text as continuous).[24]

Interestingly, all but one of the nine F errors falling within ten lines of an addition to or omission from F of at least a line in length are categorized by Walton as genuine common errors, as distinct from errors arising from the collator's ambiguous or faulty marking of Q, and it seems to me probable that the anomalous instance has been misclassified and that F's slight modification of the Qa reading owes nothing to any authoritative source.[25] This variant is Walton's number 8 (pp. 155–6), where F reads 'commands, tends, ser- uice', Qa 'come and tends seruise', and Qb 'commands her seruice' (TLN 1378–9; E4ᵛ; 2.4.102). Walton takes Walker's common-sense view that Qb's straightforward reading is a genuine correction; this granted, F's attempt to make sense of Qa could be compositorial.[26]

Our conclusion – that the occurrence of four (or five) QF errors in 4.2 is connected with the unusual number and extent of F's omissions in this scene – is thus supported by the proximity of most other QF errors to F omissions or additions. I shall in due course try to explain why this should have happened.[27] But we can already confidently conclude that the disposition of errors common to Q and F does nothing whatsoever to support Walton's interpretation of the fluctuating incidence of variants between the two texts.

Walker's Theory

Since Walton's theory cannot adequately account for the comparative paucity of QF variants within the later part of Act Three and most of Act Four, we may revert to a consideration of Walker's view that variants within this section of the text are trivial because Q here suffers from less memorial contamination than at the beginning and end of the play.

There is some evidence that for Acts Three and Four of Q the copy was, if not 'less corrupt' (a formulation that begs the crucial questions), at least 'cleaner or more finished'. The following table shows for each act (a) the number of entry and exit directions completely missing from Q but supplied by Duthie, and (b) the total number of necessary entry and exit directions.[28]

Table (z):	Missing SDs:	17	7	9	5	12
	Total SDs:	35	23	33	29	28
	Percentage missing:	49	30	27	17	43

Act Four is the least defective, Acts One and Five are the most.[29] Speech prefixes and stage directions for Albany and Cornwall in Q tell the same story. These two men are sometimes given their actual names, sometimes confusedly designated 'Duke':

1.4 *Duke* (Albany) seven times
2.1 *Cornwall* twice; *Duke* (Cornwall) four times
2.2 *Duke* (Cornwall) sixteen times
2.4 *Duke* (Cornwall) nine times
3.5 *Cornwall* six times
3.7 *Cornwall* eighteen times
4.2 *Albany* seven times
5.1 *Albany* seven times
5.3 *Duke* (Albany) once; *Albany* twenty-two times; *Duke* (Albany) ten times

Thus the designation 'Duke' is used in 1.4, 2.1, 2.2, 2.4, and 5.3; but only the unambiguous names 'Cornwall' and 'Albany' are used in 3.5, 3.7, 4.2, and 5.1. The latter four scenes are all among those in which QF variants are fewest. In the 'Duke' scenes Duthie's 'memorial' variants occur at the rate of one per 18 lines; in the 'Cornwall' and 'Albany' scenes they occur at the rate of one per 62 lines. My list of synonym substitutions not due to misreading reveals the same disparity: one per 8 lines, one per 25 lines. By contrast, variants due to misreading in Q occur at similar rates within the two sections: one per 11 lines, one per 10 lines.[30]

It seems possible, therefore, that copy for Q was to some degree heterogeneous. However, in assessing the merits of Walker's theory, our crucial question is whether supposedly 'memorial' variants really are most frequent when Goneril and Regan are on stage. It is easy to demonstrate that they are not.

In those fourteen scenes from which Goneril and Regan are entirely absent Duthie's 'memorial' variants occur at the rate of one every 23.8 lines. In the other scenes they occur at the rate of one every 20.0 lines. This difference is insignificant. Disregard the opening and closing scenes, in both of which the sisters participate, and it virtually disappears: the rate for Goneril-and-Regan scenes falls to one in every 22.5 lines. Nor does my list of synonym substitutions not due to misreading give support to Walker's claim. In scenes from which Goneril and Regan are absent the rate of such variants is one in every 9.8 lines, while in the other scenes it is one in every 8.2 lines. Disregard 1.1 and 5.3, and the rate for Goneril-and-Regan scenes drops from one in 8.2 lines to one in 10.1.

Nine scenes of *King Lear* contain more than 100 lines. Among them only 2.2, in which Regan takes part, has a heavier concentration of Duthie's 'memorial' variants than 1.2 and 3.4, in which neither sister is on stage.

Walker pointed to the sudden increase in QF variants upon the entry of Lear and his train, including Goneril and Regan, at 1.1.33 (B1ᵛ; TLN 37–8), but within 2.4, which in her view suffered more memorial contamination than any scene except 1.1 and 5.3, the incidence of variants bears no relation to the presence of Goneril and Regan on stage.[31] Neither sister is present until line 126 (E4ᵛ; TLN 1403) when Regan enters, to be joined by Goneril at line 187 (F1ᵛ; TLN 1476); both remain until the end of the scene, line 309 (F3; TLN 1613). The section in which neither is present is thus almost exactly the same length as the section in which both are present; yet the former contains seven of Duthie's 'memorial' variants, the latter six.[32]

Admittedly, that part of Walker's theory which implicates the boy actors who had played Goneril and Regan is something of a refinement on her basic postulate of a contaminating transcript from foul papers, but she was unable to find a correlation between 'bad' text and the presence of any other character – which is not surprising, since the scenes in which variants are relatively few (3.5–4.5, 4.7–5.2) employ the whole cast except France, Burgundy, and Curan. Curan's presence is limited to the beginning of 2.1, France's and Burgundy's to the second part of 1.1. In 1.1 QF variants are certainly not less frequent or significant before France and Burgundy enter (at line 187, B3ᵛ, TLN 202–3). An actor who doubled minor roles would not meet the demands of Walker's theory, because the less variant section of the text parades a full complement of extras – servants, soldiers, and attendants, besides a messenger (a gentleman in Q) and a doctor (a gentleman in F).

The more general objections to Walker's hypothesis are well known. The most telling is the improbability, remarked by Greg, 'that a couple of boys should have been able to get hold of the foul papers, still more that they should have found an opportunity to transcribe them in the playhouse, and if they were able to convey them to some more private and convenient place, there would be less need for haste and therefore less temptation to rely on memory'.[33] Moreover, transcription, even with some reliance on memory, seems altogether inadequate to explain such divergences from F as we find, for example, in Lear's opening speech.[34]

Walker deserves credit for helping salvage Q's reputation, but her theory of its provenance cannot explain the pattern of QF variants. Do recent developments point towards a solution? I believe they do.

Revision

Any satisfactory theory of the relationship of the Quarto and Folio texts must take account of the make-up of the printer's copy for the Folio. It now seems certain that F was influenced, in different ways, by Q1, Q2, and a manuscript. P. W. K. Stone has recently provided grounds for believing that an edited exemplar of Q1, with alterations and additions written in, was transcribed to form a prompt-book; that this manuscript itself served as copy for Compositor B's stints of Folio *Lear*, but that Compositor E set instead from an exemplar of Q2 that had been corrected by reference to this postulated manuscript.[35] Stone's evidence for Compositor E's use of Q2 has been reinforced by subsequent investigations, and now appears irresistible.[36] Stone's argument that B set from handwritten copy is also persuasive, though not yet of the same order of certainty. It depends upon the observation that misreadings tend to accumulate in parts of Folio *Lear* set by Compositor B. For instance, Q's 'armes' is preferred to F's 'names' (H3[v]; 4.2.17; TLN 2285) by almost every modern editor, and the F variant looks like a misreading. Conceivably the Folio compositor, intending to set 'armes', set 'rames', and this was subsequently miscorrected; though no such press variant is recorded by Hinman, the accident may have happened during an earlier stage of proofing.[37] But misreading seems more likely. Another Folio error in 4.2 ('threat-enrag'd' for Q's 'thereat inraged', H4; TLN 2319; 4.2.75) and at least half a dozen elsewhere appear to have arisen in the same way. Duthie was criticized by Greg for the frequency with which, in his 1949 edition, he postulated misreading of the playhouse manuscript by the collator, and consequent miscorrection of the copy of Q that he was attempting to bring into agreement with the manuscript: as Greg insisted, this sort of mistake 'cannot have been other than exceptional'.[38] But if errors of misreading already existed in the prompt-book, a collator comparing it with a copy of Q2 might have *transferred* them to his copy of Q2, rather than – as Duthie so implausibly supposed – perpetrating them himself, despite the aid to correct decipherment afforded by the printed text.[39] Consequently, apparent misreadings do not provide decisive evidence of the direct use of manuscript copy (though the fact that such errors cluster in Compositor B's stints remains suggestive).

Whatever Compositor B had in front of him when he set his stint of *King Lear*, the cluster of errors shared by Q and F in 4.2 seriously complicates our interpretation of the copy for the Folio. If B did work directly from the manuscript, those errors must have stood in the manuscript itself. But even if B worked, as did E, from a marked-up copy of Q2, one cannot credibly attribute to the collator's inattention the appearance of five shared errors within twenty lines, especially when those lines show so much evidence of the collator's careful intervention. We can only conclude that, though at least one and perhaps both Folio compositors worked from a marked-up copy of Q2, the prompt-book itself must somehow have been contaminated or influenced by Q1. Stone's suggestion – that an exemplar of Q1 was transcribed and revised to form a new prompt-book – therefore does not require us to accept either his uncertain conclusions about Compositor B's copy, or his implausible account of the origins of Q itself, or of the date and authorship of the Folio alterations.

Given the complex make-up of F copy, all the observed facts related to fluctuation in the rate of QF variants might be covered by a theory of revision. Let us assume that Q was set from Shakespeare's autograph and that 3.5 to 5.2 (roughly) of the manuscript was more finished than the rest of the play. Foul papers need not, after all, be uniformly 'foul', but can include relatively clean passages, either because of authorial transcription or because of greater ease in composition. Let us also suppose that Shakespeare, several years after the original composition of *Lear*, carried out revision by first annotating a copy of Q1.[40] It would be natural enough for him to rework most thoroughly the beginning and end of the play, attending less fully to the middle section where revision was now mostly a matter of deletion. We have seen that the bulk of the F cutting is of the

relatively invariant Acts Three and Four. Chapman's *Bussy
D'Ambois* supplies a suggestive parallel: the most substantial cut in
the 1641 text is in a scene in which variants are especially few (2.2).
Authors often think of cutting and rewording as alternative forms of
improving their work. They are also understandably solicitous about
the least nuances of beginnings and endings. For the dramatist
obliged to set a train of events in motion and bring them to a
conclusion, Aristotle's notorious tripartite division of a play's plot
has its practical realities. The first and last scenes of *Bussy D'Ambois*
are, like those of *King Lear*, among the most variant.

In revising Q, Shakespeare would be anxious to correct downright
errors throughout, but might overlook those not glaringly obvious,
especially in passages where his chief concern was simply to add or
delete. And to Qa's more or less indifferent variations from copy, as
restored in Qb, he might often be indifferent himself. Thus, faced in
4.2 with Qa's 'My foote vsurps my body' he might realize that 'foote'
ought to be 'foole', and yet be no less content with 'My' and 'body'
than some modern editors have been, even though Qb's 'A' and 'bed'
were the words he had once written. Similarly, Qa's 'whistle',
'seemes', and 'Iustices' are intrinsically quite acceptable, even though
probably not, on the evidence of Qb, the readings of the manuscript
copy for Q.[41] To a collator, mechanically transferring readings from
a manuscript to an exemplar of Q, all variants would necessarily have
been equal; but to the author, working on Q without recourse to
anything but his own memory and creative imagination, Qa readings
that were, strictly speaking, 'wrong' (in that they were compositorial
misrepresentations of the Q manuscript copy) would not always have
seemed so.

Shakespearian revision on an exemplar of Q would also explain
why QF variants due to misreading in Q remain frequent in parts of
the play where other variants are few (pp. 315–20 above).
Shakespeare would fairly consistently have corrected Q's misreadings, but his other alterations to the Q text would naturally cluster
within certain sections of the play.

Another feature of the variation between Q and F is most
satisfactorily accounted for by the theory of revision. In a recent
interview the actor Donald Sinden spoke of the reasons behind the
progressively increased cutting towards the end of the text for the
Royal Shakespeare Company's 1976 production of *King Lear*.
Audiences, he explained, will tolerate near the beginning of a play

longueurs that are unacceptable after an hour or so, when it becomes vital to maintain pace.[42] So it is significant that 80 to 85 per cent of the lines peculiar *to Q* fall within the last three acts, whereas 80 to 85 per cent of the lines peculiar *to F* fall within the first three acts. This means that both sets of changes to F – additions and deletions – shift the play's fulcrum slightly closer to the beginning. F's lightening of the later half of the play accords with the general view that the manuscript behind it had undergone intelligent theatrical cutting. But the distribution of matter peculiar to F is not easy to explain on the assumption that Q is memorially corrupt and that Q's 'omissions' are losses due to negligence and forgetfulness. Why should Act Four, where only one in fifty lines is missing from Q, be so much luckier than the rest of the play, where the proportion is one in twenty? But if the lines peculiar to F are mostly later additions, made in association with F's cuts, the pattern makes sense: Act Four, the most heavily cut act, is also the act to which least has been added, and this is precisely the point in any play where audience attention is likely to sag if the tempo drops. As Gary Taylor has demonstrated (in 'War', pp. 28–30), the F changes within 3.6 to 4.3 increase momentum, reduce Lear's time offstage, and intensify the narrative expectation of war.

E. A. J. Honigmann, challenging in 1965 the then prevailing eagerness to explain virtually all dialogue variation between substantive texts of Shakespeare plays as due to corruption, showed, with a wealth of detailed illustration, that where we have two texts of a poem or play, variants produced by authorial revision in one may closely resemble variants produced by corruption in the other.[43] Anyone who cares to examine successive autograph manuscripts of literary works can confirm this observation.[44] The wellnigh universal tendency of revising authors to vary phrases that are exactly repeated in an early version of their work, to shift words, phrases, lines, and longer passages from one part of their poem, story, or play to another, to emphasize by repetition certain key words and images, to work their utterance into more tidy metrical and rhetorical shape, to cut, paraphrase, enrich, and expand, and at times to tamper out of mere caprice, inevitably creates apparent evidence in the original text of anticipation, recollection, transposition, synonym substitution ('vulgarization'), omission, interpolation, and even metrical breakdown – all the traditional stigmata of a memorial report. Since much of the variation between Q and F can be proved due to revision,

Duthie's list of variants suggestive of memorial error in Q is best reinterpreted as consisting largely of Q readings later altered. I have been concerned so far with the distribution of QF variants and have mentioned their abundance in Act One. A careful examination of their character reveals that several in the opening scene are interrelated and that the Folio changes, which stress the political implications of Lear's fatal mistake, move the play further away – in wording, characterization, and dramatic concern – from its *Leir* source material. Corruption in Q could not have produced systematic differences that entail closer adherence to an early dramatization of the Lear story.

Variation in Act One, Scene One

As evidence of authorial revision in *Lear* Honigmann cited cases in which the absence from Q of small phrases present in F leaves Q metrically superior. As he argued, this phenomenon could hardly be the result of corruption in Q, since 'it seems unlikely that the men behind Q would repeatedly conform *by accident* to a pattern to which they proved themselves utterly insensitive'.[45] He deduced that Shakespeare himself introduced as afterthoughts the phrases that render F metrically less regular than Q. One of these examples will provide a convenient starting point for discussion of a few variants in 1.1.

At 1.1.245 Lear affirms to Burgundy his refusal to grant Cordelia a dowry: 'Nothing, I haue sworne, *I am firme*' (TLN 269; B4). I have italicized the metrically redundant phrase, which appears only in F. This highlighting of Lear's intransigence enriches some characteristically Shakespearian paradoxes centred on the idea of firmness. Lear is not, as Lady Macbeth accuses her husband of being, infirm of purpose, but he is mentally and physically infirm, and his very firmness with Cordelia and his firmness, or stubbornness, about his abdication are evidence of his mental infirmity. In his 'vnstooping firmenesse' (the phrase occurs in *Richard II*, Q 1597, A3ᵛ; 1,1.121) Lear is 'stoop[ing] to folly' (*Lear*, B3; 1.1.149). Shakespeare plays on these ideas. Lear warns Burgundy of Cordelia's supposed 'infirmities' (B3ᵛ; TLN 221; 1.1.202), of which the sole manifestation is the firmness of her response to his love test. Regan, alluding to her father, speaks of 'the infirmitie of his age' (B4ᵛ; TLN 318; 1.1.293), and Goneril of his 'infirme and cholericke yeares' (C1; TLN 323; 1.1.298–9).

At 2.4.105–6 Lear, with unconscious irony, considers the possibility that ill health is an excuse for Cornwall's failure to attend him: 'Infirmitie doth still neglect all office' (E4ᵛ; TLN 1382). This from the king who has abdicated so as to 'Vnburthen'd crawle toward death' (TLN 46; 1.1.41)! By 3.2.20 he sees himself as 'a poore infirme weak & | Despis'd ould man' (F4; TLN 1675).

The way in which Lear's blend of firmness and infirmity initiates the action is notably different in the Q and F versions of his opening speech. Q reads:

> The map there; know we haue diuided
> In three, our kingdome; and tis our first intent,
> To shake all cares and busines of our state,
> Confirming them on yonger yeares,
>
> > (B1ᵛ; 1.1.37–40)

F reads:

> Giue me the Map there. Know, that we haue diuided
> In three our Kingdome: and 'tis our fast intent,
> To shake all Cares and Businesse from our Age,
> Conferring them on yonger strengths, while we
> Vnburthen'd crawle toward death. Our son of *Cornwal*,
> And you our no lesse louing Sonne of *Albany*,
> We haue this houre a constant will to publish
> Our daughters seuerall Dowers, that future strife
> May be preuented now.
>
> > (TLN 42–50; 1.1.37–45)

'Shake off' meaning 'discard, rid oneself of' is common in Shakespeare, according to Schmidt's *Lexicon*, but *OED* cites no instance of 'shake' meaning 'discard' when not followed by 'off' or 'from'. So I interpret Q's 'of' in 'of our state' as primarily 'off', which gives a neat opposition with 'on' in the next line. In seventeenth-century English 'of' and 'off' were less clearly differentiated than they are today, and 'of' as a spelling of 'off' turns up in several Shakespearian good quartos.[46] Q's 'state' compresses several relevant meanings, including the political and the personal – not just Lear's kingdom, rule, and status, but his physical condition. F unfolds the implications in 'state', partly by developing the hint in Q's 'Confirming'. The Latin root was more fully present in the word for Shakespeare than for most modern readers, as is clear from such passages as 'whose strength | I will confirme with oath' in *Cymbeline*

(TLN 1221; 2.4.63–4) and 'Confirmd, confirmd, O that is stronger made, | Which was before bard vp with ribs of yron' in *Much Ado About Nothing* (Q 1600, G1; 4.1.150–1). F makes the latent content of 'Confirming' explicit by altering the semi-redundant 'yeares' to 'strengths', this change prompting the addition of 'while we | Vnburthen'd crawle toward death', which elaborates the personal motive to the point where Lear presents his abdication as almost a renunciation of the world, as he resigns himself to the second childhood ('crawle') of Jaques' last Age of Man. And of course F's 'Age' has already made explicit what in Q was conveyed in the antithesis between 'yonger yeares' and one sense of 'our state'. Having made manifest the latent content of 'Confirming', F can replace it with the more idiomatic 'Conferring', which stresses the act of donation, instead of suggesting (as does Q's verb) the ceremonial ratification of a decision already announced.[47]

The firmness of Lear's resolve is further stressed by F's 'fast intent', where Q has 'first intent', and by F's added 'constant will', each F variant implying that Lear has made up his mind and will brook no objections. Q's 'first' would be an easy misreading of 'fast', but may be defended as acknowledging, in conjunction with Q's plural 'purposes', that there are several linked reasons for the calling of this assembly: Lear is announcing his abdication, dealing with Cordelia's suitors, apportioning the kingdom, and calling for protestations of love.

F's added lines addressed to Cornwall and Albany clarify Lear's political motives – the wish to avoid civil war. Duthie thought their absence from Q the result of an actor's failure to remember them, yet in order to leave no trace of them at all an actor would have had to forget not only his words but also the simple gestures towards the Dukes that the words clearly require and that serve to acknowledge the presence of the two husbands and to single them out momentarily as the objects of audience attention. Besides, a theatrical function similar to that of these F-only lines is performed by another F-only line a little later in the scene:

> *Lear.*   . . . but now our ioy,
> Although the last, not least in our deere loue,
> What can you say to win a third, more opulent
> Then your sisters.
> *Cord.* Nothing my Lord.
> *Lear.* How, nothing can come of nothing, speake againe.
> (B2; 1.1.82–90)

> *Lear.*   . . . Now our Ioy,
> Although our last and least; to whose yong loue,
> The Vines of France, and Milke of Burgundie,
> Striue to be interest. What can you say, to draw
> A third, more opilent then your Sisters? speake.
> *Cor.* Nothing my Lord.
> *Lear.* Nothing?
> *Cor.* Nothing.
> *Lear.* Nothing will come of nothing, speake againe.
>
>   (TLN 88–96)

In Q, up until the point where Cordelia is told to speak, the names of all parties affected by Lear's procedure, and the relationships between them, are conveyed with the utmost economy. Cordelia's name is disclosed only through her use of it in asides. France, Burgundy, Albany, and Cornwall are mentioned once. F precedes these references with the F-only lines naming Cornwall and Albany, and follows them with the F-only line naming France and Burgundy, and thus helpfully identifies husbands and suitors twice.[48] In this second passage, the metonymy whereby Lear alludes to the princes in terms of their fertile lands places Cordelia's marriage in a political context (while at the same time beautifully adumbrating fruitful union). As Duthie says of the line and a half wanting in Q, 'An abridger would not gain sufficient from such a short omission to justify his trouble in adapting line [TLN 89; 1.1.83]'.[49] Certainly no theatre person, making deliberate cuts, would want to save five seconds at the expense of clarity in presentation to the audience. On the other hand, only by a very strange accident could a reporter's memory have failed to retain two brief passages that each carry visual cues, and that, though separated by some forty lines, are complementary in the contribution they make to the exposition in this opening scene.

I shall have more to say about this passage, but want first to revert to Lear's initial speech. A consequence of the late insertion of TLN 46–50 is the overloading, with fourteen syllables, of F's line 'May be preuented now. The Princes, *France & Burgundy*' (TLN 50; 1.1.45), where the text rejoins that of Q. E. A. Abbott notes that in Shakespeare's verse 'polysyllabic names often receive but one accent at the end of the line in pronunciation',[50] but none of the thirty lines that he cites is as long as this line in F, and there is no other fourteen-syllable line in *Lear*. Here again, as with 'I am firme' (TLN 269;

1.1.245), we have what appears to be an extrametrical afterthought.

A word of immense thematic significance, 'Nature', is insinuated, with some straining of syntax, at the end of Lear's first speech (TLN 58; B1ᵛ; 1.1.53). In F's addition to the scene of other key words we glimpse Shakespeare as conscious artist filling out those patterns of repeated words, ideas, and images with which twentieth-century criticism has familiarized us. The initial exchange between Lear and Cordelia is made more resonant by F's two extra tollings of that 'Nothing' which reverberates throughout the rest of the play, and Kent's parting words to Cordelia, 'The Gods to their protection take the[e] maide' (B3; 1.1.182), subtly foreshadow 'vnaccomodated man' (G2–G2ᵛ; TLN 1886–7; 3.4.106–7) once 'protection' has been altered to the Folio's slightly precious 'deere shelter' (TLN 196). Any one of these variants might be explained as due to corruption in Q, but it is not easy to believe that within the play's opening lines misfortune consistently discriminated against key words.

Another such thematic image is first introduced in the Folio's version of Lear's prelude to the love test. F's parenthetical spelling-out of the full political import of his abdication –

> (Since now we will diuest vs both of Rule,
> Interest of Territory, Cares of State)
> (TLN 54–5; 1.1.49–50)

– further amplifies Q's excessively condensed 'To shake all cares and busines of our state'; it also introduces, in 'diuest', the play's imagery of clothing and nakedness.

But the surest proof of revision is the interrelation between this parenthesis and three variants in the speeches of Kent. At 1.1.149 (B3; TLN 159) Kent urges Lear, 'Reuerse thy doome' (in Q), 'reserue thy state' (in F). Here Q conflates two passages from the old *Leir* play, in which Kent's counterpart, Perillus, referring to the disinheriting of Cordella, protests at 'this ruthlesse doome', and the King says, 'Cease, good my Lords, and sue not to reuerse | Our censure, which is now irreuocable.'[51] Greg showed that as Shakespeare wrote *King Lear* 'ideas, phrases, cadences from the old play still floated in his memory below the level of conscious thought, and now and again one or another helped to fashion the words that flowed from his pen'.[52] Duthie suggested that an actor's memory of Kent's words, as accurately rendered in F, was here distorted by his recollection of *Leir* – hence the Q version.[53] An actor may conceivably have taken part in both *Leir* and *Lear*, and his recollection of the former might possibly be strong enough to upset his memory of the latter; but since such an explanation is highly speculative, whereas we *know* that Shakespeare was familiar with the old play, it is far more reasonable to suppose that the memory of Shakespeare himself conflated the lines from *Leir* to produce a phrase that he himself had used in three of his early plays.[54] These considerations lead us back to Samuel Johnson's belief: 'I am inclined to think that *Reverse thy doom* was Shakespeare's first reading, as more apposite to the present occasion, and that he changed it afterwards to *Reserve thy state*, which conduces more to the progress of the action.'

The 'stoops'/'falls' variant earlier in the line bears witness to the same process. Kent says in F:

> Think'st thou that dutie shall haue dread to speake,
> When power to flattery bowes?
> To plainnesse honour's bound,
> When Maiesty falls to folly, reserue thy state,
> And in thy best consideration checke
> This hideous rashnesse
>
> (TLN 156–61; B3; 1.1.146–51)

Most editors prefer Q's 'stoops', which parallels 'bowes'. But 'falls' alliterates neatly with 'folly', and as Charles H. Gold has insisted, 'The Elizabethan doctrine concerning the fall of princes is a real and persuasive argument in favour of the Folio reading. The King, highest in the hierarchy of men, occupied a position which made his actions of the utmost importance to the rest of society. When Lear refuses to accept his responsibility and abdicates his position, chaos is come again.'[55] This simplistic appeal to the 'Elizabethan World Picture' nevertheless makes its point. In conservative tradition, as Gold declares, a king's abdication approximated a fall in the theological sense, a veritable sin. So the implications of the F verb fit well with the idea in 'reserue thy state', meaning 'retain thy royal dignity and power'; the F phrase expresses Kent's concern with Lear and his kingdom, which is why it 'conduces more to the progress of the action' (as Johnson put it) – that progress towards war which the Folio cuts in Acts Three and Four do so much to accelerate. Q's 'Reuerse thy doome' has an entirely different meaning, 'more apposite to the present occasion': it relates to Kent's obvious indignation at Lear's unfairness to Cordelia. Thus Gold's convincing argument in favour of 'falls' depends for its validity upon his acceptance – which is perfectly justified of course – of F's 'reserue thy state'. 'Falls' *is* the more appropriate verb in F; but in Q 'stoops', which suggests doddering old age (compare 'ould man', B3, 1.1.146), is better suited than 'falls' would be to Lear's error of judgement about Cordelia. F can afford to sacrifice the imputation of senility here because it has already interpolated 'crawle toward death' at TLN 46.

Both F variants in TLN 159, 'falls' and 'reserue thy state', emphasize the magnitude of Lear's *political* folly. Moreover, in Kent's final outburst F's 'reuoke thy guift' evidently refers to Lear's bestowal of the kingdom upon Goneril and Regan and their husbands, whereas Q's 'Reuoke thy doome' (which again echoes the *Leir* lines quoted above) presumably refers to Lear's judgement on Cordelia (TLN 178; B3; 1.1.164). Again the F version stresses Lear's more momentous blunder. In *Leir* Perillus is concerned at this stage only with the King's injustice to Cordella; so both the purport and wording of Kent's remonstrances strongly suggest that Shakespeare began by following his source and later revised so as to presage the broader repercussions of Lear's misjudgements.

Even the removal from F of Q's 'one bearing a Coronet', in the stage direction that marks Lear's entry (B1ᵛ; TLN 37; 1.1.33), works to the same effect. As Greg pointed out, if Shakespeare was responsible for Q's direction 'there is subtlety in the provision he makes. When Lear says to his "Beloued Sonnes" Cornwall and Albany "This *Coronet* part betweene you", he is bidding them share the executive office only; he retains on his own head the *crown* as symbol of "The name, and all th'addition to a King". This touch is lost in F, in which, since no provision is made, we must suppose that Lear takes the coronet from his own head to part between the Dukes.'[56] Perhaps this is to infer too much from an unremarkable *lacuna* in a stage direction, but the other four variants we have just examined seem undeniably the products of purposeful change in F, not accidental change in Q.

The major difference between the Q and F versions of the love test is that F, by spelling out Lear's motives, making him aware of the gravity of his actions, and foreshadowing their consequences, renders him more culpable, human, and forgivable. The behaviour of Q's Lear partakes of the brisk arbitrariness of myth and fairy-tale. F's Lear enunciates, if somewhat confusedly, the reasons for his actions, and is explicit about the full extent of his abnegation of power.

Q yields another echo of *Leir* where F does not, in the initial
exchange between Lear and Cordelia that I have quoted above. Over
three centuries Q's 'last, not least' has attracted the majority of
editors, who have argued no less plausibly in favour of their choice
than defenders of F in favour of theirs. The Q statement 'Although
the last, not least in our deere loue' provides a parallel with 'our
second daughter? / Our deerest *Regan*' (Bl^v–B2; 1.1.67–8). In F all
the weight of Lear's special fondness for Cordelia is placed on the
expression 'our Ioy', and 'Although' is less overtly logical. Q draws
on two widely separated passages in *Leir*, 'our deare loue' (used by
Leir as he rebukes Cordella for refusing to flatter him) and 'to thee
last of all, / Not greeted last, 'cause thy desert was small', with which
Leir turns to thank Gallia's courtier Mumford at the end of the
play.[57] Shakespeare's memories of these phrases evidently combined
with a reminiscence of his own 'Though last, not least in loue' (*Julius
Caesar*, TLN 1411; 3.1.189) to create the Q line, which he later
modified in order to incorporate the dramatically useful allusion to
France and Burgundy. In 4.4 Cordelia herself echoes Q Lear's 'our
deere loue' as she justifies her taking up of arms in defence of 'loue,
deere loue, and our ag'd fathers right' (I1^v; TLN 2380; 4.4.28).[58]

Conclusion

This brief discussion of a few interrelated variants, mainly from
passages that Duthie analysed as evincing Q's memorial corruption,
supports our earlier conclusions concerning the distribution of
variants. Above all, it shows how drastically an adjustment in our
expectations can alter the interpretation of what, as textual critics, we
observe. There was, in fact, a notable contradiction in the old attitude
to revision. Duthie, claiming that at the end of Lear's second speech
in Q we encounter a 'reading which we can confidently declare to be
non-Shakespearian', argued:

The word 'Nature' here [in F only] is of vital importance: by asking which of
his three daughters loves him most Lear is trying to discover in which of them
natural affection, the feelings binding kindred together, in a word, Nature, is
strongest. 'Nature' may be said to be a key word in this play: it is about
'Nature'. And here is the word, in a most apt context, in a context which
indeed calls for it, as the climax of Lear's first major speech. I have no doubt
that this represents Shakespeare's intention from the beginning, and
that . . . the quarto is corrupt. The conclusion of the speech is wrecked.[59]

It need hardly be said that Duthie's confidence that a key word cannot be introduced in revision, but must necessarily appear within a dramatist's first version of such a speech, is utterly unwarranted.[60] But my real reason for quoting Duthie's remarks is that they create a catch-22, because elsewhere he quoted with approval Chambers's forceful declaration that he could not 'reconcile with any reasonable conception of Shakespeare's methods of work a revision limited to the smoothing out of metre and the substitution of equivalent words, without any incorporation of any new structure or any new ideas'.[61] Duthie agreed that in revising his text Shakespeare would not have made exclusively trivial modifications; yet when, as at the end of Lear's first speech, he found F providing an additional concept that obviously enriches the meaning, he denied that it could be the result of revision. In other words, only variants of some importance could testify to revision, but if F contains something of importance that Q lacks, then it must have been in the text from the start but dropped from Q. It would be hard to argue the case for revision on those terms.

The prejudice against the notion of revision in *Lear* that could betray Duthie into such irrationalities was shared not only by Chambers, but by nearly all the most able textual critics of their time – Greg, Walker, and Kittredge among them. In order to sustain their attitude they had to ignore signs noted by Johnson close on two centuries before, neglect a convincing brief demonstration by R. H. Cunnington in 1910 that F-only passages are not accidental omissions from Q, and dismiss Granville-Barker's conviction, firmly grounded in practical experience of the theatre, that certain F cuts and additions represent Shakespeare's second thoughts, Q and F affording 'alternatives', so that 'to adopt both versions may make for redundancy or confusion'.[62] The Shakespearian scholar who looks back beyond current orthodoxies will often enough light upon forgotten truths in need of rediscovery and new formulation. That Shakespeare revised *King Lear* I take to be such a truth.

NOTES

1. For the first three bad quartos see W. W. Greg, *The Shakespeare First Folio* (Oxford, 1955), pp. 225–8, 299–309, 334–5; and for Q *Henry V*, Gary Taylor, 'Corruption and Authority in the Bad Quarto', in Stanley Wells and Gary Taylor, *Modernizing Shakespeare's Spelling, with Three Studies in the Text of 'Henry V'* (Oxford, 1979), pp. 124–62.
2. J. K. Walton (*The Quarto Copy for the First Folio of Shakespeare* (Dublin, 1971), pp. 116–17) examines and rejects the case made out by Richard E. Hasker ('The Copy for the First Folio *Richard II*', *Studies in Bibliography*, 5 (1952), 53–72) for some use of Q5.
3. Walton, *Quarto Copy*, pp. 242–5.

4. Stanley Wells, 'The Copy for the Folio Text of *Love's Labour's Lost*', *Review of English Studies*, 33 (1982), 137–47.

5. In the present volume, pp. 207–9, John Kerrigan plausibly argues that they are. There is a good discussion by Nicholas Brooke in the introduction to his Revels edition (1963) of the play, pp. lx–lxxiv. But my count of variants in *Bussy D'Ambois* is from the convenient textual appendix to Maurice Evans's New Mermaids edition (1965), pp. 113–26.

6. '*King Lear* – the 1608 Quarto', *Modern Language Review*, 47 (1952), 376–8; *Textual Problems of the First Folio* (Cambridge, 1953), pp. 37–67.

7. G. I. Duthie, ed., *Shakespeare's 'King Lear': A Critical Edition* (Oxford, 1949).

8. However, Paul Werstine shows (pp. 248–73, above) that she exaggerated the habitual inaccuracy of the Folio compositor(s) involved. Werstine's demonstration undermines Walker's account of the copy for Q just as seriously as it does her account of F.

9. *The Copy for the Folio Text of 'Richard III'* (Auckland, 1955), pp. 133–55; *Quarto Copy*, pp. 269–81.

10. Leo Kirschbaum, in his review of Duthie's 1949 edition (*Review of English Studies*, NS 2 (1951), 168–73), mounted a particularly devastating attack on his hypothesis about Q, and Duthie himself (in his New Cambridge edition of *Lear* (1960), p. 132) later abandoned it. Duthie had disposed of shorthand in *Elizabethan Shorthand and the First Quarto of 'King Lear'* (Oxford, 1949).

11. The lists are on pp. 46–67, 121–64. In *Folio Text of 'Richard III'* Walton's calculations were based on 329 pairs of variants, but in *Quarto Copy* (see p. 273) he excluded four involving speech prefixes. My references will be to Walton's presentation of his case in *Quarto Copy*.

12. On the more inclusive count I obtain proportionally fewer variants in Act Five than in Acts One to Three.

13. Walton excluded errors in F supposed to have arisen from a compositor's misinterpretation of the collator's correction of Q.

14. Walton does not give the raw figures upon which his Table (h) lines-per-variant are based. But the count for Table (g) variants is presented in *Folio Text of 'Richard III'*, p. 137 (four speech prefix variants must be subtracted from the total for Act Five; see *Quarto Copy*, p. 273), and the approximate number of Table (h) variants can be obtained by dividing the figures for lines per variant in each act into the number of common QF lines in each act in Duthie's edition, which Walton uses. Such a calculation yields a grand total of 926, which agrees with Walton's 'about 930'. Table (g) variants occur at the following rate per act: 126, 70, 57, 34, 38; and the remaining Table (h) variants thus: 160, 122, 96, 125, 98. These are the two distributions compared by chi-squared significance testing. Chi-squared = 27.4, 4 degrees of freedom, probability = less than 0.001. There is a simple description of the chi-squared test in Max Hammerton, *Statistics for the Human Sciences* (1975), pp. 64–72. Chi-squared is a standard formula for evaluating the statistical significance of the difference between expected and observed frequencies, the 'expected' frequencies being calculated as simple arithmetical proportions.

15. This list was made several years ago, and were I to repeat the exercise today many of my judgements would doubtless differ. My figures must be regarded as approximate, but my earlier criteria were consistently applied, and the subjective element in them was greatly reduced by my dependence on Duthie's notes. Duthie of course assumed that Q and F were witnesses to a *single* version of *Lear*.

16. Walton assumed that the Folio compositors worked from an annotated exemplar of Q1 in which the inner forme of sheet H, and the outer forme of sheets E, G, and K, were in the uncorrected state.

17. I have pointed out that Walton's Tables (g) and (h) are incompatible on his own theory. So perhaps I should compare the distribution of misreading variants with the distribution of Table (h), rather than Table (g), variants. If we were to subtract my misreading variants from those processed in Table (h), the table would read: 3.5, 5.1, 4.7, 5.9, 3.6. If we take this as indicative of a collator's changing efficiency, then in Act Four he was correcting no more than 59 per cent of the errors in his copy; which means that Act Four contains about 100 to 110 graphic errors, 40 to 45 of which were taken over into F.

18. If set throughout from Q2: 14.4, 9.5, 9.5, 9.4, 11.5. Ignoring variants between F and Q in only one of its states: 16.6, 9.8, 11.9, 9.6, 12.3.

19. W. W. Greg, *The Variants in the First Quarto of 'King Lear': A Bibliographical and Critical Inquiry* (Oxford, 1940); Fredson Bowers, 'An Examination of the Method of Proof Correction in *Lear*', *The Library*, V, 2 (1948), 20–44.

20. That early stages of proofing did take place is demonstrated by Blayney, *Origins*, I, 188–218.

21. However, Thomas Clayton makes out a good defence of Qa's reading, 'Old Light on the Text of *King Lear*', *Modern Philology*, 78 (1981), 347–67.

22. It would be unsafe to assume that he left the line completely unchanged and that the compositor was responsible for the alteration of 'foote' to 'Foole': the best the Q2 compositor could do in setting from Qa was change 'body' to 'head'!

23. 'Whistle', for example. In 'Four New Readings in *King Lear*' (*Notes and Queries*, 227 (1982), 121–3), Gary Taylor cites three new examples of possible error common to Qb and F; two of these, 'Tombe' (TLN 1409; E4^v; 2.4.131) and 'returne' (TLN 864; D2^v; 1.4.340), are close to substantial F additions.

24. Where an F omission or addition ends a scene, the first ten lines of the next scene are classified as category (a) text; but I completely ignored 4.3, which is in Q only.

25. Of Walton's nine straightforward common errors we would expect only two or three – (760 ÷ 2825) × 9 – to fall within category (a) text by chance alone.

26. However, the change might be authorial, if Shakespeare began his revision on a copy of Q1 which contained the Qa reading here. See Gary Taylor's discussion (below, pp. 364–5) of revisions apparently prompted by Q1 errors.

27. *2 Henry IV* presents in 4.1 a curious parallel to 4.2 *Lear*, combining unusually extensive additions to F with a paucity of QF variants and an exceptional number of errors common to Q and F. Also, perhaps coincidentally, both F *Lear* and F *2 Henry IV* contain many 'supererogatory hyphens' (Duthie, 1949, p. 192) in the stints of both compositors (B and E in *Lear*, B and J in *2 Henry IV*), and 4.2 Q *Lear* and 4.1 Q *2 Henry IV* are further linked by displaying more than their share of the total number of press corrections. See Walker, *Textual Problems*, p. 106 ('For some reason . . . from the quarto'); also pp. 100, 104–5. For a list of F cuts see A. R. Humphreys's new Arden *2 Henry IV* (1965), p. lxx; he notes F's 'unexpected hyphens' on p. lxxiv, n. 2. Q *2 Henry IV* was evidently set from foul papers, but the provenance of F, and its relation to the printed Q, are in dispute.

28. See Duthie's list on pp. 109–15 of his 1949 edition.

29. Duthie also details misassigned speech prefixes in Q (*Lear*, 1949, pp. 84–90). Their distribution per act is 4, 4, 0, 0, 6. My figures reckon a related series as one instance only. Of course, some of Q's attributions may be defended; so in this case we should perhaps speak of QF variation, rather than of undoubted defects in Q, as we may do when considering the omission of necessary stage directions.

30. All these figures are to the nearest whole number. They are for variants between F and Q in both of its states.

31. Walker, *Textual Problems*, pp. 43–4, 47.

32. In the middle section, where Regan is on stage, the rate of occurrence is roughly the same – four of Duthie's 'memorial' variants in about sixty lines.

33. Greg, *First Folio*, p. 382.
34. It might be suggested that Q was set from damaged foul papers that had been repaired by memorial reconstruction: the first and last scenes, which Walker considered most corrupt, would be written on vulnerable outer leaves of the original manuscript. Beaumont and Fletcher's *Philaster* survives in two texts: Q1 (1620) is generally inferior to Q2 (1622), and offers a widely divergent version of the first and last few hundred lines of the play; it seems clear that missing manuscript leaves were replaced by the patchwork of a theatre hack. The topic is discussed in Andrew Gurr's Revels edition (1969), pp. lxxiv–lxxxiv. However, nobody who denies revision in *Lear* should be especially eager to invoke the parallel with *Philaster*, because although Q1 of that play does suffer from corruption, 'comparison of Q1 and Q2 suggests also that they derive from different states of the authors' copy' (Gurr, p. lxxviii). An objection to any theory envisaging damage to the outer leaves of *Lear*'s foul papers is that within the first thirty-three lines variants between Q and F are few and trivial, and yet there seems to be nothing in the least unShakespearian in the wording of this prelude to the main action. *Lear*'s second speech, in which the QF variants are highly significant, would have shared a single manuscript leaf – and in part a single side – with the opening prose lines. Moreover, significant variation continues through most of the first half of the play: we are not dealing in *Lear* with isolated patches of major variation, but with a narrowing and broadening stream of variants (though this dries up into little more than a trickle for several scenes of Acts Three and Four). Joseph S. G. Bolton, 'Wear and Tear as Factors in the Textual History of the Quarto Version of *King Lear*', *Shakespeare Quarterly*, 11 (1960), 427–38, pointed out that some of Q's more significant divergences from F occur at approximately fifty-line intervals, and since most dramatists of the time penned about fifty lines on a manuscript page, he suggested that the lower edge (for example) of some leaves of the manuscript that served as Q copy had been torn, so that the last lines on both sides had disappeared until recovered by memory or guesswork. Because a prompt-book is the only manuscript likely to have suffered such damage, Bolton proposed (in the face of overwhelming evidence to the contrary) that the manuscript copy for Q into which corrupt readings had been imported as it grew illegible was a prompt-book. He listed nineteen Q 'omissions', of at least half a line, that occur within 41 to 58 lines of another Q 'omission'. But clearly many F-only passages might fall into these positions by chance. Bolton admitted that more than half of the F-only passages do *not* occur in the expected positions. Examining Q *Lear* I found that eighteen of the *stage directions* occur within 40 to 50 lines of another stage direction, and that the figure might be raised to twenty-eight if the permissible range were extended to 36 to 56. About one-third of Q's stage directions thus occur at Bolton's 'significant' intervals purely by chance. I conclude that chance alone would account for his evidence. Moreover, the fact that F-only passages are almost all structurally related either to other F-only passages or to Q-only passages argues strongly against accident as the cause of their absence from Q.
35. See Gary Taylor, pp. 354–67 below, and the remarks in my Appendix.
36. Stone, *Textual History*, especially pp. 254–80. Stone's case for Compositor E's use of Q2 is strongly confirmed by Gary Taylor, 'The Folio Copy for *Hamlet*, *King Lear*, and *Othello*', *Shakespeare Quarterly*, 34 (1983), 44–61; T. H. Howard-Hill ('The Problem of Manuscript Copy for Folio *King Lear*', *The Library*, VI, 4 (1982), 1–24) provides evidence that E was not setting from annotated Q1. My own collation of Q1, Q2, and F suggests that Stone is right, but the precise nature of the mixture for different sections of F copy may be indeterminable. (See Appendix.)

37. Charlton Hinman, *The Printing and Proof-Reading of the First Folio of Shakespeare*, 2 vols. (Oxford, 1963), I, 304–12.
38. *Modern Language Review*, 44 (1949), 399.
39. Gary Taylor makes the same point about misreadings in F *Troilus*, in '*Troilus and Cressida*: Bibliography, Performance, and Interpretation', *Shakespeare Studies*, 16 (1983), 99–136.
40. This supposition is further defended by Gary Taylor (below, pp. 354–95).
41. Editors repeat Greg's pronouncement (*Variants*, p. 147) that 'Iustices' is 'slightly ludicrous', but gloss Qb's 'Iustisers' as 'judges', which 'Iustices' also means. Is Greg's point that 'Iustices' is the more concrete word, evoking wig and gown?
42. Donald Sinden and J. W. R. Meadowcroft, 'Playing King Lear', *Shakespeare Survey 33* (Cambridge, 1980), p. 84.
43. E. A. J. Honigmann, *The Stability of Shakespeare's Text* (1965).
44. It is instructive to consider 'Kubla Khan', a poem allegedly written with a fluency which even Shakespeare might have envied. Coleridge's original version is preserved in the Crewe MS. (See John Shelton, 'The Autograph Manuscript of "Kubla Khan" and an Interpretation', *Review of English Literature*, 7 (1966), 32–42.) Comparing this with the printed version, incorporating the poet's minor revisions, we find a dozen substantive variants. It is not hard to guess why Coleridge made the twelve changes: he eliminated undesirable repetition of trivial words, subtly improved sound effects, enriched and clarified the meaning; but a scholar who had no means of knowing that the Crewe MS was Coleridge's original and who thought that it reported later corruptions of the original as preserved in print, could cite the following apparent evidence: two 'anticipations', one 'recollection', two enfeebling synonym substitutions, an incorrect numeral ('six' for 'five'), two singular nouns instead of plurals, a distorted name, and a grammatical solecism.
45. Honigmann, *Stability*, pp. 124–5.
46. *Romeo and Juliet* (1599) I3, 4.1.78; *Hamlet* (1604–5) N4, 5.2.57; *A Midsummer Night's Dream* (1600) F3ᵛ, 4.1.65.
47. Gary Taylor, *To Analyze Delight: A Hedonist Criticism of Shakespeare* (unpublished manuscript); Thomas Clayton (above, pp. 123–6). Taylor offers a brilliant critical analysis of the QF differences in Lear's conduct of the love test. My own account is restricted to a few of the points in an argument for revision that I evolved some fifteen years ago. Of course 'Confirming' may be a misreading here and at 1.1.82 (F 'conferr'd on', TLN 88; Q 'confirm'd on', B2), but it would have been a surprisingly happy error that so succinctly encapsulated the idea made explicit in F's 'strengths' and the added F line that follows. It also seems unlikely that the same mistake would have been made twice.
48. F is alone in having Lear speak Cordelia's name after their exchange: 'How, how Cordelia?', where Q has the testy 'Goe to, goe to' (TLN 100; B2; 1.1.94).
49. Duthie, *Lear* (1949), p. 27.
50. E. A. Abbott, *A Shakespearian Grammar*, third edition (1870), §469.
51. *The History of King Leir 1605*, ed. W. W. Greg, Malone Society Reprint (Oxford, 1907), lines 505–6, 567. See Taylor (below, pp. 367–76) for a full treatment of such echoes.
52. Greg, 'The Date of *King Lear* and Shakespeare's Use of Earlier Versions of the Story', *The Library*, 20 (1939), 397.
53. Duthie, *Lear* (1949), pp. 125–6.
54. *Titus Andronicus*, 3.1.24; *Romeo and Juliet*, 3.3.59; *The Two Gentlemen of Verona*, 3.1.224–5.
55. Charles H. Gold, 'A Variant Reading in *King Lear*', *Notes and Queries*, 206 (1961),

141. It is worth adding that 'folly falne' (folly-fallen) occurs in *Twelfth Night*, TLN 1279 (3.1.68).

56. Greg, *First Folio*, pp. 384–5, n. 27.

57. Malone Society *Leir*, lines 286, 2657–8.

58. There is a striking foreshadowing (reminiscence?) of *Lear* in Shakespeare's great Sonnet 124: 'Yf my deare loue were but the childe of state, | It might for fortunes basterd be vnfathered' (Q 1609, H2ᵛ), which almost certainly, in my view, belongs to the seventeenth century.

59. Duthie, *Lear* (1949), p. 25.

60. If the duplications in *Love's Labour's Lost* (1598) are authorial, they show Shakespeare inserting 'key words' into second versions of passages that in their original form lack vitality and rhetorical shape. There is a fine discussion by J. V. Cunningham, '"With That Facility": False Starts and Revisions in *Love's Labour's Lost*', in *Essays on Shakespeare*, ed. Gerald W. Chapman (Princeton, 1965), pp. 91–115. And if J. Dover Wilson, in his New Cambridge edition (1924) of *A Midsummer Night's Dream*, pp. 80–6, was right in his interpretation of the mislineation in Q (1600) at the beginning of Act Five, Shakespeare's revision there added much that is central to the play's themes.

61. E. K. Chambers, *William Shakespeare*, 2 vols. (Oxford, 1930), I, 298; as quoted by Duthie, New Cambridge *Lear* (1960), pp. 124–5.

62. R. H. Cunnington, 'The Revision of *King Lear*', *Modern Language Review*, 5 (1910), 445–53; Harley Granville-Barker, *Prefaces to Shakespeare* (1930; two-volume edition 1958), I, 329: 'On the whole . . . I recommend a producer to found himself on the Folio. For that it does show some at least of Shakespeare's own reshapings I feel sure' (p. 332). Cunnington had been partly anticipated by Koppel in 1877, but my knowledge of Koppel's arguments is restricted to what can be gleaned from H. H. Furness, Variorum *Lear* (Philadelphia, 1880), pp. 364–7.

APPENDIX

Printer's Copy for Folio *Lear*

THE combined efforts of Stone, Taylor, and Howard-Hill (as in p. 343, note 36 above) have established that Folio Compositor E was setting from marked-up Q2 copy. Stone and Taylor demonstrate the strong influence on Compositor E's stints of Q2's punctuation, and Howard-Hill the significant lack of influence of Q1's spelling. The question arises whether Compositor B was also setting from marked-up Q2 copy, but was characteristically less conservative than E in his treatment of its punctuation.

I have three reasons for thinking Stone probably right in his contention that Compositor B set his stints of *Lear* from manuscript based on Q1, rather than, like Compositor E, from an exemplar of Q2 that had been corrected with reference to such a manuscript.

(1) In quantity and quality the 'indifferent' variants linking F with Q2 are far more impressive for Compositor E's stints than for Compositor B's, as Taylor's careful analysis makes clear.

(2) If Compositor B was setting from Q2, he reproduced only 1 of the 47 semi-colons that it contains but Q1 does not, and only 16 of the 45 colons. The corresponding figures for Compositor E are 45 out of 65, and 53 out of 62. (I am relying on Stone's data.) Yet Compositor B was willing to set a great many colons, and a fair number of semi-colons, in his stints of F *Lear*. For example, the Fool's prophecy is peculiar to F, and the first 11 lines, at the foot of rr2^v, set by Compositor B (TLN 1734–44) contain 2 colons and 7 semi-colons. But perhaps Compositor B's normal practice was to restrict his setting of colons and semi-colons almost entirely to places where his copy had lighter punctuation? The available data do not support such a conjecture.

First we must supplement Stone's figures with those for colons and semicolons *shared* by Q1 and Q2. There are not many of these, because Q1's within-speech punctuation is almost confined to commas. Within Compositor E's stints 4 of 8 Q1–2 semi-colons and 7 of 9 Q1–2 colons (and all 5 Q1–2 full stops) reappear in F. Within Compositor B's stints the figures are none of 6 Q1–2 semi-colons, and one of 3 colons (and 2 of 4 full stops). This means that only 1 of 9 Q1–2 colons and semi-colons reappears in Compositor B's stints of F. When we add these figures to Stone's for stops in Q2 but not Q1, we find that if Compositor B was setting from marked-up Q2 copy he reproduced only 18 of its 102 semi-colons and colons.

For comparison there are figures available for Compositor B's treatment of copy punctuation in sample pages of *1 Henry IV* (set from Q5), *Titus Andronicus* (set from Q3), *Romeo and Juliet* (set from Q3), *Troilus and Cressida* (set from Q1), and in that final portion of *Richard III* which is generally agreed to have been set from Q3. The figures, from Gary Taylor's as yet unpublished *Toward a Text of Shakespeare's 'Richard III'*, are consistent from play to play. In total, Compositor B reproduced 28 of 54 copy semi-colons and colons. The difference between this control sample (28 agreements, 26 disagreements) and Compositor B's stints of F *Lear*, assuming use of Q2 copy (18 agreements, 84 disagreements), is highly significant from a statistical point of view (chi-squared = 18.25, 1 degree of freedom, probability = less than 0.0001). This strongly suggests that Compositor B was not setting from marked-up Q2 copy.

The one weakness in this argument is that Taylor's figures for the *Richard III* study do not discriminate between copy colons retained in F and copy semi-colons retained in F. So it remains just possible that (a) Compositor B was more reluctant to transmit copy semi-colons than copy colons, and that (b) Taylor's samples contain many more retained copy colons than retained copy semi-colons. This would help explain the discrepancy between our control sample and Compositor B's stints of *Lear*, where Q2 semi-colons, though not less frequent than Q2 colons, are far less likely to reappear in F.

(3) William S. Kable, 'Compositor B, the Pavier Quartos, and Copy Spellings', *Studies in Bibliography*, 21 (1968), 131–62, listed 126 spellings that normally reflect known copy in the Pavier Quartos of 1619, printed like the First Folio in Jaggard's shop. Kable's claim that the Pavier Quartos were set throughout by Folio Compositor B has been completely discredited by John F. Andrews, 'The Pavier Quartos of 1619: Evidence for Two Compositors' (unpublished Ph.D. dissertation, Vanderbilt University, 1971); Peter W. M. Blayney, ' "Compositor B" and the Pavier Quartos: Problems of Identification and their Implications', *The Library*, V, 27 (1972), 179–206; and Richard Knowles, 'The Printing of the Second Quarto of *King Lear* (1619)', *Studies in Bibliography*, 35 (1982), 191–206. But Kable's list, however erroneous the assumptions on which it was constructed, does appear to be tolerably reliable as a list of spellings that usually reflect copy when set by Compositor B: S. W. Reid, 'Some Spellings of Compositor B in the Shakespeare First Folio', *Studies in Bibliography*, 29 (1976), 102–38, has confirmed the reliability of several items. Kable himself found that all but 2 of 31 supposedly copy-reflecting spellings in Compositor B's stints of F *Love's Labour's Lost* did in fact occur in his Q copy, and in the course of some rough checking I have found similarly close matches between B's stints of F and the known Q copy for *The Merchant of Venice* and *Much Ado About Nothing* (42 agreements, 4 disagreements), *Troilus and Cressida* (25 agreements, 10 disagreements), and the final section of *Richard III*, where Compositor B is acknowledged to have been setting from Q3 (23 agreements, 5 disagreements). In *Troilus*, 5 of the disagreements cluster within TLN 778–1003, and 3 of the others involve a single repeated word, 'intreat'. In Compositor B's stints of *King Lear* there are 56 agreements and 11 disagreements with Q1, 38 agreements and 29 disagreements with Q2; 18 times F agrees with Q1 against

Q2, but F never agrees with Q2 against Q1. Given all the reservations that must be made about Kable's list – what we need is a new list based solely on Compositor B's treatment in F of known Q copy – this is dubious evidence for the influence of Q1, but it does rather strongly tell *against* any influence of Q2.

It is worth pointing out one implication that Stone's theory of F copy has for an analysis of the distribution of QF variants. Compositor B set most of the text of Acts Three and Four of F *Lear*, and Compositor E set most of the text of the remaining Acts. If Stone is right about the make-up of F copy, this means that most of the text of Acts Three and Four was set from a manuscript prompt-book dependent on Q1 (this being the kind of copy assigned to Compositor B) and most of Acts One, Two, and Five from an exemplar of Q2 corrected with reference to this manuscript (this being the kind of copy assigned to Compositor E). All manuscript variants not altered by Compositor B would thus have been transferred to F within B's stints, but if the correction of Q2 by reference to the prompt-book manuscript was imperfect, all manuscript variants within Compositor E's stints would not have reached the copy from which he was setting, and so would not have been transferred to F. So in Acts One, Two, and Five the prompt-book may have contained even more variants from Q as originally printed than is indicated by the amount of QF variation. And this would imply that the number of misreading variants between Q and the prompt-book was more constant from act to act than between Q and F, and the number of other variants even less so.

Finally, it should be added that it may well be possible to find alternative explanations of the association between QF common errors and added or deleted passages in *Lear*, without imperilling my argument that the fluctuating variation between texts largely reflects the amount of authorial revision. For example, any person whose attention was shuttling back and forth between a Quarto and a manuscript that contained some material not in Q and lacked some material that was in Q (a copyist or compositor working from both forms of the play at once, or a collator correcting Q with reference to the manuscript) might be especially prone to perpetuate Q errors at points where the two texts diverged. Howard-Hill's theory of F copy for *Lear* envisages just such a person – a collator-scribe, with both prompt-book and copy of Q2 at hand, attempting concurrent collation and transcription. He believes that 'by scanning first the quarto and then the manuscript to locate additions and corrections, the scribe would produce the melange of forms which characterizes the Folio text'. J. M. Nosworthy, *Shakespeare's Occasional Plays* (1965), pp. 128–63, argued that a similar feat of conflation must have been performed by the *compositors* who set F *Hamlet*.

But the essential point in my rebuttal of Walton's case for attributing all fluctuations in the incidence of QF variants to fluctuating efficiency of annotation, is that different kinds of QF variants are differently distributed. It is those variants least readily explained as scribal or compositorial for which the Act One and Four rates are most dissimilar; and the difference is that Act One has many more variants than Act Four of the kind that *must* be due either to memorial error in Q or to revision in F. (And in examining Walker's theory I give reasons for discounting the first of these two possibilities.)

King Lear
The Date and Authorship of the Folio Version

GARY TAYLOR

If the First Folio text of *King Lear* does indeed represent a deliberate
revision or adaptation of the version printed in the Quarto, then we
must seek not one date of composition, but two. The second period of
composition could have occurred any time between the completion of
the manuscript draft lying behind the Quarto and the day, sometime
in 1623, when two compositors began setting *King Lear* among the
Folio Tragedies. For the last seven years of this period Shakespeare
was dead; for perhaps three before that, he had been in retirement.[1]
The question 'When was the play rewritten?' thus inevitably raises the
question 'Who rewrote it?'. Indeed, even to speak of '*the* date' and '*the*
authorship' of the redaction presumes something we have no right to
presume: that all the changes between the Quarto and Folio versions
were made at the same time and by the same man. Those who object to
the division of the *Lear* kingdoms have not been slow to challenge that
assumption. Under the pressure of the work of Warren, Urkowitz,
Stone, and Blayney,[2] with their collective vindication both of the
distinctive coherence of the Quarto text and (excepting Stone) of its
apparent derivation from authorial copy, the centre of gravity in the
Lear debate has begun to shift: where before the Quarto was
suspected as a memorial construct and the Folio respected as the
descendant of a reliable (if slightly abridged and sophisticated) official
prompt-book, now the Quarto is itself becoming respected as the
direct descendant of an authorial manuscript, and the Folio challenged as a derivative, truncated, corrupt, and mangled bastard: a
thwart disnatured thing, of uncertain parentage. Handy-dandy:
which is the justice, which the thief?

Questions about the integrity and authority of the Folio text are
entirely legitimate. One may be somewhat disconcerted to see a
defence of the honesty of both texts lead to no more than a reversal of
opinion as to which is the liar; one may question the rational basis of
the editorial devotion to a single text, when that devotion can so
readily switch the object of its veneration; one may take exception to

the alacrity with which academics attribute textual corruption (whether they find it in the Quarto or in the Folio) to Shakespeare's fellow actors. Nevertheless, genuine uncertainties exist. Although the Folio version of the play must have been completed by 1623, all our other evidence for the date of *King Lear* pertains to only the first, original period of composition. Similar questions bedevil the issue of authorship. The Quarto text is specifically attributed to Shakespeare, whereas the Folio's is merely included in a collection which, most people now believe, contains at least one collaborative text (*Henry VIII*) and another which suffered posthumous adaptation (*Macbeth*).[3] The Quarto text appears to have been set directly from an authorial manuscript, whereas the Folio derives (perhaps at one remove) from a theatrical transcript, which could therefore have suffered unauthorized theatrical alteration as well as scribal corruption. The internal evidence for the authorship of the Folio alterations has never been investigated. Moreover, critical defences of the integrity, coherence, or even superiority of the Folio alterations by no means prove that Shakespeare made them: Shakespeare was not, after all, the only competent dramatist alive in England at some time between 1605 and 1623, and a critic as respected as Dr Johnson once regarded Nahum Tate's adaptation of Shakespeare's ending as an improvement.

Previous investigators, postulating the verbal authority of the Folio, have repeatedly castigated the Quarto merely for differing from it. But if we refuse to make this illogical assumption, and instead examine the Quarto on its own terms, we are equally obliged to examine, critically, the evidence, or lack of evidence, for the authenticity of the Folio variants. We have no right to assume Shakespeare's responsibility for them: rhetorical questions (even my own[4]) will not solve the problem. The evidence for the play's date, the evidence for its authorship, and – integral to both – the evidence for its relationship with its sources, all need re-examining. If there are two versions, there may well be two different patterns in the use of the play's sources, and perhaps evidence for two widely-separated dates of composition; if the Folio redaction is by another hand, there should be two different patterns of authorial characteristics. Dating the alleged Folio redaction is thus more than an exercise in establishing the chronology of the Shakespeare canon; it has become central to establishing whether that canon contains one version of *King Lear*, or two.

Any attempt to solve this problem must examine several disparate and difficult kinds of evidence: there is no single direct high-speed line of argument which will take us to our destination. I shall have to change trains repeatedly; some of the stages of the journey may seem interminable; some of the geography will be unfamiliar. But, reduced to its simplest outlines, what follows is a series of interrelated investigations of discrete kinds of evidence. I begin by examining the relationship between the Folio text and certain press variants in the Quarto. This is the most difficult part of the argument, but it is important, and I have tried to make it intelligible. When reconsidered in the light of recent evidence about what kind of text the Folio compositors actually had in front of them, these press variants apparently demonstrate that someone began rewriting *King Lear* on an exemplar of the printed Quarto text – an object which, of course, did not itself exist until 1608. Other arguments, considered in subsequent sections, buttress this conclusion. I survey the evidence for the influence, in both texts, of the play's various acknowledged sources ('Sources of Original Composition', pp. 367–76); I then explore the possibility that the Folio text may have been influenced by other, later sources ('Possible Sources of the Redaction', pp. 376–86). Next I examine a species of internal evidence (the use of rare words) which seems to provide a reliable guide to the chronology of Shakespeare's plays (pp. 386–93). Each of these investigations independently suggests that the manuscript consulted in printing F must have been prepared several years after the manuscript consulted in printing Q, and that Q was set directly from an authorial manuscript. In short, all of the available 'objective' evidence for dating *King Lear* identifies two distinct periods of composition, one in 1605–6 (Q), another in 1609–10 (F).

But though there were two periods of composition, there appears to have been only one author. In the last half of the essay (pp. 395–422), I concentrate on determining the authorship of the Folio's variations from the Quarto: first by an examination of image clusters, then by a survey of linguistic criteria used to distinguish Shakespeare from a number of other Jacobean playwrights. All of this evidence is compatible with Shakespeare's authorship of the redaction, and incompatible with redaction by any other identifiable Jacobean dramatist. After a consideration (and rejection) of P. W. K. Stone's argument against Shakespearian authorship, I also attempt to evaluate the hypothesis (central to the traditional case for conflating Q and F) that certain Folio interpolations, alterations, and omissions were made by playhouse agents, without Shakespeare's consent. Finally, I survey a variety of important literary and dramatic differences between Q and F, including some already individually canvassed by other critics, in an effort to provide a comprehensive working model of the strategy of the Folio redaction. This final section ('The Pattern of Revision', pp. 422–7) should, I hope, interest any critic of the play; but it is, necessarily, only one part of the larger argument that all the Folio alterations must be considered elements of a single process of redaction, begun three to five years after the play's original composition.

Finding the answers may be a complex and arduous business, but the questions themselves are simple, and so important to our understanding of the play(s) and the playwright that they deserve the effort they demand. Were there two periods of composition? If so, when did the second take place, who undertook it, and why?

Bibliographical Evidence

I have argued elsewhere that *King Lear* shows pervasive signs of the influence and stimulus of *Eastward Ho*, the 1605 collaboration by Jonson, Marston, and Chapman; if this perceived influence is real, the original composition of Shakespeare's play can be confidently dated no earlier than September 1605, after the publication of *King Leir* and *Eastward Ho*.[5] This dating would confirm that Gloucester's phrase 'These late eclipses in the Sunne and Moone' (C2; TLN 433; 1.2.103) alludes to those of 17 September and 2 October (old style). In what follows I will assume that Shakespeare completed his first version of *Lear* sometime between October 1605 and February 1606; this is, in fact, the traditional date.

Steven Urkowitz has suggested that the Folio alterations were made almost immediately, in the period between the completion of Shakespeare's first draft (preserved in the Quarto) and the première of the play (*Revision*, p. 147). This period provides the most obvious opportunity for authorial second thoughts, and Urkowitz's theory has the further advantage of supposing that only one prompt-book of the play was ever prepared. But this date can, I think, be positively ruled out. To begin with, the more successful Urkowitz and others are in convincing us of the extent and importance of the alterations, the less likely it becomes that Shakespeare would have entertained, so soon after completion, such a fundamental reworking of the play. The evidence of the rest of the canon reinforces these doubts: though there are nine other plays which survive in two texts each, one from foul papers and the other from a good theatrical manuscript (including several in which critics have discerned authorial second thoughts), in no other play are the changes so broad and deep, so extensive or integral to the dramatic structure.[6]

These doubts about the plausibility of an early date for the Folio redaction are confirmed by bibliographical evidence specific to *King Lear* itself. The proof is logically simple: the Folio text inherits certain apparently unauthoritative features of a document not in existence until 1608. The detailed evidence which supports this conclusion is, necessarily, rather less amenable to summary description. W. W. Greg's systematic survey of Quarto press variants first demonstrated a bibliographical link between Q1 and F; but new kinds of bibliographical evidence, only recently assembled and evaluated, rule out Greg's own explanation for this link. To arbitrate between the remaining possibilities, we must consider certain textual variants in gruelling detail; but such an investigation demonstrates, fairly conclusively, that the Folio text represents a later redaction of the version represented by the Quarto.

Forty years ago, W. W. Greg showed that the Folio text is in some way dependent upon the printed text of the Quarto: it repeats one or more Q1 errors and – more important – it reproduces a succession of unauthoritative Q1 press variants.[7] These press variants result from last-minute proof-correction undertaken while Q1 was actually being printed; consequently, some surviving copies of Q1 have the uncorrected state (Qa), others the corrected state (Qb), of these pages.[8] Moreover, any one copy of Q1 would almost certainly have some pages in the corrected and others in the uncorrected state; no single surviving copy consists entirely of corrected or entirely of uncorrected pages, but of a mix of each. Partly for this reason, it is possible for Peter W. M. Blayney to identify the copy of Q1 now in the New York Public Library as that once owned by Charles Jennens (*Origins*, II); equally, Greg can demonstrate that the 1619 Pavier reprint (Q2) was printed from a particular (lost) copy of Q1, one in which sheets D, G, and H stood in their uncorrected state. Neither Blayney's identification nor Greg's depends upon any conclusions about the authority or validity of the press corrections in Q1 itself; both involve no more than the recognition of a purely mechanical pattern, governed by the exigencies of early printing practice, and as such they can hardly be disputed. Greg's proof that the Folio has been in some way contaminated by the actual *printed* text of one of the early quartos is almost – though not quite – equally indisputable. If a press correction made in Q1 were authoritative, F's agreement with this correct reading would of course prove nothing about its relationship (or lack of relationship) with Q1; likewise, if a press correction in Q1 were *un*authoritative, we could infer nothing from F's agreement with the reading in the uncorrected state (or something similar to it). Greg's demonstration of F's derivation from or contamination by the printed text of Q1 therefore depends not only upon the mechanical pattern of variants, but also to some extent upon an interpretation of the authority of those variants. Fortunately, Q1 contains such an exceptional abundance of press variants, and their bibliographical interpretation is for the most part so straightforward, that the Folio's dependence in part on some exemplar of the printed Quarto text cannot be (and has not been) disputed.

The question still remains, *which* text of the Quarto: Q1 (1608) or Q2 (1619)? Greg thought he could pinpoint the influence on F of certain unauthoritative Q1 press variants not carried over into Q2: that is, the lost exemplar of Q1 from which Q2 was printed appears to have had a slightly *different* mix of corrected and uncorrected states than the quarto which influenced F. Greg therefore concluded that F had been contaminated by Q1 rather than Q2. The only plausible explanation for this fact, under the traditional assumption that there was only ever one authoritative version of *King Lear*, is that the Folio compositors were themselves working directly from an exemplar of Q1, one which had been extensively altered by reference to an authoritative manuscript. Greg's reconstruction of the derivation of the Folio text can be easily visualized thus (ignoring for a moment the relationship between the two lost manuscripts):

GREG'S STEMMA

Unfortunately, the recent work of P. W. K. Stone, T. H. Howard-Hill, and myself has made it unequivocally clear, on the basis of a whole range of objective tests, that the Folio compositors were *not* working directly from an exemplar of Q1.[9] They were instead working from a marked-up copy of Q2, or from some marked-up combination of Q2 and Q1, or from some combination of marked-up Q2 and a manuscript. In particular, Folio Compositor E was clearly working from a marked-up copy of Q2. The difficulty that this creates can be easily imagined, once we recognize that at least two *different* copies of Q1 (here identified as copy X and copy Y) have left their mark upon the Folio text:

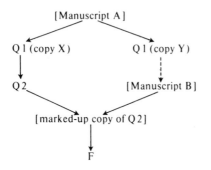

Three different sources have clearly contributed to F: a copy of Q2, copy Y of Q1, and Manuscript B. The nature of Greg's evidence (to which I will turn in a moment) makes it difficult to envisage how copy Y could have influenced F unless it had first contaminated Manuscript B.[10] We must therefore either (*a*) reject Greg's evidence that Folio *Lear* has been influenced by Q1 press variants which were not transmitted to Q2, or (*b*) explain how the authoritative manuscript consulted in printing F came to be contaminated by errors in the printed text of a book not published until 1608.

Greg's interpretation of the evidence seems to me clearly correct. Greg himself, of course, had no reason to be partial toward explanations which demolished his own belief that there was only ever one 'true' text of *King Lear*, and I see no reason to doubt the essential objectivity of his account of the relevant variants. The two variants central to Greg's own case for the direct influence of Q1 on F occur at 1.4.343 (D2^v; TLN 867) and 5.3.47 (K4^v; TLN 2990). Though Greg gave the first of these considerable weight, in isolation it is disputable. Even if, as seems likely enough, Qa's 'alapt' is an error for 'ataxt' (Greg's conjecture) rather than 'attaskt' (Qb), the variants 'ataxt' and 'attaskt' are indifferent, and must have been considered so by the Q1 press-corrector himself; consequently, the Folio's agreement, or more properly part-agreement ('at task'), with Qb could have resulted from authorial revision or compositorial substitution.[11] However, at least one objection to Greg's reconstruction here is actually removed if we assume (as Greg of course did not) that *Lear* was revised. According to Greg, someone annotating an exemplar of Q1 for use as printer's copy for F did not notice that this exemplar of Q1 read 'attaskt' where the manuscript had 'ataxt'; quite independently of this oversight, the error 'attaskt' was itself further corrupted, during the printing of F, to 'at task'. But if, as appears from a variety of purely bibliographical evidence, this annotator were instead marking up a copy of Q2, he had in front of him not the sensible 'attaskt' but the nonsensical 'alapt', which it would be most implausible to suppose that he overlooked. But in the course of 'correcting' Q2 by reference to his manuscript, he could himself easily have contributed to the eventual error in the printed text of F, in one of two ways: either he misread the manuscript 'attaskt' as 'at task', or the manuscript itself had, at some point in its transmission, acquired this misreading. Either explanation presupposes, of course, that the manuscript either contained a reading which derived from an unauthoritative press variant in Q1, or independently introduced the same variant.

The variants at 1.4.343 remain, in themselves, inconclusive (though they are better evidence if *Lear* was revised, than if it was not). But another variant on this page, not discussed by Greg, reinforces the first, as evidence that F has been contaminated by Q1. At 1.4.340 (D2ᵛ; TLN 864), Qb apparently leaves standing the error 'returne' (for conjectured 'retinue'), instead miscorrecting Qa 'after' to 'hasten'. F follows Qb in both places, but achieves metrical regularity by changing 'now' to 'no, no'.[12]

Manuscript (conjecture):	and after your retinue, now	my Lord
Qa, Q2:	and after your returne, now	my Lord
Qb:	& hasten your returne, now	my Lord
F:	And hasten your returne; no, no, my Lord

Again, the manuscript consulted in preparing printer's copy for F seems to have been influenced, at some stage in its transmission, by an unmetrical and palaeographically implausible 'correction' in Q1, a press variant only two lines above the suspicious 'attaskt'.[13] Thus, in two cases within three lines F reproduces a suspicious press correction in Q1; and since, in each case, the Folio compositor's printed copy (Q2) had the alternative reading, if the Q1 press correction is indeed an error then that error has somehow contaminated some other source consulted in the preparation of the Folio text. Since we have no evidence that anything but Q2 and a manuscript were used in preparing the printer's copy for F, the errors (if they are errors) could only have come from the manuscript.

Greg's second example is even more difficult to dismiss: Qa and F1 both omit the phrase 'and appointed guard', supplied in Qb. The press-corrector clearly did not invent this phrase; he must have retrieved it from the manuscript. The Folio thus agrees here with an accidental omission in the uncorrected state of Q1; Q2, the Folio compositor's copy at this point, contains the three words added in Qb.[14] Someone must therefore have deliberately crossed out the three words as they stood in Q2, presumably because the three words were not in his manuscript – in which case his manuscript must have been influenced, at some stage, by a copy of Q1 containing the uncorrected state of the outer forme of sheet K.

In fact, however we interpret this press variant, it demonstrates conclusively that the Folio text of *King Lear* represents a later version of the play. There are two possibilities. Madeleine Doran at one time tried to explain this Folio agreement with an error in Qa by arguing that the three words were ambiguously or marginally placed in the manuscript behind Q, and that this ambiguity resulted in their being overlooked by both the original Q compositor and the scribe who prepared the prompt-book.[15] This explanation applies, of course, only if Q was printed from Shakespeare's foul papers, which would also lie behind the eventual prompt-book: the agreement in error of Qa and F would then derive from an ambiguity in their common ancestor.

DORAN'S STEMMA (*modified by new Q2 evidence*)

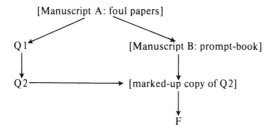

[Manuscript A: foul papers]

Q1   [Manuscript B: prompt-book]

Q2 ⟶ [marked-up copy of Q2]

F

But if Q1 were instead printed from a memorial reconstruction, the manuscript from which it was printed would have no direct relationship with Shakespeare's foul papers; to explain the common omission of these words in both Qa and F, one would have to posit an absolutely incredible coincidence.[16] Therefore, if Q1 *were* a 'bad' quarto (as Greg believed), this variant would establish, almost incontrovertibly, that someone undertook a redaction of the play after 1608, for some reason beginning that redaction from a copy of Q1, presumably because no better text was available. This is, essentially, Stone's hypothesis, though he does not himself recognize the importance of this variant.[17]

STONE'S STEMMA (*simplified*)[18]

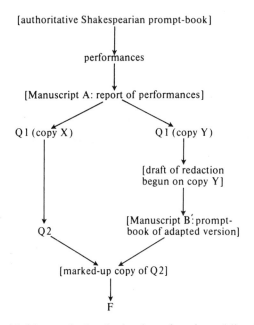

[authoritative Shakespearian prompt-book]

performances

[Manuscript A: report of performances]

Q1 (copy X)   Q1 (copy Y)

[draft of redaction begun on copy Y]

Q2   [Manuscript B: prompt-book of adapted version]

[marked-up copy of Q2]

F

One can avoid this conclusion (redaction after the publication of Q1) only by positing that the common error originates in the ambiguity of a common ancestor; this defence in turn presumes that Q1 was printed from an authoritative manuscript; if Q1 was printed from an authoritative manuscript, then in order to account for the massive differences between Q and F one must accept that someone rewrote the play extensively at some point between the completion of that manuscript and the preparation of the prompt-book behind F. In other words, either explanation forces one to the conclusion, on purely bibliographical evidence, that the Folio *must* represent a deliberate redaction of the Quarto.

The date of that redaction, as distinct from its existence, depends upon our interpretation of the Folio's agreement with Qa at 5.3.47. Once the existence of two versions is accepted, Doran's hypothesis (ambiguity in the foul papers) can be supplemented by Stone's (that the three words were deliberately cut, in the rewriting). Nevertheless, both explanations seem to me unconvincing: both presume the coincidental omission of a three-word phrase, required by the metre – an omission, moreover, which could not have resulted from any of the common sources of such errors (haplography, eyeskip, memorial omission of common short words). If Doran is right, the half-line must have been either an afterthought added in the margin of the manuscript, or an undesirable first shot ambiguously deleted. This hypothesis therefore presumes a particular and otherwise indeterminable process of composition, combined with the supposition that the results of that process were inadequately and misleadingly indicated on the paper, and also the supposition that both an Okes compositor and a scribe were identically misled – which in turn virtually presumes that Shakespeare did *not* prepare his own fair copy of the foul papers behind Q (in which case, when and how did he make his revisions?).[19] Though such a sequence of events can hardly be dismissed as impossible, it certainly can be described as relatively improbable. Stone's alternative is equally unattractive: it presupposes that the adapter deliberately excised the same three sensible and metrically necessary words that had been accidentally omitted by a compositor. Stone's excuse for this cut is that the phrase creates an ambiguity:[20]

> To send the old and miserable King
> To some retention, and appointed guard,
> Whose age has charmes in it, whose title more,
> To pluck the common bossome . . .

Stone points out that 'guard' might be wrongly taken as the antecedent of 'Whose age', as 'retention' alone could not be (*Textual History*, pp. 237–8). In the first place, this ambiguity is more apparent than real, in that 'the old . . . King' makes it fairly obvious whose 'age' and 'title' is being discussed; in the second place, such ambiguities abound in Shakespeare's work, to a degree that makes it impossible to believe that he (or his contemporaries) would have been disturbed by it; in the third place, anyone absolutely intent on removing the ambiguity could easily do so by transposing the two lines beginning with 'To' ('To some retention and appointed guard | To send the old and miserable King, | Whose age . . .'). The ease of this alternative solution to the supposed problem, a solution which does not result in the creation of a relatively rare incomplete part-line in the middle of a speech, makes it extremely difficult for me to believe that the Folio agreement with Qa's error results from artistic choice.[21]

The simplest and most plausible explanation remains Greg's, that F's agreement with this error in Q1 is the consequence of F's derivation from a copy of Q1 containing the uncorrected state of outer K. Greg has been proved wrong only in his belief that this derivation resulted from the direct use of Q1 by the compositors setting F. Since Q1 was *not* the compositor's copy for this portion of F, it follows that Q1's influence at 5.3.47, 1.4.343, and 1.4.340 *must* have been exerted on the actual manuscript. This in turn means that at some point someone must have completely transcribed the text of Q1, and that this transcription directly influenced the manuscript which was used or consulted in preparing the Folio text. But why would anyone have transcribed Q1, and why should this transcription have influenced the theatrical text used by Jaggard in 1623? Though there are a few cases where part of a printed text is known to have been subsequently transcribed (though usually only to patch an existing but defective text[22]), the most economical and plausible explanation for this very peculiar state of affairs is that the process of rewriting was actually begun on or from a copy of Q1 – in which case, of course, the rewriting could not have been begun before 1608, when Q1 was printed.

A re-examination of other Quarto press variants confirms this interpretation. In sheet D, for instance, Greg's own evidence for the influence of Qb on F led him to reject two Q1 press corrections which have every appearance of being authoritative, and which had been preferred by most earlier editors, but which F rejected in favour of the Qa alternative: Qb 'poyse' for Qa/F 'prise' (D4ᵛ; TLN 1063; 2.1.120), and Qb 'lest' for Qa/F 'best' (D4ᵛ; TLN 1066; 2.1.123). On Greg's hypothesis the Folio collator must have deliberately struck out the Qb readings here, and transcribed 'prize' and 'best' from his manuscript; but we now know that 'prize' and 'best' actually stood in Compositor E's Q2 copy, so the collator need only have overlooked them (as he easily could have done). Greg presumes that all of the Folio agreements with suspicious press variants in Q1 derive from a single source, the use of Q1 copy by the Folio printers, but this hypothesis has been ruled out by subsequent bibliographical investigations, and in any case leaves two variants in sheet D difficult to explain. The alternative hypothesis, that Folio agreements with suspicious press variants in Q1 derive from two sources (Q2 copy, and a manuscript influenced by Q1), not only explains all the new bibliographical evidence, but also accounts for these two apparent anomalies in Greg's own analysis.

All the preceding examples have been taken from passages set, in the Folio, by Compositor E, because in E's case the dependence upon Q2 is manifest. In B's stints there is, with the exception of one column (rr6^{v}b), less evidence of dependence on Q2, and some reason to believe that in places he was working directly from the manuscript. Given the current state of information, complete confidence is impossible, but two anomalies at least deserve mention. First, the Folio shows unmistakable evidence of derivation from the uncorrected state of sheet H; B set all of the Folio text corresponding to this Quarto sheet. If B was indeed working from manuscript (as seems, for at least part of this sequence, highly probable[23]), then the series of agreements between Qa and F can only be explained by assuming that Qa influenced that manuscript. In particular, as MacD. P. Jackson has pointed out (above, pp. 321–9), the cluster of agreements between F and Qa in twenty lines of F 4.2 seems in itself to establish Qa's influence upon the Folio's manuscript, regardless of whether Compositor B himself was using printed copy. Second, for sheet I there are no press variants in the surviving copies of Q1; but one Q2 reading has sometimes been defended on the grounds that it represents such a variant, preserved in the exemplar of Q1 from which Q2 was itself set. All surviving copies of Q1 read:

> *Lear.* No seconds, all my selfe, why this would make a man
> of salt to vse his eyes for garden waterpots, I and laying Autums
> dust.
> *Lear.* I will die brauely like a bridegroome, what?
>
> (I4^v; 4.6.194–8)

Between these two speeches Q2 interposes a speech by the Gentleman, fitting it in on the last line of Lear's first speech:

> of falt to vfe his eyes for garden water-pottes, I and laying Au-
> tumnes duft.   *Gent.* Good Sir,
> *Lear.* I will dye brauely like a Bridegroome. What, I will bee

(13ᵛ)

This is, of course, precisely what a press-corrector would have to do,
if he discovered the error in Q1, and did not want to increase the
number of lines on a page already set in type. But F reads differently:

> *Lear.* No Seconds? All my selfe?
> Why, this would make a man, a man of Salt
> To vse his eyes for Garden water-pots. I wil die brauely,
> Like a smugge Bridegroome . . .

(TLN 2638–41)

Greg advances two arguments against the supposition that Q2 here
represents the survival of an otherwise lost Q1 press correction. But
one of these is retracted in his own postscript (*Variants*, p. 192); the
other is that the passage is rewritten in F (p. 189). This second point
has, of course, no validity, unless one assumes, a priori, that *Lear* was
never rewritten – an assumption Greg consistently, and uncritically,
makes. If one does not make that assumption, Q2's added speech is
most plausibly explained as a necessary press correction which
happens not to be represented in any of the handful of surviving
copies of Q1, while F might easily arise from redaction in a
manuscript in some way contaminated by the uncorrected state of
Q1's sheet I.[24] Certainly, if we accept the authority of Q2's addition,
then the manuscript must have been contaminated by Q1, because B
was at this point either working directly from that manuscript, or
from a copy of Q2 (in which the addition must have been deliberately
struck out, because it was not in the manuscript).

The supposition that the process of redaction which culminated in
the Folio text began on or from a copy of Q1 thus rests not only upon
what seems to me the most plausible interpretation of the variants at
1.4.340, 1.4.343, and 5.3.47, but upon a whole series of links between
F and variant sheets of Q1. And Stone provides yet more evidence for
this hypothesis, in the form of variant readings where the Folio text
seems to result from an attempt to make sense of a Q1 error: the writer
either did not know or did not remember (or did not care to preserve)
what probably stood behind the Quarto misreadings, and instead
slightly rewrote the passage, thereby making sense of it – but a sense

slightly different from that which seems to have been originally intended.[25] One can dispute some of the readings which Stone cites as evidence, and occasionally one can find a rather similar variant in other texts where this textual hypothesis cannot be credibly invoked;[26] but for a significant number of variants this seems to me the most plausible and probable explanation of the Folio reading. In any case, these variants simply reinforce the purely bibliographical evidence that a transcription of Q1 must be postulated as an ancestor of the theatrical text underlying F1.

Why would anyone setting out to rework *King Lear* begin from a copy of Q1? There seem to me only two attractive explanations for this procedure. Stone proposes that the company's prompt-book was lost in the fire which destroyed the Globe in 1613. This hypothesis explains the need for a new prompt-book; if – unlike Stone – we assume that Shakespeare's own foul papers had already left the company's hands (to serve as printer's copy for Q1), then the company would have possessed neither prompt-book nor foul papers, and so might reasonably have resorted to Q. Of course, this reconstruction virtually presupposes that Shakespeare did not himself contribute to the Folio redaction; it also assumes, more objectionably, that the company would have felt that Q1 *needed* adapting, verbally and theatrically, before it could be used as a prompt-book. Alternatively, the redaction may be Shakespeare's, in which case we have no need to postulate the loss of the original prompt-book. Sometime after 1603 Shakespeare began to spend less time in London acting, and more time in Stratford with his family.[27] If, at some point in or after 1608, he had decided to revise *Lear* during one of these sojourns in Stratford, he could hardly have taken the prompt-book with him: the company might need it in his absence, or he might lose it, and in any case he had no advance guarantee that the company would approve of his mutilating it. If he could not take the prompt-book, and could not take the foul papers (which had been sold), the only text of his play he could have taken with him was an exemplar of Q1 – printed, he would have known, from his own foul papers. He could annotate, revise, blot, and dirty a copy of Q1 as much as he wanted, without committing himself or the King's Men to anything; and if, when he had finished, the result seemed to him worth presenting to his fellow sharers as a new version of the play, then at some point he or someone else would have had to transcribe a new fair copy from Shakespeare's own heavily marked-up exemplar of Q1.

This second reconstruction is, I believe, what actually happened.[28] However, as yet we have no evidence which allows us to arbitrate between Stone's hypothesis and my own, and for the moment we need not choose between them, because either accounts for the evidence that the Folio redaction began from an exemplar of Q1. My own hypothesis may be visually summarized thus:

PROPOSED STEMMA

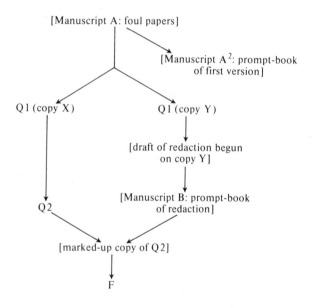

[Manuscript A: foul papers]

[Manuscript A^2: prompt-book of first version]

Q1 (copy X)

Q1 (copy Y)

[draft of redaction begun on copy Y]

Q2

[Manuscript B: prompt-book of redaction]

[marked-up copy of Q2]

F

The conclusion that the Folio represents a new version of the play, and one begun from an exemplar of Q1, provides a simple explanation for the complex and apparently conflicting evidence as to the nature of the Folio copy – evidence impossible to account for on the assumption that there was only ever one 'true' text of Shakespeare's play. More particularly, this evidence firmly dates the Folio redaction sometime after the publication of Q1, in January 1608 (new style).[29] Since we know from the Stationers' Register that a version of the play was performed at court in December 1606, this means that at least thirteen months must have separated the première of the first version and the commencement of work on the second. In fact, this may be a rather serious underestimate, since (as I have said) the original version was probably completed by early 1606 – which would leave a minimum two-year gap between the two periods of composition.

Sources of Original Composition

But even assuming a gap of only thirteen months, and assuming furthermore that Shakespeare himself was responsible for the Folio redaction, we have no reason to expect that the sources which influenced the original composition of the play would also strongly influence its revision. Indeed, if it could be shown that the Folio additions and alterations were repeatedly indebted to verbal details in the same sources which clearly left their mark on the Quarto text, the traditional hypothesis of a single ur-text would be strongly reinforced. One can go even further: if Q1 was indeed a 'bad quarto' (as the traditional view alleges), suffering from memorial corruption or some other form of unauthorized transmission, then the Folio variants should be consistently closer to the known sources, as happens unmistakably in other plays surviving in bad quartos. And if on the one hand we would not expect the original sources to be much in evidence in the additions and alterations of the revised text, on the other it is at least possible that new sources for that revision might be found, sources which show no signs of having influenced the original composition.

None of the dozens of parallels I have recently pointed out between *Eastward Ho* and *King Lear* occur in portions of the text unique to the Folio; several, however, occur in passages unique to the Quarto. Generally this is true of all the play's recognized sources. Of the forty-odd parallels Greg counts between Shakespeare's play and the anonymous *King Leir*,[30] or the dozens Muir collects from Harsnet,[31] or those singled out by Bullough in these and other accepted sources,[32] virtually none is unique to F. Where Quarto and Folio differ, the earlier text is consistently closer to the source.

Of Greg's alleged parallels with *Leir*, only one is even arguably closer to F: Leir's 'Why how now, Minion, are you growne so proud?' (*Leir* 285). F at about the same point has 'How, how *Cordelia*? Mend your speech a little' (TLN 100; 1.1.94), where Q has 'Goe to, goe to, mend your speech a little' (B2). But, aside from the fact that 'how, how' is not 'how now', Q itself (but not F) has already used *Leir*'s 'how' in Lear's preceding speech ('How, nothing can come of nothing, speake againe'). What happens between Q and F is simply a repositioning of the interjection, a postponement of Lear's first emotional burst – which hardly presupposes consultation or memory of the original source.

Bullough, among his notes, adds two more passages from *Leir* which he compares to lines found only in F.

> Wherefore, my Liege, my censure deemes it best,
> To match them with some of your neighbour Kings . . .
> By whose vnited friendship, this our state
> May be protected 'gainst all forrayne hate.
>
> (*Leir* 51–5)
>
> And pale grym death doth wayt vpon my steps
> (*Leir* 227)

The first of these Bullough compares to Lear's desire to prevent 'future strife' (TLN 49; 1.1.44), a motive made explicit only in F. But to prevent that strife Shakespeare's Lear intends only to 'publish' his daughters' dowers, not to ally himself by marriage to foreign kings: Cordelia's proposed betrothal to France or Burgundy is never given an explicit political motive, in either text. Albany and Cornwall are in any case not kings but dukes in Shakespeare's play, and already married; Lear hopes to prevent civil war rather than foreign invasion. As for Bullough's second alleged parallel, it bears only the vaguest resemblance to Lear's expressed intention to 'crawle toward death' (TLN 46; 1.1.41); the images could hardly be less alike.

Of Muir's collection of parallels from Harsnet (including many, from 3.6 and 4.1, which are omitted from the Folio), only a handful show possible Folio cognizance of the source. One is the word 'meiney' (TLN 1311; 2.4.35), where Q has 'men' (E3ᵛ). But Q's line is itself metrically defective ('They summond vp their men, straight tooke horse'), and a compositor could easily have misread the rare word 'meinie' as the common one 'menne', thereafter normalizing its spelling to 'men'. No more is involved than a simple confusion of minims (*nn* for *ini*). Likewise with some of the names of the devils. Harsnet has Smolkin, F Smulkin (TLN 1919; 3.4.140), Q snulbug (G2ᵛ); Harsnet has Fliberdigibbet, F Flibbertigibbet (TLN 1895; 3.4.115), Q *fliberdegibek* (G2ᵛ state b; *Sriberdegibit* G2ᵛ state a; Q2 *Sirberdegibit* F4ᵛ) and *Stiberdigebit* (H3; 4.1.61; *not in* F); Harsnet has *Frateretto*, F *Fraterretto* (TLN 2004; 3.6.6), Q *Fretereto* (G3ᵛ). Nonce names like these are exceptionally easy for a compositor to misread, especially if he is working from foul papers in an unfamiliar hand. This explains why Q gets the names wrong; perhaps more difficult to see, given the hypothesis that the revision began on Q itself, is why F gets them 'right'. But even F does not exactly reproduce the Harsnet form; in the case of *Fliberdigibbet* – since we cannot determine whether F derives from the corrected or uncorrected state of this Q forme[33] – it is even debatable which text is closer to Harsnet: all three occurrences of the name in Q have Harsnet's medial *d* where F has *t*. On the other hand, the correction of *Fretereto* to *Fraterretto* and the half-correction of Q 'snulbug' to 'Smulkin' do look like evidence of a memory of the Harsnet form; but if a nonce name is likely to mislead a compositor, it is equally likely, by virtue of its very singularity, to stick in the memory of someone who has once learned it, or been struck by it. Whether that someone was Shakespeare himself, or an actor, we have no way of determining.

Alternatively, one could also explain the Folio corrections '*Fraterretto*' and 'Smulkin' by assuming that, after the redaction had been transcribed from a marked-up copy of Q1, that transcription was itself compared, at some stage, with a prompt-book of the original version. This seems to me a cumbersome and otherwise unnecessary hypothesis; even if such a comparison were undertaken, I doubt that '*Fretereto*' or 'snulbug' would have been caught by it. If the writer was Shakespeare himself, no such process of consultation, or renewed familiarity with Harsnet, need be presumed; if some other dramatist, it must be. But whatever its implications for the authorship of the redaction, or for the textual prehistory of F, this half-return to Harsnet's form for two devils' names does not in any way embarrass the conclusion that there are two distinct versions of the play, the second produced thirteen months or more after the first. After all, Shakespeare echoed Harsnet as late as *The Tempest*;[34] to suggest that Shakespeare could have partially recalled a queer devil's name from Harsnet's book, years after he read it, need strain no one's credulity – especially as he would in the interim have heard the name repeatedly in performance. Moreover, the very grotesqueness of the Q distortion could have drawn his attention to it, and thereby cued his memory.

For the two other Folio parallels mentioned by Muir, the Quarto text is again explicable as a misreading of the same word: 'Conspirant' (TLN 3090; 5.3.136) where Q has the evident nonsense 'Conspicuate' (L1ᵛ), and 'ruffle' (TLN 1604; 2.4.301) where Q has 'russel' (F3). Of course this last is hardly a very persuasive parallel anyway: Shakespeare needn't have read Harsnet for 'ruffle', which in any case appears once elsewhere in a passage common to Q and F (H1; TLN 2107; 3.7.41). Typographically, moreover, 'ruffle' would be an easy error for 'ruffle', since the ffl and ffl ligatures were adjacent in the typecase.

One other probable source for the vocabulary of *King Lear* is Florio's 1603 translation of Montaigne: Muir collects a number of unusual words and parallel passages which betray Florio's possible influence. None of the parallel passages occurs only in the Folio, and of the list of parallel words – which 'should be received with caution', as Muir himself warns – only two seem potentially significant: 'bastardizing' (TLN 461; 1.2.133; Q 'bastardy', C2^v) and 'interest', from the verb 'interess' (TLN 91; 1.1.85; *not in Q*). But even if we accept these as borrowings from Florio's translation, Montaigne was a major influence on Shakespeare from *Hamlet* on, one of the most famous borrowings coming as late as *The Tempest*. Moreover, the word 'interess'd' also occurs in a passage of Holinshed that Shakespeare almost certainly read when working on *Macbeth*.[35] The two minimal links with Montaigne are thus of no value in establishing the date of the Folio variants.

Since none of the play's other acknowledged sources produces any links unique to the Folio text, we are left with six words in Harsnet (all explicable as the correction of misreadings in Q) and three alleged parallels with *King Leir* (none at all convincing). Anyone familiar with the wealth of specific verbal links with the known sources will appreciate the paucity of this evidence. And against this, even if we ignore the multitude of cases where Q passages clearly indebted to *Leir* or Harsnet or *Eastward Ho* are simply omitted in F, we can set at least ten cases where, when the two texts differ, Q is closer to the acknowledged sources than F. Some of these ten can be quickly dismissed as errors, or possible errors, in F itself: it would be foolish to base a textual hypothesis on Q's agreeing with Harsnet on 'wind' (E3; 2.3.12) where F has 'Windes' (TLN 1263), or Q's agreeing with *Leir* on 'kingdomes' (B1; 1.1.4) and 'messenger' (E3; 2.4.2) where F has 'Kingdome' (TLN 7) and 'Messengers' (TLN 1275), or Q's agreeing with *Eastward Ho* in the image of 'gale' (E1^v; 2.2.79) where F has 'gall' (TLN 1152) – especially as three of these Folio readings were set by Compositor E, who (as Paul Werstine demonstrates above, pp. 263–4) had a particular weakness for errors involving the addition or omission of terminal s. But other parallels are less easily discounted.

(1)   Q   With shady forrests (B1ᵛ; 1.1.64)
      F   With shadowie Forrests (TLN 69)
     FLORIO: shady forrests[36]

(2)   Q   Although the last, not least in our deere loue, (B2; 1.1.83)
      F   Although our last and least: to whose yong loue,
                  The Vines of France, and Milke of Burgundie,
                  Striue to be interest. (TLN 89–91)
     LEIR: Doth our deare loue make you thus peremptory? (286)
                        . . . to thee last of all,
           Not greeted last, 'cause thy desert was small (2657–8)

(3)   Q   Reuerse thy doome (B3; 1.1.149)
      F   reserue thy state (TLN 159)
     LEIR: Cease, good my Lords, and sue not to reuerse
           Our censure . . .
           Whose deeds haue not deseru'd this ruthlesse doome
                                  (505–6, 567)

(4)   Q   lets hit together (Cl; 1.1.303)
      F   let vs sit together (TLN 328)
     LEIR: Yet will I make fayre weather, to procure
           Conuenient meanes, and then ile strike it sure (1155–6)

(5)   Q   who is it that can tell me who I am? *Lears* shadow?
                                   (D1ᵛ; 1.4.230–1)
      F   Who is it that can tell me who I am?
           Foole. Lears shadow. (TLN 743–4)
     LEIR: *Leir.* Cease, good *Perillus*, for to call me Lord,
           And think me but the shaddow of my selfe. (1110–11)

(6)   Q   In his annoynted flesh rash borish phangs, (H1ᵛ; 3.7.58)
      F   In his Annointed flesh, sticke boarish phangs. (TLN 2130)
     WARNER: *ha Curre, auaunt: the Bore so ras[h]e thy hyde*[37]

(7)   Q   nay no tearing Lady, I perceiue you know't [. . .] know'st
           thou this paper?
           Gon. Aske me not what I know. *Exit. Gonorill.*
                             (L2; 5.3.158–62)
      F   No tearing Lady, I perceiue you know it [. . .] *Exit [Gonerill]*.
           [. . .] know'st thou this paper?
           Bast. Aske me not what I know. (TLN 3115–9)
     LEIR: Knowest thou these letters? *She snatches them & teares them*
               Rag. Think you to outface me with your paltry
               scrowles? (2586–7)

Of these, the first is of uncertain value, since Shakespeare did not need Florio for a conventional epithet like 'shady' for forests. Likewise, if *Leir* were not so obviously a major source for *Lear* the fourth example (noted by Bullough) would never have been seen as a parallel at all – though it is worth noting that in *Leir* one sister (Ragan) speaks the lines, in the context of promising to treat her father as the other has done, while in *Lear* also one sister (Gonorill) speaks the line, in the context of urging the other to come to some agreement about how to treat their father.[38] The remaining parallels seem to me rather difficult to dismiss. Two of them (nos. 2 and 3) have already been discussed in detail by Jackson (above, pp. 336, 339). In the second, the lines are spoken by the same character in both plays; in the third, both 'the purport and wording' of Q are markedly closer than F is to *Leir*. The significance of the last example derives from the fact that, in *Leir*, Ragan is Albany's wife, and so – in this context – the equivalent of Goneril in Shakespeare's play. Q thus agrees with *Leir* here in having Albany ask his wife if she recognizes the letter, and in having the wife reply; in F the question is answered by (and so presumably addressed to) Edmund.

One other Quarto link with the sources is the variation in the spelling of three names. Though Q (like F) prefers the spelling *Lear*, using it 208 times, it also uses *Leir* (which never appears in F) 4 times. Similarly, Q like F strongly prefers *Regan* (94 times); but unlike F, Q twice has *Ragan*, an alternative spelling used in several of Shakespeare's sources. Finally, Q clearly prefers *Gonorill* (25 times, to 1 *Gonerill*); F without exception adopts the *e* spelling, used in only one of Shakespeare's potential sources (*The Mirror for Magistrates*). Of course, the fact that a theatrical prompt-book apparently regularized the names of these three characters need not surprise us, or alter our view of F; but that Q, supposedly a memorial text, preserves variant spellings which occur in Shakespeare's known sources certainly *should* surprise us. Like all the other evidence, the variation in these names shows Q's dependence upon and apparent familiarity with sources which exercise no independent or renewed influence upon F.

Another variant which shows Q closer to a possible 'source' occurs at 1.4.166, where Q has 'Fooles had nere lesse wit in a yeare' (D1), F substituting 'grace' for 'wit' (TLN 680). Capell first pointed out that Q echoes Lyly's *Mother Bombie* (1594, repr. 1598): 'Gentlemen had neuer lesse wit in a yeere' (2.3.76).[39] Certainly *Mother Bombie* cannot be considered, on the evidence of this single parallel, a source for *King Lear*. On the other hand there is one other clear (and another possible) case of indebtedness to Lyly in *Lear*, and yet another in *Timon of Athens*, almost certainly written at about the same time (see below); and these three or four cases appear to be the very last instances of Shakespeare drawing upon Lyly's work.[40] Moreover, it seems not to have been noticed that there are other parallels in the immediate context of the *Mother Bombie* line: Lyly's line is spoken by a 'foole' (2.3.75), 'an idiot of the newest cut' (2.3.47), to a 'scholler' (2.3.51), who begins by complaining of 'a father' who 'seekes to place affection by appointment, & to force loue by compulsion' (2.3.2). The line in *Lear* is also spoken by a fool, criticizing a father guilty of a similar fault; and his rhyme proceeds to link its initial generalization to a statement about scholars ('wise men') and intellectual fashions:

> Fooles had nere lesse wit in a yeare,
> For wise men are growne foppish,
> They know not how their wits doe weare,
> Their manners are so apish.
> (D1; TLN 680–3; 1.4.166–9)

In addition, Lyly's adjacent dialogue also contains references to dirt (2.3.56), poultry (2.3.56), and crusts (2.3.67) – with which compare, in *Lear*, dirt (D1; TLN 677; 1.4.162), eggs (D1; TLN 670–4; 1.4.155–9), and crusts (D1ᵛ; TLN 710; 1.4.198).[41] It thus seems to me that Shakespeare was indeed influenced by Lyly here, probably unconsciously; if so, Q is (again) closer to his sources than F.

Some of these parallels between Q and the sources have been noticed before. G. I. Duthie observes that Q's 'Ragan' and 'Gonorill' are forms deriving from Shakespeare's sources;[42] this presumably does not embarrass him because he has already postulated (in order to explain Q's 'Reuerse thy doome') that those who made the memorial reconstruction of Shakespeare's play had also acted in its anonymous predecessor.[43] But Duthie does not offer any evidence for this hypothesis, beyond the very anomalies in question; he also leaves unmentioned and unexplained the remarkable coincidence that the hypothetical reporter(s) never confused the two plays except in respect to a very few incidental verbal details, in which (happily) the Q variants make excellent sense as they stand. In other words, this hypothetical reporter produces exactly the same pattern of dependence evident elsewhere in the text in the work of the known author.

The hypothetical reporter also shows a happy acquaintance with *Mother Bombie* and *Albion's England*. In the latter case (no. 6 above, p. 371), Duthie follows Greg in regarding Folio 'sticke' as an editorial sophistication of the authoritative Q reading 'rash' (p. 194). The venerable principle *praestat difficilior lectio* ('the more difficult reading takes precedence') justifies an editor in assuming that an agent of transmission is unlikely to invent such a rare usage as 'rash'; but that principle does not justify the assumption that authors, in revising their own work, never substitute a familiar word for an arcane one.[44] Even Kenneth Muir, who emends to 'rash', conjectures that Shakespeare might have revised to 'sticke' for reasons of euphony (fle*sh* ra*sh* boari*sh*);[45] an even better reason for the change is the very rareness of the verb 'rash', which makes it almost inevitable that a listener will initially understand the word as an adjective, and so be bewildered when no verb is subsequently forthcoming. In the theatre a listener cannot stop the play, or ask for a line to be repeated, in order to puzzle out its syntax. There is nothing intrinsically wrong with the Folio word; there is more than one apparent reason for an author's preferring it to 'rash' (and of course authors sometimes make verbal revisions for *no* apparent reason); and there is no evidence that the agents responsible for the Folio text regularly engaged in such sophistication. Compositor B, who set this page, may occasionally have made unconscious memorial substitutions, or conscious corrections of what appeared to be nonsense; but there are no parallels for his deliberately making a change like 'rash' to 'sticke'.[46] Nor have parallels been offered for such sophistications in the work of the theatrical scribes responsible for other Shakespearian texts.[47] Thus, in order to explain away Q's agreement with Shakespeare's sources, one is driven to postulate an extraordinary reporter, for whom there is no other evidence, and an extraordinary sophisticater, for whom there is no other evidence. In fact, in the second instance, in order to establish the general unreliability of the Quarto, one is forced to assert the particular unreliability of the Folio – in spite of the fact that the Folio reading in question is, in itself, sensible and apt.

All these verbal parallels have been remarked upon by earlier scholars, who themselves believed that the play was completed in only one period of composition (and whom, therefore, we have no reason to suspect of undue bias in favour of the thesis that the Folio represents a deliberate redaction). The Folio is closer to the known sources for only five rare words (meiney, Fraterretto, Smulkin, Flibbertigibbet, Conspirant), and possibly two others from a source Shakespeare is known to have reread later in his career (bastardizing, interest); in all of the first five, F's apparent 'return' to the source can be explained as the result of its correction of an obvious misreading in Q itself. On the other hand, even if we disregard the many parallels with the sources in Q passages wholly omitted by F, Q is closer to those very sources in *at least* four passages (2, 3, 5, 7, above, p. 371), where the differences between Q and F are difficult or impossible to dismiss as mere errors in F. The Quarto also shows, in its variant spellings for three names, further familiarity with those same sources, in a manner characteristic of authorial manu- scripts but most uncharacteristic of memorial reconstructions. In other words, Q's occasional differences from the sources can be accounted for by kinds of error common to normal textual transmis- sion; those in F require either extraordinary corruption or deliberate rewriting. Equally important, the passages unique to F show no dependence on the known sources of the play. It is a considerable understatement to say that this should not have happened if Q were merely a corrupt version of the original text, properly preserved (though with some abridgement) in F. In plays like *Richard III* and *Henry V*, the very bulk of verbal correspondences between Shakespeare's sources and the Folio texts makes it almost indis- putable that the quartos either have suffered serious corruption in transmission, or else stand at some remove from Shakespeare's initial composition (or both). The same class of evidence for *King Lear* supports no such conclusion; indeed, the very paucity of links between Folio *Lear* and Shakespeare's sources suggests, if anything, the *opposite* conclusion – that the Folio, not the Quarto, stands at some remove from the original act of composition. Certainly, nothing in the pattern of source-dependence justifies the orthodox description of Quarto *Lear* as a 'bad' or 'doubtful' text; nor is that pattern easily explicable on the assumption that the Folio alterations were made very soon after completion of the first draft. In other plays, like *Troilus and Cressida*, where the authorial revision seems to have been almost immediate, the second thoughts display as much familiarity with and influence by the original sources as does the first draft.[48]

Moreover, one way of describing a number of Folio departures from the Quarto is in terms of a redaction freeing the play from an excessive dependence on materials uppermost in Shakespeare's mind in late 1605. Thus, in 1.2, the Folio omits Edmund's mock prognostication (which would almost certainly have been satirically topical, after the extraordinary double-eclipse that autumn), while adding Gloucester's genuine and felt perception of impending chaos (C2ᵛ; 1.2.144–51 versus TLN 439–44; 1.2.109–14). In the central scenes, the most heavily-cut passages are Edgar's ravings (obviously influenced and almost certainly in part inspired by Harsnet) and the mad trial (the scene most heavily indebted to *Eastward Ho*). Likewise, in the treatment of the war between Cordelia and her sisters the most obvious and significant Folio change is the virtual disappearance of reference to France, and to foreign military invasion (Taylor, 'War', *passim*; Urkowitz, *Revision*, pp. 71–4, 93) – part of the story dramatized at length in *King Leir*. Whether we regard these changes as improvements (as I do), or as desecrations of an original organic whole, they all suggest a mind at some remove from Shakespeare's reading in 1605.

Possible Sources of the Redaction

If the Folio additions and alterations to Q were indeed composed sometime in 1608 or after, and if they show no signs of indebtedness to the same sources which clearly influenced Q, then we might expect them to show indebtedness to *other* sources, which did *not* influence Q; and if Shakespeare was himself responsible for the alterations, those other sources might be ones which show evident traces in his later plays.

Unfortunately, it is easier to formulate this expectation than to confirm it. The Folio-only passages do not include new narrative material or major, structurally important incidents; they do not consist of new scenes, but of alterations here and there. Some of those alterations, like Regan's supposition that Goneril simply 'restrained the Riots' of Lear's followers (TLN 1419–24; 2.4.140–5), do no more than expand upon material already in Q; others – like Lear's indignant repetitions of 'inform'd' (TLN 1373–4, 1379; 2.4.98–9, 103), or the juxtaposition of Jupiter and Juno (TLN 1295–6; 2.4.21–2) – because of their commonplace or traditional nature are by definition untraceable to any single definite source. Moreover, only a small proportion of the phrases in any of Shakespeare's work ever can be accounted for by such parallels. In the nature of the case, then, we can expect to find relatively little evidence. Moreover, even if we found new sources, they could *prove* a later date of composition only if they were by authors who died before 1605 (and thus could not have been influenced by memories of *Lear* itself), and whose work was not published until 1608 or after, with an explicit statement in the preface that the work was *not* circulated in manuscript during the interim. And if one wanted to prove by such means Shakespeare's personal responsibility for the redaction, we would also need to know that only he ever had access to the material – a condition itself incompatible with the others. I need hardly say that such conditions will never be satisfied. And given the limits of the material, it also seems to me most unlikely that one could ever establish, on the basis of Folio *Lear* alone, Shakespeare's knowledge of a source he elsewhere shows no cognizance of.

I have therefore limited myself to a survey of works which Shakespeare is believed, on other grounds, to have read between 1605 and the end of his career, concentrating on the areas or passages in those books which seem to have immediately influenced the later plays. I have found no parallels with any of the sources for what I regard as Shakespeare's last five plays: *Cymbeline*, *The Tempest*, *Henry VIII*, the lost *Cardenio*, and *The Two Noble Kinsmen*. This of course does not mean that such parallels nowhere exist; I may simply have missed them, or failed to cast my net sufficiently wide. On the other hand, the same kind of search did turn up several interesting verbal parallels with the sources of the group of plays from *Macbeth* to *The Winter's Tale*.

I have already mentioned the verb 'interess', which occurs only once in Shakespeare's work, in Folio *Lear*, and which Shakespeare might have picked up from Florio's translation of Montaigne or Holinshed's treatment of Macbeth. There are two other cases of a similar kind. One is Regan's line at 5.3.76, only in F (TLN 3019): 'Dispose of them, of me, the walls is thine'. As no walls appear in this part of the play, or in its treatment of the battle, the allusion to them here is surprising. Shakespeare may have been influenced by *King Leir*, where the climactic battles in Scenes 27 to 32 centre on the taking of Dover (though 'the walls' are never specifically referred to); alternatively, he may have been thinking of the succession of dramatized sieges in *Macbeth*, *Antony and Cleopatra*, and *Coriolanus* (and their sources). Likewise with the 'Seruants, who seeme no lesse, |

Which are to France the Spies and Speculations | Intelligent of our State' (3.1.23–5), in a passage which occurs only in F (TLN 1632–4). There is one parenthetic reference to spies in *King Leir*, Scene 7, when the Gallican King and Mumford enter disguised as pilgrims, and Mumford twice addresses the King as 'my lord'.

> KING. My Lord agayne? then let's haue nothing else,
> And so be tane for spyes, and then tis well.   (588–9)

The point here is the danger of disguised foreigners being arrested as spies, though they are in fact none; nor are they servants. Against this we can set an explicit passage in Holinshed, and its parallel in *Macbeth*:

> Makbeth had in euerie noble mans house one slie
> fellow or other in fee with him, to reueale all that
> was said or doone within the same
> > (Bullough, VII, 500)

> There's not a one of them but in his house
> I keepe a Seruant Feed.
> > (TLN 1414–15; 3.4.130–1)

There are spies scattered throughout Plutarch, and Shakespeare's only dramatization of a fifth column in another country is the Adrian–Nicanor scene in *Coriolanus* (4.3) – which is also the only dramatization of such spies in the surviving drama of the period between 1604 and 1623.[49] As in the other examples, then, F here seems to me closer to Shakespeare's later reading and later preoccupations. But such parallels are necessarily ambivalent, carrying a different weight with converts than with those unconvinced that there are two versions.

Another possible parallel is the word 'latch'd' (TLN 988; 2.1.52; Q 'lancht' D4), from the rare verb meaning 'catch; pull or strike swiftly off, out, up'. G. I. Duthie defended the Folio reading with a parallel from Stewart's *Cronicles*, a possible source for *Macbeth*; Kenneth Muir rejected it, because 'even if Shakespeare read Stewart when writing *Macbeth* there is no evidence that he had read it before he wrote *King Lear*'.[50] Commentators continue to disagree about Shakespeare's use of Stewart, and the Folio reading could be an error; but the reading and the parallel make excellent sense if the Folio redaction postdates *Macbeth*.

All but one of the remaining parallels are from North's Plutarch, which clearly influenced *Timon of Athens, Antony and Cleopatra, Coriolanus,* and (probably) *Pericles* and *The Winter's Tale.*[51] Shakespeare also read North for *A Midsummer Night's Dream* and *Julius Caesar,* but scholars have detected no signs of his influence from 1599 until this group of later plays, and none in Quarto *Lear.*[52]

The parallels with Folio *Lear* are all associated with the sources for *Coriolanus,* and with three of Plutarch's *Lives* which appear neither to have influenced any other Shakespearian play except *Coriolanus,* nor to have been dramatized by any other Jacobean playwright.[53] The Life of Phocion is the only known source for the name Nicanor (*Coriolanus* 4.3; North, pp. 811–12); its most interesting parallel with Folio *Lear* is in the line 'there is difference betwext manhood & manhood' (North, p. 798) – with which compare Goneril's 'Oh, the difference of man, and man' (TLN 2295; 4.2.26).[54] The Life of Lucullus is one of two possible Plutarchan sources for the name Adrian (*Coriolanus* 4.3). Despite expectations that he would lead the opposition to Pompey, after returning from his campaigns in the Middle East Lucullus 'sodainly gaue ouer all dealinges in thaffayres of the commonwealth . . . and therefore determined from thenceforth to liue quietly all at his ease, after so great paynes, trauailes, and troubles . . . And surely some were of his minde, and liked this great chaunge of his maruelous well: bicause he did not as Marius did' (North, p. 573). Plutarch goes on to contrast Lucullus with Cicero and Scipio too, and discusses the wisdom of retirement for 'a man whose youth & strength is gone and decayed' (North, p. 573). This is a point Plutarch also makes in his Lives of Agesilaus (the source of the name Cotus, in *Coriolanus* 4.5) and Crassus.

But it is in the Life of Marius (to which Shakespeare would have been referred by the Lucullus) that Plutarch dramatizes most fully the folly of clinging to power in advanced age, and it is Marius who provides a series of links with passages unique to Folio *Lear.* Three passages in this Life appear to have influenced *Coriolanus.*[55] Another passage could hardly fail to remind a reader of Shakespeare's *King Lear* (the more so if that reader were Shakespeare himself): in his old age, 'aboue three score and fiue yeare olde', having been driven from Rome, hunted, and abandoned by all his followers,

Marius finding him selfe all alone, & forsaken of euery man, lay on the ground a great while, and sayd neuer a word: yet at the length . . . got vp . . . and painefully wandred vp and downe, where was neither way nor pathe at all, ouerthwart deepe marisses and great ditches, full of water and mudde, till he came at the length to a poore old mans cotage . . . and fallinge at his feete, besought him to helpe to saue and succour a poore afflicted man . . . Marius . . . . stripping him selfe starke naked, went into a part of the marishe where the water was full of myre and mudde, and there was founde.

(North, p. 473)

Several other passages are also reminiscent of *Lear*:

so vnfortunate and miserable an end as he made, through his choller . . . which like boysterous windes made him to make shipwracke of all, in a most cruell, bloody, and vnnaturall age.

(North, p. 452)

[Marginal note: 'Horrible cruelty of women':] some [slue] their fathers, other their husbandes or their brethren . . . and afterwards slue them selues. And they say, that there was a woman hanged . . .   (North, pp. 466-7)

There is also extended treatment of 'the great vnthankefull parte [Marius] had played' (p. 467) in relation to Metellus, who was originally his patron, but was eventually banished and almost killed as a result of Marius's dishonest machinations.

We thus have a general probability that Shakespeare reread much of Plutarch during this period of his career, a specific probability that Shakespeare read the Life of Marius sometime before the completion of *Coriolanus*, and specific reason to infer that Marius (especially in the context of related comments in the lives of Lucullus, Agesilaus, Crassus, and Phocion) might have strongly reminded Shakespeare of certain central elements in *King Lear*.

The apparent echoes of the Life of Marius in Folio *Lear* are thus particularly intriguing. We have already seen that the Folio changes Q's 'shady forrests' (paralleled in Montaigne) to 'shadowie Forrests' (TLN 69; 1.1.64). In Plutarch, the barbarian invaders that Marius is sent to defeat 'dwelt in the furdest partes of the earth, adioyning vnto the great Occean sea, in a darke shadowed contrie, couered with wonderfull forestes' (North, p. 457), 'a cold contry, shadowed altogether with woddes and trees' (North, p. 466). The Britain Lear divides is also, of course, 'adioyning vnto the great Occean sea', and the play is clearly set in a pre-Christian barbarian world contemporary with pre-Christian Rome. However, this parallel – if it is one – depends upon a single word, where the difference between Q and F could result from nothing more exciting than a copyist's or compositor's error ('shady' for 'shadowy'). Such objections do not apply to a far more striking parallel between a passage in Plutarch and Goneril's outburst to Albany – a description of Lear which his conduct in the preceding scene, or in the sources, has done nothing to substantiate:

> A hundred Knights?
> 'Tis politike, and safe to let him keepe
> At point a hundred Knights: yes, that on euerie dreame,
> Each buz, each fancie, each complaint, dislike,
> He may enguard his dotage with their powres,
> And hold our liues in mercy.
>
> (TLN 843–8; 1.4.322–7)

This is exactly what Marius does, on his final return to Rome, after his humiliation:

> he came into Rome with a garde about him, of the veriest rascalls, & most shamelesse slaues . . . and they for the least word he spake, or at the twinckling of his eye, or at a nodde of his head made to them, slew many men through his commaundement.
>
> (North, p. 477)

These two links in Act One are made more remarkable by the fact that another of the Folio's major changes is its provision, on Lear's first entrance, of a greater emphasis upon – and new reasons for – his abdication:

> Q   and tis our first intent,
> To shake all cares and busines of our state,
> Confirming them on yonger yeares, . . .
>
> (B1ᵛ; 1.1.38–40)

> F   and 'tis our fast intent,
> To shake all Cares and Businesse from our Age,
> Conferring them on yonger strengths, while we
> Vnburthen'd crawle toward death. Our son of *Cornwal*,
> And you our no lesse louing Sonne of *Albany*,
> We haue this houre a constant will to publish
> Our daughters seuerall Dowers, that future strife
> May be preuented now . . .
> (Since now we will diuest vs both of Rule,
> Interest of Territory, Cares of State) . . .
>
> (TLN 43–50, 54–5; 1.1.38–45, 49–50)

In Q, as in Shakespeare's sources for the Lear story, Lear's abdication is either an unexplained misjudgement or a given, a postulate accepted for the sake of a salutary myth; in F, as in Plutarch, abdication is not only explicable and precedented, but in many ways noble, more noble than the continued grasping power-hunger of Marius and Crassus. Not that the revision accepts Plutarch's perspective whole-heartedly, or with it entirely replaces the earlier view; instead, by superimposing it on the Q version, F produces a new and more complex synthesis.[56]

One last possible influence on Folio *Lear* is a book apparently echoed in *The Winter's Tale*, George Puttenham's *The Arte of English Poesie* (1589). As H. S. Wilson pointed out, Puttenham's last chapter (Book Three, chapter 25) seems to have informed Shakespeare's discussion of grafting (*Winter's Tale* TLN 1903–8; 4.4.92–7); several other passages also appear to have influenced that play.[57] Book Three also contains a pseudo-Chaucerian poem which Shakespeare echoes and parodies in the Fool's prophecy:

> *When faith failes in Priestes sawes,*
> *And Lords hestes are holden for lawes,*
> *And robberie is tane for purchase,*
> *And lechery for solace*
> *Than shall the Realme of Albion*
> *Be brought to great confusion.*
>   (Puttenham, Bb4–Bb4ᵛ)

When Priests are more in word, then matter;
When Brewers marre their Malt with water;
When Nobles are their Taylors Tutors,
No Heretiques burn'd, but wenches Sutors [. . .]
Then shal the Realme of *Albion*,
Come to great confusion:
      (TLN 1736–9, 1746–printing the last two lines
      as one; 3.2.81–6. Riverside transposes the last
      two lines to follow, as here.)

Shakespeare's own prophecy draws upon his audience's familiarity with a genre of which Puttenham's is only one prominent example; but this example does occur in a book Shakespeare seems clearly to have been reading during the composition of *The Winter's Tale*, one which apparently influenced him directly nowhere else in his career. Moreover, several unnoticed links between Shakespeare's prophecy and Puttenham strengthen the conviction that the latter did indeed influence the former. To begin with, Shakespeare's and Puttenham's are the only early versions of the closing couplet which read 'Realme' rather than 'londe'.[58] And Shakespeare's unique refashioning of the prophecy's first line also seems clearly indebted to Puttenham's context. Puttenham quotes the poem as an example of the rhetorical figure *merismus*, which he calls 'the Distributer': 'when we may conueniently vtter a matter in one entier speach . . . and will rather do it peecemeale . . . for amplification sake' (Bb3ᵛ). This is of course a recipe for speeches 'more in word, then matter', and after quoting the prophecy Puttenham remarks, 'he might haue said as much in these words: when vice abounds, and vertue decayeth in Albion, then &c.' (Bb4ᵛ). Puttenham then immediately quotes another prophecy, utopian rather than denunciatory, which concludes '*Priest still preaching, and praying for our heale:* | *Then blessed is the state of a common-weale.*' Again, Puttenham's comment is 'All which might haue bene said in these few words, when euery man in charge and authoritie doeth his duety, & executeth his function well, then is the common-wealth happy' (Bb4ᵛ). Puttenham thus follows his reference to the priest in the pseudo-Chaucerian prophecy with another reference to a '*Priest . . . preaching*', framed by two comments on speeches characterized by excessive verbal amplification of simple propositions. Shakespeare's 'Priests . . . more in word, then matter' are easily suggested. Equally important, Puttenham – like Shakespeare – places a prophecy whose conditions could never be satisfied immediately after one whose conditions always are. In this respect, as in the others, Puttenham is unique as a possible precursor of Shakespeare's prophecy.

Puttenham not only quotes the two poems but comments upon them, and Shakespeare's modification of the prophecies may have been stimulated by those comments. Puttenham seems blind to the irony of both prophecies: his paraphrases of their content ignore the implicit contemporaneity of the first, and the implicit unattainability of the second. 'When vice abounds, and vertue decayeth in Albion' does not summarize the first prophecy, because only by the figure of *merismus*, only by the actual list of specific vices, does the original anonymous poet suggest 'When vice abounds (as it does today) . . . in Albion, &c.' Shakespeare makes this contemporaneity unmistakably clear by abandoning evaluative abstract criticisms for concrete topical ones. One might dispute whether, at any given time, '*robberie is tane for purchase*', but diluted beer and inflated sermons are with us always, As John Kerrigan demonstrates (above, pp. 221–3), Shakespeare's reference to heretics would have been particularly apposite at any time from 1608 to 1611; the allusions to venereal disease and the fashion-mongering of the nobility both reflect notorious social preoccupations of the period. Shakespeare's choice of examples for his *merismus* thus ensured that an audience would perceive the irony Puttenham did not—and do so by means of the very rhetorical figure Puttenham was analysing. Shakespeare's treatment of the second prophecy does the same. One might dispute whether 'euery man in charge and authoritie' will ever execute 'his function well'; but the unlikelihood of pickpockets avoiding crowds is manifest. Moreover, Shakespeare's choice of examples can be read as an implicit reply to the poem in Puttenham.

> When euery Case in Law, is right;
> No Squire in debt, nor no poore Knight;
> When Slanders do not liue in Tongues;
> Nor Cut-purses come not to throngs;
> When Vsurers tell their Gold i'th'Field,
> And Baudes, and whores, do Churches build,
>   (TLN 1740–5; 3.2.87–92)

Shakespeare's vision of Utopia says nothing about 'euery man in charge and authoritie'; political beatitude instead depends, in his vision, upon the reformation of every level of society. The Fool's prophecy thus reinforces Lear's denunciation, earlier in the scene:

> Tremble thou Wretch,
> That hast within thee vndivulged Crimes
> Vnwhipt of Iustice. Hide thee, thou Bloudy hand;
> Thou Periur'd, and thou Simular of Vertue
> That art Incestuous. Caytiffe, to peeces shake
> That vnder couert, and conuenient seeming
> Ha's practis'd on mans life. Close pent-vp guilts,
> Riue your concealing Continents . . .
>   (TLN 1704–11; F4ᵛ; 3.2.51–8)

These earlier denunciations can, of course, be directed (overtly or ambiguously) to the audience itself; they thus prepare, in both content and theatrical form, for the Fool's speech at scene's end. The same theme is elaborated in Poor Tom's panoramas of social vice and mad Lear's diagnosis of a world in which 'None do's offend' because all do. Shakespeare's modification of the prophecy thus makes good dramatic sense, and for that very reason one cannot be sure that Puttenham's comment prompted it; however, one can say that

Shakespeare's prescription for Utopia gains an entirely relevant extra dimension if read as, in part, a reply to Puttenham's.

Finally, Shakespeare might have been influenced by two other passages in which Puttenham discusses prophecies. In chapter 19 of Book One, Puttenham dismisses 'Magicians and mockers' who 'get their liuings' by 'vaine and deceitfull arts taking vpon them to reueale the truth of accidents to come', events 'such as can not possibly be knowne because they be not yet' (F4^v). This is very much Shakespeare's own attitude, both here and elsewhere in *Lear*. Puttenham proceeds to discuss 'Sir *Thomas Moores Vtopia*, resting all in deuise, but neuer put in execution, and easier to be wished then to be performed' (F4^v) – an attitude toward Utopia explicit in the second half of the Fool's prophecy. Puttenham then speaks of a 'ditty . . . of the Isle of great *Britaine*', particularly of the adventures 'of king *Arthur* and his knights of the round table' (G1–G1^v). The conjunction of magicians, prophecies, and King Arthur within this brief chapter could easily have reminded Shakespeare of Merlin's prophecies, to which he alludes at the end of the Fool's speech. Another such passage occurs in the third book, not long after Puttenham's quotation of the pseudo-Chaucerian prophecy which the Fool draws upon. There Puttenham notes that 'all our old Brittish and Saxon prophesies' are so ambiguous 'that turne them on which side ye will, the matter of them may be verified' (Ff3^v). This again easily suggests Merlin. Shakespeare in *1 Henry IV* refers to 'the dreamer Merlin and his prophecies' (F2; TLN 1680; 3.1.148), but editions of Chaucer naturally do not attribute the 'Albion' poem to Merlin, and to my knowledge only one manuscript (that in Trinity College, Dublin, dating from the mid fifteenth century) does so. Puttenham thus seems as likely as any potential source to have suggested the link between Merlin and this prophecy.

Certainly, the availability of this further association between Puttenham and the Folio addition increases the probability that whoever wrote that addition had been influenced by Puttenham – as Shakespeare had been between 1609 and 1611. Of course, we cannot determine whether Puttenham influenced *The Winter's Tale* or Folio *King Lear* first; but it seems likely that its influence on both texts was exerted at approximately the same time. One would therefore expect the revision of *Lear* (if by Shakespeare) to have immediately preceded or followed the composition of *The Winter's Tale*. And this link between Folio *Lear* and *The Winter's Tale* is even more remarkable if, as I believe, *The Winter's Tale* immediately followed *Coriolanus*.[59] If we exclude the two dubious cases dependent upon single words ('interess', 'latch'd'), all the possible parallels for material unique to Folio *Lear* are found in the sources to these two adjacent plays.

Parallelography, as Greg called it, is perilous. But Greg himself used it; used it, in fact, to help date *King Lear*. When all allowances have been made for the limits both of this evidence in particular and of source evidence in general, it seems to me that there remains enough to establish a probability that the Folio-only passages are indebted to works Shakespeare read after the original composition of *King Lear* and before the composition of *Cymbeline*. The congruence of this source material is at least suspicious. And if the suspicion is justified, it would suggest that the revision of *Lear* took place after *Coriolanus* and before *Cymbeline*: after Shakespeare's last tragedy, heavily concerned with war and politics, and just before another foray via Holinshed into early British history. The bibliographical evidence, of initial revision directly on to a copy of Q1, is consonant with this date, as is the absence of clear Folio links with the sources of the original composition (approximately four years earlier). So is the evidence of vocabulary.

Evidence of Date: Vocabulary

Eliot Slater, in a recent investigation of the entire canon, has extensively tested the hypothesis that the rarer elements of Shakespeare's vocabulary–specifically, words that occur in his work from two to ten times – show a statistically significant correlation with the accepted chronology of the plays.[60] The psychological explanation of this phenomenon is that words of a relatively low frequency of use tend to pass in and out of a writer's active (as opposed to his potential) vocabulary. In this respect vocabulary resembles most of a playwright's other working materials: just as he used rhyme and doggerel more often in his early work, wrote fewer history plays after than before 1600, and concentrated on dramatic romance from about 1607, so it should hardly surprise us that Shakespeare used certain words more frequently in some periods than in others. There is in fact nothing new or unorthodox about this perception.[61] A. C. Bradley, for instance, tried to prove that *King Lear* was written soon after *Othello* by showing that they had a number of unusual words in common.[62] However, Bradley simply noticed a handful of unusual expressions present in both plays, and offered this as evidence of proximity of composition, without attempting to discover whether his personal selection was representative or, in the context of the whole canon, significant. Since Shakespeare almost certainly used a few words in his first play which happen to recur nowhere else but in his last, no haphazard collection of individual parallels can provide trustworthy evidence of a chronological relationship. The vocabulary of Shakespeare's plays might, theoretically, bear *no* relationship to their chronology; if such a relationship *does* exist, we can only hope to discern it by surveying that vocabulary systematically, comprehensively, objectively – and statistically.

Literary scholars do not, in general, trust statistics, partly for the excellent reason that statistics are often stupidly used, but partly because literary scholars sometimes lack the patience to distinguish the stupid statistics from the sensible ones, and so tend to dismiss them all. Nevertheless, the difficulties of evaluating statistical evidence should not be allowed to obscure the validity and value of such evidence, when properly used. No scholar can disregard Charlton Hinman's analysis of recurring types in the First Folio, even though it depends upon specialist techniques which few literary critics are in any position to question.[63] Sceptics cannot content themselves with making vaguely (or vehemently) hostile remarks about the relevance of statistics to literary composition;[64] one must instead either challenge the accuracy of the new data, criticize the statistical evaluation of those data, or offer some other convincing explanation for the apparent chronological pattern.[65]

I can, therefore, see no reason to dismiss the potential validity of statistical evidence *per se*, and no gross implausibility in the suggestion that Shakespeare's vocabulary preferences gradually evolved during the course of his writing life. If they did, and if Folio *Lear* represents a later redaction (by Shakespeare or someone else) of the Quarto, then the vocabulary of the two texts should reflect these different dates of composition. Likewise, if Q represents only a memorially-contaminated text of the original dialogue, essentially preserved in F, then Q's vocabulary should be markedly simpler and less Shakespearian than that of F. Indeed, one of the most convincing demonstrations of a class of contaminated texts – 'bad quartos' – is Alfred Hart's statistical examination of the differences between the vocabulary of those texts and the vocabulary of the rest of the

Shakespeare canon.[66] Hart, notably, did *not* include Quarto *Lear* –
for the excellent reason that, considered in the light of such evidence,
Quarto *Lear* shows no signs of memorial transmission. Those who
deny that Quarto *Lear* was set directly from Shakespeare's foul
papers must, among much else, explain why its vocabulary differs so
radically from that of other memorially-contaminated quartos.

Hart's test examines the total vocabulary of single texts in relation
to the total vocabulary of the remainder of the canon, comparing the
pattern of word usage in that single text with certain *constant* features
of Shakespeare's vocabulary; Slater instead confines himself to the
rarer elements of those total vocabularies, setting the pattern of rare
word usage in one text against the shifting background of
Shakespeare's *changing* vocabulary preferences. Hart sets out to
determine whether the pattern in one text belongs in the Shakespeare
corpus; Slater, to determine where it belongs. Both techniques
depend upon the systematic application of certain rules about what
constitutes a 'word';[67] both also depend, to some small degree, upon
the objectivity of a previously edited text and corpus. Hart's test,
encompassing the entire vocabulary, would hardly be affected by a
handful of editorial decisions about compositorial or scribal error;
Slater's, confining itself to a much smaller sample, might be. Slater's
vocabulary compilations are based upon the Bartlett concordance
compared with the Spevack concordance;[68] this means in effect that
he can rely upon the editorial judgement of the Globe and Riverside
editions, supplemented (when those two disagree) by the New
Shakespeare edition of Dover Wilson.[69] But there are, as yet, no
proper editions of the two different versions of *King Lear*. I have
therefore had to draft such editions myself, in order to test the
difference between their respective vocabularies; and while I have
tried to base editorial decisions on editorial considerations, the Folio
sample is so small that my own subjective judgements about when it
needs emending might be sufficient to bias the sample. Appendix I
therefore contains a summary of all emendations I have assumed in
running this vocabulary test, and a full account of their (minimal)
effects on the results.

The vocabulary evidence is summarized in Appendix II. The
vocabulary of the entire Quarto text tends to confirm a date of
original composition between *Othello* and *Macbeth*, either just before
or just after *Timon of Athens*.[70] On the other hand, the vocabulary
unique to the Folio would appear to have been written later than Q,

or by another writer.[71] It does not have significant links (as Q does) with the plays from *As You Like It* to *Othello*;[72] its strongest links are with the four plays *The Winter's Tale, Cymbeline, The Tempest* and *Henry VIII*.[73] The excess of links between the Folio-only material and these four last plays would happen by chance only about one time in two hundred.

Three peculiarities in the distribution of the rare vocabulary point even more strongly to the same conclusions. Neither the rare vocabulary of Q, nor that unique to F, has any remarkable number of links with *Macbeth, Antony and Cleopatra*,[74] *Pericles*, or *Coriolanus*. Between Q *Lear* and *Macbeth*, for instance, the number of links above expectation has a chi-squared value of only 2.12; the comparable figure for Q *Lear* and *Cymbeline* is 9.64, for Q *Lear* and *The Tempest* 4.45.[75] *Macbeth*, moreover, has a higher figure than any of the three following plays (*Antony, Pericles* and *Coriolanus*). This is surprising: we would expect Q *Lear* to have stronger links with plays *c*.1606–9 than with plays *c*.1609–13. However, if the play was extensively reworked by Shakespeare, *c*.1609–10, then we would expect its language to re-enter his active vocabulary again, in a way which would significantly increase the number of vocabulary links between *Lear* and the plays he wrote *after* its revision. The chi-squared value for the number of links between Q *Lear*'s vocabulary and that of *Cymbeline, The Winter's Tale*, and *The Tempest* is 13.413;[76] the odds against this being coincidental are enormous (1 in 4,000). In particular, there is only about one chance in 800 of the link with *Cymbeline* being accidental. And if *Cymbeline* followed *The Winter's Tale*, the links between Q *Lear* and Shakespeare's last two uncollaborative plays are even more remarkable: such links would occur by chance only once in over 7,500 times ($\chi^2 = 14.615$). On the traditional hypothesis, of a single version of *Lear* composed in 1605 or 1606, this remarkable link between *Lear* and the late romances is quite inexplicable; but it would be a natural consequence of Shakespeare's having extensively revised the play at some point after *Coriolanus* and before *Cymbeline*.

A distinction here between the vocabulary common to both texts and that unique to Q reinforces this conclusion. Rare words in passages omitted or altered in the revised version would not have been recopied and (in the process) positively re-endorsed; consequently they would stand less chance of re-entering Shakespeare's active vocabulary. If the play was revised by Shakespeare sometime in or after 1608, one would expect the vocabulary unique to Q to have fewer links with the late work than does the vocabulary common to Q and F. And this is exactly what happens. The seven plays from *As You Like It* to *Othello* have approximately the same number of rare words (4,938) as the eight from *Macbeth* to *Henry VIII* (4,934); the rare words in Q but not F have 108 links to the group before and 97 to the group after, while for the vocabulary common to Q and F the corresponding figures are 620 to 632.

The other peculiarity in the evidence best explained by the hypothesis of revision is the distribution of those rare words which occur both in the vocabulary unique to F and in the vocabulary of Q. Unusual words occurring both in Q and in the passages unique to F tend to come, in F, in the immediate vicinity of their appearance in Q. (See Appendix III). The rare words which occur in passages unique to Q show no such relationship with the vocabulary of the remainder of Q; nor do the rare words in passages unique to the Folio text of *Troilus and Cressida* bear any such relationship to the vocabulary of the Quarto text of that play; nor do the rare words in major passages present in the (authoritative) Folio text of *Richard III*, but omitted (probably because of theatrical cutting) from the un-authoritative Quarto text of 1597.[77] In these other plays, the smaller vocabulary sample – that unique to Q *Lear*, or F *Troilus*, or F *Richard III* – was presumably written at the same time as the rest, or fairly soon after; consequently there is no reason to expect that the larger sample specifically influenced the smaller; instead, both were products of the particular state of a given mind at a given time. The vocabulary unique to Folio *Lear* departs from this pattern in exactly the way we would expect if it reflected later revision: its specific links with the main body of *Lear* suggest a mind being fitfully influenced by the (earlier) vocabulary of the text it has just been reading, revising, and copying. Indeed, exactly the same pattern as in Folio *Lear* occurs in the so-called fly scene (3.2) of *Titus Andronicus*, which is generally regarded as a later Shakespearian addition, since it is present in F but not Q, and shows various internal signs of being later work.[78]

To summarize: the vocabulary evidence for Quarto *Lear* points clearly toward the accepted date of the play's composition, and (in contrast to the vocabulary unique to the Folio text) has strong links with plays certainly or probably written between 1600 and 1604. The Folio-only vocabulary strongly corresponds, instead, with Shakespeare's last three romances and *Henry VIII*. As we would expect if the Quarto version of the play were subsequently revised by Shakespeare, its rare vocabulary apparently 'resurfaces' later (about the time of *Cymbeline*); moreover, Quarto words retained in the Folio text have much stronger links with the late plays than words not so retained. The actual distribution of such rare words in both texts likewise suggests that the Quarto represents a single homogeneous period of composition, and that the Folio instead preserves two distinct layers of usage.

Such evidence remains, necessarily, suggestive and supportive rather than conclusive: though the patterns of vocabulary linkage seem unlikely to have resulted from chance, they might reflect something other than chronology. For instance, for a few plays Slater's vocabulary evidence does not seem compatible with other, reliable external and internal evidence for the date of composition, and the two texts of *King Lear* might happen to represent another such exception. Nevertheless, one cannot lightly dismiss the agreement of all these vocabulary patterns in suggesting a later date of composition for the Folio text. Equally important, these patterns need not by themselves 'prove' anything, because they merely confirm the documentary evidence of the two early texts themselves, that there do indeed exist two distinct versions of the play. At the very least, then, we can conclude that no defence of conflation can be made on the basis of the 'objective' evidence of word usage, and that the available internal evidence suggests instead that the Folio version dates from several years after completion of the Quarto.

To this statistical evidence of Shakespeare's use of rare words throughout both texts of *Lear*, and in the canon generally, can be added the specific evidence of a single peculiar word in Folio *Lear* which appears nowhere else: *intrince*.

> Like Rats oft bite those cordes in twaine,
> Which are to intrench, to inloose
> $\qquad$ (El^v; 2.2.74–5)

> Like Rats oft bite the holy cords a twaine,
> Which are t'intrince, t'vnloose
> $\qquad$ (TLN 1147–8; the uncorrected state
> $\qquad$ reads 'holly')

John Upton first suggested, in 1746, that the Folio's 'intrince' was a contraction of *intrinsicate*, which occurs in *Antony and Cleopatra* (Cleopatra addressing the asp):[79]

> With thy sharpe teeth this knot intrinsicate,
> Of life at once vntye
>
> (TLN 3556-7; 5.2.304-5)

The connection between the two passages is manifest. But, as Stone objects, in contrast to the lines in *Antony*, those in *Lear* 'present an image of tightly-bound *cords* (which cannot be unloosed) rather than of entangled *knots* (which cannot be unravelled)'; consequently 'intrince', in the sense 'intrinsicate, entangled', is 'scarcely apt to the context' (*Textual History*, p. 53). Stone defends this interpretation of *Lear* by pointing to a reference, in the source-play *King Leir*, to Aesop's fable of the lion and the mouse:

> The silly mouse, by vertue of her teeth,
> Releas'd the princely Lyon from the net.
>
> (642-3)

Stone argues that Q itself makes perfectly good sense, if *to intrench to inloose* is emended to *to* [i.e. 'too'] *intrencht to vnloose*, an emendation which seems to me both plausible and attractive.[80] So interpreted, Q is (again) closer than F to the play's acknowledged sources. Equally important, however, F's alteration seems to result from association with a passage in a play (*Antony and Cleopatra*) almost universally believed to postdate the original composition of *King Lear*.[81] As the word *intrinsicate*, though rare, is recorded at least three times before 1605, Shakespeare could have produced a contracted form of it, in 1605, before he had himself used it in 1606-7; but given Q's relation to a passage in *King Leir*, and the bibliographical and other evidence for revision in or after 1608, the more plausible explanation is surely that Shakespeare only invented the contraction *intrince* after himself using, in a strikingly similar context, the rare word *intrinsicate*. This would place the redaction after *Antony and Cleopatra*, and suggest that Shakespeare was himself the man responsible.

Given the cumulative evidence so far for revision some time before the composition of *Cymbeline*, one other peculiarity is worth mentioning. I have noticed the way in which the vocabulary of Q *Lear* 'resurfaces' in *Cymbeline*, and Kenneth Muir has noticed that the same thing happens in respect to sources: for *Cymbeline* as for *Lear*, Shakespeare made use of Holinshed's *Chronicles* (for pre-Christian Britain), *The Faerie Queene*, *Albion's England*, *The Mirror for*

Magistrates, and a dramatic romance dating from the 1580s or 1590s. It is also worth noticing that *The Mirror for Magistrates*, which Shakespeare was rereading for *Cymbeline*, is the only one of Shakespeare's sources for *Lear* which uses the form *Gonerill*, consistently adopted in the Folio in the place of Q's preferred *Gonorill* (see p. 372 above). Moreover, before or during the composition of *Cymbeline* Shakespeare was reading the first book of Holinshed's *Chronicles* and the anonymous *Frederyke of Jennen*; both works prominently feature women (Boadicea and 'Frederycke') who actually *lead* an army – as does Cordelia in the Folio, but not the Quarto, of *King Lear*.

Evidence of Date: Style

A proper test of the metrical differences between Quarto and Folio *Lear* must await a complete re-examination of the methodology and validity of metrical tests for dating the Shakespeare canon.[82] In the interim, an impressionistic illustration of the stylistic difference between Quarto and Folio *Lear* is provided by their alternative versions of one of Kent's speeches to the Gentleman in 3.1. Here, and often elsewhere, the Folio seems to me markedly closer to the widely-recognized grammatical and linguistic complexity of Shakespeare's 'late style', a style usually said to commence with *Macbeth* and *Antony and Cleopatra*.[83]

```
Q                    there is diuision,
        Although as yet the face of it be couer'd,
        With mutuall cunning, twixt Albany and Cornwall[.]
        But true it is, from France there comes a power
        Into this scattered kingdome, who alreadie
        Wise in our negligèce, haue secret feet
        In some of our best Ports, and are at point
        To shew their open banner, now to you,
        If on my credit you dare build so farre,
        To make your speed to Douer, you shall find
        Some that will thanke you, making iust report
        Of how vnnaturall and bemadding sorrow
        The King hath cause to plaine,
        I am a Gentleman of blood and breeding,
        And from some knowledge and assurance,
        Offer this office to you.
                (F3ᵛ; 3.1.19–21, 30–42)
```

F   There is diuision
(Although as yet the face of it is couer'd
With mutuall cunning) 'twixt Albany, and Cornwall:
Who haue, as who haue not, that their great Starres
Thron'd and set high; Seruants, who seeme no lesse,
Which are to France the Spies and Speculations
Intelligent of our State. What hath bin seene,
Either in snuffes, and packings of the Dukes,
Or the hard Reine which both of them hath borne
Against the old kinde King; or something deeper,
Whereof (perchance) these are but furnishings [–]
(TLN 1628–38; 3.1.19–29)

Q contains four complete sentences, and two clearly-signposted changes of direction: *But true it is* (contrasting with the 'mutuall cunning' which covers the real division with apparent unity) and *now to you.* F has only two sentences, one incomplete; its new ending to the first sentence is a qualifying clause ('Who haue . . . Seruants') itself containing three further qualifiers ('as who . . . who seeme . . . Which are'). Moreover, in the Folio there is no clear signposting of the connection between the first and second sentences, or of the exact direction of the sentences themselves: one need only compare 'from *France* there comes a power' and 'If . . . you dare . . . , you shall' and 'I am a Gentleman' (all making the basic structure of the Quarto sentences immediately clear) with the ambiguity and complexity of the Folio syntax. The imagery of the two passages seems to me equally distinct. The Quarto's images ('scattered kingdome', 'secret feet', 'open banner', 'on my credit . . . build', 'vnnaturall and bemadding sorrow', 'of blood and breeding', 'knowledge and assurance') are hardly remarkable in form or content, except perhaps for the unintended incongruity of 'secret feet'. By contrast, the Folio's images ('Thron'd and set high', 'Spies and Speculations', 'snuffes, and packings', 'hard Reine', 'furnishings') include three remarkable doublings and two characteristic puns ('State', 'Reine'), as well as being compacted into a briefer interval, and linked by a subterranean process of association. The phrases 'great Starres' and 'set high' lead naturally to the idea of 'looking down upon' (hence 'Spies and Speculations'), but also summon up associations with astrology ('Speculations | Intelligent of our State'); 'Seruants' and 'Spies' naturally co-exist with 'snuffes, and packings'; 'packings' not only relates to 'furnishings' but also, more immediately, to the horse imagery of 'Reine'. The Folio passage, as a consequence of such features, gives an impression of stylistic density which is entirely typical of the late plays – and markedly atypical of Kent.[84]

I would not care to base a textual hypothesis upon no more than such impressionistic analyses of diction; but the peculiarity of Shakespeare's late manner has been perceived by many generations of critics and readers, and it is at least worth noting that the style of the Folio's changes accords perfectly well with the hypothesis of Shakespearian revision not long before the composition of *Cymbeline*.[85]

Internal Evidence for Authorship

We can now directly address the problem of authorship. It is certainly suggestive that the passages unique to F show exactly the pattern of style and unusual vocabulary that we would expect if they were indeed by Shakespeare and were indeed composed at the period which seems most probable on other and quite unrelated grounds. Admittedly, this could count as definitive proof only if we were able to undertake similar chronological studies of other dramatists, since it is always possible that the Folio evidence might fit equally well the vocabulary of Fletcher or Middleton *circa* (say) 1618. But even if (as seems inherently unlikely) that did prove to be so, such a result would only establish an equal case, on vocabulary alone, for Fletcher or Middleton. It would not *disprove* Shakespeare's authorship, but only make another attribution *possible*, on the basis of that single test. Moreover, it would also leave unexplained the abrupt resurgence of the Quarto *Lear* vocabulary in *Cymbeline*. It is the convergence of different kinds of evidence, all pointing to what we would expect if Shakespeare undertook a revision of *King Lear* between *Coriolanus* and *Cymbeline*, that argues most strongly for his responsibility for the redaction.

Before I examine the linguistic evidence for the chief rival claimants for authorship of the Folio alterations, however, one other piece of vocabulary evidence deserves mention. Two passages unique to F contain image clusters common elsewhere in Shakespeare's work. E. A. Armstrong has shown that in Shakespeare's works a goose often appears as part of a chain of associated ideas including disease, bitterness, seasoning, and restraint.[86] One such cluster occurs in Q itself, between 2.2.74 and 2.2.97 (E1^v–E2; TLN 1147–

72): Goose, cackling, plague, sawcy, cordes. But another such cluster occurs between 2.4.41 and 2.4.64 (E3ᵛ–E4; TLN 1317–37): sawcily, wild Geese, blind, Dolors, Stockes.[87] The three central elements in this cluster, however, occur only in F. Moreover, although the stocks are verbally specified (2.4.64) only after the Folio insertion (2.4.46–55), Kent is in them from the beginning of the scene; and when he alludes, in the last line before the insertion, to the 'shame which here' he suffers (2.4.45), there can be no doubt as to the reference. So, in the five lines before the Folio insertion, whoever was rewriting the text would have encountered 'sawcily' and a clear reference to the onstage 'stocks' in which Kent is restrained; he then wrote a passage containing 'wild Geese', 'blind', and 'Dolors'. Moreover, the same Folio addition contains elements of another irrational image cluster evident elsewhere. 'When Shakespeare used "stew" of cooking it conjured up images of the brothel, evil smells and beastliness' (Armstrong, p. 113); the brothel, in turn, generated images of disease (p. 114). In the speech which immediately precedes the Folio addition Kent describes Oswald (Goneril's *stew*ard) as 'a *reeking* Post, | *Stewd* in his hast' (E3ᵛ; TLN 1305–6; 2.4.30–1; my italics); he also describes him behaving 'sawcily' (E3ᵛ; TLN 1317; 2.4.41). Then, in the added Folio speech, appear the words 'wild Geese', 'blind', 'that arrant whore, nere turns the key toth' poore', and 'Dolors' (punning on 'dollars'). This single added speech of the Fool's thus contains two striking Shakespearian image clusters.[88] And a third appears in another Folio addition. Armstrong notes that the context of most of Shakespeare's late uses of the interjection 'hum!' contains death or sleep imagery;[89] one such (TLN 1828; 3.4.47) occurs only in F.[90] This single added word could arguably have been omitted from Q accidentally; consequently it is less useful than the added speech in 2.4 as evidence of Shakespeare's hand in the redaction. Nor are three such clusters sufficient to prove Shakespeare's authorship of all the Folio alterations, since it is at least conceivable that another author might consistently make the same irrational associations. But those who wish to propose some rival claimant would first have to demonstrate that he does share these imaginative peculiarities. And even that would be no more than negative evidence: it would make the rival's claim as good as Shakespeare's, in this one respect, but no better.

Given the small size of the sample, how would one go about establishing a positive claim to non-Shakespearian authorship? The evidence of parallels with the work of other dramatists, always difficult, is almost certainly useless here. This may seem a peculiar assertion for me to make, after myself examining possible parallels in Shakespeare's sources, but there is an essential distinction between the two kinds of evidence. In the case of the sources, I was testing material Shakespeare is known to have read in a given period, to see whether it seems in any way to have influenced the alterations in F; there can be no question whether Shakespeare influenced North, or vice versa. Any parallels between F and other dramatists would be crippled by just this uncertainty – the more so in that the two likeliest suspects, Massinger and Fletcher, the major dramatists of the King's Men after Shakespeare's retirement, are themselves notorious for their Shakespearian borrowings.[91] This leaves us entirely dependent on linguistic evidence of one kind or another. Fortunately, a great deal of work has been done on linguistic tests for the attribution of work to Middleton, Fletcher, and Massinger, and we can look briefly at Folio *Lear* in relation to some of the criteria now commonly used to distinguish their work from Shakespeare's.

The presence of Fletcher can be quickly dismissed, so far as linguistic evidence is concerned.[92] The four most important tests Cyrus Hoy used in distinguishing Fletcher's work from Shakespeare's are: Fletcher's phenomenally greater preference for *ye*, Shakespeare's equally marked preference for *hath* and *doth*, and Fletcher's greater preference for *'em*. *Ye* is found only 7 times in Folio *Lear* (as opposed to 37 and 71 times in Fletcher's shares of *The Two Noble Kinsmen* and *Henry VIII*); *'em* only 9 times (as opposed to 45 occurrences of *them*). Shakespeare's preferred *hath* and *doth* occur 49 and 13 times respectively (as opposed to no more than 6 and 3 times respectively in any one play of Fletcher's). These gross figures lend no support whatever to a claim for Fletcher's authorship of the redaction. However, it might be objected either that Fletcher merely left most of the Q forms as he found them, or that his presence has been obscured either by an intervening scribal transcript or by the Folio compositors themselves. Thus, 6 of the 7 Folio uses of *ye* are either not in Q or depart from that text's *you*; and Compositor B has a known tendency to reduce the frequency of *ye* in the texts he set, as does Edmund Knight, later bookkeeper of the King's Men. However, these facts in themselves are hardly sufficient to explain away the deficiency of *ye* forms in F. In the first place, if Fletcher five times altered Q *you* to *ye*, then he must have been transcribing the whole text – and transcription in any case seems required, at some stage, by the very extent of the revisions. And if Fletcher were transcribing, one would expect a great many more uses of *ye*, regardless of Q's practice. As for Compositor B, if we are to attribute the reduction wholly to him, he left only 3 of the forms standing in the portion of *Lear* he set – as opposed to 22 in *Henry VIII*. There are, moreover, only 4 in E's stints. We have no reason to suspect that E would have systematically removed them, but have instead good general evidence of E's extreme conservatism in preserving copy forms.[93] In any case, *ye* occurs 8 times in *Coriolanus* (apparently set from autograph copy[94]), so that the 7 appearances in F *Lear* are hardly suspicious. As for *'em*, 6 of these are departures from or not in Q; but the total of 9 for F still remains well below the 15 in *Coriolanus*, or the minimum of 25 in Fletcher's other work. All but one Folio *doth* could be derived from Q; but 8 of its 49 uses of *hath* are not in Q. In short, the linguistic evidence gives no indication of Fletcher's presence. Nor do we find, in passages unique to F, any of the peculiar constructions or rhetorical patterns characteristic of his work.[95]

Middleton can be even more quickly dismissed, on the basis of the absence or abnormally low frequency of a whole range of words and contractions common in his work but not Shakespeare's: *has, does, h'as, h'ad, ha', 'tas, 'em, I'm, e'en,* and *ne'er*.[96] As for Massinger, whom Stone (*Textual History*, p. 127) specifically proposes as author of the Folio alterations, he is perhaps the least defensible of all.[97] In Massinger's fifteen unaided plays, *ye* occurs only twice; as we have already seen, the Folio introduces 6 of these not in Q. *Has* appears only 5 times in all Massinger's work, and 13 times in Folio *Lear*. *I'th'* is found only 18 times in 5 late (post-1625) plays of Massinger, and in none of these more than 7 times; it occurs 25 times in Folio *Lear*. The contraction *o'th'*, which never appears in Massinger's work, occurs 24 times in Folio *Lear*.[98]

There seems to me little historical plausibility in ascription of the redaction to Jonson (as Stone himself concedes). The Folio contains no examples of Jonson's preferred *'hem*, but has 9 of the alternative *'em* (7 added to Q); it likewise has no instances of his preferred *i'the*; none of his distinctive *yo'* or *h'has*, and only 2 of *ha'* (both in dialect, and both taken over from Q). Only one of Jonson's distinctive traits puts in any appearance at all: his preferred *o'the* occurs once (TLN 701; 1.4.188), in contrast to 14 occurrences of the alternative *o'th'*.[99] Jonson clearly cannot be given responsibility for the Folio redaction.

Fletcher, Middleton, and Massinger are the only inherently plausible candidates for the authorship of the Folio changes: Fletcher and Massinger as the major dramatists for Shakespeare's company after his retirement, Fletcher and possibly Middleton as playwrights who collaborated with Shakespeare late in his career, Middleton as the one playwright suspected of having adapted another Folio play (*Macbeth*) after Shakespeare's retirement.[100] The linguistic evidence strongly contradicts an ascription to any of these men, or to Jonson.

Any serious alternative candidate for authorship of the Folio redaction would, it seems to me, have to satisfy two minimal historical criteria: he must have written tragedy, history, or tragicomedy at some stage in his career, and he must also have had some association with the King's Men. Even if we restrict ourselves to dramatists who satisfy at least one of these two criteria, only three candidates remain.[101] One is George Chapman, who never to our knowledge wrote anything for the King's Men, and who (with one debatable exception) apparently wrote no plays after 1613. Anyone familiar with Chapman's idiosyncratic tragic diction will find it difficult to credit him with the Folio version of *Lear*. The linguistic evidence also argues strongly against his presence.[102] Chapman's own plays and poems contain only 3 occurrences of *among*, as against 56 of *amongst*; Folio *Lear* has 3 of the former and only 1 of the latter. It also uses *between* 8, and *betwixt* only 3, times; Chapman's known work instead prefers *betwixt* by 106 to 5. These two violations of overwhelming preferences should in themselves be sufficient to rule out Chapman's hand in the redaction; in both cases, moreover, Folio *Lear* corresponds with Shakespeare's own preferences.

Both of the other candidates, Nathan Field and John Webster, wrote tragedy or tragicomedy and were strongly associated with the King's Men in the years between Shakespeare's retirement and the publication of the First Folio. Field, however, was a mediocre dramatist, best known for his two comedies; his only experience with tragicomedy was in a work of collaboration. These facts hardly encourage the hypothesis that Shakespeare's company entrusted to his hands the adaptation of a tragedy by their most successful dramatist. Nor are any of Field's linguistic peculiarities present in F. Like Chapman he strongly prefers *betwixt* (16 to 0, in his two unaided plays); he also uses *whil(e)st* 10 times, and *while* thrice, whereas Folio *Lear* has *whil(e)st* only once, against 3 uses of *while* and one of *whiles* (which Field never uses). Nor does Folio *Lear* contain his favourite interjection *pish* (8 occurrences in each of Field's unaided plays).[103]

Webster, as a tragic dramatist of stature who on at least one other occasion adapted a play for the King's Men, is easily the most attractive of these three candidates, on extrinsic grounds – though still less attractive than Fletcher, Massinger, or Middleton.[104] But the linguistic evidence decisively rules him out. Like Fletcher and Massinger, Webster strongly prefers *yes* (88 times) to *ay* (16); Folio *Lear*, conforming to Shakespeare's general usage, instead strongly prefers *ay* (19, to 8 *yes*). The Folio's 3 uses of *betwixt* also tell against Webster, who in his three unaided plays never uses *betwixt* at all, although *between* occurs 28 times. Webster elsewhere uses *'em* only 3 times, against 213 occurrences of *them*; Folio *Lear* has the contraction 9 times, and the full form only 45. *Ye*, which occurs no more than twice in any of Webster's plays, is used 7 times in Folio *Lear*.

Finally, one other category of vocabulary evidence reinforces Shakespeare's claim. As several modern scholars have demonstrated, Shakespeare's genuine works all include an unusually high proportion of new or rare vocabulary.[105] Since these studies have been based upon the number of rare words as a proportion of the total number of lines in the work, we must restrict ourselves to an examination of such words in the approximately one hundred and twenty lines actually added by the Folio. These lines include eleven words which appear nowhere else in the canon: *able* (*verb*), *buzz* (*noun*), *disquietly*, *enguard*, *furnishings*, *hurtless*, *interess'd*, *malt*, *rich* (*verb*), *unburdened* (*adjective*), and *unfitness*. They also contain ten words which appear only once or twice in Shakespeare's other works: *brewer*, *champain*, *crawl*, *divest*, *hollowness*, *Merlin*, *prediction*, *pygmy*, *smug*, and *unsubstantial*. If we include other occurrences of a word in *Lear* itself, we would have to remove 'prediction', but we could then include 'houseless' and 'machination'. In either case, or even if we exclude the proper name 'Merlin', the proportion (one rare word to every eleven, twelve, or thirteen added lines) is decidedly high – and typically Shakespearian.

If Shakespeare was not himself responsible for the Folio redaction of *King Lear*, it must have been the work of an exceptionally insignificant Jacobean dramatist, with no known association with the King's Men and no known proficiency in serious historical or tragic drama, who nevertheless shared all of Shakespeare's linguistic preferences, whose vocabulary exactly corresponded with Shakespeare's in 1609–10, who shared Shakespeare's taste for new and rare vocabulary, who like Shakespeare had mastered a variety of different verbal styles (from the rhymed couplets of the Fool's prophecy to the imagistic and syntactical complexity of Kent's altered speech in 3.1, from the authoritative prose of the additions in 1.2 and 4.6 to the comic prose of added speeches in 2.4 and 3.6), and whom the best critics for centuries have mistaken for Shakespeare himself.

Potentially Spurious Variation

Stone bases his rejection of Shakespeare's authorship on claims that the Folio alterations and additions are extraneous, ill-conceived, or poorly written. Such arguments have been heard before, of course, about other parts of the canon; but one would think that in the late twentieth century a disintegrationist would feel some obligation to base his case on more objective evidence. I, for one, do not accept that the redaction *is* inferior; nor do the other contributors to this collection. But even if there were general and widespread agreement on the inferiority of the Folio version, that need not affect Shakespeare's claim to authorship. Revisions need not be improvements, even when made by Shakespeare – and a long-standing, by no means extinct tradition of criticism regards the last works as a distinct falling-off from the period of 'the four great tragedies'. *Cymbeline* itself, Dr Johnson's 'unresisting heap of imbecility', is probably the most puzzling play in the canon. If Shakespeare revised *Lear* just before writing *Cymbeline*, some readers might well find the revision little to their taste. As in James Joyce's fantasia about works with letters for titles, we might soon find ourselves being asked, 'Have you read his F?' and answering 'O yes, but I prefer Q' – without ever doubting that F is indeed 'his'.

Stone does offer two kinds of authorship evidence which require some comment. First, he points to a number of places where a Folio reading apparently results from an attempt to make sense of a corrupt reading in Q; in several such cases the Folio solution cannot possibly represent what lies behind the Quarto error. Therefore, argues Stone, the Folio correction must have been made by someone who did not *know* what the original reading was; therefore that someone was not Shakespeare (*Textual History*, p. 114). But this assumes that Shakespeare remembered every line he ever wrote – and that, having remembered it, he would be loath to tinker with it as the fancy struck him. These are wholly unwarranted assumptions.

Dickens, for instance, sometimes recast passages in proof on the basis of printer's errors. In Dickens's case, moreover, the original manuscript was written only weeks or days (rather than years) before he corrected, or imaginatively 'miscorrected', the proofs.[106] James Joyce also rewrote lines as a result of printer's errors. In each of the following examples, a manuscript reading (MS) has been corrupted by the printer (PE), and the printer's error subsequently revised by Joyce (RV).[107]

MS: The widow Dignam
PE: The widow woman
RV: Mrs Dignam, widow woman,

MS: the fatfolds of Bloom's haunches
PE: the fat folds of Bloom's haunches
RV: the fat suet folds of Bloom's haunches

MS(Bloom in the role of Napoleon): He places a hand in his waistcoat opening calmly.
PE: He places a hand in his waistcoat, opening calmly.
RV: He places a hand in his waistcoat, posing calmly.

MS: the smooth tapstep walk
PE: the smooth [unread] walk
RV: the smooth mincing walk

Since, in Joyce's case as in Dickens's, we possess the original manuscript, the printer's proof containing the error, and the author's revision on that proof, there can be no real doubt that the error helped to generate, or was alone responsible for generating, these revisions. In another case the printer prompted Joyce to a revision which, in context, is clearly inferior to the original text. (I italicize the affected words.)

MS: On a step a gnome totting *away rubbish* crouches to shoulder a sack of rags and bones.
PE: On a step a gnome totting *among rubbish* crouches to shoulder a sack of rags and bones.
RV: On a step a gnome totting *among a rubbishheap* crouches to shoulder a sack of rags and bones.

Many more examples could be given, from Joyce and other modern writers.[108] *Ulysses* itself provides a particularly interesting parallel to *Lear*: because Joyce's revision in proof was so extensive, alongside some cases where revision clearly *does* relate to a printer's error there occur many others where it *might*.

Verbal revisions based upon printer's errors in Q thus tell us nothing about the authenticity of Folio variants. Moreover, Stone's insistence that Shakespeare cannot have been involved in the alteration of Q leads him into further difficulties elsewhere, in trying to account for the number of *good* corrections this same 'adapter' made, working from Q, and apparently without recourse to any more authoritative manuscript. Some of these corrections are difficult to attribute to anyone who did not know the original. Stone is thereby forced to conjecture that the adapter, working in 1618 or after, had managed to retrieve the actual manuscript used as printer's copy for Q1 in 1608; but that, having somehow procured this manuscript, he then used it only sporadically. Such a reconstruction explains one improbability by resort to two. What the evidence requires – a writer surprisingly familiar with the original text, but sometimes misled by a Q1 error, or taking a Q1 error as his excuse for verbal tinkering – is simply and satisfactorily supplied by the hypothesis that the writer was Shakespeare himself, working (initially) from a copy of Q1.

Stone's other argument rests on two Folio passages which, he contends, allow us confidently to date the Folio redaction after Shakespeare's retirement or death. The first of these need not detain us long:

Pla[t]e sinnes with Gold, and the strong Lance of Iustice, hurtlesse breakes: Arme it in ragges, a Pigmies straw do's pierce it. None do's offend, none, I say none, Ile able 'em; take that of me my Friend, who haue the power to seale th'accusers lips.

(TLN 2608–12; 4.6.165–70)

This hardly need refer, as Stone alleges (*Textual History*, pp. 122–5), to the Overbury scandal. Compare Claudius's

> In the corrupted currents of this world,
> Offences guilded hand may sho[u]e by iustice,
> And oft tis seene the wicked prize it selfe
> Buyes out the lawe.
> (*Hamlet* Q2: I1ᵛ; TLN 2333–6; 3.3.57–60)

Such commonplaces tell us nothing about the date or authorship of the Folio redaction of *Lear*. But Stone's other example, from the Fool's prophecy, requires a more extensive examination, which John Kerrigan conducts elsewhere in this volume (pp. 221–3); he concludes, on what seem indisputable grounds, that the line in question could as easily have been written before 1612 as after 1617.

Stone's and Kerrigan's evidence therefore gives us either a *terminus a quo* (1618) if the redaction was not Shakespeare's, or a *terminus ad quem* (1612) if it was. Bibliographical evidence indicates that the redaction cannot have taken place before 1608. Therefore if, as the authorship evidence indicates, Shakespeare was himself the reviser, we can confidently date the revision 1608–11. All the other evidence is easily compatible with this conclusion, and suggests that the chronological limits might reasonably be narrowed to 1609–10.

Shakespeare's responsibility for the Folio additions and alterations thus seems to me to be strongly supported by all the available evidence. Nevertheless, such evidence as is available can, in the nature of things, only establish the date and authorship of the *bulk* of the Folio redaction; the possibility that individual variants date from a later or earlier period, or result from interference by one or another unauthorized agent, cannot be ruled out. To take an obvious instance: if Q was printed from Shakespeare's foul papers, and F from the prompt-book of a revised version not undertaken until several years later, then there must once have existed a prompt-book of that earlier version; since that earlier prompt-book would almost certainly have differed from the foul papers in a number of respects, in certain details the revision prompt-book consulted in the printing of F may have been anticipated by the prompt-book of the original production. Thus, at 2.1.36, Q has the direction '*Enter Glost.*' (D3^v), where F has '*Enter Gloster, and Seruants with Torches*' (TLN 970). In both texts Gloucester interrupts Edmund's third subsequent speech, ordering someone to 'pursue' and 'go after' Edgar. Urkowitz suggests that, in Q, Gloucester's instructions are 'directed to offstage pursuers' (*Revision*, p. 27). But Q, characteristically of a foul-paper text, often fails to supply necessary entrances and exits; in particular, on eight other occasions it calls only for the entrance of one or more main characters, omitting to mention others who clearly enter at the same time.[109] F, characteristically of a prompt-book, supplies almost all such necessary directions. The variants at 2.1.36 thus probably reflect a difference in the provenance of the two manuscripts rather than a change of authorial intention, and editors or interpreters of Q *Lear* would be justified in supplying the attendants from F.

Many variants in stage directions clearly or arguably belong in this category; they could not influence or be detected by the foregoing evidence of a later date for the Folio redaction as a whole. Likewise, a few of the verbal revisions in F might have originated in

Shakespeare's first fair copy, or in the prompt-book of the first production. Naturally such early revisions would be almost impossible to differentiate from later ones, but two potential examples will illustrate the editorial problem. I have argued above ('Censorship', pp. 102–9) that the Folio omission of 1.4.140–55 (C4ᵛ–D1) resulted from censorship, and that the passage almost certainly disappeared before the play was ever performed. More conjecturally, the Folio addition of the Fool's last speech, 'And Ile go to bed at noone' (TLN 2043; 3.6.85), might also date from the first production. Although Shakespeare, in the course of composing 3.6, may not yet have firmly decided what to do with the Fool in the rest of the play, by the time he prepared the first fair copy – or, if not then, certainly by the time rehearsals began – he must have realized that 3.6 was the character's last appearance. The Folio's added line serves the obvious dramatic function of providing the Fool with a much more prominent and enigmatic exit from the scene and the play – a dramatic function pertinent to either text.[110] It would therefore not surprise me if this particular addition dates from the play's first prompt-book – though of course this cannot be proved, and Shakespeare in that earlier prompt-book might just as easily have given the Fool a *different* extra line.[111]

Such uncertainties only affect the dating of particular revisions; they matter much less than several unanswered questions about the authority of whole categories of Folio variant. The Folio text may contain actors' interpolations, theatrical alterations made for practical reasons, errors and sophistications accumulated during the course of its transmission. Such corruptions could be substantial without markedly affecting the evidence already examined for the date and authenticity of the revision as a whole: a scattering of corruptions and interpolations might not influence the statistical tests at all, or some might cancel out the effect of others; stage directions have not been included in any of the foregoing tests, which have also excluded the categories of vocabulary and usage most susceptible to sophistication. Most important of all, the date and 'authorship' of an omission can never, in the absence of external evidence, be established with complete certainty, and the Folio text omits approximately 300 lines present in Q.

Shakespeare himself referred to 'clownes' who 'speake . . . more then is set downe for them' (Q2 *Hamlet* G4; TLN 1887–8; 3.2.39–40), and on at least one occasion Caroline actors officially confessed to just such an offence.[112] That actors sometimes spoke more on stage than authors intended can therefore hardly be doubted. But the nature of this evidence itself undermines the assertion that such liberties in performance can have affected many of the surviving texts of English Renaissance drama.[113] Hamlet's clown speaks more than is 'set downe' for him; in the case of Jonson's *The Magnetic Lady*, the King's Men delivered lines for which neither the author nor the censor could be blamed, because they were apparently *not* in the licensed playbook. We have no evidence, and no reason to believe, that the licensed book was altered to incorporate such theatrical interpolations; indeed, to do so would have been illegal, since it would have implied the sanctioning by the Master of the Revels of material he had not seen. Only if for some reason a new book were required *could* such interpolations be added, though even in these circumstances we have no evidence that they *would* be. In some cases, notably *Othello*, we can determine that a new book was made, or the original at least heavily altered, solely or partly in order to bring it into conformity with the 1606 *Acte to Restraine Abuses*;[114] but for *Lear* there is no evidence of such interference (beyond the omission of a single 'Fut'), and in any case the original book may not even have been prepared before that Act came into being. Whatever our hypothesis about Q and F, then, we cannot postulate the preparation of a new or altered prompt-book for such reasons. More particularly, the substantial evidence for Shakespearian revision, *c.*1609–10, indicates that a new book must have been prepared at that time (and resubmitted to the Master of the Revels); by that date the Act had already been in force for three or four years. Since Shakespeare appears to have been heavily involved in the preparation of this second book, any actors' interpolations accepted into it at that time must presumably have had his sanction. Nothing in the external record, or in the nature of the Folio text, gives us any right to postulate the preparation of a third prompt-book, or to postulate that F was printed from anything other than the second book itself. We know, after all, that prompt-books existed, and any play of Shakespeare's presumably existed in this form at one time; but hypotheses involving transcripts of one kind or another require the creation of manuscripts which were not necessary and which may well in many or most cases never have existed at all. Consequently, when a text has characteristics which accord with the assumption that it was indeed printed from a prompt-book, then the burden of proof rests heavily upon those who wish to establish that it was printed from something else. In this case I can see nothing in F which would militate against its use in the theatre.[115] But even if a copy of the book, rather than the book itself, was forwarded to the printer, we have absolutely no evidence that the copyist would have been expected, or intended, or even able, to include in it material unauthoritatively spoken on stage.

The determinable history of the manuscript consulted in the printing of F thus gives us no reason to expect F to contain actors' unauthorized interpolations. Nor is this category of corruption easily defined, in relation to individual variants. How is an actor's interpolation distinguishable from an authorial addition? In the case of Greek tragedy, the theatrical manuscripts from which all surviving copies derive were not themselves collected until 75 to 150 years after the composition of the plays; in such circumstances no one can deny the possibility that the texts which survive may have suffered extensive theatrical adaptation, or verbal alterations designed to make the language more intelligible to much later audiences, or additions which had become traditional in posthumous revivals. These conditions, however, obviously have little pertinence to Shakespeare. Moreover, although the wholesale adaptation of several Greek tragedies – including interpolations of entire episodes – can be demonstrated with some confidence, in the absence of external evidence individual interpolations remain virtually impossible to detect.[116] However confident the rhetoric, when an editor labels something an actor's interpolation he is doing no more than declaring that he does not like it. Such declarations naturally tell us more about the editor than the text. For instance, Stone dismisses Gloucester's 'And that's true too' (TLN 2936; 5.2.11) as a 'stopgap' which is vacuous to the point of 'fatuity' (*Textual History*, pp. 69–70). Derek Peat, in contrast, regards it as a paradigm of the play's tragic method, and Martha Andresen sets it in the context of a series of moralizing *sententiae* throughout the play.[117] Although Peat and Andresen do not relate their judgements to the authenticity of the Folio text, those judgements have as much editorial validity as Stone's. Stone also considers that some of F's added 'nonsense syllables', like 'Sa, sa, sa, sa' (TLN 2645; 4.6.203) and 'O do, de, do, de, do de' (TLN 1839; 3.4.58–9), might have resulted from the adapter 'inventing nonsense gratuitously' (*Textual History*, pp. 247–8);[118] but again, these additions could easily be defended by reference to the play's preoccupation with both human bestiality and the unalterable insufficiency of human language. In each case Stone's objection seems to me less convincing critically than the defence of F's addition; more important, though, even if Stone's subjective reaction were widely shared, it could not establish one origin (actor's interpolation) rather than another (authorial revision) for an addition which is dramatically sensible and defensible.

Given that suspicions of theatrical interpolation depend entirely upon such dubious critical assertions, they cannot constitute, in themselves, reliable evidence for the stages of a text's transmission. That is, we cannot postulate – on the basis of nothing more exacting or secure than our own hunches that certain words or passages have been interpolated by actors – a special stage or agency of transcription which could have introduced such changes. Yet editors of Shakespeare repeatedly do just this. Dover Wilson's belief that Folio *Hamlet* was printed from a transcript of the prompt-book, rather than from the prompt-book itself, has no other foundation:[119] an entire crucial stage of transmission has been pulled out of a hat in order to supply a magical scribe who high-handedly relied on his own comprehensive memories of the verbal minutiae of performance rather than merely copying the text in front of him.[120] To justify his claim that the actors have interpolated various words and phrases, the editor himself interpolates a scribe into his stemma of the text's transmission – a scribe for whom there is no other evidence, and who behaves in every respect like a revising author, except that some of his revisions do not appeal to the editor in question.

The illegitimacy of this editorial procedure has been obscured by three apparent precedents for the situation it postulates. Greek dramatic texts unquestionably suffered from later theatrical tampering; Shakespeare's own texts underwent heavy verbal adaptation after the Restoration; theatrical adaptation of earlier plays occurred throughout the lifetime of Shakespeare and the King's Men. These precedents are all illusory. John Kerrigan has demonstrated that theatrical adaptation before the Restoration was markedly distinct from authorial revision, that both activities regularly occurred, and that the differences between Quarto and Folio *Lear* clearly define Folio *Lear* as an authorial redaction (above, pp. 213–15). After the Interregnum, however – forty years after the printing of the First Folio – this earlier distinction between revision and adaptation completely collapsed, and collapsed as the result of factors similar to those which led to the contamination of our surviving texts of Greek drama: fundamental changes in theatrical and intellectual fashion combined with a marked decline in the quality of new writing for the theatre.[121] The decline in new writing led in both cases to a heavy demand for revivals, and an equally heavy dependence by new playwrights upon techniques and material inherited from their acclaimed predecessors; the changes in fashion necessitated minor and in some cases major adaptation of the old plays, adaptations which a lesser breed of dramaturge was on hand to supply, 'improving' his predecessors and making their extravagant or obsolescent language acceptable and intelligible to later generations of theatre-goers.[122] As a result, for both Restoration England and fourth-century Greece we have documentary evidence that play texts were subjected to agents of transmission who could, would, and regularly did alter the texts themselves, in bulk and in detail, to satisfy or reflect contemporary (and from our standpoint contemptible) theatrical taste. We have no reason whatever to infer a similar brief for any theatrical scribe who may have copied *King Lear* (or *Hamlet*) between 1610 and 1623.

Proponents of interpolation must therefore demonstrate not simply that a given addition is 'unworthy of Shakespeare' (whatever that means), but specifically that Shakespeare was *incapable* of writing it. A suspected interpolation must therefore be demonstrably worse than any of Shakespeare's own lapses. Moreover, some plausible explanation must be offered for the interpolation's presence in the manuscript consulted in printing F. If we accept that that manuscript was the company's prompt-book, then we must explain why, when, and in what circumstances the prompt-book was altered to incorporate it; if we believe that the manuscript was instead a transcript of the prompt-book, we must first provide independent evidence that such a transcript existed, and then explain how and why the transcriber included the interpolation. Until such conditions are satisfied, I see no reason to suspect that Folio *Lear* has suffered from unauthorized theatrical interpolation.

The one Folio addition most often suspected as an interpolation, the Fool's prophecy (TLN 1734–49; 3.2.79–96), has been defended at length by John Kerrigan (above, pp. 218–30); the relationship between this addition and a book Shakespeare was apparently reading in 1608–10, Puttenham's *Arte of English Poesie* (above, p. 382), reinforces Kerrigan's arguments for the speech's authenticity. In any case, the underlying assumption – that the company's clown could get away with anything – hardly seems warranted for the period in which this alleged interpolation took place. Even if (as seems to me debatable) Robert Armin originally played the Fool's part, he left the King's Men sometime in 1610.[123] Shakespeare was not only still alive in 1610, but still a sharer and still writing a play a year for the company; Armin could thus hardly have forced the interpolation behind Shakespeare's back or without his consent.[124] In particular, Shakespeare's apparent revision of *Lear* may not even have been finished when Armin left, or announced his intention of doing so. Someone must, of course, have played the Fool after 1610; but no subsequent company comedian had the independent reputation, or the resulting power, that men like Tarlton, Kempe, and Armin undoubtedly possessed.

Theatrical interpolation thus seems most unlikely to have contaminated the Folio text. Many of the same considerations argue against the possibility of unauthorized theatrical alterations. Between the original composition of *Lear* and the publication of the First Folio the King's Men moved into the Blackfriars (1609) and into the Second Globe, after the burning of the first (1613–14). Neither event need have affected Folio *Lear*. We have no evidence that *Lear* was ever even performed at either the Blackfriars or the Second Globe; nor is anything in Q beyond the resources of these theatres, or anything in F beyond those of the First Globe. Nor do the resources of the company show any signs of gradual diminution or prolonged crisis.[125] This must be emphasized because, although unauthorized changes in staging usually consist of spectacular embellishments, in the case of *Lear* denigrators of the Folio text have been driven to assume the reverse: that the posthumous theatrical alterations made the play *less* spectacular, and sprang from a poverty rather than a superfluity of resources. Of course, the opposite assumption must be made to explain the Hecate scenes in *Macbeth*, supposedly added in the same few years when *Lear* was being pared to accommodate a struggling company; but editors seem unperturbed by the apparent contradiction, or by the lack of either general or specific evidence for their presuppositions about the company which purportedly adapted *Lear*.

Most commonly, editors assert that Folio *Lear* has in places been cut in order to diminish the number of roles.[126] This allegedly explains F's excision of Q's conversation between Gloucester's two servants (H2; 3.7.99–107), F's alteration of 4.6.187 from *Enter three*

Gentlemen (I4ᵛ) to *Enter a Gentleman* (TLN 2630), F's substitution of 'Gentleman' for 'Doctor' in 4.4 and 4.7 (Il–Ilᵛ, Klᵛ–K2ᵛ; TLN 2349–81, 2745–843), and F's elimination of an onstage appearance for Edgar's trumpeter (L1ᵛ; TLN 3067; 5.3.117). But in fact these variants do not affect the number of actors which the King's Men would have needed to perform *Lear*, because in each case the affected roles could easily be doubled by a number of other available actors.[127] Such doubling was the norm of pre-Restoration professional practice, and in either text *Lear* requires less doubling, and a smaller cast, than many other plays of Shakespeare.[128] Moreover, of the four alleged examples, the first (3.7.99–107) may not actually even save any doubling, since the two characters are probably required on stage whether or not they speak;[129] the second (4.6.187) seems to me almost certainly the result of a simple misreading;[130] and the third saves an actor's appearance only in one of the two scenes (4.7, where Q calls for both a Gentleman and the Doctor). Moreover, if the Doctor and the Gentleman were conflated solely to save an actor, then the role sacrificed would surely have been the Gentleman rather than the more dramatic and identifiable Doctor. This in itself strongly suggests that other motives lay behind the change. Finally, the omission of Edgar's trumpeter saves the King's Men nothing at all, since the trumpeter is still required off-stage, and was almost certainly one of the company's regular musicians. By keeping him offstage the Folio leaves Edgar's dramatic entry uncluttered by supernumeraries, raising no irreverent questions about where he got a trumpeter, emphasizing instead his solitary singularity, his learned and earned self-reliance.

The Doctor/Gentleman variant occurs in a scene, 4.7, which also contains a change in staging widely dismissed as unauthoritative: having dispensed with the Doctor, F then has Lear carried on stage in a chair (rather than being discovered in a bed), and removes the call for offstage music (K2; TLN 2771; 4.7.23). G. K. Hunter summarizes these apparently interrelated variants by saying that 'There is [in F] recurrent evidence of a desire to simplify the staging. In IV. 7 both the music and the Doctor are gone, the latter replaced (as in IV. 4) by an easier-to-use Gentleman.'[131] Hunter here echoes Capell, who believed that the Folio's 'mode of bringing in Lear, was a meer stage convenience; and for that conveniency too, those folio's sunk the speech' calling for offstage music. But in the first place, it should be noticed that F's staging calls for the onstage presence of at least two extra actors, to carry in the chair; thus Hunter *et al.* first castigate F for removing one character from this scene because of 'a penury of actors' (Malone), then further castigate it for 'a meer stage convenience' (Capell) which in fact demands at least two more actors. The modern editor simply inherits the unresolved contradictions of his eighteenth-century predecessors. In fact, the King's Men suffered from no shortage of musicians, and no demonstrable reluctance to use them;[132] doctors are required in six other plays of Shakespeare (*Wives, Macbeth, Pericles, Cymbeline, Henry VIII*, and *Kinsmen*), and in at least eight other King's Men plays first performed between 1614 and 1621;[133] beds are specifically called for in *2 Henry VI, Romeo, Othello*, and *Cymbeline*, not to mention Fletcher's *The Wild-Goose Chase* (4.3; dated 1621) and *The Spanish Curate* (4.5; dated 1622).[134] The original Q staging can, therefore, hardly have incommoded the company; nor is F's alternative in any way un-Shakespearian. Sick or disabled persons are carried onstage in chairs at *1 Henry VI* 2.5.0 (TLN 1069) and 3.2.40 (TLN 1470), *2 Henry VI* 2.1.65 (TLN 796), *3 Henry VI* 4.3.27 (TLN 2258; King Edward, who has insisted on sleeping in his chair), *Othello* 5.2.282 (N1; not in F), and *The Two Noble Kinsmen* 5.4.85 (M4).

The chair in 4.7 brings with it several dramatic advantages. Most important, as Granville-Barker noted, when Lear 'comes to himself it is to find that he is royally attired and as if seated on his throne again. It is from this throne that he totters to kneel at Cordelia's feet.'[135] The suggestion of a throne can be (and in production has been) easily made;[136] the visual parallel with the first scene can be made even more striking if Regan and Goneril in 1.1 kneel when they offer Lear their protestations of love. Kent's presence also reinforces the parallel, and the suggestion of a throne lends a particular poignance to Kent's suggestion that Lear is 'in[his] owne kingdome' (TLN 2835; K2ᵛ; 4.7.75). The old man in a chair, helpless, surrounded by at least three other figures, may also remind an audience of Gloucester, bound and tortured in a chair – especially when Lear says, 'I am bound | Vpon a wheele of fire' (TLN 2795–6; K2; 4.7.45–6). Lear's pain, like Gloucester's, is real; but in 4.7 the attention to tears and eyes, the pricking with a pin, the old man supported by others as he leaves the stage, express a world of feeling diametrically opposed to the cruelties of 3.7. And in addition to its thematic value, the chair has more immediate dramatic merits too. Unlike someone propped up in bed, a character sitting in a chair can, however weak, easily move to kneel, as Lear apparently does at 4.7.58 (K2ᵛ; TLN 2812), when

Cordelia says 'You must not kneele'. Moreover, unlike a character discovered in a bed, a character in a chair can be carried downstage, which gives an audience a decidedly better view of his face. F's staging thus facilitates an audience's attention to the dramatic, emotional, and intellectual heart of the scene: Lear's reactions on awakening, and his recognition of Cordelia. Excising the music serves the same function: it leaves the silences truly silent, filled only with the deep specific emotions of three characters rather than the generalised ready-made emotion of off-stage instruments. The 'meer stage convenience' makes the scene harder on the performers by making its success entirely dependent on their resources, rather than those of the music room. As a result, the Folio makes up in painful actuality for what it loses in moody musicality.

Q's alternative, by contrast, emphasizes symbolic properties – an attendant doctor, music, Lear rising from his bed like a man from his grave – at the expense of the central dramatic relationship. No one would wish to deny the pertinence of these symbols, or their parallels in Shakespeare's late plays; one can understand their attraction for critics primarily committed to literary rather than dramatic values. Nevertheless, they remain peripheral to this scene: Shakespeare exploits their resonances much more fully and dramatically in *Pericles*, *The Winter's Tale*, and *Cymbeline*. To accept F's directions here one need only assume that Shakespeare, in 1606, decided that he would develop the dramatic potential of literal and figurative rebirth in future plays, and so altered the staging of this scene in *Lear*; or assume – as seems to me more likely – that, in 1609 or 1610, realizing that he had since exploited that potential better elsewhere, Shakespeare retrospectively altered the staging of the scene in *Lear*. To reject F's directions here one must instead first assume that Shakespeare insisted upon retaining the scene's symbolic accoutrements despite their awkward effect on the dramatic realization of Lear's awakening to Cordelia, and then in addition assume that the company deliberately disregarded Shakespeare's wishes, either from the beginning or after he had died. Either position imposes upon its advocate an assumption about Shakespeare's attitude to his art; in either case Shakespeare must have been choosing, not between the demands of expedience and those of art, but between conflicting demands, both artistic in origin. The first explanation – that Shakespeare made the changes – is simpler, allows Shakespeare two opportunities for a change of mind, does not assume the worst about

Heminges and Condell (whom at least three other actors entrusted with the faithful execution of their wishes, after their deaths[137]), and seems to me more consonant with what we know about Shakespeare's character and career. But whether or not I am right in regarding this first explanation as intrinsically more probable, the Folio text itself remains our *only* evidence of Shakespeare's own attitude; attempts to discredit that evidence simply assume what they must prove, that Shakespeare disapproved of the change. Editors who dismiss the Folio's staging as an unauthorized simplification are merely dressing biographical speculation in the robes of 'the new bibliography'.

Like the eighteenth-century assumption that the text of F has suffered unauthorized alteration in the theatre, the eighteenth-century assumption that it has suffered extensive corruption in the course of its transmission proves on examination demonstrably implausible. Paul Werstine's analysis of the two Folio compositors (above, pp. 247–312) establishes that relatively few Folio variants are likely to have arisen in the printing-house, and at least suggests that the scribe who prepared the manuscript was neither incompetent nor irresponsible. Certainly, the scribe either interfered with his text less than did Ralph Crane and the anonymous scribe who prepared the Folio text of *2 Henry IV*,[138] or his interference was of a remarkably invisible variety. Moreover, the evidence that Shakespeare himself began his revision on a copy of Q1 absolves the printer of blame for much of the carelessness of collation evident in the Folio's retention of unauthoritative Q1 press variants; some and perhaps most of that carelessness must be Shakespeare's, and therefore embedded in the manuscript the printer consulted.[139] Nor do we have any reason to postulate an agent, at some stage in F's transmission, bent upon simplifying Shakespeare's language. This hypothetical figure, whom Duthie called 'Scribe E', owes his continued existence to editorial interpretations of two variants – rash/sticke (H1ᵛ; TLN 2130; 3.7.58) and dearne/sterne (H1ᵛ; TLN 2135; 3.7.63);[140] he has been effectively dematerialized by a reconsideration of those two variants from three quite different but mutually-supporting perspectives: Paul Werstine's (above, p. 286), Randall McLeod's (above, p. 160), and my own (above, p. 374). Like other Folio texts, and particularly those set from theatrical or other scribal copy, Folio *Lear* probably preserves little of Shakespeare's own spelling and punctuation – though in at least one case it does contain what seems, on good evidence, to have been a peculiar Shakespearian form.[141] Certainly, in *King Lear* as elsewhere, the Folio sophisticates a few recurring forms, sporadically altering 'beside' to 'besides', 'sometime' to 'sometimes', 'a' to 'he', 'yond' to 'yon', and 'farther' to 'further'.[142] Such sophistications are, however, as easy to identify as to correct. Stone alleges that someone involved in preparing the manuscript from which F was printed tried to impose upon the text an un-Shakespearian metrical regularity. However, Stone also alleges that in other places Folio alterations *disrupt* the metrical regularity of Q; he thus asks us to believe in an agent who was, simultaneously, culpably attentive to metre and culpably inattentive to it.[143] All the examples of metrical disruption could, moreover, easily be paralleled in other Shakespearian texts, and we cannot rule out the possibility that, in other places, 'mellifluous and honey-tongued Shakespeare' might himself have smoothed the metre of passages left rough in his foul papers.

We can be sure that the Folio text of *Lear* has suffered the usual, relatively small amount of sophistication and compositorial error; but we have no reason to suspect – and much evidence to deny – that it has suffered extraordinary corruption, or grievous bodily harm, in the course of its transmission into print.

Folio Omissions

We are left, finally, with the problem of omissions – although in fact 'excisions' would be a better word, since most of the passages in question must have been removed deliberately. The question is, who removed them?

As I have argued above, the Folio's excision of certain passages present in Q cannot be credibly attributed to economies in casting (p. 411), and only one major cut can be plausibly related to censorship (pp. 102–9). It also seems most unlikely that the text was cut simply because it was too long.[144] Even a fully conflated text of *Lear* contains no more lines than Q1 of *Richard III*, a text almost universally accepted as a report of that play as actually performed – as performed, moreover, on a provincial tour. Likewise, Folio *Hamlet*, apparently derived from the official playbook, contains over 300 lines more than a fully conflated text of *Lear*. Folio *Troilus* is slightly longer than a conflated *Lear*, and Folio *Othello* not much shorter; both texts were probably printed from the official playing text.[145] Since the company played Shakespearian texts longer than the conflated *Lear*, we have no right or reason to infer that the approximately 300 lines absent from the Folio text were sacrificed 'for the sole purpose of short'ning' (Capell), victims of a mere uncritical demand for a briefer play. The other members of the company might have asked Shakespeare to shorten the text; but we have no proof that they did, no criteria which would allow us to infer that they must have, and no reason to assume that Shakespeare would have felt obliged to satisfy such a request, even if it had been made. Nor can we take it for granted that Shakespeare ever intended the finished play to contain all the material present in his foul papers (from which Q appears to have been printed). Other texts printed from foul papers – notably *Love's Labour's Lost* and *Romeo and Juliet*, and also perhaps *Henry V* – contain passages which clearly seem to have been abandoned in the course of composition, and subsequently disregarded or rewritten or replaced;[146] given the anomalies of character and plot created by certain passages in 4.3 (Urkowitz, *Revision*, pp. 53–4), Shakespeare *may* have decided to abandon all or part of this short scene long before he even finished Act Four.

Regardless of who suggested the excisions, Shakespeare must have made or acquiesced in any such changes in the original prompt-book (1605–1606) or the revised one (1609–10). Only changes made after Shakespeare's retirement or death could be confidently dismissed as unauthoritative.[147] But once the book had been made and the actors had learned their parts, little purpose would be served by un-authorized minor abridgements of the text. It has sometimes been suggested that Albany's part was abbreviated in F because of the incapacity of an actor who subsequently inherited the role.[148] But such speculations have no more foundation than Theobald's conjec-ture that the Folio's changed attribution of the final speech was due to the popularity of the actor playing Edgar. The only actor we can securely identify with a particular role in *Lear* is Burbage, who played the title part;[149] Burbage died in 1619, and would have had to be replaced (if *Lear* was ever performed between 1619 and 1623). No one in the company was as talented an actor as Burbage; and yet Lear's role is no less strenuous and commanding in F than in Q. By contrast, even in Q Albany's role is not exceptionally demanding; any actor incapable of giving it a passable performance could hardly have become a sharer in the most acclaimed theatrical company of the age; no 'hired man' incapable of playing it is likely to have been hired very often, or to have had the text mutilated to fit the Procrustean bed of his incompetence. This mythical ineptus has not left his mark on any other text, or any other theatrical record of the period; we do not know (as we do for Lear) when or if the original interpreter of Albany left the company; nor do we have any evidence that the King's Men ever altered roles to accommodate particular actors.[150]

Those who strain at a gnat may swallow camels whole; nevertheless, it is astounding that editors who will argue scrupulously over the positioning of a colon, or examine hundreds of spellings in order to determine how many compositors set a text, have nevertheless accepted the validity of an entire textual hypothesis based upon such a pyramid of unsubstantiated and improbable speculation. Equally astounding is the repeated assertion that an error in F 'proves' or 'confirms' that the official prompt-book originally included 4.3. The Folio, which removes the scene, accordingly numbers 4.4 as 4.3, 4.5 as 4.4, and 4.6 as 4.5; however, it identifies the last scene of the act as 4.7 ('*Scaena Septima*'). According to Madeleine Doran, W. W. Greg, G. I. Duthie, G. K. Hunter, and others, this error establishes – or at least 'suggests' – that the omission of 4.3 must have postdated the preparation of the manuscript, and must therefore be without Shakespearian authority.[151] This 'proof' disregards the obvious fact that numerical errors of this kind (vi/vii) are easy enough to make, by misreading or memorial substitution; such a Folio error could have been made either by Compositor E, or by the printing-house scribe (who annotated E's Q2 copy), or by the theatrical scribe who prepared the manuscript. Prompt-books usually or at least very often did not contain scene numbers at all;[152] this suggests that the error, and all F's scene-numbers, may well have originated in the printing-house rather than in the theatre. In any case, there are similar errors, apparently unrelated to textual dislocation, in *Tancred and Gismond* (where Act Four is described as 3.1), in Crane's manuscript of Middleton's *The Witch* (which skips from 5.1 to 5.3), in *The Devil's Charter* (where Act Three has two Scene Twos), and in *Promos and Cassandra* (where Act Two has two Scene Fours, followed by Scene Five and then Scene Nine). Even if we limit ourselves to the First Folio, in *Love's Labour's Lost* and *King John* '*Actus Quartus*' occurs twice (the second in error for '*Actus Quintus*'), and act or scene divisions are variously botched in *The Taming of the Shrew*, *King John*, *Henry V*, *1 Henry VI*, *Richard III*, and *Cymbeline*. The numerical error at TLN 2743 of Folio *Lear* thus, demonstrably, proves nothing about the circumstances under which 4.3 was removed. If the Folio had correctly numbered the first two scenes and then misnumbered the remaining four (4.4–4.7), that would indeed suggest that 4.3 once stood in the prompt-book, though even then one could hardly prove that Shakespeare himself did not make the change after the book was prepared; but one simple error in one of the subsequent scene-numberings, four scenes later, tells us nothing about the Folio's excision of 4.3.

The major Folio excisions thus cannot be convincingly explained as the results of censorship, or limits of cast, or changes of cast, or the need to shorten an unacceptably lengthy text; nor can we demonstrate, or even reasonably infer, that any of them postdate Shakespeare's retirement. Some of them, moreover, like the heavy abridgement of 4.2, can hardly have been dictated by hack-theatrical considerations: exchanges of abuse – especially between husband and wife – have always constituted one of the easiest, cheapest, and most obvious sources of vulgar theatricalism, on stage as in life. Those who attribute other Folio cuts to a stage-manager's impatience with static poetic narratives should feel some discomfiture in having to assign the excisions in 4.2 to the same anonymous philistine. The Folio's heavy abridgement of 3.6 should embarrass conflationists even more. Not only is the omitted material 'dramatic' in the simplest sense; it also largely consists of speeches from Edgar and the Fool. As John Kerrigan demonstrates (above, p. 217), unauthorized theatrical adaptations regularly padded the role of a fool or clown; Folio *Lear* instead diminishes it. The 'sullen and assumed humor of Tom of Bedlam', similarly diminished by the Folio, was actually singled out and *advertised* on the title page of Q – a distinction otherwise reserved for characters like Falstaff, Pistol, and ancient Gower, whose contemporary dramatic impact cannot be doubted. Poor Tom and the Fool can thus hardly be characterized as likely targets for a stage-manager's blue pencil; nor does the mad trial in particular recommend itself as the victim of a Jacobean impresario's surgical depredations. As Alfred Hart remarked long ago, madmen were enjoying a theatrical vogue:[153] mad, 'distracted' characters or bedlamites appear in *The Atheist's Tragedy* (1611; performed by the King's Men?), *The White Devil* (1612), *The Two Noble Kinsmen* (1613; King's), *The Duchess of Malfi* (1614; King's), *Bartholomew Fair* (1614), *The Nice Valour* (1616; King's?), *The Mad Lover* (1617; King's), *The Old Law* (1618), *The Virgin Martyr* (1620), *The Pilgrim*

(1621; King's), *The Duke of Milan* (1621; King's), and *The Changeling* (1622). Such evidence makes it decidedly unlikely that the mad trial was removed for vulgarly theatrical motives.[154]

Other excisions seem directly related to nearby additions. Stanley Wells cites two such passages, where a Folio addition seems designed to replace material from Q which F has removed (above, pp. 14–16); Urkowitz and I have both discussed another, the alternative versions of Kent's long speech in 3.1 (quoted above, p. 393; Taylor, 'War', 31–2; Urkowitz, *Revision*, 67–79). Elsewhere in this volume (pp. 83–5) I have discussed a fourth, which occurs in 1.2: Gloucester's added lines (TLN 439–44; 1.2.109–14) about the effects of 'these late Eclipses' resemble, in basic content if not tone, Edmund's omitted lines (C2^v; 1.2.144–52) on the same subject, and it appears that someone added Gloucester's lines at the same time he cut Edmund's.

In relating these four excisions to four nearby additions I am of course making a critical judgement; nevertheless, these excisions seem worth distinguishing from the others, because in each the Folio does arguably replace what it removes, because in each conflation produces a redundant and/or awkward text, and because the critical issues at stake remain, in each, relatively local and well-defined. Moreover, if we accept the probability that one, some, or all of these four Folio excisions were made by Shakespeare at the same time that he was adding material elsewhere, and if we accept that the abbreviation of 3.6 and 4.2 is most unlikely to have been prompted by 'illegitimate' theatrical considerations, then how can we claim that the other Folio cuts could *not* have been made by Shakespeare? The case for conflating Q and F has always rested upon the assumption that Shakespeare would never, as an artist, have chosen to cancel something he had once written. The evidence that some at least of the Folio excisions were made by the reviser renders this assumption all the more difficult to maintain in relation to the others. In fact, given the cumulative evidence that F's alterations and additions represent a late Shakespearian revision of Q, to dismiss the Folio excisions we must not only assume that Shakespeare never cut his own work, but in particular assume that he did not do so even when engaged in a substantial redaction of his own earlier play. The evidence of press variants, sources, vocabulary, and style all suggests that Shakespeare reworked the text several years after its original composition. On the other hand, F contains no signs at all of theatrical interference; moreover, to explain certain of its features as the result of unauthorized interference one must presuppose a series of events and implausible procedures for which we have no evidence and no parallels.

This conclusion – that Shakespeare must be presumed responsible for all the Folio excisions – can be reached before we have even begun to try to interpret the intentions behind those cuts, or their possible relation to other variants. I emphasize this point because several recent defences of the integrity of F have been based upon attempts to demonstrate that its excisions, additions, and alterations all contribute to a significantly and consistently altered interpretation of the play, or at least of certain characters in it. Hostile critics have been quick to deny the validity of such procedures, arguing that 'It is not surprising that modern critics find purpose and significance in any set of variants; it would be surprising if they could not', or that 'However a text comes about, it has meaning. Chop the pages of *King Lear* up with scissors, throw the pieces in the air, collect them as they fall, and we shall have a text with meaning. But what sort of meaning?'[155]

Few of us would claim to be immune to the charge of having occasionally squeezed 'organic coherence' out of the most unpromising literary pustules. But scepticism about the validity of critical interpretation damages the case for conflation far more than the case for revision, because the case for conflation depends entirely upon a subjective assertion that the play makes better sense if we combine material from both early texts. The belief that *King Lear* exists in two versions rests upon the simple, demonstrable, unalterable fact that there are two early texts of the play, which differ substantially from one another; these two texts represent our only documentary evidence of Shakespeare's intentions; no contemporary document or witness alleges that the two texts were ever meant to be combined, or that either misrepresents Shakespeare's work. It is the conflationist who demands that we disregard the early witnesses, and it is therefore the conflationist who must demonstrate the inadequacy of those documents; if critical arguments about organic coherence are *ipso facto* inadmissible, no conceivable defence of the conflated text remains.

The case for revision, on the other hand, does not even need to prove that the Folio encourages a different interpretation of the action or any of the characters. The Folio might well do so; I personally think that, in certain respects, it does. But we cannot simply postulate or require that an author's revision of his own work will always spring from or impose an altered interpretation of his material. Revision might just as easily arise – as in practice it often, demonstrably, does – from a desire to communicate the original interpretation more effectively. We simply do not know why or how Shakespeare would have revised his own work. Yet defenders of the conflated text repeatedly castigate F because it does not conform to their own convictions about how Shakespeare worked. Philip Edwards, criticizing Urkowitz's interpretation of the differences between Q and F in Albany's role, objects that 'if Shakespeare *had* wished to refashion Albany's part it is certain that he would have *re-written* at least one speech'.[156] As it happens, I share Edwards's dissatisfaction with Urkowitz's interpretation of Albany; yet it is Edwards, not Urkowitz, who bases his textual hypothesis upon an unproven and unprovable assertion about Shakespeare's working habits.

Conflationists regularly berate both F and Q for not satisfying their notions about Shakespeare's methods of composition. For example, Brian Vickers, discussing the variant at 2.4.19–22 (reproduced and discussed by Stanley Wells, above, p. 14), describes Q's alternative as 'flat and dull, reading less like an authorial revision than a poor actor's memory'.[157] Quite apart from the apparent confusion about which text should contain Shakespeare's second thoughts, this claim rests nakedly upon a hunch that the felt superiority of F results from an actor's debasement (in Q) of what Shakespeare first wrote (in F), rather than upon Shakespeare's improvement (in F) of what Shakespeare first wrote (in Q). Vickers's assertion that F here improves upon Q relies upon no criteria that I can discern; his explanation of F's alleged superiority, however, clearly originates in a desire to exonerate Shakespeare from responsibility for the alleged relative inferiority of Q. This desire to protect Shakespeare quickly leads to the denial, in practice, that he could ever have revised his own work. For if a revision improved upon the original, then the original would seem to that extent inferior and therefore unworthy of Shakespeare's genius; if, on the other hand, a revision apparently weakened the original, the revision itself would seem to that extent inferior and therefore unworthy of Shakespeare's genius. Two texts could thus both be Shakespearian only if the revision did not noticeably weaken or improve upon the original, in which case it would hardly have been worth undertaking; but since Shakespeare's genius would never have been tempted by something not worth undertaking, this possibility too must be effectively dismissed. The conflationist thus defines 'Shakespeare' in a way which makes it logically impossible for 'Shakespeare' ever to have revised his own work: his definition 'fills the whole of logical space, leaving no point of it for reality.'[158]

The Pattern of Revision

Attempts to deny that F's excisions relate to its additions and alterations have, in large part, confined themselves to attacks on the subjectivity of the critical procedure which alleges such a relationship. Some dissenters have, however, objected less to the method itself than to its application in particular cases. To begin with, much of the argument has involved alleged differences in the presentation of certain characters. Character criticism is, of course, intellectually unfashionable at the moment, and more than one scholar has expressed unease about the reliability of such 'interpretations' as evidence for a textual hypothesis. But studies of pervasive imagery and themes could hardly be expected to differentiate two strata of composition. Any attempt to investigate whether scattered Folio variants interrelate must therefore find other elements of the play which recur in a widely recognized, significant, formal pattern – and 'characters' are an obvious field for exploration. But even those who accept the potential value of such interpretations may be perturbed by differences between the interpreters themselves. To take only the most obvious example, Warren ('Albany and Edgar') and Urkowitz (*Revision*, pp. 80–128) clearly disagree over how to interpret Albany, in either text. Such disagreements should hardly surprise us: critics disagree, sometimes fundamentally, about the conflated text, and recognition that Shakespeare wrote two versions of *King Lear* instead of one will not and should not produce sweet unanimity about the meaning of either, or the meaning of the differences between them. Nevertheless, such disagreements do generate understandable disquiet, in so far as they create the impression that the case for relating certain variants depends entirely upon our accepting a particular interpretation of the character or action in question: for instance, Michael Warren's misgivings about Edgar's self-satisfied sententiousness in Q, or Urkowitz's determinedly negative view of Albany in F.

One can nevertheless accept the interrelatedness and interdependence of the variants affecting these two characters without committing oneself to the specific interpretations of Albany and Edgar defended by Warren and Urkowitz. These two critics have perceived and, I believe, demonstrated a clear difference between Q and F in the *structure* of the two roles; in each case this demonstration has been accompanied by an *interpretation* of that role, as it appears in each text. These two activities should, so far as possible, be disentangled. Interpretation of character necessarily depends to a considerable degree upon a reader's or actor's perception of the tone in which a series of printed words should be spoken; descriptions of structure, by contrast, largely depend upon an analysis of plot, sequence, and the dramatic disposition of mass – features of a text about which much more agreement can be expected and achieved. To begin with, structures can exist, can be recognized, without being interpreted at all. Many of the changes in Acts Four and Five do clearly centre upon 'the two most serious structural difficulties in the entire play: the anticlimax in the first half of Act IV, and the hiatus in the middle of the last scene' ('War', p. 34). In 3.6 and 4.1 the Folio abbreviates the presentation of madness, which has already been dramatized at considerable length; abbreviation of this material inevitably throws the political plot, which has been running in tandem with it, into greater relative prominence; the remainder of Act Four further emphasizes this political narrative by means of a series of extensive cuts and alterations. Whether all these differences alter or improve or debase the meaning of the play may be debatable; but that they have a cumulative and considerable impact on its structure can hardly be denied.

The very word 'structure' implies an organization of mutually-supporting parts: a change in the interpretation of Albany and Kent logically need have no effect on the interpretation of Edgar, but a change in the structure of these two other 'survivor' roles would almost certainly change the structural function of the third. Likewise, it does not seem accidental that in the first two acts the Folio, by adding and reattributing speeches, expands the roles of both Albany and Cornwall, while at the same time adding, in Lear's explanation of his own 'darker purpose', explicit anxiety about 'future strife' between the Dukes. Or – to take a more debatable example – can it be no more than a coincidence that the Folio both softens the initial presentation of Goneril (as Randall McLeod argues) and makes Cordelia not only stronger but harsher too (as Beth Goldring argues)? Of course, as this last example illustrates, even the analysis of structure can sometimes depend on or shade into critical interpretation, and the distinction collapses if pressed too hard. But a concentration on structure, besides offering what might be a more widely acceptable description of the Folio variants, might also enable us to see the relationships between aspects of the revision hitherto treated in isolation.

Folio *Lear*, when compared to the Quarto, unmistakably diminishes both Albany and Kent in the last half of the play; it also removes the conversation of two servants after Gloucester's blinding, and Edgar's soliloquy before it. These excised passages consist, almost entirely, of explicit moral commentary by a variety of bystanders. Since most literary criticism also consists of explicit moral commentary by a variety of bystander, one can understand why we as critics have been so reluctant to admit that Shakespeare may have regarded such material as dispensable; however, the cuts not only have an obvious dramatic value, but a marked effect upon an audience's perception of the plot. For one thing, by depriving an audience of the consolations of sententiousness, the Folio makes this portion of the play much darker (as did Peter Brook, in some cases by similar means).[159] At the same time, by diminishing Kent and Albany, two spokesmen for moral values who survive the play, and by removing entirely Gloucester's two servants (who endorse the same values), the Folio throws a greater relative emphasis on the other characters who champion these values and/or survive. Three roles in particular profit, structurally, from these excisions: Lear, Cordelia, and Edgar. Lear's long absence between 3.6 and 4.6 is abbreviated; Cordelia's return comes earlier and becomes stronger; Edgar, the only one of these three beneficiaries to survive, becomes by default the play's prime medium of moral continuity, the most important agent and witness of the denouement. These changes of emphasis would occur simply as a result of the excisions, whether or not the roles of Lear and Cordelia and Edgar were themselves altered at all. But of course those roles *are* altered. Lear's reappearance in 4.6 is expanded and, as Roger Warren has argued (above, pp. 45–56), given greater prominence and impact by the cuts in 3.6. Cordelia – who, as Beth Goldring has argued (above, pp. 148–50), has been made a markedly stronger character in the Folio's version of the first scene – returns to England actually leading an army; in 4.7 she unequivocally dominates the reunion with her father, a reunion no longer effected (as in Q) partly through the medium of a semi-magical, harmony-wielding 'Doctor'. But the Folio's strengthening of Edgar's role, especially in 5.3, is both more noticeable and more important than these changes in Cordelia and Lear. To Michael Warren's admirable account of the Folio's magnification of Edgar, largely at Albany's expense, I have nothing to add;[160] but neither he nor Urkowitz remarks on the fact that Edgar fills the role of chief moral survivor much more comfortably than either Albany or Kent. Albany and Kent both suffer, but marginally and almost comically: one might say that Kent is stocked for impertinence, and Albany cuckolded for impercipience. Kent, who has no essential dramatic function left after 3.4, has to be repeatedly resuscitated artificially in order to stay in the play at all. In any text of *King Lear* Albany remains, until the last scene, peripheral;[161] even then, when he dominates the political situation, he attracts relatively little of an audience's attention or emotion.[162] Edgar, on the other hand, is the play's second-longest part, even in Q.[163] Unlike Albany, Edgar is duped only once, and that early in the play; the Folio, moreover, labours to make Edgar's initial *naïveté* more credible and creditable than it was in Q.[164] Unlike Albany, Edgar not only suffers, but suffers alongside and with and like Lear; unlike Albany (who essentially stages a *coup d'état*, after Edmund wins the battle), Edgar himself fights and overcomes first Oswald and then Edmund; unlike Albany, Edgar recognizes his own potential for depravity, and forgives first his father and then his brother; unlike Albany's, Edgar's name had strong and favourable historical associations for a Jacobean audience.[165]

As a representative of moral continuity Edgar has one further advantage over Albany: he has not been party to the power struggles which followed Lear's abdication, nor was he party to the division of the kingdom. Urkowitz's negative reading of Albany largely depends upon Albany's participation and/or acquiescence in the political developments before and after Lear's abdication; once F strips him of much of the moral indignation he expresses in Q, Albany's political stance becomes much harder to determine with any confidence, and so becomes susceptible to more sinister interpretations. Whether or not we accept Urkowitz's negative reading of Folio Albany (I do not), there can be no denying that the Folio excisions not only diminish the role, but also inevitably obscure and to some degree darken its moral tone.

This change seems to me directly related to the Folio's markedly altered dramatization of the war. The Folio variants towards the end of Act Three and throughout Act Four have the effect of accelerating and clarifying the movement towards war; they also alter the nature of this conflict, turning the foreign invasion of Q into something indistinguishable from civil war. This has two consequences. In the first place, the Folio's accelerated narrative momentum, combined with its sharper focus upon the counteraction represented by Cordelia, encourages an audience's expectation that the promised battle will resolve the plot, to the discomfiture of Lear's enemies; at the same time, by making Cordelia's resistance an armed uprising rather than a foreign invasion the Folio removes the last vestige of an 'explanation' for her eventual unexpected defeat. In short, the Folio deliberately raises our hopes higher in order, apparently, to dash them lower. In doing so it enacts, through the experience of the audience itself, one of the play's major themes: the untrustworthiness of prophecy, the utter unreliability of expectation.[166] But the Folio changes do more than that. In 'The War in *King Lear*' I described the Folio's consistent excision of references to French participation in the final conflict as 'removing an extraneous political complication'; that now seems to me an unfortunately negative way of saying that the Folio translates a somewhat irrelevant foreign invasion into the incarnation of a civil chaos set in motion by Lear's abdication. In Shakespeare's source play, Leir marries his daughters to neighbouring kings in order to protect his kingdom from invasion; at the end of the play the husband of one of those daughters invades Leir's kingdom in order to restore him to his throne. Like *Leir*, Quarto *Lear* ends in foreign invasion. But in the Folio, Lear divides his kingdom 'that future strife [between his sons-in-law] | May be preuented now' (TLN 49–50; 1.1.44–5); this very action precipitates political chaos and eventually civil war. Besides adding Lear's political explanation for his abdication, F also adds Goneril's description of the hundred knights who 'enguard his dotage' (TLN 842–8; 1.4.322–7), Kent's description of the spies in the households of both Dukes (TLN 1631–8; 3.1.22–9), the Fool's prophecy of 'the Realme of *Albion*, | Come to great confusion' (TLN 1734–49; 3.2.79–96), and Gloucester's lament that 'We haue seene the best of our time. Machinations, hollownesse, treacherie, and all ruinous disorders follow vs disquietly to our Graues' (TLN 441–4; 1.2.112–14). In Q Kent is banished for objecting to Lear's disinheritance of Cordelia, in F for objecting to his abdication. Far more insistently and powerfully than the Quarto, the Folio emphasizes Lear's division of the kingdom, and the division within the kingdom it precipitates. And this is a division which Edgar, unlike Albany, can credibly promise to heal.

In strengthening Edgar the Folio therefore strengthens the promise of moral continuity after the tragedy. Naturally, that promise remains subordinate to the crushing present pain of Cordelia's death, and Lear's; the undertaste of hope arguably only sharpens the bitterness. But in giving greater emphasis to the young promising survivor Edgar, the Folio clearly complements the new emotional complexity evident in Lear's own altered final moments. That complexity in its turn has been anticipated and prepared by Folio alterations elsewhere in Lear's own part and in the final scene.[167] In Q, we can compare Lear's final moments either with Gloucester's, whose heart 'burst smilingly', or with Edgar's description of the despairing Kent, bellowing with grief, then recounting 'the most pitious tale . . . That euer eare receiued' until his 'strings of life, | Began to cracke' (L2ᵛ–L3; 5.3.213–18). The Quarto makes Lear's death unmistakably closer, emotionally as well as temporally, to the second of these two moments. It is as though an audience were being offered a preview of two potential, alternative endings to the play: one like Gloucester's, in which Lear would be restored to his kingdom, and die exhausted by past grief and present joy – or one like Kent's, in agony unrelieved by hope. The old *Leir* play would have encouraged audiences to expect the first; Shakespeare instead – in the Quarto – gave them the second.[168] But the Folio cuts this description of Kent entirely, and at the same time makes Lear's death strikingly similar to Gloucester's, with the essential and painful difference that Lear's final reunion with his dearest child remains as illusory (in this world) as Gloucester's is real.

Some sense of hope, transcendence, spiritual consolation, the Folio ending nevertheless surely offers. Nor should this surprise us if, as I have suggested, the Folio redaction dates from 1609–10. A. C. Bradley once wondered what *King Lear* would have been like if Shakespeare had taken up the story later in his career, for instance at about the time when he was writing *Cymbeline*;[169] the answer has, I think, been staring us in the face for three and a half centuries, in the form of the Folio text. Certainly, the interrelated changes in the Folio's dramatization of the ending of *King Lear* produce an effect strikingly similar to the resonant emotional complexity of the most memorable scenes in *The Winter's Tale* and *Cymbeline*.

Conclusions

I thus regard the doubts about Shakespeare's responsibility for the redaction as unproven and unprovable. Against them we can set a pattern of stylistic evidence, image-clustering, source references, linguistic preferences, and bibliographical dependence, all coinciding with exactly what we would expect if Shakespeare had himself revised *Lear* between the completion of *Coriolanus* and the beginning of *Cymbeline*. We can also point to an occasion: the opening of the Blackfriars, in the winter of 1609–10. That opening would not of course have compelled Shakespeare to revise any of his plays; but it might have *permitted* it, the opportunity to advertise the play as 'with additions and revisions' compensating for the trouble involved in preparing a new prompt-book and new actors' parts. At least, if Shakespeare for any reason wanted to return to the play, I see no reason to dismiss – at this stage in his career, and particularly at a juncture when the company so clearly needed him – the possibility that the King's Men would have been willing to restage it. For both Shakespeare and the company, the opening of the Blackfriars would have provided an opportunity and an excuse. Why Shakespeare might have wished to return to the subject we will never know. But his preoccupation with fathers and daughters in the late romances – particularly his return in *Cymbeline* to early British history, and to the story of a daughter who disobeys her father, marries, sojourns in the wilderness, and returns at the end in the company of an invading (but eventually defeated) army – hardly make a return to *King Lear* psychologically implausible.[170]

This essay has ranged over a considerable body of evidence, and it has necessarily dealt with relative probabilities rather than certainties. But it can be said with some confidence that the relation of Q and F to Shakespeare's sources is incompatible with the traditional view that both represent defective witnesses to a lost and whole original; it *is* compatible with the hypothesis that F represents a later revision or adaptation of Q. Likewise the bibliographical evidence – that the manuscript consulted in the printing of F itself derived from an exemplar of Q – is incompatible with the traditional hypothesis, and itself virtually establishes redaction in or after 1608. The Folio alterations suggest a number of possible influences in works Shakespeare was reading up to the composition of *The Winter's Tale*; I have found no such parallels in the works he is known to have read thereafter. The statistical evidence of rare-word usage confirms the traditional dating of the play's original composition, as represented by Q; the discrepancy between the vocabulary unique to the Folio and that present in Q accords with the hypothesis of late Shakespearian revision; certain features of this vocabulary evidence suggest a particular link with *Cymbeline*. On strong linguistic evidence Massinger, Fletcher, Middleton, Jonson, Chapman, Field, and Webster – the only candidates of any plausibility, on historical grounds – can each be ruled out as the author of the Folio alterations; the same evidence exactly accords with the hypothesis of late Shakespearian revision. The more subjective evidence of image clusters, style, and subject matter also suggests Shakespearian authorship and a particular proximity to *Cymbeline*. The Folio text shows no signs of having suffered from incompetence or abnormal interference in the printing-house, or (with two exceptions) from censorship, or from the attentions of a high-handed scribe; allegations that Shakespeare's company altered the text without his knowledge or against his will prove, on examination, not only unsubstantiated but historically implausible as well.

My conclusions, then, on the basis of the evidence available, are that *King Lear* was originally composed in late 1605 to early 1606, and was then revised, by Shakespeare himself, probably in 1609–10. That the play was revised, and that Shakespeare was responsible for the revision, seem to me incontestable; the exact dating in relation to *Cymbeline* is, necessarily, less well established. On the other hand, the cumulative evidence that the revision is significantly later than the original composition does seem sufficient to rule out the possibility that Folio *Lear* represents the only prompt-book of the play ever prepared: the first version, which exists in foul-paper form in Q, therefore must have been given a theatrical production of its own, well before the major revision preserved in the Folio. We are thus faced, certainly not with two corruptions of a single *Ur-Lear*, not even with an earlier draft alongside a final theatrical text, but with two *King Lears*, both representing what the author regarded, at the time, as the play's final form, and both of which presumably received full theatrical production by Shakespeare's company in Shakespeare's lifetime.

NOTES

1. See S. Schoenbaum's *William Shakespeare: A Compact Documentary Life* (Oxford, 1977), p. 279. Given the evidence of Shakespeare's continued visits to

London, however, it would have been impossible for the company to produce a new adaptation of *King Lear* without his knowing about it; but whether he would have objected is of course debatable.

2. Like Stone (*Textual History*), Blayney doubts the authority of many of the Folio alterations (see for instance the remarks quoted by Goldring, pp. 143–4, above).

3. However, the presence in *Macbeth* of material also present in Middleton's *The Witch* does not in itself establish whether the material was originally written for one play rather than the other; the compelling new evidence of Middleton's hand in *Timon* (see n. 70) means that the possibility of his collaboration in the original composition of *Macbeth* must be reconsidered.

4. 'If Aristophanes could revise his *Clouds*, and Euripides his *Hippolytus*, why not Shakespeare his *King Lear*?' ('War', p. 34).

5. 'A New Source and an Old Date for *King Lear*', *Review of English Studies*, 33 (1982), 396–413. *Leir* was entered in the Stationers' Register on 8 May 1605.

6. The nine are: *Much Ado About Nothing*, *Love's Labour's Lost*, *A Midsummer Night's Dream*, *The Merchant of Venice*, *Richard II*, *Troilus and Cressida*, *Titus Andronicus*, *Hamlet*, and *Othello*. Only in the last two does the extent of alteration arguably approach that in *Lear*; and the revision of *Othello* seems to postdate the play's first performance by at least two years. (See below, n. 114.) For evidence of Folio consultation of a promptbook for *Love's Labour's Lost*, see Stanley Wells, 'The Copy for the Folio Text of *Love's Labour's Lost*', *Review of English Studies*, 33 (1982), 137–47; for a re-examination of the complicated situation in *Troilus*, my '*Troilus and Cressida*: Bibliography, Performance, and Interpretation', *Shakespeare Studies*, 16 (1983), 99–136. More problematic are the cases of *1* and *2 Henry IV*, where the Folio texts may not reflect actual theatrical practice (but see Werstine's discussion of *1 Henry IV*, above, pp. 248–60). Several plays occur in good texts and 'bad' quartos (*The Merry Wives of Windsor*, *The Taming of the Shrew*, *Henry V*, *2* and *3 Henry VI*, *Richard III*, *Romeo and Juliet*, and *Hamlet*); but the more extreme variation between some of these texts is probably due to corruption in transmission. My own views on two of these plays are contained in The Oxford Shakespeare edition of *Henry V* (Oxford, 1982), and *Toward a Text of Shakespeare's 'Richard III'* (forthcoming). For the problem of authorial revision generally, see E. A. J. Honigmann's *The Stability of Shakespeare's Text* (1965).

7. *The Variants in the First Quarto of 'King Lear': A Bibliographical and Critical Inquiry*, Supplement to the Bibliographical Society's Transactions, No. 15 (1940).

8. In fact the unit of correction is the forme, not the page or sheet; however, this distinction does not affect the interpretation of the evidence here.

9. Stone, *Textual History*, pp. 129–40, 257–80; Howard-Hill, 'The Problem of Manuscript Copy for Folio *King Lear*', *The Library*, VI, 4 (1982), 1–24; Taylor, 'Folio Copy for *Hamlet, King Lear*, and *Othello*', *Shakespeare Quarterly*, 34 (1983), 44–61; Taylor, 'Censorship' (above, p. 115, n. 29); Jackson, 'Fluctuating Variation' (above, pp. 328–9, 346–8). Blayney also believes that 'F's ancestry is now known to include Q2' (*Origins*, I, 245); he promises to discuss the matter fully in Volume II.

10. I assume that 'Manuscript B' was indeed a manuscript, rather than (say) an annotated and interleaved copy of Q1, in use as a prompt-book. The amount of annotation required on Q1 in order to generate a text verbally resembling F would produce something so messy that its utility as a prompt-book would be much impaired. Nor would anyone in the theatre have much motive for making indifferent changes like 'that' to 'which'. A printer might do such things because he had been told to reproduce all of the words in manuscript B; but a theatrical

manuscript is functional, not committed to any such ideal of reproductive accuracy. Likewise, indifferent variants could easily be introduced in the course of a complete transcription; but it is much less plausible to suppose that a theatrical scribe would interpolate the same variants on to an already messy bundle of marked-up printed and interleaved manuscript pages. Nor does it seem likely that the Master of the Revels would accept the submission of such a mess for his perusal; and since the only purpose of such an operation would be to replace a lost or damaged or worn-out prompt-book, the result would presumably need to be resubmitted for licensing (as with the examples I discussed above, p. 110, n. 4). Finally, if the King's Men had supplied Jaggard with such a marked-up exemplar of Q1, there would have been no reason for him to transfer its readings on to a copy of Q2, since Compositor E could have been supplied with marked-up printed copy by using the Q1-based prompt-book itself. (See, for further discussion, Taylor, 'Folio Copy'.)

11. Greg himself, in a footnote, recognized the actual indifference of this variant: 'The press-reader presumably read the manuscript "ataxt" correctly, but assumed that *tax* was only another and inferior spelling of *task*. The two verbs were used synonymously at the time, and in III.ii.16 [F4; TLN 1671] the Quarto again substitutes [sic] "taske" for [Folio] "taxe"' ('The Function of Bibliography in Literary Criticism Illustrated in a Study of the Text of *King Lear*' [1933], in *Collected Papers*, ed. J. C. Maxwell (Oxford, 1966), p. 291, note 2).

12. See my 'Four New Readings in *King Lear*', *Notes and Queries*, 227 (1982), 121–3. George Walton Williams, in a forthcoming review of textual studies in *Shakespeare Survey 36* (1983), does not find my conjecture 'retinue' plausible, but agrees that the Qb reading 'hasten' for Qa 'after' is 'unlikely' to represent the original manuscript reading.

13. In the intervening line occurs yet another suspicious Q 'correction', again reproduced by F. At 1.4.341 (D2ᵛ; TLN 865), Qb alters 'mildie' to 'milkie'. Greg recognized that 'mildie' was a legitimate word, and Stone (*Textual History*, p. 216) argues that it should be preferred, because rarer, and because a compositor would probably not misread *k* as *d* in a fairly common word. Although Stone's argument would strengthen my own case, I feel compelled to reject it, because 'mildnes' occurs only two lines below (D2ᵛ; TLN 868; 1.4.344), which renders Qa's word not only lame but explicable by contamination. Moreover, though 'milkie' may not in itself be an unusual word, 'milkie gentlenes' is a decidedly rarer collocation than 'mildie gentlenes'.

14. Since the Folio copy for this page is so crucial, and since at least two earlier critics have suggested the possibility that both Q1 and Q2 were used for F (A. S. Cairncross, 'The Quartos and the Folio Text of *King Lear*', *Review of English Studies*, 6 (1955), 252–8; Letitia Dace, 'Prolegomena to a New Edition of *King Lear*' (unpublished Ph.D. thesis, Kansas State University, 1971), pp. 189–200), I have checked all the accidentals of F here against Q1 and Q2. The Folio departs from the spelling and capitalization practice of Q1 K4ᵛ 31 times; in the same lines it departs from Q2 only 17 times. This confirms the very strong punctuation, spelling, and substantive evidence throughout F for Compositor E's use of Q2.

15. *The Text of 'King Lear'* (Stanford, 1931), p. 101.

16. Stone recognizes the need for a common ancestor, but contends that the adapter acquired, ten or more years later, the corrupt and confused manuscript from which (he believes) Q was printed. This is most implausible. His further suggestion, that the original prompt-book was lost in the Globe fire (*Textual History*, pp. 96–9), had already been considered, and convincingly rejected, by Letitia Dace in 'Prolegomena to a New Edition of *King Lear*' (an important work, to which Stone does not refer), p. 66.

17. Stone does not accept the evidence of this press variant because he believes that another Folio agreement with a reading in the *corrected* state of outer K makes it necessary to believe that the Folio manuscript was influenced by Qb. This other reading, Qb's substitution of 'to boot, to boot' for Qa's 'to saue thee' (K1; TLN 2674; 4.6.226), occurs in a portion of text set by Folio compositor B, whom Stone believes to have been setting directly from manuscript (*Textual History*, pp. 250–1); Blayney agrees that Qb is unsatisfactory (I, 250–2). But, as I have pointed out elsewhere, all of the eight significant substantive agreements with Q2 in B's stints fall in the single column which contains this very reading (rr6ᵛb), the last column that B set before E took over to the end of the play ('Folio Copy', 49–50). There is thus very strong reason to believe that B was setting from Q2 copy in at least the second column of rr6ᵛ; since Q2 there agrees with Qb, F's apparent derivation from Qb need tell us nothing about the underlying manuscript.

18. This stemma does not take account of Stone's conjecture that, in addition to Q1, the adapter acquired access to the manuscript from which Q1 was printed [A]; this implausible complication plays no necessary part in the dilemma I am here addressing. Likewise, in common with the other stemmas, this one does not deal with the possibility that only one of the Folio compositors (E) worked from printed copy: 'marked-up Q2 copy' may be taken as shorthand for a possibly complex mix of copy, which at least consisted in large part of an annotated exemplar of Q2.

19. See her review of Greg's *Variants: Review of English Studies*, 17 (1941), 468–74.

20. Q sets the first two lines of this quotation as one.

21. For the rarity of Shakespearian part-lines in the middle of speeches see Fredson Bowers, 'Establishing Shakespeare's Text: Notes on Short Lines and the Problem of Verse Division', *Studies in Bibliography*, 33 (1980), 74–130.

22. See for instance Akihiro Yamada, 'The Seventeenth-Century Manuscript Leaves of Chapman's *May-Day*, 1611', *The Library*, VI, 2 (1980), 61–9.

23. A comprehensive check of spelling evidence on rr5 (see 'Folio Copy', pp. 53–5) suggests that B used manuscript copy for at least that page, on which occur the five Folio agreements with suspicious Qa variants discussed by MacD. P. Jackson (above, pp. 321–4, 329–30).

24. After reaching this conclusion I was pleased to discover that Blayney (*Origins*, II) has provided further evidence that Q2's added speech may well derive from a press-correction in Q1; he accepts it into his own edited text (as did many eighteenth- and nineteenth-century editors). G. Blakemore Evans also includes the speech in his *Riverside* edition; he defended this choice in a review of the 1960 new Cambridge edition (*Journal of English and Germanic Philology*, 60 (1961), p. 326). P. A. Daniel (in his introduction to the Praetorius Facsimile (1885), p. xiv) seems to have first suggested this explanation for Q2's line. For a similar situation, where material added in a later reprint has been universally adopted as authoritative, see *Richard III* 1.1.101–2 (TLN 106–7), where Q2 (A3) adds two speeches not in Q1 (A3).

25. Some of Stone's examples are much more convincing than others, i.e. 1.2.13 (pp. 51–2), 5.3.142–6 (pp. 68–9), 5.3.123 (p. 186). In the third example, Q reads 'yet are I mou't | Where is the aduersarie' (L1ᵛ), and F 'Yet am I Noble as the Aduersary' (TLN 3075); Stone accepts the seventeenth-century manuscript respelling 'ere' for Q 'are' (Bodleian 2), but also conjectures 'moot' for 'mou't'. This second emendation is unnecessary, since 'ere I mou't' (i.e. 'before I move it') makes perfectly appropriate sense. For two more possible examples see Appendix I, 4.1.74 and 4.4.2 (and Addenda).

26. For instance *Troilus and Cressida* 2.3.242–3, where Q has 'Fam'd be thy tutor, and thy parts of nature, | Thrice fam'd beyond all thy erudition' (E3); F has 'Fame be thy Tutor, and thy parts of nature | Thrice fam'd beyond, beyond all erudition' (TLN 1450–1). F's 'Fame' is universally corrected to Q's 'Fam'd', but editors reject Q's unmetrical version of the second line. However, the assumption that Q is an error for F forces one to conclude that Q's line contains *two* serious and unrelated errors (omission of 'beyond' and interpolation of 'thy'); it would be much easier to suppose that Q's line should have read 'Thrice fam'd beyond [be] all thy erudition'. An editor who preferred this conjecture could then claim that F's variant represents an unauthorized improvement, deriving from the printing error in Q; it seems to me more likely that both readings (F, and my reconstruction of Q) are authorial, and that authorial revision here merely happens to occur in the same line as a printing error in one text. Nevertheless, in *Lear* the number of such cases, combined with the evidence from press variants, seems to me sufficient to justify the hypothesis of redaction from (initially) a copy of Q1.

27. Shakespeare is named in the cast-list for *Sejanus* (1603), but not in those for *The Alchemist* (1610) or *Catiline* (1611). See also T. W. Baldwin, *The Organization and Personnel of the Shakespearean Company* (Princeton, 1927), pp. 261–3.

28. For another probable instance of a Jacobean playwright making revisions on a copy of the printed quarto, see John Kerrigan's essay (above, p. 235, n. 57); for an adapter working in the same way, see his discussion of *The Fleire* (pp. 198–202). I strongly suspect that Chapman did the same for his successive revisions of the *Iliad*. See Addenda.

29. For evidence that the printing of Q was completed in January, see Blayney, *Origins*, I, 78–85.

30. 'The Date of *King Lear* and Shakespeare's Use of Earlier Versions of the Story', *The Library*, IV, 20 (1939), 377–400.

31. 'Samuel Harsnett and *King Lear*', *Review of English Studies*, 2 (1951), 11–21.

32. *Narrative and Dramatic Sources of Shakespeare*, 8 vols. (1957–75), VII (1973), 269–420. References to *King Leir* are to Bullough's text.

33. Greg (*Variants*, p. 164) persuasively contends that Qa *the* for Qb *this* at 3.4.12 (G1; TLN 1792) must be an error; but as this column of F (rr3a) clearly seems to have been set from an annotated copy of Q2, F's agreement with Qa is of no significance, since Q2 also has 'the'. F's preservation of the Qa error might therefore derive either from its Q2 copy, or from a manuscript deriving at some remove from a copy of Q1 containing the uncorrected state of this forme; as a result, no decision can be reached, as Stone realizes (*Textual History*, p. 250). Moreover, the Fliberdigibbet variant occurs on rr3ᵛ of F, set by Compositor B either from manuscript or an annotated copy of Q2: we therefore know neither whether B's copy was Q2 or manuscript, nor whether the manuscript derives from Qa or Qb.

34. Muir compares Harsnet's 'mow, and mop like an Ape, tumble like a Hedgehogge' (p. 136) with Caliban's 'Sometime like Apes, that moe and chatter at me, | And after bite me: then like Hedg-hogs, which | Lye tumbling' (TLN 1048–50; 2.2.9–11).

35. 'The sonnes of king Malcolme were aided . . . to obteine the crowne of Scotland, wherevnto they were interessed' (Holinshed, *The Third volume of Chronicles* (1586), p. 21). *OED* cites this as the first instance of 'interess', *v.* 1. It occurs in the English section of the Chronicles, parallel in time to the Scottish material directly drawn on for *Macbeth*; but Shakespeare clearly made use of this English material, for information about Siward and Edward the Confessor.

36. The 'vtmost limmits of knowen Countries, are set downe to be ful of thicke marrish grounds, shady forrests, desart and vncouth places': *The Essayes or Morall, Politike and Millitarie Discourses of Lo: Michaell de Montaigne . . . done into English By . . . Iohn Florio* (1603), p. 315 (sig. Ee2). This passage is in chapter 12 of the second book, '*An Apologie of* Raymond Sebond'.

37. Qb reads 'annoynted' for Qa 'aurynted', which suggests a manuscript spelling 'anoynted'. The Qa 'aurynted' suggests that the compositor was thinking either of 'orient' (sometimes spelled 'aurient', and meaning vaguely 'lustrous, pearl-white') or of a compound like 'aureate' ('golden', but more generally 'brilliant'; compare Macbeth's 'his Golden Blood'). However, neither of these seems likely, since there are no examples of 'oriented' as an adjective in this sense, or of 'aureant', and in either case the accentuation would be wrong. Greg is therefore probably right in calling Qb 'Certainly correct' (*Variants*, p. 168). For the parallel with Warner editors cite Robert Nares, *A Glossary . . . of Words, Phrases, Names . . . in the Works of English Authors, particularly Shakespeare . . .* (1822), referring to Warner's *Albion's England* (1586), Book 7, Chapter 36; but Book 7 is not included until the 1592 edition, and the copies I have examined of the 1592, 1596, 1597, 1602, and 1612 editions all agree in reading 'rase'. Nares does not record which edition he is quoting (p. 418). He might be reporting a press variant; however, the fact that he quotes 'rashed' for *Richard III* 3.2.11 (TLN 1807) suggests that he is treating 'rase' (the Folio reading there) as a spelling of 'rashe'. *OED*'s division of senses is not helpful here: it gives the required meaning under *race v.*[2] 2, *rase v.*[1] 1, and *rash v.*[2] 1, then lists the passage in *Lear* under *rash v.*[1] 3; 'To dash (things *together*, or one thing *against*, *in*, or *through* another)'. Its only pre-*Lear* examples for this sense are both Scottish. Nares is thus probably right in treating the passages in *Albion's England* and *Lear* as examples of the same word. Bullough regards *Albion's England* as a 'Possible Source' for the main plot of *Lear*.

38. For a defence of F's reading 'sit' here, see McLeod (above, pp. 162–3).

39. *The Complete Works of John Lyly*, ed. R. W. Bond, 3 vols. (Oxford, 1902), III, 191. Doran (pp. 55–6) noted the link with Lyly, and thought the variant was evidence of an authorial manuscript for Q. The sentiment has been dismissed as proverbial, but *King Lear* and *Mother Bombie* in fact provide the only recorded examples (see R. W. Dent, *Shakespeare's Proverbial Language: An Index* (Berkeley, 1981), F535).

40. Kenneth Muir, *The Sources of Shakespeare's Plays* (1977), pp. 9 (*Lear*) and 219 (*Timon*). *Mother Bombie* also includes a parallel for the Fool's 'Cry you mercy I tooke you for a ioyne stoole' (G4, 3.6.52; *Bombie*, 4.2.28); however, this phrase is proverbial (Dent, M897), and would be of no value if there were not already two links with Lyly elsewhere in *Lear* (both, like this one, involving the Fool, and one the same character in *Mother Bombie*, Silena). For Shakespeare's overall indebtedness to Lyly, see among others G. K. Hunter's *John Lyly: The Humanist as Courtier* (1962), pp. 298–349, and A. R. Humphreys's new Arden edition of *Much Ado About Nothing* (1981), pp. 19, 25–6, 222–8.

41. In addition, *Mother Bombie* was performed entirely by boy actors; Lear's fool was probably also a boy's part (see below, n. 123) – and in any case he is consistently *called* a 'boy'.

42. *Shakespeare's 'King Lear': A Critical Edition* (Oxford, 1949), p. 366.

43. Duthie, p. 126. The acceptance of this argument is especially astonishing in the case of modern editors (like Muir, Duthie himself, and G. B. Evans) who follow Greg in dating Shakespeare's play in late 1604 or early 1605: Greg's argument (in 'The Date of *King Lear*') is largely based on the assumption that the old chronicle *Leir* is unlikely to have been revived in 1604–5. Duthie's reporter is therefore

confusing Shakespeare's play with one not acted for ten or twenty years – and one we have no reason to associate with Shakespeare's company. See Addenda.

44. The principle of deference to the more difficult reading originated in the editing of classical texts, particularly the New Testament: it was naturally assumed that the Holy Spirit is not given to second thoughts, while the agents of his transmission across the intervening centuries self-evidently had, on occasion, the strongest motives for tampering with his account. See J. H. Bentley, 'Erasmus, Jean le Clerc, and the Principle of the Harder Reading', *Renaissance Quarterly*, 31 (1978), 309–21.

45. *King Lear*, ed. Kenneth Muir, new Arden Shakespeare (1952). Muir claims that *sticke* 'is probably an actor's substitution, or a sophistication'. But how did an actor's substitution find its way into the prompt-book? It is supposedly Q which contains actors' substitutions, not F; Muir here postulates memorial corruption in F in order to save the theory of memorial corruption in Q.

46. For B's errors, see Paul Werstine's essay (above, pp. 263–7).

47. Eleanor Prosser, in *Shakespeare's Anonymous Editors: Scribe and Compositor in the Folio Text of '2 Henry IV'* (Stanford, 1981), alleges that both Compositor B and the scribe were repeatedly guilty of such gross intrusion; but her accusations are not supported by B's work elsewhere, and even if she is right about the scribe in question (which I doubt), he was clearly *not* a theatrical scribe; moreover, as has always been recognized, the Folio text of *2 Henry IV* is unique in a good many other respects.

48. The Prologue, added in the Folio, is clearly and heavily indebted to the same sources as the rest of the play: see *Troilus and Cressida*, ed. H. N. Hillebrand and T. W. Baldwin, New Variorum Shakespeare (Philadelphia, 1953), pp. 2–6. On the Prologue's status as a later addition see Taylor, '*Troilus and Cressida*'.

49. The Lives of Cato Utican, Nicias, Marius, and Coriolanus all contain spies, foreign and domestic. Besides *Coriolanus*, the only play written between 1605 and 1623 known to contain such spies is the anonymous *Two Wise Men and All the Rest Fools* (1619): see Thomas L. Berger and William C. Bradford, Jr., *An Index of Characters in English Printed Drama to the Restoration* (Englewood, Colorado, 1975).

50. Duthie, pp. 137–8; Muir, *King Lear*, *loc. cit.*

51. For *Pericles*, see MacD. P. Jackson, 'North's Plutarch and the name "Escanes"', *Notes and Queries*, 220 (1975), 173–4; for *The Winter's Tale*, see J. H. P. Pafford's new Arden edition (1963), Appendix I, note I, and his note to 5.1.156 (Smalus).

52. *Timon* is sometimes dated 1608–9, on the grounds that it makes use of Plutarch's lives of Antony and Alcibiades (the latter Plutarch's Greek counterpart to Coriolanus); but we have no way of knowing whether he read this material for *Timon* before or after he read it for the two late Roman plays. It therefore seems to me that one must accept the evidence for an earlier date for *Timon*, in which case Shakespeare may have begun reading Plutarch again before he began composition of *King Lear*. However, (*a*) although it seems to me that *Timon* probably preceded *Lear*, we cannot be sure that it did, even if it belongs *c*. 1604–6; (*b*) given the evidence for collaboration with Middleton – see below, n. 70 – we cannot be sure that Shakespeare, rather than Middleton, had been reading Plutarch at the time of *Timon*'s composition; (*c*) even if Shakespeare had begun dipping into Plutarch again, before he turned to *Lear*, he clearly became much more deeply engrossed in Plutarch later, from about 1606–9, and Quarto *Lear* itself shows no signs of Plutarch's influence. Thus, although evidence of Folio links with Plutarch cannot in itself *prove* that the Folio passages in question belong to a later period of composition, they do suggest such a conclusion.

53. See Berger and Bradford, *An Index of Characters*. Subsequent references to North are to the pagination of *The Liues of the Noble Grecians and Romanes, compared together by . . . Plutarke . . . Translated . . . into Englishe, by Thomas North* (1579).

54. This may be proverbial. M. P. Tilley (*A Dictionary of the Proverbs in England in the Sixteenth and Seventeenth Centuries* (Ann Arbor, 1950), D332) lists a parallel in 1672; but before that the only recorded versions are of 'There is a difference between Peter and Peter' (1612, 1631; both English translations of Spanish works). In *The Two Noble Kinsmen* the jailer's daughter exclaims 'Lord, the Diffrence of men' (D2; 2.1.53–4); most scholars regard this scene as Shakespeare's. But even if Fletcher wrote it, this might be only one of several possible echoes of *Lear* in Fletcher's part of the play; compare 'The little Stars, and all' (Gl^v; 3.4.2) and 'Would I could finde a fine Frog' (Gl^v; 3.4.12), both spoken by the jailer's daughter, mad, and lost in the wood. The daughter's part of the plot also echoes the description of Ophelia's drowning.

55. Like Caius Martius, Caius Marius was a great soldier who made a mess of things in peace time, eventually precipitating civil war in Italy, being driven from Rome, and returning at the head of an invading army. Also like Martius, Marius was 'vehemently against' the distribution of corn *gratis* (North, p. 453; *Coriolanus* TLN 1808 ff.; 3.1.113 ff.); likewise, as with Martius, 'The common people, they were ready to haue fallen vpon [Marius], and to haue killed him: but the noble men being offended for the iniury they had offred him, gathered together about him to saue him' (p. 468). These similarities can be accounted for by Shakespeare's knowledge of Plutarch's Life of Coriolanus; but three other details of Shakespeare's play do not derive from that Life (or from any of the play's other known sources). Given the evidence that Shakespeare was reading widely in Plutarch at this time, and given also the general and specific similarities between the two historical figures, it seems reasonable to suggest that these details might derive from passages in Plutarch's Life of Marius. The three relevant passages are: (1) 'For sayd he, either things will amend, and the people then repenting them selues of the wrong they haue done me, will call me home again:' (p. 469; compare the similar comments between Coriolanus and his friends on the occasion of his banishment at TLN 2452–3, 2480–4; 4.1.15, 40–4); (2) 'he made more earnest sute for the sixt Consulshippe . . . seeking the peoples goodwilles by all the fayer meanes he could to please them, humbling him selfe vnto them, not only more then became his estate and calling, but directly also against his owne nature, counterfeating a curteous populer manner, being cleane contrarie to his disposition' (p. 467; compare Coriolanus's scathing characterization of the kind of politician his mother and the other patricians expect him to become, at TLN 1490–2, 2100, 2219; 2.3.99–101, 3.2.15, 111, etc.); (3) 'For that corage and boldnesse which he had in battell against the enemy, he lost it quite when he was in an assembly of people in the city: and was easily put out of his byase, with the first blame or praise he heard geuen him' (p. 467). This last character trait, pivotal in Coriolanus's banishment (3.3) and death (5.6), is not in Plutarch's accounts of either incident, or in his description of Coriolanus's character.

56. For further discussion of the Folio changes in the presentation of Lear in the first scene, see Clayton (above, pp. 123–6), Jackson (above, pp. 332–9), and Taylor (above, p. 96). If the Folio revision does date from 1610, Shakespeare would have been much closer to his own decision to 'abdicate' and retire to Stratford than he had been in 1605.

57. H. S. Wilson, '"Nature and Art" in *Winter's Tale* IV.iv.86 ff.', *Shakespeare Association Bulletin*, 18 (1943), 114–20; Wilson's main parallel (on L11^v) is reprinted and discussed by Muir, *Sources*, pp. 276–7; Puttenham is also

conveniently available in the edition by G. D. Willcock and Alice Walker (Cambridge, 1936, repr. 1970), which indicates the original page-breaks. Willcock and Walker note Puttenham's early influence and popularity; Pafford's edition of *The Winter's Tale* includes it among 'books which would be known to an educated person of Shakespeare's day' (p. xxxvi). My own examination of the book has turned up several apparent parallels not noted by Wilson. The play's known sources contain no hint of the episode in which Autolycus tricks the Old Shepherd by pretending to be a courtier who can help him receive a hearing before the king (TLN 2596–2693; 4.4.714–812). Puttenham tells a similar story involving 'a louer of wine and a merry companion in Court' who meets by chance with 'an honest plaine man of the country' who is 'rich' and has 'a fayre yong damsell of eighteene yeares old to his daughter, that could very well behaue her selfe in countenance & also in her language'. The countryman asks the courtier 'which way he were best to worke to get his suite, and who were most in credit and fauour about the king, that he might seeke to them to furder his attempt'; the courtier promises to do so, and is given twenty crowns; 'perceyuing the plainnesse of the' countryman, he plays a trick on him, but in the end the fair daughter 'found so great fauour' with the king, and the trick turned to everyone's advantage. This story occurs at the very end of Puttenham's Book Two (Q2ᵛ), and its similarities with the Autolycus episode are, I believe, difficult to dismiss. The rest of the most interesting parallels come from Book Three. As an example of the figure of 'Extenuation', Puttenham notes 'to say . . . of an arrant ruffian that he is a tall fellow of his hands' (Bb2ᵛ); Shakespeare three times reiterates this joke, when the Clown insists on his right to call Autolycus 'a tall Fellow of thy hands' (a phrase Shakespeare uses nowhere else), though knowing he is no such thing (TLN 3172, 3173, 3175; 5.2.164, 165, 167). In the next paragraph Puttenham discusses the use of this figure 'for a Courtly maner of speach with our . . . inferiours'; this is of course the basis of the whole scene in Shakespeare, with the two shepherds rejoicing in their new social superiority over Autolycus, a status which gives them the right to call him 'a tall fellow of his hands': 'If it be ne'er so false, a true Gentleman may sweare it' (TLN 3170–1; 5.2.162–3). Puttenham later draws particular attention to the 'improper' and 'vncouth' phrase '*flouds of graces*' in an unnamed, unquoted poem, complaining 'I haue heard of *the flouds of teares*, and *the flouds of eloquence*, or of any thing that may resemble the nature of a water-course, and in that respect we say also, *the streames of teares* . . . but not *the streames of graces*' (Ff1ᵛ). Only once does Shakespeare describe grace in terms of liquid – in *The Winter's Tale*: 'You Gods looke downe, | And from your sacred Vi[a]ls poure your graces' (TLN 3333–4, reading 'Viols'; 5.3.122). Book Three also contains discussions of decorum of dress, in relation to distinctions of class, and of country versus city life (Iilᵛ; compare *Winter's Tale* TLN 1805–12, 1821–3; 4.4.7–14, 21–3); of the propriety of disguising 'an ill featured face . . . because euery man may decently reforme by arte, the faultes and imperfections that nature hath wrought in them' (Ii2ᵛ; compare TLN 1914–15; 4.4.101–2), and of lifelike sculpture in relation to the distinction between nature and art (Ee2, L11ᵛ, L12ᵛ). Noticeably, all these passages link the last half of Puttenham to the last two acts of *Winter's Tale*. More generally, of course, the play's widely-recognized preoccupation with the art of nature and the nature of art makes some link with Puttenham plausible enough.

58. The poem first appeared in print in 1477–8, at the end of Caxton's edition of Chaucer's 'Anelida and Arcite'; from thence it was taken into the first collected edition of Chaucer's *Works* (1532), and reprinted (verbally unchanged) in 1542, c.1550, 1561, 1598, and 1602. In all these editions it appears toward the end of the

The Division of the Kingdoms

prefatory material, after the Table of Contents, without a title or distinctive heading; it can easily be overlooked. George Steevens noted the parallel with Puttenham; W. J. Craig's Arden edition (1901) referred to the poem's pseudo-Chaucerian status; Muir's new Arden edition (1952) first quoted the version in William Thynne's 1532 Chaucer edition; Dover Wilson and G. I. Duthie, in their New Shakespeare edition (Cambridge, 1960), first asserted that 'Sh[akespeare] probably found it in Thynne's *Chaucer* (1532)'. Wilson and Duthie offer no evidence for this assertion and do not note that Puttenham's wording is closer to Shakespeare's (or that Shakespeare apparently read Puttenham). Shakespeare of course had read Chaucer for both *A Midsummer Night's Dream* (1595?) and *Troilus and Cressida* (1602?), but there is no evidence of his having done so again before 1613 (for *The Two Noble Kinsmen*).

For the wider currency of the basic genre of 'Merlinesque prophecy', see Terence Hawkes, 'The Fool's "Prophecy" in *King Lear*', *Notes and Queries*, 205 (1960), 331–2. Hawkes quotes one early manuscript version; the fullest catalogue of manuscript texts is in Carleton Brown and R. H. Robbins, *The Index of Middle English Verse* (New York, 1943), 3943 and 3986, as supplemented by R. H. Robbins, ed., *Historical Poems of the Fourteenth and Fifteenth Centuries* (New York, 1959), p. 316. Robbins prints the Dublin manuscript version, dating from *c*. 1461 (p. 121). All the published texts, and the unpublished ones I have seen, have 'land' in place of Puttenham's and Shakespeare's 'realm'. (The new version discussed and reprinted by John P. Cutts - in *English Language Notes*, 9 (1972), 262–5 - dates from the 'middle of the seventeenth century' and is itself clearly influenced by Shakespeare's version.) Puttenham often reworded or adapted or simply misremembered poems he quoted as examples (see Willcock and Walker, pp. 320, 322), so there is nothing surprising about his departure here from all other known versions of the prophecy.

59. 'The Shakespeare Canon: New Evidence for Chronology and Authorship' (forthcoming). My own conclusions depart from the 'traditional' chronology of the late plays only in placing *Pericles* before rather than after *Coriolanus*, and *The Winter's Tale* before rather than after *Cymbeline*. The evidence for dating the revision of *Lear* is not, however, dependent on this chronology.

60. 'The Problem of *The Reign of King Edward III*, 1596: A Statistical Approach' (unpublished Ph.D. thesis, University of London, 1981). Several published articles deal with the distribution of such vocabulary evidence for specific works: 'Shakespeare: Word Links Between Poems and Plays', *Notes and Queries*, 220 (1975), 157–63; 'Word Links with "The Merry Wives of Windsor"', *Notes and Queries*, 220 (1975), 169–71; 'Word Links with "All's Well that Ends Well"', *Notes and Queries*, 222 (1977), 109–12; 'Word Links Between "Timon of Athens" and "King Lear"', *Notes and Queries*, 223 (1978), 147–9; 'Word Links from *Troilus* to *Othello* and *Macbeth*', *The Bard*, 2 (1978), 4–22. The article on *Timon* and *King Lear* was of course based upon a conflated text of the latter. Dr Slater very kindly provided me with extracts of his thesis in advance of its completion, and with much valuable advice on my own examination of vocabulary in *Lear*.

61. For a test similar to Slater's, but involving a much smaller vocabulary sample, see G. Sarrazin, 'Wortechos bei Shakespeare', *Shakespeare Jahrbuch*, 33 (1897), 121–65, and 34 (1898), 119–69.

62. See Note R, 'Reminiscences of *Othello* in *King Lear*', in *Shakespearean Tragedy* (1904).

63. *The Printing and Proof-Reading of the First Folio of Shakespeare*, 2 vols. (Oxford, 1963). It is a measure both of Hinman's care and of the specialist nature of his techniques that no part of his case analysis was significantly revised until Paul

Werstine's 'Cases and Compositors in the Shakespeare First Folio Comedies' (*Studies in Bibliography*, 36 (1982), 206–34), almost two decades later.

64. For a recent example of this dismissive polemic see Margot Heinemann's discussion of recent studies of the Middleton canon in her *Puritanism and Theatre: Thomas Middleton and Opposition Drama under the Early Stuarts* (Cambridge, 1980), pp. 284–9.

65. I emphasize that alternative explanations must themselves be convincing. See for instance E. D. Pendry's comments in *Shakespeare Survey 32* (Cambridge, 1979), p. 237, and MacD. P. Jackson's reply in *Notes and Queries*, 226 (1981), p. 146. Pendry's review also refers dismissively to Slater's article on word-links between *Timon* and *Lear*, suggesting that these may have less to do with date than with 'similarity of theme' (p. 236). But similarities of theme can be found between almost any two Shakespeare plays: the resemblances between *Lear* and *Titus Andronicus* have been often noticed, and *Shakespeare Survey 33* (Cambridge, 1980) contains articles arguing for *Lear's* strong similarities to *Taming of the Shrew* and *As You Like It*, yet *Lear* has no remarkable word-links with any of these plays. Moreover, although such similarity might account for the specific word-links between *Timon* and *Lear*, they could not possibly explain the fact that both show a strikingly similar overall relationship to the plays before and after 1604–6. Finally, since Slater has demonstrated a basic chronological distribution to the rare vocabulary of the canon as a whole, *ad hoc* explanations for the links between particular plays can hardly outweigh the initial presumption that they result from chronological proximity.

66. *Stolne and Surreptitious Copies: A Comparative Study of Shakespeare's Bad Quartos* (Melbourne, 1942).

67. In my investigation, as in Slater's, no proper nouns or words beginning with a capital letter are included. Different parts of speech (noun, verb, adjective, adverb, etc.) were taken to be different words even if identically spelled; however, different inflexions of a word (declension of nouns, conjugation of verbs, superlative of adjectives) were not taken to constitute a difference. Words hyphenated in modern editions were taken as one word; components of such compound words were therefore not separately examined. Homonyms with radically different meanings were taken to be different words. While these rules are sensible and fairly clear-cut, in practice difficulty arises over three points: determining whether certain past participles are verbs or adjectives, determining whether present participles are verbs, adjectives, or nouns, and determining what differences in meaning are sufficient to warrant a distinction between two identically spelled words. Slater himself (having to canvass the complete works) is naturally somewhat inconsistent in his treatment of all three questions; indeed, in respect to the third no hard-and-fast rule is possible. I have treated all gerunds in prepositional phrases as nouns (from *tithing* to *tithing*); all past and present participles preceded by articles or adjectives or prepositions and followed by nouns, as adjectives (the *reuenging* Gods, a *grac'd* Pallace); past and present participles governing dependent clauses, as verbs (*thredding* darke ey'd night); past participles using the auxiliary verb *to have*, as verbs (haue you *madded*). Past participles using the auxiliary verb *to be*, but without a clear passive function (i.e. followed by the preposition *by*), and past participles used in apposition without being locked into a clear adjectival construction, are the most difficult to assess; I generally treat such participles as verbs, unless there are strong contextual reasons for considering them adjectives.

68. John Bartlett, *A Complete Concordance or Verbal Index to Words, Phrases and Passages in the Dramatic Works of Shakespeare* (1894); Marvin Spevack, *The Harvard Concordance to Shakespeare* (Cambridge, Mass., 1973). Bartlett is based

upon the Globe edition of 1891, Spevack on the Riverside. Slater's tests are restricted to vocabulary in the dramatic canon, in which he does not include any of *The Two Noble Kinsmen* or *Sir Thomas More* (these limitations deriving from his partial dependence on Bartlett). Slater considers the first two acts of *Pericles* separately from the last three, but does not differentiate the vocabulary of suspect passages in *Timon of Athens* (see below, n. 70), *Macbeth* (the Hecate scenes), or *Henry VIII* (Fletcher's share). I have compiled links with *The Two Noble Kinsmen*, and differentiated the suspect passages in all the probably collaborative late plays (see Appendix II); but these figures cannot be statistically evaluated. In the absence of Slater's figures for the total number of word-links in these works or parts of works, we cannot determine how many links with *Lear* to expect, or how much weight to assign to any excess of links we observe; moreover, inclusion of the works Slater excludes would push the number of occurrences for some words over his cut-off figure of ten.

69. Slater's articles do not make it clear that he uses the New (Cambridge) Shakespeare, rather than the so-called old Cambridge edition, as his adjudicator; moreover, he uses this only when Bartlett and Spevack differ (i.e. where both agree against Wilson he does not consult the latter). I have myself consulted only Spevack, as the more reliable concordance, and one based on an extremely conservative edition.

70. Metrical, vocabulary and stylistic tests all place *Timon* and *Lear* in conjunction, *Timon* being if anything slightly earlier; this merely confirms a long-standing critical judgement that the two plays are related. For Slater's vocabulary tests, see n. 60, above; for the metrical evidence, see Karl Wentersdorf, 'Shakespearean Chronology and the Metrical Tests', *Shakespeare-Studien*, ed. W. Fischer and K. Wentersdorf (Marburg, 1951), 161–93; the stylistic evidence will be discussed in 'The Shakespeare Canon'. David Lake's *The Canon of Middleton's Plays* (Cambridge, 1975) and MacD. P. Jackson's *Studies in Attribution: Middleton and Shakespeare* (Salzburg, 1979) strongly support earlier conjectures that *Timon* is a work of collaboration by Shakespeare and Middleton; R. V. Holdsworth's exhaustive investigation of *Timon* – 'Middleton and Shakespeare: The Case for Middleton's Hand in *Timon of Athens*' (unpublished Ph.D. thesis, University of Manchester, 1982) – further corroborates these claims, as does my own 'The Shakespeare Canon'. This proposed division of authorship in *Timon* strengthens the evidence for the play's proximity to Q *Lear*.

71. The rare vocabulary unique to the Folio text does not, however, have an exceptional number of links with the suspect passages in *Timon* and *Macbeth* (Middleton), or *Henry VIII* and *The Two Noble Kinsmen* (Fletcher): see Appendix II.

72. Q has 728 links with the *As You Like It* to *Othello* group, against an expected 629; F has only 56, which is actually below the chance expectation of 57.9. If the F vocabulary were composed at the same time as Q, it should have a proportionate excess of links with this group: which would mean 69 links, instead of only 56. Because of the small size of the Folio sample the observed discrepancy does not attain statistical significance – it would occur by chance about one time in twelve – but it remains noticeable that F does not share Q's excess of links with the 1600–1604 group. Q also has strong links with the *Macbeth–Henry VIII* group (731 observed, to 629 expected); so does F (66 observed, to 57.9 expected).

73. The rare vocabulary unique to F has 44 links with these four plays, against an expected 29.14; this excess has a chi-squared value of 7.57.

74. J. Leeds Barroll's 'The Chronology of Shakespeare's Jacobean Plays and the Dating of *Antony and Cleopatra*' (in *Essays on Shakespeare*, ed. Gordon Ross Smith (Pennsylvania, 1965), 115–62) argues for an earlier date for *Antony* (late

1606, or even 1605); in which case, as he points out, it could even antedate *Lear* (p. 153). But Barroll's dismissal of metrical tests is based upon Chambers's use of them; he never mentions the more sophisticated collective test devised by Wentersdorf (see note 70, above), which puts *Antony* clearly after *Lear* and *Macbeth* – as does Slater's rare vocabulary test and my own stylistic test. Likewise, I agree with Barroll that the evidence for dating *Macbeth* in early-to-mid 1606 is circumstantial, but the independent agreement of these three statistical tests is difficult to dismiss. It seems safe to assume that both plays follow closely the original composition of *Lear*, and that consequently it should have closer links with them than with the late romances.

75. For a brief explanation of chi-squared see Jackson (p. 341, n. 14), to whom I am grateful for repeated advice on statistical matters.

76. I exclude *Henry VIII* because of its presumed collaborative character, which could distort the figures: one would need to know how many rare words occurred in each author's stint to determine whether *Lear* has any exceptional relationship with the vocabulary of the Shakespearian portion.

77. The *Troilus and Cressida* evidence depends upon acceptance of my contention that F represents the revised state of the text (see note 6). Since Q *Richard III* is almost universally accepted as a 'bad' text deriving from theatrical performances, the likeliest explanation for its omission of several long passages is that they were cut in performance; though it remains possible that they represent later additions. See W. W. Greg, *The Editorial Problem in Shakespeare* (2nd ed., Oxford, 1951), pp. 80–1; D. L. Patrick, *The Textual History of 'Richard III'* (Stanford, 1936), pp. 124–32; and Antony Hammond's new Arden edition (1981), pp. 333–5.

78. See Taylor, 'The Shakespeare Canon', and Eugene M. Waith's forthcoming Oxford Shakespeare edition of *Titus*.

79. *Critical Observations on Shakespeare* (1746), p. 327.

80. Emendation of Q's *inloose* to F's *vnloose* seems required in any case, and assumes no more than the easiest minim misreading. Omission of the final *-t* in *intrencht*, immediately before the initial *t-* in *to*, would also be very easy: compare, among many examples, *A Midsummer Night's Dream* (Q1) 'about [t]expound' (G1ᵛ; 4.1.207) and *Troilus and Cressida* (Q1) 'Must [t]arre' (C4; 1.3.390).

81. See note 74 for Barroll's contention that *Antony* might conceivably precede *Lear*.

82. I am at present engaged in a re-examination of metrical licences and dating evidence throughout the canon, in conjunction with work on the Oxford Shakespeare; but this will not be completed for several years. Moreover, Blayney will be extensively discussing metrical and lineation problems in Q1 (*Origins*, II), and it seems best to postpone further discussion until after the publication of his findings.

83. Like all editors since Pope I have rearranged the verse in the quotation from Q, which treats 'Into . . . negligēce' as one line, and consequently misdivides the next three lines, until by treating 'now . . . farre' as one line it returns to regularity.

84. For a stimulating and persuasive analysis of the increasing dissociation of style and character in Shakespeare's late work, see Anne Barton's 'Leontes and the spider: language and speaker in Shakespeare's Last Plays', in *Shakespeare's Styles: Essays in honour of Kenneth Muir*, ed. Philip Edwards, Inga-Stina Ewbank, and G. K. Hunter (Cambridge, 1980), pp. 131–50. Urkowitz sees Kent's involuted style here as the dramatic motive for the Gentleman's suspicion of him (*Revision*, pp. 75–6); Sheldon P. Zitner ('*King Lear* and Its Language', in *Some Facets of 'King Lear': Essays in Prismatic Criticism*, ed. Rosalie L. Colie and F. T. Flahiff (Toronto, 1974), p. 7) sees it as a means of overcoming 'the impression of his dress and situation'. The explanations are not incompatible; but

it seems to me that the language remains actually and dramatically anomalous, as Kent adopts this style elsewhere only in 2.2, when he is *satirically* imitating a courtier. The Gentleman's interruption of Kent need be motivated by no more than a sense of urgency about finding the king: the product of impatience, not suspicion. Richard Knowles denies that the Gentleman's 'I will talke further with you' is, as Urkowitz contends, 'a conventional code for breaking off a conversation' – see his review in *Modern Philology* (1981), p. 199. But an exact parallel occurs at *Macbeth* 1.5.71 (TLN 426: 'We will speake further'), and there are similar speeches at *Ado* 2.3.205, *All's Well* 1.3.127, *Henry V* 2.4.113, and *Othello* 4.2.244, in all of which an intention to hear or speak or consider further clearly signals a desire not to do so now. Indeed, compare Regan's 'We shall further thinke of it' with Goneril's 'We must do something, and i'th' heate' (TLN 331–2; B2; 1.1.307–8). Furthermore, in the recent BBC production of *Lear*, which retains the Quarto lines, the Gentleman's speech is clearly and naturally played as an interruption.

85. For an extremely detailed substantiation of the felt differences between late and early style, see Dolores M. Burton's *Shakespeare's Grammatical Style* (Austin, 1973).

86. E. A. Armstrong, *Shakespeare's Imagination: A Study of the Psychology of Association and Inspiration*, rev. edn. (Lincoln, Nebraska, 1963), pp. 57–65.

87. F actually reads 'wil'd Geese' (TLN 1322); Compositor E had already set 'wil'd' for Q1–2 'wild(e)' at TLN 1612 (F3; 2.4.308). For E's frequent misuse of apostrophes, see Werstine (above, p. 290, n. 53).

88. Stone calls this added speech 'an obvious interpolation', which is 'clumsily misplaced here between Kent's account of his mistreatment by Regan and Cornwall and Lear's vehement reaction to it' (*Textual History*, p. 241). But speeches by the Fool have already been interposed, twice, between a provocation and Lear's extreme response to it (TLN 726–9, 735–7; D1ᵛ; 1.4.214–7,224–5). One might claim that an adapter noticed and copied this unusual dramatic technique, but its use here cannot be regarded as any less dramatically appropriate or effective than the examples, common to both texts, in 1.4.

89. Armstrong, pp. 44–6, 218. It is worth noticing that the late instances of *hum* where these associations do not appear are all in *Timon*: 3.3.1, 3.3.9 (where Armstrong admitted that it isn't present at all) and 2.2.195 (where it is 'distant'). Lake, Jackson, and Holdsworth all assign 3.3 to Middleton, and Holdsworth regards this section of 2.2 as questionable (on other grounds). The image clusters which Armstrong does find in *Timon* all occur in passages assigned to Shakespeare by all three scholars (see Armstrong, p. 228).

90. F spells 'Humh'. The interjection is spelled 'humh', 'hum', and 'hem' elsewhere in Shakespeare; there are no apparent differences in nuance between these forms.

91. See D. M. McKeithan, *The Debt to Shakespeare in the Beaumont and Fletcher Canon* (Austin, 1938); D. J. McGinn, *Shakespeare's Influence on the Drama of his Age Studied in 'Hamlet'* (New Brunswick, N. J., 1938); A. H. Cruickshank, *Philip Massinger* (Oxford, 1920), pp. 77–80, 163–8; and T. A. Dunn, *Philip Massinger: The Man and the Playwright* (1957), pp. 203–10. Though Fletcher and Massinger both borrowed heavily from *Hamlet* and *Othello*, both are surprisingly free of echoes of *Lear* (surely impossible, if either were responsible for the Folio redaction).

92. For Fletcher and Shakespeare, see Cyrus Hoy, 'The Shares of Fletcher and his Collaborators in the Beaumont and Fletcher Canon (VII)', *Studies in Bibliography*, 15 (1962), 71–90.

93. For E's exceptional conservatism in preserving the details of his copy, see Paul

Werstine's essay in this collection, Taylor's 'Folio Copy', and Howard-Hill's
The Problem of Manuscript Copy for Folio King Lear'.

94. The most thorough recent discussion of copy for *Coriolanus* is in Philip
Brockbank's new Arden edition (1976), pp. 2–7; this endorses the traditional
hypothesis.

95. See Hoy, pp. 82–4.

96. Jackson, *Studies in Attribution*, pp. 56–8. Nor is Folio *Lear* at all characteristic of
Middleton in its use of oaths and exclamations (Jackson, pp. 67–79).

97. In a footnote Stone quotes extensively from T. A. Dunn's discussion of
Massinger's style (*Textual History*, pp. 127–8); these selections are decidedly
misleading, and anyone who reads Dunn's full discussion (*Philip Massinger: The
Man and the Playwright*, pp. 202–66) will have little inclination to attribute the
Folio redaction of *Lear* to Massinger. For instance, 'Massinger's style was much
less flexible and much more reduplicating than perhaps any of his contemporaries' (p. 211); yet *Lear* contains none of his favourite words (p. 211) or
images (pp. 212–13), and is only once echoed in the entire Massinger canon. (The
single echo, in *A New Way to Pay Old Debts* (1625), is of a passage present in both
Q and F: 'I will tread this vnboulted villaine into morter' (El^v; TLN 1138–9;
2.2.65–6), 'I will helpe | Your memory, and tread thee into mortar' (*New Way*,
(1.1.88).)

98. Cyrus Hoy, 'The Shares of Fletcher and his Collaborators in the Beaumont and
Fletcher Canon (I)', *Studies in Bibliography*, 8 (1956), 129–46.

99. Cyrus Hoy, 'The Shares of Fletcher and his Collaborators in the Beaumont
and Fletcher Canon (VI)', *Studies in Bibliography*, 14 (1961), esp. pp. 58–
64.

100. For Fletcher's and Massinger's association with the King's Men, see *The Plays
and Poems of Philip Massinger*, ed. Philip Edwards and Colin Gibson, 5 vols.
(Oxford, 1976), I, xv–xlv. Massinger did not become the company's chief
dramatist until 1626, after Fletcher's death (I, xxii); until after 1623, almost all his
known work for the King's Men was in collaboration with Fletcher (the only
exception being his collaboration with Field on *The Fatal Dowry*, and his first
unaided work, *The Duke of Milan*). As G. E. Bentley demonstrates, 'alterations of
and additions to the revived plays in the repertory of a company were the usual
work of the regular dramatist at the theatre. Consequently, when the name of the
attached dramatist for a company is known, we have a strong suggestion of the
identity of the author of the revisions made in that company's plays during his
incumbency' (*The Profession of Dramatist in Shakespeare's Time, 1590–1642*
(Princeton, 1971), p. 257). This argues against Massinger, who held this position
only after the publication of F; from Shakespeare's death to 1626 Fletcher held it.
The connection between collaboration and redaction (Bentley, p. 235) also would
argue for Fletcher, or for Middleton, on the ground that a playwright who had
collaborated with Shakespeare in his lifetime might have been regarded as having
some warrant for 'posthumous collaboration'.

101. Between 1616 and 1623 the only tragedies or tragicomedies not written by the
authors here considered (Fletcher, Massinger, Middleton, Jonson, Chapman,
Field, Webster), are: H. Shirley, *The Martyred Soldier* (before 1627; Queen
Anne's?); W. Rowley, *All's Lost by Lust* (1619–20?; Prince's); J. Day and
T. Dekker, *Guy of Warwick* (1620; unknown); T. Dekker and P. Massinger, *The
Virgin Martyr* (1620; Red Bull); T. Dekker, J. Ford, and W. Rowley, *The Witch of
Edmonton* (1621; Prince's Men). See Alfred Harbage, *Annals of English Drama
975–1700*, revised by S. Schoenbaum (1964).

102. The following account of linguistic preferences for Chapman, Field, and Webster
is taken from Lake, *The Canon of Middleton's Plays*, pp. 252–3.

103. Folio *Lear* is also exceptionally low in its use of *ye* (7 times, as opposed to 15 and 22 in Field's two plays); nor does it display his fondness for speeches in unison, or for 'grammatical inversions that generally accomplish the purpose of relegating some form of the verb to the end of the sentence or clause' (Cyrus Hoy, 'The Shares of Fletcher and his Collaborators in the Beaumont and Fletcher Canon (IV)', *Studies in Bibliography*, 12 (1959), 92–7).

104. For Webster's hand in adapting Marston's *The Malcontent* for the King's Men, see Kerrigan (above, p. 205). In the decade preceding the publication of the Folio Webster wrote *The Guise* (1614–23; unknown company), *The Duchess of Malfi* (1612–14, revised 1617–23; King's Men), and (with Middleton) *Anything for a Quiet Life* (1621?; King's Men). He seems also to have collaborated with Ford, Rowley, Dekker, Massinger, and Heywood; Carol Chillington has recently suggested that he is the famous Hand D in *Sir Thomas More* ('Playwrights at Work: Henslowe's, not Shakespeare's, *Book of Sir Thomas More*', *English Literary Renaissance*, 10 (1980), 439–79). In addition to his talent for tragedy, association with the King's Men, and record of hack-work, Webster is also well known for his imitations and echoes of Shakespeare's plays (including *Lear*). However, Webster was never the King's Men's attached dramatist (as Shakespeare, Fletcher, and Massinger were, in turn); his only known adaptation for them arose from the special circumstances of their retaliatory theft of a rival company's play; moreover, since Marston (the original author) was still very much alive, Webster might well have collaborated with him in adapting the play.

105. See Sarrazin, 'Wortechos bei Shakespeare'; Hart, *Stolne and Surreptitious Copies*, pp. 28–40, and 'Vocabularies of Shakespeare's Plays', *Review of English Studies*, 19 (1943), 128–40; Jackson, *Studies in Attribution*, pp. 148–58. (The last is the most helpful.) Jackson notes that 'For most Shakespeare plays the rate of words occurring only once or twice elsewhere is about one in 12 lines' (p. 158, n. 21).

106. Philip Gaskell, *From Writer to Reader: Studies in Editorial Method* (Oxford, 1978), pp. 142–55. As Gaskell observes, this situation creates the nasty editorial problem of whether to accept the author's first thought, or the revision necessitated by fortuitous intermediate corruption; but in *Lear*, since many other revisions were being made at the same time, it seems fairly clear that one should not (and probably could not) distinguish editorially between revisions made because of errors in Q and revisions made spontaneously.

107. I am grateful to Hans Walter Gabler (General Editor of a critical edition of the works of Joyce, in progress) for supplying me with these examples, all taken from the 'Circe' chapter of *Ulysses*.

108. See for instance Hans Zeller, 'A New Approach to the Critical Constitution of Literary Texts', *Studies in Bibliography*, 28 (1975), pp. 251–6. The entire article is an important statement of the editorial problems created by authorial revision.

109. '*Enter Lear.*' (C3ᵛ; 1.4.7; attendants required), '*Enter Lear.*' (D2ᵛ; 1.5.0; Kent and Fool required), '*Enter the Duke of Cornwall.*' (D4; 2.1.85; Regan required, attendants possibly), '*Enter Edmund with his rapier drawne, Gloster[,] the Duke and Dutchesse.*' (El; 2.2.46; attendants required), '*Enter King.*' (E3; 2.4.0; Fool and Gentleman required), '*Enter Duke and Regan.*' (E4ᵛ; 2.4.126; Gloucester certainly, servants probably, required), '*Enter Cornwall, and Regan, and Gonorill, and Bastard.*' (G4ᵛ; 3.7.0; servants required), '*Enter Cordelia, Kent and Doctor.*' (K1ᵛ; 4.7.0; Gentleman required). In each case F supplies the missing names in its direction.

110. The line may echo George Wilkins's *The Miseries of Enforced Marriage*, a play Shakespeare probably read before or while composing the Quarto version of *King Lear*. (See 'A New Source and an Old Date', pp. 408–12.) However, the particular Wilkins parallel for the Fool's exit line in Folio *Lear* ('Few else do lie abed at

noone, but Drunkards, Punks, & knaues') does not in itself constitute much to go on, since both the idea and the phrasing were more common than has sometimes been realized. (See Kerrigan, pp. 228–9; Tilley, B197; Michael Cameron Andrews, '"And I'll Go to Bed at Noon"', *Notes and Queries*, 223 (1978), 149–51; and Hilda Hulme, *Explorations in Shakespeare's Language: Some problems of word meaning in the dramatic text* (1962; repr. 1977), pp. 70–2. Reading North's Plutarch I came across at least a dozen references to people going to bed at midday or in the afternoon.) All the other Wilkins parallels with *Lear* are in Q.

111. Even if this particular seven-word addition dates from 1605–6 rather than 1609–10, one could still legitimately argue – as John Kerrigan does (above, pp. 218–30) – that the added line better fits F's version of the character than Q's. When Shakespeare came to rethink the Fool's part three or four years later he would have begun that reconsideration assuming an ending for the role which had been no part of his original design; as a consequence, the Fool's role in F might be markedly more consonant with the new exit line than the role in Q had been.

112. Bentley, *The Profession of Dramatist*, pp. 164–5.

113. Interpolations made in performance could find their way into reported texts; these are discussed in Wells and Taylor, *Modernizing Shakespeare's Spelling, with Three Studies in the Text of 'Henry V'* (Oxford, 1979), pp. 148–52.

114. Nevill Coghill persuasively argued that Shakespeare himself revised *Othello* at some point in or after 1606 (*Shakespeare's Professional Skills* (Cambridge, 1964), pp. 164–202); E. A. J. Honigmann strengthens and develops this argument in 'Shakespeare's Revised Plays: *King Lear* and *Othello*', *The Library*, VI, 4 (1982), 142–73.

115. For a summary of the evidence that the manuscript was – as is almost universally supposed – a prompt-book, or something indistinguishable from it, see W. W. Greg, *The Shakespeare First Folio: Its Bibliographical and Textual History* (Oxford, 1955), pp. 384–6. Greg does not mention two apparent errors in stage directions. For an explanation of that at 4.6.187 (TLN 2630), see below, n. 130. At 1.5.0 (TLN 874), F apparently brings in the Gentleman 47 lines before he is needed. But, as Charles Jennens noted in his 1770 edition, 'Go you before to *Gloster* with these Letters' could well be addressed to this Gentleman, before Lear turns to Kent with the instruction 'acquaint my Daughter no further with any thing you know, then comes from her demand out of the Letter' (TLN 875–7; D2ᵛ; 1.5.1–3). This interpretation disposes of the notorious difficulty about Kent being sent to Gloucester to deliver a letter to Regan, explains the distinction between 'these Letters' and 'the Letter', and justifies the Folio stage direction. (I see no reason to assume, as Jennens did, that any words are missing from the text here.)

116. See D. L. Page, *Actors' Interpolations in Greek Tragedy: Studied with Special Reference to Euripides' 'Iphigeneia in Aulis'* (Oxford, 1934). Page's own catalogue of 'Some Characteristics of Histrionic Interpolation' (116–21), includes 'spectacular innovations', 'melodramatic interpolations', 'topical interpolations', 'explanatory interpolations', 'expansive interpolations', and 'interpolations prompted by scenic exigencies'. The Hecate scenes in *Macbeth* are obvious candidates for the first category; but the 'little eyrie' addition in Folio *Hamlet* – which everyone regards as Shakespeare's – is the only topical addition I can think of in Shakespeare. Like most scholars, I remain unconvinced by C. J. Sisson's claim – in *New Readings in Shakespeare*, 2 vols. (Cambridge, 1956), I, 188–91 – that 'The Lady of the *Strachy*, married the yeoman of the wardrobe' (*Twelfth Night*, TLN 1054–5; 2.5.39–40) represents a later interpolation made for the sake of a topical dig at William Strachey and David Yeomans. Three of Page's categories – melodramatic, explanatory, and expansive – invoke critical

judgements of uncertain value in texts where authorial revision is certain or suspected. For 'scenic exigencies' (which in Page's example involves a desire to avoid dangerous or inconvenient stage mechanisms), see pp. 410–14. For a more recent survey of interpolations in one Greek tragedian's corpus, see Oliver Taplin's important (and helpfully indexed) *The Stagecraft of Aeschylus: The Dramatic Use of Entrances and Exits in Greek Tragedy* (Oxford, 1977).

117. Derek Peat, ' "And that's true too": *King Lear* and the Tension of Uncertainty', *Shakespeare Survey 33* (Cambridge, 1980), 43–53; Martha Andresen, ' "Ripeness is All": Sententiae and Commonplaces in *King Lear*', *Some Facets of 'King Lear'*, pp. 145–68. Urkowitz also defends the Folio addition (*Revision*, p. 44).

118. Stone here echoes Capell; see Urkowitz, above, p. 35.

119. *The Manuscript of Shakespeare's 'Hamlet' and the Problems of its Transmission*, 2 vols. (Cambridge, 1934), I, 22–87. The assumption that there was only ever one 'Manuscript of Shakespeare's *Hamlet*' of course begs the question. See also Harold Jenkins, 'Playhouse Interpolations in the Folio Text of *Hamlet*', *Studies in Bibliography*, 13 (1960), 31–47; though he impugns many more passages as 'interpolations', Jenkins's method does not differ substantially from Wilson's. In his new Arden edition (1982), Jenkins rejects Wilson's hypothesis of a 'playhouse transcriber with a too active memory', but does not himself offer any explanation for the presence of such interpolations in F (pp. 63–4).

120. An identical illogic underlies Alice Walker's theory that Q derives from a transcript of foul papers, corrupted by the over-confident memories of the two actors making the transcription (*Textual Problems of the First Folio* (Cambridge, 1953), pp. 37–67). As Folio *Hamlet* shows many signs of prompt-book copy, so Quarto *Lear* shows every sign of foul paper copy; Wilson and Walker in each case invent a stage of transcription to account for what each regards as a series of gratuitous memorial errors. Walker's attempt to foist the same schema upon *Othello* has been widely rejected; but editors seem not to have realized that what will not do for *Othello* won't do for *Hamlet* or *Lear* either.

121. For theatrical conditions in fourth-century Greece see Page, pp. 1–20.

122. For instance, the Smock Alley prompt-book of *Lear* in the Folger Library, dating from the late seventeenth century, alters 'gasted' (D4; TLN 991; 2.1.55) to 'frighted'; 'pight' (D4; TLN 1002; 2.1.65) to 'bent'; 'meiney' (TLN 1311; 2.4.35) to 'servan[ts]'; 'tender-hefted' (TLN 1455; 2.4.171) to 'tender'. Several other unusual expressions were either altered or omitted (as happened in the other Smock Alley prompt-books, too).

123. William A. Ringler, Jr, argues (plausibly I think) that Armin played Edgar ('Shakespeare and His Actors: Some Remarks on *King Lear*', in *Shakespeare's Art from a Comparative Perspective*, Proceedings of the Comparative Literature Symposium (Lubbock, Texas, 1981), 183–94. For Armin's departure, see Jane Belfield, 'Robert Armin, Citizen and Goldsmith of London', *Notes and Queries*, 225 (1980), 158–9. Armin died in 1615.

124. Armin was, in any case, markedly different from Tarlton in his attitude towards authors and texts, and unlikely to have attempted to interfere with Shakespeare's wishes: see F. W. Sternfeld, *Music in Shakespearean Tragedy* (1963), pp. 98–125. Significantly, Richard Brome's *The Antipodes* (1638) specifically identifies this tendency for clowns to add to their written parts as something which used to be done 'in the days of Tarleton and Kempe' (2.2.40–9) – the latter of whom had abandoned the stage by 1599. Such testimony hardly encourages the belief that *Lear* suffered from such debasement *c*.1614–22.

125. See G. E. Bentley, *The Jacobean and Caroline Stage*, 7 vols. (Oxford, 1941–68), I, 2–8. Bentley also records (I, 15–16) a letter of protection, given by Herbert in 1624, to twenty-one 'Musitions and other necessary attendantes' 'imployed by

the Kinges Ma[ties] seruantes'; this does not include boys or the sharers, and is addressed to 'all Mayo[rs], Sheriffes, Justices of the Peace, Bayleiffes, Constables, knight Ma[r]shalls men, and all othe[r] his Ma[ties] Office[rs] to whom it may or shall apperteyne'. As Bentley says, 'that at the end of 1624 . . . at least thirty-five men and an unknown number of boys had an active part in the theatrical business of the King's men . . . is a fair measure of its prosperity' (I, 16) – the more so as this letter is clearly designed to cover provincial touring, when we might expect the company to be at less than full strength.

126. Doran, *The Text of 'King Lear'*, pp. 76–8; Duthie, pp. 8–9; Greg, *The Editorial Problem*, p. 100, note 1; Stone, *Textual History*, p. 111.

127. The two servants in 3.7 could not double eleven other roles, present in 3.7 itself or in 3.6 and 4.1; some of these eleven roles could themselves be doubled, however, while F's own excisions in 3.6 and 3.7 reduce other doubling possibilities. In 4.6 the two gentlemen affected could double anyone except Gloucester, Lear, Edgar, and Oswald. In 4.7 the Doctor could double any role but the nine present in 4.7 and the adjoining scenes.

128. The most recent extensive discussion of Elizabethan doubling practices and their relevance to Shakespearian texts is in Wells and Taylor, *Modernizing Shakespeare's Spelling*, pp. 72–123.

129. F calls ambiguously for 'Seruants' at 3.7.0 and 3.7.27 (TLN 2059, 2088); one is subsequently killed resisting Cornwall. How many F intended to remain at scene's end, to 'Turne out that eyelesse Villaine' and 'throw this Slaue | Vpon the Dunghill' (TLN 2174–5; 3.7.96–7), is debatable; but it seems to me likely that at least two would be needed. Certainly editors cannot arbitrarily decide that only one was present, and then on the basis of that assumption castigate F for niggardliness in the provision of attendants.

130. It seems most unlikely that one gentleman would stay behind to chat with Edgar, unless others were present to pursue Lear; Lear asks 'Masters, know you that?' (TLN 2642; 4.6.200), to which the Gentleman answers 'we obey you' (TLN 2643; 4.6.201), and although both these plurals could conceivably include Edgar and Gloucester, it seems almost certain that they refer to a plurality of gentlemen. (These points, and others, are made in Philip Edwards's review of Urkowitz's *Revision*: *Modern Language Review* (1982), 694–8.) I therefore assume that arabic '2', or roman 'ii' or 'iii', was misread as 'a', and as a consequence either *Gentlemen* was misread *Gentleman*, or *Gent.* mis-expanded to *Gentleman.* In fact if the manuscript read (ambiguously) 'Enter Gent.', the compositor might easily have assumed that the singular was meant, and supplied 'a' himself. 'Gent.' occurs in entrance directions at *Measure for Measure* 1.2.115 (TLN 206: '& 2 Gent.') and *Two Noble Kinsmen* 4.2.54 (I4; '*and Gent.*'), both apparently printed – like Folio *Lear* – from scribal transcripts. Editors regularly emend copy-text 'gentlemen' to 'gentlemen' at *Midsummer Night's Dream* 3.2.299 (E4), *Merchant of Venice* 2.6.58 (D2[v]), and *Richard II* 1.1.152 (A4); the reverse error apparently occurs at *Hamlet* 5.2.107 (N2), and the comparable 'Gentlewoman' for correct 'Gentlewomen' at *Antony and Cleopatra* 2.2.206 (TLN 919).

131. *King Lear*, ed. G. K. Hunter, New Penguin Shakespeare (Harmondsworth, 1972), p. 319. C. J. Sisson likewise defends Q's staging by arguing that F's entrance 'may have been an additional direction inserted upon performance on a stage without a "study" ' (*New Readings in Shakespeare*, II, 242). Virtually all editors agree in preferring Q's music to F's stillness.

132. The use of music on the Shakespearian stage has been extensively studied in this century, mostly by historians of music. The best survey remains Sternfeld's *Music in Shakespearean Tragedy*. For the increase in musical accompaniment associated with the move to the Blackfriars, see Alfred Harbage, *Shakespeare and*

the Rival Traditions (New York, 1952); the Folio's elimination of music from 4.7 clearly goes against the theatrical fashion of the period, and can hardly be attributed to the actors. See also n. 125 for the number of musicians regularly employed by the company.

133. *The Duchess of Malfi* (1614), *The Widow* (1616), *Thierry and Theodoret* (1617), *The Knight of Malta* (1618), *Rollo Duke of Normandy* (1619), *The Custom of the Country* (1620), *The Double Marriage* (1620), *The Duke of Milan* (1621). Dates and attributions to the King's Men are from Harbage and Schoenbaum, *Annals*; for the presence of doctors, see Berger and Bradford, *Index of Characters*. Five of the Shakespearian plays also appear to have remained in the King's Men repertoire during this period. Both *Henry VIII* and *Kinsmen* date from 1613, and most editors believe that the Folio text of *Macbeth* represents an adapted, post-1616 revival; *Merry Wives* may have been performed at Court in May 1613 (see H. J. Oliver's new Arden edition (1971), p. x); for performances of *Pericles*, see F. D. Hoeniger's new Arden edition (1963), pp. lxv–lxvi.

134. A scene in John Ford's *The Lovers Melancholy* (King's Men, 1628) explicitly calls for a staging almost identical to the Quarto version of 4.7: '*Soft Musicke. Enter Melander (in a Coach) his haire and beard trimd, habit and gowne chang'd. Rheticas and Corax, and Boy that sings*' (L2ᵛ; 5.1). As Melander is a sleeping, mad old man here reunited with his daughter, Corax a doctor, and Rhetias a blunt servant who has kept in communication with the absent daughter, Shakespeare's influence on Ford can hardly be doubted; since Ford was in London from 1602 on, he could have witnessed the original staging (or have read the Quarto). Equally, it is clear that Ford here calls for – and was apparently given – a stage effect which the King's Men allegedly refused to give Shakespeare. This seems, to say the least, unlikely. For further examples of beds called for in King's Men plays, see Irwin Smith, *Shakespeare's Blackfriars Playhouse: Its History and Its Design* (1966), pp. 365–6.

135. *Prefaces to Shakespeare*, 2 vols. (1958), I, 298.

136. Trevor Nunn's 1968 production at Stratford-upon-Avon also had Lear carried in for the first scene, and emphasized the parallel with 4.7 by blocking and properties.

137. Bentley, *Jacobean and Caroline Stage*, II, 410. Burbage, Heminges, and Condell were, of course, the only London acquaintances Shakespeare named in his will; all three are associated with him from the beginning of his career.

138. For Crane, see T. H. Howard-Hill, *Ralph Crane and Some Shakespeare First Folio Comedies* (Charlottesville, 1972); for *2 Henry IV*, Matthias A. Shaaber's New Variorum edition (Philadelphia, 1940), pp. 503–4, 513–15.

139. See Jackson's discussion, above, pp. 321–5, 329–30.

140. Duthie, pp. 17, 194; Greg, *Editorial Problem*, pp. 99–100. Duthie also mentions the variant 'eare-bussing'/'ear-kissing' (D3ᵛ; TLN 936; 2.1.8), but admits that this could result from a simple misreading. Greg may be right in thinking F 'squints' a sophistication of 'squenies' or 'squenes' (TLN 1897; G2ᵛ, 'queues' (Qa), 'squemes' (Qb); 3.4.117), but this too could arise from misreading (e/t), assisted as at 2.1.8 by the unfamiliarity of the original word.

141. As Greg noted in his British Academy Lecture 'Principles of Emendation in Shakespeare' (1928; reprinted in *Aspects of Shakespeare*, ed. J. W. Mackail (Oxford, 1933), pp. 128–201; see p. 197), the Folio's spelling 'Somnet' at TLN 2499 (4.6.57) is recorded only twice elsewhere, both in Q2 *Hamlet* (D2; 1.4.70 and H4ᵛ; 3.3.18). These are also Shakespeare's only other uses of the word, and Q2 *Hamlet* is widely accepted as a foul-paper text. Q1 *Lear* at this point has 'sommons' (I3), presumably a misprint for the same form – perhaps, as Stone suggests (*Textual History*, p. 185), in the plural. Stone does not explain how the Folio compositors, consulting a manuscript with no Shakespearian authority,

corrected Q1 by supplying a peculiarly Shakespearian form; nor does he explain how that form found its way into the manuscript behind Q1, which he regards as a reported text.

142. See Werstine's discussion, above, pp. 276–81.

143. For accusations of metrical padding, see *Textual History*, pp. 117, 238, 242, 246, and 247; for metrical ineptitude, pp. 53–4, 245, and 246.

144. Honigmann, in 'Shakespeare's Revised Plays', notes that the 160 lines cut from Folio *Othello* would save only eight minutes of playing-time (a point made by Coghill, *Shakespeare's Professional Skills*, pp. 177–8); he also quotes W. W. Greg's summary of the nature of cuts in surviving manuscript plays: 'the cuts make no great impression on the length of the play and appear to have been usually made on what may be called local grounds . . . There is little indication of a desire to reduce plays to a standard length' (*The Shakespeare First Folio*, p. 146).

145. *Henry V, 2 Henry IV, Coriolanus* and *Cymbeline* are also longer than Folio *Lear*; but these others do not, apparently, derive from playhouse copy.

146. For the duplications in *Love's Labour's Lost* and *Romeo and Juliet*, which are universally recognized, see for instance Greg, *Editorial Problem*, pp. 61, 127; for that in *Henry V*, see my Oxford Shakespeare edition (1982), p. 16.

147. For an important argument towards the common-sense conclusion that 'the integrity of the work of art' derives from 'those intentions which are the author's, *together with those others of which he approves or in which he acquiesces*' (my italics), see James Thorpe's 'The Aesthetics of Textual Criticism', in *Art and Error: Modern Textual Editing*, ed. Ronald Gottesmann and Scott Bennett (Bloomington, 1970), pp. 62–101.

148. Brian Vickers, *Shakespeare Quarterly*, 32 (1981), p. 405. Granville-Barker made a similar suggestion (*Prefaces to Shakespeare*, I, 332). This conjecture has been independently mentioned to me twice in the last two years, as an explanation for F's cutting; both proponents were scholars of some eminence, and one an editor. Tieck seems to have offered the same explanation for the omission of 4.3: see H. H. Furness's New Variorum edition (Philadelphia, 1880), p. 360.

149. See the elegy reprinted by E. K. Chambers, *The Elizabethan Stage*, 4 vols. (Oxford, 1923), II, 309.

150. It has been claimed that the absence of a song in the Quarto text of *Othello*, and the attribution of a song in Folio *Twelfth Night*, are due to alterations made because of the lack of a boy who could sing the songs; but for *Othello* see Coghill (n. 114 above), and for *Twelfth Night* see Robert K. Turner, Jr., 'Act-End Notations in Some Elizabethan Plays', *Modern Philology*, 72 (1975), 238–47.

151. Doran, *Text of 'King Lear'*, p. 70 ('bibliographical proof'); Duthie, p. 418 ('must'); Greg, *Shakespeare First Folio*, p. 388 ('suggests . . . apparently'); Hunter, *King Lear*, pp. 320–1 ('suggests'); etc.

152. W. W. Greg, *Dramatic Documents from the Elizabethan Playhouses*, 2 vols. (Oxford, 1931), II, 210–12.

153. *Stolne and Surreptitious Copies*, p. 147. Hart himself conjectures that the trial 'perhaps . . . did not play too well on the stage', but includes discussion of this Folio cut in a paragraph otherwise devoted to censorship. On the latter see my discussion above (pp. 88–101).

154. This statement is not intended to contradict Roger Warren's argument (pp. 46–8, above) or my own (pp. 88–101, above) that 3.6 may have been abbreviated because it did not 'work' in performance. At the crudest level the scene's surface effectiveness can hardly be doubted. Noticeably, the director and cast of the 1982 BBC production of *King Lear*, though generally receptive to many Folio cuts, were astonished that the mad trial was cut; one actor called it 'the sort of change

an author would have to fight to get his cast to accept'. Tony Church, in the 1982 Santa Cruz production of the Folio text, also preferred 3.6 with the mad trial included (though he accepted the necessity for removing it, in that production). Such testimony from contemporary professionals encourages one's confidence that the abbreviation of 3.6 was not initiated by the company against Shakespeare's wishes. Warren and I only question whether, in performance, the mad trial can successfully communicate, in whole or part, all of the higher significance critics regularly attach to it. By definition, the theatrical bogeymen of the editorial imagination don't care tuppence about such 'higher significances': anyone concerned about success at this aesthetic level would be indistinguishable from the author.

155. The first quotation is from an eminent scholar at the Cambridge seminar (see Preface), who prefers to describe himself as 'an elderly gentleman at the other end of the table'; the second is from Edwards's review of Urkowitz's *Revision*. My thanks to the former for permission to quote him. (Another scholar has recently told me that, 'If Shakespeare cut the dialogue of the servants at the end of 3.7, the less Shakespeare he.')

156. See preceding note. Edwards here echoes Delius ('On the Quarto and Folio of *King Lear*', *Transactions of the New Shakspere Society*, 1875–6, pp. 125–47), who also argued that if Shakespeare himself had really revised the play, we should have found more emphatic traces of that revision than mere omissions of certain passages. Delius, however, makes this point about the whole play, thereby ignoring or dismissing Folio additions and alterations; Edwards, more plausibly if no less illogically, restricts his claim to the treatment of Albany. In reply to Edwards one might note – among others – Scott Fitzgerald's plea for permission to alter a few words in the plates of a projected second edition of *Tender is the Night*, because 'sometimes by a single word change one can throw a new emphasis or give a new value to the exact same scene or setting' (quoted by D. F. McKenzie in *The Library*, V, 14 (1959), p. 209).

157. *Shakespeare Quarterly*, 32 (1981), p. 405.

158. Ludwig Wittgenstein, *Tractatus Logico-Philosophicus*, trans. D. F. Pears and B. F. McGuinness (1961; rev. 1974), p. 35 (Proposition 4.463). For an example of such reasoning see Furness: 'in any drama by Shakespeare, it is much more easy to say why a certain passage should not be omitted, than to give a reason why it should. The presence of any passage in a play of Shakespeare's, is presumptive evidence that it is required; and to prove that it is not, lies upon those who approve of its excision. So perfect and so unerring a master was Shakespeare, that any abridgement of his plays is likely to be clumsy; it is easier to maintain, that a piece of clumsy work was done by any one rather than by Shakespeare. As Delius . . . truly says, "assuredly, Shakespeare did not himself think any passage in his *King Lear* superfluous, otherwise he would scarcely have inserted that which his editors might deem needless"' (Variorum, pp. 363–4).

159. Brook cut Act Four heavily; notoriously, he cut the conversation of the servants after Gloucester's blinding; in 4.7 he removed the Doctor and the music, and had Lear wake in a chair. (He also made many alterations with no textual authority, and it is doubtful whether he cared that certain of his changes were anticipated by the First Folio: in 3.7, for instance, he not only cut the closing dialogue but had Gloucester left alone on stage by indifferent servants, removing the furniture.)

160. Warren's account should, however, be supplemented by John Kerrigan's description (above, pp. 226–8) of the way the Folio alters the Fool's part in Act Three, thereby differentiating it more clearly from Edgar's, and at the same time subordinating the Fool to Edgar, in Lear's consciousness and our own.

161. Albany bears an uncomfortable resemblance to Roderigo. Like Roderigo, he spends most of the play being duped by a character whose evil intentions are obvious to an audience; like Roderigo, in the fourth act he seems to realize what has been happening, and determines to abandon his previous allegiance; like Roderigo, by doing so he could prevent the catastrophe; like Roderigo, he is somehow persuaded, offstage, to yield to bad advice one last time. Tolstoy's Pierre Bezukhov – also a duped, cuckolded aristocrat – demonstrates that such a role *could* be made an intriguing, intelligible, sympathetic centre of dramatic consciousness; but Shakespeare did not have a novelist's luxury of time in which to develop such a figure.

162. Why then did Shakespeare give Albany the last speech, in what appears to have been his first version of the play (Q)? Perhaps because: Albany was the highest-ranking survivor; Albany represented Scotland, and so may have been intended to compliment King James, who besides being a Scot had a son who was the current Duke of Albany; Edgar may have been intended for an actor (Armin) whose talents best suited its eccentric and mutable, rather than its heroic and moral, aspects; Edgar's historical associations were, though potent, chronologically impossible.

163. Spevack, *A Complete and Systematic Concordance to the Works of Shakespeare*, 9 vols. (Hildesheim, 1968–80) III, 946–1017. Edgar has 11.426 % of the play; his closest rival is Kent (10.277 %). These figures of course refer to the conflated text, but F drastically diminishes Kent's part, so Edgar's place seems secure. (Albany, incidentally, has less than 4 %, even with all the lines F excises.)

164. See W. D. Moriarty, 'The Bearing on Dramatic Sequence of the Varia in *Richard the Third* and *King Lear*', *Modern Philology*, 10 (1913), p. 12.

165. See F. T. Flahiff, 'Edgar: Once and Future King', in *Some Facets of 'King Lear'*, pp. 221–37, on the historical associations of Edgar's name. See also Daniel Seltzer: 'if any vocal and emotional line closely follows Lear's for emphasis, not contrast, it is that line of emotion written for Edgar' ('*King Lear* in the Theatre', in *On 'King Lear'*, ed. Lawrence N. Danson (Princeton, 1982), p. 185).

166. See John Kerrigan's discussion (above, pp. 223–6).

167. See Thomas Clayton's discussion (above, pp. 128–38).

168. The change of title, if authoritative, may be significant in at least one respect: the Quarto title, The 'True Chronicle Historie', would have had the advantage of not giving away Shakespeare's drastic departure from all previous accounts, in turning the story into a tragedy for both Lear and Cordelia. By the time of the revision, of course, Shakespeare could have counted less on the element of surprise; there would thus have been no reason *not* to advertise the play as 'The Tragedie of King Lear'.

169. *Shakespearean Tragedy*, p. 252.

170. For new evidence that the Folio revision dates from after the acquisition of the Blackfriars, see my 'The Structure of Performance: Act-intervals in the London Theatres, 1576–1642' (forthcoming).

APPENDIX I

Emendations Affecting Rare Vocabulary
in the Two Texts of 'King Lear'

1. *Emendations Made*

MOST of the Quarto/Folio variants which must or might be emended do not affect the vocabulary test: the words involved appear either less than two times (cadent F; accent (*a*.) Q; accens'd Stone conj.) or more than ten (oft/often, man/mad, etc.), or else they involve distinctions (changes of tense, inflection, or number) or categories (proper nouns) which the vocabulary test systematically ignores. The following list only includes cases where (*a*) a word would have been included in the vocabulary sample if an emendation had not been made, or (*b*) a word included in the sample would not have been if an apparent error in Q or F had been emended differently, or not at all.

The italicized variant or emendation is the one I have accepted in compiling the vocabulary test; where two readings are italicized (as at 1.2.13), one would be accepted in editing Q, and the other in editing F. The variants and emendations, and in some places the discussion of them, are followed by statistics for the variants or emendations if these fall within the criteria of the rare vocabulary test, to show how inclusion or exclusion would have affected overall results. For plays where collaboration has been suspected I have provided line numbers for the *Lear* parallels, except in the case of *Macbeth*, where none of the links occur in the suspected Hecate interpolations. I have also included, in brackets, a note of parallels with *Kinsmen* or the poems, though these have not been included in the actual tabulations, for reasons explained above (n. 68). Attribution of an emendation to Blayney indicates that it occurs in his edited reference text of Q, to be included in Volume II of *Origins*; Blayney kindly provided access to his 1979 typescript of this text. Agreement of Blayney and Stone therefore indicates that they independently arrived at the same conclusion.

In most cases there is no real doubt about the required reading in both texts: Poor Tom does not stick 'Pies' in his arms, but 'Pins'. In the case of Quarto press variants generally – which consume a large proportion of the following list – the choice of reading, though sometimes difficult, seldom creates a difference between Q and F: one either accepts the variant which F endorses, or emends F because it takes over what seems to be an error in Qa or Qb – the result being, in either case, to produce the same reading in both texts. The only notable departures from traditional editorial practice are ten new readings (proposed by Stone, Blayney, or myself), in which meaningless readings in Q are emended to produce something other than the obvious alternative (in F, or in Q's own press-corrections). These ten readings – at 1.2.13, 1.4.340, 2.4.131,

3.7.59, 4.1.74, 4.2.45, 4.4.2, 4.6.247, and 5.3.148 – are based upon the new postulate that Q may not after all be trying to look like F, and therefore that in any given instance F may be unconsciously accepting a Q press-correction, or deliberately revising the text under the stimulus of nonsense in Q.

Finally, the following account of emendations and accepted readings is based upon my own preliminary draft editions of the two texts of *King Lear* for the Complete Oxford Shakespeare, as of 1 March 1982; these decisions are, therefore, not final, and may not exactly reflect the texts as eventually published. (See Addenda.)

1.1.220   Q: for voucht (B4)   F: fore-voucht (241)
Q could easily be an alternative representation of the same word or words in F; and F's word itself would be excluded from the vocabulary test only because in it *vouch'd* occurs as part of a compound. It would therefore seem artificial to regard this as a substantive difference between the two vocabulary samples.
Vouched (*a*.): TMP

1.2.13   Q: stale dull lyed (C1)   F: *dull stale tyred* (347)
STONE, BLAYNEY: *stale dull-eyed* (for Q)
Dull-eyed: MV, PER (1.2.2)

1.2.123   Q: spirituall (C2)   F: *Sphericall* (452)
Q's error could easily represent a misreading of the spelling 'spiricall' (for which see *OED*, 'sphere').
Spherical: ERR, H5
Spiritual: 1H6, H5, WT, H8 (2.4.117, 3.2.132, 3.2.140)

1.4.114   Q: gull (C4ᵛ)   F: *gall* (644)
Gall would not be included in any case, and Q's *gull* never occurs after *Timon*. Stone defends *gull*, in the senses 'deception' and 'simpleton' (224); but this disregards *to me*, and Q would be an exceptionally easy misreading of *gall*.
Gull (*sb*.): R3, ADO, 1H4, H5, TN (3), OTH, TIM (2.1.31)

1.4.228   Q: weaknes (D1ᵛ)   F: *weakens* (741)
Weaken (*v*.): TRO, OTH, (TNK 5.4.52)

1.4.229   Q: lethergie (D1ᵛ)   F: *lethergied* (742)
Lethargy (*sb*.): 2H4, TN, TRO, OTH, COR, WT

1.4.300   Qa: vntender (D2ᵛ)   F: *vntented* (819)
Qb: *vntented* (D2ᵛ)
Untender (*a*.): LR (1.1.106), CYM

1.4.340   Qa: *after* (D2ᵛ)   F: *hasten* (864)
Qb: hasten (D2ᵛ)
My retention of Qa is defended in 'Four New Readings in *King*

Lear', *Notes and Queries*, 227 (1982), 121–3. Since F alters the remainder of the line on the basis of Qb, one must accept Qb in an edition of F; but since it has been passively accepted by the reviser, and so tells us nothing about his active vocabulary at the time, *hasten* has not been included among rare vocabulary originating in F.

Hasten: TGV, ROM, HAM, AWW, LR (4.2.16), ANT, WT, (TNK 4.3.100), (SON)

1.4.340	Q: returne (D2ᵛ)	F: *returne* (864)

TAYLOR: *retinue* (for Q)
See preceding note.
Retinue: 2H4, LR (1.4.202)

1.4.341   Qa: mildie (D2ᵛ)   F: *milkie* (865)
Qb: *milkie* (D2ᵛ)
See n. 13.
Milky: HAM, TIM (3.1.54)

2.1.120   Qa: prise (D4ᵛ)   F: prize (1063)
Qb: *poyse* (D4ᵛ)
See pp. 362–3.
Poise (*sb.*): 3H6, TRO, MM, OTH, (TNK 5.4.81)

2.2.1   Qa: deuen (E1)   F: *dawning* (1076)
Qb: *euen* (E1)
Stone and Greg disagree on the time of the action; it is sometime in the night but near to dawn, and given the flexibility of dramatic time either Q or F is acceptable.
Dawning (*sb.*): H5, HAM, MM, CYM

2.2.75   Q: inloose (E1ᵛ)   F: *vnloose* (1148)
Unloose: 2H6, (LUC), H5, TRO, MM, H8 (2.4.148)

2.2.78   Q: *Reneag* (E1ᵛ)   F: Reuenge (1151)
Editors adopt Q; F makes little sense in context, and would be an easy misreading.
Renege (*v.*): ANT

2.2.79   Q: *gale* (E1ᵛ)   F: gall (1152)
Editors adopt Q. If F is correct, it represents a significant departure from the imagery of the source passage in *Eastward Ho* (see n. 5).
Gale (*sb.*): 3H6, SHR

2.2.109   Q: dialogue (E2)   F: *dialect* (1185)
None of *dialogue*'s recorded meanings seems to make sense here.
Dialect: MM
Dialogue (*sb.*): LLL, JOHN, ADO, TN, TRO, AWW

2.2.132 Qa: Stobing (E2ᵛ)   F: *Stocking* (1211)
    Qb: Stopping (E2ᵛ)
    Stock (*v.*): LR (2.4.188)

2.2.143 Qa: contaned (E2ᵛ)   *Not in F*
    Qb: temnest (E2ᵛ)
    CAPELL: contemn[d]est
    BLAYNEY: *contemned* (I, 247–8)
    Contemned (*a.*): JOHN, TN

2.2.160 Qa: *say* (E2ᵛ)   F: saw (1237)
    Qb: saw (E2ᵛ)
    Say means 'saying'; Qb looks like a sophistication, followed by
    Q2 and so F. See Stone, p. 218.
    Saw (*sb.*, 'saying'): (LUC), 2H6, LLL, AYLI (2), HAM, TN

2.3.16 Qa: Pies (E3)   F: *Pins* (1267)
    Qb: *Pins* (E3)
    Pie (*sb.*, 'pastry'): TIT, SHR, ROM, 2H4, MWW, TRO, AWW,
    WT, H8 (1.1.52)

2.3.17 Q: seruice (E3)   F: *Farmes* (1268)
    Farm (*sb.*): SHR, R2, H5 (2), HAM

2.4.31 Q: *panting* (E3ᵛ)   F: painting (1307)
    Editors adopt Q.
    Pant (*v.*): 1H4, TN, TIM (5.4.11), LR (5.3.244), ANT

2.4.35 Q: men (E3ᵛ)   F: *meiney* (1311)
    See p. 368.
    Meiney: COR

2.4.131 Qa: fruit (E4ᵛ)   F: Tombe (1409)
    Qb: tombe (E4ᵛ)
    TAYLOR: *scrine* (for Q and F)
    See note to 1.4.340.
    Shrine: 2H6 (3), ROM, MV, CYM, (LUC)

2.4.137 Qa: deptoued (E4ᵛ)   F: *deprau'd* (1415)
    Qb: depriued (E4ᵛ)
    STONE, BLAYNEY: *deplored* (for Q)
    Depraved: (*a.*): TIM (1.2.140)

2.4.276 Q: lamely (F2ᵛ)   F: *tamely* (1576)
    Shakespeare's other uses of these words confirm that Q is
    probably only the result of an easy t/l misreading.
    Tamely: 2H4, H8 (3.2.279)
    Lamely: R3, TGV, AYLI, TIM (4.1.25)

3.4.6 Qa: crulentious (G1)   F: *contentious* (1786)
    Qb: tempestious (G1)

Qa is generally regarded as a misreading of F's word, and Qb as a proof-corrector's guess.
Tempestuous: 1H6, TIT
Contentious: TMP, (TNK 5.3.125)

3.4.117   Qa: gins (G2^v)   F: *giues* (1896)
           Qb: *giues* (G2^v)
           'Gin ('begin'): HAM, MAC (2), PER (3.2.94), CYM, TMP, (VEN (2), PP)

3.4.117   Qa: pin- | queues (G2^v)   F: Pin, squints (1897)
           Qb: pin, | squemes (G2^v)
           Like other recent editors I have accepted Greg's conjecture *squenes* (a dialect form or spelling of *squinies*).
           Squiny (*v.*): LR (4.6.137)

3.4.118   Qa: harte lip (G2^v)   F: *Hare-lippe* (1897)
           Qb: *hare lip* (G2^v)
           Hare-lip: MND

3.4.122   Q: O | light (G2^v)   F: *a-light* (1902)
           Alight (*v.*): SHR, MV, TIM (1.2.175)

3.6.25   Q: broome (G3^v)   *Not in F*
           Like other editors I have accepted Capell's emendation *bourne*.
           Bourn (*sb.*): HAM, TRO, LR (4.6.57), ANT, PER (2: 4.4.4), WT, TMP
           Broom: MND, (TNK 4.1.107)

3.6.70   Q: Bobtaile *tike* (G4)   F: Bobtaile tight (2027)
           Editors prefer Q, F making no apparent sense.
           Tike: H5 (?)
           Tight: SHR, ANT, TMP

3.7.59   Qa: lou'd (H1^v)   F: *bare* (2131)
           Qb: lowd (H1^v)
           STONE, BLAYNEY (*conj.* Greg): *bow'd*
           It is difficult to see any explanation for Qb unless *bow'd* was intended (in Q).
           Bow'd (*a.*): LLL, ROM, H8 (2.3.36)

3.7.61   Qa: steeled (H1^v)   F: *Stelled* (2133)
           Qb: *stelled* (H1^v)
           Steeled (*a.*): 1H6, (SON), H5, MM

3.7.86   Q: vnbridle (H2)   F: *enkindle* (2162)
           Shakespeare elsewhere only uses the adjective *unbridled*, and one does not easily 'unbridle . . . sparks'; Q is probably a misreading.
           Enkindle (*v.*): JN, JC, TRO, MAC

4.1.4   Q: experience (H2)   F: *esperance* (2182)
Q makes little sense; it apparently mistakes a rare word for a common one. Also, despite Stone (p. 226), *experience* is metrically anomalous.
Esperance: 1H4 (2), TRO

4.1.10   Qa: poorlie, leed (H2)   F: poorely led (2189)
Qb: *parti, eyd* (H2)
Poorly: (SON, LUC), R2, H5, TRO, MAC, CYM

4.1.61   Q: Mobing (H3)   Not in F
THEOBALD: Mopping
DUTHIE: *Mocking*
Mocking (*sb.*): LLL, AYLI, TIM (1.1.35)

4.1.74   Q: firmely (H3)   F: *fearfully* (2259)
Stone defends Q as being 'more suited to the image' (p. 221), but it is unmetrical and unparalleled in Shakespeare in this sense. However, it would also be an unlikely misreading of F's 'fearfully'; I therefore propose to emend Q to *sawcely*, Q's spelling at 1.1.21, B1 (see *OED*). This restores the metre, easily explains Q's misreading, and makes good sense ('insolently' – often much stronger than modern usage). Shakespeare elsewhere links the word with several others also present in this passage: compare 'deepe searcht with sawcie *lookes*' (LLL 1.1.85, my italics), 'so sawcily against your *High*nes' (LR 2.4.41, my italics), and '*confin'd*, bound in | To sawcy doubts' (MAC 3.4.23–4, my italics). *Saucy* is also specifically used of presumptuousness in confronting the sea (*OED* a.[1] 2d, citing *Sonnets* and *Troilus* among others).
Saucily: LR (1.1.21, 2.4.41), (LUC)
Firmly: 2H6, 3H6, SHR (3), TIT, MWW, LR (5.3.101)
Fearfully: ROM, JN, MV, 1H4, H5, PER (4.2.117), (VEN, PP, SON)

4.2.29   Qa: whistle (H3ᵛ)   F: whistle (2300)
Qb: *whistling* (H3ᵛ)
Greg's claim (*Variants*, p. 172) that the proverb always uses the verbal substantive is not correct; consequently there is little reason to regard Qb as a sophistication. The Folio is clearly indebted to the uncorrected state of sheet H.
Whistle (*sb.*): H5, PER (3.1.8), TMP, (TNK 3.5.39)
Whistling (*sb.*): 1H4

4.2.45   Qa: beniflicted (H4)   Not in F
Qb: benifited (H4)
I have assumed Qa is a misreading of manuscript *benefacted*, and

Qb an unauthoritative 'correction'. See *Notes and Queries*, 227
(1982), 121–3.
Benefit (*v.*): WT, H8 (1.2.80)

4.2.49   Qa: Humanly (H4)   *Not in F*
           Qb: *Humanity* (H4)
           Humanely: COR, TMP
           Humanity: 1H6, HAM, TRO, OTH, TIM (3: 1.1.273, 3.6.105,
           4.3.300), ANT, CYM

4.2.56   Qa: noystles (H4)   *Not in F*
           Qb: *noyseles* (H4)
           Noiseless: AWW

4.2.57   Qa: threats (H4)   *Not in F*
           Qb: threat (H4)
           JENNENS: *to threat*
           Like other editors I have no faith that Jennens's solution
           represents what Shakespeare wrote, but no convincing alter-
           native either. (But see Addenda.)
           Threat: TIT, LR (Q 4.2.75), WT

4.2.68   Qa: now (H4)   *Not in F*
           Qb: *mew* (H4)
           Mew (verb or interjection, i.e. 'the sound of a cat'): 1H4, HAM,
           MAC

4.2.75   Q: *threat inraged* (H4)   F: threat-enrag'd (2319)
           Editors adopt Q.
           Threat: TIT, LR (Qb 4.2.57), WT

4.2.87   Q: tooke (H4ᵛ)   F: *tart* (2334)
           Tart: ANT, (TNK 3.3.26)

4.3.16   Q: streme (H4ᵛ)   *Not in F*
           POPE: *strove*
           Stream (*v.*): ROM, R2, JC, AWW

4.4.2   Q: vent (I1)   F: *vext* (2352)
           'Vent' does not make sense, but is implausible as an error for
           'vext'; Stone's 'vehement' is even more implausible. But *ract*
           (= racked) presumes an easy misreading in Q, makes good sense,
           and is supported by one of the play's most sustained patterns of
           imagery (tortured bodies). An even easier emendation, graphi-
           cally, would be 'rent', but 'torn in two' does not seem as plausible
           a description of the sea; nor does it explain 'mad' as well. See also
           n. 25.
           Vexed (*a.*): ROM, JN, AWW, COR, CYM, TMP, H8
           (3.2.104)

4.6.57   Q: sommons (I3)   F: *Somnet* (2499)
          Summit: HAM (2)
          Summons (*sb.*): R2, HAM, OTH, LR (5.3.121), MAC (2), TMP,
          H8 (2.4.220)

4.6.83   Q: *coyning* (I3ᵛ)   F: *crying* (2530)
          Editors adopt Q. (But see Addenda.)
          Crying (*n.*): ROM (2), JN, ADO

4.6.184–5 Q: shoot . . . fell (I4ᵛ)   F: *shoo* . . . *Felt* (2626–7)
          Emending Q to *fells* in place of F's *Felt* would not affect the
          vocabulary pattern.
          Shoe (*v.*): MV
          Fell (*sb.*, 'animal skin'): AYLI, LR (5.3.24), MAC

4.6.225   Qa: beniz (K1)   F: *benizon* (2673)
          Qb: *benizon* (K1)
          Benison: MAC, LR (1.1.265), PER (2.ch.10)

4.6.247   Qa: battero (K1)   F: *Ballow* (2964)
          Qb: bat (K1)
          STONE, BLAYNEY (*conj.* Furnivall): *battone*
          Bat (*sb.*, 'club'): COR (2)

4.7.35   Q: iniurious (K2)   F: *Enemies* (2784)
          CAPELL: *injurer's* (for Q)
          Injurer: JN

5.1.3   Qa: *abdication* (K3)   F: *alteration* (2849)
          Qb: alteration (K3)
          Stone (p. 251) is surely right to prefer Qa as the rarer and more
          pointed reading; Greg concedes 'that the copy must have been
          rather confused to allow of such a misreading' (*Variants*, p. 177).
          F's agreement with Qb could result from inadequate correction
          of Q2 copy.
          Alteration: 1H6, (SON), 2H4, OTH, TIM (4.3.462), COR, WT (2)

5.3.24   Q: The good shall (K4)   F: *The good yeares shall* (2966)
          As a word appears to have dropped out of Q, there seems little
          justification in inventing an alternative to F's variant (i.e. Stone's
          gorecrows). See Addenda.
          Goodyear: ADO, 2H4, MWW

5.3.57   Qa: sharpes (K4ᵛ)   Not in F
          Qb: *sharpnes* (K4ᵛ)
          Sharpness: AWW, ANT, (TNK, 4.2.30)

5.3.83   Q: *attaint* (L1)   F: *arrest* (3028)
          F does not make much sense and almost certainly results from
          contamination; editors adopt Q.

Attaint (*sb.*): ERR, H5, TRO
Arrest (*sb.*): 2H6, R2, HAM, MM

5.3.148   Q: oreturnd (L2)   F: *ore-whelme* (3103)
STONE: returne to (for Q)
TAYLOR: *oreturne* (for Q)
Stone's double emendation is unmetrical and implausible, but Q
clearly represents something other than F. *Oreturn* produces the
same construction as in F, with minimal emendation.
O[v]erturn (*v.*): 1H4, 2H4, H5

5.3.292   Q: foredoome (L4)   F: *fore-done* (3259)
Q2: fore-doom'd
Foredoom is nowhere else recorded in this sense, and would be an
easy misreading of manuscript *foredoone.*
Foredo (*v.*): MND, HAM (2), OTH, LR (5.3.256)

2. Dubious Variants

A number of differences between Q and F could easily have resulted from
common or easy misreadings or printing errors: this does not mean they *did,*
but they certainly *could* have, and consequently any account of the vocabulary
differences between the two texts must make allowance for the possibility that
certain apparent differences may be spurious. The following words, which I
have included in the vocabulary samples, might be dismissed as such errors.
The first column gives the word; the second, its line reference; the third, the
word of which it might be a misreading (or the error which might have led to
its creation in one text or omission from the other); the fourth, a list of the
other plays in which the questionable word occurs. Cases already discussed in
the preceding section are not included.

QUARTO

equalities	1.1.5; B1	qualities	JN, ANT
fenced (*v.*)	4.6.282; K1^v	seuer'd	3H6 (2), AYLI, TIM, PER
imediate (*a.* = proximate in place)	5.3.65; L1	immediacy	2H4 (2), HAM, AWW
lancht (*v.* = lance)	2.1.51; D4	latch'd	R3, R2, ANT
russel	2.4.301; F3	ruffle	MWW, MM, CYM
warbling (*v.*)	2.1.39; D3^v	Mumbling	LLL, MND, AYLI

Totals: 1H6–JC: 10   AYLI–OTH: 5   TIM: 1   MAC–H8: 4

FOLIO

Champains	1.1.64; 69	(eyeskip)	TN

compact (*a.*)	2.2.118; 1194	coniunct	ERR, TIT, MND, AYLI, MM, LR (Q)
Conferring (*v.* = transfer)	1.1.40; 45	Confirming	AWW, TIM, TMP
conferr'd (*v.* = transfer)	1.1.82; 88	confirm'd	AWW, TIM, TMP
daub (*v.*)	4.1.54; 2241	dance	R3, 1H4, LR (Q)
grac'd (*a.*)	1.4.246; 755	great	MAC
intelligent	3.7.11; 2070	intelligence	LR (Q), WT
iarring (*a.*)	4.7.31; 2783	warring	1H6, SHR
nicely	5.3.45; 3100	(eyeskip)	R2, H5 (2), TN, LR (Q), PER, COR, CYM
ruffle	2.4.301; 1604	russel	TIT, JC, LR (Q)
shadowy	1.1.64; 69	shady	TGV, (TNK)
smug	4.6.198; 2641	(single word omission)	MV, 1H4
strain'd (*a.*)	1.1.169; 183	straied	(SON), MV, 2H4, TRO, (TNK)
thredding (*v.*)	2.1.119; 1062	threatning	R2, COR
vnbutton	3.4.107; 1888	on bee true	1H4, AYLI

Totals: 1H6–JC: 19   AYLI–OTH: 8   TIM: 2   MAC–H8: 8

APPENDIX II

Rare Vocabulary in the Two Texts of 'King Lear'

CHART 1. *Lear* and the Shakespeare Canon

	QF	Q-only	Q-total	F-only
1H6	737	62	9	71	11
2H6	814	68	6	74	7
3H6	614	52	13	65	3
R3	782	76	13	89	4
ERR	416	48	5	53	3
TIT	642	48	8	56	5
SHR	602	88	6	94	8
TGV	372	39	2	41	6
LLL	709	86	11	97	9
ROM	657	71	15	86	7
R2	626	60	8	68	11
MND	568	76	12	88	10
JOHN	642	57	11	68	7
MV	535	42	8	50	4
1H4	730	90	15	105	7
2H4	743	74	6	80	4
MWW	532	53	10	63	7
ADO	434	43	7	50	6
H5	836	86	8	94	12
JC	385	35	5	40	2
AYL	571	84	10	94	4
TN	555	70	13	83	5
HAM	1075	139	24	163	11
TRO	901	98	17	115	13
AWW	594	62	19	81	9
MM	486	81	8	89	11
OTH	654	86	17	103	3
TIM	486	88	15	103	9
LR (Q-only)	103	23			1
(QF)	610		23		20
MAC	567	80	10	90	8
ANT	638	68	17	85	2
PER	495	60	11	71	5
COR	697	77	17	94	7
WT	698	90	14	104	12

	QF	Q-only	Q-total	F-only
LR (F-only)	74	20	1	21	
CYM	732	117	14	131	10
TMP	554	85	7	94	10
H8	553	55	7	62	12

NOTES: The first column gives the name of each play, in a generally-accepted chronological order. (Where the order of composition of other plays would affect the interpretation of the *Lear* evidence, it has been discussed in the text or the notes.) The second column gives the total number of rare words in that play; all figures, except as modified by *King Lear* and *Troilus and Cressida* (see below), are based on Slater. The third column gives the number of occurrences, in other plays, of rare words which originate in Q, but are repeated in F; the fourth, the number of such occurrences for rare words which occur in Q but not F; the fifth column, combining three and four, gives the figures for all the rare words in Q. The sixth column gives similar figures for the rare words present in F but not Q.

The revision of *Lear* has here been provisionally placed between *The Winter's Tale* and *Cymbeline*, on the assumption that the two romances were composed in that order (see p. 438, n. 59); if *Cymbeline* was composed first, the revision would be most convincingly placed immediately after *Coriolanus*.

Since Slater's vocabulary test was originally based on the vocabulary of whole plays, it seemed advisable to test whether it worked as well for *parts* of plays. I have therefore examined the rare vocabulary of the fly scene (3.2), added to the text of *Titus Andronicus* by F, and widely suspected as a later addition; the deposition scene (4.1), not present in Q1 of *Richard II*, but widely regarded as an integral part of the original composition, omitted from Q for reasons of censorship; and the Folio alterations and additions to the Quarto text of *Troilus and Cressida*. After compiling the data for these samples, I have then adjusted Slater's figures for the whole play accordingly (i.e. subtracting from his figures for *Richard II* and *Titus* the rare vocabulary added by F's major inserts, adding and subtracting from his figures for the conflated text of *Troilus*), in order to be able to compare the rare vocabulary of the Folio additions and alterations to that of the original Quarto text. These plays should therefore provide a useful control on the data for *King Lear*. In each case, the figures exactly correspond with orthodox opinion about the date of composition of the Folio-only material.

In *Titus Andronicus*, the Quarto has 417 links with the first tetralogy, but only 197 with the next group of plays (*Errors, Shrew, Two Gentlemen, Love's Labour's Lost*); the fly scene has 27 links with the first tetralogy, and 25 with the second group. If the fly scene were composed at the same time as the rest of the play, it should have only 12.75 links with the second group, instead of 25. There is only one chance in 50 that this discrepancy is coincidental. Moreover, like Folio *Lear* the fly scene in *Titus* has remarkable links with a later group of plays, but no such exceptional links with an earlier group. Quarto *Titus* has 417 links with the first tetralogy, against an expected 260.6; the discrepancy has a chi-squared value of 92.49, which makes it virtually certain that *Titus* (if by Shakespeare) dates from the same years as *Henry VI* and *Richard III*. The fly scene, by contrast, has only 27 links with these plays, against an expected 16.4 ($\chi^2 = 5.46$). For the next group of plays, Q *Titus* has 197 links, just barely above the predicted figure of 185.5, and statistically insignificant; but the fly scene, with 25 links to this group, has an excess that would occur by chance less than one time in a thousand ($\chi^2 = 12.492$). On the other hand, the deposition scene in *Richard II* has a pattern of links almost identical with the play as a whole. With ten preceding plays (*1 Henry VI* to *Romeo*), the deposition scene has 49 links; with the eight after (*Dream* to *Henry V*), only 29. It should have only 45.9 links with the preceding plays; the difference is insignificant. As for *Troilus and Cressida*, the rare vocabulary added in the additions and alterations of F has 20 links with the six preceding plays (*Ado* to *Hamlet*), and 23 with the seven following (*All's Well* to *Macbeth*); if these alterations dated from the same time as the original composition, they should have 20.75 links with the preceding group, instead of only 20. The difference is, again, clearly insignificant.

CHART 2. *Lear* and Plays of Dubious Authorship

		Q (total)	F (only)
TIMON	Middleton	34	3
	Shakespeare	69	6
MACBETH	Middleton	0	0
	Shakespeare	90	8
PERICLES	1–2	23	1
	3–5	48	4
HENRY VIII	Fletcher	23	4
	Shakespeare	39	8
KINSMEN	Fletcher	56	7
	Shakespeare	60	4

The Folio-only sample is too small for the figures for links with any single play to have any statistical significance; figures for parts of plays are, correspondingly, even less reliable.

APPENDIX III

Internal Links in 'King Lear', 'Troilus and Cressida', 'Richard III', and 'Titus Andronicus'

1. Rare words occurring both in Q *Lear* and in the Folio additions and alterations.

	Q	F
bewray	3.6.111	2.1.107 (Q betray)
compact (a.)	1.2.7	2.2.118
daub (v.)	2.2.66	4.1.54
disaster (n.)	1.2.120	1.1.174
dotage	1.4.293	1.4.326
fitly	1.1.200	1.2.169
foot (v.)	3.4.120, 3.7.45	3.3.13
hollowness	1.1.154	1.2.113
houseless	3.4.30	3.4.26
intelligent	3.5.11	3.1.25
intelligent	3.5.11	3.7.11 (Q intelligence)
legitimate	1.2.16, 18, 19, 21	1.2.18
nicely	2.2.104	5.3.145
prediction	1.2.140	1.2.110
prescribe	1.1.276	1.2.24
ruffle (v.)	3.7.41	2.4.301 (Q russel)
sulphurous	3.2.4	4.6.128

Interestingly, *none* of the rare words in Q which link with added F vocabulary occur in Acts Four and Five. In 11 of 17 cases (italicized above), the occurrence in F follows that in Q. (I include here *houseless*, since the word in F occurs only four lines before the occurrence common to both texts, and is part of a sentence interrupted and then resumed.) On 4 occasions, the additional Folio use of the word occurs in the same scene as its use in Q; in the cases where the F use follows that in Q, the 11 Folio uses are separated by a total of 50 scenes from the 11 Quarto uses, for an average of only $4\frac{1}{2}$ scenes' separation. In at least two of the cases where F's additional use anticipates that in Q (bewray, ruffle), the F word might have been suggested by the Q variant at that point (betray, russel); on another occasion (foot), the F word comes in an added passage clearly related to subsequent cuts and alterations, which might therefore have been written after alterations elsewhere in Act Three.

2. Rare words occurring both in vocabulary unique to Q *Lear*, and in passages common to Q and F.

	QF	Q-only
advancement	2.4.200	5.3.68
aright	1.4.239	4.3.53
arraign	5.3.160	3.6.20
arraign	5.3.160	3.6.40
bastardy	1.2.10	1.2.133
benediction	2.2.161, 4.7.57	4.3.43
bourn	4.6.57	3.6.25
cart (sb.)	1.4.223	5.3.38
contemn (v.)	4.1.1, 4.1.2	4.2.32
eyeless	3.7.96, 4.6.227	3.1.8
imperfect	4.6.5	4.3.3
invade	1.1.144, 3.4.7	5.1.25
recreant	1.1.166	1.1.161
retinue	1.4.202	1.4.340
rustle	3.4.95	2.4.301
scourge (v.)	1.2.106	5.3.172
slack (v.)	2.4.245	2.4.136
saucily	1.1.21, 2.4.41	4.1.74
squiny	4.6.137	3.4.137

In contrast to Section 1, the occurrences in the first column are, here, scattered throughout all five acts. In 11 of 19 cases the occurrence unique to Q follows that common to Q and F (including *recreant*, which precedes the QF occurrence by only five lines); though the gross proportion is marginally lower than that for Section 1, this is less significant than the scattered distribution of the links. In the cases where the Q-only use follows that common to both texts, the 11 Q-only uses are separated by a total of 110 scenes from the (nearest) uses common to Q and F, for an average of 10 scenes' separation – more than double the average for F. A similar pattern emerges if we compare the distribution of links with all these rare words, regardless of whether the single-text occurrence precedes or follows that common to both texts. In that case the average separation for Q-only vocabulary (Section 2) is 8.1 scenes; that for F-only vocabulary (Section 1), only 4.235. The discrepancy here between Q and F would occur by chance only about one time in twenty. Since we have no reason to suspect distinct strata of composition in Q, the distribution of links there is presumably random; which suggests that the distribution of links with F's rare vocabulary is *not* random.

3. *Troilus and Cressida*: rare words occurring both in Q and in Folio additions and alterations.

	Q	F
composed (*a.*)	5.2.170	4.4.17
godly	2.2.32, 4.4.80	1.3.30
hedge (*v.*)	3.1.60	3.3.158
massy	2.3.17	Prologue
pavilion	1.3.305	Prologue
skittish	3.3.134	Prologue
strained (*a.*)	4.4.24	4.5.169

Only 2 of 8 times does the Folio occurrence follow that in Q. The figures here are perhaps distorted by the fact that F's major addition is a Prologue, which necessarily comes before anything in Q. In any case it is generally believed that the authorial revision in *Troilus*, whether from Q to F (as I believe; see n. 6) or F to Q, took place very soon after completion of the first draft; consequently there is no reason to expect the new vocabulary of the revision to be more influenced by the vocabulary in immediately preceding scenes or passages, than by the vocabulary in the whole of the (immediately preceding) first draft. If this pattern is typical of authorial revision between first draft and prompt-book, then it gives further reason for believing that the Folio revision of *Lear* took place some time after the initial composition.

4. Rare words occurring in major passages of *Richard III* omitted by Q, and elsewhere in the play.

	QF	F-only
commanding	4.4.104	2.2.128
exhale	1.2.58	1.2.165
pent (*a.*)	4.1.34	1.4.258
promotion	1.3.79	4.4.314
repay	4.2.119	2.2.92
retail (= pass down)	3.1.77	4.4.335
stander-by	1.3.209	1.2.62
ungoverned	3.7.110, 4.4.392	2.2.127
unwillingness	4.1.57	2.2.92

Only 3 of 9 times does the use in a major addition follow that elsewhere in the text; only once (*exhale*) are the two passages even close to one another. As it is generally assumed that the major Folio additions represent material cut in performance (and therefore not present in the theatrically-derived text of Q), we would not expect them to show stronger links with preceding rather than following parts of the play; nor do they. The difference from Folio *Lear* is again noticeable.

5. Rare words occurring in the Fly Scene (3.2), and elsewhere in *Titus Andronicus*.

buzz (*v.*)	4.4.7
coal-black	4.2.99, 5.1.32
lament (*sb.*)	3.1.218
melody	2.3.12, 4.4.86
square (*v.*)	2.1.100, 2.1.124
stump (*sb.*)	2.4.4, 5.2.22, 5.2.182
tyrannize	4.3.20

It is generally assumed that the so-called 'fly scene' is a later addition: it does not appear in Q (apparently set from foul papers) but only in F (which draws upon a theatrical manuscript). Four of the seven rare words in this scene which occur elsewhere in *Titus* are used before 3.2; they are separated from 3.2 by a total of only ten scenes, for an average of only $2\frac{1}{2}$ scenes' separation. The fly scene thus provides the closest parallel to the pattern of rare-word links in Folio *Lear*.

SELECT BIBLIOGRAPHY

T HIS list does not attempt to be comprehensive, but simply to provide readers with a checklist of the most important modern textual scholarship on *King Lear*. Most of these works are referred to in the preceding essays; the five asterisked items, which are frequently mentioned, have usually been identified by short titles only.

As elsewhere in this volume, place of publication is London, unless otherwise specified.

*Blayney, Peter W. M., *The Texts of 'King Lear' and Their Origins*, 2 vols. (Cambridge), Volume I, *Nicholas Okes and the First Quarto* (1982), II (forthcoming). Short title: Blayney, *Origins*

Cunnington, R. H., 'The Revision of *King Lear*', *Modern Language Review*, 5 (1910), 445–53

Doran, Madeleine, *The Text of 'King Lear'* (Stanford, 1931)

—— 'Elements in the Composition of *King Lear*', *Studies in Philology*, 30 (1933), 34–58

Duthie, George Ian, *Elizabethan Shorthand and the First Quarto of 'King Lear'* (Oxford, 1949)

—— *Shakespeare's 'King Lear': A Critical Edition* (Oxford, 1949)

Greg, W. W., 'The Function of Bibliography in Literary Criticism Illustrated in a Study of the Text of *King Lear*' [1933] and 'Time, Place, and Politics in *King Lear*' [1940], in *Collected Papers*, ed. J. C. Maxwell, (Oxford, 1966)

—— *The Variants in the First Quarto of 'King Lear': A Bibliographical and Critical Inquiry*, Supplement to the Bibliographical Society's Transactions, no. 15 (1940)

—— *The Editorial Problem in Shakespeare: a survey of the foundations of the text* (second edn., Oxford, 1951)

—— *The Shakespeare First Folio: Its Bibliographical and Textual History* (Oxford, 1955)

Honigmann, E. A. J., *The Stability of Shakespeare's Text* (1965)

—— 'Shakespeare's Revised Plays: *King Lear* and *Othello*', *The Library*, VI, 4 (1982), 142–73. [Half of this important article, which appeared after this volume had gone to press, is devoted to a review and critique of recent *Lear* studies, which endorses the findings of M. Warren, Urkowitz, and Taylor, and argues against Stone's attack on the authenticity of many Folio variants.]

Howard-Hill, T. H., 'The Problem of Manuscript Copy for Folio *King Lear*', *The Library*, VI, 4 (1982), 1–24

Kirschbaum, Leo, *The True Text of 'King Lear'* (Baltimore, 1945)

Moriarty, W. D., 'The Bearing on Dramatic Sequence of the Varia in *Richard the Third* and *King Lear*', *Modern Philology*, 10 (1913), 451–71

*Stone, P. W. K., *The Textual History of 'King Lear'* (1980). Short title: Stone, *Textual History*

*Taylor, Gary, 'The War in *King Lear*', *Shakespeare Survey 33* (Cambridge, 1980), 27–34. Short title: Taylor, 'War'

—— 'The Folio Copy for *Hamlet, King Lear*, and *Othello*', *Shakespeare Quarterly*, 34 (1983), 44–61

*Urkowitz, Steven, *Shakespeare's Revision of 'King Lear'* (Princeton, 1980). Short title: Urkowitz, *Revision*

*Warren, Michael J., 'Quarto and Folio *King Lear* and the Interpretation of Albany and Edgar', in *Shakespeare, Pattern of Excelling Nature*, eds. David Bevington and Jay L. Halio (Newark, Del., 1978), 95–107. Short title: M. Warren, 'Albany and Edgar'

Walker, Alice, *Textual Problems of the First Folio* (Cambridge, 1953)

INDEX OF PASSAGES DISCUSSED

BECAUSE of the variety of quotation and reference, both in this book and in the related studies, a three tiered system of indexing has been developed employing the numbering system of *The Riverside Shakespeare*. Entries appear under (a) the act and scene number for a whole scene; (b) a block of lines that may represent a specific speech or segment of action within that scene; and (c) a line or lines within that speech or segment. For example, a person wishing to gain information about 3.1.23–5 would need to consult the entries (a) under the scene (3.1), (b) under the major segment (3.1.17–42), and (c) under 3.1.23–5 to be sure to have checked all the references. Passages discussed in notes are not separately indexed if they simply carry on discussion of a passage in the context to which they are keyed.

Passages Discussed in Recent Two-Text Studies

We are grateful to Scolar Press for permission to index Stone, *Textual History*; to Cambridge University Press for permission to index Taylor, 'War'; to Princeton University Press for permission to index Urkowitz, *Revision*; and to University of Delaware Press and Associated University Presses for permission to index Warren, 'Albany and Edgar'. Citations in this index are recorded by the first letter of the author's surname; thus:

Stone, *Textual History*	S
Taylor, 'War'	T
Urkowitz, *Revision*	U
Warren, 'Albany and Edgar'	W

The references to Stone, Taylor, and Warren have been adjusted to conform with the lineation of *The Riverside Shakespeare*; accordingly, some discrepancies will be observed when this index is used to consult those works.

1.1	T 29; U 139	71–4	S 44
5	S 213	72	S 64
33	S 108; U 105	74	S 64, 191
38–45	U 81–2	76–7	S 38
38	S 224	82–120	U 30
40	S 178	82	S 178
40–1	S 67	84–5	S 117, 239
40–5	S 117, 238	88–9	S 117, 239
45	S 67, 68, 254	91–3	S 26
49–50	S 117, 238	100	S 224
55	S 134	104	S 233
59	S 190–1	110	S 15, 191
64–5	S 117, 239	116–28	U 30
69	S 18	118	S 247

Passages Discussed in The Division of the Kingdoms

Recurring indifferent variants (a/he, ah/oh, and/if, and/which, beside/besides, doth/do's, farther/further, has/hath, my/mine, more/mo, naught/nought, sometime/sometimes, that/where, that/which, that/who, thine/thy, toward/towards, 'twas/it was, who/which, yea/ha, yea/O, yon/yond, you'll/you will) are discussed on pp. 276–81, and in the Addenda (variants involving terminal *s*); another group of such variants (among/amongst, between/betwixt, does/doth, e'en/even, 'em/them, has/hath, I'm/I am, i'th/in the, ne'er/never, o'th/o'the/of the, while/whiles/whilst, ye/you, yes/ay) is discussed on pp. 397–400. None of the individual occurrences of these variants is indexed below. There is a discussion of the pattern of revision throughout the play on pp. 422–7.

ADDENDA

'KING LEAR AND CENSORSHIP' (Taylor). Michael Warren, in a forthcoming note (given as a seminar paper at the 1983 Shakespeare Association of America conference), argues that Folio 'crying' (TLN 2530; 4.6.83) is a sensible alternative to Q's 'coyning' (I3ᵛ) rather than – as has heretofore been almost universally assumed – a mere error. If this is true (and I find Warren's argument convincing), then the deliberate alteration of Q may have resulted from censorship. Certainly, 'they cannot touch mee for coyning, I am the king himselfe' might have been perceived (like the passage at 1.4.140–55, discussed on pp. 102–9) as a jibe at the King himself. *Touch* clearly means 'rebuke, reprove, censure' (*OED*, *v.* 9). The verb *coin* was used '*esp.* in a bad or depreciatory sense' to mean 'To fabricate, invent, make up (something specious, pretentious, or counterfeit)' (*v.*¹ 5b; 1561 +); it could also mean 'feign, dissemble' (*v.*¹ 7, citing *The Revenger's Tragedy*). Either of these meanings could be enough in itself to provoke censorship; the sexual sense, 'beget children' (for which see Colman, p. 188, and Muir's new Arden note), might not have been considered particularly decorous, either. Moreover, even the precise technical use of the verb might at various times have caused offence. In November 1604 James had issued a major proclamation on coinage, introducing many new coins; this was the culmination of several initiatives since his succession, aimed at uniting the currencies of his two kingdoms (a reform which the English were clearly reluctant to accept). Furthermore, a debasement of the coinage was proclaimed on 16 July 1605 (see Rogers Ruding, *Annals of the Coinage of Great Britain and its Dependencies*, 3rd. edn., 3 vols. (1840), I, 364). Thereafter, nothing of significance happened to the currency until a further debasement on 23 November 1611 (Ruding, I, 365–6); this, however, seems too late to have influenced the censor, since the Folio revision was almost certainly completed and submitted a year or more before. If the change was made in deference to censorship – which seems to me fairly likely – then it was probably made in 1605–6 (like the omission of 1.4.140–55) rather than later (like the omission of 'Fut').

'FOLIO EDITORS AND COMPOSITORS' (Werstine). On the basis of type-recurrence evidence, Hinman assigned the last 10 lines or so of column rr3b in Folio *Lear* to Compositor B, not E (II, 279). This assignment was overlooked in my description of the compositors' stints on p. 273, ll. 6–8. Affected, too, is n. 63 on p. 291, which should have indicated that B, not E, set TLN 1853–61. On pp. 276 (l. 2) and 285 (l. 5), the number of E's lines in *Lear* should read 1867, not 1877. On p. 312, the line '1860j/of the/o'th'' should be deleted. Otherwise, my argument has not to my knowledge been affected by this oversight.

Blayney's thorough bibliographical analysis of Q has concluded (*Origins*, I, 151–87) that a second compositor (Okes C) helped the main workman (Okes B) by setting I3ᵛ.16–I4ᵛ.26, H4ᵛ.18–I1ᵛ.25, K1ᵛ.3–K2ᵛ.1 (or 4.3.0– 4.4.29, 4.6.96–212, 4.6.271–4.7.56, 5.3.121–end, according to the line-numbering of *The Riverside Shakespeare*). Blayney's research makes it possible to compare the work of the four compositors in relation to a frequent source of variation between the texts, and a frequent type of compositorial error: variants involving the addition or deletion of terminal *s*. (Line counts include lines found in the Folio but not the Quarto.)

No. of lines common to Jaggard's B and Okes's B	1271
No of -s variants	36
Frequency	1/35 ll.
No. of lines common to Jaggard's E and Okes's B	1565
No. of -s variants	55
Frequency	1/28.5 ll.
No. of lines common to Jaggard's B and Okes's C	164
Variants	6
Frequency	1/27 ll.
No. of lines common to Jaggard's E and Okes's C	302
Variants	0

If most or all of the -*s* variants between Q and F originated with Jaggard's compositors, a very hefty majority should occur in E's stints (see p. 264, above). But E in fact set, proportionally, no more than B (1/34 ll. each). Nor can this discrepancy in the Jaggard evidence be accounted for by Okes's workmen. Okes C (1/78 ll.) *seems* less prone than Okes B (1/31 ll.) to introduce -*s* variants; but if Okes C were indeed reliable, why does the highest concentration of -*s* variants in the whole of *Lear* occur in the lines common to him and Jaggard B, who is known to be (in this respect) fairly reliable? The only reasonable inference from these figures would appear to be that some agency other than Okes's and Jaggard's compositors is responsible for a significant proportion of the terminal *s* variation between the two texts. (Whether that agency is an author or a scribe is, of course, impossible to determine.)

'FLUCTUATING VARIATION' (Jackson). There is no significant relation between the compositorial shares in Q (as determined by Blayney) and the relative frequency of any Q/F variation discussed in my essay; so the Q compositors cannot have been responsible for the fluctuations. Blayney does suggest that the change within 5.3 from '*Alb.*' to '*Duke.*' speech prefixes (on L3) may be due to type shortage (*Origins*, I, 141–2), but he offers no explanation of the larger pattern in prefixes for the two dukes that I note on p. 326.

'DATE AND AUTHORSHIP OF THE FOLIO VERSION' (Taylor). Shakespeare's decision to begin the revision on an exemplar of Q1 (p. 367, above, and p. 433, n. 28) might also have been influenced by the theatrical practice of marking up quartos. See the Edinburgh copy (JA 297) of Q1 (1613) of *The White Devil*, the Chicago copy of Q4 (1604?) of *A Looking Glasse for London and England* (described by C. R. Baskerville, 'A Prompt Copy of *A Looking Glass for London and England*', *Mod. Phil.*, 30 (1932), 29–51), and C. J. Sisson, 'Shakespeare's Quartos as Prompt-copies', *RES*, 18 (1942), 129–43. Sisson shows that Q *Lear* was used for regulating provincial performances (*c*.1610); this reinforces my suspicions that, if the original *Lear* prompt-book had been lost in the Globe fire (as Stone suggests), the King's Men would have been happy enough to use Q1, without substantial revision.

The parallel between *The Winter's Tale* and Puttenham noted by H. S. Wilson (see p. 382, above) was in fact first identified by William Lowes Rushton, in *Shakespeare and 'The Arte of English Poesie'* (Liverpool, 1909), pp. 118–21. Rushton also noted the 'tall fellow of his hands' parallel (pp. 34–5; see p. 437, n. 57, above). Most of the other parallels in Rushton's short book seem illusory, but there is one interesting link with *Coriolanus* (pp. 148–51); otherwise the most plausible connections all involve, as one might expect, Shakespeare's early plays. (For another such link, see the note on 'Alarbus' in Eugene Waith's forthcoming Oxford Shakespeare edition of *Titus Andronicus*.)

The absurdity of combining Greg's argument for dating the original composition of *Lear* with Duthie's explanation for Q's links with *Leir* (p. 434, n. 43) is compounded when the same editors accept Alice Walker's hypothesis that one or two boy actors provided the printer's copy for Q. These three modern editors of *King Lear* thereby postulate (without, of course, ever articulating the interrelationship of their assumptions) that the Quarto text of *King Lear* was contaminated by a boy actor's memory of his own performance in a play which had not been performed for ten to fifteen years.

My rather vague final conclusions about the date of the *Lear* revision ('1609–10') may be clarified by a record of certain related specific dates which I had assumed but did not mention in my discussion (pp. 428–9). Edward Wightman was condemned to death on 14 December 1611; he and Bartholomew Legate (condemned 21 February 1611/12) both went to the stake in March. The revision therefore presumably dates from before December 1611. Simon Forman, who died in September 1611, saw a performance of *Cymbeline* at the Globe in the spring, probably in April–May (he saw other performances on 20 and 30 April, and 15 May); if, as the evidence suggests, the revision precedes the composition of *Cymbeline*, it must be earlier than spring 1611. If *Cymbeline* influenced *Philaster*, *Cymbeline* itself probably dates from before May 1609, at or after which time *Philaster* was written: see Andrew Gurr's Revels edition (1969), xxvii–xxviii. *Philaster* had clearly been completed by October 1610; if *Cymbeline* influenced it, then the revision of *Lear* can be firmly dated between January 1607/8 and summer 1610. However, if (as seems to me more likely) *Philaster* influenced *Cymbeline*, then *Cymbeline* could have been written no earlier than May 1609, and could have been finished as late as April 1611; the revision of *Lear* might have been completed as late as (say) January 1610/11. Two other dates encourage the later (May 1609–January 1611) rather than the earlier (January 1608–summer 1610) of these two ranges. Henri IV of France was assassinated by a religious fanatic on 14 May 1610; the Fool's allusion to heretics would have been particularly topical in the following months. Moreover, although the King's Men had planned to move into the Blackfriars playhouse for over a year, the closing of London theatres because of plague made it impossible for them to begin performing there before December 1609, and perhaps not until January–February 1609/10 (Smith, *Shakespeare's Blackfriars Playhouse*, p. 248; Barroll, 'Chronology of Shakespeare's Jacobean Plays', pp. 132–3). Public performances had, however, clearly resumed by April 1610. If partly intended for performance in the company's new playhouse, Folio *Lear* might have been written before December 1609, but it could hardly have been performed before then. The long-awaited opening of the Blackfriars in early 1610, and the assassination of Henri IV in May, encourage me to believe that Folio *Lear* was not completed and performed before May–June 1610. Such a date is difficult (though not quite impossible) if *Cymbeline* influenced *Philaster*; it would require us to believe that the revision of *Lear* was completed, *Cymbeline* written, and then subsequently *Philaster* written, between 14 May and 8 October 1610. The exact date of the *Lear* revision therefore depends (if the foregoing analysis is correct) upon whether *Philaster* influenced, and *The Winter's Tale* preceded, *Cymbeline* – matters which I shall be discussing elsewhere. Here it will suffice to record my opinion that Folio *Lear* was probably completed between early June and December of 1610.

The opportunity for further editorial work on the text of Quarto *Lear* has led me to suggest new solutions to four cruces which were (or now would be) included in Appendix I. The net effect of these four changes would be to increase the Quarto's links with plays from 1600–4 by two, and its links with plays from 1606–13 by one: they thus reflect, and if anything marginally reinforce, the statistical conclusions already reached.

3.6.23–4   Q1: wanst thou eyes, at tral madam (G3ᵛ)   *Not in F*
           Q2: wantst thou eies at triall madam,
           TAYLOR: *wantst thou eyes, at trol madam?*

Q2's triple emendation is generally accepted, but leaves the passage difficult. The anomalous punctuation might come from foul papers, *trial* might have been misread *tral*, or the Q1 compositor might accidentally have omitted the *t* from *wantst* and the *i* from *trial*; but Q2 has simply guessed at the most obvious emendation suggested by the context. The usual interpretation of Q2 as 'do you want to be the object of admiring glances even at your trial' is strained and dubiously pertinent; it provides no obvious cue for Tom's song. The meaning suggested by Q1's punctuation – 'wantst thou eyes?' – is much more pointed and intelligible: it could be addressed to Lear (staring as though he were blind), or to a joint-stool Gonorill (the stool having, of course, no eyes), or to Kent or the Fool ('Don't you have eyes? Can't you see the fiend I'm talking about?'). Q1's 'wanst' could be the second person singular of the verbs *won*, *wean*, or *wain*, but it is difficult to see much pertinence in any of these. It might also, conceivably, represent a euphonic spelling of *wantst*; but elsewhere the *-tst* spelling is reduced by omitting the second *t*, not the first ('wants' rather than 'wanſt' with an ſt ligature). It therefore seems likely that Q2's 'wantst' for 'wanst' is correct, but that its removal of the comma is unwarranted.

The real difficulty is Q2's 'at triall madam'. To suggest that the compositor again simply omitted a letter seems to beg too much of coincidence, especially as this assumption requires us to repunctuate the passage in a less satisfactory way; it would be more reasonable to suppose that, here as elsewhere, the compositor has simply set nonsense because he could not make out the sense. If 'trial' were in his copy, he should have had little difficulty deducing it from the context. 'K.D.' conjectured 'worse than eyes at trol-madam' (*Notes and Queries*, 1905), and though the first part of this conjecture can be disregarded, 'trol' for 'tral' is attractive. Shakespeare refers to the game troll-madam at *Winter's Tale* 4.3.87 (TLN 1755); *OED* has examples (without hyphen, and with the spelling 'trol') from 1572 on. Moreover, *trol* could also mean 'to chant merrily or jovially' (*v.* 10, *vbl. sb.* 2) and 'to angle for fish with a running line' (*v.* 13), two senses which suggest both the form and the content of Edgar's next lines. Troll-madam was apparently often played (see *OED*) by making holes 'in the end of a bench'; Edgar and the Fool have just been instructed to sit on what is most probably a bench. The players tried to roll 'pummetes or Bowles' or 'pellets' into these holes; in other words, to play the game one needed several small balls – like eyeballs, which Edgar has just asked someone if they lack ('wantst thou eyes?'). Finally, Shakespeare several times elsewhere uses *at* before the name of a game, meaning either 'on the occasion of playing' or 'occupied with, engaged in' (Schmidt, *Shakespeare-Lexicon*, I, 62). Edgar could thus be understood to mean 'do you lack-or-desire eyes? Are you playing troll-madam?' or 'do you lack eyes with which to play troll-madam?'. It is difficult to believe that all of the connections between *troll-madam* and the context are coincidental; Shakespeare refers to the game elsewhere; emendation to *trol* seems to me to

make better sense; it involves less alteration of Q1; and the error it does assume (*trol* misread as *tral*, in a phrase the compositor did not understand) is much more typical of Q1 *Lear* (which is full of such nonsense) than is the typographical error assumed by Q2. (Blayney notes that, in terms of purely *typographical* error, Q1 is printed as well or better than F: *Origins*, I, 112, 210.)
Troll-madam: WT

3.7.17   Q: questrits (H1)
         F: *Questrists* (2076)
         TAYLOR: *questants* (for Q)
Stone (p. 50) conjectures 'questrels' (also in BM2), but the meaning 'squires' here requires the further emendation of *after him* to *after em* in the next line, and in any case puts an unlikely emphasis upon the knights' train, rather than the search for Lear. Shakespeare uses 'questant' at *All's Well* 2.1.16 (TLN 613); Q's 'questrits' could arise from an easy minim misreading. Q cannot be a typographical error for F's word, because the compositor would have needed an ft ligature; likewise, Q is an unlikely misreading of F's (elsewhere unrecorded) word.
Questant: AWW

4.2.57   Qa: slayer begin threats (H4)   *Not in F*
         Qb: state begins thereat
         STONE: slyre biggin threats
         JENNENS: state begins to threat
         TAYLOR: *flaxen begin threats*
Stone places 'some confidence' in *biggin* (*Textual History*, p. 184); to his defence of it may be added the fact that the word could be spelled 'begin' (*OED*), and is used elsewhere by Shakespeare (*2 Henry IV* H3ᵛ; TLN 2550; 4.5.27). But *slyre* is a Scottish word, not recorded before 1621; paleographically, it is a more difficult emendation than Qb's own. If 'biggin' (spelled 'begin') is right, then 'flaxen' seems a much likelier emendation of Qa 'flayer'. As Stone observes, Qa is likelier than Qb to approach what the compositor saw in the manuscript, and 'flaxen biggin' requires only a single easy emendation of Qa. Qb, aside from being nonsensical in itself, presupposes both the misreading of 'state' as 'slaier', and metathesis of terminal *s*. Jennens' emendation, almost universally accepted, adds to these implausibilities the assumption that 'to' was either omitted by the author, or accidentally omitted in both states of the line in Q. Qb looks like guesswork; Jennens's emendation looks like guesswork squared.
thereat: TIT, LR (Q 4.2.75), WT
biggin: 2H4
flaxen: HAM

5.3.24   Q: The good shall (K4)   F: The good yeares shall (2966)
         TAYLOR: The *goodier* shall

Though the substance of F's emendation seems legitimate, it is noticeable that all Shakespeare's other uses of the word (goodyere), and all the other examples cited by *OED* and editors, are in the singular: that 'the goodye(a)re' could mean 'the devil' seems clear enough, but that 'the goodye(a)res' meant 'devils' has never been substantiated. Moreover, this Folio page was set by Compositor E, who is notorious for adding terminal *s* to words in his copy. F's plural is thus doubly suspicious. The plural is also chiefly responsible for creating an ambiguity ('the good yeares' = good times) which seems impossible to reconcile with the context, but sufficiently plausible at first hearing to confuse a listener.

In defence of F, Muir suggested that Shakespeare was thinking of Pharaoh's dream (Genesis 41), but there the 'good ears' which symbolized 'good years' were themselves *devoured by* the lean ears; they did not devour anything. Biblical allusion seems most unlikely. It also seems unlikely that Shakespeare regarded 'goodye(a)re' as two words. Elsewhere, Shakespeare's early texts always treat 'goodye(a)re' as one word, running it together or hyphenating its two components: Folio *Lear* probably prints it as two words because Compositor E was working from annotated Q2 copy, with 'yeare' added in the margin for insertion, and Compositor E interpreting this (naturally enough) as a complete word rather than a suffix. And if, as Shakespeare's usage elsewhere suggests, 'goodye(a)re' was written as one word in Q's copy, then it is relatively unlikely that the Quarto compositor omitted *part* of it accidentally. This suggests two possibilities. First, the syllable omitted might have been some word other than 'yeare'; if so, we have little evidence which would enable us to reconstruct it. Alternatively, the word may have been spelled 'goodier'; Dryden uses this spelling, and *Merry Wives* has 'good-ier' (TLN 509; 1.4.122). The Q compositor might have regarded 'goodier' as nonsense, and so set 'good', the only part of the word he could make sense of.

Goodyear: ADO, 2H4, MWW